THE
ACADEMY *of* MANAGEMENT
ANNALS

THE
ACADEMY *of* MANAGEMENT
ANNALS

VOLUME 1

EDITED BY

JAMES P. WALSH ✦ ARTHUR P. BRIEF

Lawrence Erlbaum Associates
Taylor & Francis Group

New York   London

Lawrence Erlbaum Associates
Taylor & Francis Group
270 Madison Avenue
New York, NY 10016

Lawrence Erlbaum Associates
Taylor & Francis Group
2 Park Square
Milton Park, Abingdon
Oxon OX14 4RN

Printed in the United States of America on acid-free paper
10 9 8 7 6 5 4 3 2 1

International Standard Book Number-13: 978-0-8058-6220-1 (Hardcover)

Visit the Taylor & Francis Web site at
http://www.taylorandfrancis.com

and the LEA and Routledge Web site at
http://www.routledge.com

Contents

Preface

A few years ago, the Academy of Management's Board of Governors decided that our field would really benefit from an annual assessment of what we know and do not know in our various research domains. All mature fields of inquiry take stock of their work in this way. It was time to act. To make a long story short, the *Academy of Management Annals* was born. It is to be a compendium of comprehensive and critical research reviews. They provide respected and intelligent syntheses of not only our contemporary understandings but also how we reached them. Written by and for scholars, these reviews say as much about our future work as they do about our past efforts. They also stand as testimony to our many accomplishments.

We are extraordinarily honored and humbled to serve as the first editors. Fortunately, we are not alone. Our Editorial Committee is comprised of some of our field's most distinguished and generous scholars; the talent and good cheer of the Academy of Management's professional staff is unmatched; and our editor at Taylor and Francis is absolutely first rate. We are as indebted to these wonderful folks as we are to our distinguished colleagues who accepted our invitation to contribute to this inaugural volume.

These first chapters reflect the broad reach of our field. We are pleased to publish reviews of corporate control, nonstandard employment, critical management studies, physical work environments, public administration, team learning, emotions in organizations, leadership in health care, creativity at work, business and the natural environment, human resource management in a world of distributed work, and bias in performance appraisals.

This is a beginning. Future volumes will continue to honor the breadth and depth of our scholarship. We will also continue to rely on our field's best and brightest to do this work. We sincerely hope that the *Academy of Management Annals* will come to be known as the go-to resource for structuring what is taught in our classrooms and for guiding the conduct of our research. Again, we are privileged to be able to contribute to this important new initiative.

ARTHUR P. BRIEF
UNIVERSITY OF UTAH

JAMES P. WALSH
UNIVERSITY OF MICHIGAN

Contributors

Paul S. Adler
Marshall School of Business
University of Southern California
Los Angeles, California

Susan J. Ashford
Ross School of Business
University of Michigan
Ann Arbor, Michigan

Luca Berchicci
Ecole Polytechnique Federale
  de Lausanne
Lausanne, Switzerland

Ruth Blatt
Ross School of Business
University of Michigan
Ann Arbor, Michigan

S. Trevis Certo
Texas A&M University
College Station, Texas

Atira Cherise Charles
Arizona State University
Tempe, Arizona

Catherine M. Dalton
Indiana University
Bloomington, Indiana

Dan R. Dalton
Indiana University
Bloomington, Indiana

Thomas A. D'Aunno
INSEAD
Fontainebleau, France

James R. Dillon
Harvard University
Cambridge, Massachusetts

Amy C. Edmondson
Harvard University
Cambridge, Massachusetts

Hillary Anger Elfenbein
Haas School of Business
University of California, Berkeley
Berkeley, California

Kimberly D. Elsbach
University of California, Davis
Davis, California

Linda C. Forbes
Franklin & Marshall College
Lancaster, Pennsylvania

Benjamin M. Galvin
Arizona State University
Tempe, Arizona

Elizabeth George
Hong Kong University of Science and
Technology
Kowloon, Hong Kong

Mattia J. Gilmartin
Independent Consultant

Michael A. Hitt
Mays Business School
Texas A&M University
College Station, Texas

Andrew C. Inkpen
Thunderbird School of Global
  Management
Glendale, Arizona

Steven Kelman
Harvard University
Cambridge, Massachusetts

Andrew King
Dartmouth College
Hanover, New Hampshire

John Paul MacDuffie
Wharton School of Business
University of Pennsylvania
Philadelphia, Pennsylvania

Michael G. Pratt
University of Illinois at
  Urbana-Champaign
Champaign, Illinois

Loriann Roberson
Arizona State University
Tempe, Arizona

Kathryn S. Roloff
Harvard University
Cambridge, Massachusetts

Eric W. K. Tsang
University of Texas at Dallas
Dallas, Texas

Hugh Willmott
Cardiff University
Cardiff, U.K.

1

The Fundamental Agency Problem and Its Mitigation:
Independence, Equity, and the Market for Corporate Control

DAN R. DALTON
Kelley School of Business, Indiana University

MICHAEL A. HITT
Mays College of Business, Texas A&M University

S. TREVIS CERTO
Mays College of Business, Texas A&M University

CATHERINE M. DALTON
Kelley School of Business, Indiana University

Abstract

A central tenet of agency theory is that there is potential for mischief when the interests of owners and managers diverge. In those circumstances, and for a variety of reasons, managers may be able to exact higher rents than are reasonable or than the owners of the firm would otherwise accord them. While that foundational element of agency theory is secure, other elements derived directly from agency theory are far less settled. Indeed, even after some 75 years of conceptualization and empirical research, the three principal approaches that have long been proposed to mitigate the fundamental agency problem remain contentious. Accordingly, we provide a review of the fundamental agency problem and its mitigation through independence, equity, and the market for corporate control.

Introduction

Agency theory is secure among the pantheon of conceptual/theoretical foundations that inform research in corporate governance. Indeed, agency theory not only predates other influential theories, including resource dependence (e.g., Pfeffer & Salancik, 1978; Selznick, 1949; Thompson & McEwen, 1958; Zald, 1969), the resource-based view (e.g., Barney, 1991; Barney, Wright, & Ketchen, 2001; Wernerfelt, 1984), and institutional theory (e.g., DiMaggio & Powell, 1983; Meyer & Rowan, 1977; Oliver, 1991; Rogers, 2003; Scott, 1995), but remains the dominant perspective on which governance research relies.[1]

A variety of comments may underscore that view. Bratton (2001; see also Bratton, 1989) described Berle and Means' impact on legal scholarship "as a paradigm that dominated the field" and their book, *The Modern Corporation and Private Property*, as "a singular event in the last century of academic corporate law" (p. 739). Shapiro suggested that agency theory represents a "new zeitgeist" and "the dominant institutional logic of corporate governance" (Shapiro, 2005, p. 279).

Gilson (1996) observed that "the intellectual mission of American corporate governance took the form of a search for the organizational Holy Grail, a technique that bridged the separation of ownership and control by aligning the interests of shareholders and managers" (p. 331). Roe (2005; see also Mizruchi, 2004; Roe, 1994), too, shared a similar perspective that "the core fissure in American corporate governance is the separation of ownership from control" and that "separation is the foundational instability of American corporate governance" (p. 9). Perhaps it is Davis (2005) who provided the most succinct summary of the role of agency theory: "This solution to managerialism became perhaps the dominant theory of the public corporation" (p. 145).

The pivotal notion that focuses this manuscript is the central tenet of agency theory: that there is potential for mischief when the interests of owners and those of managers diverge. In those circumstances, and for a variety of reasons, managers may be able to exact higher rents than would otherwise be accorded them by owners of the firm. While we are confident that this foundation of agency theory is unavoidable and intractable, other elements derived directly from agency theory are far less settled. Indeed, even after some 75 years of conceptualization and empirical research, the three fundamental means of mitigating the agency problem (e.g., independence, equity, and the market for corporate control) remain contentious.

The voluminous research on agency theory was propelled largely by the major challenge of how to solve the fundamental agency problem. How can an organization, through its owners and its stewards, minimize the posited tendency for managers to inappropriately leverage their advantage when managers' interests are not consonant with those of owners?

Early on, three principal approaches were developed to minimize the agency problem. One, the "independence" approach, suggested that boards of directors, comprised to be independent of management, can monitor managers and assure that their interests do not diverge substantially from those of owners (Fama, 1980; Fama & Jensen, 1983a, 1983b; Jensen & Meckling, 1976; Mizruchi, 1983; see also Chandler, 1977). Another method, the "equity" approach, proposed that managers with equity in the firm were more likely to embrace the interests of other equity holders and, accordingly, to direct the firm in their joint interests (Fama & Jensen, 1983b; Jensen & Meckling, 1976). Lastly, there was the notion of the "market for corporate control," which set forth the principle that corporate markets may operate to discipline managers who inappropriately leverage their agency advantage. In such cases, self-serving executives may subject the firm to acquisition by other firms (Fama & Jensen, 1983a; Jensen & Ruback, 1983; Manne, 1965). While these three corporate governance approaches are rational in principle, the efficacy of these approaches in practice remains subject to debate.

Accordingly, in subsequent sections of this manuscript, we provide a multidisciplinary overview of agency theory with an emphasis on the three mechanisms through which the fundamental agency problem may be mitigated: (a) independence, (b) equity, and (c) the market for corporate control. In addition, we consider the impact of the current regulatory compliance climate (e.g., Sarbanes-Oxley, the guidelines of the listing exchanges [e.g., NYSE, NASDAQ], the Securities and Exchange Commission [SEC], and the Justice Department) on agency theory and corporate governance.

We do recognize the daunting scope of our project. We did, however, enjoy a substantial advantage as we greatly benefited and borrowed liberally from the reviews and discussions of agency theory that preceded us (e.g., Bradley, Schipani, Sundaram, & Walsh, 1999; Bratton, 1989, 2001; Eisenhardt, 1989; Finkelstein & Hambrick, 1996; Hillman & Dalziel, 2003; Jensen, 1998; Kim & Mahoney, 2005; Mizruchi, 2004; Moe, 1984; Stigler & Friedland, 1983; Walsh & Seward, 1990). Similarly, our task was facilitated by an extraordinary body of work that provided a broad overview of corporate governance (e.g., Corley, 2005; Daily, Dalton, & Cannella, 2003; Daily, Dalton, & Rajagopalan, 2003; Davis, 2005; Denis, 2001; Gaa, 2004; Hambrick, Werder, & Zajac, in press; Hermalin, 2005; Shleifer & Vishny, 1997; Williamson, 2005).

The attention to agency theory provides an imposing literature. Accordingly, the commentary and research on which we rely is representative of that body of work, but is by no means exhaustive. On virtually every point, we could have cited more broadly and credited more examples of outstanding and relevant work. We regret that, in this manuscript, we have not directly represented all of the work contributing to the ubiquity and influence of agency theory. We apologize, too, that we have often sacrificed detail, along with some texture, as we focus largely on the more recent work. We should also note that our review is largely U.S. centric, as the vast majority of relevant work on agency theory has that character. That said, in subsequent sections, we do address some adverse implications of that reliance.

Brief History of Agency Theory

The corporate form of organization, replete with limited liability, perpetual life, and efficient markets for transfers of ownership, first appeared some 400 years ago (e.g., Baskin & Miranti, 1997; Gourevitch & Shinn, 2005; Hermalin, 2005; Micklethwait & Wooldridge, 2003). In 1600, Elizabeth I chartered the East India Company, which in many ways was the prototype of the publicly traded, multinational enterprise.[2] From the onset, however, the corporation and its enablements were not uniformly embraced. Sir Edward Coke (1552–1634) observed that corporations "cannot commit treason, nor be outlawed or excommunicated, for they have no souls." Some years later, that sentiment was unabated. Lord Chancellor Edward Thurlow (1731-1806) noted, "Corporations have neither bodies to be punished, nor souls to be condemned, they therefore do as they like" (from Micklethwait & Wooldridge, 2003, p. 33).

This negativity would seem to be based largely on principle. Adam Smith, however, in *An Inquiry into the Nature and Causes of the Wealth of Nations* (1776; from Hutchins' translation, 1952), provided a rather practical discussion of an inherent problem attendant to joint stock companies—the consequences of owners appointing others as the stewards of their wealth. Moreover, Smith's perspective presaged the development of what would become known as agency theory. He suggested that managers of other people's money cannot be expected to "watch over it with the same anxious vigilance" one would expect from owners, and that "negligence and profusion, therefore, must always prevail, more or less, in the management of the affairs of such a company"[3] (p. 324).

In the United States, the acceptance of corporations was similarly uneven. As noted by Bradley and Wallenstein (2006, p. 47), most Americans believed that "big business was bad business" and had extreme reservations about the concentration of economic power that would accrue to such organizations. Accordingly, early corporations were subject to severe constraints on their scale and their range of activities. Such limitations, however, became essentially moot in 1886 when the Supreme Court ruled that a private corporation was a natural person under the Constitution of the United States[4] (Bradley & Wallenstein, 2006; see also Bradley et al., 1999; Cole, 2005; Krannich, 2005).

This decision was the catalyst for an unprecedented expansion of the corporate form of organization in the United States. By 1919, corporations employed more than 80% of the U.S. workforce. Perhaps more notably, prior to this time, the charters of most corporations in the United States included a unanimity rule through which corporate voting was essentially a direct democracy, the "equivalent of a New England town meeting" (Skeel, 2005, p. 77). At that time, at least in principle, there was no separation of ownership from control (Bradley & Wallenstein, 2006; Skeel, 2005). That would soon change. With the resulting increase in scale and complexity of American corporations, wrought by this new laissez faire environment, also came more opportunities for mischief (Skeel, 2005).

Berle and Means—The Modern Corporation and Private Property

In 1932, Adolph A. Berle and Gardiner C. Means published *The Modern Corporation and Private Property*. Shortly after, in a review, it was noted, "This book will perhaps rank with Adam Smith's *Wealth of Nations* as the first detailed description in admirably clear terms of the existence of a new economic epoch" (Frank, 1933, pp. 989–990). Some 50 years later, Stigler and Friedland (1983), in recounting this review, observed that "thus only a 'perhaps' separated Berle and Means from equality with [what had been referred to as] the most important book in the history of the world"[5] (p. 241).

While there has been extensive commentary on the contributions of Berle and Means' (1932) work (e.g., Berle, 1959; Bratton, 1989, 2001; Mizruchi, 2004; Stigler & Friedland, 1983), the basic proposition they set forth is easily recounted. Through the 19th century, the owners of business enterprises also comprised their management. The presiding officer of a given enterprise was usually its principal owner. Berle and Means (1932), however, reported that through the late 1800s and into the early 1900s, this concentration of large-scale ownership had substantially diminished. The large corporation was now owned by so many shareholders that individual shareholders rarely held a substantial fraction of corporations' stock. As the largest private businesses became incorporated, the ownership of these businesses often passed from private owners to a much more dispersed market ownership (Coffee, 2001; Roe, 1994).

In parallel with the diminution of ownership, influence through the redistribution of firms' equity was a transfer of direct oversight of firms' operations. Owners no longer presided over these firms; instead, professional managers increasingly held those roles. In this transition is the foundation of what became "agency theory." These professional managers, who control the firm, may not have interests that are consonant with those of the owners of the firm.

Mizruchi (2004; see also Bogle, 2005) explained that virtually all commentators have acknowledged this basic phenomenon underlying Berle and Means' thesis—the separation of ownership from control in large U.S. corporations—and the potential for mischief to which we have referred. Shleifer and Vishny (1997) underscored the gravity of the agency problem and noted that evidence for concomitant excesses is robust. Little could they, or any of us, predict the stark lessons of the agency problem that would accrue in the few years following their review.

The more formal development of agency theory would trail Berle and Means by more than 40 years. In addition to Berle and Means, other influential themes that informed agency theory emanated from the work of Alchian and Demsetz (1972, 1973), Coase (1937, 1960), Demsetz (1964, 1966, 1967, 1983), Holmstrom (1979), Ross (1973), Spence and Zeckhauser (1971), and Williamson (1964).[6] Most observers would agree, however, that Jensen and Meckling (1976) presided over the inauguration of agency theory (e.g., Denis, 2001; Walsh & Seward, 1990). As noted, a series of influential work followed describing potential interventions that might mitigate the agency problem (e.g., Fama, 1980; Fama & Jensen, 1983a, 1983b; Jensen & Ruback, 1983; Mizruchi, 1983)—independence, equity, and the market for corporate control. In the spirit of Walsh and Seward (1990), who deftly structured their seminally inclusive compendium along similar dimensions, we review each in turn.

Independence of Boards of Directors and Their Leadership Structures

From the earliest discussions of the fundamental agency problem, theorists were aware that boards of directors, as the stewards of the shareholders, would not be effective monitors of management if this relationship was tainted by self-interest (Fama, 1980; Fama & Jensen, 1983a, 1983b; Mizruchi, 1983; Jensen & Meckling, 1976). Jacobsen (1996), in what he referred to as the "classic articulation" on this point, cited Chief Justice Layton (1939) in *Guth v. Loft, Inc.*[7]

> Corporate officers and directors are not permitted to use their position of trust and confidence to further their private interests…A public policy, existing through the years, and derived from a profound knowledge of human characteristics and motives, has established a rule that demands of a corporate officer or director, peremptorily and inexorably, the most scrupulous observance of this duty, not only affirmatively to protect the interests of the corporation committed to his charge…The rule that requires an undivided and unselfish loyalty to the corporation demands that there shall be no conflict between duty and self-interest. (p. 985)

In subsequent years, conceptualization and empirical research addressing this issue of board independence focused on two elements of boards' structure. One of these is the composition of the board, specifically the extent to which the board is comprised of members who may be reasonably independent of firms' CEOs.[8] A second aspect is the leadership structure of the board. For this, the issue is the extent to which CEOs simultaneously serve as board chairperson, a structure that is believed to compromise the board's monitoring function.

The Composition of the Board of Directors

A fundamental responsibility of the board is to monitor the management of the firm (for compendia, see Dalton, Daily, Johnson, & Ellstrand, 1999; Deutsch, 2005; Finkelstein & Hambrick, 1996; Gervurtz, 2004; Hermalin & Weisbach, 2003; Johnson, Daily, & Ellstrand, 1996; Lorsch & MacIver, 1989; Zahra & Pearce, 1989; Zald, 1969). Some have repeatedly argued that the boards' willingness and ability to do so are partly or largely related to members' independence. An early example in an article entitled "Directors Who Do Not Direct" (Douglas, 1934; see also Karmel, 2005) underscores that point. For many years, board members were grouped into three categories: (a) inside directors, (b) affiliated directors,[9] and (c) outside directors (e.g., Daily, Johnson, & Dalton, 1999).

An *inside director* is an officer of the firm. An *affiliated director* is not in the employ of the firm, but has substantive linkages to the firm (e.g., a consultancy relationship, a relative of the CEO, a key supplier to the firm). *Outside directors* are not in the employ of the firm—other than in their capacity as directors—and have no substantive relationship with the firm. Inside directors and affiliated directors are not considered independent and their capacity to dispassionately evaluate the CEO has been subject to derision. Outside directors are independent.

These terms—inside, affiliated, and outside directors—are used less frequently today. With the passage of the Sarbanes-Oxley Act (SOX) of 2002[10] and the related guidelines of the listing exchanges (e.g., New York Stock Exchange [NYSE][11] and NASDAQ[12]), the expression "independent" director is now used to capture the notion of an outside director and "nonindependent" director now subsumes the notions of inside and affiliated directors.

Irrespective of these categories, there is no consensus that the differences in boards' independence, in the past or present, results in improved corporate performance. For some observers, the debate is basic: Boards, regardless of their composition, are *never* independent. For other observers, the difference in perspective is not a function of whether boards could, in principle, be more or less independent; rather, the issue is a collision of theories.

Boards are never independent? Consider, first, the former position, which Galbraith (2004) has rather succinctly captured, referring to the notion that boards can be independent as an "accepted fraud," and that "alleged directors in any sizable enterprise are fully subordinate to the management" (p. 28). This is an enduring view (e.g., Davis & Thompson, 1994; Frederickson, Hambrick, & Baumrin, 1988; Gilson & Kraakman, 1991; Hermalin & Weisbach, 1998; Shivdasani & Yermack, 1999). It has been suggested that board members, irrespective of any notion of independence, are selected—and retained—because they are sympathetic with the CEO (e.g., Solomon, 1978; Wade, O'Reilly, & Chandratat, 1990; Westphal & Zajac, 1995).

Even when directors may have been independent early in their board tenure, some observers are not convinced that this disposition will persist. Bhagat and Black (1999), for example, suggested that "independent directors often turn out to be lapdogs rather than watchdogs" (p. 4). Some have also observed that "at the end of the day, most independent directors get neutralized in one fashion or another" (Hermalin & Weisbach, 1998, p. 88; see also Smale, Patricof, Henderson, Marcus, & Johnson, 1995). A promising approach that might have forestalled such neutralization assessed independence in a novel way (e.g., Boeker, 1992; Daily & Dalton, 1995; Wade et al., 1990). Referred to as "interdependence," the concern is not whether a director is employed by or affiliated with the firm. Instead, the emphasis is on when a board member joined the firm. If board members are appointed to the board under the tenure of the current CEO, they would be considered interdependent, as they may have some sense of loyalty to the CEO, who almost certainly played a major role in appointing them. Board members appointed by a prior CEO, however, are presumably less loyal to the current CEO and are accordingly more independent. This supposition, however, has received very little empirical attention. Alternatively, Sutton (2004) proposed that *no* director is independent after he or she has served five years or more on any given board. It has also been suggested that board members having substantial wealth associated with their board service (e.g., salary, stock options, restricted shares) may be increasingly more dependent as that wealth increases (e.g., Bebchuk & Fried, 2004; Dalton, 2005b). If so, this is a troubling observation, as the compensation of directors has continued to increase dramatically in the last several years (e.g., Conference Board, 2005a; Cook, 2005; National Association of Corporate Directors, 2006; Sherman & Sterling, LLP, 2005; Spencer Stuart, 2005b).

Beyond this, one series of research underscores the abilities of CEOs and boards to moderate the influence of "independent" directors. Walsh and Seward (1990), for example, provided an outstanding overview of the "tactics" available for neutralizing internal control mechanisms. Westphal and colleagues (e.g., Westphal, 1998, 1999; Westphal, Boivie, & Ching, 2006; Westphal & Khanna, 2003; Westphal & Milton, 2000; Westphal & Stern, 2006, 2007; Westphal & Zajac, 1994, 1995), too, have provided fascinating insights into how "independence," often perceived by management and the board as outlying, deviant behavior, can be moderated. Examples of these approaches include cooptation, personal and social influence, reciprocity, demographic consistency in selection, and between-firm referrals that are consonant with prevailing board predispositions and cultures.[13]

Other dynamics may abate one's confidence in boards' independence. Consider, for example, the practice of interlocking directorates (see Mizruchi, 2004, for an extended discussion; see also Domhoff, 2006; Mizruchi, 1996). Justice Brandeis (1914) provided an early opinion of this tactic: "The practice of interlocking directorates is the root of many evils. It offends laws human and divine" (Mizruchi, 2004, p. 35). Perhaps, but many will agree that having a reciprocal interlock (wherein an officer of Company A is on the board of Company B and an officer of Company B is on the board of Company A) may not constitute best practice with regard to independence. Suppose, further, that these board members are CEOs of their respective companies (e.g., Core, Holthausen, & Larcker, 1999; Fich & White, 2005; Hallock, 1997).[14] In those circumstances, one of these CEOs may be uncomfortable judging the other. There may be a related independence issue with CEOs serving on boards, irrespective of reciprocal interlocks, particularly because CEOs comprise the largest category of board members (Spencer Stuart, 2005b). Again, the issue is whether a CEO on a given outside board is willing to effectively monitor another CEO, who is probably the chairperson of that board.

A Collision of Theories

Even for those who find the "boards are *never* independent" perspective to be a bit exaggerated, there remains a serious disconnect in the conceptual/theoretical foundations on which one might rely with regard to board independence. Those with concerns about the independence of boards would suggest, for example, that (a) inside directors report directly to the CEO, and that (b) their positions, salary, and perquisites are attributable to the CEO. Accordingly, no sensible inside director would contradict or criticize the CEO/board chairperson (e.g., Baysinger & Hoskisson, 1990; Weisbach, 1988). Moreover, affiliated directors, whose very positions on the board and whose business relationships with the firm are essentially held hostage by the CEO, are also incapable of disinterested judgment (e.g., Wade et al., 1990; Westphal & Zajac, 1995). Accordingly, in the interests of independence, the number of inside and affiliated directors on the board should be minimized.[15]

A reliance on resource dependence (e.g., Pfeffer & Salancik, 1978; Selznick, 1949; Zald, 1969) or a resource-based perspective (e.g., Barney, 1991; Barney et al., 2001; Wernerfelt, 1984), however, may lead some theorists to a disparate view, and a concomitantly different strategy. Consider the interlocking CEO board membership example. As noted, this is a threat to independence under agency theory tenets. By the standards of resource dependence, however, it is a classic expression of establishing collective structures for managing enterprise dependencies (Pfeffer & Salancik, 1978[16]; see especially chapter 7). Consider, also, the example regarding CEOs and senior officers serving on others' boards. Here again, an agency perspective may consider this a threat to independence, an unrealistic expectation that officers with these credentials will criticize others with similar portfolios and responsibilities serving on these boards. By contrast, the networking potential and innovation diffusion potential of such arrangements would likely be highly valued by the standards of resource dependence (e.g., Booth & Deli, 1996; Davis, 1991; Davis & Greve, 1997; Geletkanycz & Hambrick, 1997; Stearns & Mizruchi, 1993).

A brief review of the consequences of SOX and the requirements of the listing exchanges may provide some texture for another conceptual disconnect. Since the passage of SOX, the number of inside and affiliated directors has decreased dramatically. On average, the number of inside directors, senior officers serving on the board, has decreased from slightly over three inside directors on the board to 1.65 (Daily, Dalton, & Certo, 2004).[17] Because all CEOs serve on the board and are inside directors, we know that there is, on average, less than one (.65) non-CEO director on boards. Representation of affiliated directors is down radically as well. In 2001, for example, 39% of boards had at least half their membership comprised of inside and affiliated members; that percentage is now 17.3% (National Association of Corporate Directors, 2005). Lastly, many of these inside and affiliated board members have not been replaced; over a similar period, the total number of directors on the average board has decreased from 13.3 to 10.7 (Spencer Stuart, 2005a).[18]

As noted, many observers would suggest that these changes toward board independence through the reduction in inside and affiliated directors are utterly consistent with an expectation for improved board monitoring. Paradoxically, others would argue that, because of these changes, boards have never been more dependent (Dalton, 2005b; Lorsch, 2005[19]). Inside and affiliated directors did have one element in common—the advantage of firm-specific and/or industry-specific knowledge/information. Granted, they were often officers of the firm, consultants, former officers, suppliers, customers, bankers, and attorneys, but they were all well acquainted with the firm and with the industry.

That directors of these types are currently and decidedly out of favor will be troublesome to those who embrace the resource-based view. As noted by Barney (1991), one means of establishing a competitive advantage is through "the training, experience, judgment, intelligence, relationships, and insight" (p. 101) of individuals within the organization, presumably including senior officers and board members.

What, then, is the inflection point between these theories that do not, at once, seem complementary? The spate of independent directors has many advantages—especially through an agency lens—but their lack of firm-specific, industry-specific knowledge places them in jeopardy. As directors, on whom will they depend for the information necessary to dispatch their stewardship responsibilities? The foremost source will be the management of the firm, especially CEOs in their roles as members of the board, and probably its chair. Surowiecki (2004) pointed out that the most efficacious approach to bias people's judgment is to render them dependent for information. With less knowledgeable board members, then, are some CEOs enabled to leverage this opportunity to provide purposefully selective information?

These are nontrivial discrepancies. Perhaps a review of the literature addressing the relationship between the composition of boards of directors and firm performance will provide some foundation for assessing which arguments are best grounded.

Composition of the Board and Firm Performance

The composition of boards of directors is addressed by a distinguished tradition of research, extended discussion, narrative reviews, and meta-analyses. Fortunately, we can easily group a summary of this body of work into two categories. In the first group are those who suggest that there is no evidence of systematic relationships between board composition and corporate financial performance (Bhagat & Black, 1999, 2002; Coles, McWilliams, & Sen, 2001; Dalton, Daily, Ellstrand, & Johnson, 1998; Hermalin & Weisbach, 2003; Kaufman & Englander, 2005; Walsh & Seward, 1990). A second group (Rhoades, Rechner, & Sundaramurthy, 2000; Wagner, Stimpert, & Fubara, 1998) reports very modest, if any, relationships between board composition and some aspects of financial performance.[20] Three of these studies are extensive meta-analyses (Dalton et al., 1998; Rhoades et al., 2000; Wagner et al., 1998) comprised of some 259 samples with a combined "n" size of over 61,400.[21]

At least two levels of consistency are present in all of these reviews and discussions. First, they provide no evidence of systematic relationships between these variables. Second, most of the authors have not forsaken their commitment to affirm these relationships. Rather, time after time, we observed future-oriented discussions that emphasize other factors and moderating influences that might have better informed the relationships of interest. Accordingly, we discuss a few other aspects of this board composition/performance relationship that researchers may consider in future iterations of related work.

For instance, a misspecification issue may exist. It has been demonstrated that there are no fewer than 19 different operationalizations of "board composition" reflected in the extant literature (Daily et al., 1999). There were three operationalizations of inside director proportion, eight of outside director proportion, and eight for affiliated director proportion. Notably, through a structural equation confirmatory factor analysis, only four psychometrically sound factors could be identified,[22] and six of the individual measurements of director "proportion" had to be eliminated from the solution. Accordingly, some imprecision may have been introduced in prior operationalizations that likely hindered our collective ability to more robustly statistically combine and assess the prior literature.

Moreover, there are contemporary dynamics of board composition that may importantly inform aspects of independence that the current literature does not reflect. Consider, for example, the proliferation of "emeritus" directors about whom very little is known (for an overview, see Dalton & Daily, 2003).[23] Are they independent? Whether nominally so or otherwise, would recently appointed emeritus directors feel some gratitude toward the CEO and/or the board for having declared them "directors for life"?

Another example is the executive committee of the board. Under SOX guidelines and those of the listing exchanges (e.g., NYSE, NASDAQ), the audit, compensation, and nominating/corporate governance committees must be totally comprised of (and derivatively chaired by) independent directors. Those guidelines, however, do not apply to other committees (e.g., environmental and public policy, finance, M&A, technology) of the board. This is usually of little consequence, because relatively few companies have established these committees. The clear exception is the executive committee; in fact, 46% of *Fortune* 500 firms have executive committees (Dalton & Dalton, 2006). Consider, for example, that an executive committee could be comprised of three people,[24] none of whom need be independent.

The authority of executive committees is also crucial to the notion of independence, and varies greatly across firms. Consider, for example, Procter & Gamble, for which the "board may…limit or qualify the powers of the committee at any time, and may rescind any action of the [executive] committee."[25] Alternatively, consider the authority of the executive committee for American Express: "All acts done and powers conferred by the Executive Committee shall be deemed to be and may be certified as being done or conferred under authority of the Board of Directors."[26]

The point is not that these firms, or any of the hundreds that we could have cited, would leverage these enablements. It is notable, however, that an executive committee could be configured in such a way to render the board "independence" issue moot. Obviously, the elements attendant to an executive committee may inform board leadership structure as well.

Board Leadership Structure

The second key element of board independence is the manner by which the roles of CEO and chairperson of the board are structured.[27] In one option, referred to as "CEO duality," one person holds the positions of both CEO and board chairperson; alternatively, these roles may be held separately by two individuals (e.g., Dalton et al., 1998; Davidson, Jiraporn, Kim, & Nemec, 2004; Finkelstein & D'Aveni, 1994). Even near the onset of agency theory, Fama and Jensen (1983a, 1983b; see also Mizruchi, 1983) were uncomfortable with the combined structure and argued that it would compromise the ability of the board to reasonably monitor the CEO.

The basic issue is the awkwardness attendant to a board's evaluation of the CEO's practices, policies, and performance when the CEO serves as the presiding officer of the board (e.g., Jensen, 1993, 2005b; MacAvoy & Millstein, 2003). This has been noted as the functional equivalent of the "CEO grading his own homework" (Brickley, Coles, & Jarrell, 1997, p. 190). Others, too, have endorsed a similar perspective and strongly advocate that the roles of CEO and board chairperson should not be combined (Coombes & Wong, 2004; Monks & Minow, 2004). In fact, it has been suggested that a fundamental omission of SOX was its silence on a requirement to separate the CEO/chairperson roles (Green, 2004).

Others, however, remain unconvinced (Baliga, Moyer, & Rao, 1996; Daily & Dalton, 1997; Finkelstein & D'Aveni, 1994; Lorsch & Zelleke, 2005). Brickley and colleagues (1997) suggested, for example, that a board's optimal choice to adopt a dual or unitary board leadership structure is not theoretically obvious. Consider, for instance, unity of command, a timeless concept advocating that any person in an organization should be accountable to one, and only one, individual (see, e.g., Finkelstein & D'Aveni, 1994 for an extended discussion).

The provenance for unity of command is impressive, varied, and long-standing. In an admittedly different context, for example, we learn that "No man can serve two masters" (Mathew 6:24). In the *Federalist,* Alexander Hamilton (1788) enthusiastically endorsed the notion of unity of command (see Brickley et al., 1997, pp. 195–196). A more recent articulation of this perspective can be observed in the United States Marine Corps Officer Training Manual, in which it is noted, "Unity of command means that all the forces are under one responsible commander. It requires having a single commander with the requisite authority to direct all forces employed in pursuit of a unified purpose" (Dalton, 2005a).[28]

Clearly, the separation of CEO and chairperson of the board roles does not have this character. In that case, there is not a single presiding officer; there are two. With this, there may be the incalculable loss of having a single leader with whom both internal and external parties can interact. In such cases, everyone knows who is in charge and, critically, who is accountable (e.g., Brickley et al., 1997; Lorsch & Zelleke, 2005). On the subject of the separate CEO/board chairperson structure, Brickley and colleagues (1997, p. 194; with credit to Alchian & Demsetz, 1972), raise an interesting question: "Who monitors the monitor?" Must we now be concerned about separate chairpersons' leverage to extract inappropriate rents as a function of their position? Perhaps a review of the empirical evidence will inform a choice of CEO duality or the separate structure.

Leadership Structure of the Board and Firm Performance

An impressive body of literature, narrative reviews, and meta-analyses is dedicated to the issue of CEO duality. Notably, this work can be easily and uniformly summarized. There is no evidence of substantive, systematic relationships between corporate financial performance and board leadership structure (Baliga et al., 1996; Boyd, 1995; Brickley et al., 1997; Coles et al., 2001; Dalton et al., 1998; Faleye, 2006; Kang & Zardhoohi, 2005).[29]

While this level of consistency is unusual in any literature, we should note that none of the literature on which we have relied in this section has dismissed the conceptual/theoretical basis for such a relationship. Instead, there is continuing attention to a host of other variables that might moderate/mediate such relationships and inform under what circumstances we might more robustly observe them.

It that spirit, we discuss some elements that might facilitate such efforts. Under the broad rubric of "independence," there is some potential for misspecification that, if addressed, may inform future research. Consider, for example, that a leadership structure with a separate CEO and board chairperson is *not* necessarily indicative of independence. In fact, in the clear majority of cases (67%), the person who is the "separate" board chairperson is the former CEO of the company (Spencer Stuart, 2005b). Actually, even the "67%" is understated, because the misspecification is broader yet. Not only are these "independent" chairpersons former CEOs, they are also company founders, former CEOs of acquired/merged companies, or persons otherwise connected to the focal company beyond their service as directors and members of the board (Monks & Minow, 2004).

Consider the implications of this specification issue: Of the firms that comprise the S&P 500, 29% have a nominally separate CEO/board chair structure (e.g., two persons are serving in these roles). Of these, though, "only 9% of the boards…have a truly independent chair" (Spencer Stuart, 2005a, p. 9). Obviously, then, to the extent to which an interest in "independence" from an agency perspective has driven much of the research in this space, it has been largely misspecified in that research.

Even without relying on an agency perspective, a substantive problem exists. Consider, again, the notion of unity of command. Given the statistics as shared, we may now have one of the great ironies of corporate governance and a distressingly common scenario. When the separate chairperson is not independent, potential agency issues exist, but unity of command is wholly compromised as well. Not only would there be confusion about the authority vested in the chairperson as compared to the CEO, but there would also be uncertainty about the influence of the former CEO—now chairperson—on the new CEO. This may be perilously close to the worst case scenario.

Consider the predicament in which the board finds itself. Not only must it manage an agency relationship with the firm's CEO, but in many cases, it is subject to another agency relationship with a prior CEO/founder of the firm.[30] Additionally, a former CEO in the role of board chairperson may not be independent in a formal sense.[31] This would signify the addition of another inside member of the board, something that, consistent with our prior discussion, boards are trying to minimize. This would also mean that the new chairperson could not serve on the audit, compensation, or nominating/corporate governance committees of the board.

One additional aspect of contemporary board governance must be considered in the design of a new generation of research regarding board leadership structure: the role of the lead or presiding director. Our discussion here will be necessarily brief. While there is some commentary,[32] we are not aware of any research on the topic. As noted, approximately 70% of larger publicly traded corporations (e.g., *Fortune* 500; S&P 500) have retained the combined CEO/board chairperson structure. Notably, 96% of those that have retained the dual structure have appointed a lead director, less often referred to as a "presiding director." This individual would have, for example, the responsibility of chairing executive sessions,[33] serving as a liaison between the independent directors of the board and the firm's management, and establishing the agenda for board meetings. In principle, then, we can envision the lead director as a person to moderate some of the agency concerns implicit in a structure whereby the CEO is also the board chairperson. We are not, however, persuaded. The roles of chiefs of staff, various liaison officers, and their equivalents are commonplace, and we should not dismiss their influence. Whether those positions provide true oversight for their associated presiding officer(s) in a corporate governance context, however, is a separate matter that remains an open question.

It may be fair to say that previous research has not captured many of these elements. For us, then, agency perspectives related to separating the CEO from the board chairperson remain decidedly unsettled.

Equity Ownership

A second area of corporate governance research that has been largely framed in the agency theory tradition is the relationship between the ownership structure of the firm and financial performance. Agency theorists developed this ownership structure/performance relationship in the 1970s and 1980s (Fama & Jensen, 1983a, 1983b; Jensen & Meckling, 1976). In fact, Jensen and Meckling (1976) referred to agency theory as "a theory of ownership" (p. 309). Agency-based research suggests that the equity owned by both insiders (e.g., officers and directors of the firm) and outsiders (e.g., institutional investors, large blockholders) may importantly influence firm performance. Summarizing this stream of research, Dalton, Daily, Certo, and Roengpitya (2003) referred to two perspectives regarding the effects of equity and firm performance: *Alignment* refers to the effects of insider ownership, and *control* refers to the effects of outsider ownership. As will be developed, the alignment and control foci are neither independent nor are they necessarily complementary. In the following sections, we review the theoretical rationale underlying these relationships as well as the empirical evidence related to the relationship between the several ownership categories and firm performance.

Inside Ownership and Firm Performance

Insider equity. Early in the development and refinement of agency theory, Jensen and Meckling (1976) suggested that equity ownership aids in aligning the interests of executives with those of shareholders. According to this perspective, the utility of managers will at times diverge from the preferences of shareholders. Perhaps chief among these diverging interests is the role of risk-taking (e.g., Beatty & Zajac, 1994; Wright, Ferris, Sarin, & Awasthi, 1996). Executives with much of their human capital (and, in some cases, financial capital) tied up in their firms are apt to behave in a risk-averse manner. In contrast, shareholders may diversify their holdings across multiple firms, resulting in a more risk-neutral position.

Jensen and Meckling (1976) proposed a positive relationship between manager ownership and firm performance as a means for closing the risk gap. They suggested that as executives' ownership stakes decline, their "fractional claim on outcomes falls," resulting in executives increasingly apt "to appropriate larger amounts of the corporate resources in the form of perquisites" (p. 313).[34] While Jensen and Meckling focused primarily on perquisite consumption as a risk of decreased insider equity holdings, Demsetz and Lehn (1985, p. 1156) suggested that managers with low levels of equity may prove more inclined to shirk their duties.[35] Similarly, Shliefer and Vishny (1997; see also Jensen, 1986[36]) highlighted other, more costly outcomes such as investing free cash flow into diversifying activities and pet projects beyond rational limits, activities which generally are not in shareholders' interests.

This proposed and intuitively appealing relationship between insider equity and firm performance provided a theoretical foundation for a substantial body of empirical work. Demsetz and Lehn (1985) provided one of the earliest rigorous empirical examinations of the relationship between insider ownership and firm performance. Consistent with the premises of agency theory, they suggested that the relationship between insider equity and firm performance is interdependent. Their research, accounting for this endogeneity, revealed no systematic relationship between insider ownership structure and firm performance.

Another influential study proposed a curvilinear relationship between insider ownership and performance. Morck, Shleifer, and Vishny (1988) suggested that managerial equity ownership is beneficial at low levels, but negative at higher levels. They reasoned that as insider ownership increases, it affords managers greater power that may facilitate their entrenchment.[37] Specifically, they found that when managers own between zero and 5% and greater than 25% of outstanding shares, there is a positive relationship between ownership and performance, as measured as Tobin's Q. In the intermediate ownership range of 5% to 25% of insider ownership, the relationship is negative.

In recent years, alternative methodologies have further assessed the relationship between insider equity and firm performance. Dalton and colleagues (Dalton, Daily, Certo, & Roengpitya, 2003), for example, relied on meta-analysis to quantitatively summarize extant research and reported negligible relationships (see also Bhagat, Black, & Blair, 2004; Hermalin & Weisbach, 1988). This result is consistent with another meta-analysis (Sundaramurthy, Rhoades, & Rechner, 2005) that reported no relationship between executive holdings and corporate financial performance. Relying on panel data, Himmelberg, Hubbard, and Palia (1999), too, concluded that there is no discernible relationship between managerial equity ownership and firm performance.[38]

Demsetz and Villalonga (2001) investigated the concept of endogeneity in these relationships, earlier proposed and tested by Demsetz and Lehn (1985). Relying on a two-stage, least-squares methodology, they, too, found no statistically significant relationship between management equity ownership and firm performance. In addition, they examined potential nonlinearity in this relationship and found no support for this perspective.[39]

Another aspect of insider equity may forever cloud the agency theory-based linkage between the equity holdings of officers and board members and the performance of the firm. Prior to SOX, the basic notion of "ownership" of this equity was not always what it seemed. In many companies, both high-ranking officers and directors were subject to a requirement to hold a certain level of equity in the firm. Even so, these officers and board members did not directly purchase this equity. Instead, the firm loaned officers and board members sufficient funds to fulfill the equity requirement. Furthermore, the firm subsequently forgave these loans (e.g., Dalton & Daily, 2001; Henderson & Spindler, 2005; Knutt, 2005). SOX Section 402, however, explicitly forbids companies to extend such loans to officers and directors. Equity obtained in this manner does not reflect the spirit of linking shareholder interests with those of the officers and directors of the firm.

Executive compensation. Similar to the relationship between insider equity and firm performance, agency theory provides a theoretical foundation for the study of the relationship between executive compensation and firm performance. As Jensen and Murphy (1990) noted, "Agency theory predicts that compensation policy will tie the agent's expected utility to the principal's objective...therefore, agency theory predicts that CEO compensation policies will depend on changes in shareholder wealth" (p. 242). Consistent with this theoretical rationale, a substantial literature has examined this relationship. In one of the earliest comprehensive examinations of CEO incentives, Jensen and Murphy (1990) found that CEO wealth changes by $3.25 for every $1,000 change in shareholder wealth. In a meta-analysis of this relationship, Tosi, Werner, Katz, and Gomez-Mejia (2000) confirmed Jensen and Murphy's findings, noting that firm performance accounts for approximately 5% of the variance in total CEO compensation.

In recent years, the popularity of equity-based compensation, particularly stock options, as a device for linking managerial and investor incentives has gained importance (e.g., Conyon, 2006). Consistent with agency principles, higher equity-based components of compensation should help align the interests of executives with those of shareholders. In fact, Hall (2000) suggested, "Options are the best compensation mechanism we have for getting managers to act in ways that ensure the long-term success of their companies and the well-being of their workers and stockholders" (p. 122).

Several studies have supported the benefits of equity-based compensation (for an excellent review, see Core, Guay, & Larcker, 2003). Mehran (1995), for example, found a positive relationship between firm performance and the proportion of equity-based executive compensation. Moreover, studies have supported a positive market reaction to equity-based executive compensation. Morgan and Poulsen (2001), for example, found that the stock market reacts positively to the announcement of performance-sensitive compensation plans. In related research, Certo, Daily, Cannella, and Dalton (2003) noted a positive relationship between CEO stock option compensation and IPO firm valuations (see also Sanders & Boivie, 2004).

Other work, however, has not been uniformly supportive of an agency-prescribed relationship. Several recent studies have highlighted the potentially deleterious effects of stock options. Bergstresser and Philippon (2006), for example, found that the use of discretionary accruals to manipulate corporate earnings was more pronounced when the CEO's total compensation package was tied more closely to stock and stock options. In a related study, Burns and Kedia (2006) noted a relationship between the sensitivity of the CEO's option portfolio to stock price and the propensity to misreport corporate earnings.

Denis, Hanouna, and Sarin (2006, p. 467; see also Becher, Campbell, & Frye, 2005; O'Connor, Priem, Coombs, & Gilley, 2006) referred to the "dark side" of incentive compensation in a study that established a relationship between such compensation and securities fraud allegations. Others, too, have noted a series of arguably untoward activities that seem to be related to incentive-based compensation, including the timing of options grants (Aboody & Kasznik, 2000; Callaghan, Saly, & Subramanian, 2004; Lie, 2005; Yermack, 1997), options backdating (Heron & Lie, 2007; Narayanan & Seyhun, 2005), and options repricing (Carter & Lynch, 2004; Chen, 2004; Chidambaran & Prabhala, 2003; Daily, Certo, & Dalton, 2002).

Taken together, then, the evidence regarding CEO compensation as a monitoring mechanism remains unsettled. Bebchuk and Fried (2003) commented on the state of empirical findings, noting that "the problem with current arrangements…is that the generous compensation provided executives is linked only weakly to managerial performance. This pay-performance disconnect is puzzling from an optimal contracting view" (p. 82). Based on extant findings, some scholars have commented that executive compensation may be more a part of the agency problem than a resolution to it (Bebchuk & Fried, 2003; see also Finkelstein & Hambrick, 1989; Jensen & Warner, 1988; Sanders, 2001; Stultz, 1988).

Outside Ownership and Firm Performance

Some have also applied agency theory to examinations of the relationship between outsider equity and firm performance. As previously noted, Berle and Means (1932) observed an increasing separation of ownership and control, whereby dispersed outside shareholders lacked the incentive, and arguably the ability, to effectively monitor management.[40] In contrast, more concentrated ownership provides both the incentive and power for shareholders to monitor management (Shleifer & Vishny, 1986). Several categories of external equity holders may be in the best position to exercise such influence.

Blockholders. Shleifer and Vishny (1986) suggested that the presence of large-block equity holders positively influences firm market values.[41] Empirical evidence supporting this proposed relationship, however, remains decidedly mixed. Mikkelson and Ruback (1985) found positive excess returns surrounding the announcement date of outsiders acquiring large equity positions in firms (see also Holderness & Sheehan, 1985).[42] In contrast, McConnell and Servaes (1990) found no relationship between blockholder ownership and Tobin's Q. A recent investigation reported no association between blockholder ownership and prior or subsequent firm value (Thomsen, Pedersen, & Kvist, 2006).

A recent meta-analysis (Dalton, Daily, Certo, & Roengpitya, 2003) may best capture the uncertain nature of the relationships between blockholder equity and firm performance. The authors noted several positive relationships with firm performance (e.g., Tobin's Q, industry-adjusted return on equity [ROE], shareholder returns), as well as several negative relationships between blockholder equity and firm performance (e.g., return on assets, ROE, return on sales). The magnitude of these relationships, however, was not of practical consequence. An earlier review, too, concluded that concentrated ownership was not associated with firm performance (Walsh & Seward, 1990).

An interesting complication that potentially affects research results is a lack of consensus regarding how to capture the concept of a blockholder. While the baseline for such a determination is the 5% equity ownership rule used by the SEC, *who* is included as a blockholder is not uniform across studies. Demsetz and Villalonga (2001), for example, noted that blockholders may include executives, directors, and/or independent outsiders. The inclusion or exclusion of a given individual or group can dramatically affect study findings. As noted by Bhagat and colleagues (2004), "Ownership of a large block of shares by an officer or director might have a different effect from ownership of a similarly large block by a pension fund or mutual fund" (p. 3). Combining different categories of blockholders, then, renders interpretation of empirical findings problematic (e.g., Holderness, 2003).

Another interesting complication is attendant with blockholder ownership studies framed from an agency theory perspective. Shleifer and Vishny (1997) highlighted the potential for large blockholders to extract rents from smaller shareholders. Villalonga and Amit (2006, p. 387) referred to this situation as the "Agency Problem II." Large-block shareholders may, for example, install and entrench ill-qualified executives or directors. Gilson (2006) succinctly summarized this conflict suggesting that "Public shareholders will prefer a controlling shareholder as long as the benefits from the reduction in managerial agency costs exceed the detriment of the controlling shareholder's extraction of private benefits"[43] (p. 1652).

Here, too, then, the evidence regarding the relationship between blockholder ownership and firm performance is inconclusive. As Holderness (2003) noted, "First, it has not been definitely established whether the impact of blockholders on firm value is positive or negative. Second, there is little evidence that the impact of blockholders on firm value—whatever that impact may be—is pronounced" (p. 9).

Another interesting aspect of blockholder equity for which there is no consensus is the impact of family equity holdings (e.g., Miller & Le Breton-Miller, 2005a,b, 2006a,b). As noted by Villalonga and Amit (2006; see also Anderson & Reeb, 2003; Claessens, Djankov, Fan, & Lang, 2002; Cronquist & Nilsson, 2003; McConaughy, Walker, Henderson, & Mishra, 1998), "The evidence on this point is scant and inconclusive" (p. 387). Villalonga and Amit (2006) underscore a potential conflict within the tenets of agency theory. One perspective is that large equity holdings by founding families would mitigate the fundamental agency problem because of families' obvious incentives to monitor firms' management (Berle & Means, 1932; Jensen & Meckling, 1976); however, large equity positions by founding family members may also facilitate the expropriation of wealth from minority shareholders in favor of controlling shareholders. We would also note the greater potential for mischief when the founding family holds large equity positions and a family member is the presiding officer of the firm, or the chairperson of its board, or both.

Institutional investors.   Another category of external equity holders that has been subject to considerable academic scrutiny is that of institutional investors. Institutional investors are equity holders who file 13F SEC filings and include bank trusts, insurance companies, investment companies (mutual funds), investment advisors (brokerage firms), pension funds, and endowments with at least $100 million in equity (Bushee, 1998; Grinstein & Michaely, 2005). Academic interest in the influence of institutional investors on firm performance reflects the increasing importance of institutional ownership, particularly in the United States. While 55 years ago, institutional investors owned a modest 3% of U.S. common stocks, these same owners now own 66% of U.S. equities (Bogle, 2005). In addition, institutional ownership accounts for approximately 75% of the trading in equities listed on the NYSE (Karmel, 2004).

This category of equity holders has been proposed as a resolution to the agency problem. Pound (1988), for example, has suggested that institutional investors may monitor managers more effectively than other equity holders because they have greater expertise and can monitor at a lower cost than individual shareholders. As compared to individual equity holders, whether internal or external, institutional investors are typically far better positioned to build concentrated ownership positions in their portfolio firms. Moreover, institutional investors rely on several coordinating mechanisms (e.g., Institutional Shareholder Services, Investor Responsibility Research Center) to enable their monitoring effectiveness; access to these mechanisms may improve monitoring even when the ownership stakes of these investors are not particularly large (Grinstein & Michaely, 2005).[44] Importantly, institutional investors often have access to critical inside information not available to other investors.[45]

Not all observers are as enthusiastic about the efficacy of institutional investors' monitoring. In contrast to other investors, institutional investors serve as fiduciaries for their clients. As agents for their own clients, institutional investors are subject to a latent divergence of interests that may arise because of their own agency relationships, thus potentially influencing their investment patterns (Gompers & Metrick, 2001).[46] In fact, Bogle (2005) suggested that "the massive substitution of fiduciary ownership for personal ownership is one of the major challenges of twenty-first-century capitalism" (p. 128). One commonly mentioned disadvantage of the nature of this relationship is that institutional investors may act more as traders than investors and, thus, encourage myopic behavior among portfolio firms (e.g., Graves & Haddock, 1990).[47] Strine (2006) summarized these complex issues by suggesting that "the conflicts facing institutional investors are not only deep, but also diverse" (p. 1765).

A number of scholars have examined the extent to which institutional investor equity and firm performance are linked (for overviews, see Blair, 1995; Kang & Sorensen, 1999; Zeitlin, 1974). Gompers and Metrick (2001), for example, found a positive relationship between institutional investor holdings and firm performance. In framing their study, they suggested two alternative explanations for this relationship: (a) institutional investors are smarter than other investors are, or (b) the growth in the institutional share of the market created an increase in demand (and, subsequently prices) for the types of stocks favored by institutions.[48] Based on their findings, the authors concluded that the increase is due primarily to the demand for shares favored by institutions; they did not find evidence to support the claim that institutional investors are "smarter" than other types of investors.

Supportive studies notwithstanding, based on a meta-analysis of the relationship between institutional investor equity holdings and firm financial performance, Dalton, Daily et al. (2003) concluded that there is no positive relationship between institutional ownership and either market- or accounting-based measures of performance (see also Sundaramurthy et al., 2005 for similar results).[49] In summarizing the body of evidence, Bainbridge (2003) suggested that there was no support for a relationship between firm performance and institutional ownership.

As compared to blockholder equity studies, scholars have focused on distinguishing different categories of institutional investors. Such distinctions are important because various types of institutional investors may exhibit differing investment preferences and objectives (e.g., Grinstein & Michaely, 2005). Brickley, Lease, and Smith (1988), for example, distinguished between "pressure-resistant," "pressure-sensitive," and "pressure-indeterminate" institutional investors to reflect that different investors have alternative propensities to monitor management. Pressure-resistant institutional investors are most likely to monitor firm management and advance shareholder-oriented policies and actions. Support for the monitoring role of institutional investors is found in an inverse relationship between pressure-resistant institutional investor equity and CEO compensation (David, Kochhar, & Levitas, 1998), as well as a greater propensity to challenge management on antitakeover amendments (Brickley et al., 1988). Moreover, pressure-resistant institutional investors are likely to pressure management outside of its risk comfort zone, as evidenced by the positive association between pressure-resistant institutional investor equity and firm innovation (Kochhar & David, 1996). Similar situations may influence other outcomes as well.

Bushee (1998), for example, created a number of measures of institutional investor portfolios to account for different investment time horizons.[50] He found that dedicated institutional investors (e.g., those that exhibit low portfolio turnover, concentrated ownership, and low trading sensitivity to earnings) are associated with more long-term firm outcomes (e.g., research and development [R&D] spending).[51] In addition, executives are more likely to reduce R&D when institutions with high levels of portfolio turnover hold large stakes in the firm. Research conducted by Hoskisson and colleagues supports these findings. Hoskisson, Hitt, Johnson, and Grossman (2002), for example, found that pension funds take a longer term view and, thus, their equity holdings in firms are related to greater innovation. Alternatively, they found that mutual fund managers take a shorter term view and are much more likely to turn over their investments in firms. They search for short-term returns. Similarly, Tihanyi, Johnson, Hoskisson, and Hitt (2003) found that both pension funds' and mutual funds' equity investments were related to broader investments in international diversification, but the investments by these two types of institutional investors were made for different reasons, still in keeping with the short- and long-term concerns. These findings suggest that institutions with high levels of portfolio turnover may encourage myopic behavior on the part of the executives of the portfolio firms; yet, some institutions take a longer-term perspective and encourage appropriate executive behaviors.

Some have also argued that many institutional investors have little interest in the oversight of those companies in which they hold equity positions (e.g.,

Bogle, 2005; Hawley & Williams, 2000; Kim & Nofsinger, 2006). Kim and Nofsinger (2006), for example, noted that some 40% of equity funds annually turned over their portfolios at a rate greater than 100%. Hawley and Williams (2000) suggested that many institutional investors have adopted an indexing approach in which the performance of a broad cross section of companies rather than attention to any given company drives their investment strategy. In either case—high portfolio turnover or indexing—the effects of attempts to discipline individual companies are, at best, modest.

Private pension funds (the holdings of which greatly exceed those of public pension funds), too, may have little interest in assuming an activist role. Corporations engage private pension funds to manage their pension programs. At some risk of understatement, an activist posture towards a client company by a given private pension fund will likely undermine its relationship with that firm. Beyond that, such a posture is unlikely to provide a strong testimonial for other corporations to choose that pension fund for its services.

Also, these various funds (e.g., mutual funds, pension funds) are subject to a host of regulations that restrict the amount of equity that they can hold in any given company, as well as their ability to network with other funds (e.g., Camera, 2005; Hawley & Williams, 2000; Kim & Nofsinger, 2006; Rehman, 2006; Strine, 2006). While diversification guidelines may be admirable, they have the effect of reducing the potential influence that might otherwise have been brought to bear against companies in which these regulated funds hold equity.

Setting all of these points aside, however, there remains a substantial moral hazard associated with adopting an activism strategy. Given the obvious conjointment of institutional investors and large-scale corporations (75% of the equity in *Fortune* 500 firms is held by institutions; Karmel, 2004), what is the expected outcome when a given fund decides to pursue a more aggressive oversight role? If the campaign is successful, all funds holding equity in the "target" firm enjoy the benefits, but only the activist fund bears the costs. If the campaign is not successful, there are no benefits for anyone, but the costs remain unshared.

In sum, then, the extensive literature examining relationships between equity ownership and firm financial performance yields little support for the mitigation of the fundamental agency problem. Having established the questionable efficacy of independence and equity ownership as corrective mechanisms for the agency problem, we turn our attention to the final corrective mechanism designed to resolve agency problems and thus mitigate the costs of the fundamental agency problem: the market for corporate control.

Market for Corporate Control

The market for corporate control is thought to become operative when other forms of corporate governance fail. This mechanism operates to discipline managers who have created excessive agency costs due to managerial self-interest. The market for corporate control is based on the efficient market hypothesis,[52] and it suggests that the market will correct for excessive agency costs when managers make strategic decisions designed to satisfy their own self-interest, and thereby cause others to undervalue the firm's assets in the equity market. In an efficient market, the assets are devalued (stock price declines) because the firm's future prospects are downgraded based on managerial inefficiency, shirking of responsibilities, or malfeasance (Hawley & Williams, 2000). When the stock price declines, the firm becomes vulnerable to a hostile takeover. In this circumstance, another management team identifies the firm as undervalued, engages in a hostile takeover of the firm, and changes the management and strategies of the firm in an effort to enhance the value of the assets (Bebchuk & Fried, 2004).

Rationale for the Market for Corporate Control

Henry Manne (1965: 112) is generally credited with introducing the expression "the market for corporate control"[53] and an influential discussion of the concept. Indeed, he noted that his "paper will constitute an introduction to a study of the market for corporate control." Since that seminal work, Michael Jensen has been one of the more ardent spokespersons for the market for corporate control. In a series of articles, he explains the value of the market for corporate control, referring to it in the 1980s as a revolution (Jensen, 1984, 1986, 1987, 1988, 1989, 2005a; see also Fligstein, 1990; Jensen & Ruback, 1983; Walsh & Ellwood, 1991). Jensen and Chew (2000) argued that the series of takeovers during this period broke the reins of entrenched management that had controlled corporations in the United States since the 1930s. This entrenched management, they suggested, made many decisions that were not in the best interests of shareholders. During the revolution, however, smaller, more focused companies often gained control of a large amount of corporate assets. These companies, in turn, provided significant equity capital to shareholders.

Jensen (1984) suggested that takeovers help to protect shareholders from poor managers and signal to executives the need to manage the firm's assets in the best interests of shareholders rather than in their own self-interest. This is important because Jensen (and most financial economists) has argued that shareholders are the most important constituency of firms as the bearers of residual risk. Thus, he suggested that the market for corporate control is a powerful means to achieve restructuring of assets so that the corporation can deploy them in more productive and value-creating ways. Essentially, Jensen and Ruback (1983) proposed that the market for corporate control involves a contest in which managerial teams compete to manage specific corporate assets. In so doing, the new management teams use their recently acquired control of the assets to more efficiently allocate resources and eliminate overcapacity and inefficiencies, which characterized many mature industries and conglomerate firms in the 1980s. At the time, the market for corporate control was relatively successful, with corporate takeovers generating positive returns for acquired firms' shareholders and, on average, maintaining value for acquiring firms' shareholders (Jensen & Ruback, 1983).

As noted by Jensen (1987), the market for corporate control includes many possible actions in addition to hostile takeovers, such as voluntary mergers, leveraged buyouts, stockholder buyouts, spin-offs, split-ups, divestitures, asset sales, and liquidations.[54] Among these types of actions, the leveraged buyout (LBO) has received a significant amount of attention in practice and the scholarly literature. LBOs involve the use of significant debt to buy the equity of the firm and take it private. Approximately 90% of the purchase of equity is financed through debt and 10% is financed through the acquirer's equity. LBOs have been used by specialized buyout firms (e.g., Kohlberg, Kravis, & Roberts; Hicks, Muse, Tate, & Furst) seeking opportunities, by individual corporate raiders (e.g., Carl Icahn, Kirk Kervorkian), or by firms' managers (referred to as a management buyout [MBO]).

One persuasive argument made by Jensen (1986) is that the use of debt plays a significant role in reducing agency costs because it constrains managerial discretion. In fact, he suggested that debt is a plausible substitute for dividends to shareholders because it increases firm value by disallowing decisions that are not in shareholders' best interests. Jensen was especially critical of firms holding large cash flows greater than the profitable investment opportunities available. Firms with such cash flows should pay them out in dividends to shareholders rather than horde them internally (Jensen, 1986). Significant debt reduces large cash flows and requires managers to focus their investments on profitable opportunities.

Jensen (1987) also recognized that while these restructurings were positive for many shareholders, they had significant negative effects on many other stakeholders, such as employees and suppliers of the acquired firm. Restructurings require significant organizational change to meet the new market conditions, manage increased levels of debt, and develop new contracts with managers, employees, suppliers, and even with customers. Jensen acknowledged that these changes often involve a shift of resources from some areas in the firm to new uses, the closing of some plants and facilities, layoffs of middle managers and other employees, and reduced compensation for many. Given the substantial effects on many stakeholders, takeovers and, derivatively, the market for corporate control itself, have been subject to significant scrutiny and have experienced heavy criticism from politicians, public officials, labor unions, the media, and other prominent spokespersons. Thus, while some have championed the market for corporate control as perhaps the ultimate means of corporate governance for controlling agency costs (Jensen, 1989; Rappaport, 1990), the actions taken under its auspices have created other problems and eventually led to a reduction in its importance.

Criticisms of the Market for Corporate Control

The market for corporate control suffered considerable criticism, especially during and shortly after the revolution it spawned in the 1980s. Among the concerns were that the excessive diversification and inefficiencies in firms were caused partly because of laws, regulations, and the prevailing finance/economic theories (not all the result of agency problems). Another issue was that the market for corporate control became active only when other means of corporate governance had failed. It was also suggested that new wealth was not created by the takeovers or related actions; instead, they only redistributed it. There was also the interesting "agency" irony that some institutions and corporate raiders used the market for their own advantage, creating a second set of agency costs. In addition, the heavy use of debt created a unique set of problems that led to the demise of several LBO companies. Beyond that, the significant cost of downsizings and asset sell-offs caused substantial problems for many stakeholders of acquired firms, outside of the value received by the shareholders.

Several national laws restricted the manner in which firms could grow. In particular, the Sherman Antitrust Act of 1890 outlawed most forms of cartels, and the Celler-Kefauver Act of 1950 limited vertical and horizontal mergers (Davis, 2005). As a result, firms were disallowed from holding too much market power over their competitors, whether gained through organic growth or acquisition, increasing the attractiveness of diversification. Furthermore, prior to 1980, the equity markets assessed growth with great favor, much as they do today. As a result, executives seeking growth opportunities often ventured outside their firm's primary industries. The prevailing view of control in finance in the 1960s and 1970s, which suggested that financial synergies could be achieved across diversified product businesses through the internal allocation of capital (Davis, 2005), supported this diversification. These arguments were based on the notion that executives inside the firm have unique information and insights on each of the businesses and can thus more efficiently allocate capital to the best opportunities than could external sources of capital because they experienced information asymmetries (Hoskisson & Hitt, 1994).

As a result, the inefficient, highly diversified conglomerates of the 1980s were caused less by agency problems than by laws, regulations, and the prevailing research and practice in the use of financial controls. Unfortunately, these conglomerates were largely ineffective, suggesting the difficulty in creating financial synergies across diversified businesses in practice. Thus, corrections were needed, which led to the actions taken in the market for corporate control, along with voluntary actions to downscope these firms thereby increasing their focus and efficiency (Hoskisson & Hitt, 1994).

The market for corporate control has been described as a "blunt instrument" for resolving serious performance failures (Hawley & Williams, 2000). The extremely poor performance of firms at the time the market for corporate control becomes active serves as evidence of the failure of other governance mechanisms. Thus, the market for corporate control does not prevent performance failures; rather, it is used to correct them after they have already occurred, thereby rendering it effective ex post rather than ex ante. We would concede, however, that an active market for corporate control and a viable threat of takeover may dampen some opportunistic behavior.

While this is not a concern for many efficient market adherents, it is notable that the actions in the market for corporate control do not create new wealth; rather, they redistribute wealth primarily to the acquired firm's shareholders. Jensen and his colleagues argue that this is a highly positive outcome because shareholders bear the residual risk and should receive the rewards. In fact, Jensen argued against distribution to other stakeholders, even suggesting that we should not expect managers to consider all stakeholders in their decisions, as it is too complex for them to do so. Attempting to consider the interests of multiple stakeholders only creates more ambiguity for managers and will result in poorer decisions. He extolled the fact that it is difficult to identify any actions taken in the market for corporate control that cause harm to other shareholders. Yet, the redistribution comes from assets used for other purposes, including compensation formerly paid to managers and employees (e.g., reductions in pension plan reserves and/or benefits), funds dedicated to suppliers and, perhaps, services for customers. These actions and outcomes have caused significant criticism from stakeholders harmed by actions in the market for corporate control.[55]

Walsh and Kosnik (1993) studied the companies targeted by eight major corporate raiders during the 1980s revolution to which we have referred. They found that more than half of the companies targeted by these raiders outperformed the market during the two years prior to the raiders' revelation of their interests in taking over the firm. Jensen (1986) argued that some of the firms targeted for takeovers show positive performance outcomes prior to the takeover, but evidence other problems, such as significant cash flows that executives should be paying in dividends rather than holding. However, Walsh and Kosnik (1993) also studied the turnover of officers and directors in the companies taken over by these raiders. In the firms performing at a high level prior to takeover, they found no evidence of a disciplining effect for officers and directors.[56]

These findings complement Kosnik's (1987) earlier work on greenmail. Greenmail involves a corporate raider buying a significant equity interest in a firm threatening a takeover. Rather than pursue the takeover to its conclusion, however, the raider sells the stock acquired to the targeted firm for a premium. Thus, corporate management avoids a takeover and the corporate raider extracts a generous profit on the transaction, yet, shareholders lose value in cases where the firm's managers pay greenmail to corporate raiders, as the premium is paid out of corporate coffers.

As suggested previously, Jensen extolled the efficacy of using debt to constrain managers' actions and thereby control agency problems. In fact, in his 1989 article on the eclipse of the public corporation, he argued that the practice of LBOs constituted a new form of highly efficient organization that would lead to excellent performance. Yet, a major criticism of the market for corporate control is based on the fact that a number of LBO firms experienced performance problems, causing several of them to subsequently be restructured once again (e.g., DeGeorge & Zeckhauser, 1993; Ippolito & James, 1992; Muscarella & Vetsuypens, 1990).

These unsatisfactory performance outcomes exist for several potential reasons. Consider, for example, that the large amounts of debt involved in LBOs frequently force managers to emphasize short-term returns in an attempt to pay down the significant debt costs. Others have emphasized short-term returns for showing positive results in order to sell the company quickly. Unfortunately, emphasizing short-term returns produces decisions that are unlikely to prepare the organization for the longer term. Finally, high debt levels greatly increase bankruptcy risk. Bankruptcy risk and debt costs are higher for many LBO firms because they are often financed by junk bonds with very high relative interest rates. Thus, while heavy use of leverage may discipline managers, there are other significant costs that are borne by companies and, derivatively, shareholders.

Hitt, Harrison, Ireland, and Best (1998) compared and contrasted groups of high-performing and low-performing acquisitions. They found that high-performing acquisitions involved low-to-moderate levels of debt, whereas most of the low-performing acquisitions had high levels of debt. Similarly, Campello (2006) found that use of moderate debt led to positive product market growth, but large amounts of debt produced poor competitive performance in product markets. These empirical findings led Hitt, Harrison, and Ireland (2001) to recommend that debt be maintained at moderate levels when firms make acquisitions, as this allows the managers to exploit the synergies available from integrating the two businesses rather than take inefficient actions to cover high debt costs.

Hostile takeovers often result in costs not directly translated into financial terms. They have resulted, for example, in substantial employee layoffs and asset sales, actions that have, in turn, harmed many of the firm's stakeholders. Stakeholder theory suggests that, in addition to shareholders/owners, multiple stakeholders should be considered in any strategic action such as a takeover. This theory further implies that managers must consider and balance the competing interests of multiple stakeholders in their strategic decisions (Freeman & McVea, 2001).

Most financial economists would argue, however, that the shareholder is the only important stakeholder—or certainly, the most important one—and should thus enjoy primacy over other stakeholders. A challenge to this financial/economic perspective is that the firm may suffer in the longer term when actions cause harm to other stakeholders. Long-term financial losses are caused by the loss of valuable human capital in the form of managerial and staff layoffs, by discontent customers who turn to competitors for satisfaction, and by suppliers who no longer can trust the firm to fulfill its contractual obligations, resulting in a loss of relational capital.

Research suggests that large layoffs, often referred to as downsizing, produce negative shareholder returns (Cascio, 2002; Nixon, Hitt, Lee, & Jeong, 2004). Therefore, even most shareholders do not perceive large layoffs as in the best interests of the corporation. Recent research also suggests that there is a positive relationship between the premiums paid for an acquisition and the number of people laid off after the target is acquired (Krishnan, Hitt, & Park, 2007). Furthermore, in support of the research noted above, Krishnan and colleagues (2007) found that when firms engaged in large layoffs after making an acquisition, their subsequent performance suffered. They concluded that acquiring firms laid off employees to recoup the premiums paid, and in so doing lost valuable human capital. The loss of human capital contributed to subsequent lower firm performance.

The Demise of the Market for Corporate Control

Despite assertions that the market for corporate control is highly effective (e.g., Jensen & Ruback, 1983; for an alternative perspective, see Walsh & Seward, 1990), the market for corporate control has dissipated in recent years. The demise began in the late 1980s and early 1990s, with various (re)actions occurring on different fronts. Strong opposition from corporate managers encouraged boards of directors to enact antitakeover provisions such as poison pills, dual-class stock, and other protective mechanisms (Bainbridge, 2006; Hawley & Williams, 2000). Some state legislatures[57] passed laws that made takeovers more difficult, and court rulings (e.g., in Delaware) increased the power of boards to resist takeover attempts.[58] Equally important, however, were the indictments of Michael Milken and Drexel Burnham Lambert for securities laws violations. These indictments effectively shut down the junk bond market and thus ended takeovers funded through this vehicle (Jensen, 2005a). Finally, the collapse of the savings and loan industry, and many banks, largely eliminated the available funding for takeovers (Hawley & Williams, 2000). Perhaps Jensen (2005a) best captured the overall demise, noting that by 1990, "the era of the control market came to an end" (p. 33).

Other practice-based elements of the decline of the market for corporate control are remarkable. In principle, takeovers as a strategy to mitigate the fundamental agency problem are disciplinary (Fama & Jensen, 1983a; Jensen

& Ruback, 1983; Manne, 1965). Managers who impair the firm through mismanagement or the extraction of exorbitant rents confront a marketplace that will replace them. We acknowledge that it is a nontrivial problem to distinguish disciplinary takeovers from those propelled by strategies for nonorganic growth.[59] Still, we do not doubt that there have been largely disciplinary takeovers. We wonder, nonetheless, how that is consistent with exiting CEOs—through their employment contracts, change-of-control provisions, accelerated options, accelerated restricted shares, and related enablements—receiving hundreds of millions of dollars in "separation" pay. Moreover, we also ask how a disciplinary motive could be sensibly inferred when virtually all takeover bids are made at a premium of the target's current stock market valuation, often at least 15% or more. It is not immediately clear how nine-figure departure gratuities and premium prices for these companies constitute a model penalty. Instead, it reminds us of Kerr's (1975) classic article and admonition "On the Folly of Rewarding A, while Hoping for B."

While the market for corporate control designed to ameliorate agency problems waned in the 1990s, the appetite for acquisitions remained strong. In fact, while less ubiquitous today, hostile takeovers remain a fixture in the battles for control of assets in global markets. Thus, we examine the current trends in the market for acquisitions.

The Market for Acquisitions in the 21st Century

The market for acquisitions remains strong in the 21st century. The "popularity" of the acquisition strategy is intriguing, given the reported performance outcomes of acquisitions. Jensen (1986) reported that while target firm shareholders earn positive returns from acquisitions, acquiring firms' shareholder returns vary closely around zero. Recent research by King, Dalton, Daily, and Covin (2004) has supported these results. Their meta-analysis of studies on mergers and acquisitions found that acquiring firms generally received zero returns or suffered small negative returns. Even more compelling are the findings of Moeller, Schlingemann, and Stulz (2005). They found that from 1998 to 2001, acquiring firm shareholders lost about 12% of their investment in the firm on the announcement of acquisitions. These shareholders lost approximately $240 billion in a 4-year period, compared to about $7 billion throughout the 1980s. There are a number of potential reasons for these findings. Acquisitions can, for example, harm the internal innovation creation process (e.g., Hitt, Hoskisson, Johnson, & Moesel, 1996; Long & Ravenscraft, 1993). Hitt and colleagues (2001) argued that the lack of positive returns on acquisitions was often due to poor strategic decisions (e.g., poor choice of target firms to acquire because of weak due diligence or managerial hubris) and ineffective integration processes (c.f., Haspeslagh & Jemison, 1991). Yet, King and colleagues argued that much of the variance in acquisition performance could not be attributed to commonly suggested predictors such as relatedness of the product lines manufactured and sold by the acquiring and acquired firms.

Recent research suggests that acquisitions made for the purpose of gaining knowledge and learning new capabilities can produce positive returns (Uhlenbruck, Hitt, & Semadeni, 2006; Vermeulen & Barkema, 2001). Makri, Lane, and Hitt (2006) found that firms using a learning approach to make acquisitions build their internal science and technology knowledge, thereby increasing their innovation output. Therefore, acquisitions can be a profitable strategy when carefully designed, planned, and implemented. Yet, hostile takeovers rarely produce positive returns (Hitt et al., 2001), especially if rivals enter the bidding process. Barney (1988) explained that when a bidding contest occurs, positive returns can only be expected when private synergy exists between the acquiring and target firm.

In the last half of the 1990s and into the 2000s, we have witnessed another problem in the market for acquisitions: overvalued equity. The overvaluation of assets occurs for at least two reasons. First is the "irrational exuberance" in the market, a term coined by Alan Greenspan when he was Chairman of the Federal Reserve Board, and subsequently popularized by Robert Shiller in his book by the same name. Essentially, the Dow Jones Industrial Average tripled in value from 1994 to 1999. According to Shiller (2000), this exuberance occurred because of the new Internet technology being used in many homes and herd behavior on the part of investors. The high asset values fueled a wave of mergers and acquisitions using equity to finance the purchase of firms. This tendency may have been complemented by the "delusions of success" referred to by Lovallo and Kahneman (2003, p. 57), in which executives basically overestimate their own capabilities and exaggerate the benefits of a given initiative while discounting its costs and risks. Yet, when the "market bubble burst," many firms that had acquired others were left with overvalued assets on their books, and many shareholders lost significant value.

A second reason for the overvaluation of assets is misrepresentation of firms' assets in the accounting records, which occurred during the late 1990s at companies such as WorldCom and Enron. In this case, overvaluation results from agency problems. Executives deliberately misrepresent the firm's assets in order to maintain high equity valuations. Jensen (2005a) argued that when a firm's equity is overvalued, destruction of some or all of the core value of the firm is likely. Unfortunately, there are no immediately apparent governance mechanisms to effectively deal with these particular types of agency costs (Jensen, 2005a). The information asymmetries create difficulties for monitoring and render a market for corporate control ineffective. Executive actions leading to overvaluation of assets are driven partly by the psychology shaped by the market for corporate control in the 1980s. Since then, corporate executives have become increasingly focused on stock price, engaging in aggressive actions to increase stock price, or minimally, to ensure that it does not decrease (Denis, 2001).

While the market for corporate control is now largely inactive in the United States, evidence of its relevance exists in the global acquisition market (Shimizu, Hitt, Vaidyanath, & Pisano, 2004). Takeovers—some of hostile intent—have become increasingly common in cross-border acquisitions, especially in Europe. In the future, it will be interesting to note whether international takeovers can be identified as disciplinary in the sense of a market for corporate control.

Based on extant evidence, the market for corporate control is a coarse-grained means of controlling agency costs. The impact of the market for corporate control produced significant restructuring in U.S. industries, largely in the 1980s. It is, however, a means of last resort, employed after other governance mechanisms have failed to control or correct agency problems. Moreover, the market for corporate control produces other potential conflicts (e.g., dual effects of debt) in addition to any agency problems.

In many ways, the excesses that have driven the market for corporate control to near powerlessness can be countered. Contemporary boards need not rely on the host of antitakeover tactics, which have become de rigueur. Consider, for example, that many boards have adopted "qualified offer" guidelines,[60] a set of principles that place the board on the easily defended high ground regarding unsolicited takeover entreaties.[61] Qualified offer guidelines typically include three elements. These are critically important, because if an unsolicited takeover bid contains these elements, the target company board will consider the offer in good faith, and all poison pills and similar instruments will be nullified.

First, a qualified offer for the target's stock must be inclusive. Thus, the company mounting the takeover bid may not extend an offer for less than 100% of the stock. Through this policy, the target board precludes the bidder from paying a premium for the target stock until 51% (or whatever comprises a controlling interest) of the stock is obtained, but then not accepting the balance of the stock (thus, not paying a premium for it). In addition, a qualified offer will set forth a minimum premium (e.g., 15%, 20%, 25%, etc.) to be paid for the target's shares as of some certain date. Lastly, a qualified offer will set forth a minimum number of days for which the offer will remain in effect. This guarantees sufficient time for the board to consider the bid, secure outside expert counsel, and solicit other bids.

As is evident, when such a document is in place, allegations that a board has acted capriciously may have far less substance. Moreover, firms' managers know precisely under what circumstances the board *will* consider a bid for takeover and under what circumstances all poison pills and similar devices *will* be null and void. Such provisions facilitate an environment wherein directors are able to proactively consider multiple elements of takeover bids. The alternative is the madness of an unsolicited bid, feral constituencies, a phalanx of advisors, and the debilitating contraction of time.

We fully agree with Hawley and Williams (2000) that the market for corporate control is, indeed, a "blunt instrument" for corporate governance. Notwithstanding this idea, we concede that the market for corporate control generated some positive outcomes. Whether disciplinary in nature or otherwise, takeovers may be associated with more effective use of debt and are engines for nonorganic growth. Unfortunately, the primary legacy of the market for corporate control is, perhaps, executives' focused emphasis on increasing firms' stock price (Denis, 2001). This, as noted, is not always to good effect (Denis et al., 2006).

Conclusion

We have several objectives in this final section. We will briefly recount the results of our assessment of the fundamental agency problem and its mitigation. We also recognize that this treatise has essentially appraised the agency problem and its mitigation as a given, with no attention to those who are less comfortable with its bases and tenets. Accordingly, in fairness, we provide an overview of the posited limitations of agency theory and our comments on them. We also discuss those elements of the fundamental agency problem that are most troubling. Lastly, we share a potentially provocative perspective on the very application of agency theory—now and in the future.

Assessment of the Fundamental Agency Problem and Its Mitigation

Our assessment of the results of the empirical research and extended commentary on independence, equity, and the market for corporate control is largely invariant across the categories. There is, for example, no evidence to suggest that the independence in the composition of boards of directors is related to corporate financial performance. In addition, the literature addressing the leadership structure of the board—one person serving simultaneously as CEO and board chairperson or separating these roles—reflects no association with corporate financial performance.

With regard to equity holdings, the empirical evidence is similarly enervated. Whether one adopts an "alignment" perspective (the effects of insider ownership, e.g., officers, directors) or a "control" perspective (the effects of outsider ownership, e.g., blockholders, institutional holdings), this literature does not provide linkages to corporate financial performance. Beyond that, there are compelling arguments that the current regulatory environment does not facilitate an activist posture by institutional investors in their oversight of the companies in which they hold equity positions. Indeed, current policies would seem to restrict such initiatives. Other issues (e.g., conflicts of interests and moral hazards) would, in any case, temper institutional activism and derivatively inhibit its potential oversight roles.

Similarly, our review suggests that the market for corporate control was largely ineffective and is likely no longer active. Thus, it has done little to truly mitigate agency problems, and in fact, may have encouraged agency problems in some cases.

The reception of our assessment of the fundamental agency problem and its mitigation will, in part, be conditioned on the extent to which observers are comfortable with the relevance and application of agency theory. In this spirit, we provide an overview and discussion of the reservations that have been associated with agency theory.

Some Reservations about Agency Theory

While agency theory has been the dominant conceptual foundation for corporate governance research, not everyone has embraced it. Initially, critics averred that it was not novel (for overviews, see Bratton, 1989, 2001; Mizruchi, 2004; Stigler & Friedland, 1983; Werner, 1977, 1981). In 1914, for example, 20 years prior to Berle and Means' (1932) heralded work, Walter Lippman noted that "business…is being administered by men who are not profiteers. The managers are on salary, divorced from ownership and from bargaining" (Hawley & Williams, 2000, p. 82; see also Veblen, 1904, 1923).

Other critics suggested that Berle and Means (1932) exaggerated the extent of the decline in the concentration of economic power on which they based their work. This led to a notable comment-rejoinder-rejoinder exchange in the *American Economic Review* (Crum, 1934a, 1934b; Means, 1934). More recently, there have been concerns about the limited scope of agency theory (e.g., Cohen & Holder-Webb, 2006; Lubatkin, 2005; Lubatkin, Lane, Collin, & Very, 2005; Roberts, McNulty, & Stiles, 2005). In this perspective, critics have suggested that agency theory applies only to large, for-profit enterprises with mature capital markets and a diffuse base of shareholders. Accordingly, agency theory is purportedly ill-suited for the vast majority of business enterprises, and perhaps not applicable at all for most business enterprises based outside the United States (e.g., Lubatkin, 2005; Lubatkin et al., 2005).

Some might also argue that a relatively narrow focus has handicapped agency theory, and that other conceptual/theoretical lenses have largely subsumed it. Minimally, a more moderate perspective might suggest that agency theorists have not considered how the fundamental agency problem and its mitigation might have been informed by the broader context of corporate social responsibility (e.g., Allouche & Laroche, 2005; Bradley et al., 1999; De Bakker, Groenewegen, & Den Hond, 2005; Margolis & Walsh, 2001, 2003;[62] Orlitzky, Schmidt, & Rynes, 2003; Walsh, Weber, & Margolis, 2003), the ongoing conversation about the balance of shareholder value maximization (e.g., Berle & Means, 1932; Coase, 1937; Easterbrook & Fischel, 1983; Friedman,

1962; Jensen, 2001; Sundaram & Inkpen, 2004a, 2004b) stakeholder theories (e.g., Clarkson, 1995; Dodd, 1932; Donaldson & Preston, 1995; Freeman, 1984, 1994; Freeman, Wicks, & Parmar, 2004; Mitchell, Agle, & Wood, 1997) and stewardship (Davis, Schoorman, & Donaldson, 1977).

While these are fair criticisms, they are not dispositive. Few theories, if any, materialize de novo. An illustration that may underscore this point is found in an observation widely attributed to Sir Isaac Newton (1643–1727). In a letter written to Robert Hooke in 1675, Newton is credited with stating, "If I have seen further it is by standing on the shoulders of Giants." It seems that Sir Newton's observation was not entirely unique, as it can be traced to Bernard of Chartres. John of Salisbury, a 12th-century theologian, wrote in *Metalogicon* (1159) that "Bernard of Chartres used to say that we are like dwarfs on the shoulders of giants."[63] A close variant of this same quote from a much earlier period also exists, but with less certain provenance. Thus, if it is true that Berle and Means (1932) exaggerated somewhat regarding the issue of diffusion of ownership, we are comfortable suggesting that the intervening years have acquitted them nicely.

The focus on U.S.-based, large-scale firms is less a statement on agency theory than, more generally, on the character of corporate governance research. The vast majority of corporate governance research and commentary—whether in accounting, corporate strategy, economics, finance, law, or organizational sociology—relies on larger firms and is decidedly U.S.-centric. That agency theory may not be applicable in other contexts is not, for us, a stern indictment. Few observers would disagree that many theories are misapplied at times. Indeed, they should be occasionally misapplied and routinely reapplied; otherwise, we would not easily discover the boundaries of our theories and in what circumstances they are best practiced. Having said that, the fundamental agency problem still may be relevant to smaller scale public and private companies, as well as not-for-profits, public agencies, and a host of other enterprises. A potential for disconnect exists between the interests of those who preside over these enterprises and their principal constituencies, which may not always coincide; therein lies an agency problem.

In addition, we readily concede that one might properly regard agency theory and its mitigations as a subset of broader literatures (e.g., corporate social responsibility, shareholder value maximization/stakeholder theory, stewardship). We also accept the responsibility for our perhaps overly targeted focus on that subset. On that point, however, both the dominance of agency theory as a theoretical perspective over the last approximately 70 years and the extensive research grounded in its tenets have guided us. Even so, there are common attributes of agency theory and its mitigations and the broader lens of corporate social responsibility that are notable. With each, the empirical evidence is unconvincing, the debates concerning the adequacy of empirical protocols continue, and the search for moderators/mediators is unabated (e.g., De Bakker et al., 2005; Margolis & Walsh, 2001, 2003; Orlitzky et al., 2003).[64]

Other critical analyses of agency theory, however, are harder to rationalize. It has been argued, for example, that agency theory provides a highly simplified, even unrealistic explanation for executive and board behavior (e.g., Cohen & Holder-Webb, 2006; Hendry, 2005; Kaufman & Englander, 2005; Lubatkin, 2005; Lubatkin et al., 2005; see also Brennan, 1994; Jensen & Meckling, 1994). In this view, agency theory assumes several basic elements, including a separation of ownership from control, an attendant information asymmetry deriving from that separation, and narrowly self-interested behavior on the part of the contracting parties (Cohen & Holder-Webb, 2006; Lubatkin et al., 2005; Noreen, 1988; see also Ferraro, Pfeffer, & Sutton, 2005). Thus, it has been suggested that "the theoretical inclusion of 'self-interest' in agency theory as a vehicle that narrowly advances the interest of the individual is at best debatable and, at worse, dubious" (Cohen & Holder-Webb, 2006, p. 23; see also, Davis et al., 1997).

For us, the best compendium of this view is reflected in the work of Ghoshal (2005; see also Ghoshal & Moran, 1996; Rocha & Ghoshal, 2006). While our summary will not capture the passion and elegance of his piece and the acuity and empathy of those who commented on it (Donaldson, 2005; Gapper, 2005; Hambrick, 2005; Kanter, 2005; Mintzberg, 2005; Pfeffer, 2005), a basic tenet of Ghoshal's work is that the near-universal application of agency theory may have adverse consequences unanticipated by many of its founders and proponents. In that regard, Ghoshal (2005) noted that such a theory "Instead of controlling the opportunistic behavior of people…is likely to actually create and enhance such behaviors" (p. 85). Ghoshal firmly asserted that academic research, including agency theory, has in many instances too intensely focused on the amoral aspects of persons and organization, with a concomitantly pessimistic set of assumptions. Even so, Ghoshal conceded that systematic theory development in management should not ignore the untoward and distasteful behavior that is often present in individuals and organizations.[65]

Many observers will be comfortable with that sentiment because the sustainability of the fundamental agency problem does not require the agent to compromise all of its relationships. Obviously, not all high-ranking officers are rapacious villains determined to expropriate shareholders' and other constituencies' wealth. Still, the potential for mischief that exists with the diffusion of ownership, information asymmetry, and the availability of marginal awards has been described as intractable (e.g., Bainbridge, 2006; see also Bebchuk, 2005; Strine, 2006). This potential conflict, and its inevitability, has been aptly described outside the customary agency context. For us, some of this discussion provides both amplifications and challenges for the fundamental agency problem.

Other More Troublesome Aspects of the Fundamental Agency Problem

Arrow (1974; see also Bainbridge, 2003, 2006) persuasively argued that all complex organizations must have some means for compiling the preferences of their many constituencies and forging those into a discrete decision. It is not sensible that a large corporation be managed by consensus, as there are few enterprise equivalents of the town hall meeting.[66] Ultimately, someone has to have the authority to bind the organization to a course of action, and that centralization of authority will be an inescapable characteristic of its governance. Moreover, tensions incident to such decisions are inexorable, and not always a function of the fundamental agency problem.

Consider the disparate utilities of stakeholders. We could imagine a general preference shared by shareholders, for example, to increase the value of their shares, though few would expect to agree on how, exactly, that might be accomplished (Bainbridge, 2006). Could we anticipate that shareholders would enjoy a consensus on how to manage free cash flow? Shall the company buy back its own shares? Distribute those dollars in dividends? Invest in organic growth or nonorganic growth? We have also been reminded of the insoluble predicament faced by fiduciaries in serving their beneficiaries whose interests conflict (e.g., Bradley et al., 1999; Easterbrook & Fischel, 1991). One person's support of a strategic option in which to invest these funds (e.g., nonorganic growth), may be another's perception that funds for a CEO's "pet" project are destined to be expropriated.

Another factor may obscure our perspectives of the tensions attendant to these centralization/agency issues. Monks and Minow (2004) provided a provocative observation: No explicit decision has ever been made as a matter of policy to separate the ownership from the control of U.S. corporations. Instead, that trend was propelled by the presumably unintended consequences of the vastly increasing scale of companies, the interdependent requirements for unprecedented amounts of capital, the dispersed ownership that derived from those needs, and the overall complexity of organizations.

Many years ago, Adam Smith (from Jensen, 2005a) addressed the challenges of the corporate form and its complexities. He rather pessimistically referred to this as "…a species of warfare…which can scarce ever be conducted successfully, without such an unremitting exertion of vigilance and attention, as cannot long be expected from the directors of a joint stock company" (p. 125). Apparently, he doubted that directors could effectively discharge this task. More recently, Galbraith (2004) suggested that "guiding the large modern corporation is a demanding task, far exceeding the authority or ability of the most determined individual" (p. 26).

Other elements, too, confound our agency interpretations. Not all executives are competent (e.g., Fama, 1980; Hambrick, Finkelstein, & Mooney, 2005), nor are their competencies always suitable for the organizational context in which they serve (e.g., Finkelstein & Hambrick, 1996). Beyond that, even extraordinary executives may not enjoy munificent environments (Hambrick et al., 2005) and, if they do, they may not have the latitude to marshal resources as they wish (Hambrick & Finkelstein, 1987).[67]

Other factors noted in our review, too, are troublesome. While we will not recount them in detail, they may warrant comment. As we have noted, there is very little evidence of systematic relationships between financial performance and independence, equity, and the market for corporate control. Does this suggest, however, that research in these areas is misguided? Or that future research should be rechanneled?

Consider the quest to find a unicorn. To our knowledge, no such searches have been successful. Shall we conclude, then, that there are *no* unicorns? Alternatively, shall we decide that the various searches were incomplete, not having been conducted in the right place, or the right time, or under the appropriate circumstances? With such questions, we may be well served by heeding Kaplan's (1964) sage advice: "Wishful thinking...has its counterpart in wishful seeing" (p. 128).

Let us be clear about our equivocal unicorn. For us, the fundamental agency problem is very real and often observed. There *is* the potential for mischief, to which we have repeatedly referred when the interests of managers and owners diverge. The pivotal question is whether any of the interventions—independence, equity, and the market for corporate control—proposed to minimize agency costs is effective. Our review provides little or no evidence of systematic relationships that would sustain such a perspective. Having said that, it is unlikely that the search for such relationships will be abandoned. Instead, searches will continue in the presumably more appropriate places, times, and circumstances to which we have referred—and such searches may be useful.

Consider, for example, that there appear to be severe misspecifications of key variables and a host of seemingly relevant, but unexamined, variables that may be obscuring the mitigation of the fundamental agency problem. For some relationships, there are endogeneity concerns as well. In addition, future research on the fundamental agency problem and its mitigation will be conducted in an unfolding environment of SOX and increased oversight by the SEC and the various stock exchanges. Moreover, there is the unfamiliar landscape of abundantly funded private equity firms, hedge funds, and their partnerships (aka, "club" deals). Ironically, such enterprises operate under far less scrutiny than publicly traded companies do. Despite what would appear to be an increased agency risk, investors (individuals and institutions) are currently committing unprecedented amounts of funds to the control of these enterprises.

For us, though, there are two disturbing aspects of the fundamental agency problem and its mitigation. First is the concern about the collision of theories to which we have referred. Under the regulations of SOX and the listing exchanges, we have seen boards adopt a series of independence guidelines. Indeed, as of 2006, companies regulated by the SOX/listing exchanges provisions are 100% compliant with the majority of independent directors' guidelines, 100% compliant with the composition guidelines for audit committees, and 99.6% compliant with those guidelines for compensation committees and nominating/corporate governance committees (Spencer Stuart, 2005a). Attendant to this, however, is a radical reduction of inside directors, affiliated directors, and CEOs and other high-ranking executives serving on outside boards. By agency theory independence standards, these impressive trend lines have led to unprecedented levels of presumably independent board oversight. By the central tenets of resource dependence theory (e.g., Pfeffer & Salancik, 1978; Selznick, 1949; Thompson & McEwen, 1958; Zald, 1969), however, networking capacity has been decimated, as has the expertise-experience-reputation element of the resource-based perspective (e.g., Barney, 1991; Barney, Wright, & Ketchen, 2001; Hillman & Dalziel, 2003; Wernerfelt, 1984).

Perhaps the most troubling aspect of our review is the allegation that some agency-driven interventions have actually exacerbated the fundamental agency problem. On this aspect of agency theory, Kaufman and Englander (2005) noted that "to our bewilderment, this mantra still guides reforms for correcting the very problem it helped cause" (p. 9). They join others who underscore this view (e.g., Denis et al., 2006). We are inclined to agree with this perspective, at least on several issues.

In an earlier section, for example, we noted the excesses associated with stock options, their timing, backdating, and repricing. We could have noted similar excesses in initial public offerings (IPOs) that seem to have been guided by artificial increases in share prices (e.g., Dalton, Certo, & Daily, 2003; Hurt, 2005). From our perspective, though, the single best example of a serious agency mitigation misstep was the extension of stock options to board members (for a thoughtful discussion of an alternative view, see Hambrick & Jackson, 2000).

In 1990, only 6% of companies included stock options as an element of board members' compensation (Conference Board, 1990). By 1997, that percentage had increased to 84% (Dalton & Daily, 2001); for 2005, it is 93% (Conference Board, 2005a). Because directors set their own compensation, any form of contingent compensation visits a substantial moral hazard on them. There is a manifest problem any time that contingent compensation for officers directly informs additional compensation for directors (Bebchuk & Fried, 2004; Dalton, 2005c). As all of us have learned, through a series of sobering reports, stock options for senior officers can be associated with untoward behavior designed to increase the price of common stock to leverage those options. In principle, though, an able board can monitor this tendency and insist that these contingent rewards be pursued with reason. When boards mutually benefit from such aggressive behavior, however, that monitoring function may be impeded. Perhaps the better course is that boards' compensation should not include contingent arrangements. We wonder how the much-heralded corporate misbehavior of the late 1990s and early 2000s would have unfolded if stock options for directors were absent. Once again, we revisit the timeless forewarning of Alchian and Demsetz (1972): "Who will monitor the monitor?" (p. 782).

An Endorsement of Agency Theory and Perhaps a Provocative Perspective

Bratton (2001) suggested that Berle and Means' (1932) influence on corporate governance endures because "they diagnosed a persistent condition [that] …seems permanent and the problems themselves never seem to go away. It follows that we can predict a continuing presence for the *Modern Corporation and Private Property*…in the twenty-first century" (pp. 739–740). Certainly, the fundamental agency problem and its mitigation has been a dominant theme, providing a foundation for cross-disciplinary corporate governance research for decades. Many have and will continue to meticulously assess it, and there is much work to do.

In summary, we borrow a page from Winston Churchill, who, in a much broader context, observed that "democracy is the worst form of government except all those other forms that have been tried from time to time."[68] In this spirit, we describe agency as the worst theory of corporate governance, except all those other forms that have been tried from time to time. To this observation, however, we add a telling caveat. Our faith is in the intransigence of the fundamental agency problem and the unremitting need for its mitigation. On a continuum, we would be less concerned than Ghoshal (2005) that the quest to reduce agency costs will alone result in even more opportunistic behavior. We do, however, emphatically agree with Ghoshal (2005) on the efficacy of the universally posited mitigations of agency costs—independence, equity, and the market for corporate control: "The facts are that none of these factors have the predicted effects on corporate performance" (p. 80). We also join Ghoshal (2005; see also Daily et al., 2003) in his curiosity about why, despite the lack of empirical support, agency theory mitigations continue to dominate corporate governance research. That *is* a fair question.

We end with a provocative and potentially important question. In an earlier discussion, we noted a criticism of agency theory. The issue was its application to enterprises outside the United States. The argument is that very few countries actually have the diffusion of ownership contemplated by Berle and Means (1932). A basic tenet of agency theory is that corporate ownership became extremely diffuse such that individual shareholders had little leverage—or perhaps inclination—to assert their "control" rights. While the United States may have evolved through a period of relatively diffuse shareholdings for large-scale enterprises, a fundamental question is whether that actually remains the case today.

Consider, for example, that institutional investors hold 75% of the equity in the *Fortune* 500 (Karmel, 2004). Of the 25% or so of the equity that is otherwise held, approximately 80% of that is held in "street name"—having a brokerage firm, bank, or other nominee hold the shares in its name for the benefit of the actual investor (Borrus, 2005). This is important because individual investors do not ordinarily vote their shares held in street name. Instead, the brokers/financial institutions in which these shares are held in stewardship maintain the voting rights.

The combination of the concentration of institutional investor holdings and street name voting leads to an interesting proposition. Instead of the multimillions of voters—extreme diffusion—that many observers seem to expect for large-scale, publicly traded corporations, there are actually dramatically fewer. Consider, hypothetically, that a given *Fortune* 500 company has 35 or so institutional investors, each holding 2% of the firm's equity. This means that 35 entities are voting some 70% of the shares. For the vast majority of the balance of the shares consider that another 50 brokerage/financial institutions are voting under their street name privileges. We need not focus on the numbers in the example. The point is that instead of millions of voters, an extraordinarily diffuse group with relatively small equity positions, the reality is that the overwhelming majority of this equity is owned/voted by less than approximately 100 entities. Is this, in fact, a concentration of ownership and voting privilege not contemplated by the early articulation of what would become agency theory, or since?

A sobering irony may be implicit in this question. As noted, critics have long argued that agency theory is not applicable in most international settings because these countries do not at present have the diffusion of ownership that is a fundamental agency assumption.[69] Critics have also strongly suggested that the body of research on agency theory has been dominated by attention to large scale enterprise and may have little generalizability to other types of organizations. Setting aside generalizability, agency theory critics have yet another concern. Even if we were to more routinely conduct agency research with attention to smaller enterprises, the agency theory assumptions with regard to diffusion of equity may not be satisfied.

How large a problem do these conditions present? We know that the great preponderance of empirical work on agency theory has been conducted on the large-scale enterprise (e.g., *Fortune* 500, *S&P* 500). Is there, in fact, an issue with the concentration of institutional equity and street name voting privileges in these firms? As noted, we retain our faith in the fundamental agency problem and the mischief that may accrue when the interests of managers and owners are unaligned. With regard to the empirical evidence on the efficacy of those factors—independence, equity, and the market for corporate control—that are presumed to mitigate that mischief, we have deep and abiding concerns. With respect to the potential disconnect in the diffusion of equity assumptions contemplated by agency theory for the large scale firms, we, similar to many others, have much to consider; perhaps *reconsider* is the better word. We are certain about *one* element: There is much work to do.

Acknowledgment

We gratefully acknowledge our outside readers, Professors Donald C. Hambrick, Danny Miller, Amy J. Hillman, and Asghar Zardkoohi, for their generous counsel on this manuscript. Theirs was a substantial contribution to this work, and their willingness to share their time and expertise was a model of collegiality. We also thank Lisa Faye Miller for her expert editing of this manuscript. In addition, we wish to thank the editors, Arthur P. Brief and James P. Walsh, for their support and the opportunity to contribute to the inaugural volume of the *Academy of Management Annals* series.

Endnotes

1. Among some observers, the notion of agency theory and corporate governance are essentially equivalent (e.g., Dow & Raposo, 2005; Lubatkin, 2005; Shleifer & Vishny, 1997; Zajac & Westphal, 2004).
2. The East India Company survived for 274 years. The Hudson's Bay Company, founded in 1670, continues in business to this day (Micklethwait & Wooldridge, 2003).
3. For fascinating overviews and commentary about early principal/agent relationships relevant to that view, see Adams (1996).
4. *Santa Clara County v. Southern Pacific Railroad*, 118 U.S. 394, 397.
5. *The Modern Corporation and Private Property* has also been referred to as the most important book in the history of American corporate law (Skeel, 2005).
6. See Kim and Mahoney (2005) for an extensive summary. See also Furubotn and Pejovich (1972) for an earlier compendium.
7. *Guth v. Loft, Inc.*, 5 A.2d 503, 510 (Del. 1939).
8. We use the term *CEO* throughout to describe the presiding officer of the firm. From the standpoint of early agency theory development, this term is, strictly speaking, misplaced. The term *CEO* was not adopted until 1956, when Thomas J. Watson, Jr., president of IBM, added this designation to his title (see Capelli, Berlin, & Kendrick, 2006).
9. "Affiliated" directors have also been referred to as "gray" directors, largely in the accounting and finance literature.
10. For a summary of the key provisions of the Sarbanes-Oxley Act of 2002, see the American Institute of Certified Public Accountants (AICPA) Web site: http://cpcaf.aicpa.org/Resources/Sarbanes+Oxley/Summary+of+the+Provisions+of+the+Sarbanes-Oxley+Act+of+2002.htm, October 3, 2006.
11. For a copy of the New York Stock Exchange (NYSE) listing requirements, see www.nyse.com/regulation/listed/1101074746736.html#, October 3, 2006. For a useful summary, see www.alston.com/articles/listing%20standards%20200 4101204030137.pdf, October 3, 2006. Another extensive summary is available

at www.weil.com/wgm/cwgmhomep.nsf/files/corpgovguide_US/$file/corpgovguide_US.pdf, October 3, 2006. See also Cain (2003) for a broad history and discussion regarding listing exchange standards.

12. For a copy of the NASDAQ listing requirements, see www:nasdaq.com/about/marketplacerules.stm. For a useful summary, see www.alston.com/articles/listing%20standards%202004101204030137.pdf, October 3, 2006. Another extensive summary is available at www.weil.com/wgm/cwgmhomep.nsf/files/corpgovguide_US/$file/corpgovguide_US.pdf, October 3, 2006. See also Cain (2003) for a broad history and discussion regarding listing exchange standards.

13. Beyond the dampening influence on the selection and retention of independence-prone directors and their postselection "orientation," Westphal and colleagues (2006) have also noted that these tactics may have a serious negative impact on board opportunities for women and other minority groups.

14. Board interlocks with CEOs or otherwise are not prohibited under SOX or the guidelines of the listing exchanges. CEOs, however, in an interlock relationship, are prohibited from serving on one another's compensation committees. Also, board interlocks are prohibited between competing firms by the Clayton Act of 1914 (see Mizruchi, 2004).

15. This, of course, is a major point of emphasis for SOX and the guidelines of the listing exchanges.

16. Pfeffer and Salancik's (1978) *The External Control of Organizations: A Resource Dependence Perspective,* has recently been reissued (2003, Palo Alto, CA: Stanford University Press). We strongly recommend it to your attention, as the reissued volume includes very informative new material ("Introduction to the Classic Edition").

17. For some of these descriptive data, we rely on information provided by the Institute for Corporate Governance, Kelley School of Business, Indiana University. These data are derived from *Fortune* 500 firms' proxy statements and their corporate governance documents that are required to be available on the respective Web sites. The exact locations will vary, but will generally be found under "About Us," "Investor Relations," or "For the Investor." From there, you would generally be directed to "Governance," where the documents to which we refer will be found. We thank the Institute for Corporate Governance for access to these data.

18. This is not surprising, as many companies formally state in their governance principles (see endnote 17) that their boards will be limited to one inside director (e.g., Hewlett Packard, Altria). Full text of the principles to which we refer for Hewlett Packard can be found at www.hp.com/hpinfo/investor/govguidelines.html (October 3, 2006) and for Altria at www.altria.com/about_altria/1_5_5_corporategovernance.asp (October 3, 2006). Other firms restrict membership to two inside directors (e.g., Kraft Food, Wachovia). Full text of the principles to which we refer for Kraft Foods can be found at www.kraft.com/responsibility/governance_gov_guidelines.aspx (October 3, 2006) and for Wachovia at www.wachovia.com/file/CorporateGovernanceGuidelines.pdf, October 3, 2006.

19. In comments regarding recruiting directors with firm- and/or industry-specific knowledge of the firm at a recent corporate governance conference, Jay Lorsch noted that "because most are independent directors, you're limited on how many directors with knowledge of the company you can get on the board" (Daly, 2005).

20. The Rhoades and colleagues (2000) research, a meta-analysis, reported a corrected "r" of .04 for the relationship between board composition and financial performance. The confidence level, a useful diagnostic for meta-analyses, however, was not reported. If a given confidence interval includes zero, it suggests that the associated "r" is not statistically significant (Hunter & Schmidt, 2004). Other results of the analysis ranged from -.04 to .06. Whether statistically significant or otherwise, these results would be of modest magnitude. An r^2, for example, of the greater of the results would be .0036. The Wagner and colleagues (1998) piece, also a meta-analysis, provides an overall corrected "r" of .06. That research does provide a confidence interval that does include zero.

21. As you would expect, some overlaps in the studies and the companies comprise these samples.

22. Few observers would take much solace in knowing that there were four psychometrically sound metrics of "director proportion," inasmuch as the literature does not reflect any usage of such constructs. Instead, the literature generally relies on a single item, usually some proportion of a subset of directors (e.g., independent, inside, outside, affiliated) over the total number of directors.

23. SOX and the guidelines of the listing exchanges are silent on the issue of emeritus directors.

24. Actually, there are no SOX or listing exchange regulations regarding the size of executive committees. Such committees could, in principle, be comprised of a single member.

25. For full text of the governance documents for the executive committee of P&G, see http://www.pg.com/company/our_commitment/corp_gov/7c_committees.jhtml, October 3, 2006.

26. For full text of the governance documents for the executive committee of American Express, see http://ir.americanexpress.com/phoenix.zhtml?c=64467&p=irol-govCommComp, October 3, 2006.

27. In addition to the traditional board independence elements of board composition and board leadership structure, there is a growing literature on committees of the board. This body of work has been largely focused on the audit and compensation committees of the board (e.g., Daily, Johnson, Ellstrand, & Dalton, 1998; Defond, Hann, & Hu, 2005; Farber, 2005; Karamanou & Vafeas, 2005; Krishnan, 2005; Srinivasan, 2005; Vafeas, 2005).

28. For full text, see https://www.tbs.usmc.mil/pages/training%20corner/sho's/student%20handout/tactics/bo301.rtf, October 3, 2006.

29. As in the case of the relationship between board composition and financial performance, there is an extensive meta-analysis for the board leadership/financial performance relationship as well, comprised of 69 samples with an "n" size of 12,915 (Dalton et al., 1998).

30. We should add that there is a viable point of view that former CEOs of the company should not serve on the board at all (e.g., Monks & Minow, 2004). That perspective would presumably disqualify former CEOs as chairpersons of the board.

31. That is, he or she may not be independent by the guidelines of SOX, the relevant listing exchanges (e.g., NYSE, NASDAQ), and the corporate governance guidelines of the focal company. This would largely depend on the number of years (usually 3–5) since this person served as CEO.

32. SOX and the guidelines of the listing exchanges are silent on the matter of lead or presiding directors. For some commentary, see, for example, Conference Board (2005b) and Committee on Corporate Laws (2004).

33. An "executive session" is a meeting of a board's independent directors without the presence of the CEO or other inside directors.

34. Two recent papers examine perquisite consumption in detail. Yermack (2006) found that firms reporting personal aircraft use by the CEO underperform market benchmarks by almost 4% annually. In contrast, Rajan and Wulf (2006) highlighted the possible benefits of perquisites and suggested that "a blanket indictment of the use of perks is unwarranted" (p. 32).

35. According to Demsetz and Lehn (1985), managers alone enjoy the benefits of shirking, but the cost of shirking—presumably, poor firm performance—is borne by all shareholders.

36. Taken together, Grossman and Hart (1988) refer to such issues as the private benefits of control. Importantly, however, outside shareholders may also enjoy the private benefits of control.

37. Datta, Iskandar-Datta, and Raman (2005) found evidence contradicting this assertion. Specifically, they found a negative relationship between executive ownership and debt maturity. Their findings suggest that executives with higher levels of ownership are willing to be monitored more frequently by external debt holders.

38. Although Himmelberg and colleagues (1999) found some evidence to support a curvilinear relationship between ownership and firm performance, their inability to identify strong instrumental variables causes them to label their evidence as tentative.

39. In a similar study, Cho (1998) used simultaneous equations and found that corporate value affected ownership structure, but he did not find evidence for the opposite relationship.

40. Holderness, Kroszner, and Sheehan (1999) examined this assertion and found that managerial ownership increased from 1935 to 1995. Regarding outside ownership, Shleifer and Vishny (1997) suggested that "Even in the United States, however, ownership is not completely dispersed, and concentrated holdings by families and wealthy investors are more common than is believed" (p. 754).

41. A majority of studies define blockholders as those shareholders owning at least 5% of a firm's equity. In the United States, shareholders are required to report such holdings to the SEC. Bhagat and colleagues (2004, p. 8) provided an interesting discussion of the differences in reporting requirements when owning 5% versus 10% of a firm's equity (see also Holderness, 2003).

42. Interestingly, both studies report that these initial gains do not persist if such announcements are not shortly followed by substantive changes such as take-overs or management turnover.

43. As Holderness (2003) astutely noted, the private benefits of control enjoyed by outside shareholders do not necessarily need to come at the expense of minority shareholders. Production synergies that may result from a relationship with a blockholder (e.g., another corporation) may actually increase the wealth of minority shareholders.

44. Some observers, however, have suggested that institutions may rely too much on organizations such as the Institute for Shareholder Services (ISS) in the monitoring process (e.g., Strine, 2006). In fact, Strine (2006) argued that granting more power to institutional shareholders is equivalent to granting organizations such as ISS with more power.

45. As Grinstein and Michaely (2005) pointed out, the inside information received by institutional investors represented one of the impetuses for the recent "Fair Disclosure" regulation.

46. Karmel (2004) provided an interesting analysis regarding this topic and proposed enacting upon institutional shareholders a duty to corporations as well as shareholders.

47. Despite this common assertion that institutional investors are myopic, Hotchkiss and Strickland (2003) examined stock market reactions to earnings releases and found that the presence of institutional investors was not related to stock price stability.

48. Some evidence, for example, shows that institutional investors favor stocks with high liquidity, information flow, and volatility (Del Guercio, 1996; Falkenstein, 1996).

49. In fairness, the authors did report a significant relationship between institutional ownership and sales, but the authors questioned whether sales reflected performance as opposed to firm size.

50. Bushee's work is closely related to work by Bhagat and colleagues (2004), who used the term "relational" investing. While Bushee's notion of dedicated investors applies to institutional shareholders alone, Bhagat et al.'s concept of relational investors applies to all shareholders other than management or an ESOP who have owned more than 10% of the firm for four or more years.

51. Bushee factor analyzes nine variables to create his three composite variables of interest. See pp. 324–328 of his paper for the details of this procedure.

52. The efficient market hypothesis (EMH) has been described as the bedrock of the agency approach (Davis, 2005). Jensen (1988) suggested, "No proposition...is better documented" than the EMH (p. 26).

53. Marris (1964) is also sometimes noted as a pioneer in the early development of this concept.

54. Seward and Walsh (1996) provided an interesting insight in their research on corporate spin-offs in that activities of these types, while not addressing the market for corporate control per se, may actually be exercises in market-based corporate control.

55. As an example, Hawley and Williams (2000) suggested that approximately 150% of the takeover premium paid by Carl Icahn in the takeover of TWA was extracted from the wages of the firm's three labor unions, a redistribution of wealth from workers to shareholders.

56. Notably, Walsh and Kosnik (1993) also demonstrated that close competitors seemed to react to corporate raiders' press/rhetoric, but not necessarily to the substance of their behavior.

57. See, for example, *CTS v. Dynamics Corporation of America*, 481 US 69 (1987) in which the Supreme Court upheld Indiana's state antitakeover statute.

58. See, for example, *Moran v. Household International,* De. Ch. 490 A.2d 1059 (1985) in which the Delaware Chancery court generally upheld the poison pill.

59. We would concede that there could be an intersection as well of disciplinary motives and those for nonorganic growth.

60. Qualified offer guidelines are an example of the more generic "chewable pill," one of several tactics that may, under certain conditions, nullify poison pills.

61. Qualified offers are viewed with great favor by governance gate keeping organizations. See, e.g., Institutional Shareholder Services (ISS) at www.issproxy.com/pdf/2006USConcisePolicies.pdf, October 3, 2006.

62. Margolis and Walsh (2003; see especially Table 2) provide an outstanding, extensive compendium of the empirical research addressing corporate social responsibility and financial performance. See also Allouche and Laroche (2005) and Orlitzky and colleagues (2003) for meta-analyses of a subset of these studies. Another extensive review is provided by De Bakker and colleagues (2005).

63. See, for example, http://williampatry.blogspot.com/2006/02/standing-on-some-one-taller.html, October 3, 2006.

64. We thank James P. Walsh (personal communication) for bringing this point regarding these parallels in the weight of research and the equivocal empirical results to our attention.

65. Shortly before the publication of his piece to which we have referred, Professor Sumantra Ghoshal unexpectedly passed away. We were touched by the final comments by Professor Donald C. Hambrick (2005) in his "Response to Ghoshal," in which he noted, "Sumantra, it pains me dearly that you can't set me straight about what I've written here. We miss you, friend." Exactly right. We, too, wish that we could benefit from Sumantra's perspectives about this review of the fundamental agency problem and its mitigation.

66. The governance of some law firms, consulting firms, and accounting firms with their partnership structures may be closest to the modern day equivalent of a town hall meeting.

67. We have relied on Hambrick and colleagues (2005) for this broad discussion of executive competencies/enablements.

68. Speech at the House of Commons (November 11, 1947) in Winston S. Churchill: His complete speeches, 1897–1963, at 7566 (Robert Rhodes James Ed. 1974). We give credit to Bebchuk (2006) for bringing this to our attention.

69. This becomes a fascinating question. For the moment, let's accept that agency theory is not applicable in most international settings because most countries do not have anything near the diffusion of ownership that is a fundamental agency assumption. If, however, we also accept that most agency theory research in the

United States is based on large-scale enterprises that also do not meet the agency theory diffusion of ownership guideline, does that mean that agency theory is uniformly inapplicable both for the United States and internationally?

References

Aboody, D., & Kasznik, R. (2000). CEO stock options awards and the timing of corporate voluntary disclosures. *Journal of Accounting and Economics, 29*, 73–100.

Adams, J. (1996). Principals and agents, colonialists and company men: The decay of colonial control in the Dutch East Indies. *American Sociological Review, 61*, 12–28.

Alchian, A. A., & Demsetz, H. (1972). Production, information costs, and economic organization. *American Economic Review, 62*, 777–795.

Alchian, A. A., & Demsetz, H. (1973). The property rights paradigm. *Journal of Economic History, 33*, 16–27.

Allouche, J., & Laroche, P. (2005). A meta-analytical investigation of the relationship between corporate social and financial performance. *Revue de Gestion des Ressources Humaines, 57*, 18–41.

Anderson, R. C., & Reeb, D. M. (2003). Founding-family ownership and firm performance: Evidence from the S&P 500. *Journal of Finance, 58*, 1301–1328.

Arrow, K. J. (1974). *The limits of organization.* New York: Norton & Company.

Bainbridge, S. M. (2003). Director primacy: The means and ends of corporate governance. *Northwestern University Law Review, 97*, 547–606.

Bainbridge, S. M. (2006). Response to increasing shareholder power: Director primacy and shareholder disempowerment. *Harvard Law Review, 119*, 1735–1758.

Baliga, B. R., Moyer, R. C., & Rao, R. S. (1996). CEO duality and firm performance: What's the fuss? *Strategic Management Journal, 17*, 41–53.

Barney, J. (1991). Firm resources and sustained competitive advantage. *Journal of Management, 17*, 99–120.

Barney, J. B. (1988). Returns to bidding firms in mergers and acquisitions: Reconsidering the relatedness hypothesis. *Strategic Management Journal, 9*, 71–78.

Barney, J., Wright, M., & Ketchen, D. J. (2001). The resource-based view of the firm: Ten years after 1991. *Journal of Management, 27*, 625–642.

Baskin, J. B., & Miranti, P. J. (1997). *A history of corporate finance.* Cambridge, U.K.: Cambridge University Press.

Baysinger, B. D., & Hoskisson, R. E. (1990). The composition of boards of directors and strategic control. *Academy of Management Review, 15*, 72–87.

Beatty, R. P., & Zajac, E. (1994). Managerial incentives, monitoring, and risk bearing: A study of executive compensation, ownership, and board structure in initial public offerings. *Administrative Science Quarterly, 39*, 313–335.

Bebchuk, L. A. (2005). The case for increasing shareholder power. *Harvard Law Review, 118*, 833–914.

Bebchuk, L. A. (2006). Response to increasing shareholder power: Reply: Letting shareholders set the rules. *Harvard Law Review, 119*, 1784–1813.

Bebchuk, L. A., & Fried, J. M. (2003). Executive compensation as an agency problem. *Journal of Economic Perspectives, 17*(3), 71–92.

Bebchuk, L. A., & Fried, J. (2004). *Pay without performance: The unfulfilled promise of executive compensation.* Cambridge, MA: Harvard University Press.

Becher, D. A., Campbell, T. L., & Frye, M. B. (2005). Incentive compensation for bank directors: The impact of deregulation. *Journal of Business, 78*, 1753–1778.

Bergstresser, D., & Philippon, T. (2006). CEO incentives and earnings management. *Journal of Financial Economics, 80*, 511–529.

Berle, A. A. (1959). *Power without property: A new development in American political economy.* New York: Harcourt Brace.

Berle, A. A., & Means, G. C. (1932). *The modern corporation and private property.* New York: McMillan.

Bhagat, S., & Black, B. (1999). The uncertain relationship between board composition and firm performance. *Business Lawyer, 54*, 921–963.

Bhagat, S., & Black, B. S. (2002). The non-correlation between board independence and long-term firm performance. *Journal of Corporation Law, 27*, 231–273.

Bhagat, S., Black, B., & Blair, M. (2004). Relational investing and firm performance. *The Journal of Financial Research, 27*, 1–30.

Blair, M. M. (1995). *Ownership and control: Rethinking corporate governance for the twenty-first century.* Washington, DC: The Brookings Institution.

Boeker, W. (1992). Power and managerial dismissal: Scapegoating at the top. *Administrative Science Quarterly, 37*, 400–421.

Bogle, J. C. (2005). *The battle for the soul of capitalism.* New Haven, CT: Yale University Press.

Booth, J. R., & Deli, D. N. (1996). Factors affecting the number of outside directorships held by CEOs. *Journal of Financial Economics, 40*, 81–104.

Borrus, A. (2005, December). Investors may not want this hot line. *Business Week, 5*, 82.

Boyd, B. K. (1995). CEO duality and firm performance: A contingency model. *Strategic Management Journal, 16*, 301–312.

Bradley, M., Schipani, C. A., Sundaram, A. K., & Walsh, J. P. (1999). The purposes and accountability of the corporation in contemporary society: Corporate governance at a crossroads. *Law and Contemporary Problems, 62*, 9–86.

Bradley, M., & Wallenstein, S. M. (2006). The history of corporate governance in the United States. In M. J. Epstein, & K. O. Hanson (Eds.), *The accountable corporation* (Vol. 1, 45–72).Westport, CT: Praeger.

Brandeis, L. D. (1914). *Other peoples' money.* New York: Frederick A. Stokes.

Bratton, W. W. (1989). The new economic theory of the firm: Critical perspectives from history. *Stanford Law Review, 41*, 1471–1527.

Bratton, W. W. (2001). Berle and Means reconsidered at the century's turn. *Journal of Corporation Law, 26*, 737–770.

Brennan, M. (1994). Incentives, rationality, and society. *Journal of Applied Corporate Finance, 7*, 31–45.

Brickley, J. A., Coles, J. L., & Jarrell, G. (1997). Leadership structure: Separating the CEO and chairman of the board. *Journal of Corporate Finance, 3*, 189–220.

Brickley, J. A., Lease, J. A., & Smith, C. W. (1988). Ownership structure and voting on antitakeover amendments. *Journal of Financial Economics, 20*, 267–291.

Burns, N., & Kedia, S. (2006). The impact of performance-based compensation on misreporting. *Journal of Financial Economics, 79*, 35–67.

Bushee, B. J. (1998). The influence of institutional investors on myopic R&D investment behavior. *The Accounting Review, 73*, 305–333.

Cain, K. (2003). New efforts to strengthen corporate governance: Why use SRO listing standards? *Columbia Business Law Review, 1,* 619–659.

Callaghan, S. R., Saly, P. J., & Subramanian, C. (2004). The timing of option repricing. *Journal of Finance, 59,* 1651–1676.

Camera, K. A. D. (2005). Classifying institutional investors. *The Journal of Corporation Law, 30,* 219–253.

Campello, M. (2006). Debt financing: Does it boost or hurt performance in product markets. *Journal of Financial Economics, 82,* 135–172.

Capelli, P., Berlin, G., & Kendrick, S. (2006). Governance history: Tale of a title—The rise of the CEO. *Directors & Boards, 30,* 22–26.

Carter, M. E., & Lynch, L. J. (2004). The effect of stock option repricing on employee turnover. *Journal of Accounting & Economics, 37,* 91–112.

Cascio, W. F. (2002). *Responsible restructuring: Creative and profitable alternatives to layoffs.* San Francisco: Berrett-Koehler.

Certo, S. T., Daily, C. M., Cannella, A. A., Jr., & Dalton, D. R. (2003). Giving money to get money: How CEO stock options and CEO equity enhance IPO valuations. *Academy of Management Journal, 46,* 643–653.

Chandler, A. D. (1977). *The visible hand: The managerial revolution in American Business.* Cambridge, MA: Harvard University Press.

Chen, M. A. (2004). Executive option repricing, incentives, and retention. *Journal of Finance, 59,* 1167–1199.

Chidambaran, N. K., & Prabhala, N. R. (2003). Executive stock option repricing, internal governance mechanisms, and management turnover. *Journal of Financial Economics, 69,* 153–189.

Cho, M. (1998). Ownership structure, investment, and corporate value: An empirical analysis. *Journal of Financial Economics, 47,* 103–121.

Claessens, S., Djankov, S., Fan, J. P. H., & Lang, L. H. P. (2002). Disentangling the incentive and entrenchment effects of large shareholders. *Journal of Finance, 57,* 2741–2772.

Clarkson, M. B. E. (1995). A stakeholder framework for analyzing and evaluating corporate social performance. *Academy of Management Review, 20,* 92–117.

Coase, R. H. (1937). The nature of the firm. *Economica, 4,* 386–405.

Coase, R. H. (1960). The problem of social cost. *Journal of Law and Economics, 3,* 1–44.

Coffee, J. C. (2001). The rise of dispersed ownership: The roles of law and the state of the separation of ownership and control. *Yale Law Journal, 111,* 3–82.

Cohen, J., & Holder-Webb, L. (2006). Rethinking the influence of agency theory in the accounting academy. *Issues in Accounting Education, 21,* 17–30.

Cole, L. (2005). Reexamining the collective entity doctrine in the new era of limited liability entities–Should business entities have a fifth amendment privilege? *Columbia Business Law Review, 4,* 1–110.

Coles, J. W., McWilliams, V. B., & Sen, N. (2001). An examination of the relationship of governance mechanisms to performance. *Journal of Management, 27,* 23–50.

Committee on Corporate Laws. (2004). *Corporate director's guidebook* (4th ed.). Chicago: American Bar Association.

Conference Board. (1990). *Corporate Directors' Compensation.* New York: The Conference Board.

Conference Board. (2005a). *Directors compensation and board practices.* New York: The Conference Board.

Conference Board. (2005b). *Corporate governance handbook: Developments in best practices, compliance, and legal standards.* New York: The Conference Board.

Conyon, M. J. (2006). Executive compensation and incentives. *Academy of Management Perspectives, 20,* 25–44.

Cook, F. W. (2005). *Director compensation: NASDAQ 100 vs. NYSE 100.* New York: Frederic W. Cook & Co., Inc.

Coombes, P., & Wong, S. C-Y. (2004). Chairman and CEO: One job or two? *McKinsey Quarterly, 2,* 43–44.

Core, J. E., Guay, W. R., & Larcker, D. F. (2003). Executive equity compensation and incentives: A survey. *Economic Policy Review, 9*(1), 27–50.

Core, J. E., Holthausen, R. W., & Larcker, D. F. (1999). Corporate governance, chief executive officer compensation, and firm performance. *Journal of Financial Economics, 51,* 371–406.

Corley, K. G. (2005). The Higgs Report: Implications for our understanding of corporate governance and the non-executive director [Special issue]. *British Journal of Management, 16,* 51–54.

Cronquist, H., & Nilsson, M. (2003). Agency costs and controlling minority shareholders. *Journal of Financial and Quantitative Analysis, 38,* 695–719.

Crum, W. L. (1934a). On the alleged concentration of economic power. *American Economic Review, 24,* 69–83.

Crum, W. L. (1934b). On the alleged concentration of economic power: A rejoinder by W. L. Crum. *American Economic Review, 24,* 87–88.

Daily, C. M., Certo, S. T., & Dalton, D. R. (2002). Executive stock option repricing: Retention and performance reconsidered. *California Management Review, 44,* 8–23.

Daily, C. M., & Dalton, D. R. (1995). CEO and director turnover in failing firms: An illusion of change? *Strategic Management Journal, 16,* 393–400.

Daily, C. M., & Dalton, D. R. (1997). CEO and board chair roles held jointly or separately: Much ado about nothing. *Academy of Management Executive, 11,* 11–20.

Daily, C. M., Dalton, D. R., & Cannella, A. A., Jr. (2003). Corporate governance: Decades of dialogue and data. *Academy of Management Review, 28,* 371–382.

Daily, C. M., Dalton, D. R., & Certo, S. T. (2004). Women as directors: The inside story. *Directors & Boards, 29*(1), 36–39.

Daily, C. M., Dalton, D. R., & Rajagopalan, N. (2003). Governance through ownership: Centuries of practice, decades of research. *Academy of Management Journal, 46,* 151–158.

Daily, C. M., Johnson, J. L., & Dalton, D. R. (1999). On the measurement of board composition: Poor consistency and a serious mismatch of theory and operationalization. *Decision Sciences, 30,* 83–106.

Daily, C. M., Johnson, J. L., Ellstrand, A. E., & Dalton, D. R. (1998). Compensation committee composition as a determinant of CEO compensation. *Academy of Management Journal, 41,* 209–220.

Dalton, D. R. (2005a). If you could make one change to the governance system … Pull back the "separating roles" movement. *Directors & Boards, 30*(1), 24–26.

Dalton, D. R. (2005b). "Going private" and "going dark;" board compensation, and the downside of independence. *Directors & Boards, 2*(10), 4–6.

Dalton, D. R. (2005c). Blame the board of directors: Governance experts take on Lucian Bebchuk's arguments about shareholder power and CEO pay. *Across the Board, 42*(3), 42–46.

Dalton, D. R., Certo, S. T., & Daily, C. M. (2003). Initial public cfferings (IPOs) as a web of conflicts of interest: An empirical assessment. *Business Ethics Quarterly, 13*, 289–314.

Dalton, D. R., & Daily, C. M. (2001). Director stock compensation: An invitation to a conspicuous conflict of interest? *Business Ethics Quarterly, 11*, 89–108.

Dalton, D. R., & Daily, C. M. (2003). The enigma of the emeritus director. *Directors & Boards, 28*(1), 53–56.

Dalton, D. R., Daily, C. M., Certo, S. T., & Roengpitya, R. (2003). Meta-analyses of corporate financial performance and the equity of CEOs, officers, boards of directors, institutions, and blockholders: Fusion or confusion? *Academy of Management Journal, 46*(1), 13–26.

Dalton, D. R., Daily, C. M., Ellstrand, A. E., & Johnson, J. L. (1998). Board composition, leadership structure, and financial performance: Meta-analytic reviews and research agenda. *Strategic Management Journal, 19*, 269–290.

Dalton, D. R., Daily, C. M., Johnson, J. L., & Ellstrand, A. E. (1999). Number of directors and financial performance: A meta-analysis. *Academy of Management Journal, 42*, 674–686.

Dalton, D. R., & Dalton, C. M. (2006). Executive committees: The stealth board body. *Directors & Boards, 30*(2), 44–47.

Daly, G. (2005, October). Directors challenge value of independence standards. *Agenda*, 4.

Datta, S., Iskandar-Datta, M., & Raman, K. (2005). Managerial stock ownership and the maturity structure of corporate debt. *Journal of Finance, 60*, 2333–2350.

David, P., Kochhar, R., & Levitas, E. (1998). The effect of institutional investors on the level and mix of CEO compensation. *Academy of Management Journal, 41*, 200–208.

Davidson, W. N., Jiraporn, P., Kim, Y. S., & Nemec, C. (2004). Earnings management following duality-creating successions: Ethnostatistics, impression management, and agency theory. *Academy of Management Journal, 47*, 267–275.

Davis, G. F. (1991). Agents without principles: The spread of the poison pill through the intercorporate network. *Administrative Science Quarterly, 36*, 586–613.

Davis, G. F. (2005). New directions in corporation governance. In K. S. Cook, & D. S. Massey (Eds.), *Annual review of sociology* (Vol. 31, pp. 143–162). Palo Alto, CA: Annual Reviews.

Davis, G. F., & Greve, H. R. (1997). Corporate elite networks and governance changes in the 1980s. *American Journal of Sociology, 103*, 1–37.

Davis, G. F., & Thompson, T. A. (1994). A social movement perspective on corporate control. *Administrative Science Quarterly, 39*, 141–173.

Davis, J. J., Schoorman, F. D., & Donaldson, L. (1997). Toward a stewardship theory of management. *Academy of Management Review, 22*, 20–47.

De Bakker, F. G. A., Groenewegen, P., & Den Hond, F. (2005). A bibliometric analysis of 30 years of research and theory on corporate social responsibility and corporate social performance. *Business & Society, 44*, 283–317.

Defond, M. L., Hann, R. N., & Hu, X. (2005). Does the market value financial expertise on audit committees of boards of directors. *Journal of Accounting Research, 43,* 153–193.

DeGeorge, F., & Zeckhauser, R. (1993). The reverse LBO decision and firm performance: Theory and evidence. *Journal of Finance, 48,* 1323–1348.

Del Guercio, D. D. (1996). The distorting effect of the prudent-man laws on institutional equity investments. *Journal of Financial Economics, 40,* 31–62.

Demsetz, H. (1964). The exchange and enforcement of property rights. *Journal of Law and Economics, 3,* 11–26.

Demsetz, H. (1966). Some aspects of property rights. *Journal of Law and Economics, 19,* 61–70.

Demsetz, H. (1967). Towards a theory of property rights. *American Economic Review, 57,* 343–359.

Demsetz, H. (1983). The structure of ownership and the theory of the firm. *Journal of Law & Economics, 26,* 375–390.

Demsetz, H., & Lehn, K. (1985). The structure of corporate ownership: Causes and consequences. *Journal of Political Economy, 93,* 1155–1177.

Demsetz, H., & Villalonga, B. (2001). Ownership structure and corporate performance. *Journal of Corporate Finance, 7,* 209–233.

Denis, D. K. (2001). Twenty-five years of corporate governance research...and counting. *Review of Financial Economics, 10,* 191–212.

Denis, D. J., Hanouna, P., & Sarin, A. (2006). Is there a dark side to incentive compensation? *Journal of Corporate Finance, 12,* 467–488.

Deutsch, Y. (2005). The impact of board composition on firms' critical decisions: A meta-analytic review. *Journal of Management, 31,* 424–444.

DiMaggio, P. J., & Powell, W. W. (1983). The iron cage revisited: Institutional isomorphism and collective rationality in organizational fields. *American Sociological Review, 48,* 147–160.

Dodd, M. E. (1932). For whom are corporate managers trustees. *Harvard Law Review, 45,* 1145–1163.

Domhoff, G. W. (2006). *Who rules America? Power, politics, & social change* (5th ed.). Boston: McGraw Hill.

Donaldson, L. (2005). For positive management theories while retaining science: Reply to Ghoshal. *Academy of Management Learning & Education, 4,* 109–113.

Donaldson, L., & Preston, L. F. (1995). The stakeholder theory of the corporation: Concepts, evidence, and implications. *Academy of Management Review, 20,* 65–91.

Douglas, W. O. (1934). Directors who do not direct. *Harvard Law Review, 47,* 1305–1334.

Dow, J., & Raposo, C. C. (2005). CEO compensation, change, and corporate strategy. *Journal of Finance, 60,* 2701–2727.

Easterbrook, F. H., & Fischel, D. (1983). Voting in corporate law. *Journal of Law & Economics, 26,* 395–427.

Easterbrook, F. H., & Fischel, D. (1991). *The economic structure of corporate law.* Cambridge, MA: Harvard University Press.

Eisenhardt, K. M. (1989). Agency theory: An assessment and review. *Academy of Management Review, 14,* 57–74.

Faleye, O. (2006, January). *Does one hat fit all? The case of corporate leadership structure.* Retrieved October 7, 2006, from http://ssrn.com/abstract=394980.

Falkenstein, E. G. (1996). Preferences for stock characteristics as revealed by mutual fund portfolio holdings. *Journal of Finance, 51,* 111–136.

Fama, E. F. (1980). Agency problems and the theory of the firm. *Journal of Political Economy, 88,* 288–307.

Fama, E. F., & Jensen, M. C. (1983a). Separation of ownership and control. *Journal of Law and Economics, 26,* 301–325.

Fama, E. F., & Jensen, M. C. (1983b). Agency problems and residual claims. *Journal of Law and Economics, 26,* 327–349.

Farber, D. B. (2005). Restoring trust after fraud: Does corporate governance matter? *Accounting Review, 80,* 539–561.

Ferraro, F., Pfeffer, J., & Sutton, R. I. (2005). Economics language and assumptions: How theories can become self-fulfilling. *Academy of Management Review, 30,* 8–24.

Fich, E. M., & White, L. J. (2005). Why do CEOs reciprocally sit on each other's boards? *Journal of Corporate Finance, 11,* 175–195.

Finkelstein, S., & D'Aveni, R. A. (1994). CEO duality as a double-edged sword: How boards of directors balance entrenchment avoidance and unity of command. *Academy of Management Journal, 37,* 1079–1108.

Finkelstein, S., & Hambrick, D. C. (1989). Chief executive compensation: A study of the intersection of markets and political processes. *Strategic Management Journal, 10,* 121–134.

Finkelstein, S., & Hambrick, D. C. (1996). *Strategic leadership: Top executives and their effects on organizations.* St. Paul, MN: West Publishing.

Fligstein, N. (1990). *The transformation of corporate control.* Cambridge, MA: Harvard University Press.

Frank, J. (1933). The modern corporation and private property. *Yale Law Journal, 42,* 989–996.

Frederickson, J. W., Hambrick, D. C., & Baumrin, S. (1988). A model of CEO dismissal. *Academy of Management Review, 13,* 255–270.

Freeman, R. E. (1984). *Strategic management: A stakeholder approach.* Boston: Pitman.

Freeman, R. E. (1994). The politics of stakeholder theory. *Business Ethics Quarterly, 4,* 409–421.

Freeman, R. E., & McVea, J. (2001). A stakeholder approach to strategic management. In M. A. Hitt, R. E. Freeman, & J. S. Harrison (Eds.), *Handbook of strategic management* (pp. 189-207). Oxford, U.K.: Oxford University Press.

Freeman, R. E., Wicks, A. C., & Parmar, B. (2004). Stakeholder theory and "The corporate objective revisited." *Organization Science, 15,* 364–369.

Friedman, M. (1962). *Capitalism and freedom.* Chicago: University of Chicago Press.

Furubotn, E. G., & Pejovich, S. (1972). Property rights and economic theory: A survey of recent literature. *Journal of Economic Literature, 10,* 1137–1162.

Gaa, J. (2004). Accounting ethics [Special issue]. *Business Ethics Quarterly, 14,* 349–354.

Galbraith, J. K. (2004). *The economics of innocent fraud.* Boston: Houghton Mifflin.

Gapper, J. (2005). Comment on Sumantra Ghoshal's "Bad management theories are destroying good management practices." *Academy of Management Learning & Education, 4,* 101–103.

Geletkanycz, M. A., & Hambrick, D. C. (1997). The external ties of top executives: Implications for strategic choice and performance. *Administrative Science Quarterly, 42,* 654–681.

Gervurtz, F. A. (2004). The historical and political origins of the corporate board of directors. *Hofstra Law Review, 33,* 89–173.

Ghoshal, S. (2005). Bad management theories are destroying good management practices. *Academy of Management Learning & Education, 4,* 74–91.

Ghoshal, S., & Moran, P. (1996). Bad for practice: A critique of the transaction cost theory. *Academy of Management Review, 21,* 13–47.

Gilson, R. (1996). Corporate governance and economic efficiency: When do institutions matter? *Washington University Law Quarterly, 4,* 327–345.

Gilson, R. J. (2006). Controlling shareholders and corporate governance: Complicating the comparative taxonomy. *Harvard Law Review, 119,* 1641–1679.

Gilson, R., & Kraakman, R. (1991). Reinvesting the outside director: An agenda for institutional investors. *Stanford Law Review, 43,* 863–906.

Gompers, P. A., & Metrick, A. (2001). Institutional investors and equity prices. *The Quarterly Journal of Economics, 116,* 229–259.

Gourevitch, P. A., & Shinn, J. (2005). *Political power & corporate control.* Princeton, NJ: Princeton University Press.

Graves, S., & Haddock, S. (1990). Institutional ownership and control: Implications for long-term corporate strategy. *Academy of Management Executive, 4*(1), 75–83.

Green, S. (2004). Unfinished business: Abolish the imperial CEO. *Journal of Corporate Accounting & Finance, 15,* 19–22.

Grinstein, Y., & Michaely, R. (2005). Institutional holdings and payout policy. *Journal of Finance, 60,* 1389–1426.

Grossman, S., & Hart, O. (1988). One share-one vote and the market for corporate control. *Journal of Financial Economics, 20,* 175–202.

Hall, B. J. (2000). What you need to know about stock options. *Harvard Business Review, 78*(2), 121–129.

Hallock, K. F. (1997). Reciprocally interlocking boards of directors and executive compensation. *Journal of Financial and Quantitative Analysis, 32,* 331–344.

Hambrick, D. C. (2005). Just how bad are our theories? A response to Ghoshal. *Academy of Management Learning & Education, 4,* 104–107.

Hambrick, D. C., & Finkelstein, S. (1987). Managerial discretion: A bridge between polar views of organizational outcomes. In L. L. Cummings, and B. M. Staw (Eds.), *Research in organizational behavior* (Vol. 9, pp. 369–406). Greenwich, CT: JAI Press.

Hambrick, D. C., Finkelstein, S., & Mooney, A. C. (2005). Executive job demands: New insights for explaining strategic decisions. *Academy of Management Review, 30,* 472–491.

Hambrick, D. C., & Jackson, E. M. (2000). Outside directors with a stake: The linchpin in improving governance. *California Management Review, 42,* 108–127.

Hambrick, D. C., Werder, A. V., & Zajac, E. J. (in press). Special issue on corporate governance. *Organization Science.*

Haspeslagh, P. C., & Jemison, D. B. (1991). *Managing acquisitions: Creating value through corporate renewal.* New York: The Free Press.

Hawley, J. P., & Williams, A. T. (2000). *The rise of fiduciary capitalism.* Philadelphia: University of Pennsylvania Press.

Henderson, M. T., & Spindler, J. C. (2005). Corporate heroin: A defense of perks, executive loans, and conspicuous consumption. *Georgetown Law Review, 93,* 1835–1883.

Hendry, J. (2005). Beyond self-interest: Agency theory and the board in a satisficing world. *British Journal of Management, 16,* 55–63.

Hermalin, B. E. (2005). Trends in corporate governance. *Journal of Finance, 60,* 2351–2384.

Hermalin, B.E., & Weisbach, M. (1988). The determinants of board composition. *RAND Journal of Economics, 19,* 589–606.

Hermalin, B. E., & Weisbach, M. (1998). Endogenously chosen boards of directors and their monitoring of the CEO. *American Economic Review, 88,* 96–118.

Hermalin, B. E., & Weisbach, M. S. (2003). Boards of directors as an endogenously determined institution: A survey of the economic literature. *Economic Policy Review, 9,* 7–26.

Heron, R. A., & Lie, E. (2007). Does backdating explain the stock price pattern around executive stock option grants? *Journal of Financial Economics, 83,* 271–295.

Hillman, A. J., & Dalziel, T. (2003). Boards of directors and firm performance: Integrating agency and resource dependence perspectives. *Academy of Management Review, 28,* 383–396.

Himmelberg, C., Hubbard, R. G., & Palia, D. (1999). Understanding the determinants of managerial ownership and the link between ownership and performance. *Journal of Financial Economics, 53,* 353–384.

Hitt, M. A., Harrison, J. S., & Ireland, R. D. (2001). *Mergers & acquisitions: A guide to creating value for stakeholders.* New York: Oxford University Press.

Hitt, M. A., Harrison, J. S., Ireland, R. D., & Best, A. (1998). Attributes of successful and unsuccessful acquisitions of U.S. firms. *British Journal of Management, 9,* 91–114.

Hitt, M. A., Hoskisson, R. E., Johnson, R. A., & Moesel, D. D. (1996). The market for corporate control and firm innovation. *Academy of Management Journal, 39,* 1084–1119.

Holderness, C. G. (2003). A survey of blockholders and corporate control. *Economic Policy Review, 9,* 51–64.

Holderness, C. G., Kroszner, R., & Sheehan, D. (1999). Were the good old days that good? Evolution of managerial stock ownership and corporate governance since the great depression. *Journal of Finance, 54,* 435–469.

Holderness, C. G., & Sheehan, D. P. (1985). Raiders or saviors? The evidence on six controversial investors. *Journal of Financial Economics, 14,* 555–579.

Holmstrom, B. (1979). Moral hazard and observability. *Bell Journal of Economics, 10,* 74–91.

Hoskisson, R. E., & Hitt, M. A. (1994). *Downscoping: How to tame the diversified firm.* New York: Oxford University Press.

Hoskisson, R. E., Hitt, M. A., Johnson, R. A., & Grossman, W. (2002). Conflicting voices: The effects of ownership heterogeneity and internal governance on corporate strategy. *Academy of Management Journal, 45,* 697–716.

Hotchkiss, E. S., & Strickland, D. (2003). Does shareholder composition matter? Evidence from market reaction to corporate earnings announcements. *Journal of Finance, 58,* 1469–1498.

Hunter, J. E., & Schmidt, F. L. (2004). *Methods of meta-analysis* (2nd ed.). Thousand Oaks, CA: Sage Publications.

Hurt, C. (2005). Moral hazard and the initial public offering. *Cardozo Law Review, 26*, 711–789.

Ippolito, R. A., & James, W. H. (1992). LBOs, reversions, and implicit contracts. *Journal of Finance, 47*, 139–167.

Jacobsen, M. A. (1996). Interested director transactions and the (equivocal) effects of shareholder ratification. *Delaware Journal of Corporate Law, 21*, 91–1025.

Jensen, M. C. (1984). Takeovers: Folklore and science. *Harvard Business Review, 62*(6), 109–121.

Jensen, M. C. (1986). Agency costs of free cash flow, corporate finance, and takeovers. *American Economic Review, 76*(2), 323–329.

Jensen, M. C. (1988). Takeovers: Their causes and consequences. *Journal of Economic Perspectives, 2*, 21–48.

Jensen, M. C. (1989). Eclipse of the public corporation. *Harvard Business Review, 67*(5), 61–74.

Jensen, M. C. (1993). Presidential address: The modern industrial revolution, exit and the failure of internal control systems. *Journal of Finance, 48*, 831–880.

Jensen, M. C. (1998). *Foundations of organizational strategy.* Cambridge, MA: Harvard University Press.

Jensen, M. C. (2001). Value maximization, stakeholder theory, and the corporate objective function. *Journal of Applied Corporate Finance, 14*, 8–21.

Jensen, M. C. (2005a). Agency costs of overvalued equity. *Financial Management, 34*(1), 5–19.

Jensen, M. C. (2005b). The modern industrial revolution, exit, and the failure of internal control systems. In D. H. Chew, & S. L. Gillan (Eds.), *Corporate governance at the crossroads* (pp. 21–40). New York: McGraw-Hill Irwin.

Jensen, M. C., & Chew, D. (2000). *A theory of the firm: Governance, residual claims and organizational forms.* Cambridge, MA: Harvard University Press.

Jensen, M. C., & Meckling, W. F. (1976). Theory of the firm: Managerial behavior, agency costs, and ownership structure. *Journal of Financial Economics, 3*, 305–360.

Jensen, M. C., & Meckling, W. H. (1994). The nature of man. *Journal of Applied Corporate Finance, 6*, 4–19.

Jensen, M. C., & Murphy, K. (1990). Performance pay and top-management incentives. *Journal of Political Economy, 98*, 225–264.

Jensen, M., & Ruback, R. (1983). The market for corporate control: The scientific evidence. *Journal of Financial Economics, 11*, 5–50.

Jensen, M., & Warner, J. B. (1988). The distribution of power among corporate managers, shareholders, and directors. *Journal of Financial Economics, 2*, 3–24.

Johnson, J. L., Daily, C. M., & Ellstrand, A. E. (1996). Board of directors: A review and research agenda. *Journal of Management, 22*, 409–438.

Kang, D. L., & Sorensen, A. G. (1999). Ownership organization and firm performance. In K. S. Cook, & J. Hagan (Eds.), *Annual review of sociology* (Vol. 25, pp. 121–144). Palo Alto, CA: Annual Reviews.

Kang, E., & Zardhoohi, A. (2005). Board leadership structure and firm performance. *Corporate Governance, 13*, 785–799.

Kanter, R. M. (2005). What theories do audiences want? Exploring the demand side. *Academy of Management Learning & Education, 4*, 93–95.

Kaplan, A. (1964). *The conduct of inquiry: Methodology for behavioral sciences.* San Francisco: Chandler Publishing.

Karamanou, I., & Vafeas, N. (2005). The association between corporate boards, audit committees, and management earnings forecasts: An empirical analysis. *Journal of Accounting Research, 43*, 453–486.

Karmel, R. S. (2004). Should a duty to the corporation be imposed on institutional shareholders? *The Business Lawyer, 60*(1), 1–21.

Karmel, R. S. (2005). Realizing the dream of William O. Douglas – The Securities and Exchange Commission takes charge of corporate governance. *Delaware Journal of Corporate Law, 30*, 79–144.

Kaufman, A., & Englander, E. (2005). A team production model of corporate governance. *Academy of Management Executive, 19*, 9–22.

Kerr, S. (1975). On the folly of rewarding A, while hoping for B. *Academy of Management Journal, 18*, 769–783.

Kim, J., & Mahoney, J. T. (2005). Property rights theory, transaction costs theory, and agency theory: An organizational economics approach to strategic management. *Managerial and Decision Economics, 26*, 223–242.

Kim, K. A., & Nofsinger, J. R. (2006). *Corporate governance.* Upper Saddle River, NJ: Pearson/Prentice Hall.

King, D. R., Dalton, D. R., Daily, C. M., & Covin, J. (2004). Meta-analyses of post-acquisition performance: Indicators of unidentified moderators. *Strategic Management Journal, 25*, 187–200.

Knutt, N. (2005). Executive compensation regulation: Corporate America, heal thyself. *Arizona Law Review, 47*, 493–517.

Kochhar, R., & David, P. (1996). Institutional investors and firm innovation: A test of competing hypotheses. *Strategic Management Journal, 17*, 73–84.

Kosnik, R. D. (1987). Greenmail: A study of board performance in corporate governance. *Administrative Science Quarterly, 32*, 163–185.

Krannich, J. M. (2005). The corporate "person": A new analytical approach to a flawed method of constitutional interpretation. *Loyola University Chicago Law Journal, 37*, 61–109.

Krishnan, J. (2005). Audit committee quality and internal control: An empirical analysis. *Accounting Review, 80*, 649–675.

Krishnan, H. A., Hitt, M. A., & Park, D. (2007). Acquisition premiums, subsequent workforce reductions and post-acquisition performance. *Journal of Management Studies, 44*, 709–732.

Lie, E. (2005). On the timing of CEO stock option awards. *Management Science, 51*, 802–812.

Long, W. F., & Ravenscraft, D. J. (1993). LBOs, debt, and R&D intensity. *Strategic Management Journal, 14*, 119–135.

Lorsch, J. W. (2005). Cited in Daly, (2005). Directors challenge value of independence standards. *Agenda*, October, p. 4; see also endnote 19.

Lorsch, J. W., & MacIver, E. (1989). *Pawns and potentates: The reality of America's corporate boards.* Cambridge, MA: Harvard University Press.

Lorsch, J. W., & Zelleke, A. (2005). Should the CEO be the chairman? *Sloan Management Review, 46*(2), 71–74.

Lovallo, D., & Kahneman, D. (2003). Delusions of success: How optimism undermines executives' decisions. *Harvard Business Review, 7,* 57–63.

Lubatkin, M. H. (2005). A theory of the firm only a microeconomist could love. *Journal of Management Inquiry, 14,* 213–216.

Lubatkin, M. H., Lane, P. J., Collin, S-O., & Very, P. (2005). Origins of corporate governance in the USA, Sweden, and France. *Organization Studies, 26,* 867–888.

MacAvoy, P. W., & Millstein, I. M. (2003). *The recurrent crisis in corporate governance.* New York: Palgrave Macmillan.

Makri, M., Lane, P. J., & Hitt, M. A. (2006). *A knowledge-based approach to predicting outcomes of high technology mergers and acquisitions.* Working paper, University of Miami, Coral Gables, FL.

Manne, H. G. (1965). Mergers and the market for corporate control. *Journal of Political Economy, 73,* 110–120.

Margolis, J. D., & Walsh, J. P. (2001). *People and profits: The search for a link between a company's social and financial performance.* Mahwah, NJ: Lawrence Earlbaum Associates.

Margolis, J. D., & Walsh, J. P. (2003). Misery loves companies: Rethinking social initiatives by business. *Administrative Science Quarterly, 48,* 268–305.

Marris, R. (1964). *The economic theory of managerial capitalism.* London: Macmillan.

McConaughy, D. L., Walker, M. C., Henderson, G. V., & Mishra, C. S. (1998). Founding family controlled firms: Efficiency and value. *Review of Financial Economics, 7,* 1–19.

McConnell, J. J., & Servaes, H. (1990). Additional evidence on equity ownership and corporate value. *Journal of Financial Economics, 27,* 595–612.

Means, G. (1934). On the alleged concentration of economic power: A reply by Gardiner C. Means. *American Economic Review, 24,* 84–87.

Mehran, H. (1995). Executive compensation structure, ownership, and firm performance. *Journal of Financial Economics, 38,* 163–184.

Meyer, J. W., & Rowan, B. (1977). Institutionalized organizations: Formal structures as myth and ceremony. *American Journal of Sociology, 83,* 340–363.

Micklethwait, J., & Wooldridge, A. (2003). *The company.* New York: Modern Library.

Mikkelson, W. H., & Ruback, R. S. (1985). An empirical analysis of the interfirm equity investment process. *Journal of Financial Economics, 14,* 523–553.

Miller, D., & Le Breton-Miller, I. (2005a). *Managing for the long run: Lessons in competitive advantage from great family businesses.* Boston: Harvard Business School Press.

Miller, D., & Le Breton-Miller, I. (2005b). Management insights from great and struggling family businesses. *Long Range Planning, 38,* 517–530.

Miller, D., & Le Breton-Miller, I. (2006a). Family governance and firm performance: Agency, stewardship, and distinctive capabilities. *Family Business Review, 19,* 73–87.

Miller, D., & Le Breton-Miller, I. (2006b). Priorities, practices, and strategies in successful versus. failing family businesses: An elaboration and test of the configuration perspective. *Strategic Organization, 4,* 379–407.

Mintzberg, H. (2005). How inspiring. How sad. Comment on Sumantra Ghoshal's paper. *Academy of Management Learning & Education, 4,* 108.

Mitchell, R. K., Agle, B. R., & Wood, D. J. (1997). Toward a theory of stakeholder identification and influence: Defining the principle of who and what really counts. *Academy of Management Review, 22,* 853—886.

Mizruchi, M. S. (1983). Who controls whom? An examination of the relation between management and board of directors in large American corporations. *Academy of Management Review, 8,* 426–435.

Mizruchi, M. S. (1996). What do interlocks do? An analysis, critique, and assessment of research on interlocking directorates. *Annual Review of Sociology, 22,* 271–298.

Mizruchi, M. S. (2004). Berle and Means revisited: The governance and power of large U.S. corporations. *Theory and Society, 33,* 579–617.

Moe, T. M. (1984). The new economics of organization. *American Journal of Political Science, 28,* 739–777.

Moeller, S. B., Schlingemann, F. P., & Stulz, R. M. (2005). Wealth destruction on a massive scale? A study of acquiring-firm returns in the recent merger wave. *Journal of Finance, 60,* 757–782.

Monks, R. A. G., & Minow, N. (2004). *Corporate governance* (3rd ed.). Malden, MA: Blackwell Publishing.

Morck, R., Shleifer, A., & Vishny, R. (1988). Management ownership and market valuation: An empirical analysis. *Journal of Financial Economics, 20,* 293–315.

Morgan, A., & Poulsen, A. (2001). Linking pay to performance—compensation proposals in the S&P 500. *Journal of Financial Economics, 62,* 489–523.

Muscarella, C., & Vetsuypens, M. R. (1990). Efficiency and organizational structure: A study of reverse LBOs. *Journal of Finance, 45,* 1389–1413.

Narayanan, M. P., & Seyhun, H. N. (2005). *Do managers influence their pay? Evidence from stock price reversals around executive option grants.* Retrieved October 7, 2006, from http://ssrn.com/abstract=649804

National Association of Corporate Directors (NACD). (2005). *Public company governance survey.* Washington, DC: National Association of Corporate Directors.

National Association of Corporate Directors (NACD). (2006). *Director compensation report.* Washington, DC: National Association of Corporate Directors.

Nixon, R. D., Hitt, M. A., Lee, H.-U., & Jeong, E. (2004). Market reactions to announcements of corporate downsizing actions and implementations strategies. *Strategic Management Journal, 25,* 1121–1129.

Noreen, E. (1988). The economics of ethics. A new perspective on agency theory. *Accounting, Organizations and Society, 13,* 359–370.

O'Connor, J. P., Priem, R. L., Coombs, J. E., & Gilley, K. M. (2006). Do CEO stock options prevent or promote fraudulent financial reporting. *Academy of Management Journal, 49,* 483–500.

Oliver, C. (1991). Strategic responses to institutional processes. *Academy of Management Review, 16,* 145–1179.

Orlitzky, M., Schmidt, F. L., & Rynes, S. L. (2003). Corporate social and financial performance: A meta-analysis. *Organization Studies, 24,* 403–441.

Pfeffer, J. (2005). Why do bad management theories persist? A comment on Ghoshal. *Academy of Management Learning & Education, 4,* 96–100.

Pfeffer, J., & Salancik, G. R. (1978). *The external control of organizations: A resource dependence perspective.* New York: Harper & Row.

Pound, J. (1988). Proxy contests and the efficiency of shareholder oversight. *Journal of Financial Economics, 20,* 237–265.

Rajan, R. G., & Wulf, J. (2006). Are perks purely managerial excess? *Journal of Financial Economics, 79*, 133.

Rappaport, A. (1990). The staying power of the public corporation. *Harvard Business Review, 68*(1), 96–104.

Rehman, S. S. (2006). Can financial institutional investors legally safeguard American stockholders? *New York University Journal of Law & Business, 2*, 683–730.

Rhoades, D. L., Rechner, P. L., & Sundaramurthy, C. (2000). A meta-analysis of the effects of executive and institutional ownership. *Journal of Managerial Issues, 12*, 76–91.

Roberts, J., McNulty, T., & Stiles, P. (2005). Beyond agency conceptions of the work of the non-executive director: Creating accountability in the boardroom. *British Journal of Management, 16*, 5–26.

Rocha, H. O., & Ghoshal, S. (2006). Beyond self-interest revisited. *Journal of Management Studies, 43*, 585–619.

Roe, M. J. (1994). *Strong managers, weak owners: The political roots of American corporate finance.* Princeton, NJ: Princeton University Press.

Roe, M. J. (2005). The inevitable instability of American corporate governance. In J. W. Lorsch, L. Berlowitz, & A. Zelleke (Eds.), *Restoring trust in American business* (pp. 9–33). Cambridge, MA: MIT Press.

Rogers, E. M. (2003). *Diffusion of innovations* (5th ed.). New York: Free Press.

Ross, S. A. (1973). The economic theory of agency: The principal's problem. *American Economic Review, 63*, 134–139.

Sanders, W. G. (2001). Behavioral responses to CEOs to stock ownership and stock option pay. *Academy of Management Journal, 44*, 477–492.

Sanders, W. G., & Boivie, S. (2004). Sorting things out: Valuation of new firms in uncertain markets. *Strategic Management Journal, 25*, 167–186.

Scott, W. R. (1995). *Institutions and organizations.* Thousand Oaks, CA: Sage.

Selznick, P. (1949). *TVA and the grass roots.* Berkeley, CA: University of California Press.

Seward, J. K., & Walsh, J. P. (1996). The governance and control of voluntary corporate spin-offs. *Strategic Management Journal, 17*, 25–39.

Shapiro, S. P. (2005). Agency theory. In K. S. Cook, & D. S. Massey (Eds.), *Annual review of sociology* (Vol. 31, pp. 263–284). Palo Alto, CA: Annual Reviews.

Sherman & Sterling, LLP. (2005). *Trends in the corporate governance practices of the 100 largest U.S. public companies.* New York: Sherman & Sterling.

Shiller, R. J. (2000). *Irrational exuberance.* Princeton, NJ: Princeton University Press.

Shimizu, K., Hitt, M. A., Vaidyanath, D., & Pisano, V. (2004). Theoretical foundations of cross-border mergers and acquisitions: A review of current research and recommendations for the future. *Journal of International Management, 10*, 307–353.

Shivdasani, A., & Yermack, D. (1999). CEO involvement in the selection of new board members: An empirical analysis. *Journal of Finance, 54*, 1829–1853.

Shleifer, A., & Vishny, R. (1986). Large shareholders and corporate control. *Journal of Political Economy, 94*, 461–488.

Shleifer, A., & Vishny, R. W. (1997). A survey of corporate governance. *Journal of Finance, 52*, 737–783.

Skeel, D. (2005). *Icarus in the boardroom.* Oxford, U.K.: Oxford University Press.

Smale, J. G., Patricof, A. J., Henderson, D., Marcus, B., & Johnson, D. W. (1995). Redraw the line between the board and the CEO. *Harvard Business Review, 73*(2), 5–12.

Smith, A. (1952). An inquiry into the nature and causes of the wealth of nations (1776). In R. M. Hutchins (Ed.), *Great books of the western world* (Vol. 39, pp. 291–376). Chicago: Encyclopedia Britannica, Inc.

Solomon, L. D. (1978). Restructuring the corporate board of directors: Fond hope, faint promise. *Michigan Law Review, 76*, 581–610.

Spence, M., & Zeckhauser, R. (1971). Insurance, information, and individual action. *American Economic Review, 61*, 380–387.

Spencer Stuart. (2005a). *Spencer Stuart 2005 board index*. Chicago: Spencer Stuart. Retrieved October 7, 2006, from www.spencerstuart.com/practices/boards/publications

Spencer Stuart. (2005b). *20th Annual Spencer Stuart Survey*. Retrieved October 7, 2006, from www.spencerstuart.com/about/media/34/

Srinivasan, S. (2005). Consequences of financial reporting failure for outside directors: Evidence from accounting restatements and audit committee members. *Journal of Accounting Research, 43*, 291–334.

Stearns, L. B., & Mizruchi, M. S. (1993). Board composition and corporate financing: The impact of financial institution representation on borrowing. *Academy of Management Journal, 36*, 603–618.

Stigler, G. J., & Friedland, C. (1983). The literature of economics: The case of Berle and Means. *Journal of Law & Economics, 26*, 237–268.

Strine, L. E. (2006). Toward a true corporate republic: A traditionalist response to Lucian's solution for improving corporate America. *Harvard Law Review, 119*, 1759–1783.

Stultz, R. (1988). Managerial control of voting rights: Financing policies and the market for corporate control. *Journal of Financial Economics, 20*, 25–54.

Sundaram, A. K., & Inkpen, A. C. (2004a). The corporate objective revisited. *Organization Science, 15*, 350–363.

Sundaram, A. K., & Inkpen, A. C. (2004b). Stakeholder theory and "The corporate objective revisited": A reply. *Organization Science, 15*, 370–371.

Sundaramurthy, C., Rhoades, D. L., & Rechner, P. L. (2005). A meta-analysis of the effects of executive and institutional ownership on firm performance. *Journal of Managerial Issues, 17*, 494–510.

Surowiecki, J. (2004). *The wisdom of crowds*. New York: Doubleday.

Sutton, G. (2004). Rules for rock-solid governance. *Directors & Boards, 25*, 19.

Thompson, J. D., & McEwen, W. J. (1958). Organizational goals and environment: Goal-setting as an interaction process. *American Sociological Review, 23*, 23–31.

Thomsen, S., Pedersen, T., & Kvist, H. K. (2006). Blockholder ownership: Effects of firm value in market and control based governance systems. *Journal of Corporate Finance, 12*, 246–269.

Tihanyi, L., Johnson, R. A., Hoskisson, R. E. & Hitt, M. A. (2003). Institutional ownership differences and international diversification: Effects of boards of directors and technological opportunity. *Academy of Management Journal, 46*, 195–211.

Tosi, H. L., Werner, S., Katz, J. P., & Gomez-Mejia, L. R. (2000). How much does performance matter? A meta-analysis of CEO pay studies. *Journal of Management, 26*, 301–339.

Uhlenbruck, K., Hitt, M. A., & Semadeni, M. (2006). Market value effects of acquisitions involving Internet firms: A resource-based analysis. *Strategic Management Journal, 27*, 899–913.

Vafeas, N. (2005). Audit committees, boards, and the quality of reported earnings. *Contemporary Accounting Research, 22*, 1093–1122.

Veblen, T. (1904). *The theory of business enterprise.* New York: C. Scribner's Sons.

Veblen, T. (1923). *Absentee ownership in recent times: The case of America.* New York: B. W. Huebsch.

Vermeulen, F., & Barkema, H. (2001). Learning through acquisitions. *Academy of Management Journal, 44*, 457–476.

Villalonga, B., & Amit, R. (2006). How do family ownership, control, and management affect firm value? *Journal of Financial Economics, 80*, 385–417.

Wade, J., O'Reilly, C. A., & Chandratat, I. (1990). Golden parachutes, CEOs, and the exercise of social influence. *Administrative Science Quarterly, 35*, 587–603.

Wagner, J. A., Stimpert, J. L., & Fubara, E. I. (1998). Composition and board organizational performance: two studies of insider/outsider effects. *Journal of Management Studies, 35*, 655–677.

Walsh, J. P., & Ellwood, J. W. (1991). Mergers, acquisitions, and the pruning of managerial deadwood. *Strategic Management Journal, 12*, 202–217.

Walsh, J. P., & Kosnik, R. D. (1993). Corporate raiders and their disciplinary role in the market for corporate control. *Academy of Management Journal, 36*, 671–700.

Walsh, J. P., & Seward, J. K. (1990). On the efficiency of internal and external corporate control mechanisms. *Academy of Management Review, 15*, 421–458.

Walsh, J. P., Weber, K., & Margolis, J. D. (2003). Social issues and management: Our lost cause found. *Journal of Management, 29*, 859–881.

Weisbach, M. C. (1988). Outside directors and CEO turnover. *Journal of Financial Economics, 20*, 431–460.

Werner, W. (1977). Management, stock markets, and corporate reforms: Berle and Means reconsidered. *Columbia Law Review, 77*, 388–417.

Werner, W. (1981). Corporation law in search of its future. *Columbia Law Review, 81*, 1611–1666.

Wernerfelt, B. (1984). A resource-based view of the firm. *Strategic Management Journal, 5*, 171–180.

Westphal, J. D. (1998). Board games: How CEOs adapt to increases in structural board independence from management. *Administrative Science Quarterly, 43*, 511–537.

Westphal, J. D. (1999). Collaboration in the boardroom: Behavioral and performance consequences of CEO-board social ties. *Academy of Management Journal, 42*, 7–24.

Westphal, J. D., Boivie, S., & Ching, D. H. M. (2006). The strategic impetus for social network ties: Reconstituting broken CEO friendship ties. *Strategic Management Journal, 27*, 425–445.

Westphal, J. D., & Khanna, P. (2003). Keeping directors in line: Social distancing as a control mechanism in the corporate elite. *Administrative Science Quarterly, 48*, 361–398.

Westphal, J. D., & Milton, L. P. (2000). How experience and network ties affect the influence of demographic minorities on corporate boards. *Administrative Science Quarterly, 45*, 366–398.

Westphal, J. D., & Stern, I. (2006). The other pathway to the boardroom: How interpersonal influence behavior can substitute for elite credentials and demographic majority status in gaining access to board appointments. *Administrative Science Quarterly, 51,* 267–288.

Westphal, J. D., & Stern, I. (2007). Flattery will get you everywhere (especially if you are a male Caucasian): How ingratiation, boardroom behavior, and demographic minority status affect the likelihood of gaining additional board appointments in U.S. companies. *Academy of Management Journal, 50,* 267–288.

Westphal, J. D., & Zajac, E. J. (1994). Substance and symbolism in CEO' long-term incentive plans. *Administrative Science Quarterly, 39,* 367–390.

Westphal, J. D., & Zajac, E. J. (1995). Who shall govern? CEO/board power, demographic similarity, and new director selection. *Administrative Science Quarterly, 40,* 60–83.

Williamson, O. E. (1964). *The economics of discretionary behavior: Managerial objectives in a theory of the firm.* Englewood Cliffs, NJ: Prentice Hall.

Williamson, O. E. (2005). The economics of governance. *American Economic Review, 95,* 11–18.

Wright, P., Ferris, S. P., Sarin, A., & Awasthi, V. (1996). Impact of corporate insider, blockholder, and institutional equity ownership on risk taking. *Academy of Management Journal, 39,* 441–463.

Yermack, D. (1997). Good timing: CEO stock option awards and company news announcements. *Journal of Finance, 52,* 449–476.

Yermack, D. (2006). Flights of fancy: Corporate jets, CEO perquisites, and inferior shareholder returns. *Journal of Financial Economics, 80,* 211–242.

Zahra, S. A., & Pearce, J. A. (1989). Boards of directors and corporate financial performance: A review and integrative model. *Journal of Management, 15,* 291–344.

Zajac, E. J., & Westphal, J. D. (2004). The social construction of market value: Institutionalization and learning perspectives on stock market reactions. *American Sociological Review, 69,* 433–457.

Zald, M. N. (1969). The power and function of boards of directors: A theoretical synthesis. *American Journal of Sociology, 75,* 97–111.

Zeitlin, M. (1974). Corporate ownership and control: The large corporation and the capitalist class. *American Journal of Sociology, 79,* 1073–1119.

2

Old Assumptions, New Work:
The Opportunities and Challenges of Research on Nonstandard Employment

SUSAN J. ASHFORD

Ross School of Business, University of Michigan

ELIZABETH GEORGE

School of Business and Management
Hong Kong University of Science and Technology

RUTH BLATT

Ross School of Business, University of Michigan

Abstract

We review the literature on nonstandard work with three aims: to portray the breadth and nature of the research and theorizing to date, to document the challenges and opportunities this domain poses to both practice and theory, and to bring the study of nonstandard work more to the center stage of micro-OB. After defining nonstandard work and documenting scholarly interest in it, we discuss the literature on the experience of nonstandard workers, on managing the nonstandard workforce, as well as that on managing the interface between standard and nonstandard workers. We analyze the themes that are raised in these literatures and point to new research questions that need to be addressed. Research on nonstandard work can enhance our understanding of the nature of work, the relationship between individuals and organizations, and how organizations and individuals can undertake these new work forms.

Introduction

Alternative, nontraditional, market mediated, vulnerable, contract, freelance, e-lance, contingent, disposable, temporary, nonstandard, and telecommuting—all labels for forms of work seen with increasing frequency in the last decades of the 20th century. Standard workers, who put in set hours at a firm's location with the expectation of long careers within it, are being supplemented by multiple stripes of nonstandard workers who undertake work differently, connect to firms differently, and pursue careers with a different look (Connelly & Gallagher, 2004; Shamir, 1992). The pervasiveness of this phenomenon has led some scholars to argue that the large-company, bureaucratic model through which work has been mostly organized since World War II is becoming increasingly obsolete (Cappelli, 1999). This observation is noteworthy as many of our most influential theories also were developed in reference to a post-WWII American corporate landscape, with its munificent environment, set trade boundaries, and low levels of technology (Scott, 2004; Walsh, Meyer, & Schoonhoven, 2006). Clearly, much has changed. Organizational environments have become increasingly competitive (D'Aveni, 1994); trade boundaries are now so fluid as to represent a single global marketplace for many industries (Bartlett & Ghoshal, 1989), and technology not only has enabled new forms of work practices but also has changed the nature of work itself in many cases (Schilling & Steensma, 2001).

Many of our organizational theories are grounded in the experience of traditional, "1950s" workers who go to their company's location daily to put in a fixed number of hours each day (by clock or by normative pressures) in the full expectation of spending a career in the company's employment (Shamir, 1992). Yet, a significant class of workers does not engage work in this manner. Work can now be done virtually on one's own. Homes and coffee shops have risen in importance as hubs of economic activity. More and more individuals either work on their own and bring their products to market, work for a firm, but work out of their homes, or work for an agency and put in flexible hours (Martens, Nijhuis, Van Boxtel, & Knottnerus, 1999) at various firms within and across industries. While work in some occupations has always been organized in this manner (e.g., actors, dancers, writers, and artists), and these "new" forms of work may hearken back to a preindustrial era where guilds and markets predominated (Peipperl & Baruch, 1997), nonstandard work has now entered bureaucratic organizations in significant numbers. For some, this means the end of the organizational world as we know it. As Cappelli (1999) dramatically put it, "Career jobs are dead." The growth of this class of workers poses new management challenges for firms employing them, new effectiveness challenges for individuals choosing to work in this manner, and new challenges for our theory and research about work and workers as well.

Responding to this changing landscape, Shamir (1992) called for the creation of "a nonorganizational work psychology" to generate better understanding of the work lives of those working outside of organizational settings. Feldman, Doerpinghaus, and Turnley (1994) implored us to respond theoretically and empirically to the growing phenomenon of nonstandard workers in terms of the number of individuals working in this manner, number of firms employing them, and the amount of money involved. While large, bureaucratic organizations still dominate society (Perrow, 1991), change is clearly afoot. Yet much of the literature still implicitly assumes that standard ways of engaging with the organization are normal, and that the more nonstandard workers "look like" standard workers (e.g., by being strongly identified), the better. As Kanter (1977) argued with respect to gender, organizational roles "carry characteristic images of the kinds of people that should occupy them" (p. 250; see also Acker, 1990). The implicit expectation or desire in much of our theorizing is that employees maintain the 1950s' "organization man" terms of engagement with organizations, even as organizations themselves have abandoned it. This unacknowledged bias does not serve researchers or managers well, as it makes less likely the belief that there can be good workers who are not standard. It also marginalizes research on nonstandard workers, with some scholars viewing work done on the outside or periphery of organizational boundaries as not in the domain of our field.

We propose instead that nonstandard work is a topic worthy of study in and of itself and also is an ideal context for testing and developing theory about organizations, work, and workers. As nonstandard work becomes more prevalent in the economy, in organizations, and in individuals' career paths, we need to update our field's implicit portrayals of the nature of employees' attachment to organizations. Indeed, over the past several decades, cultural narratives about work have shifted; it is now increasingly legitimate to be nonstandard, as people take their careers into their own hands, construct their identities as professional and entrepreneurial, and view organizations in an increasingly negative light. It is time for our field to follow suit.

We set three goals for our review of the literature on nonstandard work. Our first is to portray the breadth and nature of the research and theorizing to date. Second, we aim to document the challenges and opportunities this domain poses to both practice and theory. Finally, we hope to bring the study of nonstandard work more to the center stage of particularly micro-OB, as these workers raise important and interesting theoretical issues about the nature of work, the relationship between individuals and organizations, and how organizations and individuals can undertake these new work forms. Our task is made difficult by the fragmented nature of the literature on nonstandard work. Research streams have grown largely independently by type of worker (temporary, virtual, contractors, etc.). Scholars' contributions also flow from different disciplinary perspectives, with little interaction between sociological, labor relations, psychological, and managerial or popular perspectives. The result is a literature filled with redundancies, on one hand, and theoretical gaps, on the other, as work tends to be organized around practical domains rather than theory.

This chapter proceeds in its goal of characterizing and reviewing the literature by discussing the forms nonstandard work takes, its magnitude and scholarly interest, explanations for its' prominence today, and the experience of nonstandard workers themselves. We then discuss the management challenges nonstandard workers pose for firms, whether firms are trying to manage these workers or blend a standard/nonstandard workforce. We end with some overarching conclusions about the literature and future research needs in the area.

Understanding Nonstandard Work Forms: Definitional Issues

Of the many labels used to describe this growing class of workers, we, along with Cappelli, (1999), find "nonstandard" the most descriptive as it clearly invokes a norm of "standard" work arrangements against which these workers contrast. Nonstandard workers are something "other than" standard workers, those who work on a fixed schedule, at the employer's place of business, under the employer's control, and with mutual expectations of continued employment (Broschak & Davis-Blake, 2006; Kalleberg, Reskin, & Hudson, 2000). This definition is consistent with Pfeffer and Baron's (1988) description of the three types of attachment that exist between workers and organizations: attachment based on the degree of physical proximity between employer and employee (see also Kalleberg et al., 2000); attachment based on the extent of administrative control that the employers exerts over the employee; and attachment based on the expected duration of employment. When duration of employment is limited, the organization has limited administrative control over the employee, and/or workers are not physically proximate to the organization, work is more nonstandard.

While Davis-Blake and her colleagues (Broschak & Davis-Blake, 2006; Davis-Blake, Broschak, & George, 2003; Davis-Blake & Uzzi, 1993) have used these bases of attachment to predict different outcomes of nonstandard employment, we propose that the literature would benefit from a further consideration of the ways in which nonstandard work highlights the need for theories that are pertinent to their experiences and behaviors. Since Pfeffer and Baron's (1988) theoretical conceptualization dominated the field, it seems appropriate to start our theorizing about types of nonstandard workers with their framework. As a preliminary step toward this goal, in Table 2.1 we define and give examples of nonstandard work for each of Pfeffer and Baron's dimensions. We also identify some theoretical mechanisms that possibly explain why or how this form of attachment affects workers and identify some mainstream theories used in organizational

Table 2.1 Dimensions of Attachment in Nonstandard Work and Their Implications of Theory

Dimension	Temporal Attachment	Administrative Attachment	Physical Attachment
Definition	Extent to which workers expect employment to last over the long term	Extent to which workers are under the organization's administrative control	Extent to which workers are physically proximate to the organization
Example of nonstandard worker	Temporary workers	Contract workers	Telecommuters
Theoretical mechanism	Affects workers' expectations of the future	Affects whether workers classify themselves as organizational members	Affects levels and quality of interaction
OB theories that might be affected	Organizational citizenship behavior Impression Management	Social identity Theory	Mental models

behavior that might be affected by variations in the levels and forms of workers' attachment to the organization.

Temporal Attachment

Scholars who research "contingent workers" have focused on the temporal dimension identified by Pfeffer and Baron (1988). Contingent work is "any work arrangement that does not contain an explicit or implicit commitment between employee and employer for long-term employment" (Polivka & Nardone, 1989, p. 11). A couple of definitional issues, however, limit the utility of defining work solely by the temporal dimension. First, literature on contingent work has included part-time workers (e.g., Feldman, 1990; Hulin & Glomb, 1999). In our view, however, part-time workers do not easily and unequivocally fall within the nonstandard domain. There are at least two types of part-time workers. While certain "retention" part timers do have limited work hours, they nevertheless could have expectations of employment continuity since they typically are in this work arrangement voluntarily and as a part of the organization's retention strategy (Bauer & Truxillo, 2000; Tilly, 1992). Other part-time workers form a part of a secondary labor market, work limited hours, and have no expectations of long-term employment. Given these ambiguities, we do not focus on part-time work in this review, though we occasionally reference research on part-timers to make more general points.

A second problem with defining employment relationships based on expectations for the future is that in today's uncertain work world, all workers, even standard workers, are "contingent" by this definition to some extent. The implicit commitment between employee and employer for long-term employment appears to no longer be the norm (Arthur & Rousseau, 1996; Cappelli, 1999). That said, employees do appear to differ significantly on their extent of formal and/or informal expectation for a future in the organization, with many nonstandard clearly acknowledging a limited future within an organization. This expectation may be shaped by formal organizational policy or might exist irrespective of formal policy.

Variation in expectations of longevity in employment likely affects individual behavior in organizations, but we do not yet understand how. An example of a behavior that might be affected by the limited longevity of nonstandard work is organizational citizenship behavior (Stamper & Masterson, 2002). Citizenship behaviors are typically exhibited when employees expect that the organization or its representatives will reciprocate, even if not immediately. When workers do not expect to be in an organization over a time, they are likely to reduce their citizenship behaviors. Consistent with this argument, Coyle-Shapiro and Kessler (2002) and Van Dyne and Ang (1998) found that temporary workers exhibit fewer citizenship behaviors than their permanent counterparts. However, Pearce (1993) found that temporary workers engaged in more extrarole behaviors than permanent workers, suggesting that there may be more going on. In the case of temporary workers, calculations of reciprocity might not be the only factors that affect citizenship behaviors. More work is needed for understanding how weak temporal attachment affects organizational citizenship behavior.

Similarly, when individuals expect that their association with an organization might not last for long, they may be less likely to be concerned with impression management, or how others see their performances (Barsness, Diekmann, & Seidel, 2005). Sias, Kramer, and Jenkins (1997) found support for this argument in a sample of temporary workers. They also found that these workers sought appraisal feedback less frequently, consistent with a reduced concern for how others view them. There are both advantages and disadvantages to this reduced interest in what others at work think. For individuals, less impression management may mean that they can be more authentic at work, with reduced pressure to conform to the expectations of others (Pink, 2001). On the down side, however, because they receive less feedback from others, nonstandard workers may learn and develop less than those more concerned with others' opinion of them (Ashford, Blatt, & VandeWalle, 2003). Thus, in line with their increased responsibility for their own careers, contingent workers may engage in impression management for helping them secure future positions (Arthur & Rousseau, 1996). From the firm's perspective, less impression management may mean quicker and greater accuracy in managers' knowledge of the abilities, skills, and motivations of contingent workers. In light of the relatively short history together, this speed and accuracy are important for mobilizing this workforce. On the other hand, less impression management concerns may mean lowered performance from these workers, particularly in the realm of extra-role or citizenship behaviors (Bolino, 1999). The impact of weak temporal attachment on impression management warrants further investigation.

Administrative Attachment

A second distinction raised by Pfeffer and Baron (1988) is who controls the worker administratively. In the case of self-employed independent contractors it might be the workers themselves, or it may be an agency, as is the case for contractors who are employees of a mediating agency that screens and then finds employment for them in a client organization. In the latter case, the agency participates in the control of the nonstandard worker on most issues, but some aspects of administration, such as attendance, might be the purview of the client organization. These workers tend to be treated as outsiders at their client organizations, even though they sometimes have frequent and proximate interactions with others in the organization (Kunda, Barley, & Evans, 2002), and might even represent the organization to external groups (George & Chattopadhyay, 2005). Theories that are premised on membership in a group or organization, such as social identity or self-categorization theory, may be affected by the unique situation of contract workers. For example, how do nonstandard workers reconcile the differences between perceived group membership (Stamper & Masterson, 2002) and actual group membership as they form their identification with work organizations? While the idea of multiple identities has received some attention in the social psychology literature (Cinnirella, 1997; Hornsey & Hogg, 2000; Mlicki & Ellemers, 1996; Wenzel, 2000), nonstandard workers provide a significant context in which to test theories that can help us understand how individuals manage multiple work-related identities, especially between identities that might be simultaneously and equally salient (Ashforth & Johnson, 2001).

Physical Attachment

Nonstandard workers vary in their levels of physical attachment, with some conducting work at the organization's site, others working from home a day or two a week, and others working almost entirely on their own with only infrequent contact with the organization (Pfeffer & Baron, 1988). Physically detached workers thus include those who work from home, like telecommuters, as well as those who work at client sites. The challenge for those who work remotely from their principal employer is one of managing the nature and quality of the interactions with members of the organization.

A number of organizational behavior theories are based on assumptions related to physical interactions between individuals in organizations. For instance, the research on mental models suggests that the more people interact, the more similar their mental models become (Moreland, 1999). However, this finding might not hold when people work remotely from each other, as their e-mail and phone interactions lack the richness of face-to-face contact. Levesque, Wilson, and Wholey (2001) found that in virtual teams, the longer the team operated, the further apart their mental models became. They explained this finding by suggesting that virtual team members experience less social pressures for conformity and focus instead on the task. As a result, individuals develop unique task-related skills and divergent mental models.

Insights from physically weakly attached workers can contribute and add nuance to established theory. For example, George and Chattopadhyay's (2005) research on the social identity of contract employees suggested that organizational identification can develop not only through impersonal means, such as organizational reputation, but also through personal interactions. They found that impersonal bases increase identification with the agencies who mediate contract work whereas personal bases increase identification with the client organization. Their study highlighted that weak attachment makes salient different mechanisms for developing identification with the employing and client organizations. Weak physical attachment to the agency leads to a heightened role for impersonal mechanisms and weak administrative and temporal attachment to the client organization increases the importance of personal relationships.

Our theories of work meaning also stand to benefit from reconsideration in light of weak physical attachment. Interactions with others have long been held as important means through which workers come to understand the meaning and value of their work (Salancik & Pfeffer, 1978; Weick, 1995; Wrzesniewski, Dutton, & Debebe, 2003). Yet, Blatt and Ashford (2006) found that workers who are physically (and often also temporally and administratively) detached from organizations, such as independent contractors, freelancers, consultants, and designers, make meaning through different mechanisms. Specifically, they find that independent workers make meaning by drawing on their self-knowledge and culturally available meaning units rather than through interaction with others.

These three dimensions of the relationship between workers and organizations—(a) physical, (b) administrative, and (c) temporal (Pfeffer & Baron, 1988)—are helpful for distinguishing between different kinds of workers in a world where nonstandard work forms abound. Future research on nonstandard work would benefit from a shift to an explicit consideration of these theoretical dimensions, based on aspects of the relationship between employees and organizations, rather than a focus on a particular category of workers as defined, for example, by the U.S. Bureau of Labor Statistics (e.g., "independent contractors" or "temporary employees"). Such an approach will advance understanding of how varying attachment on any one or combination of these dimensions influences important outcomes such as the development of shared cognitions (Levesque et al., 2001), organizational identification (George & Chattopadhyay, 2005), organizational citizenship behavior (Pearce, 1993), and social relationships at work (Broschak & Davis-Blake, 2006). Understanding nonstandard work through these dimensions of attachment also moves beyond simple dichotomies that distinguish "good" and "bad" nonstandard jobs (e.g., Kalleberg et al.'s, 2000, distinction between "bad" jobs that are low in wages and offer no pension or health benefits and those that are not), issues that, we believe, characterize the experience of nonstandard work rather than constituting defining feature of its form. It moves us beyond the limitations of the categories enumerated by the U.S. Bureau of Labor Statistics to portraying how people understand and experience their jobs.

Utilizing these three dimensions in empirical research, however, has its difficulties. First, although their simplicity is elegant, it can sometimes be challenging for researchers to tease them apart, since they intersect and interact in ways that make it difficult to differentiate their individual effects. For example, the current legal environment surrounding temporary employment has encouraged firms to strictly contain administrative attachment among temporary workers (to avoid coemployment claims). As a result, temporary work and administrative attachment have become more strongly linked than in the past. Similarly, the kind of "supervision" that is possible remotely means that limited physical attachment often occurs with limited administrative attachment as well (Davis-Blake, personal communication, October 2006). These difficulties may account for why Davis-Blake and her colleagues (Broschak & Davis-Blake, 2006; Davis-Blake & Uzzi, 1993; Davis-Blake et al., 2003) often referred to the degree of externalization generally rather than dimension by dimension. Their ability to theorize about the implications of different degrees of externalization is a model for future research.

Second, if being nonstandard is a matter of degree, then the question of at what point (or threshold) is someone appropriately classified as a nonstandard worker becomes pertinent. We believe that this issue is best addressed by considering two questions. First, does the individual's affiliation with a work organization place him or her at the lower end on any of Pfeffer and Baron's (1988) three dimensions of externalization? If yes, then the second question follows: Is the job traditionally conducted in a "standard" way? If both of these questions are answered affirmatively, this means that the worker is physically, temporally, or administratively weakly attached in a job that traditionally was conducted by workers who were strongly attached on any of these dimensions. Thus, the worker is nonstandard. This criterion excludes entrepreneurs, artists, and farmers, since their weak attachment to organizations has been the norm for those occupations. Likewise, it excludes those part-time workers who are in occupations that have traditionally been part time.

The second criterion we introduce suggests that the definition of nonstandard has an inherent subjective element. Indeed, what may seem standard to some employees or organizations may appear nonstandard to others. To some extent, being nonstandard is socially constructed and changes over time, as norms about employment change. This fact is reflected in the relative lack of consensus in the literature about who is included in this definition. Despite this subjective element, we believe that the definition of nonstandard work as a combination of the nature of the work arrangement along the three continua specified by Pfeffer and Baron (1988) and the fact of how work in that occupation has been traditionally arranged is a useful one.

The Magnitude of the Phenomenon and Scholarly Interest

Nonstandard work and workers no longer inhabit the fringes of the labor market. Yet estimating the number of nonstandard workers is difficult. Estimates vary and conditions change. For example in 1996, Silicon Valley, California was held up as representative and predictive of the future regarding labor trends (Carnoy, Castells, & Benner, 1997). Based on the Silicon Valley case, workers were predicted to increasingly move between organizations, filling positions on demand, or to be self-employed, providing labor to the market place (Carnoy et al., 1997). Given the technology bubble of the late 1990s, these figures and even more extravagant portrayals of the possibilities for the future seemed credible. The bubble's burst in the early 2000s, however, challenges this portrayal.

Still nonstandard work appears to be here to stay. A conservative estimate from the most recent U.S. Bureau of Labor Statistics (BLS) survey of nonstandard employment shows that in 2005, 14.8 million people, or 10.7% of the U.S. work force, were employed in a nonstandard employment arrangement. If one considered only those in contingent jobs, such as those who did not expect their jobs to last over a year, approximately 5.7 million Americans (or 4.1% of the work force) could be counted as part of this group. Although these numbers have remained consistent over a 10-year period (see Table 2.2), nonstandard work is gaining prevalence among highly paid, high skilled jobs that represent key sectors of the economy (Bendapudi, Mangum, Tansky, & Fisher, 2003). Thus, the BLS reports that in 2005, 39.9% of the individuals categorized as independent contractors were managers and professionals and that this subcategory is the fastest growing of all segments of independent workers. Less conservative estimates claim that the proportion of U.S. workers in nonstandard arrangements is as high as 33% (Houseman & Polivka, 2000). It should be noted that these BLS figures do not include individuals in part-time work.

Table 2.2 Workers in Nonstandard Work Arrangement in the United States

Year	Independent Contractors	On-Call Workers	Temporary Help Agency Workers	Workers Provided by Contract Firms	Workers with Traditional Arrangements
2005	10,342,000	2,454,000	1,217,000	813,000	123,843,000
	7.4%[1]	1.8%	.9%	.6%	89.3%
1997	8,456,000	1,996,000	1,300,000	809,000	114,119,000
	6.7%	1.6%	1%	.6%	90.1%
1995	8,309,000	1,968,000	1,181,000	652,000	111,052,000
	6.7%	1.6%	1%	.5%	90.2%

Source: BLS Reports 1995, 1997, 2005.
[1] Percentage of total number of employed workers.

Nonstandard work is not a strictly American phenomenon. In Japan, 40% of the labor force is self-employed, part time, or temporary. Similar figures hold for the United Kingdom (Carnoy et al., 1997). The Australian Bureau of Labor Statistics reported that, in 2002 and 2005, approximately 20% of the workforce was in casual employment (roughly equivalent to temporary work in the United States). Nonstandard work arrangements are gaining popularity also among firms in Canada, Europe, and parts of Asia (Allen, 2002; Connelly & Gallagher, 2004).

The size, diversity, and prevalence of nonstandard work have piqued scholars' interest. Of particular interest is the large numbers of firms that employ nonstandard workers—up to 90% of American firms (Matusik & Hill, 1998). Also, information technology makes more and more of us partially virtual— we check e-mail from home, we collaborate with others virtually, and often are just a keystroke away from work at any hour of the day or night. The nonstandardization of work now affects almost everyone's work experience.

Yet research on nonstandard work remains limited. Why do not all studies on work and workers, as a matter of course, take into account the nature of the work arrangement between workers and organizations? One explanation could be that since World War II, standard jobs were available to most of the (then White and male) American workforce, and thus, this work arrangement became the norm for how work was done (Morse, 1969). Most scholars, though they themselves might work in a virtual, nonstandard way, developed their theories of organizational behavior to describe these jobs and workers. A second, and related, explanation is that, even though since the 1920s and 1930s, there were segments of the work force in contingent, nonstandard jobs, these jobs were traditionally occupied by more marginalized members of society—women, youth, immigrants, and members of minority communities (Morse, 1969). Writing about these workers would involve taking into account not just the nature of the jobs, but also the social and political conditions associated with them. Organizational behavior scholars tended to focus their attention on the relatively less politicized population of standard workers (Martin, 2006). Third, standard employees in standard jobs have been the most accessible samples throughout most of our field's history. Researching nonstandard workers has historically been difficult due to their relatively peripheral status and intermittent physical presence in many organizations, which has made them less accessible to researchers.

However, today many nonstandard workers are not marginalized people in peripheral jobs. Independent contractors tend to be male (65% of contractors), White (89%), have at least a bachelor's degree (36%), and work in management, business, financial operations, or sales-related occupations (BLS, 2005). As a result, we need to face some of the tacit boundary conditions of our theories. For example, many of our theories focus on strong individual-organizational relationships and the desirability of such a bond (e.g., Wiesenfeld, Raghuram, & Garud, 1999). Elements of Weberian bureaucracy, such as an organizational career, assume a *future* in the organization and *membership* in the organization and thus a strong organization-employee attachment. This implies a strong individual motive to fit in (which is evidenced in the socialization literature), to belong and identify (as posited in the organizational identification literature), to impress superiors for getting ahead (a central tenet of the impression management literature), to internalize organizational values (a key assumption of the culture literature), and so on. These motives have come to be understood as important mechanisms through which organizations bring about the participation of their employees. Relaxing some of these boundary condition means that some people may not be as strongly motivated to fit in, belong, impress, and internalize organizational values. Their participation is brought about perhaps through other means.

Why the Rise in Nonstandard Work?

The rise in nonstandard work can be accounted for by firm strategic decisions, the changing nature of work, and changing employee preferences. Firms choose to employ nonstandard workers as part of their labor force for a variety of reasons (Davis-Blake & Uzzi, 1993; Uzzi & Barsness, 1998). In what is perhaps the best empirical examination of this issue, Davis-Blake and Uzzi (1993) suggested three categories of reasons why firms use nonstandard workers: costs/flexibility, feasibility, and the nature of the work being performed.

Cost/flexibility. Firms also employ nonstandard workers to stay flexible in increasingly uncertain labor and product markets by expanding and contracting their employment at will (and therefore the size of their workforce; Pfeffer & Baron, 1988). These practices allow firms to cope with increased global competition and uncertainty (Kalleberg, 2000). Theory suggests that employing nonstandard workers also allows firms to focus on their distinctive competencies by externalizing noncore work (Matusik & Hill, 1998; Pfeffer & Baron, 1988) and to curb shirking within the ranks of standard workers as the latter are pressured to perform in the presence of harder-working nonstandard colleagues (Pfeffer & Baron, 1988). Management's distrust of labor also may be an important correlate of the use of nonstandard workers. Previous research has shown that management-labor conflict, as exhibited in strikes or other forms of industrial action, has a significant positive relationship with the extent of use of contract workers (Uzzi & Barsness, 1998). Firms may employ more nonstandard workers to decrease their reliance a workforce they perceived as antagonistic. Davis-Blake et al.'s (2003) evidence suggested that the causality is reciprocal: that the use of temporary workers is also associated with standard workers' increased intent to unionize.

Feasibility. Firms cannot always employ nonstandard workers, despite a cost advantage. Feasibility is constrained by the firm's size and the level of bureaucratization of its employment practices. Davis-Blake and Uzzi (1993) found support for their argument that larger firms, and firms with bureaucratized employment practices, are more focused on maintaining workforce stability and control and therefore are less interested in using temporary workers. Their data also suggested that feasibility is constrained by the presence of powerful influence groups outside of organizations (e.g., government oversight), such that greater government oversight is correlated with lower use of temporary workers (Davis-Blake & Uzzi, 1993).

The employment of nonstandard workers is made more feasible, though, by two factors. First, the rise in the prominence and number of firms that act as employment intermediaries, such as temporary help agencies or contract companies (Kalleberg, 2000; Kalleberg & Marsden, 2005), has greatly facilitated the use of nonstandard workers. In a survey of U.S. organizations (without restrictions on size, sector, or industry), Kalleberg and Marsden (2005) found that approximately 54% used some form of employment intermediary in staffing the various activities of their organization.

Second, technology has also made nonstandard work more feasible. Whereas previously workers needed to assemble in large numbers around machinery and energy sources to coordinate their work; the advent of inexpensive communication technologies has reduced this need. Many kinds of work can now be done from almost anywhere (Kalleberg, 2000; Shamir, 1992). Technology also enables monitoring workers who are not physically present (Pfeffer & Baron, 1988). This development may increase organizations' comfort with employees conducting work off premises, making nonstandard work seem more feasible.

Nature of work. The development of information, communication, and automation technologies in the second half of the 20th century also has profoundly changed the nature of work done within organizations (Bradley, Schipani, Sundaram, & Walsh, 1999) and thus aided firms' ability to reap the cost and flexibility advantages of nonstandard work (Kalleberg, 2000; Shamir, 1992). Today, knowledge is the key factor of production and value creation. While workers were historically selected for their capacity for exertion, dexterity, and endurance, creativity and problem-solving skills are more critical in today's knowledge-based economy (Bradley et al., 1999). The result is a blurring of the divide between the functions of workers and managers (Cobble & Vosko, 2000) and a rise in work that requires considerable freedom and flexibility (Florida, 2002) for which traditional bureaucracies may be ill suited (Shalley, Zhou, & Oldham, 2004).

Given the complexity and importance of such work, however, firms may not easily let go of their control over it. In support of this observation, Davis-Blake and Uzzi (1993) found that the type of work undertaken determines employment conditions, whereby jobs high in either technical or informational complexity are less likely to be given to nonstandard workers. Thus, firms make sure that the key source of value remains within the firm. On the other hand, they find no relationship between the interpersonal complexity of a job and the use of nonstandard workers, suggesting that a wide array of jobs might be profitably structured in nonstandard work arrangements. Indeed, we are seeing firms take advantage of this fact by sending many jobs to distant locations with only minimal connection to the main body of the firm through a process of offshoring. While this practice may be nonstandard at the firm level, researchers need to carefully examine the work arrangements between the offshore firm and its workers as these may be quite standard.

Workers' preferences. According to the U.S. Bureau of Labor Statistics, in 2005, about 32% of temporary agency employees and 82% of independent contractors prefer nonstandard employment to a standard arrangement. Workers may prefer nonstandard work because of its flexibility, variety, freedom from organizational politics, and sometimes higher pay (Florida, 2002; Kunda et al., 2002). Moreover, glamorous portrayals of "free agency" further the cultural sentiment that quality of work life is higher outside of organizations (e.g., Pink, 2001). Particularly women may see nonstandard work as an opportunity to effectively combine participation in the workforce with child care or to overcome barriers to career advancement within organizations (Rothstein, 1996; Wienns-Tuers & Hill, 2002).

In sum, because nonstandard work reduces organizational costs, gives organizations and employees more flexibility, is more feasible and acceptable today, may be more consistent with important knowledge and creative work needed by today's organizations, and is aligned with many people's preferences and lifestyles, it is gaining prevalence and momentum. Its increasing prominence may be an additional source of growth for nonstandard work. That is, the more nonstandard work exists as a model of how to do work and conduct a career over a lifetime, the more legitimate it becomes as a work form and life pattern. The more legitimate it becomes, the more firms and employees will choose to engage in it. Thus, for example, it would not be surprising to see more and more jobs in the future, including jobs at the organization's core, being done in nonstandard ways and the high status and legitimacy of temporary employees that we see in high-tech occupations (Barley & Kunda, 2004) spreading to new occupations. Incrementally and over time, society changes, as do people's expectations of organizations and careers. If the number of people in nonstandard jobs increases, just what is "standard" work becomes an open question.

To understand the implications of nonstandard on the organizational behavior of nonstandard workers and on their management, a good place to start is with their experiences. These experiences have received considerably less attention than have the experience of the firms that employ them and the experience of standard workers. As such, this area is ripe with opportunities for future work.

The Experience of Nonstandard Workers

If organizations increasingly will be an agglomeration of differing types of workers, only some working in the traditional way, then we ought to look carefully at the experience of nonstandard workers, as existing research does not offer a nuanced or adequate understanding of the new world of work (Barley & Kunda, 2001). There have, though, been quite a few descriptive studies of the experience of nonstandard workers, both qualitative (e.g., Ammons & Markham, 2004; Ang & Slaughter, 2001; Baines, 1999; Barley & Kunda, 2001, Bartel & Dutton, 2001; Baruch, 2000; Brocklehurst, 2001; Cooper & Kurland, 2002; Garsten, 1999; Gossett, 2002; Jordan, 2003; Lautsch, 2002; Mallon & Duberley, 2000; Mirchandani, 1999; Olson, 1989; Parker, 1994; Rogers, 1995) and quantitative, focusing usually on nonstandard employees' attitudes (e.g., Ang & Slaughter, 2001; Benson, 1998; Dennis, 1996; DiNatale, 2001; Feldman & Bolino, 2000; Feldman et al., 1994; Howe, 1986; Kalleberg, 2000; Kalleberg et al., 2000; Katz, 1993; Krausz, 2000; Marler, Barringer, & Milkovich, 2002; Parker, Griffin, Sprigg, & Wall, 2002; Pearce, 1993; Raghuram, Wiesenfeld, & Garud, 2003; Staples, Hulland, & Higgins, 1999; Workman, Kahnweiler, & Bommer, 2003). The time is ripe for developing new theory and elaborating existing theory based on these findings. In the following section, we outline what these studies show about the experience of being a nonstandard worker with respect to control, boundaries, relationships, career, self, and choice. We also identify opportunities for both theoretical and empirical work suggested by findings in each segment.

For simplicity in this and subsequent sections, we sometimes make general statements about nonstandard workers as a group. We do recognize, however, that motivation and experience will likely vary depending on the type of nonstandard worker considered. We back our general statements with careful specification of the types of nonstandard workers examined in the studies we cite. In subsequent research, care must be taken to tailor the ideas to the specific ways in which the individual's job is nonstandard.

The Experience of Control

Nonstandard work is often associated with freedom, autonomy, and liberation from corporate control (Davenport & Pearlson, 1998; Bailey & Kurland, 2002; Pink, 2001; Storey, Salaman, & Platman, 2005). In fact, increased autonomy is one of the reasons that self-employed workers are more satisfied than their standard counterparts (Katz, 1993). At the same time, many nonstandard workers also experience great constraints, whether self-imposed or imposed by others. For example, Tietze and Musson (2003) described virtual workers' tendency to exercise self-imposed discipline. Contractors' freedom is also constrained by forces such as cyclical downtime and the structure of projects (Evans, Kunda, & Barley, 2004) and by economic concerns (Jurik, 1998). Just as with standard workers, family members, and nonwork responsibilities may likewise limit nonstandard workers' experience of freedom, particularly for telecommuters and contractors working from home (Ammons & Markham, 2004; Baines, 2002). Finally, organizations often attempt to exercise greater control of nonstandard workers by restricting their hours and duration of employment (Baruch, 2001; Broschak & Davis-Blake, 2006) and by giving them specific instructions on what they are to do and how, with little ability to negotiate demands (Ang & Slaughter, 2001). In the case of telecommuters, organizations tend to place great emphasis on scheduled meetings, reviews, and other means of monitoring (Pearlson & Saunders, 2001).

This apparent paradox suggests important research regarding the optimal combination of structure and freedom for achieving favorable outcomes among nonstandard workers. Just as organizations have a keen interest in controlling nonstandard workers, these workers need to grapple with the issue of control themselves. Following Brown and Eisenhardt (1997), who found that "semistructures," in which only some features are prescribed, are most adaptive for organizational innovation in high-velocity environments, a fruitful research stream might explore individual-level semistructures for facilitating nonstandard work. Such research could identify which elements should be tightly controlled and which should remain free, which elements should be controlled by the worker and which by the organization and which combination of freedom and constraints is experienced as most favorable by the workers themselves. Qualitative work by Ashford and Blatt (2003) began to suggest the range of tactics independent workers use to create optimal structure for the pursuit of the work, ranging from tactics that structure their time and space, to those that regulate their emotions and emotional reactions. Blatt and Ashford (2006) further examined how nonstandard workers use meaning making to facilitate staying on task and getting work done under conditions of great freedom. Considering that autonomy and freedom from organizational influence is both a common reason people enter nonstandard work (Feldman & Bolino, 2000; Kunda et al., 2002) and an important source of satisfaction (Baruch, 2000; Katz, 1993) and that a primary concern of organizations utilizing nonstandard workers is the reduced ability to control them (Ang & Slaughter, 2001; Matusik & Hill, 1998), this set of research questions merit both greater theoretical development and further empirical work.

The Experience of Boundaries

The distinction between an organizational insider and an outsider used to be relatively clear. Today the rise of nonstandard work has made it much less so (Rafaeli, 1998). Consequently, issues relatively dependent on the experience of membership, such as identification, sense of community and belonging, and socialization into the organizational culture, are rendered problematic. Indeed studies have find that contingent workers often do not feel a part of the organizations that employ them (Allan & Sienko, 1998) and are less likely to identify with them (McLean Parks, Kidder, & Gallagher, 1998; Nollen & Axel, 1996) or be committed to them (Van Dyne & Ang, 1998). This is also the case for virtual employees (Rock & Pratt, 2002; Wiesenfeld et al., 1999). In the face of blurred organizational boundaries, organization may not be the source of community (Kogut & Zander, 1996), belonging (Hogg & Terry, 2000), and identity (Dutton, Dukerich, & Harquail, 1994) that they once were.

Although people often enter nonstandard employment to better manage the work-nonwork boundary (Rothstein, 1996), ironically they may find this boundary more difficult to manage in their new work mode. Nonstandard work can blur the work-nonwork boundary, both physically, as people work from home, and temporally, as they are likely to work at all hours. Those who work at home may find it difficult to establish these boundaries, especially if they are highly involved in their work and their hours are long and irregular (Ammons & Markham, 2004; Mirchandani, 1999). They may experience the problem of "presenteeism," the inability to take time off from work, even when sick (Mann, Varey, & Button, 2000). Even the boundary between working and socializing is blurred, as nonstandard contract workers concerned about employability attend social events in the hope of making connections to facilitate future career opportunities (Kunda et al., 2002).

These observations challenge much of the research in organizational behavior that is premised on clearer distinctions. For example, the notion of "spillover" (Westman, 2001) suggests a clear boundary between work and nonwork. Herein lies an opportunity for future research. Do nonstandard workers experience boundaries as blurred or distinct? Do their actions serve to distinguish them or blur them further? Is this a source of stress or satisfaction?

The Experience of Relationships

Nonstandard work often has a substantial impact on one's relationships. For example, many have documented the feelings of isolation experienced by teleworkers (Baines, 2002; Baruch, 2001; Cooper & Kurland, 2002; Golden, 2006; Kurland & Bailey, 1999), contractors (Barley & Kunda, 2004; Feldman & Bolino, 2000), and temporary employees (Feldman et al., 1994; Rogers, 1995). However, many workers appear to adjust to this problem over time or develop strategies for dealing with it (Ammons & Markham, 2004; Baines, 1999). Another issue is the negative treatment that temporary and contract workers receive from coworkers while on site in organizations (Hudson, 2001; Smith, 1997). These experiences can lead many nonstandard workers to feel marginalized. It is perhaps because of the prevalence of exclusion that nonstandard workers are keenly attuned to how they are treated by others, with positive treatment particularly appreciated (Bartel, Wrzesniewski, & Wiesenfeld, in press; Benson, 1998; Blatt & Camden, 2006; George & Chattopadhyay, 2005; Pearce, 1993). Such relationships may also affect tangible outcomes. In Ho, Ang, and Straub's (2003) study, a positive relationship with the boss is positively related to evaluations of the nonstandard contract worker's performance. The reality of an insecure livelihood in some forms of nonstandard work (e.g., where friendship and support may coexist with competition) and the complexities of working in the home, in the case of contractors and telecommuters, can generate interpersonal tension and a greater need for social support (Baines, 1999, 2002; Trent, Smith, & Wood, 1994).

This research suggests that there may be a new set of relational rules in a complex social world where nonstandard and standard employees work alongside one another and workers work where their families live. As Lautsch (2002) wrote, nonstandard jobs entail "complex social relationships, rather than... wage contracts" (p. 41) How can nonstandard workers overcome differences in experience to create common ground for coordination, translate across disciplinary differences for communication, and develop enough trust for innovation? How do they negotiate family relations to create effective work practices?

A second research opportunity lies in understanding the community of practice that nonstandard employees develop to adapting to the nonstandard role. Numerous Web sites, online communities, associations, and networking events represent grassroots attempts by nonstandard workers to learn from each other about how to deal with these complicated relational realities (Jordan, 2003) and create community. What do they learn from each other and what can we learn from them about relationships in the new world of work? Another important area of ongoing research concerns the influence of technology on relationships patterns and the need to use technology to replace face-to-face communication (Davenport & Pearlson, 1998; Golden, 2006; Mann et al., 2000; Pratt, Fuller, & Northcraft, 2000; Wiesenfeld et al., 1999; Workman et al., 2003). Given the growing prevalence of the substitution of technology for face to face as a means of connecting even in standard work, this research has broad appeal.

The Experience of Career

Nonstandard work generally means that workers manage their own careers, rather than putting their fate in the hands of an organization (Heckscher, 2000; Hoque & Kirkpatrick, 2003; Tench, Fawkes, & Palihawadana, 2002). This fact has several implications for how nonstandard work is experienced. The first is the experience of job insecurity and the continuous search for work (Kalleberg et al., 2000; Marler et al., 2002). Temporary work is often seen as a dead-end career pattern with little or no job security (Feldman et al., 1994; Hudson, 2001). Contractors also experience significant preoccupation with maintaining their network and securing future work (Kunda et al., 2002). The second is the experience of vulnerability to market shifts stemming from nonstandard workers' closeness to and dependence on the market and forces beyond their control (Feldman & Bolino, 2000). Studies find, for example, that contractors' actions are strongly motivated by concern over income (e.g., Evans et al., 2004; Jurik, 1998).

Much has been written about whether nonstandard work is marginalizing or liberating. The research reviewed above suggests a more complicated reality, whereby even the most "boundaryless" independent contractors face economic pressures and worry about future income (Evans et al., 2004). It is time for research to focus on how to manage the complexities of personal responsibility for career, how the agency (e.g., the capacity to do otherwise; Giddens, 1984) inherent in "free agency" is best realized, and how individuals can buffer themselves against the insecurities associated with the new world of work. The latter issue is relevant for nonstandard and standard workers alike.

The Experience of Self

Nonstandard work makes identity problematic. The work lives of nonstandard workers are more likely to be marked by discontinuity, and their identities are more likely to be fragmented or liminal (Smith, 1998). Overlaid on this reality, contingent workers, contractors, and virtual workers are often marginalized, stigmatized and treated as outsiders, second-class citizens, or invisible (Barker, 1998). For example, temporary agencies often treat workers, even highly educated ones, as a bundle of skills rather than as individuals (Inkson, Heising, & Rousseau, 2001). Not surprisingly, contingent and virtual workers often do not identify with organizations and may even be resentful toward them (Feldman et al., 1994; Jordan, 2003).

Relatively little research has examined nonstandard workers' response to these experiences. A study by Jordan (1996) found that many temporary employees respond with active resistance to dehumanizing practices. Others appear to focus on re-narrating and redefining their identities in positive terms (Pink, 2001; Tietze, 2005; Zuboff & Maxmin, 2002). This mirrors the identity work of people in stigmatized occupations, who tend to develop a strong culture that positively redefines their collective identity (Ashforth & Kreiner, 1999; Peipperl & Baruch, 1997). Some research suggests that nonstandard employees turn to non-organizational sources of identity, such as occupational communities (Kunda et al., 2002). This may entail dissociation from the negative identity of being nonstandard (Chattopadhyay & George, 2001). As yet, little empirical work has offered support for these ideas, and we have limited understanding of where nonstandard workers turn to enhance their self-esteem and reduce uncertainty, two known functions of social identity (Tajfel & Turner, 1986).

The Experience of Choice

The literature portrays one key determinant of workers' response to being nonstandard as the degree of choice workers had in their standard versus nonstandard status. Indeed, Parker and colleagues (2002) argued that negative versus positive reactions to nonstandard work may depend on whether nonstandard workers entered that status involuntarily or voluntarily. McLean Parks and colleagues (1998) suggested that "the degree to which employees believe they had choice in the selection of the nature of the employment relationship" (p. 720) affects the resulting psychological contract. With increasing "voluntariness" comes increasing perceptions of justice and more extrarole behavior (McLean Parks et al., 1998). However, while the degree of choice in engaging in nonstandard work has been extensively invoked with respect to its importance in explaining the experience of nonstandard work, empirical findings have been mixed. For example, Benson (1998) found that preference for contract employment influences commitment to the employing organization but not to the host organization among temporary employees. Both Feldman, Doerpinghaus, and Turnley (1995) and Krausz (2000) found that choice in temporary work is associated with more positive attitudes toward aspects of their jobs, but Van Breugel, Van Olffen, and Olie (2005) found that choice is not associated with attitudes among temporary employees. In another empirical investigation, Ellingson, Gruys, and Sackett (1998) concluded that "the reasons leading to a choice to pursue temporary work have little relationship to performance levels" (p. 918).

The mixed findings may result from the fact that actual entry into nonstandard employment typically has both volitional and nonvolitional characteristics (Polivka, 1996) and that choice is both prospectively and retrospectively evaluated. As such choice may not be as important a variable as it first appears.

Both Jurik (1998) and Kunda and colleagues (2002) found that people face a combination of constraints (little choice) and agency (choice) in beginning to work as temporary workers and contractors. The fact that a career path is first characterized by a high degree of choice or not may not be an important determinant of subsequent attitudes. Studies find that those who *did not* choose nonstandard work still report satisfaction with the role as they come to see it as an opportunity to get away from the negative aspects of organizational employment (Jurik, 1998) whereas those who *did* choose it often report some dissatisfaction as they come to see value in their organizational pasts (Mallon & Duberley, 2000). Likewise, Marler and colleagues (2002) *expected* to find that high skills would coincide with preferences for temporary work (along the lines of a boundaryless career model), whereas low-skilled workers would prefer a standard job. However, what they found was that, while high-skilled workers prefer temporary work more than do those with low skills, only 35% express such a preference. Thus their data suggested that preference and skill level are somewhat orthogonal.

It may be more fruitful to write about how choice is construed to the self or others (narratives of choice), rather than actual choice. First, as previously stated, actual degree of choice may not be a clear-cut issue. Second, in terms of behavioral and attitudinal outcomes, narratives of choice may matter more. For example, Ammons and Markham (2004) found that those respondents who talk about working at home as a result of their choice have greater motivation to make it work. The degree of volition in their post hoc narrative—or their *perceived* choice to work in a nonstandard arrangement—has particular behavioral consequences quite independent of their actual level of choice at the time they made the decision (McLean Parks et al., 1998). Dick and Hyde (2006) similarly found that what mattered in the *choice* to engage in part-time work depended on how workers narrated it to themselves. As Weick (1996) wrote, nonstandard careers are "improvised work experiences that rise prospectively into fragments and fall retrospectively into patterns" (p. 40). What may have been a complex and messy process of choice and nonchoice when entering nonstandard employment may emerge as a coherent narrative of either choice or lack of it, each with its associated pattern of attitudes and behavioral inclinations. Blatt and Ashford's (2006) qualitative research on independent workers suggested that nonstandard workers nimbly construct and alter the meaning of their work to remain focused and positive while working in ambiguous conditions. The role of meaning making in work outcomes for nonstandard workers is a fruitful area for future research.

When considering the experience of nonstandard workers, it is important to keep in mind significant differences among the various types of workers within the category of nonstandard work (Polivka, 1996). Some of these differences have to do with status and class. Kunda and colleagues (2002) pointed out that the literature on the work of free agents focuses almost exclusively on the experience of highly skilled contractors, thereby glamorizing nonstandard work. However, these workers tend to earn premiums relative to standard employees in their occupations due to their status and skill, while other types of nonstandard workers (e.g., on call and temporary workers) are penalized (Belman & Golden, 2000; DiNatale 2001; Smith, 1997). Marler et al. (2002) labeled the first group "boundaryless" workers and the second "traditional temporary employees." They paint a somewhat glowing portrait of boundaryless workers enjoying job security rooted in their own skills and their ability to sell them. Boundaryless workers supposedly increase their security through skill accumulation and thus may not even desire a permanent job. Marler and colleagues (2002) noted that boundaryless nonstandard workers are more likely than traditional temporary employees to perceive that they have more alternatives and to expect and receive higher wages. Further, Kalleberg et al. (2000) found that, while employment in nonstandard arrangements increases the risk of bad job characteristics substantially, the self-employed and contract workers have jobs with fewer bad characteristics than do regular part timers, temporary help agency workers and on call workers or day laborers (Kalleberg et al., 2000). Our field in general knows little about the latter set of workers. The nonstandard work area might lead the way in bringing attention to issues specific to these workers.

High-quality research focused on the questions we have raised here and sensitive to the type of nonstandard worker under consideration will go a long way toward addressing Barley and Kunda's (2006) critique of this literature as focusing too much on economics and the labor market and too little on nonstandard workers' actual experiences. A focus on theory and mechanisms will also help to order the qualitative and quantitative descriptive data that do exist so that it begins to give more insights than simple description.

The Blended Workforce: A New Set of Challenges

Management increasingly faces the challenge of managing a blended workforce that includes standard and nonstandard workers performing side by side, often over some period of time. The challenges are substantial.

Attitudes and Behaviors of a Blended Workforce

Many studies have established that the employment of nonstandard workers is likely to negatively affect standard workers' attitude toward management and the organization, as well as toward their coworkers (Broschak & Davis-Blake, 2006; Chattopadhyay & George, 2001; Geary, 1992; George, 2003; Davis-Blake et al., 2003; Pearce, 1993; Smith, 1994). For example, Pearce's (1993) study of the effects of the presence of contract employees on the internal workers of a large aerospace company found that permanent employees with comparable temporary coworkers reported lower trust in the organizations than employees in permanent employee only work units. While Pearce (1993) found no difference in the self-reported organizational commitment of the internal and contract workers, the presence of temporary workers has generally been shown to be associated with poorer relations and lower trust in managers among standard workers (Davis-Blake et al., 2003; George, 2003) and with poorer supervisor-subordinate relations among all workers (Broschak & Davis-Blake, 2006).

The blending of standard and nonstandard workers also negatively affects relationships among workers in organizations. In a qualitative study of three electronics firms in Ireland, Geary (1992) found that the presence of temporary workers gives rise to tension between permanent and temporary employees. Chattopadhyay and George (2001) reported that interpersonal attraction and trust between all workers is lower as the number of temporary workers increases in work groups in three different organizations. Similarly, Broschak and Davis-Blake (2006) found that the greater the degree of blending of temporary and standard workers in a financial services organization, the worse standard workers' relationships with their colleagues.

Moreover, employing nonstandard workers affects standard workers' behavior on the job. Standard workers have been found to engage in less extrarole behaviors than contract workers (Pearce, 1993), exhibit fewer helping behaviors (Broschak & Davis-Blake, 2006), and increase their propensity to unionize (Davis-Blake et al., 2003) when nonstandard workers are added to their group.

Why All the Negativity?

Several factors may account for these negative attitudes and altered behaviors among standard employees. First, the presence of nonstandard workers may cause standard workers to question the security of their own jobs. This uncertainty may negatively affect their job attitudes (Smith, 1997) and build the sense that they have to work harder to protect their jobs from nonstandard coworkers (Geary, 1992). Permanent employees feel compelled to work overtime so that they can keep up with their temporary coworkers in one electronics firm (Geary, 1992). Geary (1992) quoted a shop steward, who said, "People complain to me about the level of overtime. But what can you do when you have 20 temps and 5 permanent people on the line? Temps feel obliged to come in at the weekend and so do permanent people as a result" (p. 263). This finding suggests that competition for resources also may help account for more negative attitudes toward organizations, managers, and coworkers among standard employees whose work groups are increasingly populated by nonstandard employees.

Nonstandard workers may alter the career mobility opportunities for standard workers as well. In a study of a large Fortune 500 utility, Barnett and Miner (1992) found that the use of temporary workers quickens the mobility of permanent employees in higher level jobs but retards the mobility of those in lower level jobs. They argued that the introduction of temporary workers reduces opportunities for advancement for lower level workers by increasing the number of potential competitors for each job while decreasing the number of individuals eligible to compete for higher levels jobs, thus eliminating the rivalry that exists for those jobs and increasing the likelihood that permanent workers advance into higher level jobs (Barnett & Miner, 1992). More recently, Broschak and Davis-Blake (2006) found that the negative effects of employment heterogeneity on employee attitudes and behaviors are particularly negative for those holding jobs that are one standard deviation below the mean job grade. The reduced mobility opportunities for these workers, as well as the resultant threat to their status, are particularly triggered by the presence of nonstandard workers.

The negative attitudes and behaviors of standard employees in response to nonstandard employees may relate to their perceptions of fairness. When standard and nonstandard workers are paid differently, standard workers may believe that the organization is unfair to the standard worker or that the organization is exploiting the nonstandard workers. In both cases, the standard workers may come to perceive the organization as untrustworthy (Pearce, 1993). George (2003) found that standard workers view the use of external workers as a violation of the psychological contract between employees and the organization. She proposed that when organizations or their representatives engage in actions that are seen to be detrimental to workers' interests, standard employees are likely to reduce their trust in the organization.

Standard workers might also resent the presence of nonstandard coworkers because they place additional role-related demands on them. In a study of staffing arrangements in a large manufacturer of photocopy and computer equipment, Smith (1994) found that standard workers believe that temporary workers do not care about work quality, and thus, the standard workers have to "organize their efforts around the expected inconsistent work of the temporary workers" (p. 299). Similarly, since the procedures used to hire temporary workers are often truncated (Christensen, 1998), the blending of standard and nonstandard workers can be associated with increased workloads for all workers. This workload increase compensates for the perceived lack of organization-specific skill of temporary workers (Pearce, 1998). Geary's (1992) case study found that temporary workers are brought in on short notice, with little screening, thus placing additional supervisory demands on standard workers. George, Chattopadhyay, Lawrence, and Shulman's (2003) study of the effects of externalization on the work of research scientists found that the greater use of temporary workers in teams is associated with scientists reporting more time spent on administrative work and less time spent on work that was meaningful to them.

Minimizing the Costs of Blending

The attitudes of standard workers toward the use of nonstandard workers are not uniform, however. There are some preliminary indicators that organizational factors can moderate the relationship between the extent to which work groups are blended and the attitudes of standard workers. Four variables have been shown to mitigate the effect of employment status heterogeneity on standard workers' attitudes. First, Davis-Blake and colleagues (2003) argued that the impact of nonstandard workers varied with the proximity of the nonstandard workers to the firm. Temporary workers, who are both physically proximate and supervised by the organization, are more disruptive to the relationship between standard workers and the organization than are contract workers, who are only physically proximate to the organization. It appears that the more similar the nonstandard worker to the standard worker, the more the standard worker is threatened by and resentful of the nonstandard worker. Broschak and Davis-Blake (2006) made a similar argument to explain their finding that temporary worker heterogeneity has a more negative effect on coworker relations than part-time worker heterogeneity does. They argued that temporary workers affect the mobility opportunities of standard workers more than do part-time workers. Also, the difference in status levels between temporary and standard workers likely triggers conflict between the two groups.

Second, the standard workers' level in the organization may buffer them from the detrimental effects of having nonstandard coworkers (Broschak & Davis-Blake, 2006). Barnett & Miner's (1992) findings that the impact of nonstandard workers on standard workers' mobility depend on the latter's organization level suggested this moderator. It may also be that workers with supervisory responsibilities feel more valued by the organization and thus are not as affected by the presence of temporary workers as those with no supervisory responsibilities (George, 2003).

Third, the relationship between the extent to which the work group is blended and standard workers' attitudes and reactions toward the organization may depend on the nature of the psychological contract between standard workers and the organization. Paradoxically, the more positive the psychological contract, the more standard workers may feel a sense of violation by the introduction of nonstandard workers into the organizational workforce. For example, in a multiorganization study of standard workers with varying levels of temporary or contract coworkers, George (2003) found, contrary to her hypothesis, that greater job security and longer term use of temporary and contract coworkers is associated with greater perceptions that the psychological contract between the standard employees and the organization has been violated, lower levels of trust in management, and lower affective commitment to the organization. She speculated that this result could be explained by Brockner, Tyler, and Cooper-Schneider's (1992) argument that the more positive the affect that individuals have toward organizations, the more severe their reactions to perceived violations of trust by the organization in comparison with those who do not have this positive affect and the related set of expectations.

Finally, standard employees' relations to the heterogeneity of the work group may depend upon the extent and nature of standard and nonstandard workers' interactions with each other. Broschak and Davis-Blake (2006) found, for example, that after controlling for group work status heterogeneity, nontask-related interactions are positively related to employee attitudes and behaviors, while task-related interactions have a negative relationship with supervisor-subordinate relations. They argued that the information and familiarity that comes from nontask-related interactions may mitigate concerns associated with the more frequent use of nonstandard workers. Task related interactions, however, are fraught with the issues and problems that differentiate between standard and nonstandard workers. Thus, task-related interactions only serve to make salient and to exacerbate the problems of blending the two groups. These studies suggested that managers can mitigate the negative effects of blending different categories of workers by managing the types of workers used, the level of standard workers put with nonstandard coworkers, and the opportunities for interaction between standard and nonstandard workers.

Existing research also leaves room for further identification of moderators of the relationship between the extent to which groups are blended and the attitudes and behaviors of workers. While Davis-Blake and colleagues (Broschak & Davis-Blake, 2006; Davis-Blake et al. 2003) argued that the effects of blending standard workers with different types of nonstandard workers will vary depending on the type of nonstandard worker (e.g., temporary, contract, or part time), no research to date has examined if this effect will vary depending on the occupations to which these standard and nonstandard workers belong. It may be that the use of such workers is more threatening in some occupations than others. For example, for occupations with tight labor markets, a firm's decision to use nonstandard workers poses a great threat to standard workers. In fact, a tight labor market may render nonstandard work more desirable, as was the case for technical contractors in the late 1990s (Barley & Kunda, 2004). In occupations with labor shortages across industries, the threat is substantially reduced.

The threat that nonstandard workers pose to standard workers could also depend on the extent to which the nonstandard workers are voluntarily in this work arrangement (Ellingson et al. 1998; Holtom, Lee, & Tidd, 2002; Tan & Tan, 2002). If they are nonstandard by choice, chances are they are not hoping to receive permanent employment in the firm and therefore are less of a threat to the standard workers' jobs.

An open question also is whether the negative effects of blending standard and nonstandard workers are asymmetrical such that standard workers are more negatively affected by the mix than are nonstandard workers. While Chattopadhyay and George (2001) were able to examine some of these asymmetries using social identity theory, future research could build on the rich research on relational demography (e.g., Tsui, Egan, & O'Reilly, 1992) to explore whether nonstandard and standard workers have differential reactions to working with each other. The asymmetry also persists in that we now know quite a bit about the effect of nonstandard workers on standard workers, but far less about what affects the perceptions and experiences of nonstandard workers as they are placed in work groups with few or many standard workers. For managers and organizations truly interested in blending the workforce, the experiences of both sides need to be fully understood and the explanatory mechanisms uncovered.

Whatever the type of nonstandard work, their increasing prominence suggests that a key issue for organizations employing or interacting with them is their management. We now turn to the managerial issues associated with employment of nonstandard workers.

Managing Nonstandard Workers

While organizations employ nonstandard workers to gain flexibility and reduce costs, the practice presents several managerial problems. Principal among them is the problem of control—how to manage the output of workers who cannot be watched closely. This problem is a growing one even with standard workers, as spans of control increase in organizations and as the knowledge and creative processes of work are less amenable to observation and direct control (Bradley et al., 1999). However, Shamir (1992) noted that organizations trying to control workers who are at home through the traditional means of bureaucratic, outcome, clan, or market control face substantial difficulties.

The difficulties of managing nonstandard workers may stem in part from implicit managerial beliefs about the relationship between commitment to the organization and productivity. Managers have traditionally held two beliefs: that workers who are committed to the organization are better workers (Mowday, Porter, & Steers, 1982) and that nonstandard workers may be less committed to the organization than workers in standard work arrangements (Gallagher & McLean Parks, 2001; Hulin & Glomb, 1999). Research indicates that they are mostly correct (Harrison, Newman, & Roth, 2006; Wheeler & Buckley, 2000), although findings have been mixed (e.g., Benson, 1998). How then does an organization gain the advantages of flexibility (with its accompanying weak commitment toward nonstandard workers), as well as the organizational benefits of a committed workforce (e.g., nonstandard workers)?

Management scholars, taking the perspective of the organization, have addressed these problems of commitment and control in four interrelated streams of research. The first, which we call *managing through job design and fit*, presents the view that the challenge of managing nonstandard workers is essentially one of managing the context in which they work. According to this view, managers can focus either on designing the job, choosing the right person, or a combination of the two, in order to increase the productivity of nonstandard workers. The second stream, building on social exchange and psychological contract theories, suggests that the key to managing nonstandard workers is to understand the factors that motivate them and to then provide them the right inducements to work. We call this approach *managing through exchange*. This approach focuses more on explicit inducements rather than the more diffused motivators that stem from a fit between individuals and jobs. The third stream of research, *management through relationships*, recognizes the growing evidence that positive relationships between coworkers can go a long way toward substituting for a positive relationship with the organization, and that managers stand to gain from facilitating the kinds of connections that make a difference. The final stream of research considers the fit between a nonstandard worker's personal identity and the values of the organization. We refer to this stream of research as *management through identity*. We discuss each of these approaches in the following section.

Management Through Job Design and Fit

One way of managing the contribution of nonstandard workers in organizations is through the jobs that are given to them. For example, Ang and Slaughter (2001) found that the jobs that organizations assign to contract workers are associated with perceptions of their trustworthiness and performance. Like Allan and Sienko (1998), they concluded that the satisfaction and performance of nonstandard workers is often a self-fulfilling prophecy. If organizations give nonstandard workers peripheral tasks, then these nonstandard workers tend to become alienated and unmotivated. But if these workers are given richer tasks, the picture can be quite different. Indeed, when nonstandard workers' jobs contain considerable autonomy, variety, flexibility, and skill utilization, they tend to be more satisfied than standard workers (Hundley, 2001; Kalleberg et al., 2000). Yet too much autonomy, when paired with extensive interdependence with others in the completion of work tasks, can prove to be too difficult to manage and has been found to reduce nonstandard workers' satisfaction (Golden & Veiga, 2005).

The characteristics of the jobs given to nonstandard workers often result from organizational attempts to achieve greater control over them. Thus researchers find that nonstandard temporary employees are more likely to be employed in jobs with less complexity and less skill utilization than permanent workers (Davis-Blake & Uzzi, 1993; Kalleberg et al., 2000). Further, because firms often employ nonstandard workers to adjust for fluctuations in workload demand (Houseman, 1997; Kalleberg, 2000), jobs with unstable demands are more often assigned to temporary or contract workers than are jobs with stable demands. Organizations also assign jobs to nonstandard workers based on whether the nature of the work is amenable to it. For example, virtual work is more or less appropriate depending on characteristics of the job such as whether much of it happens on customer sites, whether it involves rapid changes, and the extent to which it requires interaction among colleagues (Cascio, 2000; Shamir, 1992).

The degree of "fit" between the worker and the job has also been invoked as important. Thus, managers attempting to manage nonstandard work arrangements can either shape the job, chose the right person for the job, or a combination of the two. For example, virtual work arrangements might be inappropriate in the earlier stages of employment, before the employee has fully understood the culture of the workplace (Cascio, 2000). The level of congruence between the work arrangement and the individual's preferences also impacts outcomes for the individual and for the organization. Ellingson and colleagues (1998) found that if the decision to take on temporary work is more voluntary, then individuals are more satisfied with their jobs, though their performance is unaffected. Tan and Tan (2002) observed that there is a positive relationship between an individual's desire to work as a temporary worker and subsequent performance. More generally, Holtom and colleagues (2002) found that the greater the congruence between employees' preferences for full or part-time work, schedule, shift, and number of hours and the work arrangement that they have, the more positive are their work related attitudes as well as their performances. Thus, matching work arrangements to the nature of the job and employee preferences appears to be an important means for obtaining performance and satisfaction (Feldman & Gainey, 1997).

Management Through Exchange

This stream of research, building on social exchange and psychological contracts theories (e.g., Rousseau, 1995), suggests that the key to managing nonstandard workers is to understand the factors that motivate them and to then provide them the right inducements to work (e.g., McDonald & Makin, 1999). We call this approach "management through exchange" as it focuses on the conditions that affect the exchange relationship between individuals and organizations.

Several studies supported the notion that workers are responsive to the extent to which the organization meets their expectations. For example, Liden, Wayne, and Kraimer (2003) predicted that contingent workers will be more committed to organizations that provide them greater procedural justice and organizational support. This commitment, in turn, will lead them to display more citizenship behaviors aimed at these organizations. Their findings supported this theoretical framework. Ang and Slaughter's (2001) study of information systems contractors also found that contractors engage in fewer organizational citizenship behaviors and are perceived to be less trustworthy, loyal, and obedient than permanent professionals, supporting their argument that since contractors have weak ties to organizations in the form of short-term contracts, low job security, and no opportunities for advancement, they will reciprocate by having low levels of attachment to the organization. Similarly, Chattopadhyay and George (2001) and Coyle-Shapiro and Kessler (2002) found that temporary workers have lower organizational commitment and engage in fewer organizational citizenship behaviors (OCBs). They reasoned that because temporary employees do not expect long-term security and have fewer opportunities for training and career development, they may reciprocate this relatively unfavorable treatment with lower levels of OCB. Permanent employees, on the other hand, may see OCBs as less discretionary and more part of their role than temporary employees.

An interesting pattern of findings in this research stream suggests that the positive relationship between the inducements provided by the employer and OCB is stronger for temporary employees (Coyle-Shapiro & Kessler, 2002). Thus, nonstandard employment may moderate the relationship between inducements and behavioral outcomes. This finding may result from differences between standard and nonstandard workers in terms of their *expectations* of the exchange relationship with organizations. Research suggests that nonstandard temporary and contract employees perceive greater organizational support, perhaps because they do not expect as much as permanent employees (Ang & Slaughter, 2001; Pearce 1993; Van Dyne & Ang, 1998). It may be that the lower level of support nonstandard workers experience fits with their expectation levels, and thus, even though it is objectively lower than the support received by standard employees, they rate it more positively than standard employees do (Chattopadhyay & George, 2001). However, research also shows that nonstandard workers are less willing to go beyond their job descriptions on behalf of the organization (Chattopadhyay & George, 2001), suggesting that the support they receive from organizations, while noted, may not translate into a felt need to undertake OCB.

One factor influencing the terms of the exchange may be the nature of the labor market. Van Dyne and Ang (1998) used social exchange and psychological contracts arguments in their study comparing the citizenship behaviors of temporary workers and regular workers in two organizations in Singapore. Contrary to their exchange-based hypotheses, they found that temporary workers display more positive attitudes to the organization than standard workers do. They interpreted this finding in light of Singapore's tight labor market, which may have led temporary workers to see this form of work as a potential means to obtain permanent employment in organizations. These findings suggested that firms need to understand what workers want and offer it (or the possible promise of it in the future). Thus, the management implications of an exchange argument are different depending on whether nonstandard workers want to become permanent or are happy in their non-standard and temporary role (Bauer & Truxillo, 2000). There is substantial heterogeneity in what workers want. These preferences are driven not only by individual differences but also by the social and cultural norms associated with various kinds of contingent work, with some workers valuing flexible hours, others saving time on the commute, and still others income (Barley & Kunda, 2006).

Management Through Relationships

People care about relationships at work, and nonstandard workers may, in fact, care more than most. Working as a nonstandard employee is often accompanied by a sense of fragmentation, discontinuity, and confusion about one's identity and the meaning of one's work (Brocklehurst, 2001; Guevara & Ord, 1996; Kallinikos, 2003). No matter what their dimensions of weak attachment, nonstandard workers are "betwixt and between" social structures (Garsten, 1999), simultaneously both part of and outside of the social fabric of the organization. This can be an uncomfortable place to be, and other people may play an important role in helping nonstandard employees resolve, or at least cope with, these ambiguities. For example, Pratt (2000) found that in a distributed organization, personal relationships play a key role in how employees come to understand themselves, their work, and their relationships with the organization at large. Thus, he concluded, "Forming an identification with an organization is about more than creating a link with an abstract organization, it is also about making sense of the self through one's relationship with members, non-members, or both" (Pratt, 2000, p. 484; see also Rhoades, Eisenberger, & Armeli, 2001).

It is through relationships that nonstandard workers come to understand who they are relative to the organization. Their *experience* of belonging-ness (or perceived insider status; Stamper & Masterson, 2002) is sensed not through the objective details of their work arrangements but in their daily encounters with others who grant them a sense of organizational member-ship and acknowledge their claims that they belong to the social fabric of the organization (Bartel & Dutton, 2001; Blatt & Camden, 2006). These mundane acknowledgments occur despite the fact that the organization's formal work-ing arrangement may undermine it. Organizational practices, such as different colored badges and limited access to resources, remind temporary employees and contractors that they are different, if not second-class citizens (Kunda et al., 2002; Smith, 1998). By virtue of their remoteness, virtual workers often experience social isolation as well (Mann et al., 2000). Standard employees also sometimes participate in the social exclusion of nonstandard workers, for example by calling temporary employees "the temp" rather than by name, as in "Give it to the temp" or "Where's the temp?," and by avoiding socializing with them (Rogers, 2000). As Wheeler and Buckley (2000) wrote, "Because temps frequently take short duration assignments, client employees do not establish social relationships with temps; thus the temps feel further isolation" (p. 342). Standard employees may also exclude virtual workers, for example by leaving them out of the communication loop (Wiesenfeld et al., 1999).

Against this backdrop, positive relationships with coworkers can go a long way toward making nonstandard workers feel less socially isolated (Hodson, 1997). Such relationships need not be long-standing or enduring to have their positive effects. Sometimes it is enough for people to *connect*, or form a short and momentary bond (Dutton & Heaphy, 2003). Blatt and Camden (2006) found, for example, that small acts of positive connecting between temporary and permanent employees that signal inclusion, importance to others, mutual benefit, and shared emotions increases the former's sense of community at work. These positive connections serve as viable substitutes for organizational practices fostering community, as most organizational practices exclude rather than include temporary employees.

Interestingly, the sense of cohesion cultivated by positive connections among peers and between nonstandard employees and their supervisors also can strengthen the bond nonstandard employees feel toward the organization at large, which is why it may be in the organization's interest to facilitate them. Studies found that coworker solidarity is positively associated with good relations with management and commitment to the organization among standard employees (Hodson, 1997). A few studies also found this pattern among temporary and contract employees. For example, George and Chattopadhyay (2005) found that positive interpersonal relationships predict contractors' identification with the client organization, and Benson (1998) found that support from temporary employees' supervisors is a significant predictor of commitment to the client organization. Broschak and Davis-Blake (2006) found that when blending standard and nonstandard workers, social time spent with workers of the other type was associated with greater helping. Finally, Gibson and Gibbs (in press) found that creating an interpersonally psychologically safe climate is important to overcoming some of the downsides of "virtuality" (e.g., not being colocated with key coworkers).

Thus, relationships between nonstandard workers and their peers and immediate supervisors can be one key to facilitating positive organizational outcomes, such as identification and commitment, as well as nonstandard workers' personal well-being. Managers can enable the development of these relationships, thereby leveraging their potential. In fact, management may find it easier to enable positive relationships than to implement organizational practices for including and supporting nonstandard workers, simply because they are constrained by the structural features of nonstandard work and by their desire to cut costs.

Management Through Identity

A final stream of research suggested that managers of nonstandard workers can facilitate their experiences of identity, thereby aligning the identity of the individual with the interests of the organization. Chattopadhyay and George (2001) observed, for example, that temporary workers have low status in organizations and that, as a consequence, they experience low organization-based self-esteem. They found that when temporary workers work in groups dominated by permanent workers, their organization-based self-esteem is not as badly affected as when they work with mostly nonstandard workers. These findings suggested that fostering a positive work-related identity entails assigning nonstandard workers to work groups dominated by permanent workers (though, as shown in the following section, this prescription has its complications). It is important to note that the identity findings may be explained by an "opportunity" mechanism as well. Perhaps the positive effects of a nonstandard worker being assigned to a work group with standard employees are due to the fact that nonstandard workers in such groups come to believe that they have an enhanced opportunity to convert to permanent status. More research is needed to better understand this issue.

Clarifying and demonstrating organizational values can be another way to manage nonstandard workers via their identities. For example, in a study of information technology contractors, George and Chattopadhyay (2005) found that individuals identify most strongly with organizations that display values that match their own values. The more nonstandard workers see and feel the identity of the organization, the more this match can be discovered and influence subsequent attitudes and behaviors.

Themes and Issues in the Nonstandard Work Literature

In the following section, we share our general observations about research on nonstandard work. We highlight both theoretical and methodological issues in the work to date, along with our suggestions for how these can be overcome.

Using Nonstandard Work as an Attractive Context for Theory Development

Practical challenges of managing nonstandard work and interest in simply describing this emerging phenomenon, rather than theory-based research questions, have largely driven the development of this literature. As a result, the insights gained from the research have not realized the potential of this literature to contribute to the broader field of OB. Much of the research is descriptive rather than theoretical. As a result, we have a good picture of the experience of the firms employing nonstandard workers, the groups in which they are working, and a growing picture of what nonstandard workers themselves experience, but our accumulation of knowledge is slow and uneven.

The study of the phenomenon—nonstandard work—can serve as an arena for developing all kinds of midrange theories about business practice (problem-driven research) and as a means both for testing and extending foundational theories (paradigm-driven research; for a discussion of this distinction, see Davis & Marquis, 2005). Problem-driven research on nonstandard workers can focus on understanding the *whys* behind the described realities. We do not always know *why* nonstandard workers experiences are as they are. *Why* are nonstandard workers sometimes different from standard workers (or from each other) and not different at other times? A more concerted, theoretical push for developing midrange theories—theories that are moderately abstract, limited in scope, highly relevant, and easily testable (Weick, 1974)—is needed so that we can explain this multifaceted phenomenon.

Nonstandard work can also serve as a context for extending and/or identifying boundary conditions for existing theories. Yet, when theory has entered the picture in research on nonstandard workers, researchers has have tended to apply theories, such as psychological contracts (e.g., George, 2003), social exchange (e.g., Liden et al., 2003; Pearce, 1993), or internal labor markets (e.g., Barnett & Miner, 1992) to explain empirical observations without extending theory. We believe that insights gained from nonstandard workers have great potential to teach us new things about our theories. These insights can then be applied to different populations, contexts, or phenomena. We have much to gain by considering questions such as the implication of nonstandard work for how our theories construe the nature and boundary of the firm, the distribution of power within and across firms, and how differences between groups of nonstandard workers are linked to underlying psychological processes, such as coping with ambiguity, managing identity, building relationships, managing role conflict, or making choices. Our research will also benefit from cross-disciplinary intersections, such as utilizing our understanding of "bad" job characteristics (Kalleberg et al., 2000) to inform our appreciation of the challenge of constructing positive work identities (Ashforth & Kreiner, 1999) or the study of resilience (Sutcliffe & Vogus, 2003).

One goal for this chapter was to show how and why nonstandard work should be brought to the center stage of micro-OB. Recent empirical work suggested that the study of nonstandard workers might help to uncover boundary conditions for our theories. It may show us representative situations in which established relationships between constructs do not hold. For example, whereas usually the longer groups work together the more likely they are to have their mental models converge (Moreland, 1999), Levesque and colleagues (2001) found this pattern to be reversed in temporary teams, where individuals did not expect to interact in the future. Another study finds that the commonly observed negative effects of gender dissimilarity for women (Tsui et al., 1992) disappear in virtual teams where members do not interact face to face, as gender becomes less salient (Chattopadhyay, George, & Shulman, in press). In both of the previously mentioned studies, the extent and type of interaction between nonstandard workers were conceptualized as the underlying cause for the divergent results. Other features of nonstandard work, such as physical distance, administrative independence, or shortened tenure might similarly work to restrict or reverse relationships that are generally held to be true in mainstream micro-OB. Such restrictions and reversals are important in a world that will be increasingly populated by "new standard" workers who do not match our long-held picture of what is standard.

Nonstandard work is also an ideal context to study particular issues of long-standing theoretical concern to micro-organization behavior researchers. Here, the issue is the theoretical concern, not the workers or work *per se*. For example, workers holding nonstandard jobs are a great sample for studying self-regulation, since these workers operate with loose organizational controls. They are also a great sample to study ambiguity, tolerance for ambiguity, and choice. They might provide different insights into the recent focus on "self-socialization" in the socialization literature (Ashford & Black, 1996), since many nonstandard workers undertake this process regularly as they move from job to job. High status, high income nonstandard workers, with their higher levels of power, would be an ideal sample to study the concept of "i-deals" (individualized negotiated agreements about work arrangements) recently introduced by Rousseau, Ho, and Greenberg (2006).

A recent study by Barsness et al., (2005) showed the potential theoretical contribution of studies of nonstandard work. These investigators used characteristics of nonstandard work and workers to uncover general theoretical relationships relating to impression management. For example, they found that virtual workers differ from standard workers in both their motivation and opportunity for various impression-management tactics. Thus, their results informed us about impression management generally (specifically the role of motivation and opportunity), as it might unfold in a range of contexts, rather than about nonstandard workers exclusively. Thatcher and Zhu's (2006) theorizing about identity and identity enactment was a further example of what we are suggesting here. They used the realities of telecommuting to gain fresh insights into theories about identity.

Improving Theoretical Precision

In reviewing this literature, we identified a tension between general statements about nonstandard work and workers as a whole and specific consideration of the differences among such workers, for example, between temporary employees and contractors. In the following section, we argue against having separate literatures for each type of worker. However, it is important that researchers carefully consider the sample used in their research. Specifically, researchers need to be clear about how their sample differs theoretically from other nonstandard workers. For example, high status, highly paid contractors have one experience, whereas low paid temporary employees and day laborers or migrant farm workers who contract with large agricultural organizations may have an altogether different experience. Researchers need to capture the underlying theoretical differences that differentiate these groups. Clearly, status and power differences are involved, but there may be other more subtle dimensions as well. In addition, low-status jobs (e.g., day laborers) and the workers who fill them have long been considered outside the purview of organizational behavior. If we are to develop a full picture of work, both standard and nonstandard, we need to be both more precise in our theorizing and broaden the boundary of what we consider relevant to organizational behavior. Such a move would answer calls such as Martin's (2006) recent argument that our field would gain by studying traditionally marginalized groups and that the focus in business-school-based OB on managers has prevented us from gaining a sufficiently broad understanding of work and workers.

Moving Beyond Good and Bad

A predominant preoccupation of the literature on nonstandard work has been the question of whether nonstandard work is "good" (e.g., efficient for organizations and liberating for individuals) or "bad" (e.g., threatening organizational proprietary knowledge and marginalizing individuals; e.g., Felstead & Gallie, 2004; Kalleberg et al., 2000). Given that this work can be both good and bad as are its consequences, we believe a better approach may be to accept and appreciate the prevalence of nonstandard work in organizations and individual careers as a starting point for systematic theoretical and empirical research.

First, to the extent that there are negative features of nonstandard work it may be most fruitful to focus on how to transform the potentially "bad" aspects into "good." Although this question has been written about from the managerial perspective—how organizations can "make the most" of employing nonstandard workers (e.g., Cascio, 2000; Kurland & Bailey, 2002; Pearlson & Saunders, 2001; von Hippel, Greenberger, Heneman, & Skoglind, 1997), few studies have examined how individuals can make the experience of nonstandard work more positive. If more and more individuals are going to be working in this manner and if this is to be the organizational experience for greater numbers of employees, then these questions become highly relevant. What personal and social resources should they mobilize to be successful as nonstandard workers? What are their proactive strategies for adapting to frequent moves from situation to situation? Norman, Collins, Conner, Martin, and Rance (1995) studied the kinds of attributions, cognitions, and coping strategies that telecommuters use to cope with work-related problems. Likewise, Blatt and Ashford (2006) examined how meaning making helps independent workers sustain goal-directed activity. More such work is needed to understand high levels of performance, engagement, and other positive outcomes among nonstandard workers and to give aid and advice to those struggling in nonstandard roles.

Second, overcoming the simplicity of the "good versus bad" dichotomy may entail focusing the research lens on moderators, or the conditions under which nonstandard work becomes either positive or negative. The sample employed in research is one such moderator; context is another.

Capturing Context

Context is the "situational opportunities and constraints that affect the occurrence and meaning of organizational behavior, as well as functional relationships between variables" (Johns, 2006, p. 386). A consideration of context using the lenses provided by Johns suggested several ways to make sense of the ubiquitous contradictory findings in the research we have reviewed, such as on the experiences of nonstandard workers or the differences between them and standard workers.

Context shapes how organizational events are interpreted and which features of the situation are salient to those being studied (Johns, 2006). Occupation may be an important context factor that influences the meaning ascribed to work, as membership in an occupational community influences the perspective one applies to situations (Van Maanen & Barley, 1984). For example, we can learn from work that has been conducted outside of organizational settings for generations. Creative writers and artists may have quite different experiences than workers in occupations for which there is an organizational analog, such as graphic designers or computer programmers. The former may be less apt to assess their experience with reference to full-time organizational work as a comparison. Moreover, they are more likely to have well-developed narratives for making sense of their nonstandard experiences. For example, although high skill levels and training coincide with frequent mobility, low pay, and job insecurity for many artists, they tend to see it as an occupational norm and make sense of it using notions of self-actualization at work, an idiosyncratic way of life, and a strong sense of community, frames which are well-developed in the artistic occupational community (Menger, 1999). Nonstandard workers might benefit from the creation of similar overarching narratives for their occupations. Another example of a contextual feature that shapes the meaning of nonstandard work is the organization's strategic reason for hiring temporary employees (cost reduction vs. flexibility; short term buffer or hiring portal for more permanent employment) and organizational norms for how to treat temporary employees. Lautsch (2002) found that these moderate the extent to which contingent workers experience their work as positive or negative.

Context also serves as a cross-level effect, in which situational variables at one level of analysis affect variables at another level (Johns, 2006; Rousseau, 1985). Although a few studies examine the influence of variables at the organizational level of analysis, such as degree of unionization (Uzzi & Barsness, 1998) or organizational development activities (Cooper & Kurland, 2002), on variables at the individual level of analysis, such as workers' attitudes and beliefs, most studies remain at a single level of analysis. For example, a number of studies have looked at the impact of an individual-level factor—whether one works part or full time—on individual attitudes, with mixed results. Some studies find that full-time workers are more satisfied with their jobs (Hall & Gordon, 1973; Lee & Johnson, 1991; Miller & Terborg, 1979) or with their careers (Hall & Gordon, 1973) than part-time workers. Others find that full-time workers are less satisfied with their jobs (Eberhardt & Shani, 1984; Jackofsky & Peters, 1987; Lee & Johnson, 1991; Peters, Jackofsky, & Salter, 1981), or feel less commitment to the organization than part-time workers (Martin & Peterson, 1987). Still other studies show that there is no difference in the job satisfaction of full- and part-time workers (Logan, O'Reilly, & Roberts, 1973; McGinnis & Morrow, 1990).

The key to resolving these contradictory findings may lie in cross-level effects, such as the composition of the group. As relational demographers have shown, the composition of one's work group explains attitudes over and above the explanatory power of one's own demographics (e.g., Tsui et al., 1992). Thus, part-time workers in these different studies may have been comparing themselves to differing referent groups, which may explain the patterns of findings. Researchers need to conceptualize the influence of context ranging from societal, national, to the more local context effects in explaining nonstandard workers' attitudes and behaviors (e.g., Broschak & Davis-Blake, 2006; Chattopadhyay & George, 2001).

Finally, context can be seen as a configuration or bundle of stimuli (Johns, 2006). Perhaps it is not a single feature of the individual (e.g., skill level or occupation), the market (e.g., demand for certain skills and occupations), the economy (e.g., thriving, stagnating, or declining), or organizations (e.g., growing and bureaucratized) that explain the experiences of nonstandard work or the differences between standard and nonstandard workers, but particular combinations of these features. For example, skill level may interact with market demand to explain the difference between the positive experiences of highly skilled computer contractors, who were in high demand when studied by Barley and Kunda (2004), and the negative experiences of highly skilled adjunct professors who were in a field in which supply overwhelmed demand when studied by Barker (1998). The more we can build context explanations into our theorizing about nonstandard workers, the better.

Capturing Collective Processes and Broadening the Scope of Variables Considered

An additional weakness in the nonstandard literature is its individualistic nature. Research has tended to focus on the individual and his or her experience and attitudes. As a result, we know relatively little about the collective experience of nonstandard workers, the existence or nature of a nonstandard culture or collective identity, and how people are socialized into it. It is likely that nonstandard workers' interactions about their experiences contain elements of communities of practice, in which they negotiate a shared meaning of working in the way they do and strategies for dealing with common problems (Orr, 1996; Wenger, 1998). Although the importance of occupational communities is sometimes mentioned, their role in the collective experience of nonstandard work has not been empirically explored. The focus on individual attitudes also limits our understanding of collective behavioral outcomes, such as coordination, innovation, and reliability, all of which are rendered problematic when standard and nonstandard employees work together. One of the functions of organizations is to create common ground through shared meanings and shared identity (Kogut & Zander, 1996; Simon, 1976). How do people organize when they do not share a history, identity, and interpretations of the situation? These collective outcomes are a promising area of focus for future research.

Moreover, we know relatively little about the behavior of nonstandard workers as opposed to their attitudes. Most research has focused on their satisfaction, commitment, identification, and other attitudes, rather than on their concrete behavior (two notable exceptions are studies of organizational citizenship behavior among nonstandard workers; e.g., Pearce, 1993; Van Dyne & Ang, 1998; and safety behavior; Rousseau & Libuser, 1997). We do not know, for example, about their staying or leaving, their voicing or silence, or their seeking and using feedback. Beyond behaviors, emotions and emotional reactions are rarely considered as dependent variables either. Mann and Holdsworth (2003) found that teleworking is associated with significantly more negative emotions such as loneliness, irritability, worry, and guilt. These workers also experience more negative physical health symptoms than standard workers, another rarely considered dependent variable (see also Bauer & Truxillo, 2000). By broadening the range of dependent variables considered, we can capture more fully the differences between standard and nonstandard workers.

Finally, we could broaden our appreciation of the effects of nonstandard work by considering their families. While some studies have examined work-family balance issues for teleworkers (e.g., Baines & Gelder, 2003; Golden, 2006; Hill, Miller, Weiner, & Colihan, 1998) or work-family balance for part-time workers (e.g., Higgins, Duxbury, & Johnson, 2000), issues such as the impact of having a worker in the home, having a worker who works odd hours, and having a worker with an unpredictable job future all warrant more attention. It is likely that not just workers, but also their families feel the impact of the new world of work.

Increasing Methodological Rigor

The empirical studies in the nonstandard domain have varied widely in quality. A significant proportion is purely descriptive with no theory tested.

Samples sizes have ranged from lows of 10 or 12 in qualitative interview studies to highs in the 1000s in large database studies. Measurement quality also has been highly variable across studies. Finally, with some notable exceptions (e.g., Broschak & Davis-Blake, 2006; Chattopadhyay & George, 2001; Ellingson, Gruys, & Sackett, 1998), the analyses and statistical tools employed have been fairly simple. While recognizing this variability, the average quality of the empirical work in this area needs to be raised as current methodological practices will hold back the development of this literature. As we build an empirical base on the experiences of nonstandard workers, we need to be especially attentive to methodological rigor in this more emergent area of research. Several issues warrant attention.

First and most importantly, the fragmentation of the literature by type of nonstandard worker studied and across academic disciplines needs to be addressed. There may be cause to study one type of nonstandard worker or another, but there is no cause for wholly separate literatures to develop as if there were no similarity on underlying dimensions. Similarly, there is no cause for literature reviews to ignore research done in "other" areas of nonstandard work, for developing new sets of constructs without recognition of similar constructs used elsewhere and for measuring them with unique instruments. Our efforts to advance conceptually will benefit from examining literature and theory across disciplinary boundaries. As a notable example of this fragmentation, a recent review of contingent work in the *Journal of Management* (Connelly & Gallagher, 2004) did not cite any of Barley and Kunda's more sociologically oriented research on contractors (Barley & Kunda, 2004, 2006; Kunda, Barley, & Evans, 2002). Similarly, Barley and Kunda (2002; 2004; 2006) underreferenced work published in more micro and personnel outlets. Fragmentation by type of nonstandard work and fragmentation by discipline make progress difficult. Researchers in this domain need to work extra hard to cross boundaries and synthesize.

Second, if researchers are going to limit their purview to a single type of nonstandard worker, it is important that they state clearly the kind of nonstandard workers they are studying. If such a practice is followed, then future meta-analyses can help overcome the empirical fragmentation in this field because researchers can account for the type of worker studied. Careful attention to the type of nonstandard worker studied is important theoretically as well. Davis-Blake's papers with her colleagues are good models of this practice (Broschak & Davis-Blake 2006; Davis-Blake et al., 2003; Davis-Blake & Uzzi, 1993). First, these articles clearly stated which nonstandard workers they sample and then argued for the theoretical relevance of particular contrasts across specific types of nonstandard workers. For example, Davis-Blake and colleagues (2003) argued that temporary and contract workers reflect differing degrees of externalization of work and demonstrated how this difference affected outcomes.

Third, measurement consistency (using the same measure to assess the same construct across studies) has often been lacking in this fragmented literature. Also, measurement quality has sometimes been traded off to enable use of large scale data bases. Single-item scales allow a glimpse at the phenomenon, but do not allow findings to be compared to findings elsewhere in OB research.

Fourth, research in this area would benefit from greater integration across quantitative and qualitative work. Building theory explicitly from qualitative studies and using qualitative approaches to supplement quantitative findings are two ways of achieving greater integration. Ang and Slaughter's (2001) research on information systems consultants used both qualitative and quantitative data to good effect, as their qualitative data helps them explain unexpected findings in the quantitative study. This suggestion is in line with Chatman and Flynn's (2005) recent recommendations for "full cycle research" that integrates both quantitative and qualitative research and research across disciplines.

Fifth, as previously noted and as observed by Connelly and Gallagher (2004), our research on nonstandard workers is for the most part static. Studies are often "snapshot" accounts rather than longitudinal portrayals of nonstandard careers or process-oriented understanding of organizing by or involving nonstandard workers. This lack is problematic especially for research that invokes notions of the careers of nonstandard employees (e.g., boundaryless careers; Marler et al., 2002) as these most likely entail movement in and out of nonstandard and standard work in a dynamic process (Hulin & Glomb, 1999). Thus, when Marler and colleagues (2002) studied an unfolding career with a snapshot of a single data collection, their findings underrepresented the dynamic nature of the careers that they depict theoretically. We also miss how these careers are embedded in a social and cultural context (cf., Cohen & Mallon, 2001). The result is a fractured understanding. For example, the amount of time one works as a temporary employee increases employability for many clerical employees but decreases it for nonstandard academics (Barker, 1998). These findings suggested that one cannot understand the nonstandard phenomenon without considering dynamics as they unfold over time.

Causal inference is often problematic in research with data collected at one time point. Many studies in this literature slip into causal language when discussing results for data collected at one point in time. For example, when studying permanent workers' reactions to increasing proportions of nonstandard workers, researchers appear to infer that the nonstandard workers are influencing permanent workers' attitudes (Davis-Blake et al., 2004; George, 2003). However, there are other possibilities. First, causality may be reversed, whereby initial negative attitudes among permanent workers are motivating firm's to hire more temporary workers. Second, an unspecified variable such as environmental uncertainty may be causing both increasing hiring of nonstandard workers and increasing negative attitudes of permanent workers. Field experiments and longitudinal data are needed to sort out these issues.

Conclusion

The world of work, they say, is changing (Barley & Kunda, 2001). The model for how individuals interact with organizations is different now than it was in 1950 and will be different yet again 50 years hence. Our imagination about organizational behavior, about appropriate constructs, and about important processes to examine needs to expand accordingly. The more nonstandard workers exist as a model of how to do work and conduct a career over a lifetime, the more legitimate it becomes as a work form and life pattern. The more legitimate it becomes, the less counternormative it is to work in this fashion and the more people will choose to do so. Over time, society will change and people's expectations of organizations will change accordingly. An organizational behavior field that clings to an outdated model of individuals and their interactions with organizations will become anachronistic. The growth of research on nonstandard workers and the organizations that employ them is central to filling in a portrait of this new future. This literature review, with its suggestions for areas of future emphasis and research, puts us on the path toward creating that picture.

Acknowledgment

The authors are very grateful to the following people for their generous and insightful comments on previous drafts of this chapter: Joe Broschak, Prithviraj Chattopadhyay, Alison Davis-Blake, Adam Grant and Jone Pearce.

References

Acker, J. (1990). Hierarchies, jobs, bodies: A theory of gendered organizations. *Gender and Society, 4*, 139–158.

Allan, P., & Sienko, S. (1998). Job motivations of professional and technical contingent workers: Are they different from permanent workers? *Journal of Employment Counseling, 35*, 169–178.

Allen, P. (2002). The contingent workforce: Challenges and new directions. *American Business Review, 20*, 103–110.

Ammons, S. K., & Markham, W. T. (2004). Working at home: Experiences of skilled white collar workers. *Sociological Spectrum, 2*, 191–238.

Ang, S., & Slaughter, S. A. (2001). Work outcomes and job design for contract versus permanent information systems professionals on software development teams. *MIS Quarterly, 25*, 321.

Arthur, M. B., & Rousseau, D. M. (Eds.). (1996). *The boundaryless career: A new employment principle for a new organizational era.* New York: Oxford University Press.

Ashford, S. J., & Black, J. S. (1996). Proactivity during organizational entry: The role of desire for control. *Journal of Applied Psychology, 81*, 199–214.

Ashford, S. J., & Blatt, R. (2003). *On their own: Customized management of nonstandard knowledge workers.* Paper presented at the National Academy of Management Meeting, Seattle, WA.

Ashford, S. J., Blatt, R., & VandeWalle, D. (2003). Reflections on the looking glass: A review of research on feedback-seeking behavior in organizations. *Journal of Management, 29,* 773–799.

Ashforth, B. E., & Johnson, S. A. (2001). What hat to wear? The relative salience of multiple identities in organizational contexts. In M. A. Hogg, & D. J. Terry (Eds.), *Social identity processes in organizational contexts* (pp. 31–48). Philadelphia: Psychology Press.

Ashforth, B. E., & Kreiner, G. E. (1999). "How can you do it?": Dirty work and the challenge of constructing a positive identity. *The Academy of Management Review, 24,* 413–434.

Bailey, D., & Kurland, N. B. (2002). A review of telework research: Findings, new directions, and lessons for the study of modern work. *Journal of Organizational Behavior, 23,* 383–400.

Baines, S. (1999). Servicing the media: Freelancing, teleworking, and 'enterprising' careers. *New Technology, Work, and Employment, 14,* 18–31.

Baines, S. (2002). New technologies and old ways of working in the home of the self-employed teleworker. *New Technology, Work, and Employment, 17,* 89–101.

Baines, S., & Gelder, U. (2003). What is family friendly about the workplace in the home? The case of self-employed parents and their children. *New Technology, Work, & Employment, 18,* 223–234.

Barker, K. (1998). Toiling for piece-rates and accumulating deficits: Contingent work in higher education. In K. Barker, & K. Christensen (Eds.), *Contingent work: American employment relations in transition* (pp. 195–220). Ithaca, NY: ILR Press.

Barley, S. R., & Kunda, G. (2001). Bringing work back in. *Organization Science, 12,* 76–95.

Barley, S. R., & Kunda, G. (2004). *Gurus, hired guns, and warm bodies: Itinerant experts in a knowledge economy.* Princeton, NJ: Princeton University Press.

Barley, S. R., & Kunda, G. (2006). Contracting: A new form of professional practice. *Academy of Management Perspectives, 19,* 1–19.

Barnett, W. P., & Miner, A. S. (1992). Standing on the shoulders of others: Career interdependence in job mobility. *Administrative Science Quarterly, 37,* 262–281.

Barsness, Z. I., Diekmann, K. A., & Seidel, M. D. L. (2005). Motivation and opportunity: The role of remote work, demographic dissimilarity, and social network centrality in impression management. *Academy of Management Journal, 48,* 401–419.

Bartel, C. A., & Dutton, J. E. (2001). Ambiguous organizational memberships: Constructing organizational identities in interactions with others. In M. A. Hogg, & D. J. Terry (Eds.), *Social identity processes in organizational contexts* (pp.115–130). Philadelphia: Psychology Press.

Bartel, C. A., Wrzesniewski, A., & Wiesenfeld, B. (in press). Identifying from afar: Communicating organizational membership in remote contexts. In C. A. Bartel, S. Blader, & A. Wrzesniewski (Eds.), *Identity and the modern organization.* Mahwah, NJ: Lawrence Erlbaum.

Bartlett, C. A., & Ghoshal, S. (1989). *Managing across borders: The transnational solution*. Boston: Harvard Business School Press.

Baruch, Y. (2000). Teleworking: Benefits and pitfalls as perceived by professionals and managers. *New Technology, Work, & Employment, 15*, 34–49.

Baruch, Y. (2001). The status of research on teleworking and an agenda for future research. *International Journal of Management Reviews, 3*, 113–129.

Bauer, T., & Truxillo, D. (2000). Temp-to-permanent employees: A longitudinal study of stress and selection success. *Journal of Occupational Health Psychology, 5*, 337–346.

Belman, D., & Golden, L. (2000). Nonstandard and contingent employment: Contrasts by job type, industry, and occupation. In F. Carre, M. A. Ferber, L. Golden, & S. A. Herzenberg (Eds.), *Nonstandard work: The nature and challenges of changing employment arrangements* (pp. 167–212). Champaign, IL: Industrial Relations Research Association.

Bendapudi, V., Mangum, S. L., Tansky, J. W., & Fisher, M. M. (2003). Nonstandard employment arrangements: A proposed typology and policy planning framework. *Human Resource Planning, 26*, 24–40.

Benson, J. (1998). Dual commitment: Contract workers in Australian manufacturing enterprises. *Journal of Management Studies, 35*, 355–375.

Blatt, R., & Ashford, S. J. (2006). *Making meaning and taking action in knowledge and creative work: Lessons from independent workers*. Ann Arbor: University of Michigan Press.

Blatt, R., & Camden, C. T. (2006). Positive relationships and cultivating community. In J. E. Dutton, & B. R. Ragins (Eds.), *Exploring positive relationships at work: Building a theoretical and research foundation* (pp. 243–264). Mahwah, NJ: Lawrence Erlbaum.

Bolino, M. C. (1999). Citizenship and impression management: Good soldiers or good actors? *Academy of Management Review, 24*, 82–98.

Bradley, M. H., Schipani, C. A., Sundaram, A. K., & Walsh, J. P. (1999). The purposes and accountability of the corporation in contemporary society: Corporate governance at a crossroads. *Law and Contemporary Problems, 62*, 9–86.

Brocklehurst, M. (2001). Power, identity, and new technology homework: Implications for 'new forms' of organizing. *Organization Studies, 22*, 445–466.

Brockner, J., Tyler, T. R., & Cooper-Schneider, R. (1992). The influence of prior commitment to an institution on reactions to perceived unfairness: The higher they are, the harder they fall. *Administrative Science Quarterly, 37*, 241–261.

Broschak, J. P., & Davis-Blake, A. (2006). Mixing standard work and nonstandard deals: The consequences of heterogeneity in employment arrangements. *The Academy of Management Journal, 49*, 371–393.

Brown, S. L., & Eisenhardt, K. M. (1997). The art of continuous change: Linking complexity theory and time-paced evolution in relentlessly shifting organizations. *Administrative Science Quarterly, 42*, 1–34.

Bureau of Labor Statistics. (2005). *Contingent and alternative employment arrangements*. Washington, DC: Author.

Cappelli, P. (1999). Career jobs are dead. *California Management Review, 42*(1), 146–167.

Carnoy, M., Castells, M., & Benner, C. (1997). Labour markets and employment practices in the age of flexibility: A case study of Silicon Valley. *International Labour Review, 135*, 27–48.

Cascio, W. F. (2000). Managing a virtual workplace. *Academy of Management Executive, 14*, 81–90.

Chatman, J. A., & Flynn, F. J. (2005). Full-cycle micro-organizational behavior research. *Organizational Science, 16*, 434–447.

Chattopadhyay, P., & George, E. (2001). Examining the effects of work externalization through the lens of social identity theory. *Journal of Applied Psychology, 86*, 781–788.

Chattopadhyay, P., George, E., & Shulman, A. (in press). The influence of sex dissimilarity in distributive versus colocated groups. *Organization Science.*

Christensen, K. (1998). Countervailing human resource trends in family-sensitive firms. In K. Barker, & K. Christensen (Eds.), *Contingent work: American employment relations in transition* (pp. 103–125). Ithaca, NY: ILR Press.

Cinnirella, M. (1997). Towards a European identity? Interactions between the national and European social identities manifested by university students in Britain and Italy. *British Journal of Social Psychology, 36*(1), 19–31.

Cobble, D. S., & Vosko, L. F. (2000). Historical perspectives on representing nonstandard workers. In F. Carre, M. A. Ferber, L. Golden, & S. A. Herzenberg (Eds.), *Nonstandard work: The nature and challenges of changing employment arrangements* (pp. 291–312). Champaign, IL: Industrial Relations Research Association.

Cohen, L., & Mallon, M. (2001). My brilliant career? *International Studies of Management and Organization, 31*, 48–68.

Connelly, C. E., & Gallagher, D. G. (2004). Emerging trends in contingent work research. *Journal of Management, 30*, 959–983.

Cooper, C. D., & Kurland, N. B. (2002). Telecommuting, professional isolation, and employee development in public and private organizations. *Journal of Organizational Behavior, 23*, 511–532.

Coyle-Shapiro, J. A., & Kessler, I. (2002). Contingent and non-contingent workers in local government: Contrasting psychological contracts. *Public Administration, 80*, 77–101.

D'Aveni, R. A. (1994). *Hypercompetition.* New York: The Free Press.

Davenport, T. H., & Pearlson, K. (1998). Two cheers for the virtual office. *Sloan Management Review, 39*(4), 51–65.

Davis, G. F., & Marquis, C. (2005). Prospects for organization theory in the early twenty-first century: Institutional fields and mechanisms. *Organization Science, 16*, 332–345.

Davis-Blake, A., Broschak, J. P., & George, E. (2003). Happy together? How using nonstandard workers affects exit, voice, and loyalty among standard employees. *Academy of Management Journal, 46*, 475–485.

Davis-Blake, A., & Uzzi, B. (1993). Determinants of employment externalization: A study of temporary workers and independent contractors. *Administrative Science Quarterly, 38*, 195–223.

Dennis, W. J. (1996). Self-employment: When nothing else is available? *Journal of Labor Research, 17*, 645–661.

Dick, P., & Hyde, R. (2006). Consent as resistance, resistance as consent: Re-reading part-time professionals' acceptance of their marginal positions. *Gender, Work, and Organization, 13*, 543–564.

DiNatale, M. (2001). Characteristics of and preference for alternative work arrangements, 1999. *Monthly Labor Review, 124*(3), 28–49.

Dutton, J. E., Dukerich, J. M., & Harquail, C. V. (1994). Organizational images and member identification. *Administrative Science Quarterly, 39*, 239–263.

Dutton, J. E., & Heaphy, E. D. (2003). The power of high-quality connections at work. In K. S. Cameron, J. E. Dutton, & R. E. Quinn (Eds.), *Positive organizational scholarship* (pp. 264–278). San Francisco: Berrett-Koehler.

Eberhardt, B. J., & Shani, A. B. (1984). The effects of full-time versus part-time employment status on attitudes toward specific organizational characteristics and overall job satisfaction. *Academy of Management Journal, 27*, 893–900.

Ellingson, J. E., Gruys, M. L., & Sackett, P. R. (1998). Factors related to the satisfaction and performance of temporary employees. *Journal of Applied Psychology, 83*, 913–921.

Evans, J. A., Kunda, G., & Barley, S. R. (2004). Beach time, bridge time, and billable hours: The temporal structure of technical contracting. *Administrative Science Quarterly, 49*, 1–38.

Feldman, D. C. (1990). Reconceptualizing the nature and consequences of part-time. *Academy of Management Review, 15*, 103–112.

Feldman, D. C., & Bolino, M. C. (2000). Career patterns of the self-employed: Career motivations and career outcomes. *Journal of Small Business Management, 38*, 53–67.

Feldman, D. C., Doerpinghaus, H. I., & Turnley, W. H. (1994). Managing temporary workers: A permanent HRM challenge. *Organizational Dynamics, 23*, 49–53.

Feldman, D. C., Doerpinghaus, H. I., & Turnley, W. H. (1995). Employee reactions to temporary jobs. *Journal of Managerial Issues, 7*, 127.

Feldman, D. C., & Gainey, T. W. (1997). Patterns of telecommuting and their consequences: Framing the research agenda. *Human Resource Management Review, 7*, 369–388.

Felstead, A., & Gallie, D. (2004). For better or worse? Nonstandard jobs and high involvement work systems. *International Journal of Human Resource Management, 15*, 1293–1316.

Florida, R. (2002). *The rise of the creative class.* New York: Basic Books.

Gallagher, D. G., & McLean Parks, J. (2001). I pledge thee my troth…contingently: Commitment and the contingent work relationship. *Human Resource Management Review, 11*, 181–208.

Garsten, C. (1999). Betwixt and between: Temporary employees as liminal subjects in flexible organizations. *Organization Studies, 20*, 601–617.

Geary, J. F. (1992). Employment flexibility and human resource management: The case of three American electronics plants. *Work, Employment, and Society, 6*, 251–270.

George, E. (2003). External solutions and internal problems: The effects of employment externalization on internal workers' attitudes. *Organization Science, 14*, 386–402.

George, E., & Chattopadhyay, P. (2005). One foot in each camp: The dual identification of contract workers. *Administrative Science Quarterly, 50*, 68–99.

George, E., Chattopadhyay, P., Lawrence, S., & Shulman, A. (2003). *The influence of employment externalization on work content and employees' justice perceptions.* Paper presented at the 2003 National Academy of Management Meeting, Seattle, WA.

Gibson, C. B., & Gibbs, J. L. (in press). Unpacking the concept of virtuality: The effects of geographic dispersion, electronic dependence, dynamic structure, and national diversity on team innovation. *Administrative Science Quarterly.*

Giddens, A. (1984). *The constitution of society: Outline of the theory of structuration.* Cambridge, U.K.: Polity Press.

Golden, T. D. (2006). The role of relationships in understanding telecommuter satisfaction. *Journal of Organizational Behavior, 27,* 319–340.

Golden, T., & Veiga, J. F. (2005). The impact of extent of telecommuting on job satisfaction: Resolving inconsistent findings. *Journal of Management, 31,* 310–318.

Gossett, L. M. (2002). Kept at arm's length: Questioning the organizational desirability of member identification. *Communication Monographs, 69,* 385–404.

Guevara, K., & Ord, J. (1996). The search for meaning in a changing work context. *Futures, 28,* 709–722.

Hall, D. T., & Gordon, F. E. (1973). Career choices of married women: Effects on conflict, role behavior and satisfaction. *Journal of Applied Psychology, 58,* 42–48.

Harrison, D. A., Newman, D. A., & Roth, P. L. (2006). How important are job attitudes? Meta-analytic comparisons of integral behavioral outcomes and time sequences. *Academy of Management Journal, 49,* 305–325.

Heckscher, C. (2000). HR strategy and nonstandard work: Dualism versus true mobility. In F. Carre, M. A. Ferber, L. Golden, & S. A. Herzenberg (Eds.), *Nonstandard work: The nature and challenges of changing employment arrangements* (pp. 267–290). Champaign, IL: Industrial Relations Research Association.

Higgins, C., Duxbury, L., & Johnson, K. (2000). Part-time work for women: Does it really help balance work and family? *Human Resource Management, 39,* 17–32.

Hill, E. J., Miller, B., Weiner, S., & Colihan, J. (1998). Influences of the virtual office on aspects of work and work/life balance. *Personnel Psychology, 51,* 667–683.

Ho, V. T., Ang, S., & Straub, D. (2003). When subordinates become IT contractors: Persistent managerial expectations in IT outsourcing. *Information Systems Research, 14,* 66–86.

Hodson, R. (1997). Group relations at work. *Work and Occupations, 24,* 426–452.

Hogg, M. A., & Terry, D. J. (2000). Social identity and self-categorization processes in organizational contexts. *Academy of Management Review, 25,* 121–140.

Holtom, B., Lee, T., & Tidd, S. (2002). The relationship between work status congruence and work-related attitudes and behaviors. *Journal of Applied Psychology, 87,* 903–915.

Hoque, K., & Kirkpatrick, I. (2003). Nonstandard employment in the management and professional workforce: Training, consultation, and gender implications. *Work, Employment & Society, 17,* 67–689.

Hornsey, M. J., & Hogg, M. A. (2000). Assimilation and diversity: An integrative model of subgroup relations. *Personality and Social Psychology Review, 4,* 143–156.

Houseman, S. N. (1997). *Temporary, part-time, and contract employment in the United States: A report on the W. E. Upjohn Institute's employer survey on flexible staffing policies.* Kalamazoo, MI: W. E. Upjohn Institutes for Employment Research.

Houseman, S. N., & Polivka, A. (2000). The implications of flexible staffing arrangements for job stability. In D. Newmark (Ed.), *On the job: Is long-term employment a thing of the past?* (pp. 427–462). New York: Russell Sage Foundation.

Howe, W. J. (1986,) Temporary help workers: Who they are, what jobs they hold. *Monthly Labor Review, 109*(11), 45–47.

Hudson, K. (2001). The disposable worker. *Monthly Review, 124*(4), 43–55.

Hulin, C. L., & Glomb, T. M. (1999). Contingent employees: Individual and organizational considerations. In D. R. Ilgen, & E. D. Pulakos (Eds.), *The changing nature of performance: Implications for staffing, motivation, and development* (pp. 87–118). San Francisco: Jossey-Bass Publishers.

Hundley, G. (2001). Why and when are the self-employed more satisfied with their work? *Industrial Relations, 40*, 293–316.

Inkson, K., Heising, A., & Rousseau, D. M. (2001). The interim manager: Prototype of the 21st-century worker? *Human Relations, 54*, 259–284.

Jackofsky, E. F., & Peters, L. H. (1987). Part-time versus full-time employment status differences: A replication and extension. *Journal of Occupational Behavior, 8*, 1–9.

Johns, G. (2006). The essential impact of context on organizational behavior. *Academy of Management Review, 31*, 386–408.

Jordan, A. T. (1996). Critical incident story creation and culture formation in a self-directed work team. *Journal of Organizational Change Management, 9*, 27–35.

Jordan, J. W. (2003). Sabotage or performed compliance: Rhetorics of resistance in temp worker discourse. *Quarterly Journal of Speech, 89*, 19–40.

Jurik, N. C. (1998). Getting away and getting by: The experiences of self-employed homeworkers. *Work and Occupations, 25*, 7–35.

Kalleberg, A., & Marsden, P. (2005). Externalizing organizational activities: Where and how US establishments use employment intermediaries, Socio-Economic Review, 3, 389–416.

Kalleberg, A. L. (2000). Nonstandard employment relations: Part-time, temporary and contract work. *Annual Review of Sociology, 26*, 341–365.

Kalleberg, A. L., Reskin, B. F., & Hudson, K. (2000). Bad jobs in America: Standard and nonstandard employment relations and job quality in the United States. *American Sociological Review, 65*, 256–278.

Kallinikos, J. (2003). Work, human agency, and organizational forms: An anatomy of fragmentation. *Organization Studies, 24*, 595–618.

Kanter, R. M. (1977). *Men and women of the corporation.* New York: Basic Books.

Katz, J. A. (1993). How satisfied are the self-employed: A secondary analysis approach. *Entrepreneurship Theory and Practice, 7*, 35–51.

Kogut, B., & Zander, U. (1996). What do firms do? Coordination, identity, and learning. *Organization Science, 7*, 502–518.

Krausz, M. (2000). Effects of short- and long-term preference for temporary work upon psychological outcomes. *International Journal of Manpower, 21*, 635–647.

Kunda, G., Barley, S. R., & Evans, J. A. (2002). Why do contractors contract? The experience of highly skilled technical professionals in a contingent labor market. *Industrial and Labor Relations Review, 55*, 234–261.

Kurland, N. B., & Bailey, D. E. (1999, Autumn). The advantages and challenges of working here, there, anywhere, and anytime. *Organizational Dynamics,* 53–67.

Lautsch, B. A. (2002). Uncovering and explaining variance in the features and outcomes of contingent work. *Industrial and Labor Relations Review, 56*, 23–43.

Lee, T. W., & Johnson, D. R. (1991). The effects of work schedule and employment status on the organizational commitment and job satisfaction of full versus part-time employees. *Journal of Vocational Behavior, 38,* 208–224.

Levesque, L. L., Wilson, J. M., & Wholey, D. R. (2001). Cognitive divergence and shared mental models in software development project teams. *Journal of Organizational Behavior, 22,* 135–144.

Liden, R. C., Wayne, S. J., & Kraimer, M. L. (2003). The dual commitments of contingent workers: An examination of contingents' commitment to the agency and the organization. *Journal of Organizational Behavior, 24,* 609–625.

Logan, N., O'Reilly, C. A., & Roberts, K. H. (1973). Job satisfaction among part-time and full-time employees. *Journal of Vocational Behavior, 3,* 33–41.

Mallon, M., & Duberley, J. (2000). Managers and professionals in the contingent workforce. *Human Resource Management Journal, 10,* 33–47.

Mann, S., & Holdsworth, L. (2003). The psychological impact of teleworking: Stress, emotions and health. *New Technology, Work, & Employment, 18,* 196–211.

Mann, S., Varey, R., & Button, W. (2000). An exploration of the emotional impact of tele-working via computer-mediated communication. *Journal of Managerial Psychology, 15,* 668–690.

Marler, J. H., Barringer, M. W., & Milkovich, G. T. (2002). Boundaryless and traditional contingent employees: Worlds apart. *Journal of Organizational Behavior, 23,* 425–453.

Martens, M. F. J., Nijhuis, F. J. N., Van Boxtel, M. P. J., & Knottnerus, J. A. (1999). Flexible work schedules and mental and physical health. A study of a working population with non-traditional working hours. *Journal of Organizational Behavior, 20,* 35–46.

Martin, J. (2006). *Giving voice to the silenced majority in organizational theory and research.* Manuscript submitted for publication.

Martin, J. E., & Peterson, M. M. (1987). Two-tier wage structures: Implications for equity theory. *Academy of Management Journal, 30,* 297–315.

Matusik, S. F., & Hill, C. W. L. (1998). The utilization of contingent work, knowledge creation, and competitive advantage. *Academy of Management Review, 23,* 680–697.

McDonald, D. J., & Makin, P. J. (2000). The psychological contract, organizational commitment and job satisfaction of temporary staff. *Leadership and Organizational Development Journal, 21*(2), 84–91.

McGinnis, S. K., & Morrow, P. C. (1990). Job attitudes among full- and part-time employees. *Journal of Vocational Behavior, 36,* 82–96.

McLean Parks, J., Kidder, D. L., & Gallagher, D. G. (1998). Fitting square pegs into round holes: Mapping the domain of contingent work arrangements onto the psychological contract. *Journal of Organizational Behavior, 19,* 697–730.

Menger, P. (1999). Artistic labor markets and careers. *Annual Review of Sociology, 25,* 541–574.

Miller, H. E., & Terborg, J. T. (1979). Job attitudes of part-time and full-time employees. *Journal of Applied Psychology, 64,* 380–386.

Mirchandani, K. (1999). Legitimizing work: Telework and the gendered reification of the work-nonwork dichotomy. *The Canadian Review of Sociology and Anthropology, 36,* 87–107.

Mlicki, P., & Ellemers, N. (1996). Being different or being better? National stereotypes and identifications of Polish and Dutch students. *European Journal of Social Psychology, 26*, 97–114.

Moreland, R. L. (1999). Transactive memory: Learning who knows what in work groups and organizations. In L. L. Thompson, J. M. Levine, & D. M. Messick (Eds.), *Shared cognition in organizations: The management of knowledge* (pp. 3–31). Mahwah, NJ: Lawrence Erlbaum Associates.

Morse, D. (1969). *The peripheral worker.* New York: Columbia University Press.

Mowday, R., Porter, L., & Steers, R. (1982). *Organizational linkages: The psychology of commitment, absenteeism, and turnover.* New York: Academic Press.

Nollen, S. D., & Axel, H. (1996). *Managing contingent workers: How to reap the benefits and reduce the risks.* New York: Amacom.

Norman, P., Collins, S., Conner, M., Martin, R., & Rance, J. (1995). Attributions, cognitions, and coping styles: Teleworkers' reactions to work-related problems. *Journal of Applied Social Psychology, 25*, 117–128.

Olson, M. H. (1989). Organizational barriers to professional telework. In B. Boris, & C. R. Daniels (Eds.), *Homework: Historical and contemporary perspectives on paid labor at home* (pp. 215–30). Chicago: University of Illinois Press.

Orr, J. E. (1996). *Talking about the machines.* Ithaca, NY: Cornell University Press.

Parker, R. (1994). *Flesh peddlers and warm bodies: The temporary help industry and its workers.* Camden, NJ: Rutgers University Press.

Parker, S. K., Griffin, M. A., Sprigg, C. A., & Wall, T. D. (2002). Effect of temporary contracts on perceived work characteristics and job strain: A longitudinal study. *Personnel Psychology, 55*, 689–719.

Pearce, J. L. (1998). Job insecurity is really important, but not for the reasons you might think: The example of contingent workers. In C. Cooper, & D. Rousseau (Eds.), *Trends in organizational behavior* (Vol. 5, pp. 31–46). New York: Wiley.

Pearce, J. L. (1993). Toward an organizational behavior of contract laborers: Their psychological involvement and effects on employee co-workers. *Academy of Management Journal, 36*, 1082–1096.

Pearlson, K. E., & Saunders, C. S. (2001). There's no place like home: Managing telecommuting paradoxes. *Academy of Management Executive, 15*, 117–128.

Peipperl, M., & Baruch, Y. (1997, Spring) Back to square zero: The post-corporate career. *Organizational Dynamics,* 7–22.

Perrow, C. (1991). A society of organizations. *Theory and Society, 20*, 725–762.

Peters, L. H., Jackofsky, E. F., & Salter, J. R. (1981). Predicting turnover: A comparison of part-time and full-time employees. *Journal of Occupational Behavior, 2*, 89–98.

Pfeffer, J., & Baron, J. N. (1988). Taking the workers back out: Recent trends in the structuring of employment. In B. M. Staw, & L. L. Cummings (Eds.), *Research in organizational behavior* (Vol. 10, pp. 257–303). Greenwich, CT: JAI Press.

Pink, D. H. (2001). *Free agent nation: The future of working for yourself.* New York: Warner Books.

Polivka, A. E. (1996). Into contingent and alternative employment: By choice? *Monthly Labor Review, 119*(10), 55–74.

Polivka, A. E., & Nardone, T. (1989). On the definition of "contingent work." *Monthly Labor Review, 112*(12), 9–16.

Pratt, M. G. (2000). The good, the bad, and the ambivalent: Managing identification among Amway distributors. *Administrative Science Quarterly, 45,* 456–493.

Pratt, M. G., Fuller, M., & Northcraft, G. B. (2000). Media selection and identification in distributed groups: The potential cost of "rich" media. In T. Griffith, E. Mannix, & M. Neale (Eds.), *Research in managing groups and teams* (Vol. III, pp. 231–255). Stamford, CT: JAI Press.

Rafaeli, A. (1998). What is an organization? Who are the members? In C. L. Cooper, & S. E. Jackson (Eds.), *Creating tomorrow's organizations: A handbook for future research in organizational behavior.* New York: John Wiley & Sons.

Raghuram, S., Wiesenfeld, B., & Garud, R. (2003). Technology enabled work: The role of self-efficacy in determining telecommuter adjustment and structuring behavior. *Journal of Vocational Behavior, 63,* 180–198.

Rhoades, L., Eisenberger, R., & Armeli, S. (2001). Affective commitment to the organization: The contribution of perceived organizational support. *Journal of Applied Psychology, 86,* 825–836.

Rock, K. W., & Pratt, M. G. (2002). Where do we go from here? Predicting identification among dispersed employees. In B. Moingeon, & G. Soenen (Eds.), *Corporate and organizational identities* (pp. 51–71). London: Routledge.

Rogers, J. K. (1995). Just a temp: Experience and structure of alienation in temporary clerical employment. *Work and Occupations, 22,* 137–166.

Rogers, J. K. (2000). *Temps: The many faces of the changing workplace.* Ithaca, NY: Cornell University Press.

Rothstein, D. S. (1996). Entry into and consequences of nonstandard work arrangements. *Monthly Labor Review, 119*(10), 75–82.

Rousseau, D. M. (1985). Issues of level in organizational research: Multi level and cross level perspectives. In L. L. Cummings, & B. M. Staw (Eds.), *Research in organizational behavior* (Vol. 7, pp. 1–38). Greenwich, CT: JAI Press.

Rousseau, D. M. (1995). *Psychological contracts in organizations: Understanding written and unwritten agreements.* Thousand Oaks, CA: Sage.

Rousseau, D. M., Ho, V. T., & Greenberg, J. (2006). I-deals: Idiosyncratic terms in employment relationships. *Academy of Management Review, 31,* 977–994.

Rousseau, D. M., & Libuser, C. (1997). Contingent workers in high risk environments. *California Management Review, 39,* 103–123.

Salancik, G. R., & Pfeffer, J. (1978). A social information processing approach to job attitudes and task design. *Administrative Science Quarterly, 23,* 224–253.

Schilling, M. A., & Steensma, H. K. (2001). The use of modular organizational forms: An industry-level analysis. *Academy of Management Journal, 44,* 1149–1169.

Scott, W. R. (2004). Reflections on a half-century of organizational sociology. *Annual Review of Sociology, 30,* 1–21.

Shalley, C. E., Zhou, J., & Oldham G. R. (2004). The effects of personal and contextual characteristics on creativity: Where should we go from here? *Journal of Management, 30,* 933–958.

Shamir, B. (1992). Home: The perfect workplace? In S. Zedeck (Ed.), *Work, families, and organizations* (pp. 272–311). San Francisco: Jossey-Bass.

Sias, P. M., Kramer, M. W., & Jenkins, E. (1997). A comparison of the communication behaviors of temporary employees and new hires. *Communication Research, 24,* 731–754.

Simon, H. A. (1976). *Administrative behavior: A study of decision-making processes in administrative organization* (4th ed.). New York: Free Press.

Smith, V. (1994). Institutionalizing flexibility in a service firm: Multiple contingencies and hidden hierarchies. *Work and Occupations, 21*, 284–307.

Smith, V. (1997) New forms of work organization. *Annual Review of Sociology, 23*, 315–339.

Smith, V. (1998). The fractured world of the temporary worker: Power, participation, and fragmentation in the contemporary workplace. *Social Problems, 45*, 411–430.

Stamper, C. L., & Masterson, S. S. (2002). Insider or outsider? How employee perceptions of insider status affect their work behavior. *Journal of Organizational Behavior, 23*, 875–894.

Staples, D. S., Hulland, J., & Higgins, C. (1999). A self-efficacy theory explanation for the management of remote workers in virtual organizations. *Organization Science, 10*, 758–777.

Storey, J., Salaman, G., & Platman, K. (2005). Living with enterprise in an enterprise economy: Freelance and contract workers in the media. *Human Relations, 58*, 1033–1054.

Sutcliffe, K. M., & Vogus, T. J. (2003). Organizing for resilience. In K. S. Cameron, J. E. Dutton, & R. E. Quinn (Eds.), *Positive organizational scholarship: Foundations of a new discipline* (pp. 94–110). San Francisco: Berrett-Koehler.

Tajfel, H., & Turner, J. C. (1986). The social identity theory of intergroup behavior. In W. G. Austin, & S. Worchel (Eds.), *The social psychology of intergroup relations* (pp. 33–47). Monterey, CA: Brooks/Cole.

Tan, H. H., & Tan, C. P. (2002). Temporary employees in Singapore: What drives them? *The Journal of Psychology, 1*, 83–102.

Tench, R., Fawkes, J., & Palihawadana, D. (2002). Freelancing: Issues and trends for public relations practice. *Journal of Communication Management, 6*, 311–322.

Thatcher, S. M. B., & Zhu, X. (2006). Changing identities in a changing workplace: Identification, identity enactment, self-verification, and telecommuting. *Academy of Management Review, 31*, 1076 –1088.

Tietze, S. (2005). Discourse as strategic coping resource: Managing the interface between "home" and "work." *Journal of Organizational Change Management, 18*, 48–62.

Tietze, S., & Musson, G. (2003). The times and temporalities of home-based telework. *Personnel Review, 32*, 438–533.

Tilly, C. (1992). Short hours, short shift: The causes and consequences of part-time employment. In V. L. duRivage (Ed.), *New policies for the part-time and contingent workforce* (pp. 15–44). Armonk, NY: M. E. Sharpe.

Trent, J. T., Smith, A. L., & Wood, D. L. (1994). Telecommuting—stress and social support. *Psychological Reports, 74*, 1312–1314.

Tsui, A., Egan, T., & O'Reilly, C. (1992). Being different: Relational demography and organizational attachment. *Administrative Science Quarterly, 37*, 549–579.

Uzzi, B., & Barsness, Z. I. (1998). Contingent employment in British establishments: Organizational determinants of the use of fixed-term hires and part-time workers. *Social Forces, 76*, 967–1007.

Van Breugel, G., Van Olffen, W., & Olie, R. (2005). Temporary liaisons: The commitment of 'temps' towards their agencies. *The Journal of Management Studies*, *42*, 539–566.

Van Dyne, L., & Ang, S. (1998). Organizational citizenship behavior of contingent workers in Singapore. *Academy of Management Journal*, *41*, 692–703.

Van Maanen, J., & Barley, S. R. (1984). Occupational communities: Culture and control in organizations. In B. M. Staw, & L. L. Cummings (Eds.), *Research in organizational behavior* (Vol. 6, pp. 287–365). Greenwich, CT: JAI Press.

Von Hippel, C., Magnum,.S. L., Greenberger, D. B., Heneman, R. L., & Skoglind, J. D. (1997). Temporary employment: Can organization and employees both win? *Academy of Management Executive*, *11*, 93–104.

Walsh, J. P., Meyer, A. D., & Schoonhoven, C. B. (2006). A future for organization theory: Living in and living with changing organizations. *Organization Science*, *17*, 657–671.

Weick, K. E. (1974). Middle range theories of social systems. *Behavioral Science*, *19*, 357–367.

Weick, K. E. (1995). *Sensemaking in organizations*. Thousand Oaks, CA: Sage.

Weick, K. E. (1996). Enactment and the boundaryless career: Organizing as we work. In M. B. Arthur, & D. M. Rousseau (Eds.), *The boundaryless career: A new employment principle for a new organizational era* (pp. 40–57). New York: Oxford University Press.

Wenger, E. (1998). *Communities of practice: Learning, meaning, and identity*. Cambridge, U.K.: Cambridge University Press.

Wenzel, M. (2000). Justice and identity: The significance of inclusion for perceptions of entitlement and the justice motive. *Personality and Social Psychology Bulletin*, *26*, 157–176.

Westman, M. (2001). Stress and strain crossover. *Human Relations*, *54*, 717–751.

Wheeler, A. R., & Buckley, R. M. (2000). Examining the motivation process of temporary employees: A holistic model and research framework. *Journal of Managerial Psychology*, *16*, 339–354.

Wienns-Tuers, B. A., & Hill, E. T. (2002). How did we get here from there? Movement into temporary employment. *Journal of Economic Issues*, *36*, 303–311.

Wiesenfeld, B. W., Raghuram, S., & Garud, R. (1999). Communication patterns as determinants of organizational identification in a virtual organization. *Organization Science*, *10*, 777–790.

Workman, M., Kahnweiler, W., & Bommer, W. (2003). The effects of cognitive style and media richness on commitment to telework and virtual teams. *Journal of Vocational Behavior*, *63*, 199–219.

Wrzesniewski, A., Dutton, J. E., & Debebe, G. (2003). Interpersonal sensemaking and the meaning of work. In R. M. Kramer, & B. M. Staw (Eds.), *Research in organizational behavior* (Vol. 25, pp. 93–136). Greenwich, CT: JAI Press.

Zuboff, S., & Maxmin, J. (2002). *The support economy: Why corporations are failing individuals and the next episode of capitalism*. New York: Viking.

3
Critical Management Studies

PAUL S. ADLER

University of Southern California

LINDA C. FORBES

Franklin and Marshall College

HUGH WILLMOTT

University of Cardiff

Abstract

Critical management studies (CMS) offers a range of alternatives to mainstream management theory with a view to radically transforming management practice. The common core is deep skepticism regarding the moral defensibility and the social and ecological sustainability of prevailing conceptions and forms of management and organization. CMS's motivating concern is neither the personal failures of individual managers nor the poor management of specific firms, but the social injustice and environmental destructiveness of the broader social and economic systems that these managers and firms serve and reproduce. This chapter reviews CMS's progress, main themes, theoretical and epistemological premises, and main projects; we also identify some problems and make some proposals. Our aim is to provide an accessible overview of a growing movement in management studies.

Introduction

Critical management studies (CMS) might best be introduced with an illustration. In a large body of mainstream research, teamwork is presented as a means by which managers can more effectively mobilize employees to improve business performance. By reorganizing work so as better to accommodate task interdependencies, and by leaving team members a margin of autonomy in deciding how to handle these interdependencies, teamwork is often presented as a "win-win" policy, making work simultaneously more satisfying for employees and more effective for the business. Issues such as workforce diversity are studied as factors that can facilitate or impede effective teamwork, and if they impede it, research addresses how the problem can be mitigated.

In CMS research, both the practice of teamwork and the mainstream theories that inform it are seen as more problematic (see, e.g., Barker, 1993; Batt & Doellgast, 2006; Ezzamel & Willmott, 1998; Knights & McCabe, 2000; McKinley & Taylor, 1998; Proctor & Mueller, 2000; Sinclair, 1992). For example, much mainstream research either ignores, or views as pathological, the solidarity of teams in pursuing their own agendas and priorities—perhaps in resisting autocratic foremen, making work more meaningful, or simply having more fun at work. Critical research has shown how teamwork, when indeed management corrals it toward business goals, can result in the oppressive internalization of business values and goals by team members, who then begin exploiting themselves and disciplining team peers in the name of business performance and being "responsible" team players. The resulting conformism suppresses democratic dialogue about the appropriateness of the underlying values and goals. Critical studies show how teamwork routinely reinforces established class and authority hierarchies as well as oppressive gender and ethnic relations. Critical research has also sought to understand the various mechanisms that make teamwork attractive for many employees notwithstanding its negative effects. Critical research shows how discourses that are used to legitimate and enforce teamwork occlude social divisions and promote a vision of the firm as a functionally unified entity or as one big happy family. Critical research does not see the problems of teamwork as intrinsic; rather, it diagnoses the shortcomings of teamwork in practice in terms of its embeddedness in broader patterns of relations of domination, relations that operate to narrow and compromise laudable aims of increasing discretion and participation.

While issues of work organization such as teamwork form an important part of the body of CMS scholarship, CMS today addresses a wide variety of management issues in a broad range of fields—not only OB-HRM and OT, but also industrial relations, strategy, accounting, information systems research, international business, marketing, and so forth. Across these fields, the CMS use of the term *critical* signifies more than an endorsement of the standard norms of scientific skepticism or the general value of "critical thinking." It also signifies more than a focus on issues that are pivotal rather than marginal. Critical here signifies radical critique. By *radical* is signaled an attentiveness to the socially divisive and ecologically destructive broader patterns and structures—such as capitalism, patriarchy, imperialism, and so forth—that condition local action and conventional wisdom. By *critique*, we mean that beyond criticism of specific, problematic beliefs and practices (e.g., about teamwork), CMS aims to show how such beliefs and practices are nurtured by, and serve to sustain, divisive and destructive patterns and structures; and also how their reproduction is contingent and changeable, neither necessary nor unavoidable.

In developing its critical agenda, CMS has been influenced by contemporary developments beyond academia. Well-established critiques of the fundamental features of contemporary capitalism have been undercut by the decline and fragmentation of the Left since around 1970 (Hassard, Hogan, & Rowlinson, 2001). During the same period, the development of new social movements has opened new critical perspectives (e.g., Alvarez, Dagino, & Escobar, 1998). The expansion of the European Community and the rise of China, India, and other emergent economies have served to relativize Anglo-American business models and values (e.g., Dussel & Ibarra-Colado, 2006; Ibarra-Colado, 2006). Post-September 11, 2001, many certainties have been unsettled, even as others have been reinforced. A succession of major natural and social crises has brought into sharp focus issues that previously may have seemed more peripheral, issues such as business ethics, environmentalism, and imperialism. These broader developments have direct relevance for the everyday conduct of management and the everyday experience of work; yet they rarely take center stage in mainstream scholarship and teaching. CMS appeals to faculty, students, practitioners, activists, and policy makers who are frustrated by the mainstream's narrow focus.

CMS has consistently raised the concerns about the de-moralized state of management research (see Anthony, 1986)—concerns that are aired sporadically, and perhaps increasingly, by mainstream scholars. CMS has anticipated but also radicalizes the sentiments expressed recently by Ghoshal (2005):

> Academic research related to the conduct of business and management has had some very significant and negative influences on the practice of management...by propagating ideologically inspired amoral theories, business schools have actively freed their students from any sense of moral responsibility. (p. 76)

CMS radicalizes such sentiments by pointing to how prevailing structures of domination produce a *systemic* corrosion of moral responsibility when any concern for people or for the environment requires justification in terms of its contribution to profitable growth.

The following section describes CMS's progress to date—the conditions of its emergence and its growing visibility. The next three sections review in turn the common themes of research under the CMS banner and its main theoretical and epistemological premises. The fifth section sketches the landscape of CMS projects in research, education, social and political activism, and everyday management practice. The sixth discusses two key problems that are likely to shape the future theoretical agenda for CMS. The conclusion formulats some proposals for a CMS movement that we see as still in the early stages of its development.

It is impossible in the space available to address the critical work done in all the various topics and fields; our goal instead is to review the main currents of research and their theoretical backgrounds. Our review is limited to work in English.

Progress

Before analyzing the various strands of CMS, we sketch the context of business education within which it emerged and the body of knowledge to which it is counterposed. Since the recommendations of the influential Ford and Carnegie reports in the 1950s, business schools have been placed squarely within universities. The rationale for this was explicitly technocratic: Business expertise and education should be set upon an analytical, scientific foundation equivalent to that then being developed in the social sciences and in the teaching of the engineering disciplines. A positivist, value-free model of scientific knowledge was enthroned,[1] marginalizing other approaches. It promised the production of impartial, rigorous, and reliable knowledge capable of replacing the contestability of custom and practice with the authority of management's own science. Such a context, itself shaped within the broader Cold War environment of patriotic consensus, was hardly conducive to the emergence of radical critique within business schools.

Once installed in universities, business schools came into closer contact with the social sciences. These social sciences, however, were themselves evolving. The broader liberalization of advanced capitalist societies and their universities, combined with the growing disillusionment amongst policy makers with the relevance of the dry, abstract knowledge emerging from the social sciences, led to some relaxation of the grip of positivism in the late 1960s and 1970s. Across the social sciences, the established positivist hegemony began to be pluralized (but not displaced) by alternative research traditions—including varieties of Marxism, hermeneutics, and pragmatism (discussed in the following section)—that promised to draw researchers closer to the complexities and contradictions of the social world.

The effects on business schools were moderated and delayed, in part because these schools were concurrently expanding rapidly in number and size in tandem with the growth of large corporations and the associated demands for credentialed managerial labor. However, the shift within the social sciences was eventually repeated in business schools, albeit in weaker and often more compromised form. The most significant openings were in the fields of management and accounting; changes were also seen in information systems and marketing.

In this context, a number of the more established and prestigious management journals began to accommodate some heterodox research (e.g., Daft

& Lewin, 1990). This development facilitated the promotion and the recruitment of more critically oriented faculty. It also enabled the broadening of undergraduate curricula and some recruitment of critically oriented doctoral students. It has even spawned a number of management departments and business schools whose philosophy and/or faculty are explicitly "critical" in orientation (e.g., the business school at Queen Mary's, University of London, http://www.busman.qmul.ac.uk/pr/BusMgt-06.pdf) and which offer MPhil/PhD study in Critical Management (University of Lancaster Management School, http://www.lums.lancs.ac.uk/Postgraduate/MPhilCritMngt/).

CMS has been strongest in the United Kingdom. The existence of sizable numbers of U.K. academics disaffected with established management theory and practice became evident with the first Labour Process Conference in 1983, which drew most of its participants from schools of management and business. The Labour Process Conference has continued to meet annually in the United Kingdom since then, drawing between 100 and 200 participants each year. In a parallel development, the Standing Conference on Organizational Symbolism (SCOS) was formed in 1981 as a spin-off from the more mainstream European Group for Organization Studies. Whereas participants at Labour Process Conferences often took their inspiration from the Marxist tradition, members of SCOS were closer to postmodernist and poststructuralist theories (see discussion below).

A second wave of growth in the United Kingdom became visible in 1999, when an unexpectedly large number of people—over 400, drawn from over 20 countries—participated in the first CMS Conference. This conference and the biannual series it inaugurated differentiated itself from the Labour Process Conference by extending to a broader range of themes and by engaging more intensively with postmodernist and poststructuralist ideas. A listserv emerged to support this community (*critical-management*).

The United States side of the CMS movement first became visible as a workshop at the 1998 Academy of Management meetings and the concurrent formation of a listserv (*c-m-workshop*). The ensuing series of annual workshops eventually became a formally recognized Interest Group of the Academy in 2002. At the time of writing, the CMS Interest Group (CMS-IG) has 845 members, which is more than many of the older divisions. Of all the Academy groups, it has the highest proportion of non-U.S. members. Whereas in the United Kingdom the annual Labour Process Conference and the biannual CMS conference series have continued in parallel with modest overlap in participants, the U.S.-based CMS-IG has sought to encompass both "wings" in the one grouping.

Other geographic nodes of CMS have arisen too, notably in Canada, Australia, New Zealand, Scandinavia, and Brazil. Apart from the growing openness of established journals, the international development of CMS has been supported by the emergence of a number of critically oriented journals, most notably *Organization, Organization and Environment, Critical Perspectives on Accounting, Gender, Work and Organizations, Management and Organizational History,* and *Critical Perspectives on International Business.* CMS has also benefited from CMS members' creation and/or close involvement in several nonsubscription electronic journals that have actively promoted and disseminated critical work: *Ephemera, Electronic Journal of Radical Organization Theory, M@n@gement,* and *Tamara.*

Common Themes

The widespread use of the CMS label to identify alternatives to established, mainstream conceptions of management followed the publication of Alvesson and Willmott's (1992) edited collection *Critical Management Studies* (see also http://en.wikipedia.org/wiki/Critical_management_studies). However, the tradition of critical management studies goes back to older, humanistic critiques of bureaucracy and corporate capitalism (see Grey & Willmott, 2005; Smircich & Calás, 1995; Wood & Kelly, 1978) as well as to the tradition of research inspired by labor process theory, which highlights the exploitation of workers by employers (Braverman, 1974). As we shall show, these critiques of management have been elaborated, challenged, and complemented in recent years by those informed by several other streams of thought.

It would be a mistake to attribute too much unity to the CMS movement. Our chapter gives ample space to delineating its variants and internal tensions. It is nevertheless possible to discern a relatively widely shared sense of purpose. For most participants in CMS, many of the most important motivating problems are related to the capitalist core of the prevailing economic system and this core's articulation with other structures of domination (CMS scholars have also addressed the repressive features of "socialist" work organizations; e.g., Littler, 1984; Thompson, 1989; with the demise of the Soviet bloc, this question has lost its urgency, though it remains a salient question, e.g., in the study of China). The focus is reflected in the official "domain statement" of the CMS-IG (http://aom.pace.edu/cms):

> Our shared belief is that management of the modern firm (and often of other types of organizations too) is guided by a narrow goal—profits— rather than by the interests of society as a whole, and that other goals— justice, community, human development, ecological balance—should be brought to bear on the governance of economic activity.

This concern is one CMS shares to a degree with some mainstream "stakeholder" approaches to corporate governance; but CMS proponents argue that so long as the market is the dominant mechanism for allocating resources in our societies, community and government influences are forced into a subordinate role. This subordination has been reinforced by the "financialization" of contemporary capitalism, which further intensifies pressures on management to prioritize the interests of stockholders (including the executives holding stock options, of course) over all other interests (Ezzamel, Willmott, & Worthington in press; Froud, Johal, Leaver, & Williams, 2006; Lazonick & O'Sullivan, 2000). According to the domain statement, since enterprise is "guided by such narrow goals, the firm is a structure of domination"; and the "shared commitment" of CMS participants is "to help people free themselves from that domination." A more specific focus of CMS, then, is, "The development of critical interpretations of management—interpretations that are critical not of poor management or of individual managers, but of the system of business and management that reproduces this one-sidedness."

Note the emphasis upon interpretations in the plural (see Parker, 2002). This pluralism has several dimensions. First, while CMS is broadly "leftist" in leaning, it attracts and fosters critiques reflecting the concerns of a range of progressive ideologies and social movements (extending to progressive religious and spiritually informed movements). Second, while the core of CMS aims at a radical critique, there can be no sharp line dividing "really radical" from "merely reformist" criticism. The boundaries of the mainstream are not fixed but the subject of contestation: On the one hand, they expand as once critical issues and concepts are taken up in the mainstream; on the other hand, reformist criticism often opens the door to more radical change. Third, CMS accommodates diverse theoretical traditions, ranging from varieties of Marxism through pragmatism to poststructuralism. So the term *critical* does not signal a commitment to any particular school of thought, such as the Frankfurt School "critical theory" (CT; even though the latter has been an influential strand in the development of CMS; see discussion below).

We have noted that CMS proponents are motivated by concern with the role of management in the perpetuation and legitimation of unnecessary suffering and destruction, especially in the spheres of work and consumption. Many mainstream management scholars share this concern, but tend to leave it to their private, or nonprofessional lives; others feel that these misfortunes and problems are much exaggerated, view them as part of the human condition, or regard them as the inevitable price of progress. For CMS proponents, much of this suffering and destruction is remediable, and the desire to remedy it is a central motivating factor in their work. This gives rise to several common themes in CMS research, which we review briefly in the following paragraphs (drawing heavily upon Fournier & Grey, 2000; Grey & Willmott, 2005).

Challenging Structures of Domination

We have noted that CMS is distinctive in the radical nature of its critique of contemporary society. However, this radicalism would be naïve if CMS proponents did not also believe that a better, qualitatively superior form of society were possible. The implied premise of CMS is that the current form of society—capitalist, patriarchal, racist, imperialist, and productivist[2]—is but the latest in a historical sequence and that it contains within it the seeds of its possible transformation. Considering the record and prospects of advanced capitalist societies, it defies reason that the current form of society be the best humanity can do for itself with the available capabilities. The record of political experiments pursued in the name of socialism in the 20th century may not offer much hope, but abandoning the possibility of a radical change—by which we mean a change in the basic structure, not the abruptness of the process of change, which is a different issue—is not realism, as many in the mainstream might argue, but at best defeatism and at worst myopic, self-serving cynicism. Considering the relatively privileged position of academics in the social and economic order, such a stance is readily comprehensible but morally dubious if not untenable.

Diverse strands of CMS research and teaching aim to highlight the sources, mechanisms, and effects of the various forms of contemporary, normalized domination represented by capitalism, patriarchy, and so forth. This focus resonates with—and radicalizes—a long tradition of humanistic critique of the depersonalized and alienating nature of work in modern bureaucracies and corporations (e.g., Katz & Kahn, 1966), of the passivity and infantilism of mass consumption (e.g., Ritzer, 2000a; 2000b), of the unequal life opportunities afforded poor and working-class people, women, and minorities (e.g., Ehrenreich, 2001). It also brings CMS work into contact with, and similarly radicalizes, a range of research on how market relations serve mechanisms of exploitation, domination, and rent extraction (e.g., Coff, 1999).

Questioning the Taken for Granted

Challenging the taken for granted is central to the CMS mission, as it is to all oppositional activity. Opposition means subverting the tendency for social relations—such as those between management and workers or between the sexes—to become taken for granted or "naturalized." In the sphere of management, naturalization is affirmed in the common mainstream assumption that, for example, someone has to be in charge, and that managers are experts by virtue of their education and training, so it is rational for them to make the important decisions. CMS questions the self-evidence of these kinds of assumptions: Such patterns of behavior are neither natural nor eternal. CMS research portrays current management practices as institutionalized, yet fundamentally precarious, outcomes of (continuing) struggles between those who have mobilized resources to impose these practices and others who to date have lacked the resources to mount an effective challenge and thereby establish an alternative.

This theme in CMS work brings it into contact with, and radicalizes, neoinstitutional theory (e.g., on schooling, Benavot, Cha, Kamens, Meyer, & Wong, 1991), specifically with its argument that much of the structure of the world we see around us represents the taken-for-granted dominance of ideas about what things are supposed to look like, rather than any technical necessity. This theme also brings CMS into contact with international comparative research (e.g., Hall & Soskice, 2001). The discussion of different institutional structures and cultures—even if this discussion today is largely confined to different forms of capitalism—helps reveal the historically contingent character of the specific arrangements that prevail in any one place and time.

Beyond Instrumentalism

CMS proponents challenge the view, so deeply embedded in many mainstream studies of management, that the value of social relations in the workplace is essentially instrumental. (In the poststructuralist strand of theorizing discussed later, this assumption is critiqued as "performativity.") On the mainstream view, the task of management is to organize the factors of production, including human labor power, in a way that ensures their efficient and profitable application. Accordingly, people (now reclassified as "human resources") and organizational arrangements are studied in terms of their effectiveness in maximizing outputs. Goals such as improving working conditions or extending the scope for collective self-development and self-determination are not, therefore, justifiable as ends in themselves, but only if and insofar as they help improve business performance or bestow legitimacy upon oppressive practices. The assumption is sometimes explicit, for example, in the "instrumental" version of stakeholder theory (Donaldson & Preston, 1995). Sometimes, it is only implicit: As Walsh (2005) shows, it is implicit even in some of the classic, ethically framed, "normative" versions.

In the instrumentalist approach to management and organization, the goal of profitability—or, in the not-for-profit sectors, performance targets—take on a fetishized, naturalized quality. All action is then evaluated under the norms of instrumental means-ends rationality. Ethical and political questions concerning the value of such ends are excluded, suppressed, or assumed to be resolved. Instrumentalism means that other concerns—such as the distribution of life chances within and by corporations or the absence of any meaningful democracy in the workplace—are safely ignored or, at best, minimally accommodated by making marginal or token adjustments. As the result of proliferating business scandals, mainstream scholarship has become more sensitive recently to these issues; however, CMS scholars are skeptical of the mainstream argument that these scandals result from weak personal or organizational ethics: Critical research is more likely to point to the role of the broader structures within which managers and organizations function (e.g., Adler, 2002a; Knights & Willmott, 1986a; Kochan, 2002; see also materials at the Association for Accountancy and Business Affairs Web site at http://visar. csustan.edu/aaba/aaba.htm).

Instrumentalism also infiltrates the mainstream understanding of the purpose and value of research. Implicit in such thinking is the idea that research should be assessed by its contribution to the effectiveness of business management. The influence of this instrumentalist view is documented by Walsh, Weber, and Margolis (2003), who showed the unrelenting shift in North American management research away from "welfare" related concerns toward profitability concerns. The instrumentalist assumption is similarly illustrated by the demand made by the editors of many mainstream academic journals that articles conclude with a discussion of implications for managers. Research seminars often proceed on the same assumption, where the critical scholar is often confronted with the challenge, "But how does this help managers?" This assumption tethers research to a management point of view, and the concerns of other stakeholders are therefore addressed from only this narrow vantage point. There is a conflation of research *on management* with research *for managers.*

Finally, instrumentalism also dominates the mainstream understanding of the role of business education (as signaled earlier in the quote from Ghoshal, 2005, and discussed further in the following section). On the mainstream view, the study of management should simply prepare people to take their place in efforts to improve corporations' competitive performance. This vision of business education marginalizes efforts to equip students to think critically about issues of the public good and sustainability and ignores the fact that managers often feel themselves tugged in competing directions by their loyalties to various stakeholder groups and by their personal commitments to values other than profitability. Whereas instrumentalism assumes the virtue of an essentially technical training, CMS proponents argue that business education should at the very least encourage a broader, more questioning (e.g., humanities) approach that aims to provide a wider range of ways of understanding and evaluating the nature, significance and effects of doing business and managing people (French & Grey, 1996; Zald, 2002).

Reflexivity and Meaning

CMS proponents argue for the importance of reflexivity in research (Alvesson & Sköldberg, 2000; Johnson & Duberley, 2003; Woolgar, 1988). Reflexivity here means the capacity to recognize how accounts of management—whether by researchers or practitioners—are influenced by their authors' social positions and by the associated use of power-invested language and convention in constructing and conveying the objects of their research. By such reflexivity, CMS aims to raise awareness of the conditions under which both mainstream and critical accounts are generated, and how these conditions influence the types of accounts produced.

CMS scholarship has argued, for example, that research on "corporate social responsibility" or "corporate citizenship"—like claims by corporations themselves about their performance on these dimensions—should be assessed in relation to the struggles to establish the meaning of such terms (e.g., Tinker, Lehman, & Neimark, 1991). Critical scholarship asks what meanings can be attributed to such key terms as *trust, responsibility,* or *citizenship* (e.g., Knights, Noble, Vurdubakis, & Willmott, 2001). How is it that certain meanings become dominant and taken for granted? What alternative possible meanings are excluded in this process?

Power and Knowledge

The themes outlined in this section coalesce around the theme of the intimate connection between power and knowledge. Much CMS analysis is concerned with showing that forms of knowledge, which appear to be neutral, reflect and reinforce asymmetrical relations of power. This connection between power and knowledge is inevitable when researchers take existing realities as necessary givens rather than as the product of continuing struggles. It is similarly inevitable when researchers see their roles as servants of power (Baritz, 1974; Brief, 2000).

An important tendency within CMS, inspired primarily by Foucault, sees this interconnection as even deeper, using the expression "power/knowledge" to suggest the indivisibility of the relationship. On the Foucauldian understanding, power is not just a struggle between groups who have more or less of it. For Foucault, as for Gramsci (1971), power is much more pervasive; it is also a positive and not merely negative force: Power is that which enables certain possibilities to become actualities in a way that excludes other possibilities. It is, for example, what enables management scholars to assume and sustain some (e.g., mainstream) contents and identities rather than alternative (e.g., critical) ones. And inherent in the exercise of power is the unintended constitution of an Other that resists efforts to exclude or suppress it (e.g., critical scholars respond to efforts to exclude their points of view by developing critiques of managerialism).

In much HR research, for example, the problem framings, categories, and models reflect asymmetries of power between managers and workers (as noted by Nord, 1977); the Foucauldians add that HR theory is also a way of constituting and naturalizing these asymmetries (e.g., Townley, 1994). Absenteeism, for instance, is the object of a huge knowledge-power apparatus comprised of a sizable academic literature, a complex set of HRM practices, and a massive system of statistical capture and reporting. This apparatus defines absenteeism as a problem, an impediment to organizational performance. The oppressive nature of this framing has become more evident as concerns about "work-life balance" take a more prominent place in public debate. An emerging social movement is challenging the grotesque morbidity, mortality, and quality-of-life consequences of overwork and "presenteeism" (e.g., Simpson, 1998).

Theoretical Resources

The theoretical resources used by CMS can be usefully characterized using Burrell and Morgan's (1979) matrix of approaches to organizational studies. On one dimension of this matrix, forms of analysis are differentiated according to whether they focus on order, regulation, and consensus, or on change, transformation, and conflict. On the other dimension, approaches that conceive of society and organizations as objective structures are contrasted with approaches that focus on the role of agency and on (inter)subjective experience in the reproduction and transformation of social relations.

In both dimensions, the dividing lines are somewhat blurred (Gioia & Pitre, 1990; Willmott, 1993b); moreover, new theoretical currents within CMS have complicated the picture considerably. Both despite and because of these caveats, Burrell and Morgan's distinctions can be heuristically useful as a way to locate varieties of CMS and their theoretical roots.

On the first dimension, the focus on change most clearly differentiates CMS from mainstream approaches. However, two caveats are needed. First, new social movements, notably feminism and environmentalism, have considerably enriched the CMS understanding of forms of order and dimensions of change. Second, the line between order and change is fuzzy insofar as some CMS proponents leverage mainstream, regulation-oriented theories to critical, albeit reformist, purpose. As emphasized earlier, what we might call the "radical core" of CMS sees the main problems we face today as the inevitable corollaries of the prevailing form of society—a form in which market competition forces firms to treat employees and environment as mere means toward the end of profit maximization. The "reformist" variant of CMS sees the root problem not in the profit motive itself but rather in the absence of counterbalancing factors. Reformists thus argue that considerable progress could be made if the profit imperative were moderated by government regulation, by the involvement of other stakeholders in corporate governance, or simply by more enlightened values among top managers.

On the second dimension of Burrell and Morgan's matrix, CMS—in both its radical and reformist forms—has advanced both structuralist and agency-oriented theories. The main debates within CMS have been across this dimension; but connections have also been forged to their mutual enrichment. A scholarship that is motivated by opposition to domination is naturally concerned to understand both the conditioning aspects and the lived reality of this domination. As a result, critical scholarship has often engaged with the work in social theory on the structure/agency relation: Marx, pragmatist symbolic interactionism, actor-network theory, Giddens, and Bourdieu are all important in this regard. There has also been some questioning of the necessity and value of the established dualism of agency and structure as an organizing power/knowledge template, or regime of truth, for social scientific analysis, because the former tends to assume an autonomous, centered agency and the latter tends to assume an autonomous, noncontingent operation of structures. Forms of poststructuralist analysis (discussed in the following section) have sought to deconstruct the logic which asserts the foundational nature of this dualism in ways that were unanticipated by Burrell and Morgan.

The following paragraphs review the main currents of thought that have nourished CMS. We begin with those that CMS shares with more mainstream scholarship.

Leveraging Regulation-Oriented Structural Theories

CMS scholars can leverage a broad range of mainstream, regulation-oriented theories, although in doing so, it may prove difficult to articulate a radical critique. Many mainstream management theories aim to elucidate the conditions required for effective competitive performance, and critical scholars can use these theories to highlight the irrationality of organizations that sacrifice efficiency and effectiveness to preserve the prerogatives of powerful actors.

In this vein, critiques of bureaucracy, such as those that were advanced by sociologists such as Merton, Gouldner, and Blau, by psychologists at the Tavistock Institute, and by management scholars inspired by the progressive wing of the Human Relations school in the 1950s, continue to resonate in CMS research today. At a more microlevel, role stress theory has been used to show how workers lives are impaired by the role conflict, ambiguity, and overload endemic in capitalist firms. Similarly, needs-based theories of work motivation have served as a basis for critique of the alienating quality of wage work as antithetical to the need for self-determination.

Contingency theory argues that task uncertainty should lead to decentralization as a means of enabling flexible responses to volatile and unpredictable operating conditions. While mainstream theory draws instrumental conclusions from these premises, critical scholars can leverage contingency theory to point out that in practice it is common that top managers use their power to define the environment, the performance goals, and the internal organization in ways that reinforce their dominance, even at the cost of business performance (Child, 1972; Pfeffer & Salancik, 1978). Similarly, more recent theories of learning, learning organizations, and complexity show how overly bureaucratic and controlling organizations suppress learning and miss performance-improvement opportunities. Perrow (1984) used mainstream contingency theory to formulate a powerful critique of nuclear power and other systems that make inevitable devastating "normal accidents."

Resource dependency theory starts with the assumption that firms strive to preserve their autonomy; this assumption, while somewhat anthropomorphic, has the virtue of realism in suggesting that relations between and within firms reflect power concerns and not only efficiency concerns. While mainstream research draws instrumental conclusions from these premises, critical scholars invoke these same premises to advance a critique of the ideology of the market—the purported optimality and efficiency of the market as a form of economic coordination, and the purported purification of politics and power from market relations (e.g., Fligstein, 2001; Hirsch, 1975; Hymer, 1976, 1979; Mizruchi, 1996). Like the other mainstream theories, however, resource dependency theory does not give us any vantage point from which to conceptualize the historical specificity of the capitalist structure or the other prevalent structures of domination; it is therefore difficult to use resource dependency theory as a foundation for radical as distinct from reformist critique.

Leveraging Classical Sociology

Critical approaches have drawn from classical sociology to analyze management and organizations as social, rather than merely technical, phenomena, deeply implicated in the production and reproduction of structures of domination. CMS scholarship has found Weber, and to a lesser extent Durkheim, particularly useful. While mainstream scholars read these authors as conservative functionalists, their work is sufficiently rich to allow other readings that blur their location on Burrell and Morgan's matrix.

Weber is used by mainstream theory to naturalize the assumption that large, complex organizations must be organized in a bureaucratic form, even if, to many, such a form seems irredeemably alienating. CMS scholars find in Weber materials for more critical analyses. On the one hand, Weber is mobilized in the critique of market relations as vehicles for domination (of powerful firms over both less powerful employees and smaller firms) and in the critique of bureaucracy as embodying the "iron cage" of modernity and of the elevation of formal over substantive rationality (e.g., Edwards, 1979). On the other hand, some critical scholars return to Weber's argument that bureaucracy can be a bulwark against domination (e.g., du Gay, 2000; Jacoby, 1985; Perrow, 1986) and others find in Weber an inspiration for exploring the lived realities of managerial work (e.g., Watson, 1994).

Durkheim is used by mainstream research in ways that naturalize the anomic conditions of the modern world; but critical research uses Durkheim to critique these conditions and suggests that alternatives are possible (Adler & Heckscher, 2006; Bellah, Madsen, Sullivan, Swidler, & Tipton, 1985). Durkheim's later work is used by neo-institutional theory as a foundation for conceptualizing the power of shared ideas in shaping social structures and interactions: institutional arrangements that appear as natural, taken for granted can thus be shown to be shared illusions, a spell that can be broken (e.g., Biggart & Beamish, 2003). Durkheim's work on ritual affords critical insight into the social structuring of emotions in organizations (e.g., Boyle & Healy, 2003).

In these efforts, CMS often overlaps with the critical wing of neo-institutionalism (see e.g., Clemens & Cook, 1999; Hirsch, 1975, 1997). In general, however, the predominantly functionalist interpretations of classical sociology have made these traditions less attractive to critical students of management. In the main, CMS has found greater inspiration in Marx, in contemporary European thinkers such as Habermas and Foucault, in the work of pragmatists such as Dewey and Mead, and in various new social movements. We now turn to these.

Marxism and Related Theories

Marxism has for long been one of the main sources of more radical forms of structuralist critical scholarship. It has appeared in CMS in various guises, most notably as the foundation for labor process theory, but also in a range of other approaches.

Marxism Marxist theory argues that the key to understanding work organization lies in the structure of the broader society within which it is embedded, rather than in human psychology, in the dynamics of dyadic exchange, or in any timeless features of formal organizations. Social structure, in turn, is seen as fundamentally determined by the prevailing relations of production—the nature of control and property rights over productive resources. The relations of production characteristic of capitalist societies derive from the nature of the commodity (the "germ," or core, of capitalist production; Marx, 1977, p. 163). The commodity is something produced for sale rather than for direct use, and as such has two aspects: its use value—its qualitatively differentiated value as something useful to the purchaser—and its exchange value—its power to command a quantity of money in exchange. For Marx, it is the socially necessary labor time required to produce a commodity that determines this exchange value (this thesis is known as the "labor theory of value").

As a system of commodity production, capitalist relations of production have two key features. First, control and ownership of productive resources is dispersed among owners of firms who confront each other as commodity producers in market competition. Second, alongside those who enjoy such ownership is a class of nonowners who, lacking alternative access to means of production or consumption, must sell their capacity to work ("labor power") as if it were a commodity on the labor market. It is workers' propertyless condition that makes it possible to extract surplus labor from them; but how, and how much, surplus value is extracted will depend *inter alia* on class conflict. (Foley, 1986, presents Marx's basic economic theory in a theoretically sophisticated but technically simple manner.)

Marx characterized some distinctive developmental tendencies ("laws of development") of such a form of society. First, coordination by the market is intrinsically unstable: competition among firms leads to a persistent tendency to overproduction and crisis. Second, the combination of interfirm competition and class conflict leads to increasing firm size and to the replacement of labor by mechanization, and these tendencies in turn put persistent pressure on profit levels, further exacerbating crisis tendencies. Third, the basic matrix of capitalism is resistant to change: Once the market mechanism becomes predominant, this limits the efficacy of alternative mechanisms—including mechanisms that might mitigate its crisis tendencies. The dominance of market relations corrodes community, and gives capital increasing international mobility that enables it to outflank governments and thus limit governments' efforts to intervene in economic affairs. CMS has used these Marxist ideas in the study of various themes.

Analyses of class structure. Marxism asserts the unity of interests of the capitalist class in its opposition to the working class. This unity is always precarious, since capitalists also compete against their peers; but Marxism is a useful platform for studying the ongoing centripetal and centrifugal forces as they affect, for example, the structure of corporate boards, the political role of business, and the emergent global managerial class (e.g., Fidler, 1981; Murphy, 2006; Ornstein, 1984; Palmer & Barber, 2001; Useem, 1982). The Italian Marxist, Antonio Gramsci (1971), developed a sophisticated account of hegemony that has been influential in studying the class structuring of business elites and civil society (e.g., Carroll & Carson, 2003; Gill & Law, 1993; Levy & Egan, 2003).

Critique of the market. Labor markets, even apparently competitive ones, are the means by which the capitalist class asserts its monopsonist power over workers. Moreover, labor markets are typically structured to divide workers from each other, segmented into more and less exploited components, using race and gender to "divide and rule" (Edwards, 1979). Consumer markets are not the vehicle for consumer sovereignty, but means by which demand is created to satisfy artificial wants stimulated by advertising. Even where markets do function relatively competitively, the limitations of the market mechanism—externalities, instability—impose unacceptable costs on communities and nature (e.g., Adler, 2001; Benson, 1975; Marchington, Grimshaw, Rubery, & Willmott, 2005).

Critique of capitalist work organization and its ideologies. Marxist theory highlights the incompleteness of the employment contract; it thus brings into focus the exploitative role played by management practices and capitalist ideology. Work is not designed to express human needs and values, but to maximize profit and/or to safeguard the privileges and control of managerial elites. This is not (just or principally) because managers may be greedy, but because their firms must compete for investment funds and because players in financial markets direct those funds to the most profitable firms. Management innovations such as employee participation are fundamentally constrained by this systemic pressure and by the basic asymmetry of power embodied in the employment relation (e.g., as compared to a partnership or cooperative structure; Mandel, 1992). Power within firms is not merely an overlay on a rational authority structure: the firm is essentially an exercise of coercive power. Work organization, management systems, and technologies are conditioned by an imperative to extract surplus labor (e.g., Warhurst, 1998; Clegg, 1981).

Workers' experience of work.   When labor is hired and organized for the purpose of extracting a profit from its productive capacity, the meaning of work is precarious and ambiguous at best. From this perspective, workers' experience of work in the capitalist firm is one of both objective-structural and subjective-experiential alienation (Hodson, 2001). If they internalize corporate interests as their own, the alienation is even more thorough for being hidden from its subjects or cynically accommodated by them (Collins, 1995; Miller, 1975). Workers can organize to improve the terms and conditions of their employment: that has been the historic function of unions. However, unions tend to become part of the machinery of advanced capitalism, channeling workers' discontent into demands for higher wages, and suppressing demands for improved quality of life and radical change (Thompson, 1989).

The new emerges within the womb of the old.   In traditional Marxist theory, the development of the forces of production, once it reaches a certain level, renders progressively more obsolete the capitalist relations of production. The anarchy of the market—its instability and externalities—becomes progressively more costly and less tolerable. Cooperation becomes more important than competition and exploitation in facilitating the further development of the forces of production. These new forms of cooperation cannot fully flower under capitalism; nevertheless, cooperation develops, representing germs of a new form of society within the womb of the old form, and strengthening the forces for change. This view has encouraged Marxist-influenced scholars to see progressive, prefigurative significance in new forms of organization such as networks and teamwork (the influence of this logic can be seen in work by authors as diverse as Adler, 2001; Bell, 1973; Castells, 2000; Hirschhorn, 1984; Kenney & Florida, 1993; Kern & Schumann, 1984).

Marxism of course has been the object of numerous critiques, both from critical and from mainstream scholars, both in the social sciences in general and in management studies in particular. It is said that capitalism has evolved so much since Marx's day that his analysis is surely obsolete; that Marxism must be faulty if its central predictions have not yet been borne out and if efforts to build socialist societies have been such failures. By emphasizing conflict, Marxist scholarship overlooks the everyday reality of collaboration.

Marxism downplays the real margin of autonomy workers enjoy in modern society—autonomy in switching employers, in shaping their work roles, and in fashioning their identities—and the pleasures derived from work as well as consumption. Marxism gives primacy to economic interests, and this materialist view is said by some critics to understate the power of culture and values not only to shape the course of events but also to become media and fields of capitalist expansion (Willmott, 1993a). By giving considerable causal efficacy to social structures and to collective actors, Marxism is also criticized on epistemological grounds from several different quarters.

The Marxist response to these criticisms is that Marx's theory identified the basic structural features of capitalism that still characterize the most advanced economies today and that his theory predicted with remarkable prescience the main lines of its evolution: concentration and centralization of capital, acceleration of technological change, destruction of the traditional middle class and the peasantry, incorporation of women into the work force, rising education levels, expanding state sector, recurrent business cycles, imperialist expansion (or globalization), and environmental destruction (e.g., Adler, 2004; Jaros, 2005; Foster, 2000). Eagerness to see radical social-structural change led Marx and many of his followers to imagine that capitalism would have collapsed by now under the weight of its own contradictions (which it nearly did during the 1930s Great Depression and the ascendancy of Fascist regimes) or would be swept aside by a working class mobilized in revolutionary action. However, stripped of voluntaristic overoptimism and of theoretical dogmatism and overreach, Marxism continues to inspire creative critical research (Burawoy, 2003; Burawoy & Wright, 2002; Smith, 2000; Van der Pijl, 1998).

Labor Process Theory   Using key elements of Marxist theory, labor process theory (LPT) argues that the market mechanisms alone cannot regulate the labor process: Since the employment contract is incomplete, capitalists must actively control the labor process against potential worker resistance. In its earliest expressions (notably Braverman, 1974; Zimbalist, 1979), LPT argued that capitalist imperatives of labor control and cost reduction create a built-in tendency toward deskilling and degradation—fragmenting jobs, reducing skill requirements, and replacing worker autonomy with management systems. Taylorism was taken as the paradigmatic form of modern capitalist work organization.

LPT has broadened over successive generations of research. It now argues that there are a variety of managerial strategies of control beyond deskilling, such as work intensification, skill polarization, and efforts to make workers feel responsible for productivity (Littler, 1982). It also recognizes that the workplace is only one part of our complex form of society and as a result, workplace conflicts do not necessarily translate into broad social conflict (Thompson, 1990; Edwards, 1986, 1990). LPT thus acknowledges that empirically observed situations reflect a host of local factors specific to firms, markets, institutional contexts, the ideologies of the various actors, and the history of their inter-relations. However, LPT proponents argue that this variation is an outcome as well as a medium of capitalist relations of production. A persistent theme has been deep skepticism of arguments that assert upgrading trends in work or the emergence of genuinely "new paradigms" in work organization.

LPT in its more recent forms takes two steps away from classical Marx-ism.[3] First, whereas more traditional readings of Marx (e.g., Cohen, 1978)—as indeed many non-Marxist theories—give a key role to technological change as a driver of social change and a determinant of work organization, labor process theorists have been adamantly opposed to anything resembling "tech-nological determinism." LPT argues that attributing any basic causal role to technology would be to naturalize historically specific, capitalist relations of production (e.g., Burawoy, 1979, pp. 14ff, 220): Technology is itself shaped by these relations of production (e.g., Noble, 1984).

Second, in arguing that the formation of class consciousness is influenced by many factors outside the labor-capital conflict in the workplace, LPT takes its distance from more traditional Marxist-based superstructure accounts. Thus, more recent LPT research explored the role of broader changes in global political economy that constrain firm-level management policy (e.g., Thompson, 2003). It has also devoted more effort to understanding the for-mation of employees' subjective self-understandings (e.g., Ezzamel, Willmott, & Worthington, 2001; Knights & Willmott, 1989; Knights & McCabe, 2000; Stewart, 2002; Thompson & Ackroyd, 1995). In this work, LPT researchers built on Gramsci's (1971) thesis that hegemony "is born in the factory" (p. 285) and on Burawoy's (1979) observation that the interests pursued by, or attributed to, a group (e.g., "labor," "capital") are not given but are organized through practices such as the shop-floor game playing in which Burawoy par-ticipated. This line of argument opens LPT to ideas from the Frankfurt School of Critical Theory and poststructuralism (Knights & Willmott, 1989).

Marxists criticize LPT's abandonment of Marx's labor theory of value and his characterization of the laws of development of the capitalist system. They argue that these elements of Marxist theory add another, deeper layer of intelligibility to social analysis, and that without these elements, the Marxist "critique of political economy" dissolves into a theoretically weaker matrix of Weberianism (Hassard, Hogan, & Rowlinson, 2001; Jaros, 2005; Rowlinson & Hassard, 2001; Tinker, 2002). LPT proponents respond that such a move away from Marx enriches critical scholarship: It abandons some of the less easily defensible elements of Marx's theory and affords critical analysis a richer account of social structure and consciousness (Thompson & Newsome, 2004).

Other critics of LPT have argued that other conflicts (e.g., gender and ethnic-ity) are neglected by LPT even though they can be a significant basis of conflict that is not reducible to class conflict. More fundamentally, poststructuralists challenge all efforts, Marxist or otherwise, to reduce self-identity processes to the subject's ostensibly objective position within social structures (O'Doherty & Willmott, 2001). These arguments have been attacked by proponents of traditional LPT as obscuring rather than clarifying the key contradictions of capitalism (for rejoinders from different perspectives within LPT, see Thompson & Smith, 2001; Tinker, 2002).

Frankfurt School Critical Theory   Many CMS proponents have drawn inspiration from the so-called Frankfurt School tradition of CT reflected primarily in the writings of Adorno and Horkheimer (for overview, see Horkheimer & Adorno, 1972; Jay, 1973; related management research reviewed by Alvesson, 1987; Alvesson & Willmott, 1996). CT aspires to provide an intellectual counterforce to orthodox social theories that, in the name of science, legitimize the technocratic administration of modern, advanced industrial society. CT assumes the feasibility and desirability of greater autonomy for individuals, who, in the tradition of Enlightenment, are able to master their own destinies through collaboration with peers.

One of the key goals of the early Frankfurt School program of work was to explain why the revolution Marx predicted had not materialized. In the eyes of Horkheimer and Adorno (1972), and their colleagues, the proletariat had long since become divided and weakened—if, indeed, it had ever had the power and vision necessary to overthrow capitalism and establish a genuinely socialist society. Thus, the Frankfurt School's efforts have been largely directed at understanding how the working class has been disempowered by the cultural, ideological, and technological attractions of modern capitalism. To this end, they have incorporated Freudian psychoanalytic theory and other strands of sociology. CT has thus sought to remedy the relative neglect of culture and ideology in Marxian analysis, without reverting from Marxian materialism to some kind of idealism.

A key theme in CT is the critique of the authority vested in a value-free notion of science by positivist epistemology.[1] Positivism argues that knowledge simply reflects the world. According to CT, this leads to the uncritical identification of reality and rationality, and as a result, it encourages us to experience the world as rational and necessary, thus impeding attempts to change it. CT argues that positivist ideology has diffused far beyond the professional boundary of science, insofar as people are taught to accept the world "as it is," thus unthinkingly perpetuating it. CT thus sees positivism as pivotal in an ideology of adjustment, undermining our power to imagine a radically better world.

During the past two decades, the tradition of CT was carried forward by Jürgen Habermas (for overviews, see McCarthy, 1981; Finlayson, 2005). One of Habermas's central ideas was that human communication presupposes a benchmark reference point of free and equal communication embodied in what he called the "ideal speech situation." This idea has been useful to CMS scholars in understanding the ways in which forms of planning in firms and public agencies either support or suppress democratic deliberation (Forester, 1993; Burrell, 1994). Within CMS, there is some debate over whether the ideal speech situation is indeed a workable ideal or—as poststructuralists argue— just another form of hegemony (Willmott, 2003); in recent years, Habermas himself edged away from what some critics see as an unwarranted, founda- tionalist assumption. Other writers in this tradition have also had echoes in CMS, most notably Beck (1996, 2002) and Honneth (1995).

Pragmatism and Symbolic Interactionism

Pragmatism has been an important inspiration for CMS, especially for U.S. proponents. Arguably, pragmatism plays a background role for much U.S. CMS similar to the role played by Marx for U.K. CMS work (Sidney Hook, 1933/2002, famously argued that pragmatism and Marxism shared a common core; see Phelps, 1997). Two pathways of influence can be discerned.

The first pathway starts with John Dewey. Dewey has been important to CMS in two ways. First, his attention to our practical engagement with the world and his rejection of mind-body and self-other dualisms have informed research on practice, knowledge, and learning. In this, Dewey was close to Marx, Vygotsky (1962; 1978) and contemporary activity theory (Cole, 1996; Engeström, 1987). This work has had an important impact on thinking about experiential learning, including in management education (Kayes, 2002; Kolb & Kolb, 2005). It has also influenced work on ethics (Jacobs, 2004). Sec- ond, Dewey developed a powerful critique of corporate power (see Dewey, 1935/1999). Mary Parker Follett (1941/2003) carried Dewey's commitment to community and participatory democracy into organizational studies. It has been recently revived in public administration (Evans, 2000; Snider, 2000), after having been stifled as a progressive perspective by the absorption of prag- matism by logical positivism (greatly aided by Simon, 1976). Dewey's critique also lived on in C. Wright Mills. Mills stands for many CMS proponents as an exemplary public intellectual. His intellectual roots were in pragmatism, but he was also deeply influenced by Weber. His work on the middle class (*White Collar*, originally published in 1962), the ruling class (*The Power Elite*, 1956), and the tasks of sociology (*The Sociological Imagination*, 1959) displayed deep radicalism and powerful human empathy, and they continue to inspire criti- cal management research (e.g., Mir & Mir, 2002).

The second pathway of pragmatist influence starts with George Herbert Mead and the symbolic interactionist (SI) tradition of sociology that his student, Herbert Blumer (1969) codified. SI has been important in CMS research because it allows for a more "social" form of psychology and for a more "psychological" form of sociology. It rejects forms of variable analysis that assume a pregiven social world, in favor of the study of meanings and the negotiated and contested nature of social realities. Burrell and Morgan (1979) located SI in the structuralist-regulation cell of their matrix because it has often been used to study the reproduction of existing structures through everyday interaction. Nonetheless, some scholars have used it for more critical, change-oriented research. Barley's (1990) study of CT scanners in two hospitals illustrated the power of SI to make visible the role of pragmatic actors in shaping the impact of a new technology on local social structures. The critical edge comes here from revealing the contingency of the social structure, and thus our ability to change it.

The limitations of SI for the critical project lie in its lack of a theory of the broader social structures that condition local interaction. SI is a powerful lens for tracing the impact of these structures, and for showing how actions reproduce or change them; but it offers no theory of its own of the structures themselves (for overview, see Ritzer & Goodman, 2003; on efforts from within SI to respond to this critique, see Fine, 1991; 1993).

Postmodernism

During the 1990s, new streams of theory emerged in CMS, many of them collected under the umbrella headings of "postmodernism" and "poststructuralism." As noted earlier, these streams problematize the credibility of Burrell and Morgan's (1979) dimensions and the comprehensives of their framework.

The terms *postmodernism* and *poststructuralism* are used in various ways. Broadly speaking, however, postmodernism has sought to theorize the broad shift in Western societies beyond the limits of a modernist Weltanschauung toward greater flexibility and hybridity (e.g., Lyotard, 1984; on postmodernism in management research, see Calás & Smircich, 1997, 1999; Hassard & Parker, 1993; Kilduff & Mehra, 1997). It reflects and theorizes a growing disillusionment with established authorities, whether it be the authority of managers, of government, of science, or even of the figurative aesthetic in art. For postmodernists, modernity is exemplified by bureaucracy and suffers from an excess of instrumentalism: Modernity is premised on a generalized repression of spontaneity and creative imagination. In this sense, postmodernism is a new romanticism. Poststructuralism can be seen as part of a (postmodern) movement critiquing the rigidities of structuralist thinking that accord insufficient attention to contingency and undecidability. Where Marxists draw on the Enlightenment tradition of reason as a force that can enable social progress, postmodernism and poststructuralism more often draw inspiration from Nietzsche's critique of the use of reason as a mask of power. Following Nietzsche, they regard as problematic and potentially dangerous the Enlightenment's claim to secure universally valid knowledge. In their radical skepticism, these new streams of thought are responsive to, as well as reflective of, the historical demise of the left over the last two or three decades of the 20th century. We discuss postmodernism here, and leave discussion of poststructuralism to the following section on critical epistemologies.

An important feature of the postmodernist mood is its questioning of the imperialistic, totalizing claims of "metanarratives"—overarching schema that purport to order and explain broad social and historical patterns—including both Marxist and mainstream management theory. Postmodernists argue that social scientists' claims to objective truth as articulated in such metanarratives are discourses of power. Foucault was a significant influence (e.g., the selection of management studies inspired by Foucault in Calás & Smircich, 1997, Part III). Building on Nietzsche's thesis, Foucault argued that, in the modern age, power is dispersed rather than centralized and, therefore, that the presumption of being able to cleanse knowledge of power is not simply fanciful but potentially dangerous. Power functions by shaping its subjects—our self-understandings and the forms and sources of our pleasure. An informed appreciation of this process provides the most promising way to advance freedom. Teamwork, for example, is a management practice that shapes the self-identity and desires of employees, thereby engendering a new kind of subjection to an instrumental organizational regime, harnessing not only employees' bodies but also their souls. Postmodernists aim to make this subjection process less opaque and thus to facilitate resistance to it.

Postmodernism can be seen as an intensification of the modernist rejection of the confines of tradition: It is indeed more postmodern than antimodern. Postmodernism brings to our attention the limits of modernist ambitions to control every contingency. Such ambition is exemplified in both classical and progressive forms of management theory—such as in the claims of Peters and Waterman (1982) to manage and even exploit irrationality through the medium of "strong culture" and their advocacy of "empowering" teamwork (see Willmott, 1993a). Postmodernism is about releasing us from myths of modernity by celebrating serendipity and diversity—not as hypermodern instruments of "best employment practice," but as a basis for valuing all kinds of beliefs and activities that are currently marginalized, devalued, and denigrated by modernist values and associated agendas.

The focus on the more subtle mechanisms of power has been tonic for several strands of CMS, in particular labor process (Knights & Willmott, 1990) and feminist research (Calás & Smircich, 2006). The chief objection to this development—an objection that is voiced by both mainstream and critical scholars—is that if on the one hand power is so dispersed, if it is always productive as well as repressive, and if on the other hand all discourses and all assertions of "interests," including oppositional ones, are merely articulations of power, then it is difficult to distinguish emancipation from domination (see Lukes, 2005; for feminist critiques, Benhabib, 1992; Fraser, 1989). The counterargument is that it is always dangerous when someone claims to distinguish someone else's true and false interests: This opens the door to new totalitarian projects. The postmodernists' intent is not to abandon the project of emancipation, but rather to reconstitute it in the light of dark historical and creative intellectual developments of the 20th century.

Feminism

Feminism and environmentalism are intellectual movements within CMS that draw on and develop a variety of critical theories, including those previously discussed, and that have developed since Burrell and Morgan (1979) constructed their framework. The literatures in these two areas prioritize the concerns of two of the most vibrant political movements in the contemporary world. As such, feminist theory and environmental studies are particularly significant to critical management studies scholars. In both cases, there has been productive tension between liberal-reformist views and views that are more radical.

Alongside more mainstream liberal approaches, feminist theories include radical, psychoanalytic, socialist, poststructuralist/postmodern, and transnational/postcolonial variants (for a comprehensive review, see Calás & Smircich, 2006). Notwithstanding important differences, all these variants share a common goal: "Feminist theory …attempts to describe women's oppression, to explain its consequences, and to prescribe strategies for women's liberation" (Tong, 1989, p. 1). Where reformist liberal feminism advocates workforce equity and equality and investigates the role of management values and policies, the more radical perspectives advocate more fundamental change and investigate the broader patterns and structures that condition the scope of management action.

Feminist analysis has generated new theoretical insights into—and new practical approaches to—work and organizational life. In their more radical forms, these insights go to the very foundations of our understanding of formal organization: They expose the gender hierarchies and discrimination that are constitutive of current organizational forms, and suggest how organizations might function if feminist critique informed their design and governance (see Ashcraft, 2001; K.E. Ferguson, 1984; A. Ferguson, 2004; Ferree & Martin, 1995; Iannello, 1992; Savage & Witz, 1992). Feminist perspectives have been used to critique and provide alternatives to mainstream understandings of basic organizational forms such as bureaucracy (Ferguson, 1984), employment selection (Collinson, Knights, & Collinson, 1990), pay equity (Acker, 1989), leadership and management (Calás & Smircich, 1991; Wajcman, 1998), technology (Cockburn, 1991; Wajcman, 1991, 2004) culture (Martin, Knopoff, & Beckman, 1998), and more recently work-life balance (Appelbaum, Bailey, Berg, & Kalleberg, 2006; Calás & Smircich, 2006).

In addition to bringing concepts into the field that were once considered outside the domain of management theory (e.g., gender, sexuality, glass ceiling, sexual harassment, work/family balance, masculinities, and bodies), feminist theory examines organizational processes with sensitivity to the different ways people experience work and organization as a result of gendered and sexualized stratification (e.g., Hearn, Sheppard, Tancred, & Burrell, 1989). Through their work on standpoint epistemology, strong objectivity, situated knowledge, value-laden inquiry, and other alternative epistemologies (discussed further in the following section), feminist scholars have opened new epistemologies for research that exposes gender bias in science and that illuminates marginalized perspectives of women, people of color, ethnic and religious minorities and other oppressed or subaltern groups (Anderson, 2003).

For CMS scholars, feminist theory provides a rich resource for thinking about the cross-level interrelationships between subjectivity, discursive constructions, and macrostructural forces. Driven by their political commitments, more radical forms of feminism have developed some of our field's most sophisticated social theory, and have served to correct crippling gender blindness in mainstream theory.

Feminism's strengths, however, are also its limitations. Its heterogeneity has generated internal disputes that have catalyzed theoretical development; but these disputes have also slowed responses to changing historical conditions. Fraser and Naples (2004), echoing concerns of postmodernists, argue that the debates between "essentialists" and "antiessentialists" ultimately contributed to the inclusion of many more voices as these debates "usefully served to reveal hidden exclusionary premises of earlier theories" (p. 1112). They also contend that these debates "unwittingly diverted feminist theory into culturalist channels at precisely the moment when circumstances [the wave of neo-liberal globalization] required redoubled attention to the politics of redistribution" (Fraser & Naples, 2004, p. 1112). There are nevertheless important tendencies in feminist research that seek to weave together different strands of theory to address the challenges of contemporary forms of capitalism and patriarchy (see Calás & Smircich, 2006).

Environmentalism

The recently released Millennium Ecosystem Assessment (2005), a massive technical report that reflects the opinions of 1,300 distinguished scientists from 95 countries, called attention to the alarming fact that 60% of the Earth's ecosystems studied have been degraded significantly as a result of human activity. Not everyone agrees that natural systems have reached a crisis state, but the mounting evidence is increasingly convincing experts, the public, and the media that a global environmental crisis is looming.

This global environmental degradation is attributed to a variety of causes. Many analysts point to increases in human population (Brown, 2000; Kearns, 1997; National Academy of Science, 1994). Critical scholars, however, are skeptical of such apolitical explanations (for a review, see Foster, 1998). They do not see the root cause lying in population growth as much as in the way people exploit the environment for private gain with its attendant (obscenely) asymmetrical distribution of wealth and life chances. Marxist critics point to the destructive effects of decision making under the profit imperative (e.g., Foster, 2000). Other radical critics focus on the role of corporate interests in encouraging high-consumption lifestyles, anthropocentric worldviews, exploitative-patriarchal culture, and other forms of domination (e.g., Devall & Sessions, 1985; Hawken, 1993; Warren, 1997). As with feminist theories, critical environmentalism draws on a wide variety of perspectives, and it has developed several variants, notably deep ecology, social ecology, and eco-feminism (see Zimmerman, 1994).

Of particular interest to management scholars is the rise of corporate environmentalism and the assertion that effective leadership in addressing the phenomena of environmental degradation should come from the corporate sector (e.g., Hart, 1997). Long blamed for despoiling the environment, corporations and their leaders have recently launched initiatives not only to conserve resources and curb the damage but also to restore and replenish the environment. They increasingly argue that they alone have the resources, access, and expertise necessary to promote practically effective environmentalism. Mainstream scholars (e.g., Sharma, 2002) have drawn on a wide variety of frameworks to make sense of these corporate practices (for a critical review, see Jermier, Forbes, Benn, & Orsato, 2006). However, to date, the vast bulk of the scholarship on corporate environmentalism lacks the critical edge necessary to distinguish between incremental, reformist improvements and more radical innovations that come closer to matching the seriousness of the rapidly developing environmental crisis.

Taken together, several recent studies are beginning to form the foundation for a comprehensive critique of corporate environmentalism. Welford (1997) developed an early critique of the "hijacking" of the broader environmental movement by corporate capitalism. He raised questions about whether any form of corporate environmentalism can be compatible with the interests of government regulators, environmental NGOs, the broader citizenry, and the natural harmonies of the earth itself. A key orienting concept in the critical analysis of corporate environmentalism is *greenwashing*—constructing green symbolism without taking the radical steps required to deliver a full measure of green substance. Greenwashing is a central phenomenon in an era in which organizations face social pressure to address concerns about environmental degradation and resulting declines in human health. Studies on greenwashing have focused attention on how corporations contrive to convey a green image, perhaps by undertaking some highly visible campaign, but without applying the lessons of environmentalism to their business processes. Consequently, a misleading representation of corporations' environmental performance and initiatives is promoted (Athanasiou, 1996; Greer & Bruno, 1996; Tokar, 1997). Such studies highlight the role of corporate and related institutions in undermining genuine environmentalism through obfuscation and misrepresentation while supporting weak reformist programs, green marketing, and other image management techniques (e.g., Beder, 2002; Clapp & Dauvergne, 2005), on the development of theoretical perspectives on greenwashing behavior (see Forbes & Jermier, 2002; Lyon & Maxwell, 2004). Other noteworthy critical resources include Seager's (1993) ecofeminist explanation of business as usual and the ecological establishment, Newton and Harte's (1997) critique of environmentalist evangelical rhetoric, Fineman's (2000b) analysis of regulatory reinforcement, Levy's (1997; Levy & Egan, 2003; Levy & Newell, 2005) critique of environmental management, Jermier and Forbes' (2003) Marcusian CT analysis, Starkey and Crane's (2003) postmodern green narrative, Banerjee's (2003) postcolonialist analysis, and Castro's (2004) radical reformulation of the concept of sustainable development.

Tasks ahead for CMS environmentalists include the critique of green imposters and the further development of green critical theory. Another challenge lies in overcoming the tendency of environmentalists, even radically critical ones, to narrow the focus on the natural environment in a way that decouples it from the broader context of capitalism, patriarchy, racism, and imperialism.

Epistemological Premises

While some empirically oriented critical scholarship proceeds from positivist epistemological premises common in mainstream research, the drive to critique mainstream theory often prompts CMS proponents to engage with debates on epistemology that were a hallmark of Frankfurt School analysis and that have been heated within the philosophy of the social sciences (e.g., Bernstein, 1983, 1986). Within the CMS movement, there are a number of partly competing and partly overlapping epistemologies at work. We discuss here the three main families of views—standpoint theory (ST), poststructuralism, and critical realism.

Standpoint Epistemology

Many management scholars believe that value-neutral objectivity is the hallmark of properly scientific work (Simon's, 1976, position, inherited from logical positivism, is paradigmatic). While some in the CMS movement would agree, some others have embraced ST (for an overview and comparison with other epistemologies, see Anderson, 2003; for related controversies, see Harding, 2004; for discussion of the relevance to management research, see Adler & Jermier, 2005). ST challenges the idea of value neutrality, arguing that it would require scientists to do the "God trick" by adopting a "view from nowhere" (see Harding, 2004). ST argues that all phases of a research study—how we identify research issues, theorize research questions, gather and analyze data, draw conclusions, and use the knowledge produced—are conditioned to some extent by the researcher's subjective and objective place in the various dimensions of the social order—by their "standpoints" (Jermier, 1998). This assessment is broadly shared by the other two epistemologies discussed in the following section. Scholars cannot avoid or transcend these standpoints; but standpoints are frequently unacknowledged, because those in positions of power, the victors in history, are able to naturalize their own perspective.[4]

This analysis leads proponents of ST to argue that the route to deeper and arguably more objective knowledge lies not in attempting to eliminate politics from science, but in embracing politics and (consciously) adopting a standpoint that offers more rather than less insight. In a world marked by structures of domination and exploitation, research undertaken from the standpoint of the dominant elites inevitably legitimizes and naturalizes the status quo. Although all standpoints are limiting and all knowledge is partial, according to ST alternative views "from below"—that is, from the standpoint of comparatively oppressed or marginalized groups, such as workers, women, or ethnic minorities—has greater potential to generate insightful knowledge.

This argument was developed first in Marxist theory (Lukacs, 1923/1971) and then adopted by feminists and others. Marx argued that the basic structure of capitalist society ensures that subjects within it are presented with an inverted image of reality, most notably because the subjects of our world—real, living, creative people, whose development should be an end itself—appear as objects, as mere means for the self-expansion of capital. According to Marx, it is only when we take the point of view of the workers—who are now identified as producers of wealth rather than as mere factors of production—that this inversion becomes visible and a critique of the fetishizing logic of capitalism becomes possible. ST feminists have argued similarly that it is only when we take the vantage point of women that the structure and mechanisms of patriarchal domination become visible.

Many management scholars appear to think that to be a student, teacher, or researcher of management requires one to adopt the standpoint of managers and that such a standpoint gives one access to knowledge that is both objective and relevant to managers' concerns by using value-free methodology (see earlier discussion). Some advocates of this stance further argue that managers are obligated by their fiduciary responsibilities to consider social and environmental issues only insofar as they promote profit maximization. From that perspective, it would seem that CMS proponents, with their focus on social and environmental issues, are simply in the wrong field.

CMS researchers reject this logic, contesting as an ideological fantasy the neo-classical economic theory that enshrines shareholder value as the socially (Pareto-) optimal goal, and challenging the normalized role of management scholars as servants of power. Increasingly, mainstream scholars are paying attention to this critique of the narrowness of much management theory, of the blind spots in understanding that result from reliance on elite standpoints (e.g., Van de Ven & Johnson, 2006), but they generally remain wedded to a managerial standpoint, albeit now somewhat pluralized. From a CMS perspective, these concerns about "blind spots" cannot be addressed effectively without turning to more radical forms of analysis that are dedicated to remedying this blindness.

Poststructuralism

Poststructuralism comes in many forms, but is centrally concerned with the critical role of language in organizing and performing our relation to the world (Belsey, 2002; Butler, Laclau, & Zizek, 2000; Sturrock, 1993, chapter 5). It radicalizes the basic insight that there can be no theory-independent observation language. Poststructuralism recalls the value-laden nature of any assertions of facts, and rejects as authoritarian claims to objective truth—whether those claims are made by critical or mainstream scholars. But it also rejects an "anything goes" approach: To say that all knowledge claims, including its own, are historically and culturally embedded does not diminish the burden on scholars to argue in ways accepted as convincing within that historical-cultural frame.

Poststructuralism can be approached—and has garnered some of its support—via its critique of ST. ST assumes that actors who occupy a given position in the social structure have common, objective interests that will provide them with a shared perspective. Standpoint feminist research, for example, assumes the existence of a single, coherent, feminist identity that could serve as the foundation for a feminist standpoint. This assumption was challenged by Black feminists, third-world feminists, and others who asserted their own identities and points of view and who thereby questioned what they saw as the hegemony of middle-class White women in the feminist movement. This challenge was theorized by poststructuralists as demonstrating the pitfalls of attributing essential interests to women—or to social classes, or indeed to any structurally defined social category. Standpoint theorists respond that a common identity and awareness of common interests are not automatic consequences of a common structural position: The latter simply afford the opportunity to forge common identities and interests (e.g., Jameson, 1988). However, the poststructuralists challenge even this more modest causal claim, arguing that such potentiality cannot be determined by analytical fiat.

The critical value of the poststructuralist approach in organization studies is nicely demonstrated by Robert Cooper (1986; see also Willmott, 1998). Cooper drew attention to how our knowledge of organizations is framed by "method"—an endemic and powerful, yet often unacknowledged or silent, partner in the process of knowledge production. He showed that, in everyday language, the term *organization* could express two very different kinds of thinking. First, it can convey a *distal* understanding of organizations as things that exist "out there," as objective, discrete entities. On this understanding, organizations can be studied as objects possessing distinctive characteristics that can be stated as variables. This is a deeply institutionalized understanding of organization. Upon it are based diverse forms of functionalist and structuralist analysis that provide knowledge based upon what Chia (1996) termed "being-realism." In contrast, *proximal* thinking conceives of organizations as comprising diverse ongoing and open-ended activities. Researchers identify whatever boundaries or variables—or indeed, by participants themselves—are constructed and unstable, rather than more or less adequate reflections of the world "out there." Whereas distal thinking encourages an understanding of knowledge as something like a map of a comparatively well-defined objective reality, knowledge generated by proximal thinking articulates and promotes an appreciation of the precarious and incomplete processes that constitute our taken-for-granted sense of the "out there." In Chia's (1996) terminology, proximal thinking is an articulation of "becoming-realism."

In terms of its contribution to critical analysis, poststructuralist thinking is important for two reasons. First, the acknowledgement of proximal thinking provides for the possibility and legitimacy of deconstructing the claims of distal thinking, encouraging us to appreciate the dependence of the latter upon available, commonsense meanings that are idealized as "method." Second, it invites us to reflect upon the role of power in fixing, or institutionalizing, a particular way of making sense, as if this way of making sense of things had universal, observer-independent truth value and authority (Calás & Smircich, 1999; Contu & Willmott, 2003; Willmott, 2005). Needless to say, the attribution of self-evidence to a specific, orthodox way of representing the world (e.g., as organizations with structures and goals) is a powerful means of reproducing the status quo; but poststructuralists point out that the dominance of this institutionalized form of understanding can never become total, not least because any exercise of power provokes resistance (as discussed earlier). What counts as "deviant behavior" is therefore a consequence, and not simply a condition, of control. Any attempt to control or fix the meaning of any word—including words like *management* or *organization*—is inherently precarious since reality is always in excess of what is signified by any particular set of signifiers. Poststructuralists in CMS celebrate this excess and strive to widen and deepen its scope and influence, seeing it as potentially subversive and emancipatory.

Poststructuralist epistemology politicizes/ethicizes all forms of knowledge. Poststructuralists do not aim to deny or discredit the claims of science to greater objectivity; but they insist on the importance, in the actual practice of science, of assumptions and practices that are established politically rather than impartially. Critics read this "postfoundationalist" stance as a form of relativism or irrationality, which gives no greater weight to science than to alternative forms of belief (Boal, Hunt, & Jaros, 2003). Such criticism sees poststructuralist epistemology as failing an elementary logic test: When people assert that there is no objective truth, it is unclear how they can claim any objective truth value for their assertion. Poststructuralists reply that their claim is not that there is no objective truth, but rather that claims to objective truth are themselves contingent, and that an appreciation of this contingency should form an integral part of our understanding and examination of truth claims. To believe otherwise might be reassuring and beneficial to knowledge producers—placing contingency at the margins rather than the center of knowledge production lends those who don the mantle of science greater authority and renders the consumers of knowledge (e.g., policy makers) less vulnerable—but, for poststructuralists, it is a view based upon wishful thinking rather than hard-headed reflection on the centrality of politics (lower case *p*) in social practice.

Critical Realism

Critical realism is appealing to those who are critical of the mainstream's positivism but are unpersuaded or disturbed by what they see as the excessive value dependence of ST and the illogical relativism of poststructuralist epistemology. Critical realist epistemology is compatible with a broad range of political viewpoints; a growing number of CMS researchers (as well as scholars in other disciplines, e.g., economics) find critical realism to be a fruitful way to conceptualize the challenges facing the social sciences as positivism loses its plausibility and as poststructuralism challenges the established, positivist basis of differentiating science from other forms of knowledge (Archer, Bhaskar, Collier, Lawson, & Norrie, 1998; Fleetwood & Ackroyd, 2004).

Critical realism is most commonly associated with the work of Roy Bhaskar (1978; precursors and other variants are described in Verstegen, 2000). Bhaskar argued that what differentiates the practice of scientific investigation is the assumption that the object of its investigation has a real existence independent of the observer, an existence that is in principle available to objective knowledge. Where empiricism and positivism see science as finding patterns among observable facts, critical realism strives to identify the real structures that generate these facts and patterns—structures that are typically not visible to the naked eye. When scientists conduct experiments, they aim to trigger mechanisms that are attributed to the operation of these structures, and thus test their hypotheses concerning them. Critical realists understand reality to be layered: Beneath the *empirical* layer (observable by human beings), there is the *actual* (existing in time and space), and given that mechanisms may or may not be actualized, beneath the actualized lies the *real*. The real is therefore a set of structures that have causal powers from which observable events emerge.

Such a layered ontology is congenial to a critical structuralist perspective on management, where the observed regularities of organizational behavior are understood to hide as much as they reveal about the underlying social and psychological causes of domination (e.g., Tsoukas, 1994). In effect, critical realism aims to provide a basis for challenging the scientific standing of accounts that naturalize the social world by reporting its manifestations without regard for the underlying structures.

Poststructuralist critics contest the assertion that there are real mechanisms that science can detect (rather than construct; see Willmott, 1996). They argue that critical realism's universalizing claims result in an authoritarian view of science as the font of objective, impartial knowledge. Critical realists reply that science does not claim to possess objective knowledge, but that it has developed procedures that offer reasonable hope of progressing toward it. On the critical realist view, the danger of authoritarianism is forestalled by the openness of science to rational refutation and debate, thereby affirming a benign, rather than potentially malevolent, conception of rationality (Mutch, 2005; Willmott, 2005).

Critical Projects

So far, we have discussed the main theoretical traditions and epistemological orientations of CMS. We now briefly survey what CMS scholars have done with these resources in its research, pedagogy, and activism.

Critical Research

It is questionable whether there are any specifically "critical" methods or domains of research, or whether any methods or domains are antipathetic to critical research. As concerns methods, critical management studies embraces a number of epistemologies and these are compatible with very diverse research methods—quantitative as well as qualitative (see Johnson & Duberley, 2000). Nevertheless, Alvesson and Deetz (2000) provided a number of methodological pointers for the development of critical management research, arguing that these can offer important antidotes to "the managerialization of the world."

In its contributions to our knowledge of specific domains of management, CMS has addressed both conceptual and empirical concerns, often simultaneously, as it has applied different theories and methodologies to investigate and illuminate a wide range of topics. (An extensive CMS bibliography is available at http://www.criticalmanagement.org/.) In the context of this chapter, it is not possible to do more than list a small number of the more widely cited books and articles within CMS, with the aim of suggesting some starting points for the interested reader. The Appendix lists a few such entry points under each of several headings spanning most of the domains of CMS research to date.

Overall, CMS has been strongest in the area of work organization. As it developed, it has broadened to encompass a wide range of topics. The diversity of these can perhaps best be appreciated by consulting the programs of the meetings of the U.S. Academy of Management CMS-IG (see http://group. aomonline.org/cms/), the U.K.-based CMS conference (for proceedings of the first conference, see http://www.mngt.waikato.ac.nz/ejrot/cmsconference/ default.htm; for proceedings of the second, third and fourth conferences, see http://www.mngt.waikato.ac.nz/ejrot/), and the Labour Process conference (http://www.hrm.strath.ac.uk/ILPC/background/book-series.htm).

Critical Approaches to Management Education

Given that CMS is largely the creation of academics working in business schools, it is not surprising that management education is an important target of CMS intervention. In this context, as we pointed out in the previous section, CMS proponents come up against the assumption that business schools are training grounds for a business elite and that the content of research and teaching in these settings is—and must inevitably be—dominated by the demands of corporate clients. This assumption is reinforced by the AACSB and other accrediting processes, which push toward homogenization in curricula between professors within a college and among departments across universities (Jaros, 2001; Julian & Ofori-Dankwa, 2006). Understood in these terms, CMS is a misfit, if not an oxymoron.

This skeptical viewpoint is more common in the United States than in the United Kingdom. The predominant model of governance in U.S. business schools gives overwhelming weight to one key external stakeholder—the big firms that recruit most of the graduating students. This is somewhat moderated in public universities and in private schools with religious affiliations. In the United Kingdom, the weight of the corporate world is somewhat counterbalanced by stronger ties to the rest of the university and to a broader range of external stakeholders. Of these stakeholders, one of the most influential are the funding councils for the universities, which tie the resources and prestige of all departments, including schools of management and business, to formal assessments of research quality. However, even in the United Kingdom, CMS's commitment to the social good over corporate interests occasions considerable skepticism, if not opposition, from "users" who tend to assume that research should simply confirm and advance, rather than stimulate reflection upon, their priorities.

CMS proponents have proposed three main rejoinders to such evaluations (Adler, 2002b). The first rejoinder is a "militant" one: It is premised on a commitment to solidarity with the victims of corporate power and of other oppressive structures. This rejoinder embraces the oxymoron. Critically minded faculty can legitimately use their academic positions as a pulpit from which to challenge students to recognize the oppressive nature of the system they are being prepared to join. Such pedagogy may encourage some students to reconsider their career plans: A significant minority of students in business schools do in fact pursue careers outside business. Among those who do go into the business sector, such pedagogy might discourage blind implementation of corporate orders.

A second rejoinder is more "humanist" in nature. As humans who are endowed with empathy, notions of justice, and responsibilities as citizens, managers may feel profoundly ambivalent about the oppressive and exploitative dimensions of their roles. A critically oriented pedagogy can help future business leaders deal more productively with that ambivalence—productively, that is, not from the point of view of maximizing shareholder wealth, but from that of the students' personal development—helping them make more reflective choices. This view is similar to Mintzberg's (2004) position.

A third rejoinder could be labeled "progressive." On this view, managers at all levels except the most senior of levels in a capitalist corporation play a contradictory role. On the one hand, they are part of what Marx called the "collective worker," contributing expertise and assuring coordination. On the other hand, they are the agents of the intrinsically exploitative wage relation and of the coercive domination of the market. Therefore, managers, especially at lower hierarchical levels, often find themselves torn in their loyalties. A critical pedagogy can help would-be managers to become aware of this contradiction, and help them reflect on how they can position themselves relative to it.

Inspired by one or more of these rejoinders, CMS scholars have produced a number of textbooks, both basic and more advanced. Some of these are listed in the Appendix.

Political and Social Activism

One of the aspirations of critical management studies is to engage with the world to effect practical change. Many CMS scholars participate in unions, social movements, and political organizations. They also act as consultants to business, government, unions, and NGOs and as advocates in public forums. Through their scholarship, they can inform policy, connect with other activist groups across academia (e.g., critically oriented legal, accounting, and economics scholars), and reach audiences beyond their fellow academics. These engagements in turn shape CMS research, bringing to the fore new problems to study, highlighting the inadequacy of current theories, and suggesting new research strategies.

The wider university is also an important locus of CMS activism. Faculty members support student efforts to connect to social and environmental movements through student-led campus activist organizations, for example by serving as faculty advisors. Service learning courses or working with volunteer outreach projects can also serve to link students with social, political, and environmental problems. Critically oriented documentary films are frequently shown on college campuses creating openings for exchange, as do campus visits by politically progressive speakers and artists.

Notwithstanding these commitments and opportunities, the CMS movement has so far had only modest impact outside its academic home. Where critical accounting scholars have actively engaged public policy debates on accounting regulation (e.g., Mitchell & Sikka, 2005; Reform Club, n.d.), and where progressive industrial relations scholars are actively engaged in their corresponding field of practice (e.g., Kochan, 2005), other constituents of CMS have, so far, been less visible, in part because they have been focused upon challenging, and seeking to change, their immediate intellectual and professional environment. This emphasis may well shift in the future, particularly if world events continue to place in doubt the sustainability of the status quo. The neo-liberal celebration of the market over society, and the associated idolatry of the CEO would seem to be fading; the future likely holds more challenges than celebrations for business. In this context, CMS has an opportunity to acquire traction and legitimacy within academia, as policy makers and activists groups seek out management scholars whose analysis is more geared to their concerns and is less compromised by corporate involvement in, and funding, of business schools.

Relation to Everyday Management Practice

In many respects, and rather paradoxically, CMS often addresses topics and issues in ways that are less remote from the everyday worlds of practitioners than is mainstream work. CMS scores comparatively high on relevance and plausibility insofar as it acknowledges the centrality of conflicts of interest, power struggles, and contradictions—the familiar but often hidden features of contemporary work organizations. And CMS is also more inclined to make connections between topics and issues that have become fragmented and abstracted in mainstream research.

However, CMS does demand of its practitioner audience a willingness to suspend conventional wisdom and commonsense thinking—to leave the comfort zone of mainstream thinking. Consulting gurus who challenge the more backward and conservative sectors of business question and stretch this comfort zone; but these challenges typically carry tacit confirmation of the understanding that managers have a monopoly of relevant knowledge and an inalienable right to manage. CMS discourses push beyond those boundaries.

Precisely because CMS refuses to subscribe to a technocratic conception of management, practitioners and policy makers are often disoriented by, uneasy with, or downright hostile to its contribution. Privately, practitioners and policy makers may acknowledge the insights of CMS scholarship that address more directly the political realities and intractable dilemmas of management. Publicly, however, managers are often more inclined to scoff at CMS for its lack of comforting rhetoric and easy prescriptions, and/or to dismiss it as politically motivated and impenetrable (e.g., *The Economist*, 2004). Those occupying positions of privilege in corporate hierarchies are often aware of the precariousness of their authority; it is hardly surprising that they may be deeply resistant to analyses that remind them of this precariousness. Accordingly, a challenge for CMS is to resist the translation of its demanding analyses into frameworks or languages that dull its distinctive contributions while, at the same time, redoubling its determination to make a difference in the face of skeptical audiences.

Problems

As the preceding discussion has made clear, CMS is a catchall term signifying a heterogeneous body of work, a body that shares some common themes but is neither internally consistent nor sharply differentiable from more mainstream analysis. In this respect, the term is of limited use; but its fuzziness also has advantages. The fuzziness brings together a community of management scholars who share a common critical sensibility. It is a "big tent" that accommodates diverse forms of analysis—from the outrageously radical to the almost orthodox—in ways that enable both diverse internal debates and common external engagements. Looking forward, we see two main problems that are likely to shape the intellectual program of CMS.

Negativity?

As with most countermovements, CMS proponents have been more articulate about what they are against than what they are for. There are some exceptions to this generalization: some critical scholars have found considerable inspiration for their research and for their teaching in, for example, Robert Owen of New Lanark and the cooperative movement, William Morris, and Edward Filene (Jacobs, 2004; Kanter, 1972) as well as in contemporary communal experiments (Fournier, 2006; Quarter, 2000; Rothschild & Whitt, 1986). Nevertheless, the generalization is valid, and in the eyes of some scholars, both outside and within CMS, the absence of a manifesto or a set of prescriptions for change is a problem that undermines the credibility and value of CMS. Others disagree.

For many outside CMS, the habits of managerial, technocratic reasoning are deeply ingrained, and as a result, a radically critical perspective that offers little in the way of immediately actionable prescriptions can have no value. The counterargument is straightforward: The most damaging form of utopianism is arguably that which imagines that the savage injustice and destructiveness built into the core of the current social structure can be remedied by modest technocratic reform. Wars, famines, mass un- and underemployment, discrimination, and the unfolding environmental crisis—such suffering points to the need for radical, not incremental, change.

For some CMS proponents, a positive vision of a desirable future would help motivate the critique and would help overcome the counterargument that the CMS critique is utopian. Even if the ultimate goal remained ill defined, some shorter term goals might galvanize support (Fong & Wright, 2004, represent one such model). The strongest response to this argument is perhaps to note that historically recorded instances of fundamental social-structural change have typically been protracted and chaotic, and to argue that given this pattern it is neither necessary nor obviously useful to attempt to define or prescribe in detail and in advance the next stage of social evolution. While such a blueprint might help galvanize support for change among some groups in some specific moments, this reading of history suggests that major social changes proceed largely unguided by blueprints.

There is a second dimension to the negativity question: There is some debate within CMS about whether and how critical theories can address the progressive as well as oppressive aspects of capitalist development. On the one hand, some CMS proponents argue that when so much mainstream work is oriented, tacitly or explicitly, toward the defense of the contemporary form of society, the task of critique must remain essentially negative. On the other hand, others argue that if CMS cannot speak to the aspects of the prevailing system that people value, critique becomes shrill polemic (Adler, 2004). At the very least, it cannot be denied that around the world—from China to Poland—the opportunities and lifestyles associated with capitalism exert a very strong appeal. Whether the reality can sustainably fulfill the promise, —this is of course a different matter.

Materialism?

A major tension within CMS has been between structural/materialist streams, which are often Marxist inspired, and postmodernist/poststructuralist streams which place greater emphasis upon agency, language and contingency. No doubt, traces of their confluence and the associated "white water" are evident in the present text: Among the authors, there are significant divergences of view on this issue, and despite efforts to produce a well rounded and coherent paper, it would be surprising if our text did not betray these differences in some degree of unevenness in emphasis, tone, and orientation. In this respect, the chapter can be read as part of an ongoing dialogue with a series of critical commentaries on aspects of CMS (see Ackroyd, 2004; Adler, in press; Sotirin & Tyrell, 1998; Thompson, 2005).

The issue is partly generational. For older CMS proponents, the debates over Marxism and labor process theory prompted by the emergence of postmodernism, poststructuralism, and new social movements were formative. As we noted earlier, they coincided with, and in some ways reflected, a major shift in the overall political landscape, and therefore, these debates were interwoven with personal political biographies. For younger generations of researchers, however, these debates can seem remote and scholastic. Many younger scholars are more at ease with a less orthodox, more eclectic approach that favors rich diversity over rigorous consistency. For an older generation, different perspectives are associated with warring positions. For younger scholars, in contrast, points of disagreement and divergence often look less important, and the main task is to explore how they can all be mobilized, either in parallel or in creative hybrids, to advance the critical project. Diversity can be tonic.

Proposals

CMS has an ambitious objective of contributing to a progressive transformation of management theory and practice. Our survey suggests four recommendations for strengthening CMS.

First, the development of CMS will benefit from a continued diversity of forms of critique. We can take the epistemology debate as illustration. It is likely that all these families of epistemology will continue to coexist in CMS. Perhaps standpoint epistemology will appeal more strongly to those who seek to generate knowledge based on a commitment to particular issues. Perhaps critical realism will appeal more strongly to those who believe that social science should aim to deliver objective truth. And perhaps poststructuralism will appeal more strongly to those who value more reflexive and playful forms of understanding in which alternative ways of knowing are opened up rather than closed off, perhaps prematurely. However, the overall field of CMS will benefit from continued pluralism.

Second, CMS should foster vigorous debate among its different approaches. In CMS, as in any other community of research, debate inhibits the atrophying of positions and thereby acts as a potentially progressive force. At its best, debate enhances mutual understanding and respect; it challenges the parties to articulate and offer some justification of their position that may then be subjected to critical scrutiny, resulting in greater clarity for all the participants. Such debate, however, requires norms that are honored only partially and patchily in academe in general and in the CMS movement in particular.

Third, CMS should promote dialogue and debate with the mainstream. To date, such engagement has been largely one way, with conspicuously few mainstream academics being sufficiently interested or prepared to subject constituent elements of CMS to serious or sustained examination (exceptions include Donaldson, 1985; Westwood & Clegg, 2003). CMS scholarship is, however, likely to benefit from sustained efforts to engage mainstream research in dialogue. "Ghettoization" would be debilitating for the intellectual vitality of CMS.

Finally, even though these debates within CMS and with the mainstream are important, engagement with the world outside academia is, we submit, even more crucial. Those committed to advancing critical studies of management will doubtless continue to refine their theories and to debate the merits of their different approaches; the bigger challenge, however, and the one that provides the warrant for this internal debate, is to contribute more forcefully to shaping public agendas. The mainstream of the U.S. Academy of Management has become increasingly cognizant of the importance of engaging public and private policy makers (e.g., Cummings 2006; Van de Ven as cited in Kenworthy-U'ren, 2005); we argue that, following a distinctively radical path, CMS should broaden the audience to include social movements of resistance.

In this, CMS can take inspiration from Michael Burawoy's (2004) call for critical sociologists to develop a "public sociology." Burawoy distinguished mainstream and critical sociology and their respective academic and non-academic audiences. Mainstream "policy sociology" reorients "professional sociology" (mainstream academic research) toward actionable knowledge that can support the technocratic efforts of policy makers. Likewise, Burawoy argued that "public sociology" reorients "critical sociology" away from internal debates within the field and toward pubic dialogue in support of struggles for emancipation. Such public dialogue can take more traditional forms (books that stimulate public reflection and opinion columns that address current issues) or more "organic" forms (see Gramsci, 1971) that engage directly with specific communities and social movements.

Developing a better balance between such public engagement and the historically dominant form of critical scholarship that is oriented to our academic colleagues would, we believe, help CMS fulfill its promise.

Acknowledgments

We thank Jim Barker, Todd Bridgman, Marta Calás, Bill Cooke, Peter Edward, Peter Fleming, David Jacobs, Steve Jaros, John Jermier, Kate Kenny, David Levy, Richard Marens, David O'Donnell, Craig Pritchard, Linda Smircich, Paul Thompson, and Tony Tinker for their comments, even if we did not find space to incorporate them all and there remains much about the chapter with which they may disagree. We also thank the two *Annals* editors, Art Brief and Jim Walsh, for their support and suggestions.

Endnotes

1. *Positivism* is a particularly slippery term, so it is useful to explicate what we mean by it, namely an approach which assumes that (a) there is an objective external reality awaiting discovery and dissection by science; (b) scientific method gives privileged access to reality; (c) language provides a transparent medium for categorization, measurement and representation; (d) the observer scientists occupies a position outside and above reality from which he (rarely she) develops and validates robust theories about reality (Alvesson & Deetz, 2000, p. 61; see also Hacking 1981; Adorno et al., 1976).
2. Since these terms recur frequently in CMS work and in this review, we should define them. *Capitalism* is a form of society characterized by wage employment (thus domination by the class of owners, as distinct from cooperative ownership) and competition between firms (thus domination by the anarchy of the market, as distinct from democratic planning). *Patriarchy* is a form of society

characterized by the gender dominance of men over women. *Racism* is a structure of domination of one racially defined group over others. *Imperialism* is a structure of power relations in which the dominant class in one country exploits economically and dominates politically the population of other countries, even if the latter preserve formal independent sovereignty. *Productivism* is a structure of relations between humanity and the rest of the natural world in which the former destroy the latter in pursuit of their narrowly conceived self-interests, sacrificing both nature and noneconomic human values. CMS proponents often debate the nature of these structures and their interrelations but usually agree that they are all simultaneously operative today.

3. In this nuanced relation to classical Marxism, LPT is just one of several contemporary approaches that should be noted, albeit the one with the greatest impact to date on management research. We do not have space to address others, such as the anarchist Italian Autonomists (see Wright, 2002) and the efforts of the scholars around the journal *Rethinking Marxism* to develop a nondeterminist, nonreductionist form of Marxism.

4. CMS standpoint proponents, like other ST theorists, are divided on whether standpoints play similar or different roles in social versus natural sciences. Arguably, standpoints play qualitatively different roles in two domains, although even skeptics acknowledge that the case for ST in the critique of natural sciences is not easily dismissed.

Appendix   Some Studies in the Critical Spirit

1. Books
   - Alvesson & Willmott, 1996
   - Casey, 2002
   - Parker, 2002
   - Perrow, 1986

2. Edited volumes and special issues of journals
   - Academy of Management Review, 17(3) 1992. Special issue on new intellectual currents
   - *Administrative Science Quarterly*, 43(2) 1998. Special Issue on critical perspectives on organizational control
   - Alvesson & Willmott, 1992, 2003
   - Grey & Willmott, 2005
   - *Organization*, 9(3) 2002. Special issue on critical management studies

3. Books and articles on specific topics
   - Network theory: Grint & Woolgar, 1997; Law & Hassard, 1999
   - Aesthetics: Linstead & Hopfl, 2000
   - Alternative forms of organization: Ashcraft, 2001; Fournier, 2006; Luhman, 2006; Rothschild & Whitt, 1986
   - Body: Hassard, Holliday, & Willmott, 1998

- Bureaucracy: Adler & Borys, 1996; Alvesson & Thompson, 2006; Bauman, 1989; du Gay, 2000; Ritzer, 2000a,b
- Business process reengineering: Knights & Willmott, 2000
- Careers: Grey, 1994
- Class consciousness: Jermier, 1985
- Communication theory: Deetz, 1992
- Control in organizations: Clegg & Dunkerley 1980; Hyman, 1987; Jermier, 1998; Taylor, Mulvey, Hyman, & Bain, 2002; Tompkins & Cheney, 1985
- Corporate governance: Davis & Greve, 1997; Davis & Mizruchi, 1999; Lazonick, 2006; Mizruchi, 1996; Palmer, Jennings, & Zhou, 1993
- Corporate social responsibility: Marens, 2004; Margolis & Walsh, 2003
- Culture: Alvesson, 2002; Collinson, 1988; Kunda, 1992; Martin, 2001; Smircich, 1983; Watson, 1994; Willmott, 1993
- Discourse analysis: Chia, 2000; Phillips & Hardy, 2002
- Emotion: Bolton & Boyd, 2003; Fineman, 2000a; Mumby & Putnam, 1992
- Environmentalism: Jermier & Forbes, 2003; Levy & Newell, 2005; Welford, 1997
- Ethics: Jackall, 1988; Jones, Parker, & ten Bos, 2005; Neimark, 1995; Parker, 1998
- Financialization: Froud et al., 2006
- Gender: Calás & Smircich, 2006; Knights & Willmott, 1986b; Martin, 1990
- Globalization: Cooke, 2004; Hymer, 1976, 1979; Murphy, 2006
- Human resource management: Jacoby, 1985; Townley, 1994
- Identity: Pullen & Linstead, 2005
- Japanization: Elger & Smith, 1994
- Knowledge management: Adler, 2001; McKinlay, 2006; Prichard, Hull, Chumer, & Willmott, 2000
- Leadership: Calás, 1993; Smircich & Morgan, 1982
- Learning: Contu & Willmott, 2003
- Management education: French & Grey, 1996; Grey, 2004; Grey & Antonacopoulou, 2003; Reed, 2002; Summers, Boje, Dennehy, & Rosile, 1997; Whitley, Thomas, & Marceau, 1981
- Management ideologies: Abrahamson, 1997; Barley & Kunda, 1992; Gantman, 2005
- Management history: Burrell, 1997; Cooke, 1999; Jacques, 1996
- Management learning: Reynolds & Burgoyne, 1997; Reynolds & Vince, 2004.

- Masculinity: Collinson & Hearn, 1994
- Methodology: Alvesson & Deetz, 2000; Alvesson & Sköldberg, 2000; Johnson & Duberley, 2003; Prasad, 2005
- Participation and empowerment: Cooke & Kothari, 2001; Hales, 2000; Potterfield, 1999
- Political strategy: Jacobs, 1999
- Postcolonialism: Banerjee & Linstead, 2004; Prasad, 2003
- Postmodernism: Calás & Smircich, 1997; Hassard & Parker, 1993; Linstead, 2004; Thompson, 1993
- Power, politics, resistance: Clegg, 1989; Clegg, Courpasson, & Phillips, 2006; Edwards & Wajcman, 2005; Hardy & Clegg, 1996; Jermier, Nord, & Knights, 1994
- Professionals: Armstrong, 1989; Cooper, Puxty, Robson, & Willmott, 1994
- Project management: Hodgson & Cimil, 2006
- Quality management: Wilkinson & Willmott, 1994
- Race: Brief, Dietz, Cohen, Pugh, & Vaslow, 2000; Nkomo, 1992
- Resistance and misbehavior: Ackroyd & Thompson, 1999; Collinson & Ackroyd, 2006; Jermier et al., 1994
- Services: Brewis & Linstead, 2000; Sturdy, Grugulis, & Willmott, 2001
- Skills: Warhurst, Keep, & Grugulis, 2004
- Surveillance: Sewell & Wilkinson, 1992;
- Teamwork: Barker, 1993; Batt & Doellgast, 2006; Ezzamel & Willmott, 1998; Knights & McCabe, 2000; Sewell, 1998; Sinclair, 1992
- Technology in organizations: Adler, 1990; Barley, 1990; Knights & Willmott, 1988; MacKenzie & Wajcman, 1999
- Universities: Parker & Jary, 1995; Prichard et al., 2000
- White-collar work: Smith, Knights, & Willmott, 1991
- Work organization: Felstead & Jewson, 1999; Knights & Willmott, 1986a, 1989; Knights, Willmott, & Collinson, 1985; Thompson & McHugh, 2002; Thompson & Warhurst, 1998
- Work–life balance: Appelbaum et al., 2006

4. Critical studies in contiguous fields
   - Industrial relations: Ackers, Smith, & Smith, 1996; Edwards & Collinson, 2002; Harley, Hyman, & Thompson, 2005; Hyman, 1987, 1989
   - Strategy: Knights & Morgan, 1991; Levy & Egan, 2003; Levy, Willmott & Alvesson, 2003; Smircich & Stubbart, 1985

- Information systems: Hirschheim & Klein, 1989; 1994; Lyytinen, 1992; O'Donnell and Henriksen, 2002
- Marketing: Alvesson, 1994; Brownlie, Saren, Wensley, & Whittington, 1999
- Accounting: Miller & O'Leary, 1987; Tinker, 1985
- Management science: Mingers, 2006

5. Textbooks
  - Boje & Dennehy, 1994
  - Edwards & Wajcman, 2005
  - Fulop & Lindstead, 1999
  - Johnson & Duberley, 2000
  - Knights & Willmott, 1999, 2006
  - Mills, Mills, Forshaw, & Bratton, 2006
  - Mills, Simmons, & Mills, 2005
  - Thompson & McHugh, 2002

References

Abrahamson, E. (1997). The emergence and prevalence of employee management rhetoric: The effects of long waves, labor unions, and turnover, 1875 to 1992. *Academy of Management Journal, 40*(3), 491–533.

Acker, J. (1989). *Doing comparable worth: Gender, class, and pay equity.* Philadelphia: Temple University Press.

Ackers, P., Smith, C., & Smith, P. (Eds.). (1996). *The new workplace and trade unionism.* London: Routledge.

Ackroyd, S. (2004). Less bourgeois than thou? A critical review of studying management critically. *Ephemera, 4*(2), 165–170.

Ackroyd, S., & Thompson, P. (1999). *Organizational misbehaviour.* London: Sage.

Adler, P. S. (1990). Marx, machines, and skill. *Technology and Culture, 31*(4), 780–812.

Adler, P. S. (2001). Market, hierarchy, and trust: The knowledge economy and the future of capitalism. *Organization Science, 12*(2), 214–234.

Adler, P. S. (2002a). Corporate scandals: It's time for reflection in business schools. *Academy of Management Executive, 16*(3), 148–149.

Adler, P. S. (2002b). Critical in the name of whom and what? *Organization, 9,* 387–395.

Adler, P. S. (2004). Skill trends under capitalism and the relations of production. In C. Warhurst, I. Grugulis, & E. Keep (Eds.), *The skills that matter* (pp. 242–260). London: Palgrave.

Adler, P. S. (in press). Labour process theory and critical management studies: A paleo-marxist view. *Organization Studies.*

Adler, P. S., & Borys, B. (1996). Two types of bureaucracy: Enabling and coercive. *Administrative Science Quarterly, 41*(1), 61–89.

Adler, P. S., & Heckscher, C. (2006). Towards collaborative community. In C. Heckscher, & P. S. Adler (Eds.), *The firm as a collaborative community: Reconstructing trust in the knowledge economy* (pp. 11–106). Oxford, U.K.: Oxford University Press.

Adler, P. S., & Jermier, J. M. (2005). Developing a field with more soul: Standpoint theory and public policy research for management scholars. *Academy of Management Journal, 48*(6), 941–944.

Adorno, T. W., Albert, H., Dahrendorf, R., Habermas, J., Pilot, H., & Popper, K. R. (1976). *The positivist dispute in German sociology*. London: Heinemann.

Alvarez, S., Dagino, E., & Escobar, E. (Eds.). (1998). *Cultures of politics, politics of cultures, revisioning of Latin American social movements*. Boulder, CO: Westview.

Alvesson, M. (1987). *Organization theory and technocratic consciousness*. Berlin: de Gruyter.

Alvesson, M. (1994). Critical theory and consumer marketing. *Scandinavian Journal of Management, 10*(3), 291–313.

Alvesson, M. (2002). *Understanding organizational culture*. London: Sage.

Alvesson, M., & Deetz, S. (2000). *Doing critical management research*. London: Sage.

Alvesson, M., & Sköldberg, K. (2000). *Reflexive methodology: New vistas for qualitative research*. London: Sage.

Alvesson, M., & Thompson, P. (2006). Post-bureaucracy? In S. Ackroyd, R. Batt, P. Thompson, & P. S. Tolbert (Eds.), *The Oxford handbook of work and organization* (pp. 485–507). New York: Oxford University Press.

Alvesson, M., & Willmott, H. (Eds.). (1992). *Critical management studies*. London: Sage.

Alvesson, M., & Willmott, H. (Eds.). (2003). *Studying management critically*. London: Sage.

Alvesson, M., & Willmott, H. (1996). *Making sense of management: A critical analysis*. London: Sage.

Anderson, E. (2003). Feminist epistemology and philosophy of science. Retrieved October 23, 2006 from the Stanford University, Encyclopedia of Philosophy Web site: http://plato.stanford.edu/entries/feminism-epistemology

Anthony, P. (1986). *The foundation of management*. London: Tavistsock.

Appelbaum, E., Bailey, T., Berg, P., & Kalleberg, A. (2006). Organizations and the intersection of work and family: A comparative perspective. In S. Ackroyd, R. Batt, P. Thompson, & P. S. Tolbert (Eds.), *The Oxford handbook of work and organization* (pp. 52–73). New York: Oxford University Press.

Archer, M., Bhaskar, R., Collier, A., Lawson, T., & Norrie, A. (1998). *Critical realism; Essential readings*. London: Routledge.

Armstrong, P. (1989). Management, labour process, and agency. *Work, Employment, & Society, 3*, 307–322.

Ashcraft, K. L. (2001). Organized dissonance: Feminist bureaucracy as hybrid form. *Academy of Management Journal, 44*, 1301–1322.

Athanasiou, T. (1996). The age of greenwashing. *Capitalism, Nature, Socialism, 7*, 1–36.

Banerjee, S. B. (2003). Who sustains whose development? Sustainable development and the reinvention of nature. *Organization Studies, 24*, 143–180.

Banerjee, S. B., & Linstead, S. (2004). Masking subversion: Neocolonial embeddedness in anthropological accounts of indigenous management. *Human Relations, 57*(2), 221–247.

Baritz, L. (1974). *The servants of power: A history of the use of social science in American industry.* Westport, CT: Greenwood Publishing.

Barker, J. R. (1993). Tightening the iron cage: Concertive control in self-managing teams. *Administrative Science Quarterly, 38*, 408–437.

Barley, S. R. (1990). The alignment of technology and structure through roles and networks. *Administrative Science Quarterly, 35*, 62–103.

Barley, S. R., & Kunda, G. (1992). Design and devotion: Surges of rational and normative ideologies of control in managerial discourse. *Administrative Science Quarterly, 37*, 363–399.

Batt, R., & Doellgast, V. (2006). Groups, teams, and the division of labor: Interdisciplinary perspectives on the organization of work. In S. Ackroyd, R. Batt, P. Thompson, & P. S. Tolbert (Eds.), *The Oxford handbook of work and organization* (pp. 138–161). New York: Oxford University Press.

Bauman, Z. (1989). *Modernity and the Holocaust.* Cambridge, U.K.: Polity Press

Beck, U. (1996). Work risk society as cosmopolitan society? Ecological questions in a framework of manufactured uncertainties. *Theory, Culture, & Society, 13*, 3–10.

Beck, U. (2002). The terrorist threat: World risk society revisited. *Theory, Culture, & Society, 19*(4), 39–55.

Beder, S. (2002). *Global spin: The corporate assault on environmentalism.* Devon, U.K.: Green Books.

Bell, D. (1973). *The coming of post-industrial society.* New York: Basic Books.

Bellah, R. N., Madsen, R., Sullivan, W. M., Swidler, A., & Tipton, S. M. (1985). *Habits of the heart.* New York: Harper & Row, Publishers.

Belsey, C. (2002). *Poststructuralism: A very short introduction.* Oxford, U.K.: Oxford University Press.

Benavot, A., Cha, Y., Kamens, D., Meyer, J. W., & Wong, S. (1991). Knowledge for the masses: World models and national curricula, 1920-1986. *American Sociological Review, 56*(1), 85–100.

Benhabib, S. (1992). *Situating the self: Gender, community, and postmodernism in contemporary ethics.* New York: Routledge.

Benson, J. K. (1975). The interorganizational network as a political economy. *Administrative Science Quarterly, 20*(2), 229–249.

Bernstein, R. J. (1983). *Beyond objectivism and relativism: Science, hermeneutics, and praxis.* Philadelphia: University of Philadelphia Press.

Bernstein, R. J. (1986). *Philosophical profiles.* Philadelphia: University of Philadelphia Press.

Bhaskar, R. (1978). *A Realist theory of science.* New York: Harvester Press.

Biggart, N. W., & Beamish, T. D. (2003). The economic sociology of conventions: Habit, custom, practice, and routine in market order. *Annual Review of Sociology, 29*, 443–465.

Blumer, H. (1969). *Symbolic interactionism: Perspective and method.* Berkeley: University of California Press.

Boal, K., Hunt, J., & Jaros, S. (2003). Order is free: On the ontological status of organizations. In R. Westwood, & S. Clegg (Eds.), *Debating organization* (pp. 84–98). London: Blackwell.

Boje, D. M., & Dennehy, R. F. (1994). *Managing in a postmodern world*. Dubuque, IA: Kendall/Hunt Publishing Company.

Bolton, S. C., & Boyd, C. (2003). Trolley dolly or skilled emotion manager? Moving on from Hochschild's managed heart. *Work, Employment, & Society, 17,* 289–308.

Boyle, M. V., & Healy, J. (2003). Balancing mysterium and onus: Doing spiritual work within an emotion-laden organizational context. *Organization, 10,* 351–373.

Braverman, H. (1974). *Labor and monopoly capital*. New York: Monthly Review Press.

Brewis, J., & Linstead, S. (2000). *Sex, work and sex work*. London: Routledge.

Brief, A. P. (2000). Still servants of power. *Journal of Management Inquiry, 9*(4), 342–351.

Brief, A. P., Dietz, J., Cohen, R. R., Pugh, S. D., & Vaslow, J. B. (2000). Just doing business: Modern racism and obedience to authority as explanations for employment discrimination. *Organizational Behavior and Human Decision Processes, 81*(1), 72–97.

Brown, L. R. (2000). Challenge of the new century. In L. Starke (Eds.), *State of the world 2000: A Worldwatch Institute report on progress toward a sustainable society* (pp. 3–21). New York: WW Norton.

Brownlie, D., Saren, M., Wensley, R., & Whittington, R. (1999). *Rethinking marketing: Towards critical marketing acccountings*. London: Sage.

Burawoy, M. (1979). *Manufacturing consent: Changes in the labor process under monopoly capitalism*. Chicago: University of Chicago Press.

Burawoy, M. (1986). *Politics of production*. London: Verso.

Burawoy, M. (2003). For a sociological Marxism: The complementary convergence of Antonio Gramsci and Karl Polanyi. *Politics and Society, 31*(2), 193–261.

Burawoy, M. (2004). Public sociologies: Contradictions, dilemmas, and possibilities. *Social Forces, 82*(4), 1603–1618.

Burawoy, M., & Wright, E. O. (2002). Sociological Marxism. In Jonathan T. (Eds.), *The handbook of sociological theory* (pp. 459–486). New York: Plenum Books.

Burrell, G. (1994). Modernism, post modernism, and organizational analysis 4: The contribution of Jürgen Habermas. *Organization Studies, 15*(1), 1–19.

Burrell, G. (1997). *Pandemonium: Toward a retro-organization theory*. London: Sage.

Burrell, G., & Morgan, G. (1979). *Sociological paradigms and organizational analysis*. London: Heinemann.

Butler, J., Laclau, E., & Zizek, S. (2000). *Contingency, hegemony, universality*. London: Verso.

Calás, M. B. (1993). Deconstructing charismatic leadership: Re-reading Weber from the darker side. *Leadership Quarterly, 4,* 305–328.

Calás, M. B. (1994). Minerva's owl?: Introduction to a thematic section on globalization. *Organization, 1,* 243–248.

Calás, M. B., & Smircich, L. (Eds.). (1997). *Postmodern management theory*. Aldershot, U.K.: Ashgate.

Calás, M. B., & Smircich, L. (1991). Voicing seduction to silence leadership. *Organization Studies, 12,* 567–602.

Calás, M. B., & Smircich, L. (1999). Past postmodernism? Reflections and tentative directions. *Academy of Management Review, 24*(4), 649–671.

Calás, M. B., & Smircich, L. (2006). From the woman's point of view ten years later: Towards a feminist organization studies. In S. R. Clegg, C. Hardy, T. B. Lawrence, & W. R. Nord (Eds.), *The Sage handbook of organization studies* (2nd ed., pp. 284–346). London: Sage.

Carroll, W. K., & Carson, C. (2003). The network of global corporations and policy groups: A structure for transnational capitalist class formation? *Global Networks, 3*(1), 29–57.

Casey, C. (2002). *Critical analysis of organizations*. London: Sage.

Castells, E. (2000). *The rise of the network society*. Malden, MA: Routledge.

Castro, C. J. (2004). Sustainable development: Mainstream and critical perspectives. *Organization & Environment, 17*, 195–225.

Chia, R. (1996). *Organizational analysis as deconstructive practice*. Berlin: de Gruyter.

Chia, R. (2000). Discourse analysis as organizational analysis. *Organization, 7*, 513–518.

Child, J. (1972). Organizational structure, environment, and performance: The role of strategic choice. *Sociology, 6*, 1–22.

Clapp, J., & Dauvergne, P. (2005). *Paths to a green world: The political economy of the global environment*. Cambridge, MA: MIT Press.

Clegg, S. (1981). Organization and control. *Administrative Science Quarterly, 26*(4), 545–562.

Clegg, S. R. (1989). *Frameworks of power*. London: Sage.

Clegg, S. R., Courpasson, D., & Phillips, N. (2006). *Power and organizations*. London: Sage.

Clegg, S., & Dunkerley, D. (1980). *Organization, class, and control*. London: Routledge and Kegan Paul.

Clemens, E. S., & Cook, J. M. (1999). Politics and institutionalism: Explaining durability and change. *Annual Review of Sociology, 25*, 441–466.

Cockburn, C. (1991). *Brothers: Male dominance and technological change*. London: Pluto Press.

Coff, R. (1999). When competitive advantage doesn't lead to performance: The resource-based view and stakeholder bargaining power. *Organization Science, 10*(2), 119–133.

Cohen, G. A. (1978). *Karl Marx's theory of history: A defense*. Princeton, NJ: Princeton University Press.

Cole, M. (1996). *Cultural psychology: A once and future discipline*. Cambridge, MA: Belknap/Harvard University Press.

Collins, D. (1995). A socio-political theory of workplace democracy: Class conflict, constituent reactions, and organizational outcomes at a gain sharing facility. *Organization Science, 6*(6), 628–644.

Collinson, D. L., Knights, D., & Collinson, M. (1990). *Managing to discriminate*. New York: Routledge.

Collinson, D., & Ackroyd, S. (2006). Resistance, misbehavior, and dissent. In S. Ackroyd, R. Batt, P. Thompson, & P. S. Tolbert (Eds.), *The Oxford handbook of work and organization* (pp. 305–326). New York: Oxford University Press.

Collinson, D., & Hearn, J. (1994). Naming men as men: Implications for work, organization, and management. *Gender, Work, and Organization, 1*(1), 1–22.

Collinson, D. (1988). Engineering humour: Masculinity, joking, and conflict in shop-floor relations. *Organization Studies, 10,* 181–200.

Contu, A., & Willmott, H. (2003). Re-embedding situatedness: The importance of power relations in learning theory. *Organization Science, 14*(3), 283–29.

Contu, A., & Willmott, H. C. (2005). You spin me around. *Journal of Management Studies, 42,* 1645–1662.

Cooke, B. (2004). The management of the (third) world. *Organization, 11*(5), 603–630.

Cooke, B. (1999). Writing the left out of management theory: The historiography of the management of change. *Organization, 6*(1), 81–105.

Cooke, B., & Kothari, U. (Eds.). (2001). *Participation. The new tyranny?* New York: Zed Books.

Cooper, D. J., Puxty, T., Robson, K., & Willmott, H. C. (1994). The ideology of professional regulation and the markets for accounting labour: Three episodes in the recent history of the U.K. accountancy profession. *Accounting, Organizations, and Society, 19*(6), 527–553.

Cooper, R. (1986). Organization/disorganization. *Social Science Information, 25*(2), 299–335.

Cummings, T. (2006). *Quest for an engaged academy.* Paper presented at the annual meeting of the Academy of Management, Atlanta, GA.

Daft, R. L., & Lewin, A.Y. (1990). Can organization studies begin to break out of the normal science straitjacket? An editorial essay. *Organization Science, 1*(1), 1–9.

Davis, G. F., & Greve, H. R. (1997). Corporate elite networks and governance changes in the 1980s. *American Journal of Sociology, 103,* 1–37.

Davis, G. F., & Mizruchi, M. S. (1999). The money center cannot hold: Commercial banks in the U.S. system of corporate governance. *Administrative Science Quarterly, 44,* 215–239.

Deetz, S. (1992). *Democracy in the age of corporate colonization: Developments in communication and the politics of everyday life.* Albany: State University of New York Press.

Devall, B., & Sessions, G. (1985). *Deep ecology: Living as if nature mattered.* Layton, UT: Gibbs M. Smith, Inc.

Dewey, J. (1999). *Liberalism and social action.* Amherst: Prometheus Books. (Original work published 1935)

Donaldson, L. (1985). *In defense of organization theory: A reply to the critics.* Cambridge, U.K.: Cambridge University Press.

Donaldson, T., & Preston, L. E. (1995). The stakeholder theory of the corporation: Concepts, evidence, and implications. *Academy of Management Review, 20*(1), 65–91.

du Gay, P. (2000). *In praise of bureaucracy: Weber, organization, ethics.* London: Sage.

Dussel, E., & Ibarra-Colado, E. (2006). Globalization, organization, and the ethics of liberation. *Organization, 13*(4), 489–508.

Edwards, P. K. (1986). *Conflict at work: A materialist analysis of workplace relations.* Oxford, U.K.: Blackwell.

Edwards, P. K. (1990). Understanding conflict in the labour process: The logic and autonomy of struggle. In D. Knights, & H. Willmott (Eds.), *Labour process theory* (pp. 125–152). London: Macmillan.

Edwards, P., & Collinson, M. (2002). Empowerment and managerial labor strategies. *Work and Occupations, 29,* 271–290.

Edwards, P., & Wajcman, J. (2005). *The politics of working life.* Oxford, U.K.: Oxford University Press.

Edwards, R. (1979). *Contested terrain.* New York: Basic.

Ehrenreich, B. (2001). *Nickel and dimed: On (not) getting by in America.* New York: Henry Holt.

Elger, T., & Smith, C. (Eds.). (1994). *Global Japanisation: The transnational transformation of the labour process.* London: Routledge.

Engeström, Y. (1987). *Learning by expanding: An activity-theoretical approach to developmental research.* Helsinki, Finland: Orienta-Konsultit.

Evans, K. G. (2000). Reclaiming John Dewey: Democracy, inquiry, pragmatism, and public management. *Administration & Society, 32*(3), 308–328.

Ezzamel, M., & Willmott, H. (1998). Accounting for teamwork: A critical study of group-based systems of organizational control. *Administrative Science Quarterly, 43*(2), 358–396.

Ezzamel, M., Willmott, H., & Worthington, F. (2001). Power, control, and resistance in "The Factory that Time Forgot." *Journal of Management Studies, 38*(8), 1053–1080.

Ezzamel, M., Willmott, H., & Worthington, F. (in press). Manufacturing shareholder value: The role of accounting in organizational transformation. *Accounting, Organizations, and Society.*

Felstead, A., & Jewson, N. (Eds.). (1999). *Global trends in flexible labour.* London: Macmillan.

Ferguson, A. (2004). *Feminist perspectives on class and work.* From the Stanford University, Encyclopedia of Philosophy Web site: http://plato.stanford.edu/entries/feminism-class/ Accessed July 4, 2006.

Ferguson, K. E. (1984). *The feminist case against bureaucracy.* Philadelphia: Temple University Press.

Ferree, M. M., & Martin, P. Y. (1995). *Feminist organizations: Harvest of the new women's movement.* Philadelphia: Temple University Press.

Fidler, J. (1981). *The British business elite: Its attitudes to class, status, and power.* London: Routledge.

Fine, G. A. (1991). On the macrofoundations of microsociology: Constraint and the exterior reality of structure. *The Sociological Quarterly, 32*(2), 161.

Fine, G. A. (1993). The sad demise, mysterious disappearance, and glorious triumph of symbolic interactionism. *Annual Review Of Sociology, 19,* 61–87.

Fineman, S. (Ed.). (2000a). *Emotion in organizations* (2nd ed.). London: Sage.

Fineman, S. (2000b). Enforcing the environment: Regulatory realities. *Business Strategy and the Environment, 9,* 62–72.

Finlayson, J. G. (2005). *Habermas: A very short introduction.* Oxford, U.K.: Oxford University Press.

Fleetwood, S., & Ackroyd, S. (2004). *Critical realist applications in organization and management studies.* London: Routledge.

Fligstein, N. (2001). *The architecture of markets: An economic sociology of the twenty-first century capitalist societies.* Princeton, NJ: Princeton University Press.

Foley, D. K. (1986). *Understanding capital: Marx's economic theory.* Cambridge, MA: Harvard University Press.

Follett, M. P. (2003). *Dynamic administration: The collected papers of Mary Parker Follett.* New York: Routledge. (Original work published 1941)

Fong, A., and Wright, E. (Eds.). (2004). *Deepening democracy.* London: Verso.

Forbes, L. C., & Jermier, J. M. (2002). The institutionalization of voluntary organizational greening and the ideals of environmentalism: Lessons about official culture from symbolic organization theory. In A. Hoffman, & M. Ventresca (Eds.), *Organizations, policy, and the natural environment: Institutional and strategic perspectives* (pp. 194–213). Palo Alto, CA: Stanford University Press.

Forester, J. (1993). *Critical theory. public policy, and planning practice.* Albany, NY: State University of New York Press.

Foster, J. B. (1998). Introduction to bicentennial symposium on Malthus's *Essay on Population. Organization & Environment, 11*(4), 421–433.

Foster, J. B. (2000). *Marx's ecology: Materialism and nature.* New York: Monthly Review Press.

Fournier, V. (2006). Breaking from the weight of the eternal present; teaching organizational difference. *Management Learning, 37*(3), 295–311.

Fournier, V., & Grey, C. (2000). At the critical moment: Conditions and prospects for critical management studies. *Human Relations, 53*(1), 7–32.

Fraser, N. (1989). *Unruly practices: Power, discourse, and gender in contemporary social theory.* Minneapolis, MN: University of Minnesota Press.

Fraser, N., & Naples, N. A. (2004). To interpret the world and to change it: An interview with Nancy Fraser. *Signs: Journal of Women in Culture and Society, 29,* 1103–1124.

French, R., & Grey, C. (Eds.). (1996). *Rethinking management education.* London: Sage.

Froud, J., Johal, S., Leaver, A., & Williams, K. (2006). *Financialization and strategy: Narrative and numbers.* London: Routledge.

Fulop, L., & Linstead, S. (Eds.). (1999). *Management: A critical text.* London: Macmillan.

Gantman, E. R. (2005). *Capitalism, social privilege, and managerial ideologies.* Aldershot, U.K.: Ashgate.

Ghoshal, S. (2005). Bad management theories are destroying good management practices. *Academy of Management Learning and Education, 4*(1), 75–91.

Gill, S., & Law, D. (1993). Global hegemony and the structural power of capital. In S. Gill (Eds.), *Gramsci, historical materialism, and international relations* (pp. 93–124). Cambridge, U.K.: Cambridge University Press.

Gioia, D. A., & Pitre, E. (1990). Multiparadigm perspectives on theory building. *Academy of Management Review, 15*(4), 584–602.

Gramsci, A. (1971). *Selections from the prison notebooks* (Q. Hoare, & G. Nowell-Smith, Trans.). New York: International Publishers.

Greer, J., & Bruno, K. (1996). *Greenwash: The reality behind corporate environmentalism.* New York: Apex Press.

Grey, C. (1994). Career as a project of the self and labour process discipline. *Sociology, 28*(2), 479–497.

Grey, C. (2004). Reinventing business schools: The contribution of critical management education. *Academy of Management Learning and Education, 3*(2),178–186.

Grey, C., & Antonacopoulou, E. (Eds.). (2003). *Essential readings in management learning*. London: Sage.

Grey, C., & Willmott, H. C. (Eds.). (2005). *Critical management studies: A reader.* Oxford, U.K.: Oxford University Press.

Grint, K., & Woolgar, S. (1997). *The machine at work: Technology, work, and organization*. Cambridge, U.K.: Polity Press.

Hacking, I. (Eds.). (1981). *Scientific revolutions*. New York: Oxford University Press.

Hales, C. (2000). Management and empowerment programmes. *Work, Employment, & Society, 14*, 501–519.

Hall, P. A., & Soskice, D. (2001). *Varieties of capitalism: The institutional foundations of comparative advantage*. Cambridge, U.K.: Cambridge University Press.

Harding, S. (Eds.). (2004). *The feminist standpoint reader*. London: Routledge.

Hardy, C., & Clegg, S. R. (1996). Some dare call it power. In S. R. Clegg, C. Hardy, & W. R. Nord, *Handbook of Organization Studies* (pp. 622–641). London: Sage.

Harley, B., Hyman, J., & Thompson, P. (Eds.). (2005). *Participation and democracy at work: Essays in honour of Harvie Ramsay*. London: Palgrave.

Hart, S. L. (1997, January/February). Beyond greening: Strategies for a sustainable world. *Harvard Business Review*, 66–76.

Hassard, J., & Parker, M. (Eds.). (1993). *Postmodernism and organizations*. London: Sage.

Hassard, J., Hogan, J., & Rowlinson, M. (2001). From labor process theory to critical management studies. *Administrative Theory & Practice, 23*(3), 339–362.

Hassard, J., Holliday, R., & Willmott, H. (1998). *Body and organization: Toward the organization without organs*. London: Sage.

Hawken, P. (1993). *The ecology of commerce: A declaration of sustainability*. New York: Harper Business.

Hearn, J. R., Sheppard, D. L., Tancred, P., & Burrell, G. (Eds.). (1989). *The sexuality of organization*. London: Sage.

Hirsch, P. M. (1975). Organizational effectiveness and the institutional environment. *Administrative Science Quarterly, 20*(3), 327–344.

Hirsch, P. M. (1997). Sociology without social structure: Neoinstitutional theory meets brave new world. *American Journal of Sociology, 102*(6), 1702–1723.

Hirschheim, R., & Klein, H. K. (1989). Four paradigms of information systems development. *Communications of the ACM, 32*(10), 1199–1217.

Hirschheim, R., & Klein, H. K. (1994). Realizing emancipatory principles in information systems development: The case for ethics. *MIS Quarterly, 18*(1), 83–109.

Hirschhorn, L. (1984). *Beyond mechanization*. Cambridge, MA: MIT Press.

Hodgson, D., & Cimil, S. (2006). *Making projects critical*. London: Palgrave Mcmillan.

Hodson, R. (2001). *Dignity at work*. New York: Cambridge University Press.

Honneth, A. (1995). *The struggle for recognition: The moral grammar of social conflicts*. London: Polity.

Hook, S. (2002). *Towards the understanding of Karl Marx*. Amherst, NY: Prometheus.

Horkheimer, M., & Adorno, T. W. (1972). *Dialectic of enlightenment* (J. Cumming, Trans.). New York: Continuum.

Hyman, R. (1987). Strategy or structure? Capital, labour, and control. *Work, Employment, and Society, 1*(1), 25–55.

Hyman, R. (1989). *Strikes* (4th ed.). London: Macmillan.

Hymer, S. (1976). *The international operations of national firms.* Cambridge, MA: MIT Press.

Hymer, S. (1979). The international division of labour. In R. B. Cohen, N. Felton, J. van Liere, & M. Nkosi (Eds.), *The multinational corporation: A radical approach.* Cambridge, U.K.: Cambridge University Press.

Iannello, K. P. (1992). *Decisions without hierarchy: Feminist interventions in organization theory and practice.* New York: Routledge.

Ibarra-Colado, E. (2006). Organization studies and epistemic coloniality in Latin America: Thinking otherness from the margins. *Organization, 13*(4), 463–488.

Jackall, R. (1988). *Moral mazes: The world of corporate managers.* Oxford, U.K.: Oxford University Press.

Jacobs, D. C. (1999). *Business lobbies and the power structure in America: Evidence and arguments.* Westport, CT: Quorum Books.

Jacobs, D. C. (2004). A pragmatist approach to integrity in business ethics. *Journal of Management Inquiry, 13*(3), 215–223.

Jacoby, S. (1985). *Employing bureaucracy.* New York: Columbia University Press.

Jacques, R. (1996). *Manufacturing the employee: Management knowledge from the 19th to 21st centuries.* London: Sage.

Jameson, F. (1988). History and class consciousness as an unfinished project. *Rethinking Marxism, 1*(1), 49–72.

Jaros, S. (2001). A local view on transformations within the academic labour process. *Organization, 8,* 358–364.

Jaros, S. (2005). Marxian criticisms of Thompson's (1990) core labour process theory: An evaluation and extension. *Ephemera: Theory and Politics in Organization, 5*(1), 5–25.

Jay, M. (1973). *The dialectical imagination: A history of the Frankfurt School and the Institute of Social Research, 1923-1950.* Berkeley: University of California Press.

Jermier, J. (1985). When the sleeper awakens: A short story extending themes in radical organization theory. *Journal of Management, 11*(2), 67–80.

Jermier, J. (1998). Introduction: Critical perspectives on organizational control. *Administrative Science Quarterly, 43*(2), 235–256.

Jermier, J. M., & Forbes, L. C. (2003). Greening organizations: Critical issues. In M. Alvesson, & H. Willmott (Eds.), *Studying management critically* (pp. 157–176). London: Sage Publications.

Jermier, J. M., Forbes, L. C., Benn, S., & Orsato, R. J. (2006). The new corporate environmentalism and green politics. In S. R. Clegg, C. Hardy, T. B. Lawrence, & W. R. Nord (Eds.), *The Sage handbook of organization studies* (2nd ed., 618–650). London: Sage.

Jermier, J., Nord, W., & Knights, D. (Eds.). (1994). *Resistance and power in the workplace.* London: Routledge.

Johnson, P., & Duberley, J. (2000). *Understanding management research: An introduction to epistemology.* London : Sage.

Johnson, P., & Duberley, J. (2003). Reflexivity in management research. *Journal of Management Studies, 40*, 1279–1303.

Jones, C., Parker, M., & ten Bos, R. (2005). *For business ethics.* London: Routledge.

Julian, S., & Ofori-Dankwa, J. (2006). Is accreditation good for the strategic decision making of traditional business schools? *Academy of Management Learning and Education, 5*, 226–234.

Kanter, R. M. (1972). *Commitment and community: Communes and utopias in sociological perspective.* Boston, MA: Harvard University Press.

Katz, D., & Kahn, R. L. (1966). *The social pscyhology of organizations.* New York: John Wiley.

Kayes, D. C. (2002). Experiential learning and its critics: Preserving the role of experience in management learning and education. *Academy of Management Learning & Education, 1*(2), 137–149.

Kearns, F. (1997). Human population and consumption: What are the ecological limits? *Bulletin of the Ecological Society of America, 78*, 161–163.

Kenney, M., & Florida, R. (1993). *Beyond mass production: The Japanese system and its transfer to the U.S.* New York: Oxford University Press.

Kenworthy-U'Ren, A. (2005). Towards a scholarship of engagement: A dialogue between Andy Van de Ven and Edward Slotkowski. *Academy of Management Learning and Education, 4*(3), 355–362.

Kern, M., & Schumann, M. (1984). *Das Ende der arbeitesteilung? [The end of the division of labor?].* Munich: C.H. Beck.

Kilduff, M., & Mehra, A. (1997). Postmodernism and organizational research. *Academy of Management Review, 22*(2), 453–481.

Knights, D., & McCabe, D. (2000). Bewitched, bothered, and bewildered: The meaning and experience of teamworking for employees in an automobile company. *Human Relations, 53*(11), 1481–1517.

Knights, D., & Morgan, G. (1991). Corporate strategy, organizations, and subjectivity: A critique. *Organization Studies, 12*(2), 251–273.

Knights, D., & Willmott, H. (Eds.). (1986a). *Managing the labour process.* Aldershot, U.K.: Gower.

Knights, D., & Willmott, H. (Eds.). (1986b). *Gender and the labour process.* Aldershot, U.K.: Gower.

Knights, D., & Willmott, H. (Eds.). (1988). *New technology and the labour process.* New York: Macmillan.

Knights, D., & Willmott, H. (1989). Power and subjectivity at work: From degradation to subjugation in social relations. *Sociology Review, 23*(4), 535–558.

Knights, D., & Willmott, H. (Eds.). (1990). *Labour process theory.* New York: Macmillan.

Knights, D., & Willmott, H. (Eds.). (2000). *The re-engineering revolution? Critical studies of corporate change.* London: Sage.

Knights, D., & Willmott, H. (1999). *Management lives: Power and identity in contemporary organizations.* London : Sage.

Knights, D., & Willmott, H. (2006). *Introducing organizational behaviour and management.* London: Thomson Learning.

Knights, D., Noble, F., Vurdubakis, T., & Willmott, H. C. (2001). Chasing shadows: Control, virtuality, and the production of trust. *Organization Studies, 22*(2), 311–336.

Knights, D., Willmott, H., & Collinson, D. (Eds.). (1985). *Job redesign: Critical perspectives on the labour process*. Aldershot, U.K.: Gower.

Kochan, T. A. (2002). Addressing the crisis in confidence in corporations: Root causes, victims, and strategies for reform. *Academy of Management Executive, 16*(3), 139–141.

Kochan, T. A. (2005). *Restoring the American dream: A working families' agenda for America*. Cambridge, MA: MIT Press.

Kolb, A. Y., & Kolb, D. A. (2005). Learning styles and learning spaces: Enhancing experiential learning in higher education. *Academy of Management Learning & Education, 4*(2), 193–212.

Kunda, G. (1992). *Engineering culture: Control and commitment in a high-tech corporation*. Philadelphia: Temple University Press.

Law, J., & Hassard, J. (Eds.). (1999). *Actor network theory and after*. Oxford, U.K.: Blackwell.

Lazonick, W. (2006). Corporate restructuring. In S. Ackroyd, R. Batt, P. Thompson, & P. S. Tolbert (Eds.), *The Oxford handbook of work and organization* (pp. 577–601). New York: Oxford University Press.

Lazonick, W., & O'Sullivan, M. (2000). Maximising shareholder value: A new ideology for corporate governance. *Economy and Society, 29*(1), 13–35.

Levy, D. (1997). Environmental management as political sustainability. *Organization & Environment, 10*(2), 126–147.

Levy, D. L., & Egan, D. (2003). A neo-Gramscian approach to corporate political strategy: Conflict and accommodation in the climate change negotiations. *Journal of Management Studies, 40*(4), 803–830.

Levy, D. L., & Newell, P. J. (2005). *The business of global environmental governance*. Cambridge, MA: MIT Press.

Levy, D. L., Willmott, H., & Alvesson, M. (2003). Critical approaches to strategic management. In M. Alvesson, & H. Willmott (Eds.), *Studying management critically* (2nd ed., pp. 92–110). Newbury Park, CA: Sage.

Linstead, S. A. (Ed.) (2004). *Organization theory and postmodern thought*. London: Sage.

Linstead, S. A., & Hopfl, H. (2000). *The aesthetics of organizations*. London: Sage.

Littler, C. (1982). *The development of the labour processes in capitalist societies*. London: Heinemann.

Littler, C. (1984). Soviet-type societies and the labour process. In K. Thompson (Eds.), *Work, employment, and unemployment* (pp. 87–96). Milton Keynes, U.K.: Open University.

Luhman, J. T. (2006). Theoretical postulations on organization democracy. *Journal of Management Inquiry, 15*(2), 168–185.

Lukacs, G. (1971). *History and class consciousness* (R. Livingstone, Trans.). Cambridge, MA: MIT Press. (Original work published 1923)

Lukes, S. (2005). *Power: A radical view* (2nd ed.). London: Palgrave Macmillan.

Lyon, T. P., & Maxwell, J. W. (2004). *Corporate environmentalism and public policy*. Cambridge, U.K.: Cambridge University Press.

Lyotard, J. (1984). *The postmodern condition: A report on knowledge*. Minneapolis: University of Minnesota Press.

Lyytinen, K. (1992). Information systems and critical theory. In M. Alvesson, and H. Willmott (Eds.), *Critical management studies* (pp. 159–180). London: Sage.

MacKenzie, D., & Wajcman, J. (1999). *The social shaping of technology* (2nd ed.). Buckingham, U.K.: Open University Press.

Mandel, E. (1992). *Power and money: A Marxist theory of bureaucracy.* London: Verso.

Marchington, M., Grimshaw, D., Rubery, J., & Willmott, H. (Eds.). (2005). *Fragmenting work: Blurring organizational boundaries and disordering hierarchies.* Oxford, U.K.: Oxford University Press.

Marens, R. (2004). Wobbling on a one-legged stool: The decline of American pluralism and the academic treatment of corporate social responsibility. *Journal of Academic Ethics, 2,* 63–87.

Margolis, J. D., & Walsh, J. P. (2003). Misery loves companies: Rethinking social initiatives by business. *Administrative Science Quarterly, 48,* 265–305.

Martin, J. (1990). Deconstructing organizational taboos: The suppression of gender conflict in organizations. *Organization Science, 1*(4), 339–359.

Martin, J. (2001). *Organizational culture: Mapping the terrain.* Thousand Oaks, CA: Sage.

Martin, J., Knopoff, K., & Beckman, C. (1998). An alternative to bureaucratic impersonality and emotional labor: Bounded emotionality at The Body Shop. *Administrative Science Quarterly, 43,* 429–469.

Marx, K. (1977). *Capital: Vol. 1.* New York: Vintage.

McCarthy, T. (1981). *The critical theory of Jürgen Habermas.* Cambridge, MA: MIT Press

McKinlay, A. (2006). Knowledge management. In S. Ackroyd, R. Batt, P. Thompson, & P. S. Tolbert (Eds.), *The Oxford handbook of work and organization* (pp. 242–262). New York: Oxford University Press.

McKinlay, A., & Taylor, P. (1998). Through the looking glass: Foucault and the politics of production. In A. McKinlay, & K. Starkey (Eds.), *Foucault, management and organization theory* (pp. 173–191). London: Sage.

Millennium Ecosystem Assessment. (2005). *Ecosystems and human well-being: Current state and trends: Vol. 1.* Washington, DC: Island Press.

Miller, J. (1975). Isolation in organizations: Alienation from authority, control, and expressive relations. *Administrative Science Quarterly, 20*(2), 260–271.

Miller, P., & O'Leary, T. (1987). Accounting and the construction of the governable person. *Accounting, Organizations, and Society, 12*(3), 235–265.

Mills, A. J., Mills, J. C. H., Forshaw, C., & Bratton, J. (2006). *Organizational behaviour in a global context.* Orchard Park, NY: Broadview Press.

Mills, A. J., Simmons, T., & Mills, J.C.H. (2005). *Reading organization theory: A critical approach to the study of organizational behaviour and structure* (3rd ed.). Orchard Park, NY: Broadview Press.

Mills, C. W. (1962). *White collar: The American middle classes.* New York: Oxford University Press.

Mills, C. W. (1956). *The power elite.* New York: Oxford University Press.

Mills, C. W. (1959). *The sociological imagination.* New York: Oxford University Press.

Mingers, J. (2006). *Realizing systems thinking: Knowledge and action in management science.* Berlin: Springer.

Mintzberg, H. (2004). *Managers not MBAs: A hard look at the soft practice of managing and management development.* Harlow, U.K.: Pearson Education.

Mir, R., & Mir, A. (2002). The organizational imagination: From paradigm wars to praxis. *Organizational Research Methods*, 5(1), 104–124.

Mitchell, A., & Sikka, P. N. (2005). *Taming the corporations*. Basildon, U.K.: Association for Accountancy & Business Affairs.

Mizruchi, M. S. (1996). What do interlocks do? An analysis, critique, and assessment of research on interlocking directorates. *Annual Review of Sociology, 22*, 271–298.

Mumby, D. K., & Putnam, L. L. (1992). The politics of emotion: A feminist reading of bounded rationality. *Academy of Management Review, 17*(3), 465–486.

Murphy, J. (2006). Critical challenges in the emerging global managerial order. *Critical Perspectives on International Business, 2*(2), 128–146.

Mutch, A. (2005). Discussion of Willmott: Critical realism, agency, and discourse: Moving the debate forward. *Organization, 12*(5), 781–787.

National Academy of Science. (1994). *Population summit of the world's scientific academies*. Washington, DC: National Academy of Sciences Press.

Neimark, M. K. (1995). The selling of ethics: The ethics of business meets the business of ethics. *Accounting, Auditing, and Accountability Journal, 8*(3), 81–96.

Newton, T., & Harte, G. (1997). Green business: Technicist kitsch? *Journal of Management Studies, 34*, 75–98.

Nkomo, S. (1992). The emperor has no clothes: Rewriting race in organizations. *Academy of Management Review, 17*, 487–513.

Noble, D. (1984). *Forces of production: A social history of industrial automation*. New York: Knopf.

Nord, W. R. (1977). Job satisfaction reconsidered. *American Psychologist, 32*, 1026–1035.

O'Doherty, D., & Willmott, H. (2001). Debating labour process theory: The issue of subjectivity and the relevance of poststructuralism. *Sociology, 35*(2), 457–476.

O'Donnell, D., & Henriksen, L. B. (2002). Philosophical foundations for a critical evaluation of the social impact of ICT. *Journal of Information Technology, 17*(2), 89–99.

Ornstein, M. (1984). Interlocking directorates in Canada: Intercorporate or class alliance? *Administrative Science Quarterly, 29*(2), 210–231.

Palmer, D. A., Jennings, P. D., & Zhou, X. (1993). Late adoption of the multidivisional form by large US corporations: Institutional, political, and economic accounts. *Administrative Science Quarterly, 38*, 100–131.

Palmer, D., & Barber, B. M. (2001). Challengers, elites, and owning families: A social class theory of corporate acquisitions in the 1960s. *Administrative Science Quarterly, 46*(1), 87–120.

Parker, M. (Ed.). (1998). *Ethics and organizations*. London: Sage.

Parker, M. (2002). *Against management*. Oxford, U.K.: Polity.

Parker, M., & Jary, D. (1995). The McUniversity: Organization, management, and academic subjectivity. *Organization, 2*(2), 319–338.

Perrow, C. (1984). *Normal accidents: Living with high-risk technologies*. New York: Basic Books.

Perrow, C. (1986). *Complex organizations*. New York: Random House.

Peters, T. J., & Watermann, R. H. (1982). *In search of excellence: Lessons from America's best-run companies*. New York: Harper & Row.

Pfeffer, J., & Salancik, G. (1978). *The external control of organizations.* New York: Harper and Row.

Phelps, C. (1997). *Young Sidney Hook: Marxist and pragmatist.* Ithaca, NY: Cornell University.

Phillips, N., & Hardy, C. (2002). *Understanding discourse analysis: Investigating processes of social construction.* Thousand Oaks, CA: Sage.

Potterfield, T. A. (1999). *The business of employee empowerment: Democracy and ideology in the workplace.* Westport, CT: Quorum Books.

Prasad, A. (Eds.). (2003). *Postcolonial theory and organizational analysis.* Basingstoke, U.K.: Palgrave Macmillan.

Prasad, P. (2005). *Crafting qualitative research: Working in the postpositivist traditions.* Armonk, NY: M.E. Sharpe.

Prichard, C., Hull, R., Chumer, M., & Willmott, H. (Eds.). (2000). *Managing knowledge: Critical investigations of work and learning.* London: Macmillan.

Proctor, S., & Mueller, F. (Eds.). (2000). *Teamworking.* London: Palgrave.

Pullen, A., & Linstead, S. (2005). Introduction: Organizing identity, interrupting identity. In A. Pullen, & S. Linstead (Eds.), *Organization and identity* (pp. 1–19). London: Routledge.

Quarter, J. (2000). *Beyond the bottom line socially innovative business owners.* Westport, CT: Quorum Books.

Reed, D. (2002). Management education in an age of globalization: The need for critical perspectives. In C. Wankel, & DeFillippi (Eds.), *Rethinking Management Education for the 21st Century* (pp. 209–236). Greenwich, CT: Information Age Publishing.

Reform Club. (n.d.). *Open letter to AAA members from the Reform Club.* Retrieved Oct 23, 2006 from http://pegasus.cc.ucf.edu/~goldwatr/letter.html

Reynolds, P. M., & Vince, R. (2004). *Organizing reflection.* Aldershot, U.K.: Ashgate Publishing.

Reynolds, P. M., & Burgoyne, J. G. (1997). *Management learning: Integrating perspectives in theory and practice.* London: Sage.

Ritzer, G. (2000a). *The McDonaldization of society.* Thousand Oaks, CA: Pine Forge Press.

Ritzer, G. (2000b). *The McDonaldization thesis: Extensions and explorations.* London: Sage.

Ritzer, G., & Goodman, D. J. (2003). *Sociological theory* (6th ed.). New York: McGraw-Hill.

Rothschild, J., & Whitt, J. A. (1986). *The cooperative workplace: Potentials and dilemmas of organizational democracy and participation.* Cambridge, U.K.: Cambridge University Press.

Rowlinson, M., and Hassard, J. (2001). Marxist political economy, revolutionary politics, and labor process theory. *International Studies of Management and Organization, 30*(4), 85–111.

Savage, M., & Witz, A. (Eds.). (1992). *Gendered bureaucracy.* Oxford, U.K.: Blackwell/ The Sociological Review.

Seager, J. (1993). *Earth follies: Coming to feminist terms with the global environmental crisis.* New York: Routledge.

Sewell, G. (1998). The discipline of teams: The control of team-based industrial work through electronic and peer surveillance. *Administrative Science Quarterly, 43*(2), 397–428.

Sewell, G., & Wilkinson, B. (1992). Someone to watch over me: Surveillance, discipline, and the just-in-time labour process. *Sociology, 26*(2), 271–289.

Sharma, S. (2002). Research in corporate sustainability: What really matters? In S. Sharma, & M. Starik (Eds.), *Research in corporate sustainability: The evolving practice of organizations in the natural environment* (pp. 1–29). Cheltenham, UK: Edward Elgar.

Simon, H. (1976). *Administrative behavior* (3rd ed.). New York: Free Press.

Simpson, R. (1998). Presenteeism, power, and organizational change: Long hours as a career barrier and the impact on the working lives of women managers. *British Journal of Management, 9*(s1), 37–50.

Sinclair, A. (1992). The tyranny of a team ideology. *Organization Studies, 3,* 611–626.

Smircich, L. (1983). Concepts of culture and organizational analysis. *Administrative Science Quarterly, 28,* 339–358.

Smircich, L., & Calás, M. B. (1995). Introduction. In L. Smircich, & M. B. Calás (Eds.), *Critical perspectives on organization and management theory* (pp. 13–29). Aldershot, U.K.: Dartmouth.

Smircich, L., & Morgan, G. (1982). Leadership: The management of meaning. *Journal of Applied Behavioral Studies, 18,* 257–273.

Smircich, L., & Stubbart, C. (1985). Strategic management in an enacted world. *Academy of Management Review, 10*(4), 724–736.

Smith, C., Knights, D., & Willmott, H. (Eds.). (1991). *White collar work: The non-manual labour process.* London: Macmillan.

Smith, T. (2000). *Technology and capital in the age of lean production: A Marxian critique of the "New Economy."* Albany: State University of New York Press.

Snider, K. F. (2000). Expertise or experimenting? Pragmatism and American public administration, 1920-1950. *Administration & Society, 32,* 329–354.

Sotirin, P., & Tyrell, M. (1998). Wondering about critical management studies. *Management Communication Quarterly, 12*(2), 303–336.

Starkey, K., & Crane, A. (2003). Toward green narrative: Management and the evolutionary epic. *Academy of Management Review, 28,* 220–237.

Stewart, P. (2002). The problem of the collective worker in the sociology of work in the U.K. *Sociologia del Lavoro, 86*(7), 145–164.

Sturdy, A., Knights, D., & Willmott, H. (Eds.). (1992). *Skill and consent.* New York: Routledge.

Sturdy, C., Grugulis, I., & Willmott, H. (Eds.). (2001). *Customer service: Empowerment and entrapment.* London: Palgrave.

Sturrock, J. (1993). *Structuralism* (2nd ed.). London: Fontana Press.

Summers, D., Boje, D., Dennehy, R., & Rosile, G. (1997). Deconstructing the organizational behavior text. *Journal of Management Education, 21*(3), 343–360.

Taylor, P., Mulvey, G., Hyman, J., & Bain, P. (2002). Work organization, control, and the experience of work in call centres. *Work, Employment, & Society, 16,* 133–150.

The Economist. (2004, May 22). But can you teach it? *8376,* 81.

Thompson, P. (1989). *The nature of work* (2nd ed.). London: Macmillan.

Thompson, P. (1990). Crawling from the wreckage: The labour process and the politics of production. In D. Knights, & H. Willmott (Eds.), *Labour process theory* (pp. 95–124). London: Macmillan.

Thompson, P. (1993). Postmodernism: Fatal distraction. In J. Hassard, & M. Parker (Eds.), *Postmodernism and organizations* (pp. 183–203). London: Sage.

Thompson, P. (2003). Disconnected capitalism: Or why employers can't keep their side of the bargain. *Work, Employment, and Society, 17*(2), 359–378.

Thompson, P. (2005). Brands, boundaries, and bandwagons; A critical reflection on critical management studies. In C. Grey, & H. C. Willmott (Eds.), *Critical management studies: A reader.* Oxford, U.K.: Oxford University Press.

Thompson, P., & Ackroyd, S. (1995). All quiet on the workplace front: A critique of recent trends in British industrial sociology. *Sociology, 29*(4), 615–633.

Thompson, P., & McHugh, D. (2002). *Work organizations* (3rd ed.). London: Palgrave.

Thompson, P., & Newsome, K. (2004). Labour process theory, work, and the employment relation. In B. Kaufman (Eds.), *Theory and the employment relationship* (pp. 133–162). Champagne, IL: Industrial Relations Research Association.

Thompson, P., & Smith, C. (2001). Follow the redbrick road: A reflection on pathways in and out of the labour process debate. *International Studies of Management and Organization, 30*(4), 40–67.

Thompson, P., & Warhurst, C. (Eds.). (1998). *Workplaces of the future.* London: Macmillan.

Tinker, T. (1985). *Paper prophets: A social critique of accounting.* New York: Praeger.

Tinker, T. (2002). Spectres of Marx and Braverman in the twilight of postmodernist labour process research work. *Employment & Society, 16*(2), 251–281.

Tinker, T., Lehman, C., & Neimark, M. (1991). Falling down the hole in the middle of the road: Political quietism in corporate social reporting. *Accounting, Auditing, and Accountability Journal, 4*(2), 28–54.

Tokar, B. (1997). *Earth for sale: Reclaiming ecology in the age of corporate greenwash.* Boston: South End Press.

Tompkins, P. K., & Cheney, G. (1985). Communication and unobtrusive control in contemporary organizations. In R. D. McPhee, & P. K. Tompkins (Eds.), *Organizational communication: Traditional themes and new directions* (pp. 179–210). Beverly Hills, CA: Sage.

Tong, R. (1989). *Feminist thought: A comprehensive introduction.* Boulder, CO: Westview Press.

Townley, B. (1994). *Reframing human resource management.* London: Sage.

Tsoukas, H. (1994). What is management? An outline of a metatheory. *British Journal of Management, 5*, 1–13.

Useem, M. (1982). Classwide rationality in the politics of managers and directors of large corporations in the United States and Great Britain. *Administrative Science Quarterly, 27*(2), 199–226.

Van de Ven, A. H., & Johnson, P. E. (2006). Knowledge for theory and practice. *Academy of Management Review, 31*(4), 802–821.

Van der Pijl, K. (1998). *Transnational classes and international relations.* London: Routledge.

Verstegen, I. (2000). *Bhaskar and American critical realism.* Retrieved Oct 23, 2006 from http://www.raggedclaws.com/criticalrealism/archive/iverstegen_baacr.html

Vygostky, L. S. (1962). *Thought and language.* Cambridge, MA: MIT Press.

Vygotsky, L. S. (1978). *Mind in society*. Cambridge, MA: Harvard University Press.

Wajcman, J. (1991). *Feminism confronts technology*. Cambridge, U.K.: Polity Press.

Wajcman, J. (1998). *Managing like a man: Women and men in corporate management*. University Park: Pennsylvania State University Press.

Wajcman, J. (2004). *Technofeminism*. Cambridge, U.K.: Polity Press.

Walsh, J. P. (2005). Book review essay: Taking stock of stakeholder management. *Academy of Management Review, 30*(2), 426–452.

Walsh, J. P., Weber, K., & Margolis, J. D. (2003). Social issues and management: Our lost cause found. *Journal of Management, 29*(6), 859–881.

Warhurst, C. (1998). Recognizing the possible: The organization and control of a socialist labor process [Special issue]. *Administrative Science Quarterly, 43*(2), 470–497.

Warhurst, C., Keep, E., & Grugulis, I. (Eds.). (2004). *The skills that matter*. London: Palgrave.

Warren, K. J. (Eds.). (1997). *Ecofeminism: Women, culture, nature*. Bloomington: Indiana University Press.

Watson, T. (1994). *In search of management*. London: Routledge.

Welford, R. (1997). *Hijacking environmentalism: Corporate responses to sustainable development*. London: Earthscan Publications.

Westwood, R., & Clegg, S. (Eds.). (2003). *Debating organization*. New York: Blackwell.

Whitley, R., Thomas, A., & Marceau, J. (1981). *Masters of business: The making of a new elite?* London: Tavistock.

Wilkinson, A., & Willmott, H. (Eds.). (1994). *Making quality critical*. London: Routledge.

Willmott, H. (1993a). Strength is ignorance; slavery is freedom: Managing culture in modern organizations. *Journal of Management Studies, 30*(4), 515–552.

Willmott, H. (1993b). Breaking the paradigm mentality. *Organization Studies, 14*(5), 681–720.

Willmott, H. (1996). A metatheory of management: Omniscience or obfuscation? *British Journal of Management, 7*(4), 323–328.

Willmott, H. (1998). Recognizing the other: Reflections on a new sensibility in social and organizational studies. In R. Chia (Ed.), *In the realm of organization: Essays for Robert Cooper* (pp. 213–241). London: Routledge.

Willmott, H. (2003). Organization theory as a critical science? Forms of analysis and 'new organizational forms.' In H. Tsoukas, & C. Knudsen (Eds.), *The Oxford handbook of organization theory* (pp. 88–112). Oxford, U.K.: Oxford University Press.

Willmott, H. (2005). Theorizing contemporary control: Some poststructuralist responses to some critical realist questions. *Organization, 12*(5), 747–780.

Wood, S., & Kelly, J. (1978). Toward a critical management science. *Journal of Management Studies, 15*, 1–24.

Woolgar, S. (1988). Reflexivity is the ethnographer of the text. In S. Woolgar (Ed.), *Knowledge and reflexivity: New frontiers in the sociology of knowledge* (pp. 14–34). London: Sage.

Wright, S. (2002). *Storming the heavens: Class composition and struggle in Italian autonomist Marxism*. London: Pluto Press.

Zald, M. (2002). Spinning disciplines: Critical management studies in the context of the transformation of management education. *Organization, 9*(3), 365–385.

Zimbalist, A. (Eds.). (1979). *Case studies on the labor process.* New York: Monthly Review Press.

Zimmerman, M. E. (1994). *Contesting earth's future: Radical ecology and postmodernity.* Berkeley, CA: Berkeley University Press.

4

The Physical Environment in Organizations

KIMBERLY D. ELSBACH

Graduate School of Management
University of California, Davis

MICHAEL G. PRATT

University of Illinois at Urbana-Champaign

Abstract

We review empirical research on the physical environment in professional, organizational work settings (i.e., offices, meeting rooms, and design work spaces) from the past several decades. This research reveals no common elements of the physical environment (e.g., enclosures and barriers in work spaces, adjustable work arrangements, personalized work spaces, and ambient surroundings) that are consistently and exclusively associated with desired outcomes in these work settings. Instead, these elements are routinely associated with both desired and undesired outcomes. Based on these findings, we suggest that understanding the role of physical environments in organizations requires an understanding of common trade-offs in organizational life. Further, we suggest that the prevalence of such trade-offs is grounded in tensions that are inherent to the functions that physical environments serve (i.e., aesthetic, instrumental, and symbolic functions). We provide an outline of these tensions and trade-offs in relation to common elements of the physical environment, and suggest that researchers consider these tensions and trade-offs in their future research.

Introduction

Physical environments in organizations include all of the material objects and stimuli (e.g., buildings, furnishings, equipment, and ambient conditions such as lighting and air quality) as well as the arrangements of those objects and stimuli (e.g., open-space office plans and flexible team work spaces) that people encounter and interact with in organizational life (Carnevale, 1992; Davis, 1984; Hedge, 1982; Sundstrom, Bell, Busby, & Asmus, 1996). These material objects, stimuli, and arrangements distinguish the physical environment from other types of organizational environments such as the social environment (i.e., the surrounding human social structures and norms) and the purely natural environment (i.e., surroundings that are completely constructed by nature).

Physical environments play a major role in facilitating and constraining organizational action. Everything from the efficient manufacture of computer chips to the research and development of new flavors of potato chips is affected by the design and arrangement of machinery, work spaces, environmental controls, and equipment. Further, because physical environments tend to involve large objects, relatively fixed and long-lasting arrangements, and expensive installations, design decisions need to be made carefully and require a clear understanding of the effects of physical environments on organizations and their members.

In this chapter, we review research, published over the last thirty years, examining the effects of physical environments in professional work settings such as offices, meeting rooms, and design areas—the most commonly studied work settings in organizational literature. Our review includes research from both general organizational journals (i.e., *Academy of Management Journal, Administrative Science Quarterly, Journal of Organizational Behavior,* and *Organization Science)* and specialty journals that focus on the managerial implications of physical environments in organizations (i.e., *Environment and Behavior* and *Journal of Environmental Psychology).*[*]

In general, our review suggests that choosing objects and their arrangements in professional, organizational work settings is one of the most difficult tasks a manager faces. It is not difficult because there are few choices and configurations available to managers. In fact, just the opposite is true. There is a dizzying array of choices in the area of office design alone (see Elsbach & Bechky, 2007 for a review). The difficulty arises because these choices always come with both benefits and costs. As a result, managers must balance a large number of complex trade-offs when making decisions about the nature of physical environments in their organizations.

---

[*] We should note that we exclude from our review research on purely physiological effects of physical environments, such as the effects of temperature and lighting on heart rate and cognitive fatigue. We also exclude studies of the physical environment in manufacturing or production settings, such as factory floors, and in purely outdoor settings, such as road construction and farming. These effects and settings are primarily studied by engineering, design, and ergonomic scholars and tend to focus on construction and materials issues, as well as physiological issues.

By focusing on trade-offs, we differ from other reviews that have attempted to organize this rather large body of literature by examining underlying psychological "mechanisms" that may explain how individuals react to the physical environment (e.g., Baron, 1994; Oldham, Cummings, & Zhou, 1995; Sundstrom & Sundstrom, 1986). Our decision to stray from this organizing scheme was based on three rationales. First, because of their large number, a focus on mechanisms may not be parsimonious and may even call for an additional organizing scheme (e.g., a hierarchy of mechanisms). As we argue later, needs for control, the complexity of jobs, and the invocation of stereotypes are just some of the psychological mechanisms that have been linked to individuals' reactions to the physical environment. Second, past attempts to identify overriding mechanisms (e.g., "social interference") have only found mixed support (e.g., Oldham et al., 1995). Third, a mechanism perspective often begins with trying to understand characteristics of people (e.g., our human needs), with the physical environment serving merely as a context for understanding those needs. By contrast, we believe it may be advantageous to reverse this figure-ground relationship and begin with the characteristics of the physical environment itself. Thus, we employ an organizing scheme that was originally designed for explaining elements of the physical environment itself, rather than our reactions to it.

In the following sections, we discuss some of the most commonly studied elements of the physical environment in organizational settings and examine the apparent trade-offs in implementing these elements. We then describe how tensions inherent in these physical elements may explain this prevalence of trade-offs and may provide guidance for how to manage these trade-offs. We close with some guidelines for future research.

Trade-Offs in Managing the Physical Work Environment

In 1965, advice about the design of physical environments in organizations was limited to calls for office tidiness. One handbook admonished

Avoid overdecorating your desk area. When your desk, shelves, and wall space are covered with mementoes, photographs, trophies, humorous mottoes, and other decorative effects, you are probably not beautifying the office; rather you may be giving it a jumbled, untidy look. You may also be violating regulations against using nails in the walls, and so on. The proper atmosphere for a business office is one of neatness and efficiency, not hominess. (Parker Publishing Editorial Staff, 1965, p. 17)

As it turns out, this is not always good advice. On the one hand, an empty and moderately tidy office (characterized by "organized stacks" of paper work) has been shown to have strong positive effects on attributions of the occupant's friendliness, organization, and welcomeness (Morrow & McElroy, 1981). If the occupant is present, a tidy (vs. messy) office has also been shown to lead to higher ratings of sincerity, intelligence, ambition, and calmness (Sitton, 1984). In addition, a moderately tidy office has been shown to lead to higher ratings of visitor comfort in the office (Morrow & McElroy, 1981). Finally, there is evidence that a neat office is important to prospective employees who are considering joining a corporation, leading to a more positive impression of the organization and a stronger likelihood of accepting a job offer (American Society of Interior Designers, 2000).

On the other hand, research has also shown that an empty and messy (vs. empty and tidy) office leads to more positive attributions of the occupant's activity, kindness, and sociability (Sitton, 1984), as well as busyness (Morrow & McElroy, 1981). Further, if a messy (vs. tidy) office is observed when the occupant is present, observers will make more positive attributions of sociability (Sitton, 1984). Clearly, there are trade-offs to having a messy or neat office.

In a similar manner, most of the research on the elements of physical environments in organizational work settings suggests a complicated picture in which most common objects and arrangements have both positive and negative implications, making it at times necessary for managers to make trade-offs when choosing or designing physical work environments. In the following sections, we review research that illustrates and reveals these trade-offs. We organize this discussion according to the elements of physical environment that, based on our review, appear to be most commonly studied (also see Baron, 1994). These common design elements include the following: (1) enclosures and barriers in work spaces; (2) adjustable work arrangements, equipment, and furnishings; (3) personalization of work spaces, including the display of well-known symbols; and (4) nature-like ambient surroundings, including natural light, presence of plants, wood interiors, views of nature, and natural aromas. These elements and their trade-offs are discussed below and summarized in Table 4.1.

1. Enclosures and Barriers in Work Spaces

No issue in the design of physical environments in professional, organizational work settings has received more attention than the management of enclosures and barriers (i.e., partitions, walls, doors, cubicles, open spaces, and hallways that buffer workers from each other and from ambient disturbances). A number of ongoing debates about the virtues of opposing workplace designs have contributed to this attention (Elsbach, 2003). For instance, the debate between proponents of open-plan office designs (few barriers and enclosures, with work spaces separated by 5-foot high, moveable partitions) versus traditional office designs (more barriers and enclosures, with offices separated by floor-to-ceiling walls and doors) has persisted for over 30 years (Brookes & Kaplan, 1972; Hedge, 1982; Maher & von Hippel, 2005; Oldham & Brass,

Table 4.1 Trade-Offs in the Design of Physical Environments in Organizations

Dimension of Physical Environment	Generally Desired Effects	Generally Undesired Effects
High Degree of Enclosure and Barriers	Increases satisfaction for managers and professionals (Brennan, Chugh, & Kline, 2002; Carlopio & Gardner, 1992; Hedge, 1982)	Reduces satisfaction for clerical workers (Carlopio & Gardner, 1992; Zalesny & Farace, 1987)
	Increases performance and satisfaction on simple tasks (Oldham et al., 1991)	Reduces performance and satisfaction on complex tasks (Oldham et al., 1991)
	Improves perceived status of managers (Carlopio & Gardner, 1992)	Reduces task identity among clerical, professional, and managerial workers compared to open plan (Zalesny & Farace, 1987)
	Reduces fatigue and psychosomatic complaints if job accompanied by high numbers of interruptions and low screening ability of occupant (Fried, 1990)	Open plan improves speed of mission proposal design among engineers at Jet Propulsion Lab (Mark, 2002)
	Low degree of noise, distraction, and crowding leads to high perceived architectural privacy and sense of control over environment (Becker et al., 1983; Crouch & Nimran, 1989; Oldham, 1988; Oldham & Brass, 1979; Sundstrom et al., 1980; Sundstrom et al., 1994)	Use of desk as barrier between occupant and visitor signals unwelcomeness to visitor (Morrow & McElroy, 1981)
	More enclosed sides and few neighbors improve job performance of administrative and clerical employees (Sundstrom et al., 1980)	If barriers block visual intrusion, but not noise intrusion, they are detrimental to workers with poor stimulus screening abilities (Maher & von Hippel, 2005)
	Employees prefer privacy on complex and routine tasks (Sundstrom et al., 1980)	

Table 4.1 Trade-Offs in the Design of Physical Environments in Organizations (Continued)

Dimension of Physical Environment	Generally Desired Effects	Generally Undesired Effects
High Degree of Enclosure and Barriers (continued)	More privacy does not reduce social interaction compared to open plan (Sundstrom et al., 1980) Increases task feedback and trust in management (Zalesny & Farace, 1987)	
Adjustable Work Arrangements	Control over work station settings and design of work arrangements more important to job satisfaction than adequacy of physical features, actual arrangement of features, or symbolic effects of features (Carnevale & Rios, 1995) Ability to adjust and arrange work space associated with greater job satisfaction and performance (Lee & Brand, 2005) Adjustability of work space furniture, storage, and materials associated with greater environmental satisfaction and self-reported performance. Adjustable partitions associated with greater perceived privacy and better communication (O'Neill, 1994)	Adjustable workstation lighting led to worse performance on creative task than no control over lighting (Veitch & Gifford, 1996) Control over temperature led to lower job satisfaction (Paciuk, 1990) Customizable furniture and barriers are rarely adjusted by work space occupants (Hedge, 1982)
Ability to Personalize Work Space	Personalization increases ability to affirm distinctive identities and personalities (Donald, 1994; Elsbach, 2003; Wells, 2000).	Personalization of office with hobby mementoes and conversation pieces can lead to negative attributions of occupant (e.g., low status, unprofessional) (Elsbach, 2004)

Companies that allow for greater personalization have more positive social climates and moral and lower turnover (Wells, 2000)

Capacity for work space personalization and ability to control access to work space associated with high status (Veitch & Gifford, 1996)

Status markers improve job satisfaction and work space satisfaction for supervisors more than for nonsupervisors (Konar et al., 1982)

Personalization is a means to mark and defend territories (Brown, 1987)

Personalization helps to improve employee well-being (i.e., general happiness, stress and anxiety levels, and physical health) by improving job satisfaction and work environment satisfaction (Wells, 2000)

Personalization increases attachment and commitment to a place or organization (Vinsel, 1980)

Personalization increases pleasantness of surroundings for workers (Wells, 2000)

Messy offices signal busyness (Morrow & McElroy, 1981)

Messy offices signal less welcomeness, organization, and friendliness. Moderately tidy offices (organized stacks) led to most positive attributions (Morrow & McElroy, 1981)

Presence of identity-affirming artifacts may affect role perceptions and lead to behavior consistent with those roles—even if inappropriate (Rafaeli & Pratt, 1993; Weick, 1996)

Authority symbols lead to stereotyped perceptions of organization, including low degree of autonomy for workers (Ornstein, 1986; 1992)

Newer courthouse façade that looked like schema of "prison" perceived as more intimidating and more likely to lead to a conviction than courthouse façade that did not match this schema (Maas et al., 2000)

Personalization of offices accurately signals traits of openness (through high level of decoration, quantity of magazines, quantity and variety of books and CDs), conscientiousness (through cleanliness, organization, and uncluttered space), and extroversion (through highly decorated, cheerful, colorful, cluttered, and unconventional decor; Gosling et al., 2002).

Table 4.1 Trade-Offs in the Design of Physical Environments in Organizations (Continued)

Dimension of Physical Environment	Generally Desired Effects	Generally Undesired Effects
Ability to Personalize Work Space (continued)	Large, salient artifacts such as desks and high barriers are most likely to lead to status categorizations of office occupant (Elsbach, 2004)	
	Presence of status symbols (credentials and diplomas) lead to attributions of achievement orientation (Morrow & MeElroy, 1981)	
	Authority symbols (U.S. flag, restrictive sign) led to low ratings of autonomy in organization in both bank and movie industry reception area (Ornstein, 1986; 1992)	
	Empathic symbols (plants, artwork) led to higher ratings of consideration in both bank and movie industry reception area (Ornstein, 1986; 1992)	
	Reward symbols (certificates, diplomas) led to higher ratings of rewards in the organization in both bank and movie industry reception area (Ornstein, 1986; 1992)	
	Dress signals professional identities and status in organizations (Rafaeli & Pratt, 1993; Rafaeli et al., 1997)	
	Project prototypes or artifacts may be displayed and serve as boundary objects, that allow workers to communicate across functional boundaries, while affirming distinctive functional identities and legitimacy (Bechky, 2003a; Carlile, 2002)	

Personalization of offices does not accurately signal traits of agreeableness and emotional stability (Gosling et al., 2002).

Nature-Like Surroundings

Working on clerical tasks or negotiations in room with natural (vs. neutral) aroma led to higher perceptions of self-efficacy (Baron, 1991)

Working on clerical task or negotiation in room with natural aroma (vs. neutral aroma) led to higher output goals, more efficient work strategy, and preference for less confrontational modes of conflict resolution, and more concessions in negotiations (Barron, 1990).

Working in room with natural lighting and plants leads to high ratings of environmental pleasantness and satisfaction (Stone & English, 1998) and higher test scores in classroom (Wollin & Montagne, 1981)

Views of nature through windows improves satisfaction and reduces stress (Finnegan & Solomon)

Views of nature through windows reduce need to compensate by displaying visual items with nature-like images in one's office (Heerwagen & Orian, 1986)

Work areas with large numbers of plants led to low productivity on a low complexity, repetitive task, while areas with no plants led to high productivity in same task (Larsen et al., 1998)

Posters of nature scenes in work area increased perceived task demand, hostility, and depression for workers working on a high-task demand task (Stone & English, 1998)

Use of natural green color on public transit buses was seen by some observers as symbolizing identification with terrorist group, military, and garbage trucks; also made the buses hard to see at night and hot during the day (Rafaeli & Vilnai-Yavetz, 2004b)

Table 4.1 Trade-Offs in the Design of Physical Environments in Organizations (Continued)

Dimension of Physical Environment	Generally Desired Effects	Generally Undesired Effects
Nature-Like Surroundings (continued)	Office decorated with natural wood flooring and furnishings leads to more positive overall impressions of occupant (Ridoutt et al., 2002), and more natural building exterior leads to evaluative responses of "calmness" by observers (Nasar, 1994) Use of natural materials and view of the natural environment (vs. use of more manufactured, composite materials) leads to greater creative performance in an interior work space (Mitchell-McCoy & Evans, 2002) Natural green color of bus seen by some observers as pleasant and calming (Rafaeli & Vilnai-Yavetz, 2004b)	

1979). This debate was recently highlighted in an article about the simultaneous hatred for and persistence of the office cubicle:

> Reviled by workers, demonized by designers, disowned by its very creator, [the cubicle] still claims the largest share of office furniture sales—$3 billion or so a year—and has outlived every 'office of the future' meant to replace it. It is the Fidel Castro of office furniture. (Schlosser, 2006, p. 21)

One reason that barriers and enclosures appear to be such a hot topic is their visual salience and easy comparison among workers (e.g., workers may easily identify inequities in the degree of privacy they are afforded in comparison to their coworkers). Such salience makes barriers and enclosures a common signal of status and rank. Further, barriers and enclosures may demand attention because their inadequacy in buffering employees from noise and distractions has been shown to be a strong inhibitor (vs. facilitator) of work performance (Crouch & Nimran, 1989). Such negative effects tend to garner more attention than do positive effects (Fiske & Taylor, 1991). It is perhaps not surprising then, that issues related to enclosures and barriers were the top environmental concern of office workers, designers, and top executives in a large-scale survey of Canadian employees (Kelly, 1992).

In the following sections, we discuss research indicating both the generally desired and generally undesired effects of using more (vs. less) barriers and enclosures in professional work settings.

Generally desired effects of barriers and enclosures. One of the primary arguments in favor of more barriers and enclosures is that barriers and enclosures reduce unwanted intrusions and overstimulation from the environment, allowing workers to concentrate on their jobs and reducing their feelings of dissatisfaction with the work environment (Cohen, 1980; Oldham, 1988). According to proponents of this "overstimulation" theory, in work spaces that lack adequate barriers and enclosures

> the combination of excessive social interaction and small amounts of personal space . . . exposes employees to overstimulation (Desor, 1972; Paulus, 1980) . . . [and] generally evokes a negative response from individuals, both behaviorally and attitudinally, and in the workplace this likely results in employee dissatisfaction and withdrawal (Oldham, 1988; Paulus, 1980). (Maher & von Hippel, 2005, p. 220)

By contrast, adequate barriers and enclosures can be used to stop both unwanted background stimuli (e.g., noise and light), as well as interruptions from others. Further, these salutary effects of adequate barriers and enclosures on job satisfaction may be more useful to managers and professional workers than to clerical workers (Carlopio & Gardner, 1992; Hedge, 1982;

Maher & von Hippel, 2005). For managers, having control (we discuss control as an important element of the physical environment in and of itself later) over one's barriers (e.g., being able to close one's door) allows them the opportunity to "shut out" both background stimuli and noises that interfere with "heads down" or "thinking" work that they are commonly called upon to complete (O'Neill, 1994). In addition, for managers, a closed door on a private office is an effective means of discouraging others from interrupting its occupant because it signals that "thinking" work is being done. Yet, for secretarial or clerical workers, a private office may not strongly dissuade other workers from interrupting or disturbing the office occupant because these other workers assume that the clerical worker is not doing important "thinking" work and does not need privacy. In support of this argument, researchers have found that clerical workers perceive an enclosed office as less private than do managerial workers because such an office does not, in practice, afford great privacy to these clerical workers (Sundstrom, Town, Brown, Forman, & McGee, 1982).

A second benefit of barriers and enclosures is that they may help signal appropriate status levels, especially in organizations that desire such stratification of the workforce. In turn, they may improve satisfaction among high - ranking managers who value status as a component of their workplace identity (Elsbach, 2003; Sundstrom, Burt, & Kamp, 1980). In support of this reasoning, researchers have found that occupying a private, enclosed office with floor-to-ceiling walls and a door is one of the most widely recognized physical markers of status within modern corporations (Campbell, Dunnette, Lawler, & Weick, 1970). Further, researchers have found that removing barriers, through the use of an open-plan office design that provides approximately equal amounts of privacy to all levels of workers, reduces satisfaction with the work space among higher status workers (e.g., managers) while it increases satisfaction among lower status workers (e.g., clerical workers; Carlopio & Gardner, 1992; Zalesny & Farace, 1987).

A third argument in favor of barriers and enclosures is that they allow for more confidentiality in work, including the ability to have confidential conversations with other employees (Carlopio & Gardner, 1992). Thus, several studies of managerial workers have shown that a primary dissatisfaction with open office plans is the inability to hold confidential conversations, such as performance evaluations, without being overheard (Oldham & Brass, 1979; Sundstrom, Herbert, & Brown, 1982). Further, in a university setting, researchers found that students actually noticed a reduction in useful and honest feedback when speaking with faculty who occupied nonprivate versus private offices (Becker, Gield, Gaylin, & Sayer, 1983). In related research, researchers found that open-plan offices that used 5-foot partitions to separate work spaces were effective at reducing visual distractions and interruptions, but not noise distractions and interruptions (Kupritz, 1998). The fact that one can easily hear conversations through moveable partitions supports the notion that such partitions are not effective barriers for preventing others from overhearing confidential conversations.

A final benefit of barriers in the work space is that they may motivate workers to have more frequent and satisfying conversations and interactions (especially informal and unscheduled interactions) because these workers perceive that their discussions will not disturb coworkers. In this manner, Hatch (1987) found that technical workers actually increased their level of informal interaction and communication in a high-tech firm when they worked in areas that had higher (vs. lower) partitions between work spaces. Hatch proposed that this effect may have been due to the privacy that barriers allowed. Similarly, in their study of university students, Becker et al. (1983) found that students felt more comfortable dropping in, unexpectedly, on faculty members who occupied private (vs. open) offices. The researchers suggested that this effect may have been due to students' reduced worries about disrupting nearby faculty during nonscheduled meeting hours. Together, these findings support the paradoxical notion that barriers actually increase informal interaction. As Becker et al. (1983) put it, "[Informal] interaction is facilitated not by unlimited opportunities for interpersonal contact, but by the opportunity for privacy. The ability to control interaction appears to be the critical variable mediating the negative effects of reduced privacy and crowding" (p. 723).

Generally undesired effects of barriers and enclosures.   Despite the above findings, opponents of barriers and enclosures in the work environment argue that these elements prevent some specific forms of informal communication, specifically the communication of visual information (Boje, 1971; Pile, 1978). For example, researchers have found that many clerical staff dislike enclosures and barriers because they prevent visual scanning of the work environment that allows them to know who is available to answer questions or provide information (Carlopio & Gardner, 1992; Zalesny & Farace, 1987). Similarly, researchers have shown that barriers may inhibit visual information about the source of intrusive noise (Maher & von Hipple, 2005) . Further, these researchers suggest that if workers can anticipate noise, see where it is coming from, or anticipate when it will end, then the disruption is less bothersome than if they can hear the noise but cannot see its source (Maher & von Hippel, 2005, p. 226).

A second downside of barriers and enclosures is that they may inhibit collaboration in environments that require fast-paced problem solving and decision making. For instance, Mark (2002) discussed how engineers in a mission proposal design team (referred to as "Team X") were able to move their work fluidly around a "war room" at the Jet Propulsion Laboratory. This ability to fluidly change the work arrangement enabled them to follow problems in real time and simultaneously work on several issues, focusing attention on a given issue as it became most relevant. In this manner, Mark described how the barrierless war room lent itself to a constantly changing arrangement of workers:

> As soon as expertise is needed to solve a problem, team members seek out the source of the problem, possibly approaching colleagues already working on its solution, a customer with a question, or even a public display indicating an error. Others may join in the solution effort or stay at their desks calling out quick answers. Team X members routinely move between individual subsystem work, group work, and the orchestrated combined work of the entire team. . . . Activity among team members is always related to physical location, *and each one's activity is visible to everyone else in the room* [italics added]. Thus, the physical arrangement of the entire group provides indication to everyone else as to the state of the human network, which in turn conveys information about a particular mission proposal's overall design status. (pp. 91–92)

Other researchers have suggested that barriers may reduce performance on simple tasks that benefit from social facilitation effects (i.e., increased stimulation from ambient intrusions; Geen & Gagne, 1977). Evidence from more recent research on barriers and job performance suggests,however, that such facilitation may also occur on complex tasks and that ambient intrusions may actually hamper some simple tasks. Thus, researchers have found that workers in more complex jobs actually show improved performance when barriers are reduced, while those in simple jobs show decreased performance in more open work environments (Oldham, Kulik, & Stepina, 1991). It may be that the particular job processes are more important than the task type in determining the benefits versus costs of barriers in the work environment. This argument fits with research that suggests that the degree to which interruptions and distractions negatively affect job performance (regardless of task type) predicts the degree to which workers prefer private work spaces (Becker et al., 1983; Crouch & Nimran, 1989; Fried, 1990; Lee & Brand, 2005; Sundstrom, Town, Rice, Osborn, & Brill, 1994). Thus, if the job process involves a lot of focused, "heads down" thinking, whether it is a simple task (e.g., simple copy editing) or a complex task (e.g., complex research coding), a more enclosed and private work space may be beneficial. By contrast, jobs requiring less cognitive focus but more stimulation -- such as a simple sorting tasks or a complex brainstorming sessions -- may benefit from less privacy and enclosure.

A fourth downside to barriers and enclosures in the corporate work environment is that they may reduce workers' perceptions of task significance and task identity, which have been shown to be important predictors of job satisfaction (Oldham & Rotchford, 1983; Zalesny & Farace, 1987). For instance, in a study of task significance among female, clerical workers, Oldham and Rotchford (1983) found that a more open work environment produced greater perceptions of task significance (i.e., perceptions that jobs were meaningful and important to the organization). The researchers suggest that the more open environment allowed the clerical workers to compare their roles with others in the organization and helped them to become aware of their importance in the organization (which was greater than they would have thought if they had not been able to compare to others in the organization). By contrast, in a similar study of clerical workers, Oldham and Brass (1979) found that workers perceived a reduction in task significance in an open office plan. They suggest that, in this case, greater exposure to other workers allowed the clerical workers to see how their jobs were *less* important than they would have thought if they had not been able to compare to others. Thus, barriers and enclosures may inhibit a positive sense of task significance in those cases in which this significance is not readily apparent to workers.

In terms of task identity, it appears that the same mechanisms may be at work. Zalesny and Farace (1987) found, for example, that perceptions of task identity for clerical, professional, and managerial workers all increased after a move from a traditional to an open-plan office. In the open-plan office, it appears that all of these workers were able to see how they were doing a complete job versus only part of a job. Again, this may have been the case because, in the open-plan office, workers were able to compare what they did to others and could see how their jobs and outputs constituted complete tasks within the organization.

A final downside to barriers is that they may signal and reinforce undesired status and power differences between workers, especially in organizations that wish to improve collaboration and feedback across job levels and ranks. Thus, as noted earlier, the strong symbolic effects of barriers and private offices (i.e., more privacy and barriers around a person's work space are perceived to indicate that the person has higher status and more power in the organization) may be undesirable in an organization that is seeking to reduce status barriers to collaboration (Vilnai-Yavetz, Rafaeli, & Yaacov, 2005). Researchers have found that these symbolic effects are very potent, especially when they are confirmed by an office occupant's high organizational rank (Sundstrom, Town, et al., 1982).

2. Adjustable Work Arrangements, Equipment, and Furnishings

As organizations have moved toward nontraditional work arrangements that call for employees to work in many different locations or require them to reserve work spaces one day at a time (e.g., nonterritiorial or hoteling arrangements), the adjustability or customizability of one's work environment has become an essential component of work space design (Zelinsky, 2002). Much of the research on adjustable work arrangements focuses on the benefits and costs of perceiving control over one's work environment, regardless of the type of adjustments that are available (Huang, Robertson, & Chang, 2004;

Karasek, 1979, Karasek & & Theorell, 1990). We discuss these effects in the following sections.

Generally desired effects of adjustable work arrangements. Research from environmental psychology suggests that giving employees the opportunity to control task-relevant dimensions of their work environment—including control of ambient conditions (i.e., lighting, temperature, noise, air quality) as well as the ability to adjust equipment, tools, and furnishings to meet individual needs (e.g., adjustable-height chairs, adjustable tools, and customizable office arrangements)—is associated with improved job satisfaction and job performance (Carnevale & Rios, 1995; Lee & Brand, 2005). Researchers suggest several reasons for these benefits.

First, researchers have shown that the ability to adjust or adapt work space arrangements and storage areas improves job satisfaction and performance because it allows workers to adjust privacy, comfort, and ease of access to work materials in ways that fit their *specific work needs* (Lee & Brand, 2005; O'Neill, 1994). Further, training that enhances workers' ability to effectively make these adjustments (e.g., training that helps them to adjust their work station equipment and furniture) has been shown to be critical to achieving greater work satisfaction in customizable work settings (Huang et al., 2004).

Second, the positive effects of adjustability and adaptability of work arrangements may result from an innate *need for control* that all humans possess (Baumeister, 1998). By providing employees with the opportunity and ability to adjust and control their physical work environment, organizations may be helping workers to satisfy this need. As Baumeister (1998) noted,

> Broadly speaking, control and esteem are probably the two most important motivations of the self. People almost universally react badly to any major loss of either esteem or control, and they generally seem to desire and enjoy opportunities to gain either esteem or control. Both are strongly linked to happiness (Campbell, 1981; Campbell, Converse, & Rogers, 1976), and people will often augment their substantive esteem and control with inflated, exaggerated self-perceptions. (p. 713)

This argument also suggests that the perception of control (or what is often called the "illusion of control" [Langer, 1975]) may be just as important as actual control in improving employees' job and environmental satisfaction. Although not studied in relation to adjustable work arrangements, the notion that perceived control increases satisfaction has been supported by numerous studies in other contexts, including decision making (Brown, 1995), risk taking and gambling (Horswill & McKenna, 1999), and coping with threat (Taylor, 1983).

Generally undesired effects of adjustable work arrangements. While the positive effects of adjustable work arrangements appear to be commonly found, there is growing evidence that control over the work environment may have downsides. The first downside is that, while the *perception* that one has control over one's environment may be beneficial in many cases, the actual *exercise* of control can be detrimental, at least in specific instances.

For example, researchers have found that while having the opportunity to control ambient conditions (e.g., temperature, lighting) is associated with higher job satisfaction for workers, actually altering ambient conditions can be associated with poorer job satisfaction and job performance in particular cases (Paciuk, 1990; Veitch & Gifford, 1996). In one case, Veitch and Gifford (1996) found that in an experimental study of lighting and performance on creative tasks, subjects who were given choice over their lighting conditions perceived that they had more control over their environment than subjects who were not given choice over lighting conditions, but performed more poorly and more slowly on a creativity task than "no-choice" subjects. Veitch and Gifford suggested that the subjects in the "choice" condition may have felt additional pressure to perform because they were given choice over their ambient conditions. In turn, the authors suggest that this added pressure may have led to poorer performance on the creativity task.

In another case, Paciuk (1990) found that while perceptions of control over thermal dimensions of the work environment increased job satisfaction, the actual use of these thermal controls reduced satisfaction. Paciuk suggested that this effect may have resulted from poor use of temperature controls (e.g., adjusting the temperature so that it is too high or too low for comfort and effective work) and that it highlights the need for training that actually allows employees to exercise control over their work environments in an effective manner. This finding underscores our general lack of understanding about when and where to give employees control over their physical work environments. As Veitch and Gifford (1996) put it, "We do not know which features of the physical environment are the ones for which control is desired, nor can we reliably predict which experiences of the physical environment will lead to the development of such control" (p. 274).

A second downside of providing adjustable work arrangements, equipment, and furnishings to workers is that these adjustable features are often not used, and equipment and furnishings are left in their original configurations. Thus, in his study of 649 employees of an office building that had recently been converted from a traditional plan to a more open office plan, Hedge (1982) found that while furnishings and arrangements in the open plan could have been adjusted to meet specific user needs, this just was not done. As he reported,

Although the open-plan office provides extremely flexible accommodations, this study found little evidence that it was being used in this way at either the personal or the organizational level. Rather, once layout plans had been prepared, the office remained relatively static for several years. (p. 539)

The problem with this scenario is that the original configuration of the office may not have been well suited for the worker or task to which it was assigned. Yet, the presumption that the work space occupant would adjust it prevented management from checking to see if work space arrangements and equipment configurations were well suited for that occupant. Thus, a nonadjustable work arrangement may have led to a better fit for occupants of the open plan because, at least, these arrangements could have been set up correctly from the beginning.

3. Personalization of Work Areas and Display of Well-known Symbols

Personalization of work areas includes the display and arrangement of artifacts and objects according to personal choices and desires. It is important to note that when we use the term *personalization* we are not so much referring to the ability to personalize (i.e., whether or not one's corporate policies allow personalization at all) as we are to the quantity and quality of personalization (i.e., how much one chooses to display, what types of things are displayed, and how they are arranged).

As was indicated earlier in our discussion of messy desks, the notion of personalization of work areas is an issue that has been long discussed in management literature. Perhaps this is because personalization is so common among workers. In fact, research suggests that over 70% of employees personalize their work spaces (Brill, Marguilis, & Konar, 1984). We discuss the benefits and costs of such displays in the following section.

Generally desired effects of personalization and symbol display. A commonly found benefit of personalization of work environments is that such displays help employees to affirm their workplace and professional identities (Elsbach, 2003, 2004; Gosling, Ko, Mannarelli, & Morris, 2002). In fact, some researchers have defined personalization as "the deliberate decoration or modification of an environment by its occupants to reflect their *identities* [italics added] (Sommer, 1974; Sundstrom 1986)," (Wells & Thelen, 2002, p. 302). Further, expression of identity has been found to be the top-cited reason for personalization in studies of office workers (Wells, 2000). As Dittmar (1992) put it,

[Material] possessions can symbolize an individual's unique personal qualities, values, and attributes, and they can be a symbolic record of personal history and relationships (self-expressive symbols). But material possessions also locate people in social-material terms: They signify the social groups we belong to, social position, and relative wealth and status (categorical symbols). Personal attributes and social locations are integral aspects of identity, as seen by both self and others. Thus, material possessions are important means of constructing, maintaining, and expressing both personal and social identity. (p. 380)

Such personalization and the display of symbols and artifacts reinforce identity by either affirming *status* (e.g., relative rank, such as "top-management") or affirming *distinctiveness* (e.g., relative uniqueness, such as "engineer"; Brewer, 1991; Dittmar, 1992; Frank, 1985; Pratt & Rafaeli, 2001).

First, just as barriers and enclosures can be important indicators of employee status, so too can office personalization indicate and affirm the status of its displayer. Common personal artifacts that are used to indicate status include awards and diplomas, high-quality furnishings, business cards denoting rank and prestige, and expensive-looking artwork (Elsbach, 2004; Pratt & Rafaeli, 2001).

The critical link between personalization and status is especially salient when employees cannot personalize their workplace. In these conditions, individuals may engage in behaviors (sometimes illegitimate) designed to compensate for these lost status markers (Elsbach, 2003; Steele, 1973). For example, when organizations attempt to remove status markers (e.g., by assigning everyone the same type of work space, regardless of rank), employees have been shown to improvise means of determining status vis-à-vis physical markers (e.g., by supporting unspoken rules about the number of personal artifacts allowed to different levels of management; see Zenardelli, 1967). These effects have been shown to be especially strong for managers, who typically have been found to personalize with art, furniture, and photos that enhance their status rather than with artifacts that merely display personal interests (Goodrich, 1986; Konar, Sundstrom, Brady, Mandel, & Rice, 1982).

In a similar manner, personalization can help employees to affirm distinctiveness (i.e., show that they belong to a distinct social group or possess distinctive interests, knowledge, or abilities; Belk, 1988). Humans have been shown to possess a strong *need for uniqueness* (Snyder & Fromkin, 1980) or *need for differentiation* (Brewer, Manzi, & Shaw, 1993) that motivates them to affirm their distinctiveness in social situations. As a result, it is not surprising that individuals would want to affirm distinctive identities and traits at work. At least in some cases, such affirmations have been shown to be effectively cued through personalization of offices. For instance, Gosling et al. (2002) showed that office workers could effectively and accurately signal the traits of conscientiousness (through a clean, organized, and uncluttered office), openness (through an office with lots of decoration, books, and magazines), and extroversion (through an office with lots of clutter, color, and unconventional decor).

In turn, losing the ability to personalize one's work surroundings may be highly threatening to individuals. For example, Goffman (1961) described how institutions that confiscate personal possessions upon arrival (e.g., hospitals, military training camps, prisons, boarding schools, and monasteries) systematically limit the personal distinctiveness of individuals and may cause a traumatic dampening of a distinctive sense of self.

These needs for distinctiveness may sometimes be powerful enough to overshadow needs for status, especially in highly depersonalized settings. For example, in a study of high-tech workers, Elsbach (2003) found that employees who moved to a nonterritorial work arrangement—in which employees did not "own" permanent work areas, but instead reserved a different work area on a day to day basis—perceived more threat to their distinctiveness than to their status. As Elsbach noted, in the non-territorial environment,

> participants routinely reported that they were not able to display permanent physical identity markers that indicated the valued and distinctive attributes, skills, and roles they possessed and that they felt a loss of identity as a result. The most common instances of personal distinctiveness threats resulted from the absence of personal artifacts (e.g., photos, mementoes, equipment) that participants used to signal distinctiveness categorizations central to their workplace identities (e.g., parent, artist, athlete). Although these distinctiveness categorizations were relevant to participants' workplace identities, they typically involved nonjob roles, such as being a parent, that were not easily affirmed through other work-related markers like behavior or titles. As a result, personal distinctiveness categorizations were likely to be affirmed exclusively through the display of personal physical artifacts. (p. 635)

In addition to its effects on identity, personalization has also been shown to improve mood and reduce stress (Scheiberg, 1990; Wells, 2000). In one study, the most commonly reported reason for personalizing work space was the positive emotional response that workers experienced from working in a personalized environment (Scheiberg, 1990). Many others reported that their personalized surroundings helped them to relax and cope with stress. In turn, companies that allow great freedom in the personalization of individual work spaces have reported lower turnover and higher morale than companies that highly restrict such personalization (Wells, 2000). By contrast, in companies that limit or discourage personalization of work space, employees have called the work environment "sterile, impersonal, and cold" (Goodrich, 1986, p. 130).

Symbol display, more generally, can also affect cross-functional coordination via the use of *boundary objects* (Bechky, 2003a; Carlile, 2002). Star (1988) defined boundary objects as objects that, figuratively and sometimes literally, "sit in the middle" (p.47) of two or more functional areas and help to establish a shared context for workers in those functional areas. For example, Bechky (2003a) described how engineers and assemblers in a semiconductor equipment manufacturing organization used design drawings (of machines) and machine prototypes as boundary objects for problem solving during the development and testing phases of a new product launch. Bechky found that the machines were more effective than the drawings as boundary objects because they were concrete and allowed engineers to "see" the problems that assemblers were having with machine prototypes, even though they did not understand the assemblers' descriptions of these problems. By contrast, Bechky found that design drawings were too abstract and unfamiliar to assemblers to serve as a useful boundary object for problem solving.

Finally, researchers have found that personalization and symbol display may increase employees' organizational attachment and commitment (Goodrich, 1986; Hess, 1993). In a study of personalization among college dorm residents, Vinsel, Brown, Altman, and Foss (1980) found that college students who stayed in school beyond their freshman year displayed more items reflecting their commitment to their present university environment, while students who dropped out of college after their freshman year displayed more items reflecting their commitment to their previous home environment. In a similar way, employees who personalize their work environment in ways that reflect affiliation with that organization (i.e., display of mementoes with company logos, company newsletters, and project-related artifacts from work in the company) may also be likely to report higher commitment to the organization than employees who do not engage in such personalization (Pratt & Rafaeli, 2001). In these cases, the visible display of company artifacts may cause employees to feel psychological pressure to behave consistently (e.g., express organizational attachment) with their public commitments of company affiliation (Cialdini, 1993; Rafaeli & Pratt, 1993).

Generally undesired effects of personalization and symbol display. Despite the numerous benefits of workplace personalization and symbol display described, there is evidence that such displays may also have downsides. In particular, there is evidence that workplace personalization and symbol display may lead to inaccurate (Gosling et. al., 2002) and, sometimes, negative perceptions of displayers (Elsbach, 2004). Psychological and organizational research on *impression management* (Schlenker, 1980) and *first impressions* (King & Pate, 2002) has examined the role of physical markers such as décor and material wealth on initial and lasting impressions of individuals who display such markers. This research suggests that first impressions of individuals are strongly influenced by easily observable attributes that are seen early on in an encounter (Christopher & Schlenker, 2000; Greenberg, 1988; Laumann & House, 1969; Rafaeli & Pratt, 1993).

At the same time, psychological research on cognitive biases has shown that observers are prone to a number of inaccuracies in their attributions of workers who display personal artifacts. In particular, research on the actor/observer effect (Jones & Nisbett, 1972), stereotyping based on physical markers (Waibel & Wicklund, 1994), and categorizations based on "dominant representations" (Dittmar, 1992) suggest that observers may primarily attend to large and visual salient physical artifacts (e.g., prominently displayed photos, large and imposing furniture) and view those artifacts in stereotypical ways (e.g., personal artifacts are displayed as symbols of status vs. symbols of distinctive interests) and as intentional signals of a displayer's symbolic identity (vs. merely artifacts that happen to be in one's office for instrumental purposes, such as relevance to a current work project).

Because of these biases, observers may stereotype displayers of work space personalization based on a quick glimpse or brief encounter with their work setting, and in ways not intended by the displayer. For example, in a study of office workers, Elsbach (2005) found that observers were more likely than displayers to focus their attention on artifacts that were salient due to large size, novelty, or contrast (e.g., hobby artifacts, fun artifacts, awards, and provocative artifacts). Further, observers were more likely than displayers to interpret physical markers as indicators of identity in general, and of status (vs. distinctiveness) in specific.

There is also the potential for symbol display to lead to stereotyping at the organizational level. Research on the interpretation of common symbolic displays in reception areas of corporations has shown that observers interpret some types of symbols in very predictable (and often, stereotypical) ways. For instance, Ornstein (1986, 1992) found that observers interpreted authority symbols that were displayed in reception areas (e.g., U.S. flags, pictures of organizational leaders, displays of organizational logos, formally dressed receptionists, and restrictive signs) as signals that the organization provided low autonomy to workers and was characterized by a high degree of structure. By contrast, Ornstein found that observers interpreted empathic symbols in reception areas (e.g., plants, artwork, magazines, family photos, and informally dressed receptionists) as signals that the organization allowed employees greater autonomy and had a climate of higher consideration. Interestingly, these effects occurred both in a reception area of a bank and a reception area of a movie industry corporation, suggesting that these symbols were so strongly aligned with specific attributions that context did not make a difference in their interpretation.

In a similar study, Maas et al. (2000) found that while observers of photos of two courthouse facades found both to be equally pleasing aesthetically, these observers found the courthouse with a more modern and industrial look (vs. an older, more European look) to be more intimidating and to elicit greater predictions that a given suspect would receive a conviction. Observers' comments revealed that, although the modern courthouse was aesthetically pleasing, it also more closely fit observers' schemas or stereotypes of what a prison looks like. As a result, this symbolic exterior led to perceptions of the modern courthouse that were more negative.

4. Nature-Like Ambient Surroundings

Ambient work surroundings include the temperature, lighting, air quality, aroma, textures, visual stimuli, and sounds workers experience merely by their presence in the work area. Our review of research on ambient dimensions of the work setting suggests that surroundings that mimic nature—that is, what we call "nature-like" ambient surroundings (e.g., natural sunlight, natural materials such as wood in décor, the presence of plants in the work area, nature-like colors, and art depicting scenes of nature)—generally result in positive emotional and cognitive responses from those experiencing them. This finding echoes research showing that among "favorite" places identified by residents of several different countries, natural environments (e.g., woods, beaches, mountains, lakes) are mentioned by the majority (Newell, 1997). Both natural settings and nature-like built environments may be preferred by workers because they are cognitively and emotionally restorative and "freeing" (Newell, 1997). Thus, numerous studies have found that people report restorative effects of natural environments compared to unnatural built environments (Hartig, Mang, & Evans, 1991).

Yet, because of the wide variation in individual preferences and sensitivities, surroundings that are experienced as pleasant to some workers are likely to be experienced as unpleasant to others. Further, even those surroundings that are experienced as pleasant to most workers may have unintended and negative side effects because they also effect the ability of people to perform their work (Wollin & Montagne, 1981). We discuss these trade-offs of nature-like ambient surroundings in the following section.

Generally desired effects of nature-like ambient surroundings. A growing amount of research suggests that nature-like ambient stimuli are associated with job satisfaction and, in turn, improved job performance (Spreckelmeyer, 1993). For example, research on aroma in work surroundings has shown that a natural scent (e.g., a mild aroma of cotton flower) improves self-efficacy perceptions, goal setting, use of efficient work strategies, and less confrontational negotiation styles. Researchers have also shown that in classroom situations, more natural lighting and plants led to higher test scores, higher teacher ratings, and more positive ratings of the classroom than a more traditional, sterile classroom (Campbell, 1979; Wollin & Montagne, 1981). Further, several studies have shown that windows that allow views of natural settings (e.g., trees, water, lawns) are highly desired by office workers. In turn, office workers who do not have such views are less satisfied and more stressed than other workers (Finnegan & Solomon, 1981) and are likely to hang more visual materials that are nature-oriented on their walls to compensate for the lack of natural views (Heerwagen & Orians, 1986). Finally, researchers have recently found that the use of natural materials in interior design (vs. use of manufactured composite materials) led to higher ratings of creative potential for a work space and higher actual creative performance in that work space (Mitchell-McCoy & Evans, 2002).

Researchers suggest that these positive effects may be due to the effects of nature-like work surroundings on positive sensory experiences of workers, which, in turn, lead to positive mood states and arousal levels (Baron, 1994). That is, nature-like ambient surroundings lead to more positive moods (Hartig, Böök, Garvill, Olsson, & Gärling, 1996) and to higher levels of cognitive arousal (Hartig et al., 1991), both of which may improve job performance (especially on creative tasks) and job satisfaction.

Another positive effect of nature-like ambient surroundings is the positive impression that these surroundings give to observers. For example, in a study of interpersonal perception of office occupants, Ridoutt, Ball, and Killerby (2002) found that the presence of wood furniture and flooring in an office led to a more positive overall impression of the office occupant (on the dimensions of professionalism, success, honesty, caring, and creativity) compared to an occupant of an office decorated with nonnatural materials. Similarly, other studies have found that the presence of plants and wood finishes in offices are associated with perceived status of the office occupant (see Sundstrom & Sundstrom, 1986 for a review). While these effects are partly attributed to the association between quality of furnishings and status (i.e., because wood is considered a high quality, expensive furnishing, it is associated with high status), these effects may also be due to the aesthetic responses associated with natural decor. In particular, researchers have shown that built environments that are high in order and naturalness lead observers to experience a sense of "calmness" (Nasar, 1994). Such a response may indicate to observers that they are in the presence of a positive and successful other.

Generally undesired effects of nature-like surroundings. Yet, nature-like ambient surroundings may not be desirable in all settings and with all users. For instance, a naturally lit office that leads to relaxation for some workers may impose stress for others (Boubekri, Hull, & Boyer, 1991). Similarly, a rustic decor that suggests nature and openness to some may suggest an imposing masculinity to others. A vivid example of this type of effect comes from Rafaeli and Vilnai-Yavetz's (2004b) study of Israel's public transportation buses and the decision to paint them a dark green color in 1999. While some observers found the green color aesthetically pleasing and associated it with positive emotions (e.g., "I like this green color. It creates calmness. It is pleasant" [p. 680]), others found it to be just the opposite (e.g., "This color is repulsive, disgusting" and "[The color] creates fear and anxiety").

While these differences could have reflected purely personal preferences, it is likely that the symbolic meaning of the color had something to do with observers' reactions. On one hand, the green color was widely associated with nature and the natural environment. On the other hand, the green color of the bus was also commonly associated with a terrorist organization that had a long history of attacks in Israel and was also similar to the color of military fatigues and local garbage trucks. Because of these symbolic connotations, many observers' emotional reactions to the buses were fueled both by their perception of the color itself and by symbolic meaning of the color in the context of their daily lives.

A second downside of nature-like physical environments is that they may have negative effects on performance. Again, in the case of the green bus, Rafaeli and Vilnai-Yavetz (2004b) found that some drivers disliked the color because it was too dark and because it too easily blended into its surroundings, making it easier for traffic and pedestrian accidents to occur, especially at night. In addition, other drivers and riders reported that the dark green color made the bus very hot inside due to the increase in heat absorption.

Nature-like work environments may also negatively affect performance by providing a salient contrast to unpleasant task characteristics. For example, in a laboratory study involving a computer task in a small office, Stone and English (1998) found that the display of posters depicting a nature scene led to improvements in perceptions of the workplace pleasantness, but increased perceived task demand on a high-demand task and increased hostility and depression levels among participants. Stone and English argue that the nature scene made workers more acutely aware of how stressful their task was in comparison to their feelings when in nature.

A final downside of nature-like ambient surroundings is that they may induce positive moods that, in addition to creating more job satisfaction, also lead employees to have more overconfidence in their gut instincts and greater motivation to maintain their good mood by not engaging in unpleasant aspects of work (Bless et al., 1990; Isen, 1993). As a result, researchers have found that in repetitive or uninteresting tasks that require employees to follow a strict protocol (e.g., equipment testing, copy editing, some routine maintenance tasks), moderately negative (vs. positive) moods actually improve performance because they motivate employees to do a good job as a means of alleviating their negative moods, and they do not cause employees to have overconfidence in their own abilities or gut instincts (Elsbach & Barr, 1999). In support of this notion, in a laboratory clerical task, Larsen, Adams, Deal, Kweon, and Tyler (1998) found that while the laboratory "office" was rated as most attractive when it contained a large number of potted plants, participants' productivity scores on a letter identification or sorting task were lowest in this office.

Tensions Inherent in the Physical Work Environment

The mixed findings reported in the preceding sections become more understandable—and we argue, even expected—when we examine the complex nature of the objects and arrangements that comprise the physical environment in organizational settings. Specifically, we suggest that the very nature of this physical environment is fraught with different, and sometimes opposing, qualities. When these qualities come into opposition—a condition we refer to as *tensions*— they can force those attempting to alter or manage the physical environment to make difficult choices.

As we will argue, some of these tensions can be ameliorated, at least in part, through deliberate efforts to cope with various differences (e.g., functional differences) inherent in the physical environment. Building on research that concerns the management of tensions (Maybury-Lewis, 1989; Poole & Van de Ven, 1989; Pratt & Foreman, 2000), we argue that tensions in the physical environment can be handled in one of three basic ways: (1) *deletion* or *sacrifice* where one tension is satisfied but the other is not—as in the case of a classic trade-off; (2) *integration* where both tensions are addressed simultaneously (i.e., via alignment of tensions); and (3) *compartmentalization* or *segregation* where the tensions are managed by treating them separately. Segregation can take at least two forms: *spatial* (i.e., allowing different parts of the organization to focus on ameliorating different tensions) and *temporal* (i.e., meeting opposing needs at different points in time).

All of the tensions we describe are based on opposing effects between or within the *functions* that physical environments serve in organizational life. Using the framework of Rafaeli and Vilnai-Yavetz (2004a,b)*, we define these tensions as occurring between or within the instrumental (i.e., performance relevant), symbolic (i.e., meaning relevant), and aesthetic (i.e., sensory relevant) functions of physical objects and arrangements. Overall, it is our assertion that these inherent tensions in the environment can explain why researchers find so few consistently positive effects of workplace designs. We illustrate these various tensions in Figure 4.1 and discuss them below. As noted in Figure 4.1, these distinctions are important for determining whether the tensions can be successfully managed—that is, whether both "sides" of the tensions can be satisfied (i.e., through integration or segregation) or whether tensions must involve "true" trade-offs where hard choices must be made about what must go unsatisfied (i.e., sacrifices).

Interfunctional Tensions

One major set of tensions inherent in the physical environment occurs *between* the functions (i.e., instrumental, symbolic, and aesthetic) of the objects or

---

* We should point out two differences between our discussion of these elements and how they were originally used by Rafaeli and Vilnai-Yavetz (2004a,b). First, Rafaeli and Vilnai-Yavetz's focus was solely on physical artifacts. We widen this focus to include other aspects of the physical environment, such as the arrangement of those artifacts. Second, they refer to these various aspects of physical artifacts as "dimensions." However, our inclusion of arrangements of artifacts adds an intentional element to our discussion; thus, we prefer to call these aspects "functions" as they reflect various purposes or meanings of the physical environment—that is, to make production easier (instrumentality), to evoke sensory and aesthetic experiences (aesthetics), and to represent other concepts or images (symbolism).

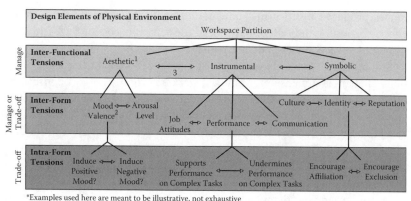

*Examples used here are meant to be illustrative, not exhaustive

---

Figure 4.1   Basic Functions[1], Forms of Functions[2] and Tensions[3] Embedded in Physical Environment— Examples Used Here Are Meant to Be Illustrative, Not Exhaustive.

artifacts in that environment. For example, the symbolic and instrumental functions of an office partition may be at odds if the partition denotes desired symbolic status to a manager, but prevents the instrumental function of private conversations required by a manager. Since any given artifact, stimulus, or arrangement in the physical environment can simultaneously serve each of these functions, it is perhaps not surprising that these functions can potentially be at odds with each other in organizations. Thus, one of the lessons of the "green bus" case previously described (Rafaeli & Vilnai-Yavetz, 2004a) is that the instrumental function of "visibility" (e.g., the ability of the buses to be seen), the aesthetic function of "color" (e.g., whether it was perceived as ugly or not), and the symbolic function of "identity" (e.g., the association of the color with specific groups or causes) of an object can undermine each other.

Increasingly, researchers are simultaneously examining the multiple functions that elements of the physical environments play. For example, Cappetta and Gioia (2006) noted the tension between *aesthetics and instrumentality* in the fashion industry (e.g., a beautiful store can be horrible to work in just as a beautiful shoe can be painful to walk in). Others have noted that the aesthetic benefits of some elements of the physical environment—such as the improved mood and job satisfaction resulting from nature-like artwork or plants in the office—may be offset by negative instrumental effects due to the contrasts workers perceive between pleasant surroundings and a menial and tedious task (see Larsen et al., 1998; Stone & English, 1998).

In other research, Pratt and Rafaeli (1997) show how the *symbolic and instrumental* aspects of professional dress (a less-studied dimension of physical environment in organizations) may also be at odds. In their study, the use of scrubs (i.e., the standard-issue garb of health professionals) by rehabilitation nurses produced positive instrumental effects by allowing nurses to more effectively deal with bodily fluids but at the symbolic cost of increasing the distance between nurses and their patients.

Still other researchers have examined how the *symbolic and aesthetic* functions of a single dimension of physical work environment may oppose each other. As noted earlier, in their study of courthouse facades, Maas et al. (2000) found that while a modern-looking courthouse was judged as "attractive," it also fit observers' schema of a prison and, thus, was viewed as more intimidating than a similarly attractive courthouse that did not fit the prison schema.

Finally, there may be times when two functions are aligned, but a third is not. Elsbach and Bechky (2007) note such interfunctional tensions in Oticon, a Danish hearing aid manufacturer. Oticon used potted and portable birch trees as a means of creating flexible boundaries in an open office design. While *symbolically and aesthetically* effective (i.e., they effectively created boundaries and created a pleasant environment), the trees failed in terms of *instrumentality* as they were unable to effectively block noise in the office.

As noted in Figure 4.1, we believe that these types of interfunctional tensions are manageable. That is, it is *possible* to align or simultaneously satisfy (i.e., integrate) the instrumental, aesthetic, and symbolic functions of objects, stimuli, and arrangements in the physical environment. For example, Elsbach and Bechky (2007) illustrated how the Lincoln and Mercury brand's flexible "team room" at the Ford Motor Company was able to align each of these functions. In this case, the adjustable design of the room facilitated collaboration (instrumental), could be used to demarcate boundaries for different groups (symbolic), and allowed team members to adjust conditions to create a positive and pleasant sensory experience (aesthetic).

Yet, there may be some factors that make the resolution of interfunctional tensions difficult. For example, organizations may lack the resources (monetary or creative) to align these functions. Lacking these resources, organizations may end up managing interfunctional tensions by segregation. For example, different functions may become fulfilled differently in different parts of the organization (i.e., spatial segregation). Thus, one's entrance lobby may largely be used to facilitate aesthetic functions, while one's work space may tend more toward the instrumental (Elsbach & Bechky, 2007). When resource constraints are extreme, however, these tensions may have to be managed via sacrifice—deleting the expression of one function for another.

Interform Tensions

Within each of the major functions, there are a variety of forms that the physical environment can take. For example, aesthetic functions may include a variety of sensory experiences such as general mood and arousal, as well as auditory, olfactory, tactile, and visual stimulation. Instrumental functions include effects on productivity, communication patterns, and job attitudes such as job satisfaction. Finally, there are also several functional divisions within the symbolic realm including the expression of culture, identity, authority, brand image and reputation, and legitimacy (Pratt & Rafaeli, 2006).

These different forms often come into conflict in terms of their effects on organizations and their members. For example, as noted earlier, Veitch and Gifford (1996) illustrated an interform tension within the function of instrumentality: Giving people choice over their lighting may increase control over the work environment (one form of instrumental function) at the expense of productivity on creative tasks (another form of instrumental function). Similarly, our early illustration of the "messy desk" reveals an interform tension within the function of symbolism. Having a tidy desk may allow one to look more intelligent, but at the cost of appearing unsociable (Sitton, 1984). Finally, in their laboratory study of clerical work, Stone and English (1998) suggested an interform tension within the function of aestheticism. Specifically, they found that adding posters to the work environment created pleasant work surroundings but led to increased hostility and depression when workers were asked to do a high-demand task in those surroundings (because the contrasts between work and surroundings become more salient).

Like interfunctional tensions, some of these interform tensions may be successfully managed via integration, especially when contextual factors are considered in the design of physical environments (Ahrentzen, 1990; Carnevale & Rios, 1995; Lee & Brand, 2005). Thus, Mark's (2002) depiction of the flexible arrangement of a team space revealed that it contributed to both successful communication and job performance in the context of high-paced problem solving. Similarly, research on boundary objects shows how the tension between the symbolic forms of identity and legitimacy may be managed. For example, Bechky (2003a) showed how machine prototypes used by assemblers and engineers in a semiconductor manufacturing equipment company allowed these two groups to both affirm distinct group identities (i.e., the engineers designed the machines but did not understand their functioning in practice, while the assemblers understood their functioning but did not understand their design) and provided legitimacy to each group when they were required to interact (working on the machine showcased why it was important to have both groups working on the same project).

By contrast, other interform conflicts may be less manageable. A good example is our discussion of messy versus tidy offices earlier. As noted, researchers have found that both messy and tidy offices lead to positive attributions of inhabitants (Sitton, 1984). On the one hand, if the occupant is present, a tidy office leads to higher ratings of sincerity, intelligence, ambition, warmth, and calmness. On the other hand, if the occupant is not present, a messy office leads to more positive attributions of the occupant's activity, kindness, warmth, and sociability. Clearly, one cannot be both present in and absent from one's office. Therefore, office occupants must decide whether they want to receive attributions of activity, kindness, and sociability (in which case they should leave their offices messy and hope observers see them empty) or if they want to receive attributions of sincerity, intelligence, and ambition (in which case they should keep their offices tidy and hope observers see them occupied).

Fortunately, even some of these apparent trade-offs may be manageable to a degree. For example, apparent trade-offs in the use of one artifact (e.g., one's desk) may be offset by looking across patterns of artifacts (e.g., group pictures on a neat desk), rather than just one (Pratt & Rafaeli, 2001). Similarly, instrumental interform tensions, such as between control and productivity, may be ameliorated somewhat with additional training (e.g., training on how to adjust lighting for different tasks). More generally, we believe that these more difficult interform tensions can often be managed via temporal or spatial segregation. For example, returning to the messy desk example, a person might intentionally vary the tidiness of his or her office depending on who is likely to see it. Thus, when prospective job candidates are visiting, you might keep your desk clean; however, you may leave it messier when meeting with a protégé and trying to establish a friendly connection. As with interfunctional tensions, resource constraints may push the resolution of these tensions toward making sacrifices. As noted in Figure 4.1, however, as we move toward intraform tensions, it becomes increasingly difficult to skirt the trade-offs imposed by the physical environment.

Intraform Tensions

A final set of tensions in the physical environment occurs within a specific form itself. Here a form of a function may have two or more different manifestations that may conflict with each other. As illustrated in Table 4.1, our review found that intraform tensions were most likely to manifest within the symbolic function.* For example, physical markers can be used to denote "territories" of organizational groups (see Brown, Lawrence, & Robinson, 2005 for review) that hold various social identities (Pratt & Rafaeli, 1997, 2001). These social identities (which are forms of the "symbolic" function of physical environments), however, may manifest in both the encouragement of *affiliation* with in-group members and *exclusion* from out-group members. To illustrate, organizational groups may differentiate from one another by designing

---

* In some instances, attempts to manipulate the aesthetic environment may lead to an intraform tension. For example, assuming different preferences among employees, any given piece of artwork will likely induce *both* positive and negative moods as some will like it and some will dislike it. Similarly, specifically tailoring a work setting to encourage performance for one functional group may also simultaneously be dysfunctional and discourage performance for another group. Unlike social identity, however, that both affiliates and excludes in *all conditions*, our review suggests that the intraform tensions in instrumentality and aesthetics were more situation dependent. Because they may not be "pure" examples of intraform tensions, we have added question marks after these examples in Figure 4.1.

physical work areas that symbolize each group's identity (e.g., work areas filled with supplies and equipment that are useful primarily to that group). These social identity markers attempt to establish—even if temporarily—who is "in" the group and, in turn, encourage affiliation among those in-group members (Bechky, 2003a; Brown et al., 2005; Carlile, 2002; Fleischmann, 2006). Yet, at the same time, these markers may also signal who is "out" of the group and, thus, they may also encourage exclusion of these out-group members. This exclusion can become a problem when members who may be assigned to work in a functional group do not identify with the physical markers used to symbolize that group's territory (e.g., if a work area has only drawing supplies and an engineer assigned to that group works in sculpting or modeling, she may feel excluded from the group). Further, such exclusion may discourage cross-functional collaboration because out-group members may feel alienated and unwelcome in the in-group's space.

Unlike the other tensions previously noted, the only way to deal with intra-form tensions is to make trade-offs and sacrifices. Thus, in the case described in the preceding section, workers may be forced to choose whether they value in-group affiliation most (in which case they should display social identity markers for their group and risk alienating out-group members) or if they prefer a more inclusive organizational culture and cross-group identification within a work space (in which case they should limit social identity markers for their group to encourage interaction with out-group members).

Taking Stock and Moving Forward

Our review suggests that the objects, stimuli, and arrangements that comprise the physical environment in corporate work environments have both powerful and complex effects in organizations. Their power is reflected in their ability to strongly shape individual behavior and interpersonal and group interactions in instrumental, aesthetic, and symbolic ways. Their complexity is evident in the myriad of trade-offs, tensions, and challenges inherent in their design and management.

By looking backward on what has been done over the past 30 or so years, we can see a few primary trends. First, the bulk of the research summarized in Table 4.1 has been more focused on the instrumental and symbolic functions of physical environments than on aesthetic functions. This is perhaps not surprising given our field's emphasis on productivity and on the "cultural turn" that has pervaded recent research in management. Second, we have only just begun to examine interactions between the physical environment and other types of environments (e.g., the social environment and natural environment). Finally, we find relatively few clear messages or guidelines about how people in organizations can successfully and proactively manage their physical environment. These historical trends offer three suggestions about where research on the physical environment should go.

1. Putting the "Physical" into the Physical Environment

Perhaps ironically, we believe that attention is needed in that area where individuals most directly (i.e., via the senses and our aesthetic sensibilities) interact with the physical environment. The incorporation of the physiological sensory experience, in general, is lacking in the organizational management field (see Heaphy, 2006, and Heaphy & Dutton, 2007, for a critique and reconceptualization). We feel that this connection between physiology and the physical environment, however, may play a critical role in organizational studies.

As noted in our introduction, the influence of environmental conditions (e.g., light and temperature) on physiological reactions (e.g., heart rate) has largely been outside the scope of organizational researchers' areas of interest. Two possible exceptions may be research on the physical environment and *stress* (e.g., Scheiberg, 1990; Wells, 2000)—although even here the emphasis tends to be on psychological stress rather than its sensory implications and manifestations (e.g., Huang, Robertson, & Chang, 2004)—and on *relaxation* (Boubekri et al., 1991; Oldham, et al., 1995; Scheiberg, 1990). But are these the only ways that physical environments effect our physiologies?

While we do not suggest that organizational researchers become physiologists, per se, we do believe that we need to look more closely at the often underexamined direct and indirect effects of the physical environment on our physiological well-being. We might, for example, take a new look at the direct effects. How might other physiological reactions—beyond various states of activation (stress vs. relaxation)—relate to how we think, feel, and act at work? We know that noxious stimuli can affect health and mood. By contrast, we know that certain aspects of the physical environment (e.g., natural light) can induce positive mood. Can we use this information to design "happier" organizations? And are there other beneficial physiological effects? Moreover, we know that our genetic "wiring" can lead to variations in our responses to ambient stimuli, but can a specific work environment "rewire" us to psychologically and physiologically respond to a given environment in either healthy (e.g., with a positive attitude and low blood pressure) or nonhealthy (e.g., with a negative attitude and high heart rate) ways?

We also expect that there are some critical indirect effects as well. For example, research suggests that social relationships have a strong influence on our physiologies, such as the functioning of our cardiovascular and immune systems as well as our neuroendocrine responses (Heaphy & Dutton, 2007). Given that the physical environment influences social relationships, we should—at minimum—expect an indirect effect of the physical environment on physiological well-being. Can we design organizations to promote healthiness? The rising cost of employee health insurance makes this a nontrivial issue.

2. Looking at Interactions Between Physical, Social, and Natural Environments

More generally, our review suggests that researchers begin to look more closely at how the physical environment interacts with other environments such as the social environment or the natural environment.* For example, in looking at the intersection of the physical and natural environment, researchers might examine how various aspects of building design (e.g., number and placements of windows and skylights, quality of artificial heating and cooling) interact with natural climate conditions (e.g. local cloudiness temperatures) to produce desired effects on job performance.

Similarly, there remains considerable room for additional research at the intersection of the physical and social environment. For example, most of the research we have reviewed has been on the social implications of physical environments from a western perspective. But how and to what degree do these insights generalize across cultures? Do different cultures relate to the physical environment in fundamentally different ways? How might ideas of *feng shui*, the Chinese art of placing objects, relate to Western notions of office design (e.g., Goodall, 2001)?

Another highly promising area concerns how the physical environment influences nonconscious cognition. Dual process theories, for example, posit that two distinct information-processing systems exist in the human body: one slower—primarily cognitive, analytical, and tied to conscious rational thought; and the other faster—strongly emotional, associative, and tied to more nonconscious intuitive process (e.g., Epstein, 2002; Dane & Pratt, 2007; Gollwitzer & Bayer, 1999). Kahneman's (2003) work in this area suggested that some properties of objects, such as their size and loudness, are automatically and unconsciously processed via a "natural assessment" (p. 701). Other aspects of physical objects, by contrast, often require the use of language and, thus, more effortful and conscious processing. By implication, dual processing theory suggests that the sensory aspects of objects in the physical environment may be processed through one type of information-processing system, while

---

* Of course, this begs the question of whether it is meaningful to see these environments as independent. For example, we cannot have the "physical" environment with its artificial barriers and symbols without having a "natural" environment that supplies the raw materials. It may even be that we cannot have a "social" environment without a physical one. As Carlile (2006) noted, "The material world, in one shape or form, always mediates human activity. People never act in a vacuum or some sort of hypothetical universe of doing but always with respect to arrangements, tools, and material objects" (p. 101). Thus, the physical environment is inexorably entwined with the other environments. Therefore, we might consider what is gained and lost by dividing the environment into these component types.

some social elements that require language to process may require another.* This leads us to wonder what impact each of these information-processing systems has on our perceptions and what might happen if the conclusions drawn from each differ.

Research at the intersection of the physical and social environments may also continue to look at the reasons *why* the physical environment influences how we think and feel. In this way, managers can come up with potential means of better managing the physical environment. For example, one of the key benefits of enclosures is that they allow for more personal and frequent communication—especially confidential communication. This effect, however, is explained by a mediator: privacy. If privacy is central—rather than high barriers and enclosures—might there be other ways of achieving it?

There may be. Researchers have found that being positioned away from major traffic areas and noise intrusions, which provides a space barrier rather than an actual partition barrier, has a stronger affect on perceived privacy than having barriers that may not completely buffer workers from noise intrusions (Kupritz, 1998). Continuing to explore the various physiological (e.g., arousal), cognitive (e.g., information overload), and emotional (e.g., disgust) mediators between our physical world and our social reactions to it will help us be more effective in finding additional avenues for attaining similar outcomes (e.g., job satisfaction, performance).

An alternative approach to examining the intersection of the physical environment with the social and natural environments would be to try to move farther away from this intersection. For example, is it possible to look more purely at the physical environment apart from the people in it or the natural environment surrounding it? Pratt and Rafaeli (2006) suggested a more archeological approach to studying the physical environment that may involve examining empty or abandoned physical environments for clues to how people work. This research could, in turn, complement existing work that examines "actor-observer" effects—that is, the difference between what is intended by the placer or objects and what is interpreted by those who interact with them in an organization (Cappetta & Gioia, 2006; Elsbach, 2005). An archeological perspective takes a further step back, adding a third-party observer perspective to the perspective of what the physical environment was intended to do (e.g., Bell, Fisher, Baum & Greene, 1990) and how employees react to it (May, Reed, Schwoerer, & Potter, 2004; Morrow & McElroy, 1981; Oldham & Brass, 1979; Sutton & Rafaeli, 1987).

---

* Kahneman (2003) does suggest that repeated exposure to more abstract features of objects or other stimuli can, over time, lead to its more automatic processing. This opens up the possibility for the influence of nonconscious thought and the physical environment even more.

3. Understanding and Managing Trade-Offs and Tensions

A third opportunity for exploration in the area of the physical environments in corporate work settings is to disentangle the reasons for the highly inconsistent effects found for various physical environment interventions, such as the use of enclosures and barriers in work spaces, adjustable work arrangements, the personalization of work, and the creation of nature-like workplace surroundings. We have attempted to disentangle these effects, at a very basic level, by identifying various tensions inherent in the physical environment. We believe, however, that additional work is needed in this area.

To begin, it would be interesting to examine whether and how different types of tensions influence the magnitude and scope of outcomes in organizational settings. For example, we would imagine that tensions involving instrumentality may be the most disruptive for an organization, and likely for the individual employee, too (depending on one's job and degree of job security). It is unclear, however, if tensions involving instrumentality and some other function have greater effects than those involving just instrumentality. Given the nested nature of the tensions, we also wonder if intraform tensions are more pernicious than interform and interfunctional tensions. Finally, it is unclear if tensions are additive or multiplicative in their effects.

In addition, we believe that researchers should look for other conditions that may exacerbate or attenuate these tensions. For example, we know that actors and observers view physical objects differently (Devine, 1989; Fiske & Neuberg, 1990; Gilbert, 1989). Because objects and arrangements in the physical environment are not only relatively permanent and visibly salient, but also have an existence that is independent of the person who designed or placed these objects in the environment (Elsbach, 2004, 2005), actor-observer dynamics in the physical environment may be even more pronounced. These dynamics, in turn, may serve to heighten inherent tensions in the physical environment. For example, if customers view a high-ranking manager's office as reflecting low status, this may worsen interfunctional tensions between the symbolic (e.g., status) and instrumental (e.g., performance) aspects of the officer's job.

Alternatively, human resource management practices may provide a means for attenuating tensions. For example, training employees about how an office design reflects not only task demands but also symbolic and aesthetic concerns may help ameliorate interfunctional tensions. Similarly, assessing aesthetic tastes may enhance the relationship between music or architecture and performance by aligning these functions. Of course, these recommendations presume that (a) there are some connections between the various functions of workplace stimuli, objects, and arrangements; and (b) that a given manager can recognize and articulate these connections.

From a more practitioner-oriented perspective, we believe that a better understanding of the inherent tensions and their degree of "manageability" can significantly enhance a manager's ability to navigate the complexity inherent in the physical environment. In particular, our review points to a general "decision tree" for those who want to better manage the stimuli, objects, and arrangements in their workplace.

To start, managers should endeavor to understand which types of tensions they are facing. Are they between or within functions (instrumental, aesthetic, or symbolic)? If they are within functions, are they between forms (e.g., job attitudes and job performance) or within forms (e.g., affiliating and excluding through the creation of territories)? To make such an analysis, however, involves the recognition that the physical environment *can* be viewed along various functions and forms. Moreover, to fully appreciate these various functions may involve bringing in very different areas of expertise to assess the situation. For example, while Rafaeli and Vilnai-Yavetz (2004a) noted that "instrumental experts" such as those who work in the physical environment (e.g., engineers, mechanics, drivers), "aesthetics experts" (e.g., product designers), and "symbolism experts" (e.g., public relations consultants) each could raise issues involving all three functional areas surrounding a particular artifact (a green bus), other types of expertise may need to be leveraged when assessing the physical environment.

If the tension is deemed "manageable," then organizations need to commit sufficient resources to resolving the issue. As Elsbach and Bechky (2007) noted, such management takes more than money. It also involves committing sufficient cognitive (e.g., creative) resources to "work smart" and understanding how you can achieve multiple functions with the same objects and arrangements. They recommend explicitly mapping out how a specific set of design features facilitates the various instrumental, symbolic, and aesthetic functions within an organization. In their example of a law firm, they map the firm's "production areas," comprised of distinct functional areas (e.g., document preparation, case mapping, mock trials, etc.), and how these physical features facilitate decision making (instrumental), affirm the status of different groups (symbolic), and allow for individuals and groups to tailor their aesthetic experiences to meet their needs (aesthetic).

If a tension cannot be resolved, either because a firm lacks resources or faces an intraform tension, then the manager's task is prioritization. Such prioritization may involve emphasizing some functions over another. For example, as we noted earlier, Elsbach and Bechky (2007) noted that certain functions may need to dominate in different parts of the organization (e.g., aesthetics in the entrance lobby). In other instances, prioritization simply involves very difficult choices and, possibly, sacrifices. For example, should temporary workers be given similar offices to full-time staff, thus symbolically communicating that they are part of the same group? Should management be cloistered on the top floor of an office building or located more centrally? To answer these types of issues, it is best that organizational leaders have a good sense of what they value, and use their physical environment as a means to enact these values.

In Closing: A Call to Action

In 1981, Franklin Becker, author of the seminal book *Workspace: Creating Environments in Organizations*, noted, "The way the physical setting is created in organizations has barely been tapped as a tangible organizational resource" (p. 130). Over 25 years later, almost the same statement could be made. In fact, during the years 1975–2005, the more mainstream organizational journals, *Academy of Management Journal, Administrative Science Quarterly, Journal of Organizational Behavior*, and *Organization Science*, published only 15 empirical papers that explicitly focused on the role of physical environments in organizations[*]. As organizations continue extend the boundaries of physical environments (e.g., "virtual" organizations, hoteling, and teleworking), the importance of understanding the role that the physical environment—and its interaction with other aspects of both organizational and nonorganizational environments—plays on how we think, feel, and work is only becoming more critical.

Acknowledgments

We would like to thank Beth Bechky, Greg Oldham, Anat Rafaeli, and Iris Vilnai-Yavetz for their comments on this manuscript.

References

Ahrentzen, S .B. (1990). Managing conflict by managing boundaries: How professional homeworkers cope with multiple roles at home. *Environment and Behavior, 22,* 723–752.

American Society of Interior Designers. (2000). Why employees stay—Or go. *Facilities Design & Management, 19,* 46–50.

Baron, R. A. (1990). Environmentally induced positive affect: Its impact on self-efficacy, task performance, negotiation, and conflict. *Journal of Applied Social Psychology, 20,* 368–384.

Baron, R. A. (1994). The physical work environment of work settings: Effects on task performance, interpersonal relations, and job satisfaction. In B. M. Staw & L. L. Cummings (Eds.), *Research in Organizational Behavior, 16,* 1–46.

Baumeister, R. (1998). The self. In D. T. Gilbert, S. T. Fiske, & G. Lindzey (Eds.), *The handbook of social psychology* (Vol. 1, pp. 680–740). Boston: McGraw-Hill.

---

[*] These 15 papers include Bechky (2003b); Carlile (2002); Elsbach (2004); Elsbach (2003); Fried (1990); Hatch (1987); Oldham & Brass (1979); Oldham, Kulik, & Stepina (1991); Oldham & Rotchford (1983); Pratt & Rafaeli (1997); Rafaeli, Dutton, Harquail, & Mackie-Lewis (1997); Rafaeli & Vilnai-Yavetz (2004b); Sundstrom, Burt, & Kamp (1980); Sutton & Rafaeli (1987); and Zalesny & Farace (1987).

Bechky, B. A. (2003a). Object lessons: Workplace artifacts as representations of occupational jurisdiction. *American Journal of Sociology, 109*, 720–752.

Bechky, B. A. (2003b). Sharing meaning across occupational communities: The transformation of knowledge on a production floor. *Organization Science, 14*, 312–330.

Becker, F. D. (1981). *Workspace: Creating environments in organizations*. Westport, CT: Praeger Publishers.

Becker, F. D., Gield, B., Gaylin, K., & Sayer, S. (1983). Office design in a community college: Effect on work and communication patterns. *Environment and Behavior, 15*, 699–726.

Bell, P., Fisher, J., Baum, A., & Greene, T. (1990). *Environmental Psychology* (3rd ed.). Chicago: Holt, Rinehart and Winston, Inc.

Belk, R. W. (1988). Possessions and the extended self. *Journal of Consumer Research, 15*, 139–168.

Bless, H., Bohner,G., Schwarz, N., & Strack, F. (1990). Mood and persuasion: A cognitive response analysis. *Personality and Social Psychology Bulletin, 16*, 331-345.

Boje, A. (1971). *Open-plan offices*. London: Business Books Ltd.

Boubekri, M., Hull, R. B., & Boyer, L. L. (1991). Impact of window size and sunlight penetration on office workers' mood and satisfaction: A novel way of assessing sunlight. *Environment and Behavior, 23*, 474–493.

Brennan, A., Chugh, J. S., & Kline, T. (2002). Traditional versus open office design: A longitudinal field study. *Environment and Behavior, 34*, 279–299.

Brewer, M. B. (1991). The social self: On being the same and different at the same time. *Personality & Social Psychology Bulletin. 17*, 475–482

Brewer, M. B., Manzi, J. M., & Shaw, J. S. (1993). In-group identification as a function of depersonalization, distinctiveness, and status. *Psychological Science, 4*, 88–92.

Brill, M., Marguilis, S. T., & Konar, E. (1984). *Using design to increase productivity* (Vol. 1). Buffalo, NY: Workplace Design and Productivity Inc.

Brookes, M. J., & Kaplan, A. (1972). The office environment: Space planning and effective behavior. *Human Factors, 14*, 373–391.

Brown, B.B., (1987). Territoriality. In D.Stokols and I. Altman (eds.), *Handbook of environmental psychology*, 505-531. New York: Wiley.

Brown, G., Lawrence, T., & Robinson, S. (2005). Territoriality in organizations. *Academy of Management Review, 30*(3), 577–594.

Brown, T. A. (1995). The Monty Hall dilemma Donald Granberg. *Personality and Social Psychology Bulletin, 21*, 711–723.

Campbell, D. E. (1979). Interior office design and visitor response. *Journal of Applied Psychology, 64*, 648–653.

Campbell, J. P., Dunnette, M. D., Lawler, E. E., & Weick, K. E. (1970). *Managerial behavior, performance, and effectiveness*. New York: McGraw-Hill.

Capetta, R., & Gioia, D. (2006). Fine fashion: Using symbolic artifacts, sensemaking, and sensegiving to construct identity and image. In A. Rafaeli & M. Pratt (Eds.), *Artifacts and Organizations: Beyond Mere Symbolism* (pp. 199–219). Mahaweh, NJ: Lawrence Erlbaum.

Carlile, P. R. (2002). A pragmatic view of knowledge and boundaries: Boundary objects in new product development. *Organization Science, 13*, 442–455.

Carlopio, J. R., & Gardner, D. (1992). Direct and interactive effects of the physical work environment on attitudes. *Environment and Behavior, 24,* 579–601.

Carnevale, D. G, & Rios, J. M. (1995). How employees assess the quality of physical work settings. *Public Productivity & Management Review, 18,* 221–231.

Carnevale, D. G. (1992). Physical settings of work: A theory of the effects of environmental form. *Public Productivity & Management Review, 15,* 423–436.

Christopher, A. N., & Schlenker, B. R. (2000). The impact of perceived material wealth and perceiver personality on first impressions. *Journal of Economic Psychology, 21,* 1–19.

Cialdini, R. B. (1993). *Influence. The new psychology of modern persuasion* (3rd ed.). New York: Quill.

Cohen, S. (1980). After effects of stress on human performance and social behavior: A review of research and theory. *Psychological Bulletin, 88,* 82–108.

Crouch, A., & Nimran, U. (1989). Perceived facilitators and inhibitors of work performance in an office environment. *Environment and Behavior, 21,* 206–226.

Dane, E., & Pratt, M. G. (2007). Exploring intuition and its role in managerial decision-making. *Academy of Management Review, 32*(1),33-54.

Davis, T. R. V. _(1984). The influence of the physical environment in offices. *Academy of Management Review, 9,* 271–283.

Desor, J. A. (1972). Toward a psychological theory of crowding. *Journal of Personality and Social Psychology, 21,* 79–83.

Devine, P. G. (1989). Stereotypes and prejudice: Their automatic and controlled components. *Journal of Personality and Social Psychology, 56,* 5–18.

Dittmar, H. (1992). Perceived material wealth and first impressions. *British Journal of Social Psychology, 31,* 379–391.

Donald, I., (1994). Management and change in office environments. *Journal of Environmental Psychology, 14,* 21-30.

Elsbach, K. D. (2005). Perceptual biases and mis-interpretation of artifacts. In A. Rafaeli & M. Pratt (Eds.), *Artifacts and organizations: Beyond mere symbolism* (pp. 61–81). Mahaweh, NJ: Lawrence Erlbaum.

Elsbach, K. D. (2004). Interpreting workplace identities: The role of office decor. *Journal of Organizational Behavior, 25,* 99–128.

Elsbach, K. D. (2003). Relating physical environment to self-categorizations: Identity threat and affirmation in a non-territorial office space. *Administrative Science Quarterly, 48,* 622–654.

Elsbach, K. D., & Barr, P. S. (1999). The effects of mood on individual's use of structured decision protocols. *Organization Science, 10,* 181–198.

Elsbach, K. D., & Bechky, B. A. (2007). It's more than a desk: Working smarter through leveraged office design. *California Management Review, 49,* 80–101.

Fiske, S., & Taylor, S. (1991). *Social cognition.* NY: McGraw-Hill.

Epstein, S. (2002). Cognitive-experiential self-theory of personality. In T. Millon & M. J. Lerner (Eds.), *Comprehensive handbook of psychology, Vol. 5: Personality and social psychology* (pp. 159–184). Hoboken, NJ: Wiley.

Finnegan, M. C., & Solomon, L. Z. (1981). Work attitudes in windowed vs. windowless environments. *Journal of Social Psychology, 115,* 291–292.

Fiske, S. T., & Neuberg, S. L. (1990). A continuum of impression formation, from category-based to individuating processes: Influences of information and motivation on attention and interpretation. In L. Berkowitz (Ed.), *Advances in experimental social psychology, 23*, 1–74. San Diego, CA: Academic.

Fleischmann, K. (2006). Boundary objects with agency: A method for studying the design-user interface. *The Information Society, 22*, 77–87.

Frank, R. (1985). *Choosing the right pond: Human behavior and the quest for status.* New York: Oxford.

Fried, Y. (1990). Workspace characteristics, behavioral interferences, and screening ability as joint predictors of employee reactions: An examination of the intensification approach. *Journal of Organizational Behavior, 11*, 267–280.

Geen, R. G., & Gagne, J. J. (1977). Drive theory of social facilitation: Twelve years of theory and research. *Psychological Bulletin, 84*, 1267–1288.

Gilbert, D. T. (1989). Thinking lightly about others: Automatic components of the social inference process. In J. S. Uleman & J. A. Bargh (Eds.), *Unintended thought*, 189–211. New York: Guilford.

Goffman, E. (1961). *Asylums.* New York: Doubleday.

Goodrich, R. (1986). The perceived office: The office environment as experienced by its users. In J. D. Wineman (Ed.), *Behavioral issues in office design*, 109–133. New York: Van Nostrand Reinhold.

Gollwitzer, P., & Bayer, U. (1999). Deliberative versus implemental mindsets in the control of action. In S. Chaiken & Y. Trope (Eds.), *Dual-Process theories in social psychology* (pp. 403–422). New York: Guilford Press.

Goodall, Jr., H. R. (2001). Writing the American ineffable, or the mystery and practice of feng shui in everyday life. *Qualitative Inquiry, 7*(1), 3–20.

Gosling, S. D., Ko, S. J., Mannarelli, T., & Morris, M. E. (2002). A room with a cue: Personality judgments based on offices and bedrooms. *Journal of Personality and Social Psychology, 82*, 379–398.

Greenberg, J. (1988). Equity and workplace status: A field experiment. *Journal of Applied Psychology, 73*, 606–613.

Hartig, T., Mang, M., & Evans, G. W. (1991). Restorative effects of natural environment experiences. *Environment and Behavior, 23*, 3–26.

Hartig, T., Böök, A., Garvill, J., Olsson, T., & Gärling, T. (1996). Environmental influences on psychological restoration. *Scandinavian Journal of Psychology, 37*, 378–393.

Hatch, M. J. (1987). Physical barriers, task characteristics, and interaction activity in research and development firms. *Administrative Science Quarterly, 32*, 387–399.

Heaphy, E. (006). Bodily insights: Three lenses on positive organizational relationships. In J. Dutton & B. Baggins (Eds.) *Exploring positive relationships at work: Building a theoretical and research foundation.* London: Erlbaum.

Heaphy, E., & Dutton, J. (in press). Positive social interactions and the human body at work: Linking organizations and physiology. *Academy of Management Review.*

Heerwagen, J. H., & Orian, G. H. (1986). Adaptations to windowlessness: A study of the use of visual decor in windowed and windowless offices. *Environment and Behavior, 18*, 623–639.

Hedge, A. (1982). The open-plan office: A systematic investigation of employee reactions to their work environment. *Environment and Behavior, 4*, 519–542.

Hess, J. A. (1993). Assimilating newcomers into an organization: A cultural perspective. *Journal of Applied Communication, 21,* 189–210.

Horswill, M. S., & McKenna, F. P. (1999). The effect of perceived control on risk taking. *Journal of Applied Social Psychology, 29,* 377–391

Huang, Y. H., Robertson, M. M., & Chang, K. I. (2004). The role of environmental control on environmental satisfaction, communication, and psychological stress: Effects of office ergonomics training, *Environment and Behavior, 36,* 617–637.

Isen, A.M., 1993. Positive affect and decision making. In M. Lewis and J.M. Haviland, eds., *Handbook of Emotion,* 261-277. New York: Guilford.

Jones, E. E., & Nisbett, R. E. (1972). The actor and the observer: Divergent perceptions of the causes of behavior. In E. E. Jones, D. E. Kanouse, H. H. Kelley, R. E. Nisbett, S. Valins, & B. Weiner (Eds.), *Attribution: Perceiving the causes of behavior* (pp. 79–94). Morristown, NJ: General Learning Press.

Kahneman, D. (2003). A perspective on judgment and choice. *American Psychologist, 58,* 697–720.

Karasek, R. A., & Theorell, T. (1990). *Healthy work: Stress, productivity, and the reconstruction of working life.* New York: Basic Books.

Karasek, R. A. (1979). Job demands, job decision latitude, and mental strain: Implications for job re-design. *Administrative Science Quarterly, 24,* 285–311.

Kelly, L. (1992). The Steelcase report on working conditions. *Worklife Report, 8,* 6–8.

King, A. R., & Pate, A. N. (2002). Individual differences in judgmental tendencies derived from first impressions. *Personality and Individual Differences, 33,* 131–145.

Konar, E., Sundstrom, E., Brady, C, Mandel, D., & Rice, R. (1982). Status demarcation in the office. *Environment and Behavior, 14,* 561–580.

Kupritz, V. W. (1998). Privacy in the work place: The impact of building design. *Journal of Environmental Psychology, 18,* 341–356.

Langer, E. J. (1975). The illusion of control. *Journal of Personality and Social Psychology, 32,* 311–328.

Larsen, L., & Adams, J., & Deal, B., & Kweon, B., & Tyler, E. (1998). Plants in the workplace. The effects of plant density on productivity, attitudes, and perceptions. *Environment and Behavior, 30,* 261–281.

Laumann, E. O., & House, J. S. (1969). Living room styles and social attributes: The patterning of material artifacts in a modern urban community. *Sociology and Social Research, 53,* 321–342.

Lee, S. Y., & Brand J. L. (2005). Effects of control over office workspace on perceptions of the work environment and work outcomes. *Journal of Environmental Psychology, 25,* 323–333.

Maas, A., Merici, I., Villafranca, E., Furlani, R., Gaburro, E., Getrevi, A., et al. (2000). Intimidating buildings. Can courthouse architecture affect perceived likelihood of conviction? *Environment and Behavior, 32,* 674–683.

Maher, A., & von Hippel, C. (2005). Individual differences in employee reactions to open-plan offices. *Journal of Environmental Psychology, 25,* 219–229.

Mark, G. (2002). Extreme collaboration. *Communications of the ACM, 45,* 89–93.

May, D. R., Reed, K., Schwoerer, C., & Potter, P. (2004). Ergonomic office design and aging: A quasi-experimental field study of employee reactions to an ergonomics intervention program. *Journal of Occupational Health Psychology, 9*(2), 123–135.

Maybury-Lewis, D. (1989). The quest for harmony. In D. Maybury-Lewis & U. Almagor (Eds.), *The attraction of opposites: Thought and society in the dualistic mode* (pp. 1–18). Ann Arbor: University of Michigan Press.

Mitchell-McCoy, J., & Evans, G. W. (2002). The potential role of the physical environment in fostering creativity. Creativity Research Journal, 14, 409–426.

Morrow, P. C., & McElroy, J. C. (1981). Interior office design and visitor response: A constructive replication. *Journal of Applied Psychology, 66*, 646–650.

Nasar, J. L. (1994). Urban design aesthetics. The evaluative qualities of building exteriors. *Environment and Behavior, 26*, 377–401.

Newell, P.B. (1997). A cross-cultural examination of favorite places. *Environment and Behavior, 29*, 495-514

Oldham, G. R., & Brass, D. J. (1979). Employee reactions to an open-plan office: A naturally occurring quasi-experiment. *Administrative Science Quarterly, 24*, 267–284.

Oldham, G. R., & Kulik, C. T., & Stepina, L. P. (1991). Physical environments and employee reactions: Effects of stimulus-screening skills and job complexity. *The Academy of Management Journal, 34*, 929–938.

Oldham, G. R., & Rotchford, N. L. (1983). Relationships between office characteristics and employee reactions: A study of the physical environment. *Administrative Science Quarterly, 28*, 542–556.

Oldham, G. R. (1988). Effects of changes in workspace partitions and spatial density on employee reactions: A quasi-experiment. *Journal of Applied Psychology, 73*, 253–258.

Oldham, G. R., Cummings, A., & Zhou, J. (1995). The spatial configuration of organizations: A review of the literature and some new research directions. *Research in Personnel and Human Resources Management, 13*, 1–37.

O'Neill, M. J. (1994). Work space adjustability, storage, and enclosure as predictors of employee reactions and performance. *Environment and Behavior, 26*, 504–526.

Ornstein, S. (1986). Organizational symbols: A study of their meanings and influences on perceived psychological climate. *Organizational Behavior and Human Decision Processes, 38*, 207–229.

Ornstein, S. (1992). First impressions of the symbolic meaning s connoted by reception area design. *Environment and Behavior, 24*, 85–110.

Paciuk, M. T. (1990). The role of personal control of the environment in thermal comfort and satisfaction at the workplace. In R. I. Selby, K. H. Anthony, J. Choi, & B. Orland (Eds.), *Coming of age* (pp. 303—312). Edmond, OK: Environmental Design Research Association.

Parker Publishing Editorial Staff. (1965). *The business etiquette handbook*. West Nyack, NY: Parker Publishing.

Paulus, P. B. (1980). Crowding. In P. Paulus (Ed.), *Psychology of group influence* (pp. 245–289). Hillsdale, NJ: Lawrence Erlbaum.

Pile, J. F. (1978). *Open office planning*. New York: Whitney Library of Design.

Poole, S., & Van de Ven, A. (1989). Using paradox to build management and organization theories. *Academy of Management Review, 14*(4), 562–578.

Pratt, M. G., & Foreman, P. (2000). Classifying managerial responses to multiple organizational identities. *Academy of Management Review, 25*(1), 18–24.

Pratt, M. G., & Rafaeli, A. (2006). Artifacts in organizations: Understanding our 'Object-ive reality'. In A. Rafaeli & M. Pratt (Eds.), *Artifacts and organizations* (pp. 279–288). Mahwah, NJ: Lawrence Erlbaum Associates.

Pratt, M. G., & Rafaeli, A. (1997). Organizational dress as a symbol of multilayered social identities. *Academy of Management Journal, 40,* 862–898.

Pratt, M. G., & Rafaeli, A. (2001). Symbols as a language of organizational relationships. B. Staw & R. Sutton (Eds.) *Research in organizational behavior* (Vol. 23, pp. 93–132). Stanford, CA: JAI Press.

Rafaeli, A., Dutton, J., Harquail, C. V., & Mackie-Lewis, S. (1997). Navigating by attire: The use of dress by female administrative employees. *Academy of Management Journal, 40,* 9–45.

Rafaeli, A., & Pratt, M. G. (1993). Tailored meanings: On the meaning and impact of organizational dress. *Academy of Management Review, 18,* 32–55.

Rafaeli, A., & Pratt, M. G., Eds. (2005). *Artifacts and organizations: Beyond mere symbolism.* Mahaweh, NJ: Lawrence Erlbaum.

Rafaeli A., & Vilnai-Yavetz, I. (2004a). Instrumentality, aesthetics, and symbolism of physical artifacts as triggers of emotions. *Theoretical Issues in Ergonomics Science, 5*(1), 91–112.

Rafaeli, A., & Vilnai-Yavetz, I. (2004b). Emotion as a connection of physical artifacts and organizations. *Organization Science, 15,* 671–686.

Ridoutt, B. G., Ball, R. D., & Killerby, S. K. (2002). Wood in the interior office environment: Effects of on interpersonal perception. *Forest Products Journal, 52,* 23–30.

Scheiberg, S. L. (1990). Emotions on display. *American Behavioral Scientist, 33,* 330–338.

Schlenker, B. R. (1980). *Impression management.* Monterey, CA: Brooks/Cole.

Schlosser, J. (2006, March 22). Trapped in cubicles. *Fortune Magazine,* pp. 21–25.

Sitton, S. (1984). The messy desk effect: How tidiness affects the perception of others. *Journal of Psychology, 117,* 263–267.

Snyder, C. R., & Fromkin, H. C. (1980). *Uniqueness: The human pursuit of difference.* New York: Plenum.

Sommer, R. (1974). *Tight spaces: Hard architecture and how to humanize it.* Englewood Cliffs, NJ: Prentice-Hall.

Spreckelmeyer, K. F. (1993). Office relocation and environmental change: A case study. *Environment and Behavior, 25,* 181–204.

Star, S. L. (1988). The structure of ill-structured solutions: Boundary objects and heterogeneous distributed problem solving. In M. Huhns, & L. Gasser (Eds.), *Readings in distributed artificial intelligence* (Vol. 2, 37–54). Menlo Park, CA: Morgan Kaufman.

Steele, F. I. (1973). *Physical settings and organizational development.* Reading, MA: Addison-Wesley.

Stone, N. J, & English, A. J. (1998). Task type, posters, and workspace color on mood, satisfaction, and performance. *Journal of Environmental Psychology, 18,* 175–185.

Strati, A. (1992). Aesthetic understanding of organizational life. *Academy of Management Review, 17,* 568–581.

Sundstrom, E., & Burt, R. E., & Kamp, D. (1980). Privacy at work: Architectural correlates of job satisfaction and job performance. *The Academy of Management Journal, 23,* 101–117.

Sundstrom, E., & Sundstrom, M. G. (1986). *Work places: The psychology of the physical environment in offices and factories.* Cambridge, U.K.: Cambridge University Press.

Sundstrom, E., Bell, P. A., Busby, P. L., & Asmus, C. (1996). Environmental psychology 1989–1994. In J. T. Spence, J. M. Darley, & D. J. Foss (Eds.), *Annual review of psychology* (Vol. 47, pp. 485–512). Palo Alto, CA: Annual Reviews.

Sundstrom, E., Herbert, R. K., & Brown, D. W. (1982). Privacy and communication in an open-plan office: A case study. *Environment and Behavior, 14,* 379–392.

Sundstrom, E., Town, J. P., Brown, D. W., Forman, A., & McGee, C. (1982). Physical enclosure, type of job, and privacy in the office. *Environment and Behavior, 14,* 543–559.

Sundstrom, E., Town, J. P., Rice, R. W., Osborn, D. P., & Brill, M. (1994). Office noise, satisfaction, and performance. *Environment and Behavior, 26,* 195–222.

Sutton, R. I., & Rafaeli, A. (1987). Characteristics of work stations as potential occupational stressors. *The Academy of Management Journal, 30,* 260–276.

Taylor, S. E. (1983). Adjustment to threatening events: A theory of cognitive adaptation. *American Psychologist, 38,* 1161–1173.

Veitch, J. A., & Gifford, R. (1996). Choice, perceived control, and performance decrements in the physical environment. *Journal of Environmental Psychology, 16,* 269–276.

Vinsel, A., Brown, B. B., Altman, I., & Foss, C. (1980). Privacy regulation, territorial displays, and effectiveness of individual functioning. *Journal of Personality and Social Psychology, 39,* 1104–1115.

Vilnai-Yavetz, I., Rafaeli, A. & Yaacov, C.S. (2005). Instrumentality, aesthetics, and symbolism of office design, *Environment and Behavior, 37,* 533-551.

Waibel, M. C., & Wicklund, R. A. (1994). Inferring competence from incompetence: An ironic process associated with person description. *European Journal of Social Psychology, 24,* 443–452.

Wells, M., & Thelen, L. (2002). What does your workspace say about you?: The influence of personality, status, and workspace on personalization. *Environment and Behavior, 34,* 300–321.

Wells, M. M. (2000). Office clutter or meaningful personal displays: The role of office personalization in employee and organizational well-being. *Journal of Environmental Psychology, 20,* 239–255.

Wollin, D. D., & Montagne, M. (1981). College classroom environment. Effects of sterility versus amiability on student and teacher performance. *Environment and Behavior, 13,* 707–716.

Zalesny, M. D., & Farace, R. V. (1987). Traditional versus open offices: A comparison of sociotechnical, social relations, and symbolic meaning perspectives. *The Academy of Management Journal, 30,* 240–259.

Zelinsky, M. (2002). *The inspired workspace: Designs for creativity & productivity.* Gloucester, MA: Rockport Publishers.

Zenardelli, H. A. (1967). Testimonial to life in a landscape. *Office Design, 5,* 30–36.

5
Public Administration and Organization Studies

STEVEN KELMAN

John F. Kennedy School of Government, Harvard University

Abstract

The study of public organizations has withered over time in mainstream organization studies research, as scholars in the field have migrated to business schools. This is so even though government organizations are an important part of the universe of organizations—the largest organizations in the world are agencies of the U.S. government. At the same time, the study of public administration, once in the mainstream of organization studies, has moved into a ghetto, separate and unequal. Centered in business schools, mainstream organization research became isomorphic to its environment—coming to focus on performance issues, which are what firms care about. Since separation, the dominant current in public administration has become isomorphic with *its* environment. In this case, however, this meant the field moved backward from the central reformist concern of its founders with improving government performance, and developed instead a focus on managing constraints (i.e., avoiding bad things, such as corruption or misuse of power, from occurring) in a public organization environment. Insufficient concern about performance among public administration scholars is particularly unfortunate because over the past 15 years, there has occurred a significant growth of interest among practitioners in improving government performance. The origins and consequences of these developments are discussed, and a research agenda for organization studies research that takes the public sector seriously is proposed.

Introduction

U.S. government organizations are an important part of the universe of organizations. The U.S. Department of Defense is the largest organization in the

225

U.S. government: Its budget ($410 billion in 2006) is noticeably larger than sales of ExxonMobil ($339.9 billion) and of Wal-Mart ($315.7 billion), the world's two largest corporations by sales (U.S. Office of Management & Budget, 2007, p. 314; Fortune, 2006a). The Department of Defense has about 3.3 million employees (2.6 million uniformed and 700,000 civilian), compared to 84,000 for ExxonMobil and 1.8 million for Wal-Mart (Department of Defense, 2002; Fortune, 2006b; Wal-Mart, 2006). If the cabinet department with the smallest budget, the Commerce Department, were a *Fortune 500* company, it would rank 367th. Beyond its size, the U.S. government has main responsibility for important problems such as protecting the environment, educating children, and finding terrorists—and for protection of values and individuals that the market undervalues or neglects (Mintzberg, 1996). Finally, the U.S. government creates the very foundation for civilized life through providing individual security and the ground rules for operation of the market. (Oliver Wendall Holmes once observed, "Taxes are the price I pay for civilization.")

The U.S. government also has serious performance problems. To be sure, government performs better than its reputation. In a survey, a sample of 1,000 professors teaching American government and modern American history courses identified rebuilding Europe after World War II, expanding the right to vote, strengthening the highway system, containing communism, and promoting equal access to public accommodations as the "government's greatest achievements" in the 20th century (Light, 2002)—no paltry collection. There is nonetheless enough truth to stereotypes of incompetent delivery and indifferent service for any but the most dyed-in-the-wool apologist to agree that in domains ranging from public education to emergency management to foreign policy decision making, government underperforms. In rich democracies, no question about government is more important than underperformance.

The argument of this review is straightforward. Improving government performance is a topic worthy of significant research attention, yet dramatically insufficient scholarly firepower is directed at it. The separation of public management research from mainstream organization studies that has appeared over past decades is the main reason such firepower has been absent. What has happened? Most obviously, mainstream researchers largely disengaged from studying government, depriving research on government performance of its largest natural source of sustenance. In addition, the smaller group of scholars who study government organizations has largely isolated itself from mainstream organization studies. This has made them less interested and less able to contribute to producing research about government performance. Because of its location mainly in business schools, mainstream research is centrally concerned with performance. With separation, pressure on those studying government to study performance has dwindled. Thus, in recent decades, public administration scholars, often proudly, have paid little attention to researching performance. With separation, public administration has also been cut off from methodological advances, particularly increased use of econometrics, lab experimentation, and computational analysis, in social psychology, sociology, and political science. Thus, methods have generally been primitive, excessively relying on case studies, using selection on the dependent variable, and producing discursive "conceptual" frameworks with weak empirical grounding or theoretical rigor—what Rainey (personal communication, August 25, 2006) has called "essayism."[1] This means research on agencies often lacks sophistication, which inhibits the ability to draw conclusions strong enough to use for improving performance.[2] It also promotes a general view that anything having to do with government organizations—including research about them—is second rate.

Given these problems, bringing the two traditions together again is a priority. With those whose work I will review, I share the idea that government should be seen as a positive force, in theory and often in practice. Government is too important not to propel the goal of improving its performance to a front rank of research attention. Insufficient concern about performance among public administration scholars is particularly unfortunate because, over the past 15 years, particularly in the Anglo-American world, there has occurred an astounding, heartening growth of interest in improving government performance among practitioners and a lively interest in techniques for how to do so. The field is therefore betraying practitioners who could use help for their efforts.

Constraints and Goals

Government underperformance is overdetermined. One explanation, which economists favor, is that agencies are protected monopolies, and thus, they lead an easy life without performance pressures (Rainey, Backoff, & Levine, 1976; Savas, 1982). Savas (1982) wrote that monopolies produce a situation where citizens are "subject to endless exploitation and victimization" and where "so-called public servants have a captive market and little incentive to heed their putative customers" (pp. 134–135). The universality of popular obloquy regarding government performance across time and place suggests that the monopoly criticism is not entirely groundless, since agencies' most obvious common feature is monopoly status. To state, however, that agencies generally lead an easy life without outside pressures is inaccurate. Pressures come from the political system and the media, not the marketplace, but that does not make them innocuous: If one asked people whether they would rather be attacked on the front page of *The Washington Post* or subjected to the punishment that firms typically mete out for poor performance, it is not obvious most would choose the former. Another explanation is that few of the best people choosing government careers do so because of an interest in managing organization performance, but rather, to influence formulation of policies such as those for AIDS or terrorism. A third explanation is that, compared with the profit metric for firms, agencies often have a hard time developing good metrics to achieve performance improvement (e.g., What should the State Department's metrics be?), or agencies have controversies about goals (e.g., Should the Forest Service cut down trees for economic use or preserve them for wilderness lovers?).

In this review, I focus on a different account, not necessarily because it has the largest effect size (researchers do not know) but because it relates to the nature of research in public administration and its relationship to mainstream organization studies. This explanation is that government underperforms because, compared with firms, government pays less attention to performance in the first place. All organizations have both goals, and constraints that put boundaries around what they may legitimately do to achieve their goals. Traditionally, in government, the tail wags the dog—constraints loom larger than goals, inhibiting good performance.

Central to understanding both government organizations and the challenge for public administration research and practice is the distinction between goals an organization has and constraints under which it operates (Simons, 1995; Wilson, 1989, chapter 7[3]). Goals are the results that an organization seeks—for firms, goals are profit, market share, or customer satisfaction; for the Environmental Protection Agency (EPA), a goal is improved air quality; and for the National Cancer Institute, a goal is better understanding of cancer. Constraints are the limits of acceptable behavior, even to meet goals,[4] for organizations and their members. For firms, constraints include respecting accounting rules, not dumping toxic wastes, and not kidnapping competitors. For agencies, constraints include officials not accepting bribes, not lying to the public, treating citizens fairly, respecting due process, and ensuring accountability to the public for agency actions.

Since constraints often embody important ethical values, such as respect, honesty, and integrity, they should be important for all organizations. Simons (1995) argued, "Every business needs [boundary systems], and, like racing cars, the fastest and most performance-oriented companies need the best brakes" (p. 84). This is particularly so in the government, where behaviors often communicate signals about societal values: Equal treatment of citizens signals the social importance of equality, and dishonesty lowers the moral tone in society (Kelman, 1993). Furthermore, an important line of research (e.g., Brockner & Wiesenfeld, 1996; Thibault & Walker, 1975; Tyler, 1990) argues that procedural fairness encourages people to accept decisions that are contrary to their personal interests. In service production, the process used to produce the service is often seen as "part of the product" (Lovelock, 1992); to this extent, a fair process may be seen as a goal, not a constraint (even here, this cannot be considered a mission goal).

At the same time, one cannot typically judge organizations (or individuals) that have only respected constraints as successful. Imagine a journalist who, during a long career, never revealed a source or fabricated evidence but who also never covered a good story. Imagine also a company that never cooked its books but that never made a sale. Furthermore, an organization (or individual) is not normally successful when it focuses significant energy on assuring that constraints are respected, because that energy is unavailable for goal attainment. If an individual spends hours each day worrying about how he or she will avoid murdering others, the person is unlikely to be successful at achieving substantive goals. Instead, a healthy organization (or individual) is one that takes constraints for granted. Firms seldom think that not kidnapping competitors is a constraint because they take the constraint for granted. (Consider, however, Russia in the early 1990s. This could not be taken for granted, and that was a reason the society was in bad shape.[5])

In the world of practice, firms usually focus in the first instance on achieving their goals: A business that does not cannot stay in business. Parsons (1960) argued that a firm is indeed an organization whose "defining characteristic is the attainment of a specific goal" (p. 63). A central fact, however, about the practice of government, across most times and places, is that, in the environment in which government operates, the opposite is closer to the truth—failure to pay attention to constraints often inflicts more pain (Wilson, 1989). This is so because, first, in government, goals are often controversial (e.g., Should affirmative action be required or free trade pursued?); everybody agrees, however, that it is wrong to lie or show favoritism. Constraint violation is therefore an easier story for media or opposing politicians to expose. Second, goal achievement is not fully under agency control and occurs over time, while constraint violation is immediate. Third, pursuing goals is about "maximizing good government," while respecting constraints is about "minimizing misgovernment" (Uhr, as cited in Gregory, 2003, p. 564); many have such limited aspirations for government that they ask only for reducing misgovernment—a standard for success that firms would find incomprehensible.[6] Fourth, agency accountability is a central value in a democracy, but this focus is a constraint because it refers not to results but only to process.[7]

All organizations should seek to maximize attainment of goals while respecting constraints. For firms, goal focus increases the probability that they will perform well and the risk that they will ignore constraints (e.g., the Enron problem; Schweitzer, Ordonez, & Douma, 2004). For government, the problem is less that constraints are violated (although the way the media cover government may produce the misimpression of common misbehavior) and more that they perform poorly (e.g., the Katrina problem).

The importance of constraints is tied to dominance of bureaucratic organizational forms in government, since rules and hierarchy are important control tools.[8] As Kaufman (1977) famously noted, "One person's 'red tape' may be another's treasured procedural safeguard" (p. 4). Combined with rules developed at the top, where those lower down are merely executing directives, hierarchy fits into the desire to subordinate unelected officials to political control (Warwick, 1975). If one cares about minimizing misgovernment rather than maximizing good government, one will be disinclined to grant officials discretion. As Theodore Roosevelt stated, "You cannot give an official power to do right without at the same time giving him power to do wrong" (Roosevelt, as cited in White, 1926, p. 144).

Public Administration and Organization Studies: From Colleagues to Strangers

The founders of public administration[9] in the first decades of the 20th century saw the field as closely tied to the general study of management. Woodrow Wilson (1887), then a young political science professor, wrote in *The Study of Administration*, the first scholarly work calling attention to public administration, "The field of administration is a field of business" (p. 209). In the field's first textbook, *Introduction to the Study of Public Administration*, White (1926) wrote that "conduct of government business" was similar to "conduct of the affairs of any other social organization, commercial, philanthropic, religious, or educational, in all of which good management is recognized as an element essential to success" (p. 5). Another early text referred to the legislature as an agency's "board of directors" and its director as its "general manager" (Willoughby, 1927). The most influential collection of essays on public administration during the 1930s, *Papers on the Science of Administration* (Gulick & Urwick, 1937), is an important collection for the history of organization studies in general. Gulick (1937b), the most influential public administration scholar of the era (and one of three members of the panel proposing a plan for executive branch reorganization to Franklin D. Roosevelt in 1937), wrote, in his essay *Science, Values and Public Administration*, "There are principles...which should govern arrangements for human association of any kind...irrespective of the purpose of the enterprise...or any constitutional, political or social theory underlying its creation" (p. 49). Fayol (1937), who worked mostly on business management, argued, "We are no longer confronted with several administrative sciences but with one alone, which can be applied equally well to public and to private affairs" (p. 101). Simon, Smithburg, and Thompson's (1950) textbook *Public Administration* stated, "Large-scale public and private organizations have many more similarities than they have differences" (p. 8). At this time, studies of public organizations were important for organization studies, tied in with Tayloristic industrial engineering and contributing to the study of organization design. Frank Goodnow, the first president of the American Political Science Association (APSA), was a public administration scholar. "In the 1930s, public administration dominated the fields of both political science and management" (Henry, 1990, p. 4). The prominence of public administration also reflected the lack of business school research at the time.

Modern organization studies grew out of industrial psychology at the beginning of the 20th century (Baritz, 1960). Industrial psychology initially addressed issues in mostly an individual context (e.g., personality tests for job applicants), but with the Hawthorne studies, it turned attention to small groups and grew within sociology after World War II. Although they did not

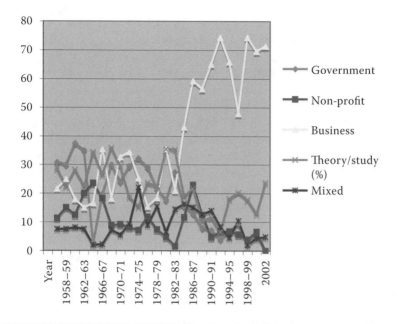

Figure 5.1   Evolution in Research on Government, Topics in *Administrative Science Quarterly*. Note: Percentages Represent Articles Where the Source of Empirical Data and/or the Theory Involved the Sector in Question. Because Not All Articles Were about Some Sector, but Rather about Organizations in General, Percentages Do Not Add up to 100%. (Material Developed by Author.)

consider themselves public administration scholars, early postwar organization studies scholars, particularly sociologists, situated important research in government, both because agencies were seen as worth studying and because access was often easier than for firms. Selznick (1953) began his scholarly career writing about the New Deal Tennessee Valley Authority. Two other classics, Blau's (1955) *The Dynamics of Bureaucracy* and Crozier's (1954) *The Bureaucratic Phenomenon,* were empirically located in government.[10]

In 1956 *Administrative Science Quarterly (ASQ)* was founded as an outlet for scholars from sociology, political science, and social psychology engaged in organization studies. Figure 5.1 displays changes in percentages of *ASQ* field-based empirical articles situated in government, nonprofits, and firms. In almost every year of its first decade, the percentage situated in government exceeded that in firms. Until the early 1980s, *ASQ* published significant research situated in government. In recent years, such research has vanished.

This transformation reflects the overwhelming migration of organization research into business schools, which in turn reflects larger social trends. Since the 1980s, the salary gap for professional/managerial work between government and industry has dramatically increased (Donahue, 2008). During this time, business was also culturally "hot." In 2003 about 125,000 students in the United States were studying for MBAs compared to one fifth that number studying for master's degrees in public administration or public policy (U.S. National Center for Education Statistics, 2006).[11] The enormous growth of wealth in the business community provided business schools funding sources unavailable to others. At the same time, ideological attacks on the desirability of government playing an active role in society and on the idea of public service, spread in academia (especially economics; e.g., Friedman & Friedman, 1980; Tullock, 1976, 1979) and politics.[12] Business schools thus became a gold mine for organization scholars, offering abundant well-paying jobs and a benign funding environment.[13] Not surprisingly (though, I would suggest, not honorably), mainstream organization studies thus by and large forgot government. To be sure, the bulk of organizational behavior empirical research—most obviously lab experiments—is "ainstitutional" in setting. However, in situating field research or considering topics for theorizing, organization studies directed attention to the world of business that was its new home, and large swathes of the field (e.g., strategy research) was squarely located in the business world.

While mainstream scholars were abandoning government, public administration scholars were administering a self-inflicted wound by isolating themselves from the mainstream. Mosher (1956) noted few connections between public administration and social psychologists studying small groups, and no use of lab studies, while also noting that, conversely, organization studies scholars (e.g., Blau and Selznick) did not cite public administration literature, although they researched government. The emergence of organization studies in social psychology and sociology created a need and an opportunity for public administration scholars to reach out (the traditional disciplinary home for public administration was political science). The field failed to do this; instead, it retreated inward. An examination of the most cited public administration research showed that in 1972 60% of citations "came from fields of study that held no particular distinction between business administration, public administration, or any other type of administration," but by 1985, this had declined to 30% (McCurdy, 1985, pp. 4–5).

The Public Administration Ghetto

Separation of public administration from mainstream organization studies has resulted in creation of a modestly sized public-sector research ghetto. The Academy of Management (2006) had almost 17,000 members. By contrast, in 2005 the Public Administration Research Section of the American Society for Public Administration (APSA, 2006) had 355 members, and the Public Administration Section of the APSA (2006) had 515 members.[14]

The ghetto is separate. In a published survey of the field, *The Oxford Handbook of Public Management* (2006), a section called "disciplinary perspectives" included law, ethics, and economics but not organization behavior/theory, social psychology, sociology, or political science.[15] One sees the result in the author index. DiMaggio is cited three times, Kramer twice, Pfeffer twice, Weick twice, and high-profile names such as Argote, Bazerman, Dutton, Hackman, Neale, Staw, and Tushman not once—even though a number of them, such as Weick, Staw, and Bazerman, situate some of their research in government. By contrast, the index is full of names that are unfamiliar in mainstream organization studies and political science—Pollitt is cited 80 times, Bouckaert 32 times, and Frederickson 17 times.

The ghetto is unequal, having only now begun to undertake a transition to modern social science methodologies that became common elsewhere after the field became ghettoized.[16] Public administration has roots in prescription and close ties to practitioners. *Public Administration Review (PAR)*, traditionally the field's most important journal, began in 1940 as the organ of the American Society for Public Administration, an association with mostly practitioner members, and thus, the journal has always needed to appeal to practitioners, inhibiting methods advance.[17] An examination of dissertations for 1981 concluded that only 42% "tested a theory or a causal statement" and that 21% had research designs even "potentially valid"; fewer than one fourth of the articles in *PAR* between 1975 and 1984 discussed relationships among variables (Perry & Kraemer, 1986). More recently, few efforts have been made empirically to evaluate the wave of public management reform, something, an empirically oriented researcher lamented, that "the academic community has not taken seriously" (Boyne, 2003, p. 2). Lynn (1996), a senior scholar critical of the field's standards, wrote that public administration failed to "develop habits of reasoning, intellectual exchange, and criticism appropriate to a scholarly field" (p. 7).

Public Administration Separatism

Public organizations are, of course, both "public" and "organizations." In its ghetto, public administration has taken a separatist turn. Like ethnic separatisms, public administration separatism defines itself by emphasizing how it differs from the larger world. This means fixating on the unique "public" part of public organizations and neglecting, even proudly, the "organization" part connecting the field to a larger world. Thus, the central separatist theme is opposition to what is designated (e.g., Peters & Pierre, 2003; Pollitt, 1990; Wamsley et al., 1990) as "generic management"—the view that organizations share enough common features about which generalizations may be made to make it useful to study agencies and firms together.[18]

A number of public administration scholars (e.g., Allison, 1986; Bozeman, 1987; Perry & Rainey, 1988; Rainey, Backoff, & Levine, 1976) have written about differences and similarities between public and private organizations. Obviously, the two are alike in some ways and different in others. Which aspect one emphasizes is not ontological but normative. This is partly because one may attach different value to ways organizations are alike or different. If one cares about performance, this directs attention to similarities, since performance drivers (e.g., determinants of successful teams or design of coordination mechanisms) are often similar. In addition, emphasizing similarity or difference is partly normative because one may criticize (and advocate reform of) some ways agencies are empirically different, if these differences impede good performance in government.

Mainstream research, centered in business schools, became isomorphic to its environment—coming to focus on performance issues, which is what firms care about. Walsh, Weber, and Margolis (2003) found individual or organization performance was far more likely to be the dependent variable in empirical papers in the *Academy of Management Journal* than institutional or societal welfare.[19] One thinks of research on determinants of team performance and successful negotiation outcomes, or of all strategy literature, which deals in various ways with determinants of firms' economic success. In addition, research on topics such as cognitive biases, organizational citizenship behavior, and escalation of commitment all involve phenomena linked to organization performance. As human resources management research has become more "strategic," it has become more associated with the impact of human resources policies on organization performance.[20]

Since separation, the dominant current in public administration has also become isomorphic with its environment. In this case, however, this meant the field moved backward from the central reformist concern of its founders with improving government performance and, instead, developed a focus on constraints. Had public administration been part of the mainstream, such isomorphism would have been tempered by exposure to a larger universe of organizations.

Development of Public Administration: A History and Synthesis

This section presents a synthesizing account of the field's development, discussing (a) the founding decades, (b) the separation from mainstream organization studies, (c) practitioner-led reforms of the last decades and reactions to them, and (d) the rise of a "public management" current. The unifying theme will be the changing relation of public administration research to performance improvement in government.

The Founding Decades

At the beginning, there was performance—or, to use that era's idiom, promotion of "economy and efficiency."[21] White's (1926) early text stated, "The objective of public administration is the most efficient utilization of the resources at the disposal of officials and employees" (p. 2). Gulick (1937) wrote, "In the science of administration, whether public or private, the basic 'good' is efficiency" (pp. 191–192). The founders of public administration were reformers, promoting good management as a means to improve government performance. White argued that growth of the state's role in society had increased interest in "the business side of government." He continued, "More and more clearly it is being understood that the promise of American life will never be realized until American administration has been lifted out of the ruts in which it has been left by a century of neglect" (White, 1926, pp. 9, 13; see also Wilson, 1887).

The founders specifically established the field in distinction to public law, which emphasized constraints. White (1926) stated "the study of administration should start from the base of management rather than the foundation of law, and is therefore more absorbed in the affairs of the American Management Association than in the decisions of the courts" (p. 2). While public law's major objective was "protection of private rights," public administration's main objective was "efficient conduct of public business" (White, 1926, pp. 4–5). Three chapters in White's text discussed legislative and judicial control of agencies, the other 28 organization design and personnel management.

Herbert Simon and Dwight Waldo: The Road Not Taken[22]

Shortly after World War II, two young scholars each published widely noted books: Herbert Simon (1947) published *Administrative Behavior*, and Dwight Waldo (1948) published *The Administrative State*. At the time, Simon was clearly a public administration scholar. His first published article (Simon, 1937) was about municipal performance measures. One cannot read *Administrative Behavior* without noticing that it is written from a public administration perspective. And three years later, Simon (Simon et al., 1950) coauthored *Public Administration*. Waldo, by contrast, received his Ph.D. (on which he based his book) in political philosophy. Each, with the iconoclasm of youth, criticized the field's founders. Each, however, urged the field in different directions, and they argued with each other over the next few years (Simon, 1952; Waldo, 1952).

The two had different subsequent histories. Simon became an icon of social science and won the Nobel Prize for economics. Waldo became an icon of public administration: The American Society of Public Administration's highest scholarly award is named after him, and 60 years later, his book was the subject of a retrospective collection titled *Revisiting Waldo's Administrative State* (Rosenbloom & McCurdy, 2006).[23] One continued an astonishingly productive career, while the other wrote little but elucidations of his first book.[24] Waldo's *The Administrative State* helped set public administration on a separatist path. Simon's *Administrative Behavior* represented a road not taken.

Simon began his book with a blistering attack on existing public administration, exemplified by Gulick, for promulgating "proverbs" regarding organization design that suffered from the double flaw of poor logic (some contradicted each other) and lack of empirical testing. Methodologically, Simon called on public administration, as a science of human behavior, to associate itself with social psychology and, more generally, to test propositions about organizations in a more scientific way. Substantively, Simon endorsed the founders' support for "efficiency" as the criterion to judge organizations, although adding a focus on making good organizational decisions was not present in the founding literature. As Bertelli and Lynn (2006) have noted, Waldo later argued—correctly, I think—that, although his attack on the founders is remembered, Simon, with his interest in science and efficiency, actually had much in common with them (p. 50). As noted earlier in this chapter, Simon also endorsed the founders' interest in common elements across organizations. Simon pointed public administration on a path that would have reached out to the emerging field of organization studies.

Waldo's critique of the founders was the opposite of Simon's. Waldo denounced the founders' preoccupation with efficiency. He also rejected their aspirations to science, not for poor execution (as with Simon) but rather for ignoring values, particularly the importance of democracy. He argued that the founders sought expert administration, questionable from a democratic perspective, and centralized hierarchy, violating democracy at work. Waldo believed the field needed to redirect attention toward the creation of "democratic administration"—greater popular participation in setting direction for agencies and greater employee participation inside them. Seen from the perspective of this review, Waldo disparaged the field's attention to how well agencies performed and urged focus instead on process—perhaps the most important constraints that government organizations face, but constraints nonetheless. Waldo's style also displayed great literary flair—a style the field sought to imitate—, but one that Simon (1952) distained as "loose, literary, [and] metaphorical" (p. 496).

In the early 1950s, Simon left public administration to transform the Carnegie Institute of Technology's business school into a research-oriented institution. March and Simon's (1958) *Organizations* was about organizations in general, with no particular government orientation. (March went to Carnegie after getting a degree in political science.) Cyert and March's (1963) *A Behavioral Theory of the Firm,* specifically dealing with business, followed. Simon's departure was a tragic loss. The field was small enough that the departure of one young, prominent figure actually made a difference, especially at a crucial time when organization studies was growing rapidly in disciplines not traditionally connected to public administration and, thus, when building new links was crucial. One may also speculate that Waldo's approach was attractive for a field traditionally close to political science but now distained by that discipline for preoccupation with "manhole covers"; that by turning to political philosophy, public administration might regain its esteem.

The Political Turn in the Road

In the view of public administration founders, a dividing line existed between "politics," where elected officials decide, and "administration," where unelected officials should hold sway (Goodnow, 1914; Wilson, 1887). In Goodnow's classic formulation, politics "has to do with policies or expressions of the state will," while administration "with the execution of these policies" (p. 1). The founders erected this separation to give unelected officials breathing room from interference from politicians who cared about patronage rather than performance.

Such a line is empirically unrealistic and normatively debatable. Empirically, career officials are strongly involved in policy formulation, as sources of substantive policy ideas and judgments about whether proposals make sense and (often) as advocates for a point of view (generally one consistent with values their agency's mission embodies). After laws are passed, political decision making by unelected officials continues. Administrative discretion is inevitable in determining specifics of regulations (Kelman, 1981)—How many parts per million of sulfur dioxide should be allowed in the air? Should auto safety regulations require airbags?—as well as for frontline "street-level bureaucrats" (Lipsky, 1980; Maynard-Moody & Musheno, 2003) deciding how to apply policies and, generally, how to treat the public. It is easy, however, to see why a policymaking role for unelected officials might be seen as problematic in a democracy. Finer (1941) proposed, as a normative matter, that the proper role of administrators toward elected officials was "subservience;" this is the most straightforward form of the democratic accountability of unelected officials. There, however, would appear to be nothing undemocratic about a congressional decision to give discretion to such officials—based on the substantive advantages this brings—as long as the decision is itself democratically made.

Following World War II, attacking the politics/administration dichotomy became a major theme in public administration, perhaps as some scholars received government experience and became involved in policymaking. Unelected officials' participation in the political process was a major element in Appleby's (1949) work and in Gaus' (1950) widely noted essay, included in the 10th anniversary edition of *PAR*, called "Trends in the Theory of Public Administration," which concluded with the flourish, "A theory of public administration means in our time a theory of politics also" (p. 168). Most importantly, a version of this theme—increasing democratic participation in administration—was central to Waldo's alternative to the founders.[25]

As public administration followed Waldo, these issues became central to the field. An analysis of public administration theory (Denhardt, 1990) concluded that the main change between the 1950s and the 1980s was a shift from "positivist" organizational research to "subjective" discussions about the relationship between administration and politics. The analysis reviewed theory articles in *PAR* between 1980 and 1985 and classified the major topics as "the role of the public bureaucracy in the governance process," "the ethics of public service" (identified as "one striking shift in the priorities of public administration theorists in the 1980s"), "citizenship and civic education," "alternative epistemologies" (mainly questioning positivism, which, some may argue, never established a firm foothold in the field in the first place), contributions "to organization theory generally," and public choice theory (Denhardt, 1990). Of these, only contributions "to organization theory generally" tied the field to mainstream organization studies.

Discussions during the 1970s and 1980s combined interest in this topic with an emerging separatism. The so-called "new public administration" (Marini, 1971) was a movement of young, politically left-of-center scholars who were influenced by the turbulence of the 1960s and who argued that agencies and the field needed to pay more attention to social equity and Waldo's "democratic administration." The new public administration was "less 'generic' and more 'public' than its forebear" (Frederickson, 1971, p. 316). The so-called "Blacksburg Manifesto" scholars of the 1980s mixed separatism with strong support for an active political role for career officials. Wamsley (1990), in the lead essay in a "Blacksburg" volume, referred to "debilitatingly irrelevant intellectual baggage" inherited from the field's founders—"(borrowing) heavily from private-sector management techniques" rather than developing "its own theories, concepts, norms, or techniques" (p. 24). The "own theories" sought mostly involved justifying officials' wide participation in policymaking:

> The popular will does not reside solely in elected officials but in a constitutional order that envisions a remarkable variety of legitimate titles to participate in governance. The Public Administration, created by statutes based on this constitutional order, holds one of these titles. Its role, therefore, is not to cower before a sovereign legislative assembly or a sovereign elected executive [but rather] to share in governing wisely and well the constitutional order. (Wamsley et al., 1990, p. 47)

Both empirical and normative inquiries regarding administrators' roles in policymaking and the public's role in administration are legitimate, and there is no reason to criticize the field's initial postwar engagement, especially given the oversimplified view that the founders had articulated. Over the decades, however, pragmatic accommodations have been made between the principle of subordination of unelected officials to democratic control and the reality of a far less passive role for them. Many of these work better in practice than in theory. Democratic participation is also, of course, a problem in our societies, but except to observe the problem needs attention, the outpouring from public administration has not generated much theoretical or empirical progress, compared to work by those formally trained as political philosophers, which few public administration scholars are. This problem, therefore, seems to represent a gigantic exercise in what Freudians call "work avoidance"—looking for things to occupy oneself other than the difficult-to-solve performance problems that the government actually faces. Moreover, this turn created ghettoization, because these issues are unique rather than shared with organization studies.

The political turn also moved the field closer to concern about constraints (especially when emphasizing limits on actions of unelected officials); public law (e.g., Davis, 1969, 1978) is preoccupied with control of administrative discretion, which is considered a grave danger. Waldo (1968) urged public administration to move away from its hostility to administrative law. Cooper (1990) noted that public law had "experienced a resurgence in public administration" during the 1970s and 1980s, another move in the wrong direction, away from performance.

Enter the "New Public Management"

Over the past 20 years, what Kettl (2005) called "a remarkable movement to reform public management has swept the globe" (p. 1; see also Peters, 2001). Hood (1991) labeled this the "new public management"; in the United States, it came to be known as "reinventing government." The movement came from practitioners and sought public sector self-renewal—a break from the preoccupation with constraints in favor of a drive to improve performance.

Public management reform began in the early 1980s in New Zealand, the United Kingdom, and Australia (Kettl, 2005). In all cases, senior politicians initiated reform. In the background of all three countries was slow growth, fiscal crisis, and a widespread view that government was trying to do more than it could afford and not doing it well enough. In the United Kingdom, Margaret Thatcher initiated management reforms as part of an antigovernment, conservative ideology, though Tony Blair continued and deepened reform after the Labour party came to power in 1997. In New Zealand and Australia, left-of-center governments introduced management reforms. In the United States, reform grew from President Clinton and Vice President Gore's effort to reposition Democrats from traditional defense of "big government," while endorsing a positive government role.

In both New Zealand and the United Kingdom, the first reform measures involved efforts to reduce government spending—New Zealand introduced accrual accounting (to account for the full budgetary cost of programs upfront), and the United Kingdom introduced the "financial management initiative" to reduce waste.[26] In all these countries, the effort then expanded to include the use of performance measurement to establish a new context for public management, whereby managers would be freed from many process rules (e.g., for hiring or budgeting) in exchange for producing improved service/cost performance—a mixture of what became called "let managers manage" and "make managers manage." Public management reform also included a new attention to the importance of agencies providing good "customer service." Finally, all three countries had significant, state-owned infrastructure (e.g., power, railroads, and water), and reform also included privatization, as well as increased "contestability" for other services to competition between in-house and outsourced production.

In the United States, Osborne and Gaebler (1992), a journalist and a former city manager, published *Reinventing Government*, which, amazingly for a book about public management, became a bestseller and then the basis for the Clinton–Gore administration's "reinventing government" initiative—formally known, tellingly, as the National *Performance* Review. In the book, the authors argued for government that was "mission driven" rather than rules driven and for using results-oriented performance measures. The authors quoted Patton: "Never tell people how to do things. Tell them what you want them to achieve and they will surprise you with their ingenuity" (Osborne & Gaebler, 1992, p. 108). They argued that government should "steer not row" or, said differently, should set policy for service delivery but have services delivered through nongovernment parties. "Reinventing government" mixed management reform with workforce downsizing. Reformers attached themselves to a law that Congress passed to begin pushing performance measurement (Kettl, 2005). An effort was made to learn from business, as in the 1997 report *Businesslike Government: Lessons Learned from America's Best Companies* (Kettl & DiIulio, 1995). [28]

Politicians' promotion of management reform was quite visible. Less visibly, however, many career officials supported or promoted the efforts. In Sweden, career officials promoted management reform as early as the 1960s (Sundstrom, 2006), and in the United States, career officials promoted introducing total quality management into agencies at the end of the 1980s (Kaboolian, 2000). Teams of civil servants making suggestions for agency improvements produced most of the 1993 Gore reinventing government report (see also Kelman, 2005).

One central theme in reform efforts has been debureaucratization. For the founders, no trade-off existed between bureaucracy's constraint-promoting role and its impact on performance. White (1926) referred approvingly to Taylor's influence on public administration (p. 12). Classic discussions of organization design recommended centralized, hierarchical, and rule-driven organizations. [29] More recent reformers, however, have seen bureaucracy as an enemy of performance for reasons similar to Mintzberg's (1979) criticism of "machine bureaucracy" and Ouchi's (2003) analysis of public school management (undertaken without awareness of its relationship to new public management).

The Empire Strikes Back

Some public administration scholars embraced reform and aligned themselves with the performance movement. A new current, calling itself "public management" in conscious self-distinction to public administration, arose with its own version of performance orientation. Particularly in the United Kingdom, a disturbing proportion of the field, however, reacted with cranky skepticism or downright hostility, often displaying nostalgia for good old days of the public sector not needing to concern itself with pesky performance demands.[30] *PAR*'s three editors who served when new public management emerged were all negative. The field's two most recent handbooks (Ferlie, Lynn, & Pollitt, 2005; Peters & Pierre, 2003) were predominantly critical. A major theme of the essays in *Revisiting Waldo's Administrative State* was skepticism about new public management, something the book's introduction noted. The sad result has been that, "unlike in the transition to the twentieth century," when public sector reform was "led by the Progressives and orthodox public administration," current transformation efforts have proceeded "largely without intellectual or moral support from academia" (Kettl, 2002, p. 21).

In reacting to reform, public administration's separatist chickens came home to roost. Practitioners had unwittingly challenged the separatist turn. Thus, new public management caused separatism to become more self-conscious and to develop a theoretical defense of the primacy of constraints over goals in government going beyond any articulated before. Perhaps the most influential in the British torrent of attack was Pollitt's (1990) *Managerialism and the Public Service*, which popularized the phrase "manageralism" in public administration discourse.[31] Pollitt initially defined this as a belief "that better management will prove an effective solvent for a wide range of economic and social ills," which, absent the overdramatization, might not appear to be an "-ism" but just the unexceptional claim that good management improves performance.[32] Pollitt did not like the implication of generic management—"the transfer...of managerialism from private-sector corporations to welfare-state services represents the injection of an ideological 'foreign body' into a sector previously characterized by quite different traditions of thought" (pp. 1–2, 11). Rhodes (2002) stated, "The coming of the New Right with its love of markets heralded lean times for Public Administration...It found its prescriptions roundly rejected for private sector management skills and marketization" (p. 107). Frederickson (1997) worried about an "excessive and uncritical reliance upon the value assumptions of business administration" (p. 194) in government. Radin (2006) saw generic management as a major flaw of the "performance movement."

British critics associated new public management with the hostility of Thatcherite Conservatism to the public sector. "Managerialism has become a steadily more prominent component in the policies adopted by right-wing governments towards their public services...[It] is the 'acceptable face' of new-right thinking concerning the state" (Pollitt, 1990, p. 11). New public management has also been linked (e.g., Ferlie, Lynn, & Pollitt, 2005) with "public choice" theory, the application of microeconomics to the analysis of government. More broadly, the critics are ideologically skeptical of business.

Pollitt (1990) complained about new public management's "favourable analysis of the achievements of the corporate sector during the last half century" (p. 7). Savoie (1994) objected to "enthusiasm...for the merits of private enterprise" (p. 146). This antibusiness tone was illustrated by an aside that Peters (2001) appended in a footnote to his comment that supporters of the "customer" metaphor see it as trying to provide "the same expectations of quality that they have when dealing with a private-sector firm": "Those of us who deal regularly with airlines and Blue Cross-Blue Shield may consider being treated like the customer of a private concern to be a threat" (pp. 45, 206).

The critics disapproved of importing business terms into government, even those that one might regard in a positive light. An example is enmity against the word *customer*, as in *customer service* (e.g., du Gay, 2000, pp. 108–111; Peters, 2001, p. 45; Pollitt, 1990, pp. 45, 139).[33] Critics have gone beyond observations (Moore, 1995, pp. 36–38) that government "delivers" not just services but also obligations (e.g., to pay taxes or to obey laws), and beyond the observation that those who may be concerned about how a service is delivered often include more than the service's immediate recipients (e.g., consumers as well as farmers are affected by farm subsidies). Instead, critics have anxieties that are more sweeping about the word *customer* as a replacement for *citizen*—that it presents an image of a passive recipient rather than an active agent or an image of one as a selfish monad receiving personal benefits rather than as a participant in a collective enterprise.

Fretting about business metaphors has occasioned resurrection of the politics/administration dichotomy in the context of concern about introduction of the idea from business that public managers should behave as "entrepreneurs" (Doig & Hargrove, 1987). Terry (1993) called a *PAR* article, "Why We Should Abandon the Misconceived Quest to Reconcile Public Entrepreneurship with Democracy," concluding that "the concept is dangerous and thus, public administration scholars should avoid using it if at all possible" (p. 393). In an unfortunate passage, Peters (2001) maintained, "It is not clear that in systems of democratic accountability we really want civil servants to be extremely creative" (p. 113). Savoie (1994) stated, "Bureaucracy is designed to administer the laws and policies set by elected politicians, and as a result, authority delegated to career officials must be handled bureaucratically in order to accept direction" (p. 330).[34]

What should one make of this? Particularly in New Zealand, some of the intellectual underpinning of reform used principal-agent and public-choice theory (though, oddly, the Labour Party instituted reforms). It is legitimate to question public choice analysis for reasons similar to those appearing in mainstream organization theory criticizing principal-agent models and other import of microeconomics into organization studies (Ferraro, Pfeffer, & Sutton, 2005; Ghoshal & Insead, 1996). People also, of course, legitimately hold different views on the overall role of business in society. It, however, is flawed to elide the concern that health care will become a for-profit enterprise, available only to those able to pay for it, using management tools to improve performance, simply because for-profit firms use those tools. As for the customer idea, it works better in practice than in theory. In reality, the alternative to treating people as customers is not typically treating them like citizens but treating them like dirt. Since frontline staffs easily understand its meaning, the word "customer" provides a powerful metaphor for driving performance improvement.

A conscious defense of the primacy of constraints over goals emerged in embrace of what frequently became referred to as "traditional" public administration values.[35] Savoie (1994) worried about "rejecting traditional public-administration concerns with accountability and control, and giving way to the business-management emphasis on productivity, performance, and service to clients" (p. 283). Peters (2001) used the phrase "cherished traditions of personnel and financial management" (p. 36) to refer to bureaucratic rules; Peters' references to "traditional" values (e.g., probity, impartiality, etc.) appear in at least six places (pp. 88, 108, 121, 125, 129, 200). Thus, the bane of government is presented as a virtue. "Performance" is also presented as a negative word. Radin (2006) boldly called a book *Challenging the Performance Movement.* Lynn (2006) characterized a salutary, if innocuous, statutory change in the legal purpose of government training that the reinventing government program promoted—changing it from providing "training related to official duties" to "training to improve individual and organizational performance"— as supporting a "darker view of reinvention" (p. 113).

The critics rejected reformers' attacks on bureaucracy and embraced constraints. Du Gay's (2000) *In Praise of Bureaucracy* lauded bureaucracy for promoting constraints, while demeaning the significance of performance goals that the bureaucracy might harm. In DuGay's book, phrases such as "probity" and "reliability" abounded. Du Gay praised bureaucracy for being "ordered, cautious," while new public management judged agencies for "failure to achieve objectives which enterprise alone has set for it" (p. 87), presumably performance and cost consciousness. "If the rule of law is to be upheld and there is to be a system of accountability within government the hierarchy becomes the crucial link between ministers and the decisions taken in their name by their numerous subordinates in the field" (Peters & Wright, 1996, p. 632). Peters (2001) mused about "a return to the bureaucratic Garden of Eden" (p. 200).

Sometimes, the tone is lackadaisical, displaying the opposite of the urgency about performance that reformers sought and evoking the atmosphere of a gentleman's club. Du Gay (2000) belittled "a 'can do' approach to the business of government" and the "dangers that the demand for enthusiasm pose" (pp. 92–93) to the traditional role of civil servants as advisors who, without displaying commitment, present ministers with options and emphasize pitfalls of proposals.[36] The literature on "public service motivation," to be discussed in the following section, argues that commitment to agency mission is an important source of motivation for good performance in government, counteracting the more meager economic incentives agencies can offer. Du Gay, however, mocked the effort of one senior civil servant "to ensure that her staff were infused with a discernible sense of 'mission'" (p. 129). Similarly, though others believe fresh blood often invigorates organizations, du Gay was skeptical of recruiting outsiders. He quoted a business manager brought in to run an agency who stated, "I don't expect to become a 'civil servant,'" and said, "Quite what benefits are meant to accrue from having someone occupying a senior position within the Civil Service who doesn't want to be a civil servant are not at all clear" (pp. 128–129).

Although many critics of new public management come from the political left, this emphasis suggests traditionalist conservatism as well. Terry (1990) cited Burke's worry about subjecting "our valuable institutions" to the "mercy of untried speculations" (p. 401). Radin (2006) fretted about "unintended consequences" of using performance measures to improve performance (pp. 16–19), which, as Hirschman (1991) noted in *The Rhetoric of Reaction*, is a classic conservative argument against change—the "perversity thesis" that "everything backfires" (chapter 2).[37]

Contemporary bureaucracy advocates should take pause that Austrian economists such as von Mises and Hayek, who advocated a very limited government role in society, favored a bureaucratic form of government organization because it promoted impartial treatment and consistency over time, which they saw as important ways that government allowed markets to work (Armbruster, 2005). For these economists, constraints loomed large because they believed government's goals should be modest. For those envisioning a more active government role, this should be disquieting.

In their defense, critics were correct to note that issues with the special contexts of government often make performance improvement efforts harder than in firms. It is also easy to sympathize with the sarcastic dismissal of guru nostrums, often taken from business bestsellers, which have formed part of public management reform. Furthermore, the bark in the critiques is often worse than the bite. Pollitt (1990) softened his antimanagerialist message considerably in his last chapters, though this is not what is generally remembered. The "alternatives" to managerialism that he presented all "place performance and quality (as defined by consumers) above unreflective rule-following or conformity to precedent"; Pollitt agreed that it might be argued that all the major alternatives point in roughly the same direction as managerialism (p. 175). Radin (2006) stated in her last chapter that the "performance movement" needed to change its ways and democratically "involve a range of actors" in establishing performance goals, but few performance measurement advocates would disagree. Du Gay (2000) stated, "The function of officials…

cannot be exhaustively defined in terms of achieving results with maximum 'economic efficiency,' 'value for money' or 'best value.' There is [sic] a host of other obligations and responsibilities imposed on state officials" (p. 144); this is not exceptional, except that earlier pages were confined to belittling concern with results. None of all this added up to the animus that animates these attacks.

Performance-Oriented Scholarship in Public Administration

Public administration has a minority performance-oriented contingent, many of them scholars at the University of Georgia and the University of Syracuse, two of the strongest U.S. public administration programs. Rainey's (2003) text *Understanding and Managing Public Organizations* took a performance-oriented approach and cited some mainstream organization literature.[38] In a lecture to the American Society of Public Administration, Ingraham (2005) stated, "Performance matters so much for government...that we *must* keep the fundamental performance promise: Our only choice is to use taxpayer and donor dollars in the very best way possible" (p. 391, emphasis in original). Ingraham, Joyce, and Donahue (2003) reported on the Government *Performance* Project (for state governments) and the Federal *Performance* Project, both foundation-funded efforts designed to provide information to inform the public, rather than to constitute research.[39] The projects measured and rated management capacity, which the authors defined as "government's intrinsic ability to marshal, develop, direct, and control its financial, human, physical, and information resources" (Ingraham et al., 2003, p. 15). Unfortunately, measurement was limited to management systems (though these included a capacity to "manage for results" by developing and using performance measures) rather than to substantive performance. To explain senior federal government manager performance, Selden and Brewer (2000) used a structural equation model with employee survey data to test Locke and Latham's (1990a; 1990b) "high performance cycle." Perry and colleagues (e.g., Angle & Perry, 1981; Lee & Perry, 2002) empirically examined issues, such as employee motivation in the public sector and the impact of information technology investments on government productivity. In a series of papers, Meier and O'Toole (2002, 2003; O'Toole & Meier, 2003) examined the influence of various managerial and organizational practices on variance in school-level performance on Texas educational tests. In the United Kingdom, a group at Cardiff University (e.g., Boyne, 2006; Boyne, Meier, O'Toole, & Walker, 2006) studied local government performance using variance across them for quantitative empirical analysis.

Public Management

Scholars interested in government performance improvement usually come from public policy schools or think tanks. During the 1970s, several universities (e.g.,

Harvard, Berkeley, Duke, Michigan, Texas at Austin, and Minnesota) established master's degree programs in Public Policy as opposed to Public Administration. The distinction involved the greater attention that public policy programs gave to the substance of policies (e.g., health or national security policy), analyzed using microeconomics, prescriptive decision theory, and econometric evaluation research. Starting at Harvard, however, these programs also began a new current in studying public organizations called "public management."

Public management was defined two ways. First, it focused on the behavior of top executives rather than on issues that were of more interest to middle or functional managers (Rainey, 1990, p. 162).[40] Second, to many, the word *management* rather than *administration* sounded more muscular, implying "a decisiveness and proactiveness that appear to be lacking in government" (p. 171). Public policy programs sought to train people "able to *move* an agency" rather than train them to play just "a custodial role" (Stokes, as cited in Lynn, 2003, p. 16).[41] Public management thus offered a new emphasis on performance. Although many U.S.-centric public management scholars had never heard the phrase "new public management," some wrote with sympathy about its ideas.[42]

The most important work in the public management tradition is Moore's (1995) *Creating Public Value*. The central concept in the book is "public value," or creation of government outputs that citizens value more than these outputs cost to produce. "The aim of managerial work in the public sector is to create *public* value just as the aim of managerial work in the *private* sector is to create private value" (p. 28, emphasis in original).

Moore (1995) criticized the expectation, perpetuated by the political system, that public managers "be faithful agents of...mandates," which "produces a characteristic mindset...of administrators or bureaucrats rather than of entrepreneurs, leaders, or executives" (p. 17). This mindset "denies the public sector the key ingredient on which the private sector specifically relies to remain responsive, dynamic, and value creating: namely, the adaptability and efficiency that come from using the imaginations of people called managers to combine what they can sense of public demands with access to resources and control over operational capacity to produce value" (p. 17).

Creating Public Value sought to promote "strategic management" in government. Broadly, this meant that "instead of simply devising the means for achieving mandated purposes, [managers] become important agents in helping to discover and define what is valuable to do. Instead of being responsible only for guaranteeing continuity, they become important innovators in changing what public organizations do and how they do it" (p. 20). Moore saw managerial discretion as "an opportunity for leadership." He specifically stated that business schools' work on corporate strategy was relevant to thinking about strategy for a public manager. A public manager's strategy, Moore argued, should have three elements—goals reflecting the public value that agencies seek to create; an account of how one can achieve support for these goals in the "authorizing environment;" and a plan to create operating capacity to achieve the goals. Since all of these jobs are in service of creating public value, Moore's greatest contribution may be expanding demands on the manager for what he or she needs to achieve good performance—not only to create operating capacity but also to participate in the political process.

Another influential book is Barzelay's (1992) *Breaking Through Bureaucracy.* The book is based on a case study of the transformation of an overhead organization in Minnesota, responsible for personnel, purchasing, information technology, and other administrative functions, into two separate organizations: (a) a fee-for-service voluntary source of purchasing and information technology services and (b) an oversight function responsible for regulatory control of these areas. Barzelay characterized public management reform as a break from the "bureaucratic paradigm" of the Progressive era in favor of a "postbureaucratic paradigm." He presented a number of contrasts between the two—the former "defines itself both by the amount of resources it controls and by the tasks it performs" and the latter "by the results it achieves for its customers" (p. 8).

Other scholars at public policy schools embraced a performance orientation that focused, more than Moore, on internal operations instead of the agency's external environment. Bardach's (1998) *Getting Agencies to Work Together* is a study of cross-agency collaborations in which agencies took joint responsibility for delivering a service (e.g., social services for people with multiple problems). His book was methodologically and prescriptively the strongest of the growing but generally weak literature on this topic. Bardach's first chapter is straightforwardly called "Creating Value Through Collaboration," and it endorses "managing for results" and managerial "purposiveness" ("a combination of public spiritedness and creativity;" p. 6). Behn's (1991) *Leadership Counts,* a case study of a successful state program training disadvantaged workers, sought to explain, in a guru-like style, management practices that help explain successful performance. Behn's (2001) *Rethinking Democratic Accountability,* an important theoretical work, argued that government agencies' accountability should change from accountability for process and rule-following—respecting constraints—to results (performance) accountability. Behn was also the most prolific of the public management scholars who wrote about nonfinancial performance measurement (e.g., 1991, 2003, 2006). Kelman's (1990) *Procurement and Public Management* had an antibureaucracy thrust similar to Barzelay. Kelman's (2005) *Unleashing Change* was a quantitative empirical study that analyzed a survey of 1,600 frontline civil servants, studying a change process in the procurement system that was part of "reinventing government" and that sought to implement ideas from Kelman's (1990) earlier book.

To this list one should also add scholars at think tanks, most prominently Kettl and Light, then of the Brookings Institution. Kettl, Ingraham,

Sanders, and Horner (1996) wrote a study on civil service reform that was subtitled "Building a Government that Works." They noted, "Government's performance can only be as good as the people who do its work," and they called to debureaucratize a system that created inflexibility and insufficiently rewarded good performance and to build a "culture of performance" along with "a culture of public service" (pp. 3–5).[43] Light's (2005) *Four Pillars of High Performance* presented research by RAND about organizational performance, although the book's orientation was not limited to government agencies.[44] Using an interesting methodology, Light asked RAND researchers to think about the organization they knew best, inquired about practices at the organization, and then used regression to develop predictors of high performance, such as delegating authority for routine decisions, investing in new ideas, and managing using performance measures, three of the seven strongest predictors. Altshuler and Behn (1997) and Borins (1998), university-based academics, wrote about determinants of government innovation using applications to the Ford Foundation/Kennedy School of Government, Innovations in American Government award program as their data source.

What should one make of the public management current? One of its remarkable features is that it has created a wedge between preoccupation with the political role of unelected officials and public administration separatism: It incorporates participation of unelected officials in the political process, but in service of better agency performance.

More generally, public management is often seen as radically departing from public administration tradition; however, I believe one should see it as the heir of the field's founders. This is an unconventional view. True, the founders advocated separating politics and administration; indeed, Moore (1995) saw this as the essence of "traditional doctrines of public administration" that he was criticizing (pp. 21, 74–76). However, their actual purpose was to argue for the *importance* of public administration: Politics and administration were to be kept separate so agencies could perform effectively, without political interference that was likely to be indifferent to competence. Furthermore, as stated earlier in this chapter, it is unfair to suggest that more recent public administration scholarship accepted this dichotomy. Second, the founders used different language, such as "economy and efficiency" rather than "performance." Barzelay (1992) contrasted "efficiency" from the bureaucratic paradigm with "quality and value" in postbureaucracy (pp. 118–121). I would argue that, although the words do indeed suggest different emphases, both worry about goals rather than constraints. Finally, the founders advocated the bureaucratic form and "scientific management," while contemporary performance advocates seek to "break through bureaucracy." However, the founders would have argued that bureaucracy would best produce the "results" that Barzelay favors—though they would not have used that language.

Lastly, virtually all public management literature uses case studies—with few using quantitative or experimental work—making it methodologically weaker than the best work coming from public administration, from both younger and older scholars. This is partly because of the focus on top leader behavior, which drives one-off accounts and partly because of Harvard Business School's influence on Harvard's Kennedy School. The literature also heavily focuses on "best practice" studies, which Lynn (1996) rightly criticized for selection on the dependent variable. The public management turn, therefore, has produced no *methodological* renewal.

Public Management: A Research Agenda for Organization Studies

A number of issues are more important in a government than in a business context because they involve organizational phenomena that are more central to agencies than to firms. For this reason, these issues have been underresearched in mainstream organization studies, though they fit comfortably into a mainstream sensibility. An organization studies research agenda that took public management seriously—and a public administration research agenda that took goals and, hence, performance, seriously—would thus increase attention to the following.

Bureaucratic organization forms. This issue has virtually disappeared from the mainstream screen since Mintzberg (1979), except for interesting work about how routines evolve (e.g., Feldman, 2000; Levinthal & Rerup, 2006; Pentland & Feldman, 2003). Bureaucratic organizations' impacts on performance and on alternatives to bureaucracy remain important to government. Research questions might, for example, include (a) interaction effects between bureaucratic structure and dispositions or between internal rules and the nature of external (e.g., media) oversight in explaining behavioral reactions to a bureaucratic environment; (b) field experiments examining performance impacts of differentially rule-bound or hierarchical environments in different decision situations and for different employees; and (c) techniques that managers might use to counteract the signal a rule-bound environment sends that one's job consists of nothing beyond following rules.

Nonfinancial performance measurement. New public management has promoted use of nonfinancial performance measures as the public sector's counterpart to profit. Some theoretical and empirical literature on the topic from public administration and economics exists (e.g., Hatry, 1999; Propper & Wilson, 2003), as does significant mainstream literature on goal setting's impact on performance (Latham, 2007). The topic needs considerable additional theoretical and empirical work (particularly fieldwork in agencies) about performance measurement as a performance-enhancing intervention in the absence of financial incentives for employees to meet goals.[45]

Public service motivation. There is evidence (e.g., Brehm & Gates, 1999; Crewson, 1997; Frank & Lewis, 2004; Houston, 2000; Jurkiewicz et al., 1998) that better performance, which is elicited by extrinsic incentives in firms, can be elicited by intrinsic rewards in government service. The general topic of motivating good performance using noncash incentives, and the specific question of how managers can encourage public service motivation (Grant, 2007), needs better empirical/theoretical work.

Rare events: Emergency management, finding terrorists.   Government agencies must frequently prepare for the unusual, seek out needles in haystacks, and display high-reliability performance. Performing well in such situations requires a mix of operational (e.g., managing surge capacity) and cognitive (e.g., noticing the unusual in the first place) capabilities. Much of the existing literature about "situational awareness" has an individual cognition, engineering flavor (e.g., Endsley, Bolte, & Jones, 2003). Snook (2000) discussed situation awareness in an organization context and, indeed, a government context (F-15 fighters accidentally shooting down Army helicopters over northern Iraq in 1994).[46] A small body of literature also exists about high-reliability organizations, from both public administration (e.g., LaPorte & Consolini, 1991; Rochlin, 1996) and organization studies (Weick & Sutcliffe, 2001). Weick and Sutcliffe's research program, I believe, should be more rigorously empirical in its examination of mindfulness and of whether trade-offs exist between routine performance and mindfulness. Tushman and O'Reilly's (1996) "ambidexterity" construct, both for emergency management and for detecting weak environmental change signals (e.g., new terrorist tactics), may be relevant here as well but needs operationalization in a government context.

Interorganizational production and governance.   In recent years, it has become common to speak of a shift from "government" to "governance" in delivering public performance. Governance involves "the processes and institutions, both formal and informal, that guide and restrain the collective activities of a group," while government is "the subset that acts with authority and creates formal obligations" (Keohane & Nye, 2000, p. 12). Kettl (2002) noted, "'Governance' is a way of describing the links between government and its broader environment" (p. 119). To some extent, this literature parallels that of organization studies about cross-firm alliances (e.g., Powell, 1990; Podolny & Page, 1998).

The overwhelming bulk of cross-boundary production occurs through contracting and other indirect policy tools that Salamon (1981; 2002) discusses, as well as through collaboration within government across agency boundaries (Agranoff & McGuire, 2003; Bardach, 1998; Huxham & Vangen, 2005; Thomas, 2003). Enough examples, however, exist—from mundane "adopt a highway" programs, to momentous public-private collaboration against terrorism—that newer forms of "collaborative governance" should not be ignored (Selsky & Parker, 2005).

Contracting is a crucial way that public services are delivered (Kettl, 1988; Kelman, 2002), and is more important in agencies than in firms. Determinants of contractor performance have received some attention in organization studies, often from a transaction-cost economics perspective (e.g., Mayer & Argyres, 2004; Mayer & Nickerson, 2005; Srinivasan & Brush, 2006). There are also a few empirical articles are about this topic in a government context (Brown & Potoski, 2003, 2006; Milward & Provan, 2003; Provan & Milward, 1995). Compared to its importance in government, this domain is underresearched. For contracting, the main question is about predictors of contractor performance; in particular, more work that is empirical and that tests the performance impact of relational/trust-based models versus principal-agent models is needed for contract management (Van Slyke, 2007), including possible impacts of moderator variables. For cross-agency collaboration, questions involve incentives for collaboration and evolution of collaborative institutions absent (in contrast to cross-firm alliances) a profit incentive, as well as collaborations' impact on performance, about which researchers know virtually nothing. Important questions about "governance" fall outside of the areas that mainstream organization theory has hitherto studied. In a world where organization studies took government seriously, however, that would be an opportunity, not a problem.

Conclusion

The agendas of those researching government and business will never be identical. Both kinds of organizations have important, unique issues. Those interested in public management, for example, care little about corporate strategy research. It is possible, however, to mix questions from mainstream organization theory creatively with the special political context of government; examples are Hammond and Thomas' (1989) work about departmentalization design decisions and broader work (e.g., Moe, 1993) about the impact of political choices regarding agency location on agency decisions.

Greater involvement in public management problems would be good for mainstream organization studies. Research access to agencies is relatively easy. Rich presence of archival and memoir data makes agencies a fruitful research location, an opportunity that some who study decision making, leadership, escalation of commitment, social loafing, and sense making (e.g., Eden, 2004; Snook, 2000; Staw, 1981) already use. Greater public sector involvement can be good for organization studies for another reason. Isolating public administration from organization studies encouraged the former to pay too much attention to constraints; it also discouraged the latter from paying enough attention to ethical issues for firms. Exposure to a public environment may encourage rebalancing. Scholars studying business may furthermore be able to adapt material that public administration scholars have developed about managing constraints to a business context.[47]

Most importantly, the public sector needs help with its performance problems. Mainstream organization studies can provide help by having mainstream scholars engage these problems and by providing public administration exposure to the mainstream to give public administration a greater dose of the performance orientation that the government needs, as well as of the contemporary methods that can generate research that is useful to help the government.

Acknowledgment

I would like to thank Bob Behn, Sandy Borins, Hannah Riley Bowles, Trevor Brown, Adam Grant, Rod Kramer, David Lazer, Todd Pitinsky, Matt Potoski, Hal Rainey, and Fred Thompson, as well as the editors, Jim Walsh and Art Brief, for helpful comments on a draft. I would also like to thank Carl Loof for helpful research assistance.

Endnotes

1. It should be noted that many outside of the field have rightly criticized the casualness about causality in regression-based analysis that marks much of mainstream organization research.
2. To be sure, mainstream organization studies have suffered ongoing bouts of anxiety (e.g., Rynes, Bartunek, & Daft, 2001) that its research is insufficiently useful to practitioners. Furthermore, of course, one should not, of course, exaggerate the successes of mainstream research in generating results conclusive enough to be used for performance improvement, though the nihilist view that we have learned nothing would also be wrong.
3. Wilson (1989) used the word *tasks* to describe what I call "goals," and Simons used the phrase "boundary systems" to describe what I call "constraints."
4. In linear programming or economics, one often speaks of maximizing goals subject to constraints.
5. A helpful way to think about the difference between goals and constraints, although it does not apply perfectly, is in terms of the common distinction in moral philosophy between "negative" and "positive" duties (Russell, 1980; Tooley, 1980). Negative duties are those that require one to refrain from some action (e.g., do not kill), and positive duties are those that require one to undertake some action (e.g., save people who are dying). Constraints can generally be respected if an organization does nothing—if an agency lets no contracts, it will not violate the constraint that contracting officials should not award contracts to relatives; if it has no program to combat terrorism, it will not risk violating the due process rights of terrorist suspects. Meeting goals almost always requires action. Simons (1995) stated, "If I want my employees to be creative and entrepreneurial, am I better off telling them what to do or telling them what not to do? The answer is the latter. Telling people what to do by establishing standard operating procedures and rule books discourages the initiative and creativity unleashed by empowered, entrepreneurial employees. Telling them what not to do allows innovation, but within clearly defined limits…Boundary systems are stated in negative terms or as minimum standards" (p. 84). One should also distinguish between constraints

and multiple goals. If the U.S. government seeks good relations with India and Pakistan (where improving relations with one may hurt relations with the other), the State Department faces multiple goals. These are not the same as constraints. Those arguing for a "stakeholder" rather than a "shareholder" view of the firm are typically arguing for the importance of goals other than shareholder wealth maximization, although sometimes they are also arguing that greater attention should be paid to constraints (e.g., accounting ethics). Thus, Freeman and McVen (as cited in Sundaram & Inkpen, 2004) argued, "The stakeholder framework does not rely on a single overriding management objective for all decisions," and Clarkson (1995, p. 112) argued, "The economic and social purpose of the corporation is to create and distribute wealth and value to all its primary stakeholder groups." In both cases, the corporation is pursuing goals—creating value that then must be distributed—not merely respecting constraints.

6. More broadly, greater attention is paid in government to mistakes than to achievements. White (1926) observed that public officials perceive that "whenever we make a mistake, some one jumps on us for it, but whenever we do something well nobody pays any attention to us. We never get any recognition except when we get 'bawled out'" (p. 243–244). Half a century later, Derek Rayner, the CEO of Marks and Spencer brought into the British government under Thatcher, noted that, in government, "Failure is always noted and success is forgotten" (Rayner, as cited in Hennessy, 1989, p. 595).

7. These are long-standing facts about government. In an earlier era (and still in many countries, especially in the developing world), constraints were often violated (e.g., by corruption or political favoritism), making respect for constraints a more natural part of the political agenda. White (1926) noted that government needed to apply a standard of consistent treatment of cases in a way unnecessary in business. The long-standing focus on constraints explains the lack of attention, until recent decades, to development of nonfinancial performance measures in government—agencies' most important counterparts to firms' profit measure—including issues of measurement and standardization (a counterpart to GAAP for nonfinancial government performance metrics).

8. The bureaucratic form has become so associated with government that, for example, Wilson's (1989) classic book on government agencies was simply titled *Bureaucracy*, and political scientists generally refer to government agencies generically by the name "the bureaucracy."

9. Over the last 30 years, a distinction has developed between those who call the field "public management" and those who continue to use the older phrase "public administration." The significance of this terminological pluralism will be discussed in a later section.

10. Lewin's (1958) early research about attitude change in groups, while not involving small groups inside government, was about how agencies might persuade people to eat odd cuts of meat during wartime rationing.

11. The second number includes students studying social work, so the real contrast is larger. The number of MBA students has more than doubled since 1980, while the number of MPA/social work students has increased by about half.

12. In 1986 one conservative columnist wrote, "We should be eternally grateful that government is stupid and bungling," and added, "I want a government that is stupid, lethargic, and low-performing." Barry Goldwater expressed a similar sentiment in *The Conscience of a Conservative* (Behn, 2005, pp. 1–2).

13. Although this will not be a major theme in this chapter because it centers on organization studies, parallel to the separation of public administration from organization studies, a separation from political science, the other discipline to which the field was traditionally connected, has also occurred. The reasons were somewhat different. During the 1950s, political science began using more sophisticated, quantitative methods; in the 1980s, the field became interested in formal modeling. This favored research on individual voting behavior or congressional roll call votes over studies of organizations because large sample sizes made them more amenable to quantitative analysis. The new political science also had little sympathy for public administration's practical approach; in their view, "public administration concerns the lower things of government, details for lesser minds"—frequently ridiculed as obsession with "manhole covers" (Waldo, 1990, p. 74; see also Fesler, 1990; Kettl, 2002). Political science, therefore, began, in effect, to shun public administration. By 1962 the American Political Science Association (APSA) report, "Political Science as a Discipline," mentioned public administration "only in passing," and the 1983 APSA compendium did not even include it as a subfield (Henry, 1990; Kettl, 2002, p. 84). Currently, most of the meager body of political science research on organizations is written in a principal-agent tradition and discusses relations between legislatures and agencies (for summaries, see Bendor, 1990; Bendor, Glazer, & Hammond, 2001). A small body of work is closer to mainstream organization studies (e.g., Miller, 1992; Hammond, 1993). Carpenter's (2001) work about the efforts of senior public managers a century ago to build operating capacity and political support has an extraordinarily modern ring, although it involved managers working long ago.

14. The Public and Nonprofit division of the Academy of Management had 497 academic members as of 2006.

15. *The Handbook of Public Administration* (Peters & Pierre, 2003) had a section called "Organization Theory and Public Administration," although the topics discussed were idiosyncratic enough to suggest lack of broad familiarity with the field.

16. Younger scholars (e.g., Heinrich, 2000; Heinrich & Fournier, 2004; Bertelli, 2006; Hill, 2006) have tried to move the field toward mainstream social science. As this chapter proceeds, the reader may note the dominance of books over articles in citations. This is because the academic culture of emphasizing papers over books—reflecting a methodological shift to bounded empirical work—is just beginning in public management.

17. Mosher (1956) noted that, for this reason, the journal was "not itself an adequate or appropriate outlet for more than a very few research reports" (p. 272).

18. The phrase "generic" is negative, suggesting bland inferiority (e.g., to call wine "generic" is an insult).

19. For research about firms, the danger—and the worry the Walsh et al. paper expresses—is that constraints are underresearched (consider the somewhat orphan status of business ethics research). I will return to this toward the end of this chapter.

20. Some organization theory literature (e.g., Meyer & Gupta, 1994) has sought to problematize the concept of "performance" in organizations.

21. The phrases do not have the same connotation: "Economy and efficiency" suggested strong emphasis on saving money, i.e., treating performance as a constant, while reducing the cost of producing it (e.g., White, 1926; Gulick, 1937), while "performance" suggests emphasis on quality as a variable. However, one early author did argue, "When we say efficiency, we think of homes saved from disease, of boys and girls in school prepared for life, of ships and mines protected against disaster" (as cited in Waldo, 1948, p. 196). Both the words "efficiency" and "performance" are alternatives to emphasis on constraints.

22. Bertelli and Lynn's (2006) work was extremely helpful in preparing this section of the review (chapters 2–3).

23. Simon received the Waldo Award in 1999, a surreal event for many reasons, including their earlier hostility. The public administration section of the APSA actually conducted a formal debate at its 2005 meeting about whether *Administrative Behavior* or *The Administrative State* was the most influential public administration book of the previous 50 years (Rosenbloom & McCurdy, 2006b).

24. Bertelli and Lynn (2006, p. 179) noted the closing sentence in Waldo (1952) stating that Simon might become a major figure "if he can resist the temptation to make a career of defense of his first book" (p. 503) and then noting that this "is the fate that awaited Waldo."

25. Somewhat later, this became a theme in political science as well (e.g., Lowi, 1969; Aberbach, Putnam, & Rockman, 1981; Gruber, 1987).

26. The United States went through a similar effort around the same time with the Reagan-era "Grace Commission," named after a corporate CEO who headed an effort led by private sector managers to identify wasteful spending produced by poor management.

27. The spread of reform might be analyzed through a neo-institutionalist lens as a fad, but the reinventing government program was launched with nary any foreign influence, and it is hard to imagine that Thatcher received her ideas from New Zealand.

28. By contrast, business managers brought in as volunteers had been responsible for the Reagan-era Grace Commission.

29. A contemporary descendent of this view is the argument for rules/standard operating procedures in terms of their roles in creating organizational capabilities (e.g., Nelson & Winter, 1982, chapter 6; March, Schulz, & Zhou, 2000).

30. The U.K. hostility is noteworthy in that these efforts have gone on long and visibly. The lack of empirical research is particularly unfortunate given the plethora of government-generated data that could be analyzed.

31. The expression recurs endlessly in the chapters in Ferlie, Lynn, and Pollitt (2005). This word occasionally appears in critical management studies theory (e.g., Clegg & Hardy, 1996), generally to mean a mainstream approach centering on managers in organizations rather than on workers or other constituencies.

32. Adding "-ism" to a common word typically warns of something ominous being hinted.

33. Another example is hostility to the idea of "entrepreneurship" among non-elected officials, a topic to which I will return in a slightly different context in the following section.

34. Other critics (e.g., Peters & Wright, 1996), however, expressed the opposite worry, that the distinction between "steering" and "rowing" in Osborne and Gaebler (1992), and hence in new public management, recreates the politics/administration divide, reducing the ability of nonelected officials to participate in policymaking.

35. The previous discussion of the founding decades of academic public administration suggests that, at least for the United States, the reference should be to traditional values in public-sector *practice* rather than to public administration *theory*.

36. The mainstream literatures on cognitive biases, groupthink, and escalation of commitment (e.g., Bazerman, 2005; Janis, 1982; Staw, 1981) indeed warns of dangers of premature commitment and inappropriate failure to consider disconfirmatory evidence. One should seek, however, to create ability for managers and organizations to reduce these problems in decision making while still taking advantage of the performance-enhancing impacts of belief in a goal. Minimally, why there should be a division of labor between career officials and politicians whereby the latter specializes in enthusiasm while the former specializes in warding it off is not clear.

37. Perverse consequences of course occur, but the appropriate comparison is not between a perfect change, without such consequences, and an imperfect one where they are found, but between an imperfect change and the status quo.

38. Rainey's master's degree is in psychology and his Ph.D. is from a public administration program housed within a business school.

39. The projects were undertaken in cooperation with *Governing* and *Government Executive* magazines respectively, both publications aimed at senior government managers.

40. An academic pecking order phenomenon was also at play here because public policy programs were generally at universities with higher standing than those with public administration programs; faculty at public policy schools occasionally stated with arrogance that public administration graduates would work for their graduates.

41. Looking back to an earlier era, Savoie (1994), a public administration separatist, wrote, "The term administration rather than management best described government operations...The role of administrator involved the applying of formalized procedures" (p. 172).

42. A new journal, broadly supporting public management reform, was revealingly called the *International Public Management Journal*; it contained a number of papers defending new public management (e.g., Behn, 1998; Gruening, 2001).

43. They therefore saw a public service culture in the service of performance not as a justification for separatism.

44. RAND also published its own collection *High-Performance Government* (Klitgaard & Light, 2005), focusing specifically on government.

45. The business literature on stakeholder management and the balanced scorecard (Kaplan & Norton, 1996) also discusses nonfinancial performance issues, but certainly for the latter, and mostly for the former (Walsh, 2005), the nonfinancial performance measures are seen as being at the service of a superordinate goal of financial performance. For public organizations, no such subordination exists; nonfinancial and financial (in a public-sector context, cost control and/or efficiency) performance measures have independent status.

46. Currently a business school academic, Snook was an Army officer and West Point instructor before writing the dissertation forming the basis for the book.

47. Public administration literature is less relevant to questions of stakeholder management and conflict resolution than one might imagine because this literature (e.g., on political management, Moore, 1995; Heymann, 1987; on public deliberation, Reich, 1990) assumes a context of decision making in a democratic political system that does not apply to firms.

References

Aberbach, J. D., Putnam, R. D., & Rockman, B. A. (1981). *Bureaucracies and politicians in western democracies.* Cambridge, MA: Harvard University Press.

Academy of Management. (2006). http://apps.aomonline.org/MemberDirectory/main.asp. Accessed June 30, 2006.

Agranoff, R., & McGuire, M. *Collaborative public management: New strategies for local governments.* Washington, DC: Georgetown University Press.

Allison, G. T., Jr. (1986). Public and private management: Are they fundamentally alike in all unimportant respects? In F. S. Lane (Ed.), *Current issues in public administration* (3rd ed., pp. 184–200). New York: St. Martin's Press.

Altshuler, A. A., & Behn, R. D. (Eds.). (1997). *Innovation in American government: Challenges, opportunities, and dilemmas.* Washington, DC: Brookings Institution.

American Political Science Association. (2006). http://www.apsanet.org/content_4715.cfm. Accessed July 26, 2006.

American Society for Public Administration. (2006). http://www.aspaonline.org/spar/members.html. Accessed July 26, 2006.

Angle, H. L., & Perry, J. L. (1981). An empirical assessment of organizational commitment and organizational effectiveness. *Administrative Science Quarterly, 26*(1), 1–14.

Appleby, P. H. (1949). *Policy and administration.* University, AL: University of Alabama Press.

Armbruster, T. (2005). Bureaucracy and the controversy between liberal interventionism and non-interventionism. In P. Du Gay (Ed.), *The values of bureaucracy* (pp. 63–88). Oxford: Oxford University Press.

Bardach, E. (1998). *Getting agencies to work together.* Washington, DC: Brookings Institution.

Baritz, L. (1960). *The servants of power: A history of the use of social science in American industry.* Middletown, CT: Wesleyan University Press.

Barzelay, M. (1992). *Breaking through bureaucracy: A new vision for managing in government.* Berkeley, CA; Los Angles; Oxford, UK: University of California Press.

Barzelay, M. (2001). *The new public management: Improving research and dialogue.* Berkeley and New York: University of California Press and Russell Sage Foundation.

Bazerman, M. H. (2005). *Judgment in managerial decision making* (6th ed.). New York: Wiley.

Behn, R. D. (1991). *Leadership counts: Lessons for public managers.* Cambridge, MA: Harvard University Press.

Behn, R. D. (1998). The new public management paradigm and the search for democratic accountability. *International Public Management Journal, 1*(2), 131–164.

Behn, R. D. (2001). *Rethinking democratic accountability.* Washington, DC: Brookings Institution.

Behn, R. D. (2003). Why measure performance? Different purposes require different measures. *Public Administration Review, 63*(5), 586–606.

Behn, R. D. (2005a). The core drivers of Citistat: It's not just about the meetings and the maps. *International Public Management Journal, 8*(3), 295–319.

Behn, R. D. (2005b). On government's compelling need for managerial competence. *Bob Behn's Public Management Report, 3*(2), 1–2.

Bendor, J. (1990). Formal models of bureaucracy: A review. In N. B. Lynn & A. Wildavsky (Eds.), *Public administration: The state of the discipline* (pp. 373–420). Chatham, NJ: Chatham House Publishers.

Bendor, J., Glazer, A., & Hammond, T. H. (2001). Theories of delegation. *Annual Review of Political Science, 4,* 235–269.

Bertelli, A. M. (2006). Motivation crowding and the federal civil servant. *International Public Management Journal, 9,* 1–23.

Bertelli, A. M., & Lynn, L. E. Jr. (2006). *Madison's managers: Public administration and the Constitution.* Baltimore: Johns Hopkins University Press.

Blau, P. M. (1955). *The dynamics of bureaucracy: A study of interpersonal relations in two government agencies.* Chicago: University of Chicago Press.

Borins, S. (1998). *Innovating with integrity: How local heroes are transforming American government.* Washington, DC: Georgetown University Press.

Boyne, G. A. (2006). Explaining public service performance: Does management matter? *Public Policy and Administration, 19*(4), 100–117.

Boyne, G. A., Meier, K. J., O'Toole, L. J. Jr., & Walker, R. M. (Eds.) (2006). *Public service performance: Perspectives on measurement and management.* Cambridge, UK: Cambridge University Press.

Bozeman, B. (1987). *All organizations are public: Bridging public and private organization theory.* San Francisco: Jossey Bass.

Bozeman, B. (Ed.). (1993). *Public management: The state of the art.* San Francisco: Jossey-Bass.

Brehm, J. O., & Gates, S. (1999). *Working, shirking, and sabotage: Bureaucratic response to a democratic public.* Ann Arbor, MI: University of Michigan Press.

Brockner, J., & Wiesenfeld, B. M. (1996). An integrative framework for explaining reactions to decisions: The interactive effects of outcomes and procedures. *Psychological Bulletin, 120,* 189–208.

Brown, T. L., & Potoski, M. (2003). The influence of transactions costs on municipal and county government choices of alternative modes of service provision. *Journal of Public Administration Research and Theory, 13*(4), 441–468.

Brown, T. L., & Potoski, M. (2006). Contracting for management: Assessing management capacity under alternative service delivery arrangements. *Journal of Policy Analysis and Management 25*(2), 323–346.

Carpenter, D. P. (2001). The forging of bureaucratic autonomy: Reputations, networks and policy innovation in executive agencies, 1862–1928. Princeton, NJ: Princeton University Press.

Clarkson, M. B. E. (1995). A stockholder framework for analyzing and evaluating corporate social performance. *Academy of Management Review, 20*, 92–117.

Clegg, S. R., & Hardy, C. (1996). Conclusions: Representations. In S. R. Clegg, C. Hardy, & W. R. Nord (Eds.), *Handbook of organization studies* (pp. 676–708). London: Sage.

Cooper, P. J. (1990). Public law and public administration: The state of the union. In N. B. Lynn & A. Wildavsky (Eds.), *Public administration: The state of the discipline* (pp. 256–286). Chatham, NJ: Chatham House Publishers.

Crewson, P. E. (1997). Public-service motivation: Building empirical evidence of incidence and effect. *Journal of Public Administration Research and Theory, 4*, 499–518.

Cyert, R. M., & March, J. G. (1963). *A behavioral theory of the firm*. Englewood Cliffs, NJ: Prentice-Hall.

Davis, K. C. (1969). *Discretionary justice: A preliminary inquiry* (reprinted in 1980). Westport, CT: Greenwood Press.

Davis, K. C. (1978). Administrative law treatise (2nd ed.). San Diego: K. C. Davis Publishing.

Denhardt, R. B. (1990). Public administration theory: The state of the discipline. In N. B. Lynn & A. Wildavsky (Eds.), *Public administration: The state of the discipline* (pp. 43–72). Chatham, NJ: Chatham House Publishers.

Doig, J. G., & Hargrove, E. C. (Eds.). (1987). *Leadership and innovation: Entrepreneurs in government*. Baltimore: Johns Hopkins University Press.

Donahue, J. D. (in press). *The other economy: American inequality and the warping of government work*. Cambridge, MA: Harvard University Press.

Du Gay, P. (2000). *In praise of bureaucracy: Weber, organization and ethics*. London; Thousand Oaks, CA: Sage.

Eden, L. (2004). *Whole world on fire: Organizations, knowledge, and nuclear weapons devastation*. Ithaca, NY, and London: Cornell University Press.

Endsley, M. R., Bolte, B., & Jones, D. G. (2003). *Designing for situation awareness: An approach to user-centered design*. New York: Taylor & Francis.

Fayol, H. (1937). The administrative theory in the state. In L. H. Gulick & L. Urwick (Eds.), *Papers on the science of administration* (pp. 99–114). New York: Institute of Public Administration.

Feldman, M. (2000). Organizational routines as a source of continuous change. *Organization Science, 11*, 611–629.

Ferlie, E., Lynn, L., and Pollitt, C. (2005). *Oxford University Press handbook of public management*. Oxford: Oxford University Press.

Ferraro, F., Pfeffer, J., & Sutton, R. I. (2005). Economics language and assumptions: How theories can become self-fulfilling. *Academy of Management Review, 30*, 8–24.

Fesler, J. W. (1990). The state and its study: The whole and the parts. In N. B. Lynn & A. Wildavsky (Eds.), *Public administration: The state of the discipline* (pp. 84–96). Chatham, NJ: Chatham House Publishers.

Finer, H. (1940). Administrative responsibility in democratic government. *Public Administration Review, 1*(4), 335–350.

Fortune. (2006a). Largest U.S. corporations. *Fortune, 153*(7), 4/17/2006, F1–F20.

Fortune. (2006b). Exxon at a glance. *Fortune, 153*(7), 4/17/2006, 77.

Frank, S. A., & Lewis, G. B. (2004). Government employees: Working hard or hardly working? *American Review of Public Administration, 34*(1), 36–51.

Frederickson, H. G. (1971). Toward a new public administration. In. F. Marini (ed.), *Toward a new public administration* (pp. 309–331). San Francisco: Chandler Publishing.

Frederickson, H. G. (1997). *The spirit of public administration.* San Francisco: Jossey-Bass.

Friedman, M. & Friedman, R. D. (1980). *Free to choose: A personal statement.* New York: Harcourt Brace Jovanovich.

Gaus, J. (1950). Trends in the theory of public administration. *Public Administration Review, 10*(3), 161–168.

Ghoshal, S., & Insead, P. M. (1996). Bad for practice: A critique of the tranaction cost theory. *Academy of Management Review, 21,* 13–47.

Goodnow, F. J. (1914). Politics and administration: A study in government. New York: Macmillan.

Grant, A. M. (2007). Relational job design and the motivation to make a prosocial difference. *Academy of Management Review, 2*(2), 393–417.

Gregory, R. (2003). Accountability in modern government. In B. G. Peters & J. Pierre (Eds.), *Handbook of public administration* (pp. 557–568). London; Thousand Oaks, CA: Sage.

Gruber, J. E. (1987). *Controlling bureaucracies: Dilemmas in democratic governance.* Berkeley: University of California Press.

Gulick, L. (1937a). Notes on the theory of organization. In L. H. Gulick & L. Urwick (Eds.), *Papers on the science of administration* (pp. 1–46). New York: Institute of Public Administration.

Gulick, L. (1937b). Science, values and public administration. In L. H. Gulick & L. Urwick (Eds.), *Papers on the science of administration* (pp. 189–195). New York: Institute of Public Administration.

Gulick, L. H., & Urwick, L. (1937). *Papers on the science of administration.* New York: Institute of Public Administration.

Hackman, J. R. (1985). Doing research that makes a difference. In E. E. Lawler, A. M. Mohrman, S. A. Mohrman, G. E. Ledford, & T. G. Cummings (Eds.), *Doing research that is useful for theory and practice.* San Francisco: Jossey-Bass.

Hammond, T. H. (1993). Toward a general theory of hierarchy: Books, bureaucrats, basketball tournaments, and the administrative structure of the nation-state. *Journal of Public Administration Research and Theory, 3*(1), 120–145.

Hammond, T. H., & Thomas, P. A. (1989). The impossibility of a neutral hierarchy. *Journal of Law, Economics, and Organization 5*(1), 155–184.

Harvard University Alumni Affairs and Development Communications. (2006). *Managing Harvard's resources.* Cambridge, MA: President and Fellows of Harvard College.

Hatry, H. P. (1999). *Performance measurement: Getting results.* Washington, DC: Urban Institute Press.

Heinrich, C. J. (2000). Organizational form and performance: An empirical investigation of nonprofit and for-profit job-training service providers. *Journal of Policy Analysis and Management, 19*(2), 233–261.

Heinrich, C. J., & Fournier, E. (2004). Dimensions of publicness and performance in substance abuse treatment organizations. *Journal of Policy Analysis and Management, 23*(1), 49–70.

Hennessy, P. (1989). *Whitehall.* London: Secker & Warburg.

Hennessy, P. (1995). *The hidden wiring.* London: Victor Gollancz.

Henry, N. L. (1990). Root and branch: Public administration's travail toward the future. In N. B. Lynn & A. Wildavsky (Eds.), *Public administration: The state of the discipline* (pp. 3–26). Chatham, NJ: Chatham House Publishers.

Heymann, P. B. (1987). *The politics of public management.* New Haven, CT: Yale University Press.

Hill, C. J. (2006). Casework job design and client outcomes in welfare-to-work offices. *Journal of Public Administration Research and Theory, 16*(2), 263–288.

Hirschmann, A. O. (1991). *The rhetoric of reaction: Perversity, futility, jeopardy.* Cambridge, MA: Belknap Press of Harvard University Press.

Hood, C. (1991). A public management for all seasons? *Public Administration, 69,* 3–19.

Houston, D. J. (2000). Public-service motivation: A multivariate test. *Journal of Public Administration Research and Theory, 4,* 713–727.

Huxham, C., & Vangen, S. (2005). *Managing to collaborate: The theory and practice of collaborative advantage.* London and New York: Routledge.

Ingraham, P. (2005). Performance: Promises to keep and miles to go. *Public Administration Review, 65*(4), 390–395.

Ingraham, P. W. (Ed.). (2007). *In pursuit of performance: Management systems in state and local government.* Baltimore: Johns Hopkins University Press.

Ingraham, P. W., Joyce P. G., & Donahue, A. K. (2003). *Government performance: Why management matters.* Baltimore: Johns Hopkins University Press.

Janis, I. L. (1982). *Groupthink: A psychological study of policy decisions and fiascoes.* Boston: Houghton Mifflin.

Jurkiewicz, C. L., Massey, T. K. , & Brown, R. G. (1998). Motivation in public and private organizations: A comparative study. *Public Productivity and Management Review, 21,* 230–250.

Kaboolian, L. (2000). Quality comes to the public sector. In R. E. Cole & W. R. Scott (Eds.), *The quality movement and organization theory* (pp. 131–153). Thousand Oaks, CA: Sage.

Kaplan, R. S., & Norton, D. P. (1996). *The balanced scorecard: Translating strategy into action.* Boston: Harvard Business School Press.

Kaufman, H. (1977). *Red tape: Its origins, uses and abuses.* Washington, DC: Brookings Institution.

Kelman, S. J. (1981). *Regulating America, regulating Sweden: A comparative study of occupational safety and health policy.* Cambridge, MA: MIT Press.

Kelman, S. J. (1990). *Procurement and public management.* Washington, DC: American Enterprise Institute Press.

Kelman, S. J. (1993) What is wrong with the revolving door? In B. Bozeman (Ed.), *Public management: The state of the art* (pp. 224–251). San Francisco: Jossey-Bass.

Kelman, S. J. (2002). Contracting. In L. M. Salamon (Ed.), *The tools of government: A guide to the new governance* (pp. 282–318). New York: Oxford University Press.

Kelman, S. J. (2005). *Unleashing change.* Washington, DC: Brookings Institution.

Keohane, R. O., & Nye, J. S., Jr. (2000). Introduction. In J. S. Nye, Jr., & J. D. Donahue (Eds.), *Governance in a globalizing world* (pp. 1–41). Washington, DC: Brookings Institution.

Kettl, D. (1988). *Government by proxy: (Mis?)Managing federal programs.* Washington, DC: Congressional Quarterly Press.

Kettl, D. (2002). *The transformation of governance: Public administration for the 21st century.* Baltimore: Johns Hopkins University Press.

Kettl, D. F. (2005). *The global public management revolution* (2nd ed.). Washington, DC: Brookings Institution.

Kettl, D. F., & DiIuilio, J. J., Jr. (1995). *Inside the reinvention machine: Appraising governmental reform.* Washington, DC: Brookings Institution.

Kettl, D. F., Ingraham, P. W., Sanders, R. P., & Horner, C. (1996). Civil service reform: Building a government that works. Washington, DC: Brookings Institution.

Klitgaard, R. E., & Light, P. C. (Eds.). (2005). *High-performance government: Structure, leadership, incentives.* Santa Monica, CA: RAND Corporation.

Kramer, R. M. (1998). Revisiting the Bay of Pigs and Vietnam decisions 25 years later: How well has the groupthink hypothesis stood the test of time? *Organizational Behavior and Human Decision Processes, 73,* 236–271.

Kramer, R. M. (2000). Political paranoia in organizations: Antecedents and consequences. In S. Bachararch & E. Lawler (Eds.), *Research in the sociology of organizations* (vol. 17, pp. 47–87). Stamford, CT: JAI Press.

La Porte, T. R., & Consolini, P. M. (1991). Working in practice but not in theory: Theoretical challenges of high reliability organizations. *Journal of Public Administration Research and Theory, 1*(1), 19–47.

Latham, G. P. (2006) *Work motivation: History, theory, research, and practice.* Thousand Oaks, CA: Sage.

Lee, G., & Perry, J. L. (2002). Are computers boosting productivity? A test of the paradox in state governments. *Journal of Public Administration Research and Theory, 12*(1), 77–102.

Levinthal, D., & Rerup, C. (2006). Crossing an apparent chasm: Bridging mindful and less-mindful perspectives on organizational learning. *Organization Science, 17*(4), 502–513.

Lewin, K. (1958). Group decision and social change. In E. E. Maccoby, T. M. Newcomb, & E. L. Hartley (Eds.), *Readings in social psychology* (3rd ed., pp. 197–211). New York: Holt, Rinehart & Winston.

Lipsky, M. (1980). *Street-level bureaucracy: Dilemmas of the individual in public service.* New York: Sage.

Light, P. C. (2002). *Government's greatest achievements: From civil rights to homeland security.* Washington, DC: Brookings Institution.

Light, P. C. (2005). *The four pillars of high performance.* New York: McGraw-Hill.

Locke, E. A., & Latham, G. P. (1990a). *Work motivation: The high performance cycle.* In Uwe Kleinbeck et al. (Eds.), *Work motivation* (pp. 3–25). Hillsdale, NJ: Lawrence Erlbaum Associates.

Locke, E. A., & Latham, G. P. (1990b). *A theory of goal setting and task performance.* Englewood Cliffs, NJ: Prentice-Hall.

Lovelock, C. H. (1992). Are services really different? In C. H. Lovelock (Ed.), *Managing services: Marketing, operations, and human resources* (2nd ed., pp. 1–16). Englewood Cliffs, NJ: Prentice-Hall.

Lowi, T. J. (1969). *The end of liberalism.* New York: Norton.

Lynn, L. E., Jr. (1996.) *Public management as art, science, and profession.* Chatham, NJ: Chatham House Publishers.

Lynn, L. E., Jr. (2003). Public management. In B. G. Peters & J. Pierre (Eds.), *Handbook of public administration* (pp. 14–24). London; Thousand Oaks, CA: Sage.

Lynn, L. E., Jr. (2006). *Public management: Old and new.* New York: Routledge.

March, J. G., & Simon, H. A. (1958). *Organizations.* New York: Wiley.

March, J. G., Schulz, M., & Zhou, X. (2000). *The dynamics of rules: Change in written organizational codes.* Stanford, CA: Stanford University Press.

Marini, F. (Ed.). (1971). *Toward a new public administration.* San Francisco: Chandler Publishing.

Mayer, K. J., & Argyres, N. S. (2004). Learning to contract: Evidence from the personal computer industry. *Organization Science, 15*(4), 394–410.

Mayer, K. J., & Nickerson, J. A. (2005). Antecedents and performance implications of contracting for knowledge workers: Evidence from information technology services. *Organization Science, 16*(3), 225–242.

Maynard-Moody, S., & Musheno, M. (2003). *Cops, teachers, counselors: Stories from the front lines of public service.* Ann Arbor, MI: University of Michigan Press.

McCurdy, H. E. (1986). *Public administration: A bibliographic guide to the literature.* New York and Basel: Marcel Dekker.

Meier, K. J., & O'Toole, L. J., Jr. (2002). Public management and organizational performance: The effect of managerial quality. *Journal of Policy Analysis & Management, 21*(4), 629–643.

Meier, K. J., & O'Toole, L. J., Jr. (2003). Public management and educational performance: The impact of managerial networking. *Public Administration Review, 63*(6), 689–699.

Meyer, M. H. & Gupta, V. (1994). The performance paradox. In B. M. Staw & L. Cummings (Eds.), *Research in organizational behavior* (Vol. 16, pp. 309–369). Greenwich, CT: JAI Press.

Miller, G. J. (1992). *Managerial dilemmas: The political economy of hierarchy.* Cambridge, UK: Cambridge University Press.

Milward, H. B., & Provan, K. G. (2000). Governing the hollow state. *Journal of Public Administration Research and Theory, 10*(2), 359–379.

Milward, H. B., & Provan, K. G. (2003). Managing the hollow state: Collaboration and contracting. *Public Management Review, 5*(1), 1–18.

Mintzberg, H. (1979). *The structuring of organizations: A synthesis of the research.* Englewood Cliffs, NJ: Prentice-Hall.

Mintzberg, H. (1996). Managing government, governing management. *Harvard Business Review, 74*(3), May/June, 75–83.

Moe, T. M. (1990). The politics of structural choice: Toward a theory of public bureaucracy. In O. E. Williamson (Ed.), *Organization theory: From Chester Barnard to the present and beyond* (pp. 116–153). Oxford: Oxford University Press.

Moore, M. H. (1995). *Creating public value: Strategic management in government.* Cambridge, MA: Harvard University Press.

Mosher, F. C. (1956). Research in public administration: Some notes and suggestions. *Public Administration Review, 16*(3), 169–178.

Mosher, F. C. (Ed.). (1975). *American public administration: Past, present, future.* University, AL: University of Alabama Press.

Nelson, M. (1982). A short, ironic history of American national bureaucracy. *Journal of Politics, 44*(3), 747–778.

Nelson, R. R., & Winter, S. G. (1982). *An evolutionary theory of economic change.* Cambridge, MA: Belknap Press of Harvard University Press.

O'Toole, L. J., Jr. (2003). Interorganizational relations in implementation. In B. G. Peters & J. Pierre (Eds.), *Handbook of public administration* (pp. 234–244). London; Thousand Oaks, CA: Sage.

O'Toole, L. J., Jr., & Meier, K. J. (2003). Plus ça change: Public management, personnel stability, and organizational performance. *Journal of Public Administration Research and Theory, 13*(1), 43–64.

Osborne, D., & Gaebler, T. (1992). *Reinventing government: How the entrepreneurial spirit is transforming the public sector.* Reading, MA: Addison Wesley.

Ouchi, W. G. (2003). *Making schools work: A revolutionary plan for getting your kids the education they need.* New York: Simon & Schuster.

Parsons, T. (1960). *Structure and process in modern societies.* Glencoe, IL: Free Press.

Pentland, B. T., & Feldman, M. S. (2005). Organizational routines as a unit of analysis. *Industrial and Corporate Change, 14,* 793–815.

Perry, J. L., & Kraemer, K. L. (1990). Research methodology in public administration: Issues and patterns. In N. B. Lynn & A. Wildavsky (Eds.), *Public administration: The state of the discipline* (pp. 347–372). Chatham, NJ: Chatham House Publishers.

Perry, J. L., & Rainey, H. G. 1988. The public-private distinction in organization theory: A critique and research strategy. *Academy of Management Review, 13,* 182–201.

Peters, B. G. (2001). *The future of governing* (2nd ed.). Lawrence, KS: University Press of Kansas.

Peters, B. G., & Pierre, J. (Eds.). (2003a). *Handbook of public administration.* London; Thousand Oaks, CA: Sage.

Peters, B. G., & Pierre, J. (2003b). Introduction: The role of public administration in governing. In B. G. Peters & J. Pierre (Eds.), *Handbook of public administration* (pp. 1–10). London; Thousand Oaks, CA: Sage.

Peters, B. G., & Wright, V. (1996). Public policy and administration, old and new. In R. E. Goodin & H-D. Klingemann (Eds.), *A new handbook of political science* (pp. 628–641). Oxford: Oxford University Press.

Podolny, J. M., & Page, K. L. (1998). Network forms of organization. *Annual Review of Sociology, 24,* 57–76.

Pollitt, C. (1990). *Managerialism in the public services: The Anglo-American experience.* Oxford: Basil Blackwell.

Powell, W. (1990). Neither market nor hierarchy: Network forms of organization. *Research on Organizational Behavior, 12,* 295–336.

Propper, C., & Wilson, D. (2003). The use and usefulness of performance measures in the public sector. *Oxford Review of Economic Policy, 19*(2), 250–267.

Provan, K. G., & Milward, H. B. (1995). A preliminary theory of interorganizational network effectiveness: A comparative study of four community mental health systems. *Administrative Science Quarterly, 40*(1), 1–33.

Radin, B. A. (2006). *Challenging the performance movement.* Washington, DC: Georgetown University Press.

Rainey, H. G. (1990). Public management: Recent developments and current prospects. In N. B. Lynn & A. Wildavsky (Eds.), *Public administration: The state of the discipline* (pp. 157–184). Chatham, NJ: Chatham House Publishers.

Rainey, H. G. (2003). *Understanding and managing public organizations.* San Francisco: Jossey-Bass/Wiley.

Rainey, H. G., Backoff, R. W., & Levine, C. H. (1976). Comparing public and private organizations. *Public Administration Review, 36,* 223–246.

Reich, R. B. (Ed.). (1988). *The power of public ideas.* Cambridge, MA: Harvard University Press.

Rhodes, R. A. W. (2002). The new public administration of the British state. In C. Hay (ed.), *British politics today* (pp. 101–126). Cambridge, UK; Malden, MA: Polity Press in association with Blackwell.

Rochlin, G. I. (1996). Reliable organizations: Present research and future directions. *Journal of Crisis and Contingency Management, 4*(2), 55–59.

Rosenbloom, D. H., & McCurdy, H. E. (Eds.). (2006). Revisiting Waldo's administrative state: Constancy and change in public administration. Washington, DC: Georgetown University Press.

Russell, B. (1980). On the relative strictness of negative and positive duties. In B. Steinbock (Ed.), *Killing and letting die* (pp. 215–237). Englewood Cliffs, NJ: Prentice-Hall.

Rynes, S. L., Bartunek, J. M., & Daft, R. L. (2001). Across the Great Divide: Knowledge creation and transfer between practitioners and academics. *Academy of Management Journal, 44*(2), 340–375.

Salamon, L. M. (1981). Rethinking public management: Third-party government and the changing forms of government action. *Public Policy, 29*(3), 255–275.

Salamon, L. M. (Ed.). (2002). *The tools of government: A guide to the new governance.* New York: Oxford University Press.

Savas, E. S. (1982). *Privatizing the public sector: How to shrink government.* Chatham, NJ: Chatham House Publishers.

Savoie, D. J. (1994). *Thatcher, Reagan, Mulroney: In search of a new bureaucracy.* Pittsburgh: University of Pittsburgh Press.

Schweitzer, M. E., Ordóñez, L., & Douma, B. (2004). Goal setting as a motivator of unethical behavior. *Academy of Management Journal, 47,* 422–432.

Selsky, J. W., & Parker, B. (2005). Cross-sector partnerships to address social issues: Challenges to theory and practice. *Journal of Management, 31*(6), 849–873.

Selznick, P. (1953). *TVA and the grass roots.* Berkeley: University of California Press.

Simon, H. A. (1937). Can municipal activities be measured? *The Municipality, 32* (December), 281–282.

Simon, H. A. (1947). *Administrative behavior.* New York: Macmillan.

Simon, H. A., Smithburg, D. W., & Thompson, V. A. (1950). *Public administration.* New York: Alfred A. Knopf.

Simon, H. A. (1952). "Development of theory of democratic administration": Replies and comments. *American Political Science Review, 46*(2), 494–503.

Simons, R. (1995). Control in an age of empowerment. *Harvard Business Review, 73*(2), 80–88.

Snook, S. A. (2000). *Friendly fire: The accidental shootdown of the U.S. Blackhawks over northern Iraq.* Princeton, NJ: Princeton University Press.

Srinivasan, R., & Brush, T. H. (2006). Supplier performance in vertical alliances: The effects of self-enforcing agreements and enforceable contracts. *Organization Science, 17*(4), 436–452.

Staw, B. M. (1981). The escalation of commitment to a course of action. Academy of *Management Review, 6*(4), 577–587.

Staw, B. M. (1984). Organizational behavior: A review and reformulation of the field's outcome variables. *Annual Review of Psychology, 35,* 627–666.

Sundaram, A. K., & Inkpen, A. C. (2004). The corporate objective revisited. *Organization Science 15*(3), 350–363.

Sundstrom, G. (2006). Management by results: Its origin and development in the case of the Swedish state. *International Public Management Journal, 9*(4), 399–427.

Terry, L. D. (1993). Why we should abandon the misconceived quest to reconcile public entrepreneurship with democracy. *Public Administration Review, 53,* 393–395.

Thibaut, J., & Walker, L. (1975). *Procedural justice: A psychological analysis.* Hillsdale, NJ: Lawrence Erlbaum Associates.

Thomas, C. W. (2003). *Bureaucratic landscapes: Interagency cooperation and the preservation of biodiversity.* Cambridge, MA: MIT Press.

Tooley, M. (1980). An irrelevant consideration: Killing versus letting die. In B. Steinbock (Ed.), *Killing and letting die* (pp. 56–62). Englewood Cliffs, NJ: Prentice Hall.

Tullock, G. (1976). *The vote motive.* London: Institute for Economic Affairs.

Tullock, G. (1979). Public choice in practice. In C. S. Russell (ed.), *Collective decision making.* Baltimore: Johns Hopkins University Press.

Tushman, M. L., & O'Reilly, C. A. (1996). Ambidextrous organizations. *California Management Review, 38*(4), 8–30.

Tyler, T. R. (1990). *Why people obey the law.* New Haven, CT: Yale University Press.

U.S. Department of Defense. (2002). DoD 101: An introductory overview of the Department of Defense. http://www.defenselink.mil/pubs/dod101/dod101_for_ 2002.html. Accessed July 26, 2006.

U.S. Office of Management and Budget. (2007). *Budget of the United States Government, Fiscal Year 2007* (Table S-2, p. 314).

U.S. National Center for Education Statistics. (2006). Master's and doctorate's degrees earned by field: 1980 to 2003: Table 290. In *Statistical abstract of the United States* (p. 188). Washington, DC: U.S. Census Bureau.

Van Slyke, D. M. (2007). Agents or stewards: Using theory to understand the government–nonprofit social service contracting relationship. *Journal of Public Administration Research and Theory, 17,* 157–187.

Wal-Mart. (2006). http://www.walmartfacts.com. Accessed July 26, 2006.

Waldo, D. (1948). *The administrative state: A study of the political theory of American public administration.* New York: The Ronald Press Company.

Waldo, D. (1952). Development of theory of democratic administration. *American Political Science Review, 46*(1), 81–103.

Waldo, D. (1968). Scope of the theory of public administration. In J. C. Charlesworth (Ed.), Theory and practice of public administration: Scope, objectives, and methods. Monograph. *Annals of the American Academy of Political and Social Science,* 1–26.

Waldo, D. (1990). A theory of public administration means in our time a theory of politics also. In N. B. Lynn & A. Wildavsky (Eds.), *Public administration: The state of the discipline* (pp. 73–83). Chatham, NJ: Chatham House Publishers.

Walsh, J. P. (2005) Book review essay: Taking stock of stakeholder management. *Academy of Management Review, 30*(2), 426–438.

Walsh, J. P., Weber, K., & Margolis, J. D. (2003). Social issues and management: Our lost cause found. *Journal of Management, 29*(6), 859–881.

Wamsley, G. L. (1990). Introduction. In G. L. Wamsley, R. N. Bacher, C. T. Goodsell, P. S. Kronenberg, J. A. Rohr, C. M. Stivers, O. F. White, & J. F. Wolf (Eds.), *Refounding public administration* (pp. 19–29). Newbury Park, CA: Sage.

Wamsley, G. L., Bacher, R. N., Goodsell, C. T., Kronenberg, P. S., Rohr, J. A., Stivers, C. M., White, O. F., & Wolf, J. F. (1990). Public administration and the governance process: Shifting the political dialogue. In G. L. Wamsley, R. N. Bacher, C. T. Goodsell, P. S. Kronenberg, J. A. Rohr, C. M. Stivers, O. White, & J. F. Wolf (Eds.), *Refounding public administration* (pp. 31–51). Newbury Park, CA: Sage.

Warwick, D. P. (1975). *A theory of public bureaucracy: Politics, personality, and organization in the State Department.* Cambridge, MA: Harvard University Press.

Weick, K. E., & Sutcliffe, K. M. (2001). *Managing the unexpected: Assuring high performance in an age of complexity.* San Francisco: Jossey-Bass.

Willoughby, W. F. (1927). *Principles of public administration with special reference to the national and state governments of the United States.* Washington, DC: Brookings Institution.

Wilson, J. Q. (1989). *Bureacracy: What government agencies do and why they do it.* New York: Basic Books.

Wilson, W. (1887). The study of administration. *Political Science Quarterly, 2,* 197–222.

White, L. D. (1926). *Introduction to the study of public administration.* New York: Macmillan.

Ziller, J. (2003). The continental system of administrative legality. In B. G. Peters & J. Pierre (Eds.), *Handbook of public administration* (pp. 260–268). London; Thousand Oaks, CA: Sage.

6
Three Perspectives on Team Learning
Outcome Improvement, Task Mastery, and Group Process

AMY C. EDMONDSON, JAMES R. DILLON,
AND KATHRYN S. ROLOFF

Harvard Business School

Abstract

The emergence of a research literature on team learning has been driven by at least two factors. First, longstanding interest in what makes organizational work teams effective leads naturally to questions about how members of newly formed teams learn to work together and how existing teams improve or adapt. Second, some have argued that teams play a crucial role in organizational learning. These interests have produced a growing and heterogeneous literature. Empirical studies of learning by small groups or teams present a variety of terms, concepts, and methods. This heterogeneity is both generative and occasionally confusing. We identify three distinct areas of research that provide insight into how teams learn to stimulate cross-area discussion and future research. We find that scholars have made progress in understanding how teams in general learn, and propose that future work should develop more precise and context-specific theories to help guide research and practice in disparate task and industry domains.

Introduction

Organizations increasingly rely on teams to carry out critical strategic and operational tasks. By implication, an organization's ability to learn—that is, to improve its outcomes through better knowledge and insight (Fiol & Lyles, 1985)—is dependent on the ability of its teams to learn (Edmondson, 2002; Senge, 1990). Teams, defined as work groups that exist within the context of a larger organization and share responsibility for a team product or service (Hackman, 1987), are a design choice for accomplishing work. In many of today's organizations, teams develop strategy, design and produce new products, deliver services, and execute other key tasks that influence organizational performance. When teams change what they do or how they do it—in support of organizational goals—an organization maintains or enhances its effectiveness in a changing world. How do teams learn, and what factors are most important to team learning? This article reports on current perspectives and findings that address these questions.

Team-learning research builds upon and complements decades of research on organizational learning in the management literature. Both topics originate from an assumption that collectives—not just individuals—can be said to learn. Many have argued that organizations must learn to succeed in a constantly changing world (Garvin, 2000; Senge, 1990), yet the topic of organizational learning has received more theoretical than empirical attention (Weick & Westley, 1993). This imbalance can be explained by at least two causal factors. First, conceptual disagreement about what it means for an organization to learn limits systematic progress (Edmondson & Moingeon, 1998; Fiol & Lyles, 1985). Second, the methodological challenges associated with measuring learning in multiple organizations at the same time are considerable. Although finding multiple teams to study is also challenging, the practical obstacles are surmountable. As a result, a growing number of empirical studies on team learning are helping to ameliorate the shortage of data relative to theory on collective learning in organizations.

Research explicitly focused on team learning emerged as a topic in the management literature in the 1990s, and expanded in volume and variety in the early 2000s and beyond. Perhaps the best known early use of the term *team learning* is found in Peter Senge's (1990) book, *The Fifth Discipline: The Art and Practice of the Learning Organization,* a managerial look at insights drawn primarily from the field of system dynamics. Although the theories and tools of *systems thinking* (the "fifth discipline") constitute the book's core contribution, team learning is presented as one of the other four disciplines enabling an organization to learn. Researchers in organizational behavior later elaborated Senge's notion that teams are the fundamental unit of learning in organizations (e.g., Edmondson, 2002; Fiol & Lyles, 1985), as described next.

In this chapter, we review selected empirical studies on team learning from three research traditions: (a) learning curves in operational settings (outcome improvement), (b) psychological experiments on team-member coordination of task knowledge (task mastery), and (c) field research on learning processes in teams (group process). Our review includes articles published in leading management-research journals, along with a few current unpublished studies that came to our attention. Given the large number of issues related, or potentially related, to team learning, including those covered in extensive literatures on team effectiveness, learning and education, organizational change, and other relevant topics, we chose to limit our focus to peer-reviewed articles in the management research literatures that explicitly used the terms *team learning* or *group learning*, and to emphasize empirical studies—those that analyzed quantitative or qualitative data collected in the field, classroom, or laboratory. Even with these criteria to narrow our search, space constraints preclude an exhaustive review of all articles that might qualify. Some will have been overlooked due to ignorance, others due to an imperfect attempt to draw a boundary that allows us to describe the studies we do include in enough detail to be useful. Thus, we have traded completeness for depth; when appropriate and possible, we have attempted to describe methods and findings in ways that allow readers to view a study's conclusions critically. Overall, our aim was to characterize the nature of research that has been conducted and to begin to assemble what is known and unknown about the theoretically and practically important topic of team learning.

Research on Team Learning

In this section, we review studies in manufacturing, social psychology, and organizational behavior that provide intellectual and empirical underpinnings for theories of team learning in the management literature. We organize our review into three reasonably distinct bodies of work, each offering unique results and implications for the future of team-learning research. One area owes its methods and intellectual roots to research on new processes in manufacturing and service operations. A second originates in the social psychology laboratory and pursues questions related to how members of small groups coordinate their knowledge and actions to accomplish interdependent tasks. The third area, situated in microlevel organizational behavior research, emphasizes interpersonal climate and group processes, and relies heavily on methods developed in organizational research on team effectiveness. Although not devoid of cross-fertilization, the three areas have remained surprisingly separate during the time in which research on team learning has developed as a distinct topic of inquiry. They offer distinct lenses on the varied phenomena of team learning; each addresses a different fundamental question, and each offers different conceptualizations of team learning. These distinctions are summarized in Table 6.1.

These areas of prior work vary in size and importance for theory on team learning. In particular, learning-curve studies that explicitly involve teams are few in number, yet this work is sufficiently distinct in approach from other team-learning research to warrant separate attention. Moreover, we learn from different approaches by including a range of methods and contexts, despite differences in relative impact. Next, in a roughly chronological sequence, we review the three areas, starting with learning-curve research, followed by psychological studies of task mastery, and then by research on learning processes in work teams in real organizations.

Table 6.1 Comparison of Three Research Streams

Concepts	Outcome Improvement	Task Mastery	Group Process
Motivating Concern	At what rate do groups improve their efficiency?	How do team members coordinate knowledge and skill to accomplish tasks?	What drives learning-oriented behaviors and processes in organizational workgroups?
Concept of Team Learning	Learning is performance improvement— usually efficiency improvement	Learning is task mastery	Learning is a process of sharing information and reflecting on experience
Dominant Independent Variables	Codified knowledge; collocation or shared ownership; team stability; knowledge sharing	Group members trained together or separately; transactive memory system; communication	Team leader behavior; psychological safety; team identification; team composition; organizational context
Dominant Dependent Variable	Rate of cost or time reduction	Performance on a novel task	Team effectiveness or learning behavior
Findings	Amount of experience working together improves team performance outcomes. In later work, how people work together and dimension of improvement affect the rate of learning.	Having coordinated ways of codifying, storing, and retrieving individual knowledge is necessary to access individual knowledge for coordinated task performance.	Team leadership and shared beliefs about team psychological safety, goals, or identity promote or inhibit team learning behaviors and, in turn, team performance.
Methods	Field research: Collection of quantitative data from teams producing a product or a service	Lab experiments: Small teams of students as subjects; random assignment to conditions to establish causality	Largely field research: Qualitative and quantitative data that provide observations of real organizational work teams

Outcome Improvement: Learning-Curve Research at the Group Level

Recent studies of learning curves in teams introduced a subfield into a long-standing body of research on improvement rates in manufacturing facilities. Since Wright's (1936) observation that unit costs decrease with experience (or cumulative volume), the learning curve has been the subject of much research in the fields of operations management, economics, competitive strategy, and technology management. Overall, this work documents a robust link between cumulative production experience and some measure of operational performance improvement (e.g., cost reduction, yield improvement, productivity improvement). Research in health care delivery similarly finds that performance on a new technology or procedure improves with increased experience (e.g., Ramsay et al., 2000). In healthcare, a service context, the dependent variable is often procedure time, an important measure of process efficiency in services. In both manufacturing and service contexts, the core theme in this work is the benefit of experience for efficiency, whether measured as cost or time.

Background. The existence of learning curves implies that organizations improve with experience, or that "practice makes perfect." Yet, some studies show homogeneous learning curves (similar slopes for the same amount of experience) across sites (e.g., Baloff, 1971; Wright, 1936), and others show heterogeneity (different rates) across sites (e.g., Dutton & Thomas, 1984; Hayes & Clark, 1985). The observation of slope differences suggested that unmeasured factors—such as how the learning process is managed—affect the rate of learning (Pisano, Bohmer, & Edmondson, 2001), such that cumulative experience is a necessary but insufficient explanatory variable. For example, Argote, Beckman and Epple (1990) analyzed historical data on shipbuilding during World War II, and found significant differences across shipyards in rates of productivity improvement. Lacking detailed process or other organizational data, the authors speculated that factors such as turnover might help explain the learning-curve differences.

More generally, many studies have analyzed longitudinal data from one or more sites producing similar products, but very few have included firsthand knowledge of sites that might help explain differences. Proposed explanations related to turnover or better management thus were inferred from a distance. A noteworthy exception can be found in Adler's (1990) study of several plants in a high-tech manufacturer. By collecting qualitative data on managerial and communication processes to supplement quantitative analysis of production data, Adler was able to attribute differences in learning curves to (a) how sites handled the development-manufacturing interface, (b) transfer processes between a primary location and sites that started up later, and (c) ongoing cooperation among sites. These ideas suggested the possibility of differences in teamwork explaining improvement rates and called attention to the cooperative nature of production work, opening up a line of inquiry explicitly focused on learning curves at the group level. Building on this insight, Argote, Insko, Yovetich, and Romero (1995) designed a laboratory experiment that showed that both turnover and task complexity reduced the benefits of team experience on task improvement.

Learning curves in teams. Learning curves in small-group production processes thus constitute a late entry into a longstanding research tradition, which thus far presents only a few articles. Selected studies are shown in Table 6.2. One of the earliest group learning-curve studies took place in a retail setting. With data from 36 pizza stores, Darr, Argote, and Epple (1995) found that unit costs improved significantly with cumulative experience, but at different rates across stores. They proposed that knowledge acquired through experience-based learning would transfer across stores owned by the same franchisee but not across stores owned by different franchisees. Communication across same-franchisee stores was presumed to be the mechanism explaining this difference, but was not measured.

Subsequent research in the manufacturing setting collected field data from 62 quality-improvement projects at a Belgian steel wire manufacturer, using a detailed coding system to assess project activities. From these data, factor analysis identified two dimensions of learning. Substantive results showed that improvement—in this case waste reduction—occurred in projects characterized by both operational and conceptual learning activities (Lapre, Mukherjee, & Van Wassenhove, 2000).

In another service setting, Pisano and colleagues (2001) showed that 16 surgical teams learned to use a radical new cardiac surgery technology at significantly different rates (where the outcome was procedure time reduction, a measure of surgical team efficiency). The authors speculated that how teams were managed affected the rate of learning and provided two case studies to illustrate this possibility.

Edmondson, Winslow, Bohmer, and Pisano (2003) examined two distinct learning curves simultaneously—procedure time reduction and breadth of use—with data on coronary artery bypass graft (CABG) surgery from 15 teams in as many hospitals. Comparing improvement for these two dimensions, the authors found that when the dimension of improvement required acquisition of *tacit knowledge* (as was the case for procedure time reduction) teams at different sites learned at significantly different rates. In contrast, for breadth of use, a dimension of improvement supported by *codified knowledge*, the learning curves were homogenous across sites. Tacit knowledge is difficult to transfer across sites, generally requiring individuals to accompany the knowledge, such as to demonstrate how to coordinate team member actions in smoother ways; whereas codified knowledge, in this case, a type of surgery, could be readily transferred without face-to-face interaction. Moreover, for improvement that relied on tacit knowledge, team composition stability was associated with faster learning. Team members that stayed together, improved more quickly. Teams with members that were quickly substituted in or out took longer.

In a similar context, Reagans, Argote, and Brooks (2005) studied joint-replacement surgery in teaching hospitals and found that increased experience working together in a team promoted better coordination and teamwork. Increased organizational experience also was found to help individuals access each other's knowledge. In short, learning by doing, the authors argued, has several pathways—including one supported by team stability and sustained coordination at the team level, and one created by increased familiarity with how one's organization works, through organizational membership stability. Selected studies are shown in Table 6.2.

Summary. Research in this area has clear methodological and conceptual similarities. The notion of a learning curve is relevant at or near the beginning of a new initiative (product or process), and learning curves document improvement with experience. Over time, learning curves flatten as new learning subsides. Studies rely on longitudinal quantitative outcome data from manufacturing or service organizations and regression analyses to model learning curves. The dependent variable is a measure of efficiency such as cost, productivity, or time. With access to data from multiple groups taking on the same learning goal, recent research has been explicit about the role of teamwork—especially communication and coordination—in fostering improvement. A common theme in this work is testing for and explaining differences in rates of improvement across teams.

Studies of learning curves in teams have built on, and added to, an established research paradigm by introducing new field-based research methods to supplement the traditional analytic approach in the learning-curve literature. Through site visits, interviews, and the collection of data on organizational variables such as worker turnover, team learning-curve research has begun to identify factors that explain differences in improvement. Core findings, summarized in Figure 6.1, suggest that team stability, knowledge sharing, common ownership, colocation, codified knowledge, and organizational experience promote efficiency improvement. In sum, the way learning is managed affects the rate of improvement.

A notable strength of research in this area is its high-quality data and emphasis on outcomes with clear practical importance. These studies thus offer refreshingly objective outcome variables and the advantage of data from multiple groups learning the same thing at roughly the same time, allowing comparability across teams despite the complexity of the contexts in

Table 6.2 Selected Studies from Learning Curve Research at the Teams Level of Analysis

Authors	Data	Context	Aspect of Team Learning	Key Findings
Adler (1990)	Cost data from three multinational plants of an electronic product manufacturer	Manufacturing plants, manufacturing–R&D interface	Cost decreases with volume following launch of new product lines	Intensive knowledge sharing between R&D and plant engineers before start up and after start up led to more rapid cost decreases.
Darr, Argote, & Epple (1995)	Cost data from 36 similar service organizations	Pizza stores, some owned by same franchisee, some not	Unit cost decreases with experience (volume)	All stores improve with experience. Stores with same owner share ideas, which do not transfer across stores with different owners.
Pisano, Bohmer, & Edmondson (2001)	Procedure time data from dozens of surgical operations	Sixteen cardiac surgery teams implementing radical new surgical procedure in leading healthcare centers	Surgical procedure time decreased with experience (number of procedures conducted)	Different teams learned at different rates. How teams were managed appeared to differ.
Edmondson, Winslow, Bohmer, & Pisano (2003)	Procedure time data and number of grafts completed in each operation	Fifteen cardiac surgery teams implementing radical new procedure for coronary artery bypass graft surgery in leading health care centers	Procedure time decreased while number of grafts (complexity or challenge of procedure) increased with experience	Different teams learned at different rates when the procedure involved tacit knowledge and same rate when it involved codified knowledge. Team stability improved rates.
Reagans, Argote, & Brooks (2005)	Procedure time and number of procedures completed (individual and team)	Joint replacement surgery in teaching hospitals	Procedure time decreased while number of procedures increased with experience	Increased experience both working on the team and within the organization improved outcomes.

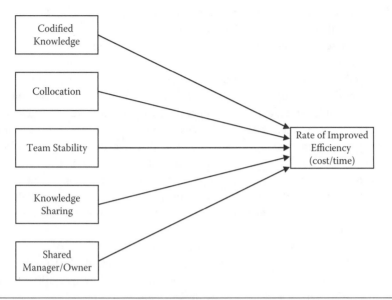

Figure 6.1   Key Constructs and Relationships in Outcome Improvement Area.

which they work. At the same time, the work focuses narrowly on efficiency improvement in repetitive operations as the measure of learning, and offers little insight into today's most prevalent team challenges related to innovation and various kinds of knowledge work that do not involve repetition of similar tasks.

Task Mastery: Coordinating Team-Member Knowledge in Interdependent Tasks

A second area of research emphasizes task mastery by teams and studies how team members learn to accomplish interdependent tasks. This area views team learning as an outcome of communication and coordination that builds shared knowledge by team members about their team, task, resources, and context. More specifically, team learning is conceptualized as task mastery, and how well a team has learned its task is a typical measure of success.

Research in this area examines how teams leverage their members' knowledge and skills to increase the quality and amount of knowledge available for task execution. A central focus in this work is encoding, storing, retrieving, and communicating information in teams (Wilson, Goodman, & Cronin, in press). Simply put, this work has found that teams with members who know what each other knows (collectively and individually) are better able to perform interdependent tasks. Although learning was not explicitly defined in most of the task-mastery papers we reviewed, researchers implicitly treated learning as an outcome best measured in terms of task performance, paying particular attention to mastering new tasks. A related area of research—on effects of shared cognitive schemas on group decision making (e.g., Gruenfeld, Mannix, Williams, & Neale, 1996; Walsh, Henderson, & Deighton, 1988)—is outside the scope of our review, but develops similar arguments and empirical results.

In general, this research focuses on the relationship between team cognitive systems and team task performance, and relies primarily on laboratory experiments for data. Researchers have assembled teams of university students, assigned them a task such as assembling a transistor radio or completing a flight simulation, and tested their ability to complete the task under different experimental conditions. Most of the teams studied in this way consisted of strangers convened to complete an isolated task before disbanding. These laboratory studies have allowed causal inferences about particular features of team learning but left open questions about how the results generalize to real-world settings.

Our review focuses on more recent research in this area, starting in 1995; (for a review of earlier research, see Klimoski & Mohammed, 1994 and Walsh, 1995). Researchers in this area have emphasized team-level cognitive constructs, using terms such as *shared mental models* (Cannon-Bowers, Salas, Converse, & Castellan, 1993), *transactive memory systems* (Wegner, 1987), and *social cognition* (Larson & Christensen, 1993), among others. Conceptually, these constructs are similar; all are team-level cognitive systems that encode, store, retrieve, and communicate knowledge and all are used to predict task performance (e.g., Hollingshead, 2001; Wegner, 1987).

Effects of knowing who knows what in a team.   Early work on transactive memory systems focused on the relationships between group training, transactive memory systems, and task performance. Liang, Moreland, and Argote (1995) studied laboratory-based experimental teams assembling transistor radios, and measured the transactive memory system (TMS) by coding videotapes of the teams assembling radios to assess: memory differentiation, task coordination, and task credibility.[1] Including factors (task motivation, group cohesion, and social identity[2]) previously related to group performance in their model, the authors found that teams that trained together developed a stronger TMS and a stronger social identity, performed better on the task (fewest assembly errors), and recalled more assembly information than teams of individuals trained separately. Furthermore, the researchers maintained that group training did not directly predict task performance, but rather its effects were mediated by the development of a TMS.

Moreland, Argote, and Krishnan (1998) conducted two follow-up studies, replicating the findings and ruling out alternative explanations. In the first, they used the same research design but added two new training conditions: (a) an individual-training condition followed by a team-building exercise, and (b) a reassignment condition in which teams trained together were shuffled into new teams prior to task execution. The results indicated that groups trained together performed better that the other three training conditions, and this relationship was again mediated by the existence of a TMS. Interestingly, groups in the team-building condition matched the group-development and social-identity scores of the group-trained condition, but still underperformed them. Groups in the reassignment condition performed no better than the individual training condition, illustrating turnover's detrimental impact on task performance.

In the second experiment, the researchers examined the content of team TMSs (complexity, accuracy, and agreement) and investigated whether social loafing would occur when teams were trained together (Moreland et al., 1998). Teams of undergraduates were trained together or individually, but instead of completing the task in teams, as anticipated, each subject was asked to complete the task alone. In advance, subjects completed a questionnaire on beliefs about their team members' task-related knowledge and skills. Although teams trained together demonstrated greater complexity, accuracy, and agreement in beliefs about each other's expertise, there were no significant performance differences between individuals trained together or apart. Thus, if social loafing had occurred when teams trained together, it did not lead to subsequent individual performance differences.

Stasser, Stewart, and Wittenbaum (1995) also sought to understand how shared cognitive representations of members' task knowledge impacted team performance. A laboratory study showed that explicit recognition of members' task-relevant expertise improved a team's task performance more than simply mentioning differences in member expertise on the team. The authors concluded that having frank knowledge of each individual's expertise—knowing who knows what—leverages a team's ability to develop informal schemas of accountability such that "experts" in a given domain are called upon to use their expertise and to store new related knowledge. Although teams in this study were not trained together, they developed shared understanding of members' expertise through explicit discussion, and achieved similar results. A later study suggested that when team members know each other, uniquely held tacit knowledge is more likely to make it into the conversation than when they are unacquainted (Gruenfeld et al., 1996).

Not surprisingly, communication has been studied as the critical mechanism explaining transactive memory and other cognitive systems development. In particular, research showed that communication was a predictor of task performance (word recall) among intimate partners (Hollingshead, 1998a, b). Moreland and Myaskovsky (2000) also studied communication, collaborative training, and TMSs, and found that teams assembling transistor radios that trained together performed no better than teams that did not train together but were given specific information on individual team member's expertise. They concluded that, although training together is an antecedent of TMS development, the underlying mechanism is not communication per se, but rather the opportunity to get to know each team member's specific knowledge and skills.

To better understand the relationship between communication and knowledge encoding in teams, Rulke and Rau (2000) compared teams that trained together and apart, and showed that the former developed better TMSs than the latter. Further, teams with the most functional TMSs—and best task performance—engaged in specific conversations about individual expertise early in the team's life and continued to have conversations about expertise over time. The authors proposed that TMS formation follows a pattern of initial expertise declaration, followed by expertise evaluation by the team, and finally expertise coordination for task execution.

Types and content of shared memory systems. Some researchers proposed the existence of multiple simultaneous TMSs in teams, such as those focused on tasks, routines, or resources (Cannon-Bowers et al., 1993; Klimoski & Mohammed, 1994). In a study of teams engaged in a flight-simulation task, Mathieu, Heffner, Goodwin, Salas, and Cannon-Bowers (2000) found statistical support for two conceptually distinct types of shared mental models, one related to task work and one related to team work. They also examined the effect of sharedness of metal models (degree of overlap in members' perceptions of team mental models) on task performance. The relationship between the degree of sharedness (for both task work and teamwork) and the outcome of task performance was mediated by team processes, including strategy formation and coordination, cooperation, and communication.

Rentsch and Klimoski (2001) likewise proposed that *schema agreement*, or sharedness, is critical for task performance. Taking their hypothesis to a field setting, they tested relationships between antecedents (such as composition), teamwork schema agreement, and team effectiveness. Antecedents, including educational similarity, teaming experience, team-member recruitment, and team size (negative), were related to team-member schema agreement, which in turn mediated the relationship between the antecedent variables and team effectiveness. In the same journal issue, Smith-Jentsch, Campbell, Milanovich, and Reynolds (2001) reported that rank and experience among navy personnel significantly predicted the overlap of shared mental models; the higher the rank or the greater the experience, the greater the degree of similarity between team-member mental models. However, the authors argued that these antecedents were not deterministic; with training, team members who had lower ranking or less experience were able to develop shared mental models similar to those of the "experts."

In addition to mental model agreement, Moreland and colleagues (1998) determined that teams with TMSs had a greater degree of complexity and accuracy in their beliefs about each other's expertise. In a field study of teams in a consumer-products organization, Austin (2003) found that transactive memory accuracy (the extent to which group members accurately identify each other's knowledge) was a better predictor of task performance (financial goal achievement) than other dimensions of a team TMS, including team knowledge, mental model convergence, and member specialization. Austin also proposed a new type of TMS related to knowledge about each team member's external relationships, and suggested that successful task performance leverages not only unique team-member knowledge but also the knowledge uniquely available to them from outside the team's boundaries. A theory paper by Brandon and Hollingshead (2004) introduced *validation* as a third dimension of a team TMS, and defined it as the extent to which team members participate in the TMS. The paper argued that TMS *convergence* (defined as high levels of sharedness/agreement, accuracy, and validation) was optimal for teams.

One study noted the difficulties of importing extra-team knowledge. Studying undergraduate workgroups in a semester-long class project, Gruenfeld, Martorana, and Fan (2000) investigated how teams leverage knowledge introduced from other teams. They found that when a team member left his or her original team to visit another ("foreign") team, the visitor's ideas were used in the foreign team, while unique ideas proposed by the foreign team's "indigenous" members decreased. In addition, indigenous team members failed to utilize their own returning member's ideas, yet they did generate more unique ideas than they did in their original formation. The authors concluded that the process of knowledge transfer between teams is complex because various team-level social influences influence how knowledge is integrated into a team's memory systems.

How shared memory systems develop. Rather than assume the team mental-model-development process was linear, researchers began to examine how members' knowledge of each other's skills and abilities evolved over time in response to changing task demands (Brandon & Hollingshead, 2004; Liang et al., 1995). Levesque, Wilson, and Wholey (2001), in a study of undergraduate students engaged in a software-development project, found that one dimension of a team's shared mental models (mental model convergence) decreased over time, while another dimension (role differentiation) increased over time. They posited that role differentiation led to an increase in specialization, prompting more independent work drawing from individual expertise, leading to less interaction, and hence less convergence in shared knowledge. They did not tie these changes over time to differences in task performance, but suggested that interaction is critical for maintaining shared mental models in a team.

Lewis (2004) also studied how a team's TMS evolves over time, building on Levesque et al.'s (2001) observation that interpersonal communication patterns developed early in a team's collaboration affected how a team's TMS matures. Lewis found that interpersonal processes such as face-to-face communication during the planning phase were particularly important for TMS maturation. A team's ability to fine-tune an existing TMS depended on the extent of face-to-face communication. Implementation-phase TMSs were positively related to both task performance and team viability, suggesting the need to maintain a TMS over the entire course of a task.

Lewis, Lange, and Gillis (2005) studied undergraduate teams engaged in three similar tasks over time. Teams were initially trained together and then asked to assemble an electronic device, a telephone. For some teams, the experimenters imposed a reshuffling in which half of the members on a team were swapped with those of another team before beginning the task, a move that effectively dismantled the TMSs. As predicted, intact teams performed better on the task than disrupted teams. Before performing the second task, assembling a stereo, some teams were again randomly reshuffled to dissolve their TMSs. Thus, for the second task, there were three groups: those with (a) intact TMSs, (b) previously intact but now dismantled TMSs, and (c) never-intact TMSs. Contrary to prediction, the results showed no statistically significant performance differences between groups on the second task. Further analyses revealed an interesting interaction effect between expertise stability and task performance; teams that developed TMSs before the first task (and whose members maintained the same domain of expertise for both tasks) performed the best. Finally, the third task called for teams to describe in writing how they would assemble an electronic stapler. Intact teams with stable TMSs showed evidence of having developed more abstract, generalized knowledge about the task and the underlying principles associated with electronic assembly, compared to those with a disrupted TMS. Developing abstract knowledge was seen as evidence of a higher order learning process, through which teams were processing and accommodating new information into their repertoire of behaviors.

Studies on team-memory systems have included few organizational variables, although some noted the likelihood that context would influence the shape of team-memory systems over time (Druskat & Pescosolido, 2002). Ren, Carley, and Argote (2006) studied the effects of organizational context in a computer simulation study of hypothetical team situations. The authors examined the effects of team TMSs on two performance outcomes: (a) time and (b) quality. The effects of a TMS on both outcomes depended on the organizational context (dynamic vs. stable)[3] and on team size. With a TMS in place, teams in dynamic contexts or of large sizes achieved improved time outcomes, while those in stable contexts or of small sizes reaped better-quality outcomes. Although all teams performed better with a TMS, the study suggested that effectiveness is contingent upon team context and size.

Barriers to task learning in teams. The extent to which a TMS is useful in a team depends largely upon how accurately it reflects reality. In addition to team size and turnover, other barriers to TMS development identified include collaborative inhibition, an observed tendency for teams to perform worse than individuals on recall tasks (Basden, Basden, Bryner, & Thomas, 1997; Hollingshead, 1998b); and mutual enhancement, a tendency to discuss shared knowledge rather than knowledge held by only one member (Stasser et al., 1995; Wittenbaum, Hubbell, & Zuckerman, 1999).

Some researchers find team mental-model building is implicitly political; members selectively negotiate content based on perceived relevance as opposed to simply adding team-member knowledge together (Walsh et al., 1988). Taken-for-granted socialized perceptions play a vital role in shaping a team's TMS. In one study, Hollingshead and Fraidin (2003) found that team members assessing their own expertise relative to others (in the absence of explicit information) relied on stereotypes about salient identity characteristics such as gender. Furthermore, when such stereotypes were activated, individuals tended to assign expertise according to stereotypes and to act in ways that fulfilled stereotypes about themselves. For example, in male-female dyads, males or females might act as knowledge "experts" in stereotypically male or female domains. The authors suggested that, without additional knowledge about individuals or an explicit effort to act against them, TMSs play a role in perpetuating harmful stereotypes. These studies thus demonstrated cognitive and social forces that inhibit TMS development. Candid information sharing in teams can be seen as difficult and yet critical for the emergence of a TMS. Table 6.3 highlights a selected subset of task-mastery studies.

Summary. This area of research recognizes that teams need a way to organize and retain a shared understanding of who knows what, and who can do what, to interact effectively to do their work. The construct of transactive memory systems captures a means for coordinating action in teams, minimizing the need for discussion. The shared knowledge embedded in TMSs allows task mastery by (a) ensuring that unique individual knowledge is used, (b) allowing specialization, (c) reducing redundant information, and (d) developing informal structures for accountability. For teams that do not require diverse member expertise or knowledge to do their work, a TMS may not be necessary. Finally, researchers suggest that TMSs require continuing communication to be maintained, an area that merits further investigation.

This work presents a few general conclusions about generic team-memory systems and task performance on novel tasks, as depicted in Figure 6.2. First, certain team characteristics, notably team size and expertise diversity, promote or inhibit TMS development, agreement, and accuracy. Second, features of the organizational context may affect TMS development. Third, barriers inhibit TMS development, such as team size and turnover. Fourth, transactive

Table 6.3 Selected Studies from Task Mastery Research

Authors	Data	Context	Aspect of Team Learning	Key Findings
Liang, Moreland, & Argote (1995)	Data on assembly quality, observations, and surveys of 30 teams	Lab: three-person undergraduate teams assembling AM/FM radios	Development of a transactive memory system (TMS)	Training together resulted in better assembly quality and predicted the development of a TMS.
Moreland & Myaskovsky (2000)	Data on assembly quality, observations, and surveys of 63 teams	Lab: three-person undergraduate teams assembling transistor radios	Teams trained together or given explicit information about each other's expertise had better assembly quality	Training together promoted TMS development, largely due to the opportunity to determine team-member specialization.
Mathieu et al., (2000)	Flight mission success (points), observations and surveys of 56 teams	Lab: two-person teams engaged in flight-simulation task	Degree of similarity of team mental models, team processes such as coordination	Team processes mediated the relationship between mental models and performance.
Lewis (2004)	Surveys of 64 teams and client organizations	Lab: four- to six-person teams of MBA students engaged in a semester-long consulting project	Development and maturation of a TMS over time	Transactive processes such as communication early in a team's existence supported the TMS maturation in later phases.

Lewis, Lange, & Gillis (2005)	Data on assembly quality, coded qualitative data, and surveys of 100 teams	Lab: three-person student teams assembling electronic devices	Applying TMSs to multiple, similar tasks	Teams with TMSs developed during training learn and apply knowledge to other similar tasks.
Ren, Carley, & Argote (2006)	Virtual experimental data from 60 computer modeled teams	Lab: computer simulation/ modeling of three-person team performing multiple tasks	Influence of environmental context on TMS development	A team's TMS is contingent on organizational environment, team size, and task characteristics.

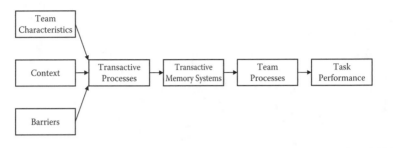

Figure 6.2   Key Constructs and Relationships in Task Mastery Area.

processes (Lewis et al., 2005) foster TMS development in the form of inter-personal interaction and communication eliciting knowledge about members' expertise (Liang et al., 1995; Moreland & Myaskovsky, 2000; Rulke & Rau, 2000; Stasser et al., 1995), and transactive processes mediate the relationship between context, team characteristics, and outcomes (Liang et al., 1995). Fifth, different types of team-level memory systems operate in teams at any given time, capturing member knowledge, task knowledge, teamwork knowledge, and knowledge about members' external relationships. Finally, team processes mediate the relationship between TMS and task performance (Mathieu et al., 2000).

Reliance on laboratory methods in this research has limited knowledge of how context affects team learning. Thoughtful discussions of TMS research methods have suggested that more field research is needed to investigate many of these lab-based conclusions (Mohammed, Klimoski, & Rentsch, 2000). In summary, this work informs us that coordinated ways of storing knowledge at the group level help teams master new tasks, and that developing shared team mental models is an essential aspect of this learning process.

Group Process: Understanding Learning Behavior in Real Teams

A third area of research conceptualizes team learning as a group process, rather than as a group or team outcome. Building on models, constructs, and methods from research on organizational learning and on team effectiveness, studies in this area typically investigate real workgroups in field settings. Team-effectiveness research typically employs an input-process-output (I-P-O) model in which group interaction processes mediate the relationship between group inputs (e.g., context, structure, composition) and group outputs (e.g., quality, innovation, performance) (e.g., Hackman, 1987; McGrath, 1984; also see Ilgen, Hollenbeck, Johnson, & Jundt, 2005, for a review). Organizational behavior researchers interested in team learning thus naturally turned to group process for evidence of learning.

A growing number of field-based studies examines learning processes in teams and how they are affected by managerial and contextual factors (such as team climate, goals, and identity) and, in turn, how they affect team performance. In its nascent stages, identifying the process of learning in real teams involved qualitative, exploratory methods (Edmondson & McManus, in press). In later work, constructs have become more formalized, and validated survey measures are growing in number. These field studies describe learning behaviors in ways that were not possible in quantitative learning-curve studies, and develop insight about organizational context not available in the psychology laboratory. In general, in this work, researchers attempt to observe or measure the processes of learning rather than relying on performance improvement as evidence that learning has occurred.

Team climate and learning behavior. Early field research on learning in teams focused on effects of leader behavior and group climate. Using a case study design with four cross-functional process-improvement teams in a large high-tech manufacturing firm, Brooks (1994) classified group processes into two types of learning behaviors: those that took place within team meetings (e.g., posing problems, sharing and discussing new ideas or information) and those that took place outside team boundaries (e.g., gathering and sharing information outside the team). In these teams, members' perceptions of the interpersonal risk created by within-team power differences appeared strongly related to learning behavior. Further, those teams lacking in learning behavior found it difficult to span team boundaries, and members "described the climate at the team meetings as 'stifling,' 'intimidating,' and 'damaging,'" with leaders "publicly ridiculing them" for voluntary contributions to meetings (p. 223). In contrast, in other teams, leaders encouraged member participation and deemphasized power differences.

In another field study, Edmondson (1996) uncovered differences across eight hospital workgroups in a specific learning behavior: speaking up about mistakes. Unexpectedly, survey data suggested that teams with better team leaders, higher quality team interpersonal process, and greater team effectiveness had higher, rather than lower, detected error rates. Interview and observational data, collected by an independent researcher blind to the surprising quantitative results, reinforced Edmondson's ex post explanation that better teams were more likely to report (rather than hide) errors, which she reasoned was essential for team learning. Just as Brooks (1994) had found, some team leaders (nurse managers, in this setting) had fostered a climate of openness that fostered willingness to engage in learning behavior.

To test this accidental finding more systematically, Edmondson (1999) studied climate and learning behavior in 53 teams of four types in a manufacturing firm, collecting both qualitative (interview and observation) and quantitative (survey) data. The study introduced the construct of *team psychological safety* to predict team-learning behavior. Psychological safety (the shared belief that a group is safe for interpersonal risk-taking) was found to mediate the effects of team leader coaching and context support on team-learning behavior. Learning behavior, in turn, mediated the effects of psychological safety on performance. Edmondson concluded that team-learning behavior helped translate effective team design and leadership into team performance.

Subsequent studies took a closer look at the effect of team leaders on learning behaviors. Edmondson (2003) described ways that team leader actions promote and inhibit psychological safety and, hence, learning behaviors in surgical teams. Effective team leaders (surgeons) fostered "speaking up in the service of learning" (p. 1419) by motivating the need for learning and deemphasizing power differences. Edmondson argued (but did not test) that learning processes should be expected to vary by team type; notably, learning in *interdisciplinary action teams*, in which real-time improvisation and coordination is critical to performance, was not likely to be explained by the same variables as in routine production teams.

Also focusing on team leaders, Sarin and McDermott (2003) surveyed 52 product-development teams in six high-tech companies and identified team-leader behaviors that facilitated team learning: involving members in decision making, clarifying team goals, and providing bridges to outside parties via the leader's status in the organization.[4] Context also mattered; team learning was more extensive when the project was important to the organization. Team size was negatively related to learning, possibly because of the additional challenge of coordinating and communicating among more people. Finally, learning was related to team performance (speed to market and innovation). Although Sarin and McDermott presented learning as a first-order outcome[5] (rather than a process), we include the study in this section because it demonstrated additional ways that team leadership promoted learning and in turn enhanced performance, a second-order outcome.

Unbundling team-learning behavior. As process studies of team learning became more numerous, researchers took a more detailed look at specific learning behaviors. Building on the observation of process differences across teams (Brooks, 1994; Edmondson, 1996), later work categorized learning behaviors to refine understanding of their effects on learning and performance outcomes. For example, in their qualitative study of surgical teams, Edmondson, Bohmer, and Pisano (2001) identified four steps of the learning process (enrollment, preparation, trials, and reflection) in which each surgical case was a "trial" from which to learn (through collective discussion, or reflection). Gibson and Vermeulen (2003) similarly conceptualized team learning as "a cycle of experimentation, reflective communication, and knowledge codification" (p. 222) in which all three processes must be present, and thus measured team learning as the product of these three factors. An exploratory study (Sole & Edmondson,

2002) of seven globally dispersed ("virtual") product-development teams in a multinational corporation discovered that team learning in this setting involved figuring out how to recognize and access situated knowledge embedded in different facilities and locales.

Related studies examined whether different types of team-learning behaviors have differential effects on team performance. A qualitative study of 12 manufacturing company teams of varying types (management, product development, service, production) identified the different implications for organizational performance of teams engaged in *incremental learning* (improvement) versus *radical learning* (innovation) (Edmondson, 2002). The article proposed that when teams responsible for innovation (e.g., developing new strategies or products) fail to learn, the organization may miss critical market opportunities that threaten future competitiveness; when teams engaged in production fail to learn, costs and other inefficiencies could threaten the organization's near-term profitability and competitiveness. Both types of teams, however, appeared to benefit from a similar process of iterating between action and reflection.

Wong (2004) surveyed 73 teams from multiple organizations and industries, measuring both *local learning* (learning from interactions within a group) and *distal learning* (learning by seeking ideas, help, or feedback from external parties). Group cohesion (strength of intrateam relationships and support) promoted both local and distal learning behaviors (as Brooks's [1994] exploratory analysis had suggested), which in turn showed differential effects on performance. Local learning predicted efficiency of team operations and mediated the effects of group cohesion on efficiency (consistent with Edmondson, 1999); in contrast, distal learning predicted team innovativeness, had a negative moderation effect on team efficiency, and actually suppressed local learning on a team. Based on these results, Wong recommended that teams responsible for task mastery should focus on local learning (and even avoid excess external contact), while those charged with innovating should focus on distal learning.

Building on team boundary-spanning research (Ancona & Caldwell, 1992), recent qualitative work identified a need for vicarious team learning with data from pharmaceutical "in-licensing" teams (Bresman, 2007). Survey data from 43 teams in six firms were then analyzed to show that several team-learning behaviors (experiential team-learning behavior, vicarious team-learning behavior, and contextual-learning behavior) were empirically distinct, and all contributed to externally rated team performance. Exploring related issues in a very different context, and arriving at different conclusions, Tucker, Nembhard, and Edmondson (2006) used surveys and interviews to study 23 process-improvement teams in hospital intensive care units, and found that *learn-what* (activities that identify current best practices, requiring boundary spanning to draw from the experiences of other teams, hospitals, or the research literature) and *learn-how* (activities that operationalize practices in the work setting) were distinct team-learning factors. Learn-how was associated with process improvement, but learn-what (the boundary-spanning behavior) was not. One possibility was that all teams studied were engaging in high levels of learn-what, restricting the explanatory power of the variable. Another possibility was that the learning in intensive care units requires more learn-how—the internally focused learning behavior—because of the importance of attention to specific work processes and relationships in producing change.

A closely related stream of research studies *team reflexivity*, "the extent to which teams reflect upon and modify their functioning" (Schippers, Den Hartog, & Koopman, in press; West, 1996, 2000). Team reflexivity has much in common with the team-learning concepts just discussed. Research on reflexivity has emphasized its positive effects on team performance (Schippers, Den Hartog, Koopman, & Wienk, 2003), consistent with other findings that show team-learning behaviors to be related to team performance or effectiveness (e.g., Edmondson, 1999). A study by Schippers and colleagues (in press) tested an intervention, in which teams of educators managing schools in Holland, trained by the author to engage in more reflexivity, subsequently showed better performance. The study stands as a preliminary but important attempt to produce the team behaviors proposed as valuable by the theory.

Shared learning goals. Several researchers have studied how common goals or purposes on a team affect learning behavior. Ely and Thomas (2001) conducted extensive observations and interviews of one team at each of three firms, in law, nonprofit consulting, and financial services. The authors analyzed their qualitative data to identify shared perspectives about interracial relations. Successful integration of diverse experiences in a team seemed to them to require an integration-and-learning perspective about team diversity—viewing diversity as a "resource for learning and adaptive change" (p. 240). Teams with an integration-and-learning perspective appeared more willing to spend time talking about, and working through, differences of opinion and conflicts. The other two perspectives (attitudes and goals related to diversity) identified were that (a) diversity can be leveraged to gain access and legitimacy in a market by matching employee-customer demographics, and (b) facing diversity requires overcoming discrimination to create fairness. The integration-and-learning perspective appeared to help team performance; teams without this perspective tended to avoid discussing different viewpoints, and stifled minority perspectives.

Two recent survey studies investigated shared goals related to learning. Bunderson and Sutcliffe (2003) measured *team-learning orientation* (an emphasis on proactive learning and skill development in a team) in 44 business-unit management teams in a large consumer-products company. The results found learning orientation to be a significant predictor of team performance (business-unit profitability) but with a curvilinear relationship, such that a mid-range level of learning orientation was optimal for performance. Further, the optimal level was higher for teams with lower prior-period performance. The authors concluded that learning orientation was useful to correct performance deficits but hurt performance if taken too far.

Surveying members of 107 teams from a variety of Chinese companies and industries, Tjosvold, Yu, and Hui (2004) found that teams with cooperative goals were more likely to engage in learning behavior[6] (than teams with competitive or independent goals) and more likely to report learning from their mistakes (measured as an outcome). Learning behavior only partially mediated this relationship.

Team identification. Team identity provides another antecedent of learning behavior in teams. Studies have investigated members' identification with their team as a moderator of the effects of context and group composition on learning; measures of interest included both overall team identification and "faultlines" between demographically overlapping subgroups of a team. First, Gibson and Vermeulen (2003) studied 156 teams in five pharmaceutical and medical products firms and analyzed survey and interview data to argue that subgroup strength (the degree to which some pairs of team members share demographic characteristics not shared with others) was an important moderator of contextual factors such as the performance management efforts of an external leader, team empowerment (autonomy), and the availability of an organizational knowledge-management system. Finding a nonmonotonic relationship between subgroup strength and learning behavior, such that a moderate level of subgroup strength was optimal for learning, the authors suggested that performance management efforts of external leaders partially compensated for either weak or strong subgroups, but that "teams with moderate subgroups display a high level of learning behavior to start with and increase this behavior much less as a result of performance management actions" (p. 228). They also reported that subgroup strength was a better predictor of performance than simple group heterogeneity (average pair-wise demographic overlap between team members). In sum, the degree of member identification with the team rather than with a particular subgroup influenced a team's ability to put its diversity to good use.

Studying a concept similar to subgroups, Lau and Murnighan (2005) measured the effect of demographic *faultlines* (dividing lines between demographic subgroups) on team-learning behavior in 79 groups of undergraduates working in assigned teams to complete a course project. Analysis of survey data suggested that team learning benefited from cross-ethnicity and cross-sex communications, but this effect was negatively moderated by faultline strength. Stronger faultlines offset, but did not entirely reverse, the positive effects of diverse communication for learning.

In a related study of 57 multidisciplinary teams in the oil and gas industry, Van der Vegt and Bunderson (2005) measured the strength of emotional identification with the team as a whole, rather than identification with subgroups. They found that collective team identification moderated the effects of expertise diversity on learning behavior and performance. Teams with stronger collective team identification were more successful at tapping the expertise diversity in the room, while those with low collective identification allowed diversity to inhibit learning behavior and team performance. The authors suggest that this phenomenon occurred because collective team identification stimulated otherwise difficult learning behaviors across expertise lines. These three studies illustrate how subgroup and faultline strength, or low identification with the team as a whole, make it harder to capture the benefits of diversity for learning.

Effects of context.   Recent studies introduce the context in which a team operates as a fundamental influence on team learning. To begin with, a team's context can present (or preclude) the opportunity to engage in learning behaviors. Examining the adoption of new routines in teams, one survey study of 90 teams from three pharmaceutical and medical-products firms measured knowledge-transfer effort to acquire new routines, as well as the knowledge acquisition outcome itself (Zellmer-Bruhn, 2003). The results showed that both process *interruptions* and *external contact* (exposure to other teams) predicted team engagement in knowledge-transfer learning behaviors, but only interruptions predicted actual knowledge acquisition. Knowledge-transfer efforts partially mediated the relationship between interruptions and knowledge acquisition, and exploratory analyses suggested that different types of interruptions affected both engagement in learning behavior and successful adoption in different ways. Interruptions in the flow of work provided opportunities to exercise reflection—creating an opening for learning to occur.

Zellmer-Bruhn and Gibson (2006) studied 115 teams in five multinational firms, collecting survey data supplemented with interview and archival data, and found that a learning outcome—"the extent to which the team created new processes and practices" (p. 509)—was more likely to occur in less-centralized organizations where teams were granted decision-making autonomy by the local and global organizations. In contrast, teams with less product-and-process discretion or those in organizations with a strategy of global integration were more likely to conform to prescribed practices and thus showed less learning behavior. Although not counterintuitive, these results are important in highlighting the necessity of considering context when measuring team-learning behavior and outcomes. Table 6.4 summarizes selected studies.

Summary. Field research on team learning has focused on group process, initially emphasizing interpersonal constructs and later expanding the lens to examine effects of multiple antecedents, including aspects of the organizational context in which teams work. Early team-learning studies established learning behavior as a mediating process between structure and performance; subsequent work examined the nature and types of learning behaviors more in more detail. Recent work has recognized that team type and context matter, but with limited systematic attention to measuring either, and future studies are likely to push the frontiers of such contingent theorizing still further. Thus, theory in this field-based work is becoming both more contextually detailed and more contingent over time, as discussed further in the next section.

Figure 6.3 summarizes our discussion of research in this area by illustrating the principal relationships found in this research, with a couple of relational alterations among variables. Although individual studies tended to assess main effects of team climate and context on learning behavior (e.g., Brooks, 1994; Edmondson, 1996, 1999, 2003; Zellmer-Bruhn & Gibson, 2006), consideration of a fuller set of studies suggests different possibilities. Thus, our summary model suggests that the influence of context on learning behavior is mediated by variables such as team-leader behavior, team goals, task characteristics, and team composition, and that intrateam climate is a moderator (Edmondson, 2003)—not a mediator (cf. Edmondson, 1999; Wong, 2004)—of the other antecedents of learning behavior. This proposal is consistent with results that show main effects on learning behavior, because the mediated and moderated effects shown here could not be tested in studies that did not measure all the variables. Figure 6.3 uses dashed lines show the untested relationships we propose, rather than solid (main effect) lines that depict previously tested relationships.

Team task (e.g., task routineness) is included in Figure 6.3, even though empirical support for task effects on team learning is limited. Although task attributes occasionally have been included in studies—for example, Edmondson (1999) included four types of team tasks and Wong (2004) measured task routineness—more commonly, task type is implicit in the choice of research setting or subjects. Not surprisingly, in these different studies, different variables explained learning (e.g., leader behavior, vicarious learning behavior, or team identification), suggesting that future research should pay more explicit attention to developing and testing theory about how task attributes affect team learning. Finally, studies rarely measure comprehensive sets of variables, such as those depicted in Figure 6.3, and so relative effect sizes of antecedents remain an area for future research.

Team learning in this area of research is a verb. Researchers observe or otherwise measure learning as group behaviors and activities, rather than inferring that learning has taken place from observed outcomes. This emphasis

Table 6.4 Selected Studies from Group Process Research

Authors	Data	Context	Aspect of Team Learning	Key Findings
Edmondson (1999)	Surveys, interviews, and observations of 51 teams	Four types of teams (functional, self-managed, cross-functional product-development or project teams) at a single manufacturer	*Team learning behavior:* asking for help, experimenting, discussing errors, and seeking information and feedback from customers and others	Team design and leadership can foster psychological safety, which enables learning behavior, and thus team performance.
Bunderson & Sutcliffe (2003)	Surveys of team leader and members; Team performance and demographic data from corporate records	Management teams of 44 operating units (equally divided among high-, average-, and low-performance) in a large consumer-products firm	*Team learning orientation:* the extent to which a team encourages proactive learning and competence development among its members	Overemphasizing learning can compromise team performance. The optimal level of learning orientation is higher for low performers, and lower for high performers.
Wong (2004)	Surveys of team members and managers in 73 teams	Teams from four organizations (a financial services firm, a hospital, an industrial company, and a high-tech company)	*Local learning:* intragroup speaking up, opinion seeking, reflection; Distal learning: seeking outside ideas, help, and feedback	Different types of team learning can have distinct antecedents and produce separate effects on performance.

Van der Vegt & Bunderson (2005)	Surveys of members and supervisors on 57 teams; archival data	Multidisciplinary teams from a company in the oil-and-gas-industry in the Netherlands	*Learning behavior:* open sharing, evaluation, and combining of the team's ideas and work	Collective team identification moderates the effects of diversity on learning behavior and performance.
Zellmer-Bruhn & Gibson (2006)	Surveys of 115 teams and their external supervisors; archival data	Wide range of teams from five multinational pharmaceutical and medical-products firms	*Learning:* "the extent to which the team created new processes and practices" (p. 509)	The autonomy granted by the organizational context can constrain or enable team innovation and learning.

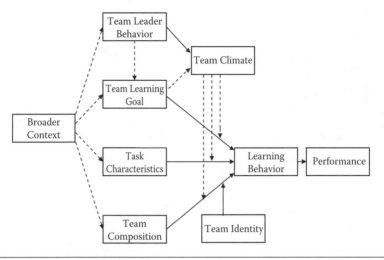

Figure 6.3   Key Constructs and Relationships in Group Process Area.

on process derives both from roots in team-effectiveness research, as well as from a reliance on field-based methods to understand how teams learn. This growing body of work also directly examined the relationship between learning behavior and performance in teams, a noteworthy endeavor for two reasons. First, the learning-performance relationship is not always positive (Bunderson & Sutcliffe, 2003; Wong, 2004); second, different types of learning are seen as relevant for different types of performance outcomes (Edmondson, 2002; Wong, 2004). In contrast, the first two areas of research position performance-type outcome measures (efficiency improvement, task mastery) as primary measures of learning.

This area also offers diverse and detailed portraits of team-learning processes that can only be obtained through field research. Qualitative data has provided the texture and detail necessary for illuminating process and clarifying mechanisms in a variety of settings, while quantitative results have strengthened confidence in a small but growing number of measures and relationships. Moreover, a growing number of studies use multilevel concepts and analytic techniques to reflect the reality of individuals nested in teams and teams nested in organizations (e.g., Edmondson, 1999; Zellmer-Bruhn & Gibson, 2006).

Limitations.   Important limitations of this work must be noted. Despite some consistent measures and themes, overall the constructs and measures of team learning and its antecedents are remarkably inconsistent across studies. For example, none of the studies of team identity, team goals, or organizational context use the same terminology or measures, although they addressed similar issues. While many studies characterized intrateam climate—usually referring to perceptions of interpersonal openness or caring about the team, climate attributes potentially captured by the term psychological safety (e.g., Edmondson, 1999; Kahn, 1990; Schein & Bennis, 1965)—climate terms and measures still show only partial convergence. In measures of team-learning behavior—the central variable in this work—we observed a trend of growing convergence as studies moved toward greater use of survey methods, but even here consistency (when the latent variable is in fact the same) would facilitate theory development (e.g., the items in *problem-solving orientation* (Tjosvold et al., 2004) related clearly to group process or learning behavior and less to goals). Consequently, it is difficult to compare results and to build knowledge. Future research would benefit from convergence on terms and measures when possible, or clarity about how and why a construct is different from competing terms. We return to this theme in our discussion section.

In conclusion, despite many insights and a growing number of studies, further conceptual development and additional empirical work are needed to better specify relationships among constructs. Few prior studies include enough variables to sort out moderating relationships, requiring some extrapolation in Figure 6.3 to include reasonable possibilities.

Discussion

In this section, we reflect on what we have learned from our review of research on team learning. We identify a small number of well-supported relationships, as well as some that are slightly more speculative. We also identify problems and limitations in this literature, and propose specific areas for improvement. In general, we call for clarity and consistency of constructs and variables, but advocate continued inclusiveness in what is considered relevant to team learning. We start by a brief review of findings, followed by an overview of research trends, and then discuss differences and similarities in the three areas of research as a foundation for discussing what the term *team learning* means.

Key Findings

Across the studies reviewed, several variables stand out as sufficiently supported in prior work to remain essential for inclusion in future research—at least within a given range of settings. These include team stability, team leader behavior, and psychological safety or other aspects of interpersonal climate. Other factors, including task attributes, need further theoretical development and empirical research; that is, we have preliminary evidence that they matter, but not enough data to know exactly how or under what conditions.

First, we consider factors that almost certainly matter. At least some studies in all three areas included *team stability* as a variable. Although stability did not affect learning in all studies, in most it did, particularly in the learning curve and task mastery areas. Moreover, the extent to which members have worked together is clearly an important issue for understanding how well they share their knowledge, skills, and actions to achieve collective aims.

For teams that have leaders, leader behavior has been shown consistently in field research to be an important factor in shaping the climate of the team and in motivating learning. Power dynamics present an important theoretical relationship with learning behavior, due to the interpersonal risks involved in asking questions or discussing mistakes, some of the activities emphasized in the group process area. Social psychologists have long recognized that people look to leaders for cues on appropriate behavior in a social setting (e.g., Tyler & Lind, 1992). The team leader is also a focal point for coordination of effort (e.g., Edmondson, 2003) a role that deserves greater attention in the future. Psychological safety, or interpersonal climate more generally, is not only importantly related to leader behavior, but also merits consideration in its own right as a focal construct in the group-process area.

With less empirical support to back our arguments, we suggest that team learning is shaped in important ways by the nature of the task. The task attributes that matter most remain undertheorized, however. Possibilities include the nature of the team's goals (short-term, achievable goals may not be conducive to extensive learning behavior, for example), as well as the *level of discretion* over task-based action encountered by a team (e.g., an assembly-line task vs. pure brainstorming), task interdependence, knowledge intensiveness, or the degree of interpersonal risk in the work (e.g., are mistakes a salient feature of the task?). The theoretical centrality of team task for learning argues that more research should investigate specific kinds of teams facing specific challenges with real-world importance. Bresman's (2007) study of pharmaceutical in-licensing teams is one such example.

The context in which a team works, such as that created by the industry or by the resources available to the team from inside and outside the organization, can have an important influence on team-learning processes and outcomes, as shown by very recent research (Zellmer-Bruhn & Gibson, 2006). Going forward, context must be investigated more systematically. In health care, for example, the intrinsic importance of goals such as patient safety contrasts with goals such as cost reduction, and could have an effect on the types of learning observed and on the role of various antecedents. Pressure (or opportunity) for innovation, change, and learning from the broader context could be an important antecedent of team goals, processes, and outcomes.

Finally, as we look for more contextually specific models, collaborations between organizational researchers and people with domain expertise present cross-fertilization opportunities. Both the learning-curve and group-process areas have been the beneficiaries of such successful collaborations with healthcare researchers. More such partnerships are needed for contextually specific research in areas like public organizations (with scholars of government), schools (with educational scholars), and top management teams (with executives).

Trends

Team-learning research exhibits two dominant trends over the past decade. First, as with many maturing literatures, the work has shifted from more exploratory and simple models that identify issues, constructs, and possibilities to more quantitative, mature, and precise models (Edmondson & McManus, in press). Thus, over time, models of team learning are more likely to include mediators that test mechanisms translating antecedents into outcomes, and moderating variables that help specify precise conditions under which particular antecedents produce a desired outcome. Models that include moderators recognize that treating all teams and all contexts the same way is unlikely to reflect the realities of team learning accurately.

Moderators tested thus far include task type (Van der Vegt & Bunderson, 2005) and industry context (Zellmer-Bruhn & Gibson, 2006); moderators suggested but not formally tested include team type (Edmondson, 2003, 1999) and knowledge tacitness (Edmondson et al., 2003). That is, some work recognizes that the fundamental challenge of learning in teams is different for different tasks. For some tasks (particularly in real work settings), multiple learning challenges are relevant, and antecedents and performance implications may be different for each.

Within this trend, the term *team* is becoming insufficiently specific as the task, context, and learning process necessarily differ—possibly in theoretically important ways—for different types of teams. For example, when task constraints or organizational strategy do not allow local autonomy, teams are less free to engage in learning behavior (Zellmer-Bruhn & Gibson, 2006). Similarly, due to the nature of their task, innovation teams will engage in more learning behaviors than routine production teams. Thus, by proposing models of team learning that are universal, we lose conceptual and predictive accuracy. In contrast, models that pertain to specific kinds of teams, identified along theoretical dimensions (e.g., knowledge versus action, expertise diversity), or specific kinds of contexts, are needed to advance team-learning research. We return to this theme, in discussing specific possibilities for new research.

Commonalities and Differences Across Areas

Although the research areas we reviewed are substantively different along several dimensions, as highlighted earlier in Table 6.1, noteworthy commonalities connect pairs of areas. First, the learning curve and group-process areas share a methodological foundation in field research, both collecting field data and examining learning challenges in real work settings in organizations. The task mastery area, in contrast, draws almost exclusively from the laboratory.

Second, the learning-curve and task-mastery areas both conceptualize learning as improved task performance. This agreement may be driven by the type of task studied—typically a (constrained) production task for which successful completion is well defined and execution is the team's primary focus. In contrast, the group-process area explores a wide array of team tasks—often unconstrained or creative, with multiple successful outcomes possible—and focuses on adaptive behaviors that enable team success in the face of uncertainty or change.

Third, despite differences in methodology and research setting, the task-mastery and group-process areas share a disciplinary foundation in the psychology of group dynamics, and both investigate how team-member knowledge and interpersonal relationships affect group outcomes. In contrast, learning-curve studies examine efficiency improvement with little attention to group member perceptions or behaviors.

The rubric of team learning—as an abstract concept—may be the only commonality tying all three areas together, as reflected in low levels of cross-area citations. As a result, researchers with a common interest in how organizational teams learn lack a coherent body of accumulated knowledge about different kinds of teams facing different kinds of challenges. A lack of shared terminology is partly to blame; however, differences across areas go deeper than word choice.

What Is Team Learning?

From one study to another—even within research areas—how team learning is conceptualized varies considerably, including task mastery, process improvement, expanded understanding, discussing mistakes and failures, experimenting, and innovation, to name a few. This variety reflects the range of phenomena and activities being studied—from product assembly to strategy formation. Although this breadth reflects the natural range of collaborative work in organizations, it limits the precision of the term *team learning*. Perhaps surprisingly, we will not try to correct this imprecision in this chapter, arguing instead that team learning should remain an encompassing rubric.

We propose that team learning is a useful abstraction that cannot be thought of as a single specific organizational phenomenon. On its own, the term *team learning* does not refer to product development, new product assembly, or more efficient cardiac surgery. The processes, antecedents, and outcomes of learning in these different team contexts can vary dramatically, requiring more precise descriptions and theories to inform practice in meaningful ways. This is consistent with our earlier point that theoretical models require greater specificity and precision about team type and organizational context—to be both more accurate and more useful.

In the paragraphs that follow, we point to methodological and disciplinary causes and implications of the proliferation of concepts, methods, and activities in this growing body of work. We then call for consistency of constructs and measures, without seeking to constrain the meaning of team learning.

Sources of conceptual variety. First, methodological choices influence how team learning is conceptualized. Methods limit data sources and study settings, which in turn determine the types of phenomena observed. Researchers using one method may be studying a legitimately different phenomenon from those associated with another method. Surveys, interviews, observations, lab experiments, and archival data each measure certain aspects of group behavior or outcomes and ignore others, regardless of what might be present in a phenomenon or research setting. For example, a large archival dataset from a production facility can reveal changes over time in operational efficiency but not in coordination of operators' skills or group discussion of errors, and so a study relying on such data is likely to measure (and thus conceptualize) learning as efficiency improvement. In this way, the varied methods discussed here support different contributions to theory about learning in teams.

Related to methods, disciplinary training is also clearly an important source of conceptual variety. For example, those trained to examine service and manufacturing processes systematically will tend to look to measures that matter to operations managers, such as time or cost. Experimental social psychologists care deeply about establishing causality, and must examine factors that can be operationalized and assessed in a short-term task. Organizational behavior researchers seek to learn from and theorize naturally occurring sources of variance in social settings, which are often subjective and imprecise. In each group, we read our own literatures and cite those who have preceded us in similar endeavors.

Away from unity. Several authors have proposed unitary definitions of team learning (Gibson & Vermeulen, 2003; Wilson et al., in press), advocating convergence on a single (but differing) concept. Our review uncovers diversity that does not lend itself to a uniform definition of team learning. We find that team learning is not a unitary concept at this point in the development of several related literatures, and we are reluctant to argue that it should be otherwise.

First, a pragmatic reason. A single concept is unlikely to cover all that constitutes team learning because the work carried out by real teams in organizations varies so broadly. Even the term *team* is imprecise, and definitions are shifting to encompass new realities (e.g., Ancona, Bresman, & Kaeufer, 2002), and whether the word *learning* refers to process or outcome has long remained ambiguous. Second, we argue that diversity is generative. The inclusion of different phenomena under an encompassing rubric can stimulate cross-fertilization among research areas that otherwise would not learn from each other. Third, our view of the inclusiveness of team learning is tied to the prior work on organizational learning, which has traditionally encompassed a range of real-world phenomena, from innovation to process improvement to planned system change (Edmondson & Moingeon, 1998). Attempting to promote a single concept of organizational learning would be unlikely to succeed after 50 years of well-known research from different schools of thought (Argyris & Schön, 1978; Huber, 1991; Levitt & March, 1988) In our view, the term team learning is sufficiently abstract that limiting it to one operational definition is impractical if not counterproductive. Instead, we argue that team learning, like organizational learning, is a useful rubric, an umbrella term encompassing a variety of loosely related theories and studies.

Toward consistency. Despite our reluctance to mandate a single definition of team learning, we strongly advocate greater consistency in constructs and measures used in empirical research. As the team-learning literature matures, theory development will be enabled by consistent terms and measures for highly similar concepts, helping researchers to clearly differentiate new findings from prior work, and enabling researcher communication and progress.

The relative simplicity of the three figures in our review belies the confusing proliferation of terms in this research. Prior work is replete with examples of close conceptual cousins called by different names and measured by sets of remarkably similar survey items. This problem is particularly prevalent in the group-process research area, as was previously noted, but also appears in the task-mastery area, where similar phenomena are variously referred to as "team mental models," "transactive memory systems," or "shared cognition."

All three areas also display confusion about the concept of learning itself. In learning-curve research, for example, reductions in product cost or production time may happen because the team learned, which is not to say that these outcomes are themselves learning. Task-mastery studies rarely make a "before" and "after" comparison, instead comparing "treatment" and "control" groups to demonstrate that certain treatments cause improvements in coordination of skills and knowledge. In the group-process area, an example of this confusion is the use of similar measures by Zellmer-Bruhn and Gibson (2006), Wong (2004), and Gibson and Vermeulen (2003) to measure learning, innovation, and experimentation, respectively.

Measures of learning also vary across studies, making it difficult to systematically accumulate evidence (see also Wilson et al., in press). Even in streams of work that agree in conceptualizing learning as a process, researchers include different types or measures of that process, and draw conclusions about learning as if it were a unitary construct. It is possible that different aspects and, hence, measures of learning might help explain disparate findings.[7] For example, if multiple learning processes operate in a team, and a study measures only one, results are unlikely to be replicated in different settings. Similarly, cases in which learning only partially mediates between antecedents and performance (e.g., Van der Vegt & Bunderson, 2005; Zellmer-Bruhn, 2003) may occur because only one aspect of learning behavior was measured. We are unlikely to agree on a single measure or definition of team learning, and so it may be more fruitful to begin to define subcategories and measures that are shared and used, going forward.

In short, given the inclusive nature of team learning, clearly specifying the phenomenon being studied may help knowledge develop systematically. Notably, studies should clearly identify whether they are examining a learning behavior or a learning outcome, and label variables accordingly (e.g., "knowledge transfer behavior," "knowledge acquisition outcome"). Many articles in the past have sought to contribute to "team learning" in general, while using a narrow measure. It might be more accurate for an article to claim to contribute to knowledge of vicarious learning in interdisciplinary healthcare teams, for example, rather than knowledge of team learning.

Convergence of terms and measures for antecedents of team learning would be particularly helpful to advance theory. The task-mastery literature has tested a variety of team characteristics as predictors of TMSs, but has not tried to consolidate them into a useful framework.[8] The variety of names for learning orientation and team identification in the group-process area was just discussed. Likewise, in the task-mastery area, little agreement exists on the overall terms to describe team mental models (Cannon-Bowers et al., 1993; Larson & Christensen, 1993; Liang et al., 1995) and definitive terms within the area such as "sharedness" versus "agreement" (Mathieu et al., 2000; Rentsch & Klimoski, 2001).

In contrast, explicit attempts to assess an alternative conceptualization of a prior variable are useful. For example, Tjosvold and colleagues (2004) expected (but did not find) that blaming orientation would curb learning behavior in teams and thus could be used as an alternative to psychological safety (Edmondson, 1999). Such efforts could help clarify the boundaries of existing constructs, or replace them if better constructs and explanations are developed. However, this refining process is limited by the variety of data sources and contexts studied; it is just as likely that Tjosvold and colleagues' (2004) Asian teams differed in important ways from Edmondson's (1999) Midwestern teams as that psychological safety is a "better" predictor. With more precision about context, discussed next, and more consistency of terms, as advocated here, future researchers can sharpen the set of variables that best explain precise phenomena of interest.

Finally, we welcome the heterogeneity studied under the team-learning rubric, but suggest that some conceptual boundaries are essential. More specifically, everything related to change is not learning. Creativity, for example, is not a conceptual match to learning. Communication is not one and the same as learning. A common theme shared by the three research areas just discussed is that learning implies some kind of positive change (created or intended by certain activities), whether in understanding, knowledge, ability/skill, processes/routines, or systemic coordination. We thus propose that conceptualizations of team learning be limited to both processes and outcomes that include this element of positive change produced by investments in developing shared insight, knowledge, or skill.

Moving Forward

Team-learning research has tackled some of the most fundamental challenges teams face—including how teams improve performance in repetitive operations, how members learn to work together on novel tasks, and how they manage the face threats implied by admitting ignorance or uncertainty. Reflecting on the articles just reviewed, we can identify useful insights about coordination and interpersonal processes for academic discussions of teams, teamwork, and learning in organizations. Little of this literature thus far has sought to solve specific practical problems (such as improving product development, enriching strategic decision making, or reducing medical errors) in which teams play a role. Although most of the research can be said to have implications for practice, managerial imperatives are rarely a driver of the questions and data selected in this work. This attribute is not unique, or even unusual, in management studies. Nonetheless, it appears to us particularly noteworthy in this instance given the potential relevance of teams and teamwork for organizational effectiveness. Thus, the question of what team-learning researchers can say to managers remains an important motivating concern. We suggest relevance should be a crucial driver of future research.

New directions for team learning research. We identify three opportunities for research that would advance knowledge ofteam learning in crucial ways. First, we call for field research designed to explore the range and nature of team-learning challenges in today's organizations. Comparative case studies of diverse situations in which teams faced a need for learning could help shape subsequent theory development and empirical research to reflect the realities of current team-based work. Lacking systematic knowledge of team-learning challenges in different industry contexts, it is difficult to identify the key variables that might serve as boundary conditions for theoretical relationships such as those depicted in Figures 6.1, 6.2, and 6.3. To illustrate, the challenges faced by cross-disciplinary, interorganizational teams in healthcare delivery (e.g., Nembhard, 2006) are likely to differ from those faced by geographically dispersed process-development teams in polymer production (e.g., Sole & Edmondson, 2002), and universal models of team learning do not capture these. Clearly, we do not seek unique models for every industry or task, but rather we hope to specify critical variables differentiating contexts and how these variables would alter existing theoretical models. In sum, we propose that field-based research to understand context-specific factors and relationships is an important next step.

Second, we call for quantitative research on samples that include more than one type of team and/or more than one type of context (varying on theoretically relevant dimensions). As just noted, despite awareness that team type is important, prior research has rarely tested its effects systematically. However, logic, together with preliminary research (e.g., Wong, 2004), suggests that focused hypotheses related to task type and to certain features of the work context could be developed. We should be able to predict effects of certain team and task variables, such as those just discussed, and to test them in studies that deliberately include variance in these dimensions of interest. Research on such samples would contribute to the development of midlevel models that are neither too narrow to be relevant to theory nor too general to be useful to practice.

Third, recognizing that team boundaries in many organizations are both temporary and permeable (Ancona et al., 2002; Edmondson & Nembhard, in press; Mortensen, 2004), we call for research on systems of teams or teamwork in organizations. As this possibility lies beyond current conceptions of team learning, we discuss it further in a section on broader implications.

The previously mentioned opportunities necessarily involve multiple methods. As our ideas and models become more mature, laboratory studies can establish causality and test proposed boundary conditions, to the extent that reasonable facsimiles of the conditions can be created and manipulated. Laboratory research can produce general statements about social phenomena but offers a limited approximation of real-world conditions; field observations uncover complexity and relevance but lack precision. These complementary strengths and weaknesses have given rise to the idea of full-cycle research, in which researchers include both lab and field research over time (Chatman & Flynn, 2005), and multimethod hybrid studies (Edmondson & McManus, in press) that integrate qualitative and quantitative data in a single project. Both of these approaches would be of value in future team-learning research.

Choosing a path forward.   Research on team learning is at a crossroads. One path forward involves more of the same—a growing number of empirical studies often introducing novel, even if conflicting, terms and approaches, published in varied journals with little cross-fertilization. Another path requires researchers to use similar terms for similar constructs, while becoming more accurate (accepting the need to make narrower claims) about a reasonably diverse and highly relevant set of real-world challenges. The latter path would likely attract more practitioner attention, while risking seeming less scholarly to some.

Broader Implications

Team-learning research has developed constructs and models that shed light on essential everyday collaborative activities in organizations. By and large, this research has investigated organizational antecedents of team learning. Here, we briefly consider team learning's consequences. We first discuss what learning in and by teams does for the organizations in which they work; in so doing, we go up a level of analysis to put these various team-learning models into a broader perspective. We then examine team learning's consequences for individuals, as well as for other teams in an organization.

We began this review with the premise that team learning has value for organizations. Much has been said about the capacity of a learning organization to create and execute superior strategy (e.g., Senge, 1990). Learning in teams is seen as a key mechanism through which learning organizations become strategically and operationally adaptive and responsive. This implies that organizations can set the stage for strategic responsiveness by putting in place factors that enable team learning. In other words, strategic and operational responsiveness is enabled top down so it can emerge bottom up.

How the learning of individual work teams translates into organizational learning is not well understood, however. It is clear that teams carry out both innovation and improvement in organizations, producing both new products (Sarin & McDermott, 2003) and processes (Tucker et al., 2006). But how are such team-learning processes and outcomes coordinated between teams to ensure that the organization's goals are met? How do teams configure and reconfigure over time to accomplish organizational work (and learning)? We know little about how coherent patterns of team learning can be created in an organization, so that individual teams learn independently in support of common organizational aims. On the one hand, left to their own devices, teams may learn in ways that do not support organizational goals. On the other hand, if senior management provides individualized learning goals to each team, the learning processes are likely to be overly scripted and constrained, to hardly qualify as learning.

The literature offers few insights into this problem. As just noted, suggestive qualitative research identified two learning types, incremental and radical, and argued that particular organizational teams were positioned to engage in one more than the other (Edmondson, 2002). Radical learning is likely to involve much higher levels of uncertainty and experiments that fail, compared to incremental learning, while ultimately being the source of much that is innovative in organizations. Incremental learning, in contrast, should involve activities that were knowable in advance and lead either to gradual improvement of work processes or mastery of known tasks (e.g., those previously executed by others). The former is akin to exploration; the latter to both exploitation (March, 1991) and execution of tasks that may be new to the team but not new to the world.

Knowledge about how teams that explore new knowledge differ from those that exploit existing knowledge, as well as what factors are essential to success in each, is also limited. Studies tend to include one type or the other, but not both. Thus, we lack data on which factors matter most for which types of teams. Research that examines the context in which team learning takes place (e.g., Zellmer-Bruhn & Gibson, 2006) is a step toward the development of such contingent and accurate models in the future. Another important area for future research is how organizations integrate radical and incremental learning effectively; despite theory recognizing the need for such balance, manifested in ambidextrous organizations (Duncan, 1976; Tushman & O'Reilly, 1996), the microprocesses through which this is accomplished remain under explored. Additional micro and mesolevel field research on these issues is needed, which could contribute to better integration of organizational and team-learning theory.

We propose attention to intraorganizational networks of teams that learn, in which an essential part of that learning involves boundary spanning to coordinate interdependent activities. Following Edmondson and Roberto (2003) we refer to this as a *team-based learning infrastructure*, and suggest that it explains how organizations can and do learn, especially when pursuing important aims for which no prior blueprint exists. An example of such an aim is patient safety in hospitals; patient safety is clearly important, but no one knows exactly how to achieve it in today's complex healthcare organizations (Edmondson, 2004). Boundary spanning occurs naturally in cross-functional teams, whose members are motivated to communicate with both team members and functional colleagues (Sarin & McDermott, 2003); the same is true in dispersed teams (Sole & Edmondson, 2002). When teams combine knowledge or adopt processes across boundaries, members become familiar with knowledge, routines, and cultures in other areas of the organizations, possibly strengthening their ability to cross such boundaries in the future. How this happens in a broader variety of organizational work teams remains understudied. Future research could investigate the durability and utility of team-based networks for the organization as a whole.

Finally, we consider two other outcomes of team learning. First, learning in teams almost necessarily plays a role in developing the knowledge and skills of individuals who compose the team (Edmondson & Nembhard, in press). Team learning thus can benefit the organization, a level up, and the members, a level down. More research is needed on how individuals benefit from their team-learning experiences in terms of intellectual, career, and personal-development goals. Second, we suggest attention to the effects of team learning on future teams that are composed of some, but not all, of the same members. Many work teams have permeable boundaries and transient membership, disbanding and reforming frequently (Ancona et al., 2002). How does one team's learning affect the team fragments that emerge in later teams? Organizations stand to benefit when ideas are cross-fertilized and diverse individuals learn to work together. For example, research reviewed in this paper identified benefits of diverse experiences on a team (Ely & Thomas, 2001; Lau & Murnighan, 2005; Van der Vegt & Bunderson, 2005), and the value of ideas an outsider can bring to a team (Sole & Edmondson, 2002). Other research, however, showed that some types of learning acquired as a team may not be portable to other group or individual contexts.[9] Such conflicting evidence merits additional research into the circumstances under which team learning's benefits are portable and whey they are not—research that would have practical implications for the design and management of teams, especially temporary project teams. A kind of "cross-functional learning" could take place in teams, so that teams composed of people with experience and similar functional composition will organize, learn, and execute their tasks more quickly and easily than those lacking such experience. These and other issues remain ripe for additional field research.

We conclude with the reminder that learning by its nature involves facing uncertainty; acknowledging ignorance; and being willing to generate variance, entertain false starts, and reach dead ends along the way. Embracing this mindset requires moving beyond traditional management tools and mindsets, which seek to organize and simplify the complex reality of organizational life by creating smaller, more certain and more predictable tasks. In this way, learning and execution are often at odds. Team learning in organizations must be recognized not as a mechanism for implementing planned change but as a strategy for tolerating forays into the unknown.

Endnotes

1. *Memory differentiation* was "the tendency for group members to specialize in remembering distinct aspects" of the task, *task coordination* was "the ability of group members to work together smoothly", and *task credibility* was "how much the group members trusted one another's knowledge" about the task, all of which characterized a strong TMS (Liang et al., 1995, p. 388–389).

2. *Task motivation* was "how eager the group members were to win the award" for task completion, *group cohesion* was "the level of interpersonal attraction among group members," and *social identity* "the tendency for subjects to think about themselves as team members rather than individuals" (p. 389).

3. *Task environment* was defined as volatile if a team frequently switched tasks; *knowledge environment* was defined as volatile if team members quickly forgot unutilized knowledge. The organizational context was rated "stable" if a team was low on both dimensions and "dynamic" if it was high on both dimensions.

4. Other leader and team characteristics did not predict learning: leader consideration, leader initiation of process structure, product complexity, and team functional diversity.

5. Survey items measured members' anticipated behavioral change on future product-development teams or on work in other areas of the organization.
6. The authors called this variable a "problem solving orientation," but the items used in the measure clearly related to what team-learning researchers have called "learning behaviors."
7. For example, two studies find opposite effects of low-to-moderate subgroup strength on learning behavior (Gibson & Vermeulen, 2003; Lau & Murnighan, 2005). Likewise, some find a learning orientation to be consistently good for performance (Ely & Thomas, 2001) while others find it good only in small doses (Bunderson & Sutcliffe, 2003).
8. As noted, Hackman's (1987) model provides an exemplar of how to cluster sets of related variables (effort, knowledge and skills, action strategies) into an actionable and theoretically useful framework.
9. Similarly, recent careers research (e.g., Groysberg, Nanda, & Nohria, 2004) found that the performance of "star employees" suffered when they moved to new organizations (and, hence, new teams).

References

Adler, P. S. (1990). Shared learning. *Management Science, 36*(8), 938–957.

Ancona, D. G., Bresman, H., & Kaeufer, K. (2002). The comparative advantage of X-teams. *MIT Sloan Management Review, 43*(3), 33–39.

Ancona, D. G., & Caldwell, D. F. (1992). Bridging the boundary: External activity and performance in organizational teams. *Administrative Science Quarterly, 37*, 634–655.

Argote, L., Beckman, S. L., & Epple, D. (1990). The persistence and transfer of learning in industrial settings. *Management Science, 36*(2), 140–154.

Argote, L., Insko, C. A., Yovetich, N., & Romero, A. A. (1995). Group learning curves: The effects of turnover and task complexity on group performance. *Journal of Applied Social Psychology, 25*(6), 512–529.

Argyris, C., & Schön, D. A. (1978). *Organizational learning: A theory of action perspective.* Reading, MA: Addison-Wesley Publishing Company.

Austin, J. R. (2003). Transactive memory in organizational groups: The effects of content, consensus, specialization, and accuracy on group performance. *Journal of Applied Psychology, 88*(5), 866–878.

Baloff, N. (1971). Extension of the learning curve—Some empirical results. *Operational Research Quarterly, 22*(4), 329–340.

Basden, B. H., Basden, D. R., Bryner, S., & Thomas, R. L., III. (1997). A comparison of group and individual remembering: Does collaboration disrupt retrieval strategies? *Journal of Experimental Psychology: Learning, Memory, and Cognition, 23*(5), 1176–1191.

Brandon, D. P., & Hollingshead, A. B. (2004). Transactive memory systems in organizations: Matching tasks, expertise, and people. *Organization Science, 15*(6), 633–644.

Bresman, H. (2007). Learning strategies and performance in innovation teams. *Academy of Management Best Paper Proceedings.* New York.

Brooks, A. K. (1994). Power and the production of knowledge: Collective team learning in work organizations. *Human Resource Development Quarterly, 5*(3), 213–235.

Bunderson, J. S., & Sutcliffe, K. M. (2003). Management team learning orientation and business unit performance. *Journal of Applied Psychology, 88*(3), 552–560.

Cannon-Bowers, J. A., Salas, E., & Converse, S. (1993). Shared mental models in expert team decision making. In N. J. Castellan Jr., *Individual and group decision making: Current issues* (pp. 221–246). Hillsdale, NJ: Lawrence Erlbaum Associates, Inc.

Chatman, J. A., & Flynn, F. J. (2005). Full-cycle micro-organizational behavior research. *Organization Science, 16*(4), 434.

Darr, E. D., Argote, L., & Epple, D. (1995). The acquisition, transfer, and depreciation of knowledge in service organizations: Productivity in franchises. *Management Science, 41*(11), 1750–1762.

Druskat, V. U., & Pescosolido, A. T. (2002). The content of effective teamwork mental models in self-managing teams: Ownership, learning, and heedful interrelating. *Human Relations, 55*(3), 283–314.

Duncan, R. B. (1976). The ambidextrous organization: Designing dual structures for innovation. In R. H. Kilmann, L. R. Pondy, & D. P. Slevin (Eds.), *The management of organization design: Strategies and implementation* (Vol. 1, pp. 167–188). New York: North-Holland.

Dutton, J. M., & Thomas, A. (1984). Treating progress functions as a managerial opportunity. *The Academy of Management Review, 9*(2), 235.

Edmondson, A. C. (1996). Learning from mistakes is easier said than done: Group and organizational influences on the detection and correction of human error. *Journal of Applied Behavioral Sciences, 32*(1), 5–32.

Edmondson, A. C. (1999). Psychological safety and learning behavior in work teams. *Administrative Science Quarterly, 44*(2), 350–383.

Edmondson, A. C. (2002). The local and variegated nature of learning in organizations. *Organization Science, 13*(2), 128–146.

Edmondson, A. C. (2003). Speaking up in the operating room: How team leaders promote learning in interdisciplinary action teams. *The Journal of Management Studies, 40*(6), 1419–1452.

Edmondson, A. C. (2004). Learning from failure in health care: Frequent opportunities, pervasive barriers. *Quality and Safety in Health Care, 13*(6), 3–9.

Edmondson, A. C., Bohmer, R. M., & Pisano, G. P. (2001). Disrupted routines: Team learning and new technology implementation in hospitals. *Administrative Science Quarterly, 46*(4), 685–716.

Edmondson, A. C., & McManus, S. E. (in press). Methodological fit in management field research. *Academy of Management Review.*

Edmondson, A. C., & Moingeon, B. (1998). From organizational learning to the learning organization. *Management Learning, 29*(1), 5–20.

Edmondson, A. C., & Nembhard, I. M. (in press). Product development and learning in project teams: The challenges are the benefits. *Journal of Product Innovation Management.*

Edmondson, A. C., & Roberto, M. R. (2003). *Children's hospital and clinics: Teaching note 5-303-071.* Boston: Harvard Business School Publishing.

Edmondson, A. C., Winslow, A. B., Bohmer, R. M., & Pisano, G. P. (2003). Learning how and learning what: Effects of tacit and codified knowledge on performance improvement following technology adoption. *Decision Sciences, 34*(2), 197–223.

Ely, R. J., & Thomas, D. A. (2001). Cultural diversity at work: The effects of diversity perspectives on work group processes and outcomes. *Administrative Science Quarterly, 46*(2), 229–273.

Fiol, C. M., & Lyles, M. A. (1985). Organizational learning. *Academy of Management. The Academy of Management Review, 10*(4), 803.

Garvin, D. A. (2000). *Learning in action.* Boston: Harvard Business School Press.

Gibson, C., & Vermeulen, F. (2003). A healthy divide: Subgroups as a stimulus for team learning behavior. *Administrative Science Quarterly, 48*(2), 202–239.

Groysberg, B., Nanda, A., & Nohria, N. (2004, May). The risky business of hiring stars. *Harvard Business Review, 82*(5), 92–100.

Gruenfeld, D. H., Mannix, E. A., Williams, K. Y., & Neale, M. A. (1996). Group composition and decision making: How member familiarity and information distribution affect process and performance. *Organizational Behavior and Human Decision Processes, 67*(1), 1–15.

Gruenfeld, D. H., Martorana, P. V., & Fan, E. T. (2000). What do groups learn from their worldliest members? Direct and indirect influence in dynamic teams. *Organizational Behavior and Human Decision Processes, 82*(1), 45–59.

Hackman, J. R. (1987). The design of work teams. In J. Lorsch (Ed.), *Handbook of organizational behavior* (pp. 315–342). Englewood Cliffs, NJ: Prentice-Hall.

Hayes, R. H., & Clark, K. B. (1985). Explaining observed productivity differentials between plants: Implications for operations research. *Interfaces, 15*(6), 3.

Hollingshead, A. B. (1998a). Communication, learning, and retrieval in transactive memory systems. *Journal of Experimental Social Psychology, 34*(5), 423–442.

Hollingshead, A. B. (1998b). Retrieval processes in transactive memory systems. *Journal of Personality and Social Psychology, 74*(3), 659–671.

Hollingshead, A. B. (2001). Cognitive interdependence and convergent expectations in transactive memory. *Journal of Personality and Social Psychology, 81*(6), 1080–1089.

Hollingshead, A. B., & Fraidin, S. (2003). Gender stereotypes and assumptions about expertise in transactive memory. *Journal of Experimental Social Psychology, 39*(4), 355–363.

Huber, G. P. (1991). Organizational learning: The contributing processes and the literatures. *Organization Science, 2*(1), 88–115.

Ilgen, D. R., Hollenbeck, J. R., Johnson, M., & Jundt, D. (2005). Teams in organizations: From input-process-output models to IMOI models. *Annual Review of Psychology, 56*, 517–543.

Kahn, W. A. (1990). Psychological conditions of personal engagement and disengagement at work. *Academy of Management Journal, 33*(4), 692–724.

Klimoski, R., & Mohammed, S. (1994). Team mental model: Construct or metaphor? *Journal of Management, 20*(2), 403–437.

Lapre, M. A., Mukherjee, A. S., & Van Wassenhove, L. N. (2000). Behind the learning curve: Linking learning activities to waste reduction. *Management Science, 46*(5), 597–611.

Larson, J. R., & Christensen, C. (1993). Groups as problem-solving units: Toward a new meaning of social cognition. *British Journal of Social Psychology, 32*(1), 5–30.

Lau, D. C., & Murnighan, J. K. (2005). Interactions within groups and subgroups: The effects of demographic faultlines. *Academy of Management Journal, 48*(4), 645–659.

Levesque, L. L., Wilson, J. M., & Wholey, D. R. (2001). Cognitive divergence and shared mental models in software development project teams. *Journal of Organizational Behavior, 22*, 135–144.

Levitt, B., & March, J. (1988). Organizational learning. *Annual Review of Sociology, 14*, 319–340.

Lewis, K. (2004). Knowledge and performance in knowledge-worker teams: A longitudinal study of transactive memory systems. *Management Science, 50*(11), 1519–1533.

Lewis, K., Lange, D., & Gillis, L. (2005). Transactive memory systems, learning, and learning transfer. *Organization Science, 16*(6), 581–598.

Liang, D. W., Moreland, R. L., & Argote, L. (1995). Group versus individual training and group performance: The mediating factor of transactive memory. *Personality and Social Psychology Bulletin, 21*(4), 384–393.

March, J. G. (1991). Exploration and exploitation in organizational learning. *Organization Science, 2*(1), 71–87.

Mathieu, J. E., Heffner, T. S., Goodwin, G. F., Salas, E., & Cannon-Bowers, J. A. (2000). The influence of shared mental models on team process and performance. *Journal of Applied Psychology, 85*(2), 273–283.

McGrath, J. E. (1984). *Groups: Interaction and performance.* Englewood Cliffs, NJ: Prentice-Hall.

Mohammed, S., Klimoski, R., & Rentsch, J. R. (2000). The measurement of team mental models: We have no shared schema. *Organizational Research Methods, 3*(2), 123–165.

Moreland, R. L., Argote, L., & Krishnan, R. (1998). Training people to work in groups. In R. S. Tindale, L. Heath, J. Edwards, E. J. Posavac, & F. B. Bryant (Eds.), *Theory and research on small groups* (pp. 37–60). New York: Plenum Press.

Moreland, R. L., & Myaskovsky, L. (2000). Exploring the performance benefits of group training: Transactive memory or improved communication? *Organizational Behavior and Human Decision Processes, 82*(1), 117.

Mortensen, M. (2004). *Antecedents and consequences of team boundary disagreement.* Paper presented at the Best Paper Proceedings of the Academy of Management, New Orleans, LA.

Nembhard, I. M. (2006, April). *When do organizations learn from each other: Interorganizational learning from health care collaborative teams.* Paper presented at the Production & Operations Society Meeting, Boston.

Pisano, G. P., Bohmer, R. M., & Edmondson, A. C. (2001). Organizational differences in rates of learning: Evidence from the adoption of minimally invasive cardiac surgery. *Management Science, 47*(6), 752–768.

Ramsay, C. R., Grant, A. M., Wallace, S. A., Garthwaite, P. H., Monk, A. F., & Russell, I. T. (2000). Assessment of the learning curve in health technologies: A systematic review. *International Journal of Technology Assessment in Health Care, 16*(4), 1095–1108.

Reagans, R., Argote, L., & Brooks, D. (2005). Individual experience and experience working together: Predicting learning rates from knowing who knows what and knowing how to work together. *Management Science, 51*(6), 869–881.

Ren, Y., Carley, K. M., & Argote, L. (2006). The contingent effects of transactive memory: When is it more beneficial to know what others know? *Management Science, 52*(5), 671–682.

Rentsch, J. R., & Klimoski, R. (2001). Why do 'great minds' think alike?: Antecedents of team member schema agreement. *Journal of Organizational Behavior, 22*, 107–120.

Rulke, D. L., & Rau, D. (2000). Investigating the encoding process and transactive memory development in group training. *Group & Organization Management, 25*(4), 373–396.

Sarin, S., & McDermott, C. (2003). The effect of team leader characteristics on learning, knowledge application, and performance of cross-functional new product development teams. *Decision Sciences, 34*(4), 707–739.

Schein, E., & Bennis, W. (1965). *How can organizations learn faster? The challenge of entering the green room.* New York: Wiley.

Schippers, M. C. (in press). Learning to learn at school: Reflexivity in school management teams and student performance. *Journal of Applied Psychology.*

Schippers, M. C., Den Hartog, D. N., & Koopman, P. L. (in press). Reflexivity in teams: A measure and correlates. *Applied Psychology: An International Review.*

Schippers, M. C., Den Hartog, D. N., Koopman, P. L., & Wienk, J. A. (2003). Diversity and team outcomes: The moderating effects of outcome interdependence and group longevity and the mediating effect of reflexivity. *Journal of Organizational Behavior, 24*(6), 779–802.

Senge, P. M. (1990). *The fifth discipline: The art and practice of the learning organization.* New York: Doubleday.

Smith-Jentsch, K. A., Campbell, G. E., Milanovich, D. M., & Reynolds, A. M. (2001). Measuring teamwork mental models to support training needs assessment, development, and evaluation: Two empirical studies. *Journal of Organizational Behavior, 22*, 179–194.

Sole, D., & Edmondson, A. C. (2002). Situated knowledge and learning in dispersed teams. *British Journal of Management, 13*(S2), S17–S34.

Stasser, G., Stewart, D. D., & Wittenbaum, G. M. (1995). Expert roles and information exchange during discussion: The importance of knowing who knows what. *Journal of Experimental Social Psychology, 31*(3), 244–265.

Tjosvold, D., Yu, Z.-y., & Hui, C. (2004). Team learning from mistakes: The contribution of cooperative goals and problem-solving. *The Journal of Management Studies, 41*(7), 1223–1245.

Tucker, A. L., Nembhard, I. M., & Edmondson, A. C. (2006). *Implementing new practices: An empirical study of organizational learning in hospital intensive care units.* Boston: Harvard Business School. (Working paper No. 06-049)

Tushman, M., & O'Reilly, C. (1996). Ambidextrous organizations: Managing evolutionary and revolutionary change. *California Management Review, 38*(4), 8–30.

Tyler, T. R., & Lind, E. A. (1992). A relational model of authority in groups. *Advances in Experimental Social Psychology, 25*, 115–191.

Van der Vegt, G. S., & Bunderson, J. S. (2005). Learning and performance in multidisciplinary teams: The importance of collective team identification. *Academy of Management Journal, 48*(3), 532–547.

Walsh, J. P. (1995). Managerial and organizational cognition: Notes from a trip down memory lane. *Organization Science, 6*(3), 280–321.

Walsh, J. P., Henderson, C. M., & Deighton, J. (1988). Negotiated belief structures and decision performance: An empirical investigation. *Organizational Behavior and Human Decision Processes, 42*, 194–216.

Wegner, D. M. (1987). Tranactive memory: A contemporary analysis of the group mind. In B. Mullen, & G. R. Goethals (Eds.), *Theories of group behavior* (pp. 185–208). New York: Springer-Verlag.

Weick, K. E., & Westley, F. (1993). Organizational learning: Affirming an oxymoron. In S. R. Clegg, C. Hard, & W. R. Nord (Eds.), *Handbook of organization studies* (pp. 440–448). London: Sage.

West, M. (1996). Reflexivity and work group effectiveness: A conceptual integration. In M. A. West (Ed.), *Handbook of work group psychology*. Chichester, NY: Wiley.

West, M. (2000). Reflexivity, revolution and innovation in work teams. In M. M. Beyerlein, D. A. Johnson, & S. T. Beyerlein (Eds.), *Product development teams* (Vol. 5, pp. 1–29). Stamford, CT: JAI Press.

Wilson, J. M., Goodman, P. S., & Cronin, M. A. (in press). Group learning. *Academy of Management Review.*

Wittenbaum, G. M., Hubbell, A. P., & Zuckerman, C. (1999). Mutual enhancement: Toward an understanding of the collective preference for shared information. *Journal of Personality and Social Psychology, 77*(5), 967–978.

Wong, S.-S. (2004). Distal and local group learning: Performance trade-offs and tensions. *Organization Science, 15*(6), 645–656.

Wright, T. P. (1936). Factors affecting the cost of airplanes. *Journal of Aeronautical Sciences, 3*(4), 122–128.

Zellmer-Bruhn, M. (2003). Interruptive events and team knowledge acquisition. *Management Science, 49*(4), 514–528.

Zellmer-Bruhn, M., & Gibson, C. (2006). Multinational organizational context: Implications for team learning and performance. *Academy of Management Journal, 49*(3), 501–518.

7

Emotion in Organizations

A Review and Theoretical Integration

HILLARY ANGER ELFENBEIN

University of California, Berkeley

Abstract

Emotion has become one of the most popular—and popularized—areas within organizational scholarship. This chapter attempts to review and bring together within a single framework the wide and often disjointed literature on emotion in organizations. The integrated framework includes processes detailed by previous theorists who have defined emotion as a sequence that unfolds chronologically. The emotion process begins with a focal individual who is exposed to an eliciting stimulus, registers the stimulus for its meaning, and experiences a feeling state and physiological changes, with downstream consequences for attitudes, behaviors, and cognitions, as well as facial expressions and other emotionally expressive cues. These downstream consequences can result in externally visible behaviors and cues that become, in turn, eliciting stimuli for interaction partners. For each stage of the emotion process, there are distinct emotion regulation processes that incorporate individual differences and group norms and that can become automatic with practice. Although research often examines these stages in relative isolation from each other, I argue that each matters largely due to its interconnectedness with the other stages. Incorporating intraindividual, individual, interpersonal, and organizational levels of analysis, this framework can be a starting point to situate, theorize, and test explicit mechanisms for the influence of emotion on organizational life.

We keep coming back to feelings, I'll have time for feelings after I'm dead. Right now we're busy. (NASA Administrator Michael Griffin, speaking about the historic Independence Day 2006 launch of the space shuttle Discovery, after discussing the horror and sadness at losing the

Columbia space shuttle in 2003, the worry leading up to the launch of Discovery, and the relief and pleasure at watching Discovery succeed; Boyce, 2006)

Introduction

This is an exciting time to be a researcher interested in emotion in organizations. In the wake of best-selling popular books (e.g., Goleman, 1995), as well as the resurgence of decades-old investigations of worker sentiments (Hersey, 1932), there has been heightened—indeed, often hysterical—enthusiasm from practitioners and academics alike. This popularization has tended to elevate the status and legitimacy of emotion as a topic of scholarly inquiry, and has lead to a near explosion of research on the topic (Barsade, Brief, & Spataro, 2003; Brief & Weiss, 2002; Rafaeli & Worline, 2001), which represents a large-scale reversal of lay beliefs that the best way to manage emotions in the workplace is not to have any. F. W. Taylor's (1911) scientific management focused on machine-like efficiency and discounted emotion because it was seen as irrational, personal, and feminine (Mumby & Putnam, 1992)—as typified in the opening quote. By contrast, researchers now celebrate the infusion of emotion into organizational life (Fineman, 1996)—with implications for individual, group, and even firm performance, as well as intricate connections to organizational phenomena as varied as justice, diversity, power, creativity, stress, culture, and others.

The explosion of research in this area has been a boon, but it has also been a mess. Popularization has led to many sweeping—yet often poorly substantiated (e.g., Goleman, 1995)—claims about the power of emotion to be harnessed for the bottom line. The academic literature has been extensive, but often only a loosely connected body of work with disparate themes all included under the banner of emotion. Often research takes existing topics within management and divides them into purportedly emotional versus nonemotional versions. At some extremes, arguments claim that nearly everything is emotion and that it now encompasses every phenomenon heretofore studied across management and organization. One question, then, is how to articulate boundaries because, for emotion to mean anything, it cannot mean everything. Another question is how to integrate the study of emotion into a coherent whole.

The present chapter is the first to organize a review of the research literature on emotion in organizations around an integration of psychologists' conceptions of the emotion process. At this point, a definition of *emotion* may—or may not—be necessary. Although we tend to think that we know emotion when we see it, researchers have proposed a wide variety of definitions, the most widely held that emotions are adaptive responses to the demands of the environment (Ekman, 1992; Scherer, 1984a; Smith & Ellsworth, 1985). However, Fridlund (1994) argued that there is no formal definition of emotion that is not tautological in some way, and he ultimately suggested that emotion is merely a social convention for discussing behavioral intentions. At its core, most theorists agree that emotion is a reaction to a stimulus and has a range of possible consequences (Frijda, 1988). Whereas emotions typically refer to discrete and intense but short-lived experiences, *moods* are experiences that are longer and more diffuse, and lack awareness of the eliciting stimulus. Moods can be created by stimuli of relatively low intensity, or can be left behind by emotions that fade so that the initial antecedent is no longer salient (e.g., Cropanzano, Weiss, Hale, & Reb, 2003; Schwarz, 1990). *Affect* is an umbrella term encompassing mood and emotion (Forgas, 1995).

The Emotion Process

The integrated process framework presented here draws on processes detailed by distinguished theorists of emotion and social judgment, including Brunswik (1955), Buck (1984), Ekman (1972), Fridlund (1994), Frijda (1986; Frijda and Mesquita, 1994), Gross (2001), Scherer (1984a; 1995), Weiss and Cropanzano (1996), and others who argued for theoretical models of emotion as an interrelated series of processes that unfold chronologically. It incorporates important contributions from psychology and allied fields such as sociology and organization studies.

The goal of this chapter is to review the existing research literature on emotion in organizations systematically in terms of this process framework. Although it is beyond the scope of the chapter to review the entire underlying literature on emotion, where possible, it includes that which is illustrative or directly relevant. It would be an overly ambitious claim for any model to account for absolutely every aspect of emotion studied within organizational settings. However, at the risk of failing, this is a first attempt to move away from characterizing the vast literature as discrete topics, and to integrate it into a single framework. To the extent that this attempt falls short, it is a starting point for further development.

The emotion process begins in Figure 7.1 with intrapersonal processes when a focal individual is exposed to an eliciting stimulus, registers the stimulus for its meaning, and experiences a feeling state and physiological changes, with downstream consequences for attitudes, behaviors, and cognitions, as well as facial expressions and other emotionally expressive cues. Further, Frijda (1988) argued that emotions automatically trigger secondary controlled responses to regulate the emotion, which Figure 7.1 illustrates in the gray, shaded area. At each stage, regulation processes allow for individual and group norms to override automatic processing (e.g., Frijda, 1986; Grandey, 2000; Gross, 2001), although this distinction can blur when practice at any of these regulated processes renders them overlearned and, thus, automatic (Campos, Frankel, & Camras, 2004; Gross, 1998b). Moving from intrapersonal to interpersonal processes, the downstream consequences of emotional experience can result in externally visible behaviors and cues that become, in turn, the eliciting stimulus for interaction partners, as depicted in Figure 7.2. Each step of the emotion process is presented in more detail in the sections below.

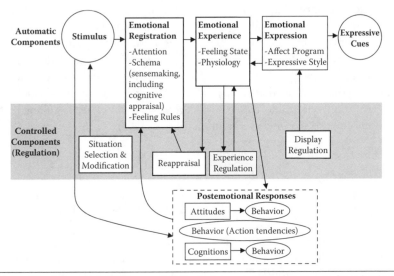

Figure 7.1 Integrated Intrapersonal Process Framework for Emotion in Organizations. *Note:* Processes with round outlines are externally visible, whereas those in rectangles are internally experienced. Copyright 2006, Hillary Anger Elfenbein.

Although common wisdom considers emotion to be chaotic and disorganized, the emotion process is orderly, carefully sequenced, and governed by empirical regularities (Frijda, 1988). Emotions unfold chronologically through a rule-governed sequence of automatic components depicted in the figures (Frijda, 1986, 1988; Gross, 2001). The controlled components in the gray box arise at specific stages but are optional and can end at any point. Not every path is possible, and the arrows in the figures identify links previously theorized and empirically documented. These steps unfold so quickly that they can appear together to represent a single phenomenon. However, for conceptual clarity I prefer to treat emotion more as an adjective than a noun: Each piece of the process is emotional, but no single piece on its own is emotion.

Although the stages are often studied in relative isolation from each other, I argue that each process matters largely because the other processes matter with which it is interconnected. For example, we care about the ability to recognize emotional cues only because an emotional expression suggests something about another person's emotional experience, which suggests something about the other's evaluations of the stimuli in his or her environment. Likewise, we care about leaders' emotional expressions because followers interpret these expressions as important stimuli.

The focus on individual and dyadic processes evidenced in Figures 7.1 and 7.2 is in no way intended to discount the emotional role of groups, organizations, and societies. Indeed, their crucial roles are infused throughout the

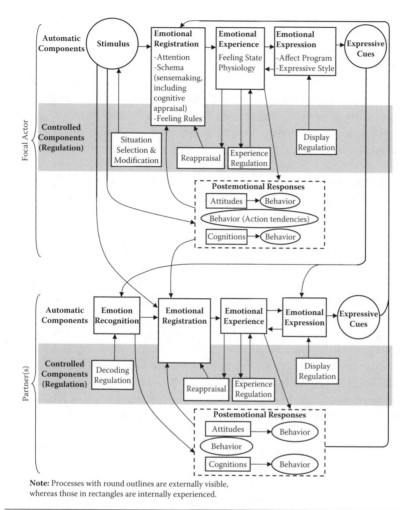

Figure 7.2   Integrated Interpersonal Process Framework for Emotion in Organizations. *Note:* Processes with round outlines are externally visible, whereas those in rectangles are internally experienced. Copyright 2006, Hillary Anger Elfenbein.

framework, first within the norms inherent in the regulated components and second within the dyadic processes that can occur en masse. Thus, the framework captures multiple levels of analysis, including intraindividual, individual differences, interpersonal, and organizational processes.

From a Stimulus to Emotional Registration and Experience

Starting with William James (1884), modern psychologists have emphasized that emotional experience follows the perception of a stimulus. More recently, Weiss and Cropanzano's (1996) affective events theory (AET) characterized emotional states in the workplace as "discrete reactions precipitated by specific events" (p. 41). Thus, Figure 7.1 begins with a stimulus.

Stimuli

A stimulus need not literally be an event that occurs, but can also be a stable feature of the environment that is salient. Indeed, any contact between a person and his or her environment can become an affective event, particularly when the environment includes other people. Kelly and Barsade (2001) argued that greater interdependence in the modern workplace makes it contain more intensely evocative stimuli. The asocial monotony of past work ensured that mostly routine events arose, whereas working closely with other people brings new and changing stimuli. Among the greatest emotional impact for workers are those events related to interactions with coworkers, customers, and supervisors—with leaders' behaviors looming particularly large (e.g., Basch & Fisher, 2000; Dasborough, 2006; Gaddis, Connelly, & Mumford, 2004; Mignonac & Herrback, 2004). Although social interactions tend to be the most salient, economic events and conditions are also important emotional elicitors (Brief & Weiss, 2002), as are a variety of environmental factors such as temperature, noise, and aromas (Isen & Baron, 1991), and physical artifacts such as colors and symbols (Rafaeli & Vilnai-Yavetz, 2004) that can be fleeting or chronic. Emotions also emerge from the act of engaging in work itself (Csikszentmihalyi, 1975; Sandelands, 1988), and from external factors that carry over to work, such as family concerns (Brief & Weiss, 2002).

Beyond mechanical tasks, we relate to our work as a series of interactions and relationships with other people (Dutton & Dukerich, 2006; Wrzesniewski, Dutton, & Debebe, 2003). Examining a range of narratives about work, Boudens (2005) found that themes of establishing and maintaining equilibrium in relationships and maintaining personal boundaries and identity tended to be particularly evocative of emotion. Positive elicitors included work-related accomplishments and overcoming obstacles, personal support, solidarity, and connectedness. Negative elicitors included inequitable situations focusing largely on nonfinancial compensation, discrimination, both covert and overt conflicts and power struggles, violations of norms and trust to the detriment of other individuals or the workplace itself, ideology-based disagreements, actual or potential on-the-job death and injury, and humiliation. In Mignonac and Herrbach's (2004) large-scale survey, the most frequent positive events were accomplishment and praise from supervisors and coworkers, and the most frequent negative events were being assigned undesired work, the departure of a well-liked coworker, interpersonal conflicts with supervisors and coworkers, and the interference with work of personal problems.

There is a long history of focusing on job characteristics and other environmental factors as important stimuli that influence workers' affective states (Hackman & Oldham, 1976; Herzberg, 1966; Saavedra & Kwun, 2000). Indeed, many emotional experiences are related to particular job functions. Haas' (1977) steelworkers spent their days in precarious positions at great heights. Call center representatives report that they face an average of 10 customers per day who are verbally aggressive (Grandey, Dickter, & Sin, 2004). Research-and-development teams frequently face technical problems, insufficient staffing, conflict among team members, and funding shortages (Pirola-Merlo, Härtel, Mann, & Hirst, 2002). They also experience the excitement of having creative ideas and seeing them recognized by colleagues (Amabile, Barsade, Mueller, & Staw, 2005). Because emotions are elicited the most strongly for our most central concerns, one's position within an organization can affect the most influential stimuli. For example, individuals low in a hierarchy express concerns about being treated kindly by others, whereas superiors express concerns about their subordinates following rules and norms (Fitness, 2000; Sloan, 2004). Annoying experiences for Disneyland theme park employees include "having children and adults asking whether the water in the lagoon is real, or where the well-marked toilets might be, or where Walt Disney's tomb is to be found, or the real clincher—whether one is 'really real'" (Van Maanen & Kunda, 1989, p. 69).

Emotional Registration

The attributes of an event may be objective, but meanings materialize (Weick, Sutcliffe, & Obstfeld, 2005). Including in Figure 7.1 an intervening stage in the process framework between the stimulus and experience does not represent a stand in the long-standing debate about the primacy of affect versus cognition. On one side, Zajonc (1998) reviewed evidence that pathways in the brain via emotional structures are faster and more direct than pathways via cognitive structures. On the other side, cognitive appraisal and related theories argue that we analyze the social environment for cues to determine our emotional experience (James, 1884; Lazarus, 1991; Schacter & Singer, 1962). However, in either case, a direct link from stimulus to experience is not tenable because—at some level, however minimal—a stimulus must be registered for it to evoke an emotional reaction. Even a subconscious level of awareness and processing is sufficient to bring a stimulus into the emotion process (Garcia-Prieto, Bellard, & Schneider, 2003; Leventhal & Scherer, 1987; Zajonc, 1998). I label the intervening stage "emotional registration" rather than appraisal in order to incorporate both this automatic subconscious processing as well as more explicit cognitive interpretation. Even so, it is worth noting that the nomenclature of "cognitive appraisal" has tended to mislead people into a false dichotomy of automatic versus controlled stimulus registration—where the term *cognitive* has suggested that appraisal is verbal, conscious, deliberate, logical, and slow (Ellsworth & Scherer, 2003). Even controlled appraisals tend to occur quickly and with little awareness because they are overlearned—after all, we practice appraising the events of greatest relevance to us, and so for relevant events the process is likely to be well practiced. Indeed, the lack of conscious awareness of the registration process—the sense that our emotional reactions are clear and free of subjective interpretation—often prevents individuals within organizational settings from questioning and evaluating their appraisals.

There are three steps within the emotional registration process: attention, schemata, and feeling rules:

Attention. The first step in emotional registration is attention—not necessarily conscious attention, but literally that the actor's sensory organs are oriented to take in the stimulus. At its most minimal, a preconscious exposure of several hundred milliseconds may be enough to register a stimulus, but not when looking elsewhere. For example, placing a physical barrier to prevent participants from seeing each other limits the impact of participants' mood on their interaction partners (Carnevale & Isen, 1986; Howard & Gengler, 2001). Attention can also include deliberate attention as people learn over time which events are ordinary—and thus ignorable—and which are worth taking notice.

Schemata. Emotional registration also involves an act of sensemaking: "What does an event mean?" (Weick et al., 2005, p. 410). In psychology, basic-emotions theorists argue that we are hardwired to code events automatically in terms of their meaning for the self (Ekman, 1992; Frijda, 1986; Scherer, 1995). The cognitive appraisal process is an ordered sequence of checklists that direct our attention soonest to the most pressing emotional challenges (Scherer, 1984). The initial rudimentary checks are "rapid automatic processing on a schematic level" (Scherer, 1995, p. 245) that do not require effort or even awareness. The earliest dimension is novelty—indeed whether a stimulus is worth noting, consciously or even subliminally (Frijda, 1986; Scherer, 1984a). Scherer (1995) argued that the next dimensions are the inherent pleasantness of a stimulus, its relevance to our goals, our potential for coping with the situation, followed by others that proceed in a conditional order based on the answers to the first set. Other theorists proposed slightly different appraisal dimensions, with the most comprehensive list including: pleasantness, attentional activity (approach vs. avoid vs. ignore), anticipated effort (active vs. passive), initial causal agent (self vs. other), current control (self vs. other vs. no one), certainty (comprehendible and predictable), perceived goal obstruction, consistency with norms or social standards, and fairness (Smith & Ellsworth, 1985). This sequence has also been described as two stages, with an initial primary appraisal of pleasantness and a subsequent secondary appraisal including all the remaining dimensions that involve more complex meaning and analysis (Lazarus, 1991). Although appraisal checks even for complex dimensions can become intuitive and automatic, we have the option to suspend the process in motion—for example, taking the time to figure out whether a colleague was serious or just kidding.

Taken together, the results of these checks distinguish among five basic families of emotion: approach (e.g., interest, hope, and anticipation), achievement (e.g., relief, satisfaction, contentment, pride, and joy), deterrence (e.g., anxiety, fear, and distress), withdrawal (e.g., sadness, shame, and resignation), and antagonism (e.g., irritation, anger, and hate; Scherer & Tran, 2001). Over time, the memory of higher order dimensions fade away as we forget about the specific event, but moods can linger on as emotions "divorced from their antecedents" (Cropanzano et al., 2003, p. 843) with only the pleasantness dimension remaining.

The emotional registration process is deeply contextualized. Being hit by a ball could be an attempted injury, clumsiness, or an invitation to play. A strategic issue facing managers could mean a threat or an opportunity (Jackson & Dutton, 1988). Indeed, evaluations along the appraisal dimensions are socially constructed, situation specific and—because they are in the eyes of the beholder—neither true or false (Zajonc, 1998). Wrzesniewski et al. (2003) argued that tasks at work do not have inherent meaning but that meaning is developed around interpersonal cues from others. Thus, there is great variability in the emotional reactions that an event can invoke. For example, Scherer and Ceschi (2000) showed that the same eliciting event—the loss of baggage for airline passengers—evoked a range of states including anger, sadness, indifference, worry, and even humor. Although strong situations such as mortal dangers may be interpreted consistently, the link between stimulus and experience needs to be flexible enough to accommodate the range and diversity of human environments.

Cognitive appraisal theory is underappreciated for its power to shed light on phenomena central to organizations. The fact that we are hardwired to appraise events along these sequential dimensions suggests that the judgments correspond to our most pressing concerns inside and outside of organizations. For example, Frost (2003) argued that individuals within organizations feel pain based on how their organizations appear to respond to events, rather than the events themselves—particularly as related to the dimensions of responsibility, fairness, certainty, control, and the ability to cope with current conditions. Likewise, procedural justice research emphasizes the importance of the fairness and control dimensions over that of valence (Lind & Tyler, 1988). In the domain of leadership, Dasborough's (2006) interview study yielded a set of categories of leader behaviors that included awareness and respect, motivation and inspiration, empowerment, communication, reward and recognition, and accountability—corresponding closely to many of the appraisal dimensions. Also, counterfactual thinking is likely to weigh heavily in the appraisal process, particularly given the inclusion of a certainty dimension, as we compare the state of the world to what we expected it might be. When consideration of such counterfactuals leads to regret, it is stronger for outcomes that were under our own control, for outcomes that resulted from action versus inaction, and for unexpected events (Mellers, 2000). Power is woven throughout the appraisal process, given that higher power actors are more likely to approach versus avoid, to be active versus passive, to act as initial causal agents, to be in control currently, and to enforce others' adherence to norms and social standards (Keltner, Gruenfeld, & Anderson, 2003). Taken together, high power provides greater flexibility to hold others accountable for negative outcomes and themselves for positive outcomes—leading to more anger and contempt versus sadness and to more pride versus gratitude (Morris & Keltner, 2000; Tiedens, 2001). The appraisal dimension of fairness connects it intricately with the concepts of justice and voice (Judge, Scott, & Ilies, 2006; Smith & Ellsworth, 1985; Weiss, Nicholas, & Daus, 1999), which, by definition, are always affective events. Sensemaking is an organizational construct that Weick et al. (2005) argued often accompanies an emotional experience. Thus, the chronologically earliest appraisal—novelty—is related to expectancy violation and thus is a precursor to macrolevel sensemaking (Weick et al., 2005). Finally, diversity can influence and be influenced by the appraisal process. It has been a challenge for researchers to reconcile the discrepant pattern of findings showing alternately that diversity is a help versus hindrance for individuals and groups (Williams & O'Reilly, 1998). More recently, Garcia-Prieto et al. (2003) argued that these conflicting findings may relate to organization members' emotional appraisals. First, diversity may have no effect if it is not perceived as novel and, thus, not to be appraised. Second, biases in interpreting ingroup versus outgroup behavior and cultural differences in implicit theories such as those regarding control, certainty, and fit with norms can feed into the judgments made for the appraisal checks. Taken together, members of diverse groups can appraise different events and can appraise the same events differently.

Feeling rules. The appraisal process, like many exercises in decision making, begins with at least some sense of the desired answer. Although the process of applying appraisal dimensions to events appears to be universal across individuals and even cultural groups (Scherer & Wallbott, 1994), exactly how one applies them is a formula all his or her own. Feeling rules refer to the chronic goals of the registration process. They include a sense of how one should feel, including an emotional category as well as features such as intensity and duration, and can be verbally described just like any other norm (Hochschild, 1979). Most often, these desired states are to experience the most positive and the least negative affect (Frijda, 1988). In this sense, the entire field of motivation is relevant to the extent that motivations are goals for particular experiences, and emotion indicates whether goals are realized (Buck, 1988). Feeling rules also include one's regulatory focus to approach pleasure versus avoid pain (Brockner & Higgins, 2001) and psychodynamic concepts such as defense mechanisms and drives, which have a role in directing the emotional appraisal process (Scherer, 1995). Some of the early pioneers of organizational behavior focused on workers' emotional needs (Maslow, 1943; Herzberg, 1966). Such needs lead us to shape our actual environment as well as our interpretation of it, in such a way to lead to our desired emotional states.

Emotional Experience

Emotional experience is the closest process in Figure 7.1 to what is colloquially described as *emotion*—the psychological and physiological sense of being affected emotionally by an event (Frijda, 1986). Ashforth and Humphrey (1995) argued, "From moments of frustration or joy, grief or fear, to an enduring sense of dissatisfaction or commitment...the experience of work is saturated with feeling" (p. 98). Large-scale qualitative studies of workplace events and narratives reveal the widest range of sentiment provoked within organizations, with positive experiences of pride, belongingness, fulfillment, relief, excitement, optimism, affection, nostalgia, empowerment, and joy, and negative experiences of disappointment, fatigue, strain, bitterness, resentment, anger, indignation, rage, embarrassment, pain, disgust, surprise, shock, regret, guilt, sorrow, fear, desperation, uncertainty, rejection, worry, and frustration (Basch & Fisher, 2000; Boudens, 2005). Workers report greater variety in their negative emotions (Dasborough, 2006), which is consistent with cognitive appraisal theory in that one need not complete the ordered checklist in the absence of pressing challenges (Scherer, 1984b).

Feelings within organizations are often mixed and ambivalent (Fong, in press; Pratt & Doucet, 2000). Multiple feeling rules can conflict, for example when high-powered women face discrepant scripts for achievement and gender (Fong & Tiedens, 2002). Further, stimuli can be complex, with multiple answers to the appraisal checks and, therefore, multiple emotions elicited. For example, organizational change is a highly complex and salient emotion-eliciting event (George & Jones, 2001; Huy, 1999). Indeed, Vince (2006) found that senior managers of a firm undergoing an acquisition experienced a range of different emotions—from anger at themselves and others to shame, agony, sadness, powerlessness, depression, and fear—based on which aspects of the multifaceted event they considered.

There is a temptation in the management literature to argue for the inherent goodness of positive emotion and the inherent badness of negative emotion. However, both result from the same emotional registration process and evolved alongside each other. Social functional theorists have long argued that even unpleasant emotions have valuable roles for social and work life (e.g., Fridlund, 1994; Keltner & Haidt, 1999). Whereas positive emotions are rewards, negative emotions are warnings and punishments (Larsen &

Ketelaar, 1989). Positive mood is crucial for daily functioning and cooperation, yet negative mood is critical for response to survival situations (Spoor
& Kelly, 2004; Zajonc, 1998). S. E. Taylor's (1991) mobilization-minimization
theory of negative emotion argued that initial mobilization processes galvanize internal resources to direct attention and behavior toward solving the
problem at hand, and over time, minimization processes attempt to soften
and repair the impact of the negative event.

Consistent with this notion that negative emotions are adaptive orienting responses, negative versus positive work events appear to loom larger for
employees. In an experience-sampling study, Miner, Glomb, and Hulin (2005)
found that the effect on workers' mood was five times stronger for negative
than positive events, in spite of positive events occurring three to five times
as often. Similarly, workers can better recall negative events and negative
events have a greater impact on them (Dasborough, 2006). Negative mood
is more likely to spill across the work-family boundary than positive mood
(Williams & Alliger, 1994), and colleagues converge more strongly in their
negative versus positive moods (Bartel & Saavedra, 2000). This may explain
the vast research literature on stress in organizational settings. Stress has been
defined as "an unpleasant emotional experience associated with elements of
fear, dread, anxiety, irritation, annoyance, anger, sadness, grief and depression" (Motowildo, Packard, & Manning, 1986), which is a type of negative
emotional experience (Scherer, 1995). Its pernicious effects result from ignoring its helpful side—stress is supposed to be a warning signal for the need
to change, but its underlying causes often do not get changed in spite of the
warning. Even anger in the workplace can be beneficial when used within its
intended role as an emotion of moral justice that provokes us to confront an
obstacle or offender to change the behavior of another (Dilorio & Nusbaumer, 1993; Morris & Keltner, 2000). However, anger is generally considered
an overly disruptive state to be regulated heavily (Dilorio & Nusbaumer, 1993;
Wharton & Erickson, 1993) and is rarely put to productive use.

Individual differences. Organizational actors carry with them their emotional history that includes traces of their past emotional experiences (Fineman, 1996). Over time, we use our emotional experiences to refine the schemas
used in stimulus registration, as we encounter events repeatedly and become
more adept at interpreting their meaning. Then, in turn, we use these repeated
schemas as a lens to interpret new events, in a process that can be self-fulfilling. The chronic experience of sadness can lead us to interpret more events as
sad, which makes us sadder. There is a reciprocal influence between emotional
states and traits, connected by our systematic interpretive lenses.

More recent theories argue that the distinction between emotional states
and traits can be blurry and that, indeed, traits merely refer to the likelihood
of experiencing particular states (Fleeson, 2001; Larsen & Ketelaar, 1991).

Everyone is capable of experiencing every emotion, but practice makes perfect. Dispositions are attribution styles incorporated into the feeling rules and schemas that we use to interpret our world. Support for this perspective comes from research showing that emotional dispositions such as negative affect, neuroticism, optimism, and extraversion influence participants' unique reactions to standardized emotion elicitors (Brief, Butcher, & Roberson, 1995; Larsen & Ketelaar, 1989; Watson & Clark, 1984), as well as evidence that affective states and their corresponding traits tend to have similar influences on resulting behaviors and cognitions (George, 1991; Lerner & Keltner, 2001). It is worth noting that, in addition to this assimilation effect that occurs when we travel a well-practiced emotional registration—whether or not it quite fits the new situation—our chronic schemas can also create contrast effects when we develop new benchmarks to evaluate stimuli not on absolute terms but with respect to recent experience (Fuller et al., 2003). In developing these benchmarks, Frijda (1988) argued that we can more easily habituate to positive experiences—thus, creating a hedonic treadmill in which ever-greater pleasure is required for positive experience—whereas the impact of negative stimuli is less malleable to recent experience.

Within organizational research, by far the most common focus on affective traits has been the appraisal dimension of intrinsic pleasantness, as examined in bipolar models of mood. In contrast with basic emotions theories, which argue that we experience distinct categories of emotion, the circumplex model of affect attempts to map these categories into a two-dimensional space. In one version, one axis refers to *valence* or *hedonic tone*—the intrinsic pleasantness of a stimulus—and the other axis refers to the level of intensity of activation (Feldman Barrett & Russell, 1999). A second version of the model rotates these axes 45 degrees so that they refer to high-low positive affect and high-low negative affect, which are defined as the tendency to experience positive and negative states, respectively (Watson, Clark, & Tellegen, 1988). Contrasting these two models has been controversial, particularly because the rotated version suggests that the experience of positive and negative states are independent—a finding that appears to be an artifact of examining only half of the circumplex by sampling exclusively from intense experiences (Cropanzano et al., 2003; Feldman Barrett & Russell, 1999). Even so, the rotated model has been highly influential and has generated extensive empirical work within organizational settings. Individuals high in positive affect are more focused externally on promoting positive outcomes, where individuals high in negative affect are more focused internally on preventing negative outcomes (Diener & Larsen, 1984; Higgins, 1998; Larsen & Ketelaar, 1989). Positive versus negative affect also map onto promotion versus prevention regulatory focus, respectively (Brockner & Higgins, 2001). Individuals high versus low in negative affect self-report more negative events, especially subjective events, and report that these events have a longer and more intense negative impact on them (Aquino, Grover, Bradfield, & Allen, 1999; Burke, Brief, & George, 1993; Grandey, Tam, & Brauburger, 2002). Likewise, individuals high in positive affect are more reactive to positive workplace events and less reactive to negative events (Frederickson, 2001; Miner et al., 2005). There is enough evidence that affective experience overlaps with self-reported perceptions of objective job characteristics—such as stressors—to suggest that positive and negative affect form a powerful lens rendering even straightforward reports of one's work environment unreliable (Bagozzi & Yi, 1990; Burke et al., 1993; Saavedra & Kwun, 2000). These differences in affective experience feed into worker's subjective well-being, perhaps tautologically given that one definition of well-being is that people "feel many pleasant and few unpleasant emotions" (Diener, 2000, p. 34).

Other affective personality traits have received less attention but are fertile ground for organizational research. In theory, every dimension of cognitive appraisal could be subject to individual idiosyncrasies in its use and overuse (Ellsworth & Scherer, 2003). For example, related to the appraisal of coping potential, individuals differ chronically in feelings of control over stressful situations (Williams & Alliger, 1994). Related to fairness, for example, individuals in economic games differ in terms of whether they prefer fair versus greedy behavior (Haselhuhn & Mellers, 2005). Given the definition of *creativity* as ideas or solutions that are both new and useful (Amabile, 1983), appraisals of novelty and goal relevance could relate to individual differences in creativity. Likewise, micromanagement could relate to appraisals of control and blame, risk behavior to certainty, obstinacy to goal obstruction, whistle blowing to social standards and norms, and old-fashioned laziness could relate to anticipated effort.

In the absence of higher order emotional appraisals, intensity is the second axis of the unrotated circumplex describing mood states. Just as there are individual differences in the predominance of positive versus negative experiences, there are also individual differences in the predominance of high versus low-intensity emotions (Feldman, 1995). Indeed, what we often mean when describing a person as *emotional* is that they experience their emotions—any emotions—intensely. There has been relatively little research in organizational settings on stable individual differences in affective intensity, with the exception of Weiss et al. (1999), who found that self-reported affective intensity predicted greater variation in actual moods as assessed by experience sampling. Classic research on arousal examined intensity of experience at the intrapersonal level (Yerkes & Dodson, 1908) and could be extended fruitfully to the interpersonal realm.

As promising as research has been on individual differences, it is important to look beyond them. Emotional experiences start with stimuli, even if personality serves as an interpretive lens. Accordingly, a great deal of variation in affective states is intrapersonal (Weiss et al., 1999)—indeed, the majority, according to recent experience-sampling studies of mood pleasantness (56%;

Miner et al., 2005) and state hostility (53%; Judge et al., 2006). This is more than sampling error. For example, variation can occur in daily cycles (Weiss et al., 1999). Strong situations can overwhelm the impact of personality. For example, some jobs are inherently more stressful than others (Motowildo, Packard, & Manning, 1986).

Physiology. Although there is a long debate regarding whether mental awareness of feeling states precedes physiological arousal or vice versa (e.g., James, 1884; Schachter & Singer, 1962; Zajonc, 1998), the two cannot easily be separated. Indeed, James (1884) argued that fear without awareness of one's heartbeat, breathing, muscle tenseness, and trembling can hardly be considered fear. Emotions induce short-term and long-term changes to bodily functioning. In the short term, psychophysiological responses are set in motion immediately upon registering a stimulus and can take a few seconds to course through the body (Zajonc, 1998). These physical changes that accompany emotional experience are responsible, for example, for the experience of anger as smoldering hot and fear as shivering cold (Scherer, 1984b). In the long term, the effects of short-term physiological changes accumulate and affect the body. Hochschild (1983) referred to "emotional stamina" as the ability to express emotion for long periods of time without negative effects on one's physiological state. For example, the increased rate of hypertension among individuals prone to stress speaks to the harmful effects of heightened physiological arousal over time. The classic stressor-stress-strain approach taken by the stress literature (e.g., Beal, Weiss, Barros, & Macdermid, 2005) can be reconciled with the emotion process model by considering the stressor as a stimulus, stress as the feeling state, and strain as the physiological effect.

The potential of psychophysiological markers of emotion to inform processes within organizations is immense and barely tapped. Ashby, Isen, and Turken (1999) proposed a neuropsychological theory of positive affect arguing that positive affect acts by increasing levels of the neurotransmitter dopamine. Heaphy and Dutton (in press) reviewed evidence that positive workplace interactions have beneficial effects on three physiological systems: the cardiovascular system that distributes oxygen and nutrients via the blood, the immune system that heals and defends the body against disease and tissue damage, and the neuroendocrine system that regulates the nervous system and biologically active hormones. Such physical changes suggest mechanisms to explain why positive relationships among colleagues, supervisors, customers, and other stakeholders (e.g., mentoring and leader-member exchange) can have beneficial consequences beyond the instrumental benefits at stake (Heaphy & Dutton, in press). Thus, psychophysiology can play a valuable role in elaborating theoretical mechanisms for organizational phenomena. Further, psychophysiological measures can be invaluable for organizational researchers. Although they usually require additional training and equipment for data collection and analysis or collaboration with experts in such methods (Heaphy & Dutton, in press), they do not require participants' awareness or willingness to report about their emotions—a great concern in research on emotion (Matthews, Zeidner, & Roberts, 2002; Scherer, 1984b).

Emotional Expression

Ultimately the very private intrapersonal emotional processes described in the previous sections are made public, as our sensemaking efforts become shared in the form of emotional expression and other postemotional behaviors. Emotionally expressive cues—depicted in the upper right corner of Figure 7.1—begin with words (Pennebaker, Mehl, & Niederhoffer, 2003), but nonverbal cues are particularly important because organizations often lack a vocabulary for discussing emotional experience (Sandelands, 1988). Nonverbal cues include facial expressions, vocal tone, body language, movement, touching, and physical distance—indeed, essentially any way that the human body can emit movement, sound, or feeling can take on an expressive quality (Allport & Vernon, 1933).

On the intrapersonal level, expression has a value in itself. Indeed, Zajonc (1998) argued that the term *emotional expression* is preemptive, implying through its very name the argument that physical cues are intended as a signal of internal states. According to *vascular efference* theory, facial cues and head movements feed back into emotional experience, via the regulation of blood flow and brain temperature (Tomkins & McCarter, 1964; Zajonc, 1998). Although this particular argument is specific to the face, afferent feedback also leads individuals to feel internal states consistent with their own vocal tones and body postures (Hatfield, Hsee, Costello, & Weisman, 1995). Even if nonverbal cues are frequently driven by internal experience, the strength of their association can lead the pathway to reverse. A further intrapersonal value to emotional expression is catharsis that helps to terminate unwanted emotional experience. Individuals may vary in the extent to which externalizers discharge emotion using visible emotional expression versus internalizers who use internal somatic activation (Buck, 1988).

On the interpersonal level, emotional expression is one of the most powerful forms of social influence (e.g., Ekman, 1972; Keltner & Haidt, 1999), inside and outside of the workplace. The modern study of emotion as communication leans heavily on Brunswik's (1955) lens model of ecological perception—embedded within the interpersonal process framework in Figure 7.2—in which properties such as emotional states are associated probabilistically with specific external cues and, in turn, these cues are perceived probabilistically by a judge trying to infer the property. Although emotional expression has often been studied in organizational settings on its own, the lens model implies that expression needs to be considered in the context of how it is perceived by others.

The influential social function perspective on emotion has emphasized its adaptive implications as communication (DePaulo & Friedman, 1998; McArthur & Baron, 1983; Morris & Keltner, 2000). Evolutionarily, the emotions with the clearest physical signals are those for which it is generally adaptive to inform others—such as fear and anger, but not boredom (Cosmides & Tooby, 2000). Keltner and Haidt (1999) outlined three mechanisms by which the communication of emotions evolved as an adaptive response to social living. First, emotional expressions efficiently convey information about reactions to our shared environment, beliefs, social intentions, and feedback toward others. Second, emotional expressions tend to evoke emotional responses in others that help to solve the problems of group living; for example, embarrassment can elicit forgiveness, and pain can elicit sympathy. Anger is intended to induce others to adjust irritating behavior—and can evoke a range of emotions from fear and guilt, if the implicit appraisal of blame is accepted, or a spiral of anger otherwise. Third, emotions can serve in operant conditioning as rewards or punishments, and promises or threats of possible future rewards or punishments. For example, male managers in a simulated employment setting offered greater praise to those female subordinates to whom they offered low tangible compensation (Vescio, Gervais, Snyder, & Hoover, 2005). Morris and Keltner (2000) described social functions of anger to punish others for misdeeds, gratitude to reward others for cooperating, guilt to spur efforts to repair relationship harm, contempt to signal to someone their lower status, and shame to signal a transgressor's regret without need for formal punishment. They argued that the social function perspective does not mean that emotions are always functional—particularly at any given level of analysis—but rather that each emotion evolved with a function that it can serve, even if it does not always do so. These functions are the reason not merely to be happy all of the time—we would lose the evolutionary value of negative emotion. Social functions help in resolving conflicts, appeasement, dividing resources fairly, and generally maintaining effective relationships (Morris & Keltner, 2000).

Emotion as spontaneous versus deliberate communication has been hotly debated (Parkinson, 2005). At one extreme, Ekman (1972) argued that expression is primarily a spontaneous readout of internal states and shows true emotion at all times except when managed with conscious effort. However, empirical evidence appears to favor more moderate positions, particularly Fridlund's (1994) behavioral ecology theory in which social audience factors heavily into emotional expression, even with internal states and conscious management held constant. Scherer (1988) distinguished between spontaneous *push factors* caused by the feeling and physiology of emotional experience—such as bodily changes like accelerated breath or shaking—versus *pull factors* caused by social intentions to communicate. He further distinguished between pull factors that convey information versus those making a specific appeal for action. For example, an expression of fear could signify frozen terror, a deliberate signal that danger is nearby, or a request to extricate the expressor from the scary situation.

Pull factors have been investigated largely under the umbrella of *display rules*, to be described in the later section on display regulation. Push factors include biologically determined affect programs as well as cultural and individual expressive style. Classic studies demonstrated that emotional expressions can be recognized across cultural groups at accuracy levels greater than chance guessing alone, which suggests that a core of expression is universal and biologically programmed (Ekman, 1972, 1992; Russell, 1994). Indeed, as most people living with pets would agree, basic emotional messages can also transcend species boundaries. However, some of the message gets lost along the way. There is an in-group advantage favoring the understanding of emotional expressions that originate from members of one's own cultural group (Elfenbein & Ambady, 2003). A recent dialect theory of emotion argued that cultural groups vary subtly yet systematically in the cues they use to express emotion and that judgments are more accurate for expressions that use a familiar style (Elfenbein, Beaupré, Lévesque, & Hess, 2007). These cultural dialects are more than the overlearned conscious management of expression, in that they develop from random variation across isolated groups and do not necessarily serve a social function. Even within cultures, individuals develop unique expressive styles. Personality theorists have examined individual differences in the intensity of expressive displays (Halberstadt, 1986; Gross & John, 1998). In addition to intensity, individuals may also differ in the particular cues they use for the same displays (Elfenbein, Foo, Boldry, & Tan, 2006).

The appearance of expressive displays may differ based on whether they are created by push versus pull factors. Spontaneous expressions are more symmetrical, more consistent in their duration, and can use different expressive cues (Rinn, 1984). Observers can detect some of these differences, most notably the difference between the Duchenne smile with both lip corner retraction and wrinkles around the eyes versus the non-Duchenne smile with only lip corner retraction—often known as the authentic versus fake smile, respectively. For example, Scherer and Ceschi (2000) found that airline employees judged the good humor of their passengers with lost baggage based on fake versus authentic smiling. Grandey, Fisk, Mattila, Jansen, and Sideman (2005) found that authentic versus fake smiling enhanced customer satisfaction and perceptions of friendliness in simulated hotel and actual restaurant settings. Push versus pull factors can also influence the channel of communication through which cues are expressed. Ekman and Friesen (1969) proposed a hierarchy of nonverbal expressive cues from the most controllable to the most leaky. They argued that facial expressions are more controllable and provide more feedback from the self and others, compared to leakier channels such as the body and voice. Voluntary cues tend to be expressed via facial expressions, whereas the cues expressed via leakier channels tend to be more spontaneous. Emotional expressions most likely fall along a continuum between push and pull factors, in that we can exhibit varying levels of intentional control. Facial expressions can give us away, and with practice even leaky channels can be controlled.

Most research on emotional expression within organizational settings focuses on its regulation, and is discussed at length in the later section on display regulation.

Emotion Regulation

Each of the emotion processes previously reviewed—from a stimulus to registration, experience, and expression—can be brought under at least partial voluntary control via emotion regulation processes that are unique to each stage (Frijda, 1988), depicted in the gray, shaded area of Figure 7.1. Gross' (2001) pioneering model of emotion regulation emphasized that there are distinct regulation strategies across the particular stages of emotion, and argued that attempts to regulate chronologically earlier tend to be more effective than those attempts later in the emotion process.

Regulating Stimuli

Although the emotion process framework starts with a stimulus in the environment, people choose their environments (Buss, 1987; Diener, Larsen, & Emmons, 1984). *Situation selection*, or limiting exposure to situations that evoke undesired emotions and increasing exposure to situations evoking desired states, is the chronologically earliest form of regulation within the emotion process (Gross, 1998a, b). Different work environments make different affective events more or less likely (Weiss & Cropanzano, 1996). At some level, every choice that an employee makes is an affective event. We use our anticipated emotions in order to guide decision making (Loewenstein & Lerner, 2003; Mellers, 2000), and thus, the decision-making process looks ahead through the emotion process and selects situations that will expose us to desired emotional experiences and avoid unwanted ones. However, this process of *affective forecasting* in anticipating our future emotions is imperfect, and suffers from biases such as over reliance on momentarily salient issues and underestimating our resilience against negative events and habituation to positive events (Gilbert, Pinel, Wilson, Blumberg, & Wheatley, 1998; Loewenstein & Schkade, 1999).

There is a temptation to review the entire organizational literatures on person-organization, person-group, and person-job fit, given the powerful influence that organizations have in choosing situations for the individuals within them. Indeed, many theorists have noted the strong component of emotion infused into organizational culture, in which different environments promote particular emotions and discourage others, often at great effort (Albrow, 1992; Ashforth & Humphrey, 1993; Ashkanasy, 2003; Fineman, 1993, 1996; Huy,

1999; Kelly & Barsade, 2001; Merton, 1952; Rafaeli & Worline, 2001; Rafaeli & Vilnai-Yavetz, 2004; Sutton, 1991; Van Maanen & Kunda, 1989). Indeed, cultural control via emotions is valuable in that it provides a tighter and deeper hold on employees than conventional bureaucratic mechanisms (Van Maanen & Kunda, 1989).

Organizational structure influences the emotional experiences of the individual. Indeed, bureaucracy developed at least partly to limit individuals' abilities to act upon their emotions when the modern workplace replaced kinship ties with standard operating procedures (Ashforth & Humphrey, 1995; Putnam & Mumby, 1993). Hierarchy creates an emotional division of labor (Ashforth & Humphrey, 1995; Van Maanen & Kunda, 1989). Any kind of delegation involves some degree of situation selection—and tasks that elicit aversive emotions are more likely to be delegated. Van Maanen and Kunda (1989) argued that higher status roles involve creating emotional stimuli for others, rather than responding to others' stimuli. Particular strategies for emotional delegation include neutralizing, which involves limiting and routinizing interpersonal contact, and buffering, which separates the emotional connections involved in front stage relationship development tasks from back stage tasks and commercial roles (Ashforth & Humphrey, 1995). Ethnographic research details, for example, how managers offload anxiety-provoking situations downward in the hierarchy, such as responsibility for 24-hour nurse staffing under resource constraints (Brooks, 2003), and conducting emotionally charged in-person eligibility interviews for social services (Garot, 2004). However, ideally, leaders also use their greater powers to buffer the effect of negative events on their followers (Pirola-Merlo et al., 2002).

Organizations have "emotionalized zones" (Fineman, 1996, p. 556) that maintain employees' equilibrium by permitting certain experiences not possible elsewhere. The need for emotional regulation can be so intense that employees benefit by releasing some of the constraints off stage, for example, using physical spaces accessible only to insiders, humor, workplace rituals, and off-site events such as parties, karaoke, and anywhere else that alcohol is served (Ashforth & Humphrey, 1995; Rafaeli & Sutton, 1987).

Although stimulus selection clearly benefits individuals and organizations in many ways, it can also lead to the proverbial ostrich putting its head in the sand. For example, service representatives sometimes choose to avoid customers to whom they should be available (Grandey, 2000).

People choose their environments, but they also shape them. *Situation modification* involves changing a situation to adjust its emotional impact (Gross, 1998a, b). Thus, emotions can be catalysts propelling us to action. For example, just as organizational change evokes emotions, so too do emotions evoke organizational change. Individuals seek to resolve discrepancies between their current and desired states of affairs (George & Jones, 2001). As emphasized by the Positive Organizational Scholarship movement (e.g., Frost,

2003; Dutton, 2003), efforts abound to improve organizations to make them safer, more fair, more rewarding, and generally more emotionally fulfilling.

Regulating Emotional Registration, Experience, and Expression.
One of the hottest areas within the study of emotion in organizations has been the regulation of emotional registration, experience, and expression. These processes are all distinct, but work together toward the common goal of reducing unwanted emotional experience and the downstream effects that this experience has on others (Gross, 1998b). These processes are discussed first individually, and then together in the context of emotional labor that spans regulation strategies.

Reappraisal. Reappraisal is regulation of the emotional registration process, with effects on the subcomponents of attention, feeling rules, and schemas (Gross, 1998b). Whereas situation selection alters one's actual exposure to a situation, attention deployment alters one's attention to it (Gross, 1998b). This can include ignoring a situation altogether or focusing on particular aspects of a complex situation. Within reappraisal, feeling rules are also altered when organizations and social partners provide guidance about which emotions are inherently desirable to experience. People often look to similar others for clues to how they should feel (Ashforth & Humphrey, 1995; Sutton, 1991). For example, Van Maanen and Kunda (1989) described a high-tech company with a familiar phrase that "it's not work, it's a celebration" (p. 80).

The most ubiquitous form of reappraisal is to alter emotional schemas, by providing new responses to the stimulus evaluations within emotional appraisal. Weick et al. (2005) argued that sensemaking is a public and social process. Workers are most open to reappraisal when events are ambiguous, multifaceted, and potentially harmful to self-interests (Ashforth & Humphrey, 1995). In such cases, leaders often pave the way by modeling reactions that signal how to make meaning of an event (Pescosolido, 2002; Pirola-Merlo et al., 2002; Yukl, 1999). Organizational examples abound of deliberate changes to the application of emotional schemas. For example, flight attendants are encouraged to see customers as small children who cannot be held responsible for unruly behavior (Hochschild, 1983). Language helps to create new schemas, such as when Disneyland refers for example to customers, police, and uniforms as guests, security hosts, and costumes, respectively (Van Maanen & Kunda, 1989). Error-management training attempts to increase learning by reappraising mistakes as opportunities (e.g., "the more errors you make, the more you learn!"; Keith & Frese, 2005, p. 681). Debt collection agencies teach their employees to reframe their interactions with sympathetic debtors as bills to be collected and to believe that angry debtors are not angry at the collector personally and, indeed, collectors are helping debtors to protect their credit history (Sutton, 1991). Social service workers consider how clients may be responsible for their own difficult situation and less needy than alternate applicants (Garot, 2004). Humor is often used as part of changing schemas. Making fun of adversity both invokes positive affect directly and also signals that one can cope with a challenging situation (Avolio, Howell, & Sosik, 1999). Making fun of colleagues changes interpretations of their worthiness. In Collinson's (1988) ethnography, machine-shop employees used humor against others to reappraise themselves as smart and powerful when, objectively, their position was treated as among the most lowly in their manufacturing organization. The value of reappraisal is to help achieve desired feeling states when initial schemas fail in that regard. For example, employees of an airline facing bankruptcy and lay-offs who took part in an intervention designed to teach reappraisal strategies reported higher positive affect, lower negative affect, and more constructive attitudes toward the bankruptcy than those randomly assigned to receive training at a later date (Neck & Manz, 1996). There is a certain dark side when organizations deliberately fill this role—indeed, Van Maanen and Kunda (1989) referred to dictating the meaning to attach to one's work as "social molestation" (p. 92).

Experience regulation. Experience regulation involves deliberate direct changes in emotional state, outside of the registration process. This includes a host of psychodynamic defense mechanisms such as suppression, denial, and sublimation, in which an opposing emotion is substituted for one deemed unacceptable. Research emphasizes the downsides of suppressing emotional experience. Control over any ongoing thought process can lead to ironic effects where the suppressed thoughts and feelings bounce back to a greater degree after the active control is lifted (Gross, 2001; Wegener, Erber, & Zanakos, 1993). Chronic supressors of emotional experience often lose touch with their emotional states (Davis & Schwartz, 1987). Suppressed emotions can cross experiential channels from subjective feeling to greater physiological arousal, which damages health over time (Gross, 1998b, 2001). Further, suppression is often imperfect and still leaks into downstream emotional processes such as expression (Ekman & Friesen, 1969). There has been relatively little organizational research attention paid to the suppression of experience—rather than emotional display—perhaps because an experience truly suppressed is no longer accessible for research. The high steel ironworkers in Haas' (1977) ethnography suppressed their fear largely through sheer will to cover it up, and even replaced it with flagrant acts of bravado. This became apparent only after a deadly accident, when incontrovertible proof of their emotions froze the ironworkers in their own fear and they literally had to be carried from the worksite. Huy (2002) reported that many managers in a stressful organizational change event expressed a need to "'psyche' themselves up" and "'blank out' negative thoughts" (p. 41). Experience regulation also includes physical behavior that feeds back into emotional states via catharsis, escalation, or direct effects on physiology—such as exercise, massage, alcohol, narcotics, chocolate, etc. For example, debt collectors angry after frustrating phone calls were encouraged to punch a desk (Sutton, 1991). Judge et al. (2006) argued that deviant behavior in the workplace acts as a kind of catharsis, in which workers feel that they have restored control after feeling frustration. Undergoing action of some kind relieves the energy potential created by emotional action tendencies that need to be discharged in some way (Loewenstein & Lerner, 2003). The social sharing of emotions serves as an opportunity for catharsis as well as reappraisal, given that venting or discussing feelings with others can give rise to new interpretations (Fineman, 1993). A whopping 75 to 84% of participants interviewed about anger experiences report that they told someone else at the time (Fitness, 2000; Sloan, 2004). Although relieving, such acts of venting can also be harmful for organizational actors. Brown, Westbrook, and Challagalla (2005) found that salespeople who vented to colleagues after losing major opportunities received lower performance appraisals from their supervisors.

Display regulation. Display regulation involves changing visible emotional expression without altering the underlying experience. Ekman (1972) coined the term display rules as "management techniques" (p. 225) that allow individuals to "decouple their expressions from their feelings" (p. 127). These are norms about what is appropriate to display and include deintensifying, intensifying, neutralizing, and masking (Ekman, Sorensen, & Friesen, 1969). As norms, they can be described explicitly and, indeed, are even laid out in many corporate manuals (Van Maanen & Kunda, 1989). Although they are conscious norms, display rules can become overlearned to the point where the expressor is barely aware of their influence (Ashforth & Humphrey, 1993; Ekman, 1984), like any other form of regulation (Gross, 1998b).

Ekman's (1972) original coinage emphasized that display rules serve social functions—the outward acknowledgment of internal feeling rules—such as maintaining harmony by suppressing negative displays in collectivist cultures. Indeed, this is a common display rule in organizations, particularly among lower power actors to whom concerns such as harmony typically fall. However, there are as many possible display rules as potential social messages to display. Wharton and Erickson (1993) categorized organizational display rules as integrative, differentiating, and masking. Integrative displays are pleasant and affiliative (e.g., customer service). Differentiating displays such as anger create social distance (e.g., police officers and bill collectors). Masking displays use neutral demeanors to demonstrate reserve and high status (e.g., clinicians and judges). A helpful heuristic for analyzing specific display rules is to use the emotion process framework and *forward-track* through the sequence. An actor's optimal display rule is one that the interaction partner recognizes and registers to create an emotional state with postemotional attitudes, behaviors, and cognitions that the actor desires. For example, high steel ironworkers suppress their displays of fear so as not remind colleagues who are trying to control their own fear (Haas, 1977). Researchers generally argue that positive displays are valuable, such as in customer service, because they create positive emotional contagion for the customer and serve as an inherently rewarding stimulus for operant conditioning (Rafaeli & Sutton, 1989) that elicits reciprocity (Tsai, 2001). However, the process framework adds another explanation, which is that a positive display provides information about the actor's beliefs along the dimensions of emotional appraisal—in particular, that there are no stimuli in the shared environment that are goal obstructing, unfair, or counternormative. By contrast, an irritated display would imply an attribution of blame, and a fearful display would imply an attribution of uncertain events. Thus, at its core, positive displays to customers are expert reassurance that they are blameless (e.g., "the customer is always right") and that the coast is clear.

Researchers have examined a number of factors that influence display rules. Rules originate with selection, training, rewards, and reinforcement—both formal and informal (Rafaeli & Sutton, 1989; Sutton & Rafaeli, 1988). Individuals bring traces of past display rules from one organization to the next (Rafaeli & Sutton, 1987). Display rules vary in their strength, and their crystallization versus flexibility to incorporate personal expressive style (Ashforth & Humphrey, 1993). For example, supervisors vary substantially in their beliefs about subordinates' emotional displays within the same industry (Tsai, 2001) and even the same organization (Wilk & Moynihan, 2005). Rules are more prevalent for high-energy states, whether positive or negative, than for low energy states (Bartel & Saavedra, 2000), thus allowing people freer reign in their subtlety. Display rules evolve over time—for example, Huy (2002) described how managers released display rules during a corporate upheaval—and they can also vary based on the time of the day, season of the year, and even the weather (Rafaeli & Sutton, 1989). For example, Sutton and Rafaeli (1988) found that convenience stores had a display rule of friendliness only during periods of light traffic. During busy periods the norm was for neutral displays signaling that the clerk was efficient and valued the customer's time. Similarly, display rule preferences can shift with experimentally induced task goals (Gaddis et al., 2004). In light of the disparate social functions served across occupational roles, display rules vary greatly across occupations. Bill collectors and drill sergeants display hostility, whereas funeral directors display sadness, and customer representatives display cheerfulness (Rafaeli & Sutton, 1987, 1989). Specified emotional displays predict financial rewards for professional group members as diverse as nurses, waitresses, prostitutes, conmen, and poker players (Fineman, 1996). Hochschild (1979) argued that display rules denote a zone of permission. Given that low power suggests lesser flexibility for agentic emotions such as anger, contempt, and pride versus sadness and gratitude (Morris & Keltner, 2000; Tiedens, 2001), these are reflected in typical display rules for women and low-level employment. Violation of such rules is a power play—because actors presume to interpret the world in a high-power manner—resulting in enhanced status if successful, but attributions of being uppity and out of control if not. Display rules vary across interaction partners, in light of different social goals. For example, nurses are expected to show warmth to patients yet flat affect to physicians, and waiters size up their customers for the demeanor they prefer (Rafaeli & Sutton, 1987, 1989). Likewise, debt collectors display sympathy to new debtors, and for long-standing debtors, they show irritation to those who are indifferent, friendly, or sad and calmness to those who are angry (Sutton, 1991). In each case, the goal is consistent with the social function of putting the debtor into a state of mind to pay the bill promptly: an agitated—yet not too agitated—state of arousal. At some level, Sutton (1991) argued, debtors pay bills merely to end the stream of collectors' phone calls, which makes the debt payment a form of stimulus selection. Display rules are so ubiquitous that even the encouragement organization wide to express authentic emotion can itself become an oppressive display rule for those who are not normally expressive (Martin, Knopoff, & Beckman, 1998; Van Maanen & Kunda, 1989).

Emotional labor.   Emotional labor (EL) is an umbrella term encompassing reappraisal, experience regulation, and expression regulation, which are considered alongside each other because actors frequently trade off among these options as strategies toward this same goal—although, in practice, most research includes only reappraisal and display regulation. The three can be difficult to distinguish because they are all manifested and monitored within organizations via external expressive cues. No one strategy is superior, as each is more suited to particular situational demands (Gross, 1998b), and skill across all these strategies tends to benefit individuals (Lopes, Salovey, Côté, & Beers, 2005). Hochschild (1979) coined the term EL as the creation of an observable expressive display to follow norms, and emphasized that EL is bought and sold for the goals of an organization rather than individual. Although Ashforth and Humphrey (1993) went as far as to argue that all expression of expected emotion during service encounters should be considered emotional labor—even genuine displays resulting from authentic experience—a key element of emotional labor is that the intimacy of human emotion is commoditized and literally part of the labor process (Domagalski, 1999), as contrasted with work feelings that are emergent from human interaction (Putnam & Mumby, 1993). Hochschild (1983) examined job classifications and estimated that one third of the U.S. workforce engaged in EL as a routine part of their jobs. Although emotional labor is often considered women's work, Glomb, Kammeyer-Mueller, and Rotundo's (2004) examination of U.S. employment classifications revealed that jobs high in EL included both stereotypically female positions (e.g., nurses, librarians, and social workers) and stereotypically male positions (e.g., police officers and lawyers). Emotional labor is particularly relevant for boundary spanners (Ashforth & Humphrey, 1993; Wharton & Erickson, 1993). Front-line personnel devote more effort to creating harmony because they interact with individuals who are not under the control of the organization, and whose needs are often at odds with those of the organization (Wharton & Erickson, 1993). EL is also more relevant for the service sector—where quality is a subjective judgment of an experience—rather than more tangible areas such as manufacturing (Wharton & Erickson, 1993). Indeed, among service workers, Pugh (2001) found no zero-order association between self-reported positive affect and objective ratings of expressive displays—suggesting widespread EL. As such, emotional labor is increasingly important to modern organizations, given the rise in the service economy (Wharton, 1993).

Given that expressive displays are the end products of emotional labor, EL serves the same social functions of the display rules discussed previously. Achieving these social functions feeds into organizations' instrumental goals such as client purchases, satisfaction, and bill payment (Ashforth & Humphrey, 1993; Côté & Morgan, 2002; Grandey, 2003; Rafaeli & Sutton, 1989). Gains from EL are especially pervasive when goals are mediated by the subjective judgments of others, as in the case of tipping by customers, jury verdicts, client referrals, and so forth (Rafaeli & Sutton, 1987). Even so, it is not helpful to make blanket statements like "emotional labor leads to better performance," because the benefit accrues only when emotional labor succeeds in eliciting the desired response from an interaction partner (Côté, 2005). Emotional displays might not match the optimal social function, for example, when a display is perceived as insincere or irrelevant, such as when a sales clerk is friendly in a store that emphasizes speed (Rafaeli & Sutton, 1989). A display may also be mismatched when forward tracking through the emotion process leads to the opposite behavior that is desired (e.g., a positive display to a debtor signals the debt is not a serious problem; Sutton, 1991).

As helpful as emotional labor may be for organizations, it often has harmful consequences for employees' performance and personal welfare, in terms of work strain leading to burnout, exhaustion, low job satisfaction, inability to stay in role, lower customer satisfaction, and lesser sense of personal accomplishment (Brotheridge & Lee, 2003; Côté & Morgan, 2002; Grandey, 2000, 2003; Rafaeli & Sutton, 1989). These negative consequences appear to be stronger for the use of display regulation versus reappraisal, which Hochschild (1983) referred to as surface acting and deep acting, and Gross (1998a) referred to as *antecedent-focused* and *response-focused regulation*, respectively. However, the empirical relationship between EL and work strain has been inconsistent. Indeed, EL may even be a welcome reprieve from boredom for jobs low in cognitive demands (Glomb et al., 2004). Côté (2005) reviewed four mechanisms previously used to explain the relationship between EL and strain: (a) emotional dissonance caused by displaying emotions that are not experienced and, thus, getting out of touch with one's own actual feelings and sense of self (Ashforth & Humphrey, 1993; Grandey, 2000, 2003; Rafaeli & Sutton, 1987; Van Maanen & Kunda, 1989); (b) vascular efference, also known as *facial feedback* (Zajonc, 1998), which helps employees' inner feelings come in line with outward display; (c) cognitive load due to the demands of maintaining self-control (Beal et al., 2005; Gross, 2001; Muraven & Baumeister, 2000), which reduces attentional resources for other tasks; and (d) the potential buffering impact of personal control. Côté argued that these four mechanisms explain some but not all empirical findings. Dissonance predicts greater strain only when self-reported measures are used for both experience and display, but not using outside ratings of display. Display requirements may be less salient to those who fit in well, potentially inflating the association of self-reported display rules and strain. Facial feedback does not explain why strain is greater for display regulation versus reappraisal, when the facial movements are largely the same for both. Likewise it does not explain strain for those who suppress negative displays. The cognitive load explanation is challenged by multiple findings that positive emotional displays often lead to lesser strain. Further, long-term employees often practice EL enough to render it automatic. Finally, personal control is a double-edged sword, where emotional labor is alternately easier for those who feel they are enacting a valued identity and those who disengage.

Côté (2005) concluded that the common thread is that strain is lower under conditions of emotional labor that are likely to elicit the most favorable responses from interaction partners. Because reappraisal produces positive expressive displays that appear more spontaneous and authentic, they are better received. By contrast, display regulation produces inauthentic and forced positive displays that elicit negative responses from observers and increase the employee's strain (see also Grandey, 2003; Rafaeli & Sutton 1989). In addition, EL may create strain by blocking the social function of negative emotion—which is an opportunity to solve a problem to which we are being alerted (Gross, 1998b; Keltner & Haidt, 1999). Because the social functions of negative emotions tend to be more immediate and pressing (Frijda, 1986), we are hardwired to respond more strongly to them (Taylor, S. E., 1991), which may explain why it creates less strain to squelch positive versus negative displays.

This large body of empirical work demonstrates that there can be personal costs to succeed at enacting display rules, but a value to success as long as the price is not too high. Researchers often extol the virtues of deep acting over surface acting for this reason (e.g., Gosserand & Diefendorff, 2005; Grandey, 2003). However, there is also a cost of success itself. Antecedent-focused strategies such as reappraisal can result in chronically inflexible or unrealistic appraisals of one's environment that cannot simply be turned off (Gross, 1998b). Although deeply acted displays may appear more authentic to the audience (e.g., Grandey, 2003), ultimately they compromise the authenticity of personal emotional experience and can contaminate one's emotional life outside of the workplace (Fineman, 1993; Hochschild, 1983; Rafaeli & Sutton, 1987; Van Maanen & Kunda, 1989). For example, employees who perform masking roles often have difficulty engaging their families at an emotionally expressive level (Wharton & Erickson, 1993). Even inside the workplace, a person who cannot convey sincere reactions misses the chance to develop a meaningful personal connection with clients, community members, colleagues, and the work itself (Grandey, 2000; Pogrebin & Poole, 1995).

Postemotional Responses

The most pervasive research interest in emotion within organizations has been its downstream consequences. In addition to their influence on general well-being and expressive behavior, emotional experiences feed into attitudes, behaviors, and cognitions, which are depicted together as postemotional responses in the dashed box within Figure 7.1. In addition to direct links between emotional states and behaviors, the model also includes indirect links to behavior that are mediated by intervening attitudes and cognitions (Eagley & Chaiken, 1998; Loewenstein & Lerner, 2003). Given the connection between emotional experience and postemotional behaviors, a question of natural interest—even obsession—to management scholars has been the influence of emotion on job performance, which is discussed at the end of this section.

The three resulting types of visible behaviors can, in turn, be considered as stimuli to feed back into the emotion registration process, as depicted in Figure 7.1. This connection is central to the James–Lang (e.g., James, 1884) and Schacter–Singer (1962) theories of emotion, in which individuals look to external behaviors and cues in order to infer their own internal emotional states. Along these lines, more recently Weick et al. (2005) argued that "action is always just a tiny bit ahead of cognition, meaning that we act our way into belated understanding" (p. 419). Just as postemotional behaviors can serve as stimuli for the self, they can also serve as stimuli for interaction partners, as depicted in Figure 7.2.

To resist imperialism of other areas within organizational studies, at this point it is important to be clear that not all attitudes, behaviors, and cognitions result from the emotion process. Thus, Figure 7.1 includes a link from the stimulus directly to postemotional responses that is depicted as unmediated by emotional registration and experience. In practice, these separate paths can difficult to disentangle; however, for theoretical reasons it is important to distinguish them.

Emotion-Driven Attitudes

The formal definition of an *attitude* is "a psychological tendency that is expressed by evaluating a particular entity with some degree of favor or disfavor" (Eagly & Chaiken, 1998, p. 269). Thus, by their very definition, attitudes are connected to the emotional dimension of valence—its association with an object. However, Eagly and Chaiken (1998) argued that emotions and attitudes are still distinct concepts and that attitudes are not merely affective reactions. Accordingly, although organizational researchers often refer to attitudes as emotions (e.g., intergroup emotions, interpersonal affect), as a field we should discourage this practice by distinguishing affect-driven attitudes from affect per se (Brief & Weiss, 2002).

Even so, given that valence is the primary dimension of emotional appraisal, the two concepts are inextricably linked. There is robust evidence for valence-consistent mood biases in organizationally relevant attitudes such as job satisfaction, performance appraisal, commitment, cohesion, intention to maintain working relationships, intention to turnover, evaluation of consumer goods, and even overall life satisfaction—although these effects can reverse if perceivers are made aware of moods that are irrelevant to the attitudes (Clore, Schwarz, & Conway, 1994; Forgas & George, 2001). Affect influences performance appraisals to be consistent with the valence of the affect (Robbins & DeNisi, 1994), particularly when the rating criteria are ambiguous (Isen & Baron, 1991). Largely an evaluation of emotional valence, leader-member exchange—the quality of subordinate interactions with their leaders—is greater under positive affect (Isen & Baron, 1991). Indeed, some have argued that an evolutionary role of emotion was to facilitate the development of interpersonal liking and rapport (Spoor & Kelly, 2004).

Affect-based versus cognition-based attitudes. There is an assumption strongly held that affect-based attitudes are stronger and qualitatively different than those formed via cognitive processing (Brief & Weiss, 2002). Zajonc (1998) argued that affective reactions are primary in determining our attitudes toward the social environment. Further, emotion-driven attitudes are stronger predictors of subsequent behavior than cognition-driven attitudes (Millar & Millar, 1996). Perhaps the inability to articulate the logic of forming an attitude leads to source amnesia, which could strengthen the feeling that the association is correct. Indeed, greater experience in a domain tends to predict greater influence of affect-based versus cognition-based attitudes on resulting behavior, suggesting that we trust our gut instincts better when that gut is better informed (Weiss, 2002).

However, in practice it is difficult to distinguish the cognitive versus affective source of attitudes. The clearest distinction comes from psychology laboratory studies in which attitudes are manipulated via subliminal priming.

Edwards (1990) found that such affect-based attitudes are expressed with greater confidence, perhaps due to affective primacy where we are prone to trust gut instincts. Further, Edwards (1990) found that attitudes undergo greater change via means of persuasion that match the initial affect-based versus cognition-based source of the attitude. In the case of nonexperimentally induced attitudes, the separation of affective versus cognitive components is less clear. Rather than presenting confirmatory factor analyses that demonstrate divergence in survey scales, the best practice is to validate scales by determining their sensitivity to experimental manipulations—although even in such cases there is usually still a substantial degree of overlap in scales measuring the two types of attitudes (Crites, Fabrigar, & Petty, 1994).

In spite of this challenge, the distinction between cognition-based and affect-based attitudes has captured a great deal of attention from organizational researchers. Ashforth and Humphrey (1995) distinguished between calculative versus affective commitment as well as transactional versus transformational leadership. Likewise, emotional attachment to a job is different from a cognitive assessment that a job is a good fit (Brief & Weiss, 2002), a topic to be discussed at greater length in the section that follows. However, attempts to separate concepts such as conflict and commitment into purportedly emotional versus nonemotional forms should be questioned closely and accompanied by firm evidence that, indeed, the source of the attitude is affect versus cognition. In the absence of such evidence that attitudes are versus are not accompanied by emotional experience, it is not clear to what extent the literature benefits from these distinctions. Often, the designation of an attitude as emotional appears synonymous for intense—such as emotional commitment (Huy, 2002)—or synonymous for having other people as the target—such as task versus emotional conflict (Xin & Pelled, 2003). In the latter cases, it may be more accurate to refer to the distinction as task versus relationship (Jehn, 1995), given that task conflict can also be emotional to the extent that we appraise it as relevant to the self. In practice, affect and cognition may be so intertwined that it is not possible to make clear empirical distinctions in the source of attitudes even if they are theoretically distinct.

Job satisfaction. For decades, particularly from the 1950s through mid-1980s, the attitude of deepest interest to organizational scholars has been job satisfaction, and indeed the early study of affect in organizations was intricately tied to job satisfaction (Brief & Weiss, 2002; Weiss & Cropanzano, 1996). Although job satisfaction was initially defined as job-related affect, Weiss and Cropanzano's (1996) AET articulated, first, that job satisfaction is an attitude rather than an emotional experience and, second, that the evaluation of one's job is not necessarily entirely affective, but also has a cognitive component to it as well. Weiss (2002; Weiss et al., 1999) argued that job satisfaction results from the three distinct factors of affective experiences, evaluative judgments, and beliefs about one's job.

A wide body of evidence connects affective experience to job satisfaction. At the trait level, job satisfaction is substantially higher for those high in trait positive affect and low in trait negative affect (Connolly & Viswesvaran, 2000; Judge & Larsen, 2001). Connolly and Viswesvaran (2000) attributed this relationship to affect-congruent interpretation of one's work environment, construct contamination in the form of overlap and method bias across self-reported questionnaires of affect and satisfaction, and the mediating role of state affect. Further evidence for the role of trait affect comes from the relative stability of individual job satisfaction over time, even in the context of major situational changes—suggesting that enduring traits can influence one's evaluative lens (Staw & Cohen-Charash, 2005). Thoresen, Kaplan, Barsky, Warren, and de Chermont's (2003) large-scale meta-analysis reported that high positive affect and low negative affect predicted higher job satisfaction, higher organizational commitment, lower emotional exhaustion, lower depersonalization, greater sense of personal accomplishment, and lower turnover intentions. Interestingly, they found nearly no difference between the influence on job satisfaction of affect as measured by state versus trait measures. Examining state affect within individuals across time, experience-sampling methods show that positive affective experience on a day-to-day basis is related to job satisfaction (Ilies & Judge, 2002; Weiss et al., 1999). Weiss et al.'s (1999) study further demonstrated that affect as well as beliefs about a job contribute independently to job satisfaction. However, they point out that even so-called cognitive beliefs may have initially been influenced by affective experiences. It appears likely that the influence of trait affect on job satisfaction is mediated by state affect, in that affective traits predict the likelihood of experiencing particular states (Fleeson, 2001; Larsen & Ketelaar, 1991) and, in turn, state affect influences job satisfaction in studies using experimental manipulations of mood. Notably, providing freshly baked cookies at the time of administering a job satisfaction survey increased scores significantly (Brief, Butcher, & Roberson, 1995), just as judgments of overall life satisfaction and a host of other social judgments can be influenced by mood inductions (Schwarz & Clore, 1983).

Interest in job satisfaction has been largely fueled by its presumed influence on workplace performance, a pursuit that has been one of the holy grails of organizational behavior—pursued for years and nearly abandoned due to decades of null results for methodological reasons (Kluger & Tikochinsky, 2001). It may be that early measures of job satisfaction that failed to tap into the attitude's affective component dampened its apparent association with performance (Staw & Cohen-Charash, 2005). Judge, Thoresen, Bono, and Patton's (2001) large-scale meta-analysis revealed a moderate association between job satisfaction and job performance—a correlation of around .30—which is higher in the case of high-complexity jobs and for global measures of job satisfaction that are more likely to tap into affective versus cognitive attitudes. This association may be dampened by moderating factors, such as turnover in the case of individuals high in positive affect who are more likely to leave jobs where they are unsatisfied (Staw, Sutton, & Pelled, 1994). The link may also be tenuous because satisfaction can lead to so many different behaviors—ranging from job engagement to leisure—as can dissatisfaction (Weiss & Cropanzano, 1996). For example, Judge et al. (2006) found that lower job satisfaction leads to more counternormative behaviors, and they argued that such deviant behavior is a form of behavioral adaptation in an attempt to restore equity and feelings of empowerment. Overall, the promise of a link to performance has fueled research on job satisfaction, which may generalize to other job-related attitudes.

Emotion-Driven Behaviors

Emotions are meant to move us. The origin of the term is the Latin word *promotionem*, to move forward, which reflects the evolutionary role for emotion to respond to survival challenges with action. *Action tendencies* are "action and the impulse for action, or their absence...One wants to hit, destroy, or retaliate, or jump and shout, to regain a lost person" (Frijda, 1986, p. 231). Each emotional experience triggers a specific automatic response corresponding to the core human theme of the emotion (Lazarus, 1991). Such action tendencies activate and prioritize our behaviors, signaling that we need to respond or no longer need to respond to aspects of the environment (Frijda, 1988). As such, they are implicit goals that signal the most evolutionarily adaptive response to a stimulus, and tend to take *control precedence* to occupy center stage above other concerns (Frijda, 1988; Frijda & Mesquita, 1994). Under intense enough emotion, individuals are considered out of control (Loewenstein & Lerner, 2003). On the one hand, action tendencies can be mapped to discrete emotional states, as emotions can be distinguished from each other in terms of the actions for which they prepare us (Frijda, 1986; Lazarus, 1991; for a review, see Grandey. 2008). On the other hand, action tendencies can also be general, changing broad goals as much as specific behaviors (Clore et al., 1994). Indeed, Scherer (1984b) argued that emotion evolved in order to decouple stimuli from behavioral responses, in order to increase flexibility in our behavioral repertoires.

The action tendencies of negative emotions are meant to address immediate problems and change circumstances for the better in the short or long term, and at the level of the individual or the community, and should be evaluated in terms of their long-term influence on reproductive success (Cosmides & Tooby, 2000; Frijda, 1986). For example, anger can serve to readjust a relationship or interaction (Morris & Keltner, 2000). Even the hot rage associated with jealousy can limit the presence of rivals for one's partner (Cosmides & Tooby,

2000). Thus, negative emotions can have positive consequences—and remain in our repertoire—when they lead us to actions that relieve the elicitor.

The action tendencies of positive emotions tend to be less specific or directed at immediate concerns. Frederickson's (2001) broaden and build theory emphasized that positive affect expands our action repertoires and encourages creativity and search, facilitating approach rather than avoidant behavior, and widens the array of behaviors that come to mind. Broadened activities include playing, pushing limits, exploring, savoring, and integrating concepts and activities from disparate sources. The broaden and build theory argues that positive affect encourages longer term adaptation and the development of durable resources such as growth and well-being, rather than an immediate focus on solving life-threatening issues. Thus, positive affect is designed to undo the damage of negative affect and return psychological and physiological states to normal levels (Frederickson, 2001). George and Brief (1992) reviewed evidence that positive moods lead to a family of *organizational spontaneity* behaviors that include helping, protecting the organization, making constructive suggestions, improving one's own development, and spreading goodwill. Further, positive mood predicts lesser absenteeism (Forgas & George, 2001). Isen and colleagues (Isen, 1987, 2001; Isen & Baron, 1991) amassed extensive research detailing the specific behaviors associated with positive affect, particularly greater creativity, greater generosity and cooperation, greater seeking of variety and small-stakes risk taking. However, they also noted that individuals in positive moods can be defensive about protecting their affective state and sometimes avoid tasks that have the potential to dampen their mood.

In examining the role of emotional experiences on behavior in organizations, it is worth noting that frequently our desired behavioral responses are blocked. Boudens (2005) wrote of workplace narratives, "In many of the stories, the narrators chose to do and say nothing about the way they felt. In some cases they simply felt constrained, not wanting to jeopardize their position or upset the balance between themselves and another coworker" (p. 1302). Constraint often arises from differences in status within the organization, particularly for the experience of anger—with those higher in the hierarchy able to confront the cause of their anger in the short term, and those lower having the option to withdraw, in both the short and long term (Fitness, 2000; Sloan, 2004). Employees' emotional traits can also influence their willingness to block these emotional action tendencies. For example, individuals lower in trait hostility appeared to engage in less deviant behavior as a function of their state hostility (Judge et al., 2006). Speaking to the potential harm to employees of such blockage, Simpson and Stroh (2004) found that there was greater felt dissonance from display rules that decreased versus increased negative displays. It may be easier to undertake an action tendency that is not felt versus to withhold an action tendency that is. This might explain why negative emotion often has harmful consequences in organizational settings, because its evolutionary goal of enabling corrective action is often thwarted.

Emotion-Driven Cognitions

Although emotion has long been considered a barrier to rationality—disruptive, illogical, biased, and weak—newer work also emphasizes its adaptive nature (Ashforth & Humphrey, 1995; Putnam & Mumby, 1993). The three main perspectives on the relationship between emotion and cognition are that emotion interferes with cognition, that emotion serves cognition, and that the two are intertwined (Fineman, 1996). All three of these perspectives are veridical.

Emotion interferes with cognition. There is a strongly held lay belief that emotion is pernicious for thinking (Forgas, 2003). Indeed, Frijda (1986) argued that emotion serves as a relevance detector, so that it is purposely disruptive. Emotion can interrupt thoughts and redirect attention to the emotion itself (Beal et al., 2005; Weiss & Cropanzano, 1996). Strong emotions can occupy cognitive capacity, including attention, reasoning and memory at the time of both encoding and retrieval (Clore et al., 1994; Schwarz, 1990). This cognitive interruption is adaptive to the extent that we need to be alerted of the need to pause and prioritize (Loewenstein & Lerner, 2003). However, it can be maladaptive to the extent that the evolutionary adaptation no longer matches our current decision making environment, to the extent that emotions are responsive to immediate influences that are not relevant to our cognitions, and to the extent that emotions can distort our evaluations of the probabilities and consequences of decisions (Loewenstein & Lerner, 2003).

Isen and colleagues (Isen, 1987, 2001; Isen & Baron, 1991) argued that even positive affect can serve as an interruption, because individuals in positive moods want to protect those moods by avoiding unpleasant thoughts. They reviewed evidence that this *affect state protection* makes losses loom larger than gains even more so than normally, and leads individuals to avoid certain types of decisions. Those high in positive affect can be overconfident and suffer to a greater degree from self-serving biases (Staw et al., 1994), for example, overestimating the extent to which others see them as valued members of their professional advice networks (Casciaro, Carley, & Krackhardt, 1999). Further, positive affect is a signal that one's objectives are already achieved (Frijda, 1988), and this signal that all is okay has the potential to make us less critical and discerning (George & Zhou, 2002).

Emotion serves cognition. As much as emotion can disrupt thinking, it can also serve it. Emotion orients and directs attention to solving problems, helps to distinguish relevant from irrelevant stimuli, and provides the motivation to reach decisions and implement them (Fineman, 1996; Loewenstein & Lerner,

2003). Indeed, newer evidence suggests that affect is an essential component of thought and decision making because we depend on somatic markers, which are internal signals about the desirability and consequences of possible actions (Damasio, 1994). Emotions benefit cognition by taking these factors explicitly into account, and are adaptive to the extent that they encompass the criteria relevant to a decision maker's future utility as well as accurate expectations about likely events and the way they would make the decision maker feel (Loewenstein & Lerner, 2003). Such affective processing can also take place implicitly, bubbling up to consciousness in the form of hunches and gut instincts that enable appropriate decision making (Fineman, 1996). Further, affect assists us to organize the categorization of social and even inanimate objects, in terms of how they make us feel (Forgas, 2003). Given these cognitive goals that are served by affect, some researchers even refer to emotionally influenced thought as "hot cognition" (Morris & Keltner, 2000).

Extensive evidence demonstrates mood-congruent influences on learning, memory, associations, social judgments, and social interaction behaviors (Clore et al., 1994; Forgas & George, 2001). Forgas' (1995) *affect infusion* model (AIM) theoretically integrated this disparate evidence by arguing under what circumstances to expect greater influence of affect on cognition. The term affect infusion indicates the intensity with which affectively loaded information influences cognitions and resulting behaviors. There are two distinct mechanisms for affect infusion: the process of thinking as well as the content of thoughts (Forgas, 1995; Forgas & George, 2001). First, affect infusion is greater for deeper thinking, constructive processing, and active elaboration versus routine, recurrent tasks. Second, affect infusion is greater when learning new information versus elaborating what one already knows (Forgas, 1995; Forgas & George, 2001). Further, AIM assumes that individuals use the simplest strategy that is capable of producing an appropriate response. Given the presence of affect infusion, it operates on cognition via three mechanisms: memory-based effects, affect-as-information, and information processing (Forgas, 2003).

The influence of affect on memory is a special case of state-dependent memory, in which we are primed more easily to access and recall information when in a similar affective state to that in which it was originally learned (Clore et al., 1994; Isen & Baron, 1991), particularly for information that is autobiographical (Clore et al., 1994). However, it is worth noting that these effects can be fragile to replicate in the laboratory and tend to appear only when affective states are strong, salient, and self-relevant and when the task calls for the active generation and elaboration of information rather than simple recall (Clore et al., 1994; Forgas, 2003).

The second mechanism for affect infusion is affect-as-information, in which we ask ourselves how we feel as a heuristic for judgments (Schwarz & Clore, 1983, 1988). Our emotions provide information about our own psychological state and the world around us—for example, with fear versus calm suggesting different assessments of the likely safety of an environment (Schwarz & Clore, 1983). Affect tends to be used more often as a source of information when the judgment itself is affective in nature (e.g., preferences and liking), for unfamiliar versus familiar domains, when little other information is available, for low versus high personal involvement, when the affect appears directly relevant versus irrelevant; under low versus high cognitive resources, under high versus low time constraints, when we have high versus low clarity about our feelings, and when judgments are overly complex for the piecemeal processing of information—in general, under the conditions that encourage heuristic processing (Clore et al., 1994; Forgas, 2003; George & Zhou, 2002; Loewenstein & Lerner, 2003; Schwarz, 1990). Although affect can be a valuable and intuitive method to access our own judgments, we can also mistake incidental preexisting feelings as relevant to new targets. Indeed, the influence of mood-as-information is stronger when we are not aware of the true source of the mood (Forgas, 2003; Loewenstein & Lerner, 2003). As such, moods can be more powerful influences than discrete emotions precisely because they are more diffuse, global, and difficult to identify the source (Schwarz, 1990).

The third mechanism for affect infusion is via information processing. Affect influences not only recall, but also the very learning and interpretation of new information (Forgas, 2003). Perceivers tend to interpret new information in a mood-congruent manner, and process new information more slowly and deeply when it is mood congruent (Forgas, 2003). In the case of positive affect, information processing is more top down, broader, more flexible and assimilative, makes more extensive use of preexisting ideas and associations but less new information, and is also less effortful, more superficial, faster, and more confident (Clore et al., 1994; Forgas, 2003). Petty and Wegener's (1998) hedonic contingency approach argued that positive moods tend to invite effortful processing for those tasks that are generally pleasant, but only simplified heuristic processing for those tasks that are potentially frustrating. Isen (1987, 2001; Isen & Baron, 1991) argued that positive affect makes connections among ideas more accessible, leads to a broader and more complex focus on problem solving, and increases flexibility to join disparate ideas together—which, taken together, generally promotes decision making that is more efficient without being sloppy. Frederickson's (2001) broaden and build theory argued that positive emotion is a signal that an environment is safe—leading to more creative and deeper processing, with a widened array of thoughts that come to mind because exploration behaviors do not need to be postponed for the sake of basic safety. Accordingly, consistent with its positive effects on playfulness and exploration in novel and unusual settings, positive affect is associated with greater creativity (Clore et al., 1994), even with a time lag of one to two days following the positive mood (Amabile et al., 2005). Further, individuals high in positive affect tend to take in wider information about the social environment, for example resulting in greater accuracy in assessing the personal networks of their colleagues (Casciaro et al., 1999).

By contrast with positive affect, information processing under negative affect is more bottom up, more systematic and detailed, more narrow and vigilant in attention, and more externally focused toward changing one's existing situation (Clore et al., 1994; Forgas, 2003; Loewenstein & Lerner, 2003; Schwarz, 1990). Because negative mood signals us that we are in an unsatisfactory or even dangerous situation, we need to process information more deeply and with greater causal reasoning to address the underlying concern (Schwarz & Clore, 1983). Although positive mood is sometimes portrayed as uniformly beneficial—and negative mood as uniformly harmful—indeed, there appear to be specific cognitive benefits to negative moods. In light of the deeper and more deliberate processing focused on social tasks, negative versus positive affect can lead to behaviors that are more polite, friendly, and elaborate (Forgas, 2003). Negative mood leads to lesser bias, for example greater accuracy in understanding the content of performance feedback and lesser susceptibility to the fundamental attribution error (Forgas & George, 2001). This is related to the *depressive accuracy* of mild and chronically depressed individuals, who show greater complexity in forming attributions and social judgments (Clore et al., 1994). There are even data suggesting a potential boost to creativity for being in a negative mood, which does not speak against the research on positive mood and creativity because Isen and colleagues' work typically contrasted positive versus neutral rather than negative states (e.g., Isen, 1987). George and Zhou (2002) found that negative emotion could increase creativity when it was rewarded, and they argued that the negative mood signaled that more effort was necessary in a task. Thus, naturally occurring negative affect can be an energizing force that motivates us for change, which can enhance creative thinking (George & Zhou, 2002). George's (2000) review concluded that every profile of mood is helpful for some cognitive settings and harmful for others. This suggests the value of focusing on congruence between the cognitive tendencies of any particular mood and the task requirements of the work setting.

In addition to positive and negative moods, some moods are mixed. Mixed emotions can serve as information that the world is in an unusual state, and one needs new solutions because the old rules may no longer apply (Fong, in press). Indeed, Fong (in press) found that experimentally induced ambivalence increased performance in a test of creativity—but found this effect disappeared if participants were also given proverbs emphasizing that mixed emotions are commonplace. Likewise, mood swings can increase creative thinking (Amabile et al., 2005).

Although most work on the influence of affect on cognition has focused on positive versus negative valence, exciting recent research has moved beyond valence to examine the role of other dimensions of emotional appraisal.

Lerner and Keltner (2001) argued that there are *appraisal tendencies*, which are cognitive tendencies akin to action tendencies that are specific to dimensions of emotional appraisal. For example, angry individuals focus on issues of blame and fearful individuals focus on issues of risk. Overall, affect is a lens through which we interpret the events around us, with a theme of addressing the underlying core relational themes of our emotions (Loewenstein & Lerner, 2003). Consistent with these appraisal tendencies, Tiedens and Linton (2001) found that emotions that are characterized by high versus low certainty—such as anger and contentment versus worry and surprise—lead to greater heuristic versus systematic processing, in the form of greater stereotyping, greater reliance on the expertise of the source of information, and less attention to argument quality. Lerner, Small, and Loewenstein (2004) theorized and found that differential action tendencies among negative emotions—with disgust to expel unwanted objects and sadness to change one's circumstances—led disgusted buyers to pay less and sad buyers to pay more for the same goods.

Emotion and cognition are intertwined. The third perspective on the relationship between affect and cognition is that they are intertwined, in the sense that much of what we consider rational is already pursued on highly emotional grounds. "Thinking and feelings are inextricably linked most of the time" wrote Ellsworth and Scherer (2003), "Certain ways of interpreting one's environment are inherently emotional, few thoughts are entirely free of feelings, and emotions influence thinking" (p. 572). Indeed, evolutionary psychologists have argued that emotion evolved as a means to coordinate functions across multiple cognitive and behavioral domains, which suggests that the distinction of affect versus cognition is to some degree arbitrary and semantic (Cosmides & Tooby, 2000).

Affect is always a critical part of the construction of thoughts and, indeed, it is problematic to separate affect from cognition (Forgas, 2003). Although emotional appraisal can be automatic and intuitive, ultimately each of the dimensions of cognitive appraisal discussed in the preceding section about emotional registration is a cognitive evaluation that is influenced by emotional processing. Thus, when we evaluate an event as positive or negative, establish its causality, its goal significance, and so forth, at some level it is not meaningful to label these evaluations as emotional versus cognitive. For example, the major elicitors of perceptions of justice are positive treatment by others who have control over a situation (Judge et al., 2006), which overlap greatly with the cognitive appraisal dimensions linked most closely to anger, such as valence, certainty, control, and responsibility. Thus, findings that justice violations are associated with anger may be due as much to semantic overlap between justice and anger versus a newly uncovered relationship. Indeed, it may be that society has constructed the neutral and rational construct of justice in order to correspond to an underlying emotional judgment (e.g., anger). For this reason, we should tread lightly in research intended to demonstrate that emotions accompany the judgments of organizationally relevant topics such as justice, status, and conflict, as such statements may be true by design. Closely related is research that aims to demonstrate that emotions mediate the relationship between such topics and outcomes of interest, because the so-called mediator may be overlapping and intertwined with the independent variable. Such studies risk reinventing core principles of the psychology of emotion. Alternately, it would be fruitful for those who propose to take an emotional perspective on a topic previously considered through a cognitive lens to examine the dimensions of cognitive appraisal as a starting point for how emotion may already be woven into our current understanding of the topic. In doing so, the strongest evidence for a unique role of emotion on outcomes arises when emotional experience becomes decoupled from its original source, and this incidental affect has powerful and often unintended consequences (Loewenstein & Lerner, 2003).

Job Performance

Ultimately, much of the research interest in emotion-driven behaviors—regardless of their pathway through Figure 7.1 directly from emotional experience or indirectly via attitudes and cognitions—relates to the influence of these behaviors on employee job performance. The earliest perspective on this issue is that emotion-driven behaviors are generally counterproductive, which drives the lay intuition that emotion gets in the way of business. If emotion evolved as an adaptation to assist with the problems of survival, perhaps solutions that were adaptive for animals and early humans are no longer appropriate for the task demands of modern organizational life (Morris & Keltner, 2000). Natural selection has been too slow to update the structure of the brain past that of the hunter gatherer (Cosmides & Tooby, 2000). To the extent that jobs increasingly require cognitive attention and processing, the cognitive load created by emotions can render them a detriment to productivity (Clore et al., 1994). Indeed, emotion appears to be a more pernicious influence on performance in more versus less cognitively complex tasks (Beal et al., 2005).

Nonetheless, researchers in organizational behavior have been driven by a vision of the happy worker as productive worker. Hersey (1932) was the first to show that productivity was higher under positive mood and lower under negative mood. Staw and colleagues' (e.g., Staw, Bell, & Clausen, 1986; Staw et al., 1994) landmark works demonstrated that individuals who self-reported more frequent positive emotional experience tended to be rated as more effective in their workplaces. Accumulated evidence now shows that, generally, high positive affect and low negative affect are associated with greater job performance, and longitudinal designs suggest that the direction of causality is more likely to begin with affect as the cause of performance as opposed to vice versa (Côté, 1999). Staw et al. (1994) theorized that positive affect is associated with better measured job performance due to (a) a direct intrapersonal effect on productivity and motivation, such as greater persistence and higher goals (e.g., George & Brief, 1996), (b) rater bias where the same level of performance may be rated more highly due to halo effects from others who are favorably inclined toward those high in positive affect, and (c) interpersonal effects where colleagues offer substantive assistance and other favorable reactions that lead to tangible performance benefits for high positive affect employees. Conversely, those under high negative affect such as stress tend to perform worse at their jobs, which is attributed to the cognitive load of attending to the source of the negative emotion (Motowildo et al., 1986). Although much of the research on affect and performance has been at the level of trait differences, in keeping with the often fleeting nature of emotional experience, promising recent work has also found that momentary changes in state affect influence individuals' productivity over time (Beal et al., 2005).

The performance implications of affect have been increasingly examined in negotiation settings. Negotiators in positive moods tend to achieve higher individual and joint outcomes, due to greater use of cooperative strategies and less use of contentious strategies, higher goals, greater development of trust, better insight, more effective exchange of information, and greater confidence (Barry, Fulmer, & Van Kleef, 2004; Carnevale & Isen, 1986; Forgas, 1998; Thompson, Nadler, & Kim, 1999). Barry and Oliver (1996) also argued that positive affect tends to benefit negotiators by increasing postsettlement compliance and the continuation of working relationships. By contrast with positive mood, negative mood appears to harm negotiation performance. Negotiators induced with negative moods are less accurate in reading their counterparts' interests (Allred, Mallozzi, Matsui, & Raia, 1996), and are more likely to reject offers that are economically superior to their alternatives (Pillutla & Murnighan, 1996).

In spite of this evidence supporting the idea of the happy worker as productive worker, the relationship between affect and performance appears complex, and depends on a number of factors such as competing effects, the role of interaction partners, constraints on behavior, and the performance context itself. In the case of competing effects, some influences of affective states can cancel each other out, yielding little apparent effects. For example, in a realistically simulated foreign exchange trading scenario, participants in pleasant moods had greater confidence yet also lower accuracy in evaluating market trends (Au, Chan, Wang, & Vertinsky, 2003). Thus, those in bad moods were the most accurate yet benefited little due to their conservative trading patterns. A further complexity in the role of individual affect on performance comes from interaction partners. For example, because negotiators tend to be attuned to their counterparts' behaviors in order to reciprocate or complement these behaviors as appropriate, it is difficult to make performance predictions based on one negotiator's emotional state in the absence of considering the partner's state as well (Butt, Choi, & Jaeger, 2005). The influence of affect on performance can also be limited due to strong situations that constrain behavior. For example, Staw et al. (1994) argued that the relationship can be dampened in jobs that require a minimum level of performance in order to maintain employment standing. Having a low power position can also serve as a constraint. Anderson and Thompson's (2004) study of negotiation simulations found that only the trait positive affect level of the higher power party was predictive of bargaining outcomes.

Ultimately, the influence of affect on performance is context dependent, based on whether there is a match versus mismatch between the response tendencies of the affect and the demands of the task at hand (Beal et al., 2005; Clore et al., 1994; Forgas & George, 2001; Weiss & Cropanzano, 1996). The demands of the task include not only productivity, but also other potentially valuable workplace outcomes such as greater extra-role behaviors and lower counterproductive acts and absences—which tend to be associated with higher positive affect and lower negative affect (for a review, see Grandey, 2008). Each affective state has its place. For example, negative affect can be beneficial for jobs that require critical scrutiny and evaluation, such as inspectors, and for jobs in which concentration is important and performance would suffer in the event of frequent social interruptions and distractions (Staw et al., 1994). Further, negative affect can be a helpful signal to exit a job with poor fit and, indeed, workers reporting more negative emotional experiences at work report greater intentions of quitting their jobs (Grandey et al., 2002). Likewise, in some contexts positive emotions can be harmful for productivity, such as when they distract workers from their tasks or foster inertia by suggesting that a job is already well done (Ashforth & Humphrey, 1995; Beal et al., 2005; Weiss & Cropanzano, 1996). Taken together, these findings suggest the value of calling attention to boundary conditions related to job requirements and demands, where particular affective states can be helpful in some tasks and harmful in others.

Emotion Recognition

This point in the review departs from intrapersonal to interpersonal emotion processes. Figure 7.2 juxtaposes an interaction partner or partners alongside the focal actor who has been considered by the previous sections and, thus, highlights a number of additional emotional phenomena of interest within organizations. The first interpersonal process to be highlighted is *emotion recognition*. Indeed, the signal value of emotional expression that was discussed earlier requires a perceiver to interpret the signal. Emotion recognition is the process of analyzing expressive cues to infer another person's emotional state. Thus, as depicted in Figure 7.2, the output of the emotion process for one person—expressive cues—can be stimulus that forms the starting point for another.

The Backtracking Process

Emotional expressions are a powerful source of information—in effect, a window into another person's inner thoughts and feelings. The larger social function of emotion recognition—beyond simply providing an assessment of another person's emotional state—is that it allows perceivers to *backtrack* and reconstruct that person's apparent emotion process. From an expression one infers a likely experience, and from the likely experience one infers the likely objective environment and the expressor's interpretation of it. Indeed, perceivers often describe emotional expressions in terms of likely eliciting events rather than emotional categories per se (Yik & Russell, 1999). Along the way, we infer details such as authenticity cues suggesting whether experience matches expression and at whom the display was intended. Related to the backtracking of emotion recognition is the forward tracking of *empathy*—which starts from a common stimulus and infers what another person is likely to feel. The goal of backtracking and forward tracking is to gain usable information about social partners' likely beliefs and future behaviors and, indeed, about the objective environment. Perceiving is for doing (Gibson, 1979); we use information from others' emotions as feedback to navigate our social worlds (Rosenthal, Hall, DiMatteo, Rogers, & Archer, 1979). Such sensitivity evolved to assist in coordinating and communicating with group members (Ekman, 1972; Spoor & Kelly, 2004). Lest this description make emotion recognition sound overly analytic, we interpret others' emotional cues quickly and automatically, without disruption by competing attentional demands (Neumann & Strack, 2000). Indeed, one often notices the value of reading emotional cues only when they are gone, for example, in computer-mediated "virtual" communication—for which new emotional channels quickly evolved such as *emoticons* and all capital writing.

Examples abound of backtracking via emotion recognition in organizational settings. Rafaeli and Sutton (1989) described an Israeli supermarket clerk being told she must be new to the job because she was smiling. The customer backtracked to conclude the clerk perceives her job as pleasant, and this is only possible if the clerk did not have the experience to develop appropriate schemas (e.g., appraisals of high certainty, unpleasant, goal obstructed) to evaluate the monotonous job. Musicians read audiences' emotions to infer performance evaluations and adjust the music accordingly (Pescosolido, 2002). Leaders recognize emotions in order to understand better how followers make sense of their environments and to gauge appropriate leadership behaviors (Huy, 2002; Pescosolido, 2002). Likewise, team members look to their leaders for performance feedback and infer that negative displays convey dissatisfaction (Sy, Côté, & Saavedra, 2005). Note that backtracking relies on a perceiver's interpretive lens. For example, union members may interpret colleagues' stress as a response to their work, whereas management sees the same stress as a defect in the workers' appraisal of coping (Fineman, 1996).

Recognizing others' emotions can influence attitudes, behaviors, and cognitions, represented together in Figure 7.1 under postemotional responses. This can be mediated by a perceiver's own emotional experience, or directly with information used in nonemotional processing. For example, emotion recognition helps to infer others' characteristics such as personality, competence, and status within an organization. The cues in facial expressions influence trait judgments (Knutson, 1996)—which is sensible for perceivers given that, indeed, many traits refer to the likelihood of experiencing particular states (Fleeson, 2001). For example, participants find more likable those who express uniquely human emotions such as admiration, love, remorse, or regret (Vaes, Paladino, Castelli, Leyens, & Giovanazzi, 2003)—as inferred by their better treatment of them. Individuals high in negative affect may give off cues of anxiety that their colleagues interpret as a signal they are passive and able to be victimized (Aquino et al., 1999). Perceivers also judge others' competence from even *thin slices* of expressive cues, and they can accurately assess everything from teacher ratings and physician effectiveness to voting behavior and communication ability (Ambady & Rosenthal, 1992). In simulated work environments and video vignette studies, participants viewing negative displays from supervisors gave lower satisfaction ratings (Glomb & Hulin, 1997; Newcombe & Ashkanasy, 2002). In terms of status, Tiedens (2001) found that participants conferred higher ratings to politicians and made higher salary recommendations for job candidates who expressed anger versus sadness, in keeping with high power as a source of flexibility to hold others accountable for negative outcomes. Likewise, in a vignette study, leaders displaying negative versus positive emotions received lower approval ratings—particularly for norm violations such as males displaying sadness and females displaying anger (Lewis, 2000). Tiedens (2001) argued that expressing anger may create a trade-off where ratings are lower for liking-related constructs such as satisfaction, but higher ratings for competence-related constructs such as status and power.

Recognizing another person's emotional state can also provide information about his or her preferences—for example, his or her bottom line in a negotiation. In several negotiation studies, participants were informed explicitly of their partners' supposed emotional state. Thompson, Valley, and Kramer (1995) showed that face-to-face negotiators who were later given a verbal statement supposedly written by their partners regarding how the outcome compared to expectations tended to report feeling the inverse affect—in keeping with naïve assumptions that one's gain comes at another's loss and vice versa. Further, participants who believed their partners were in-group members and disappointed in one round offered them more resources in the next round—suggesting they used emotion recognition to make a redress. In computer-mediated scenarios with simulated opponents, Van Kleef, De Dreu, and Manstead (2004a, 2004b) gave participants verbal statements between rounds about emotional reactions to offers that were supposedly written by their counterparts without realizing they would be read. Participants used these reaction statements to adjust their behaviors—offering less to participants already happy with the last offer and more to participants who were angry with the last offer. However, in a series of two-way interactions, these effects appeared only when participants were in a low-power position where they needed to placate their counterparts, only when they had sufficient cognitive resources, cognitive flexibility, and time available, and only when generous offers from opponents did not appear to speak for themselves. In a vignette study and a face-to-face exercise in which one negotiator was given a lesson emphasizing the value of angry versus neutral emotional display, Sinaceur and Tiedens (2006) found that negotiators in a low-power position made greater concessions to counterparts expressing anger, presumably because they were motivated to undertake the relationship repair that the angry displays suggested were necessary. Taken together, these studies suggest the great potential importance to negotiators of backtracking via emotion recognition.

The majority of quantitative research on emotion recognition in organizations has focused on accuracy and its consequences, with accuracy defined in terms of judgments that match the expressor's intended emotional state. Typical studies contain photographs of facial expressions, audiotapes of vocal tones, or video clips of body movement. Elfenbein, Foo, White, Tan, and Aik's (in press) recent meta-analysis showed that—across corporate, academic, nonprofit, foreign service, and clinical settings—greater individual-level emotion recognition accuracy generally predicted better subjective workplace effectiveness as rated by supervisors, supervisees, peers, and clients. Examining objective performance, Elfenbein et al. (in press) found that negotiators high in accuracy were better able to create value with their counterparts and also to claim value for themselves. However, emotion recognition accuracy is not always beneficial because some messages are better left unheard. Indeed, Steiner (1955) argued that accurate social perception benefits individuals only when several conditions are met: they have freedom to alter their interpersonal behaviors, when the preferences or intentions that they perceive are relevant to the task at hand, and when the resulting behavior is aligned with the group or dyadic task. Indeed, personal relationships often suffer from the accurate understanding of potentially damaging thoughts and feelings (Simpson, Ickes, & Blackstone, 1995). Negative interpersonal feelings in social situations tend to leak out through the less controllable, nonverbal channels such as vocal tone (Swann, Stein-Seroussi, & McNulty, 1992). Accordingly, people who are especially skilled at *eavesdropping* by recognizing information via leaky channels tend to have difficulty in their personal and workplace relationships—particularly when understanding leaky negative cues (Elfenbein & Ambady, 2002b). Participants in a group decision-making task who were highly accurate with a subtle test of emotion recognition were less liked by peers and less able to incorporate their own interests into the group decision (Lopes, Barsade, Nezlek, Straus, & Salovey, submitted). As valuable as sensitivity can be, sometimes a lack of sensitivity provides others with privacy from intrusion into their inner worlds, can dampen rather than amplify the daily ups and downs of work life, and can inoculate one from the influence of others' moods. Speaking to Steiner's criterion for freedom to alter behavioral responses, people who are the most capable of acting appropriately in response to others' emotions benefit the most from accurate recognition—for example, leaders who are extraverted versus introverted (Rubin, Munz, & Bommer, 2005).

The importance of individual variation in emotion recognition also raises a question about the average level: Are people generally accurate or inaccurate? On the one hand, emotion recognition is highly intuitive and automatic, and evolved as an adaptation to solve the problems of group living (Spoor & Kelly, 2004). Indeed, classic studies demonstrate we can even recognize emotions expressed by members of distant cultural groups (Ekman et al., 1969). However, the absolute accuracy rates in such studies were quite low, on average only 58% after correcting for chance guessing (Elfenbein & Ambady, 2002a)—on tasks that were carefully screened, for which participants' attention was drawn to stimuli and for which responses were multiple-choice (Russell, 1994). Perhaps more directly germane to organizational life, studies of thin slice judgments have an average correspondence with objective criteria of about .39 (Ambady & Rosenthal, 1992)—which is impressive but imperfect. Likewise, the little research that has examined accuracy in actual emotion judgments made within organizational settings suggests that observers understand much—but not all—about colleagues' affect (Bartel & Saavedra, 2000; Totterdell, Kellett, Teuchmann, & Briner, 1998). For example, Scherer and Ceschi (2000) showed that airline employees assisting passengers with lost bags could accurately detect passengers' self-reported worry and humor, but not their anger, indifference, or sadness—which are lower intensity or likely to be masked by display rules. Although accurate recognition of others' states may be adaptive, so too may be inaccuracy when Steiner's (1959) criteria for the benefit of social perception are not met. For example, controlled studies of lie detection based on expressive behavior rarely yield performance better than chance (O'Sullivan, 2005), but on a daily basis most people face only white lies that may be better left undetected (Swann et al., 1992). Ultimately, accuracy in emotion recognition is likely to be imperfect. In the act of backtracking through another person's entire emotion process, errors can enter at any point—and can accumulate.

Regulating Recognition Via Decoding Rules

Just as expressors can regulate their displays, perceivers can regulate their interpretations. *Decoding rules* (Buck, 1984) refer to norms about the appropriate recognition of others' emotions. Perceivers can choose to decode a message inaccurately or to decode a message accurately but not allow themselves to register or respond to it. Decoding rules can protect perceivers' interests when sensitivity to others' cues may be detrimental. Although less research within organizations has directly addressed decoding rules, theoretically one would expect to find them in tandem with display rules. The flip side of Hochschild's (1983) flight attendants' display rule to smile at hostile passengers could be a decoding rule to overlook their hostile behavior. In Garot's (2004) ethnography of bureaucrats, service workers developed strategies to ignore the apparently sincere displays of tearful sadness from applicants for housing subsidies who were deemed ineligible. Perceivers can also use decoding rules to assist expressors who fail to regulate their own displays properly—for example, a decision to overlook an inadvertent outburst in a meeting or tears in the locker room.

Interpersonal Influence of Emotion

Emotion is a powerful source of social influence. Hochschild (1979) included within her definition of emotional labor any actions intended to change others' emotions. Rafaeli and Sutton (1989) argued that display rules exist in order for expressive displays to influence others. Disneyland tells its employees that if they are happy at work, then the guests will be happy at play (Van Maanen & Kunda, 1989).

The opportunity to shape each other's thoughts and feelings arises via multiple pathways within the emotion process—indeed, this is where emotion becomes a dance. *Emotional contagion* is a family of phenomena that describe this social influence (Hatfield et al., 1994). A heuristic to distinguish the multiple forms of influence is to examine the emotion process framework in Figure 7.2 systematically for possible pathways—starting in each case with the circles that denote externally observable processes and tracing pathways that reach the interaction partner. Interpersonal influence can result from sharing access to the same stimuli—and registering the stimuli similarly or, in the case of empathy, judging how the stimuli would be registered by relevant others. Emotional expressions are also a powerful source of influence. Through a two-part process of *primitive efference* described by Hatfield, Cacioppo, and Rapson (1994; see also Kelly & Barsade, 2001; Lakin, Jefferis, Cheng, & Chartrand, 2003), the expressive cues of others invoke behavioral mimicry that leads, in turn, to affective experience. Given that the primitive efference pathway bypasses emotional registration, such contagion is of mood—not emotion—because it lacks awareness of the elicitor (Neumann & Strack, 2000).

However, emotional contagion can also take place via emotion recognition, where expressive cues are interpreted for their meanings and serve as stimuli to feed into emotional registration and experience. Even more consciously, perceivers can use *social comparison* to examine others' expressive cues and infer the appropriate emotion to experience (Barsade, 2002; Kelly & Barsade, 2001). Finally, postemotional responses such as instrumental behaviors—and the behaviors resulting from emotionally driven attitudes and cognitions—have a powerful influence on others. For example, it can be demoralizing when colleagues are often late or absent, even if one was initially happy at work. Among these multiple mechanisms for emotional influence, most research attention has focused on nonconscious mimicry and social comparison (Barsade, 2002; Bartel & Saavedra, 2000; Totterdell, 2000). Given the complexity of contagion, the specific mechanism generally remains untested in empirical work (cf., Howard & Gengler, 2001).

Although recent research and theory has focused on emotional contagion as a source of transferring consistent mood states (e.g., Kelly & Barsade, 2001), most of the mechanisms for emotional contagion also have the potential to invoke consistent or complementary states. For example, embarrassment might invoke forgiveness rather than more embarrassment (Keltner & Haidt, 1999). Anger directed at a low-power negotiator leads to fearful—not angry—behavior (Van Kleef et al., 2004a, 2004b). In terms of emotional appraisal, anger is an accusation of cause—which can invoke fear or apology if the accusation is accepted, but more anger if it is not. Complimentary versus consistent contagion can vary based on the perceiver's backtracking process—for example, fear may strike fear when the perceiver interprets it to be directed at a stimulus common to them, but not otherwise. The optimal form of emotional influence from the sender's perspective is to create an emotional induction for which the likely postemotional responses are consistent with the sender's preferences. Senders may prefer an audience that is happy (e.g., service representatives), fearful (e.g., politicians and police), or angry (e.g., sports coaches and drill sergeants).

A number of factors appear to influence the extent of emotional contagion. Groups can develop schemas and rules for managing members' emotional lives, which become automatic with practice. Norms can address feeling rules, display rules, and shared schemas for reappraisal, and also sensitivity to each others' emotions (Bartel & Saavedra, 2000). Indeed, Elfenbein, Polzer, and Ambady (2007) found that randomly assigned teams of full-time public service interns differed significantly in their ability to recognize each others' nonverbal expressions of emotion—even though these teams did not differ in their abilities to recognize the expressions of strangers. These findings suggested that teams varied in their person-specific learning of expressive styles and/or norms for attending to others' emotions. Thompson, Nadler, and Kim (1999) argued that groups can develop *transactive emotion*—akin to cognitive *transactive memory* (Wegener, 1986)—which are schemas consisting of metaknowledge about colleagues' emotional behaviors. Norms can be perpetuated through Attraction-Selection-Attrition processes (Schneider, 1987) favoring those whose emotion processes function similarly to existing members (George, 1990). Further, emotional contagion appears to be influenced by social closeness. Emotional contagion is greater when receivers like senders—even when liking is randomly assigned through the belief that the other had offered a token gift (Howard & Gengler, 2001).

Examples of emotional contagion abound in organizational settings. Pugh (2001) was the first to show that contagion is the mechanism responsible for the relationship between employee positive emotional displays and customer ratings of service quality by demonstrating mediation via customer positive affect. In a simulated video rental store, service employees who produced "real" versus "fake" smiles invoked greater positive emotional contagion in their customers (Hennig-Thurau, Groth, Paul, & Gremler, 2006). Tan, Foo, and Kwek (2004) demonstrated that, just as employees influence customers, customers also influence employees. Patrons of fast-food restaurants who self-reported greater agreeableness and low negative affect received greater objectively coded positive displays from employees.

Leadership factors heavily into organizational examples of emotional contagion (e.g., Ashforth & Humphrey, 1995; Hatfield et al., 1994). Conger (1991) argued that arousing affect in others is an important mechanism for transformational leaders to influence followers. Some have gone so far as to say that "put simply, management's job has become the management of emotion" (Rafaeli & Worline, 2001, p. 107), or that the modern leader is "an emotional manager" (Pescosolido, 2002, p. 584). George (2000) reviewed evidence that leader affect influences a range of follower outcomes such as prosocial behavior, retention, and group performance. This appears to be mediated by followers' affect. In a simulated work environment using intact teams, Sy et al. (2005) demonstrated that the mood randomly assigned to the leader influenced followers' moods accordingly which, in turn, influenced group process and performance. Although influence can flow in both directions and across peers (Totterdell, 2000), leaders are particularly influential senders of contagion because followers are more attentive to leaders than the reverse (Sy et al., 2005). Further, leaders tend to feel less constrained by expressive norms than followers, and greater expressiveness induces greater contagion in others (Totterdell et al., 1998). Accordingly, in general lower status individuals undergo greater shift to reach emotional convergence than their higher status peers (Anderson, Keltner, & John, 2003).

Although emotional contagion is initially a dyadic process, with a sender and a receiver, influence is reciprocal and emotional states can spread throughout groups. Indeed, in an *emotional transaction*, the sequence comes full circle, as the expressor is read by the perceivers who are themselves read by the original expressor, in a dynamically unfolding and updating series of communication acts (Rafaeli & Sutton, 1987, 1989). The convergence of group members' emotional experiences appears to be healthy and beneficial for teams (Barsade & Gibson, 1998; Kelly & Barsade, 2001). Just as closeness can facilitate the transfer of emotional states, emotional contagion also increases closeness. Spoor and Kelly (2004) argued that the convergence of affective states across group members promotes group bonds and loyalty. Accordingly, roommates and married couples who show greater convergence over time in their expressive styles also report more satisfying relationships (Anderson et al., 2003). In intact work groups, Bartel and Saavedra (2000) demonstrated significant convergence in group mood via objective behavioral cues and self-report scales. Convergence was stronger for their groups with richer histories of interaction in the form of more stable membership, greater interdependence, or more clear norms for their regulation of moods. Convergence was also stronger for negative versus positive moods, suggesting that colleagues are more sensitive and responsive to signals of potential problems. Totterdell and colleagues (Totterdell, 2000; Totterdell et al., 1998) documented mood convergence among teams of professional cricket players, nurses, and accountants—even when controlling for team performance and shared exposure to the work setting. Their data suggested a dynamic updating of mood states, given that convergence occurred within single time periods in their event sampling, which ranged between several hours and one day. Convergence was stronger for those reporting greater commitment to their teams and—speaking to changes in social closeness over time—mood linkage among the cricket players was greater when working collectively while playing defense versus working individually while playing offense. Their collective activity may have provided both greater motivation to converge as well as greater interpersonal exposure. Likewise, Totterdell, Wall, Holman, Diamond, and Epitropaki (2004) found that job-related mood was more similar for employees closer to each other in their task networks. Barsade (2002) used a simulated work task to demonstrate that a confederate's positive expressive cues led to greater teammate positive mood as self-reported and coded by outside observers. This more positive mood, in turn, led to greater cooperation and self-reported performance and lesser conflict. Although empirically groups appear to benefit from emotional contagion, Barsade (2002) argued that—at extremes—mood contagion could be dysfunctional if groups become more rigid in their responses or overcome with strong emotions.

Ultimately, emotional contagion itself can become a stimulus. Frijda and Mesquita (1994) argued that we examine the match between our experience and the appearance of those around us to determine whether our reactions are appropriate with respect to social norms. Intuitively, we understand the benefits of convergence and expect to experience it (Hochschild, 1979). Barsade, Ward, Turner, and Sonnenfeld (2000) applied to affective states the similarity-attraction paradigm, whereby it is reinforcing to be with similar others.

Surveying the top management teams of large corporations, they found that emotional similarity in trait positive affect—which influences state positive affect—predicted better self-reported team processes and even marginally better corporate financial performance. They argued that affective similarity reflects team members' initial similarities as well as their abilities to converge. The benefits of affective similarity are not limited to positive mood. Indeed, Locke and Horowitz (1990) found that similarity in dysphoria, a low-grade depression, led to more satisfying social interactions. If affective diversity makes groups comfortable, however, sometimes comfort does not help groups to meet their goals. Heterogeneous affect can be a helpful signal of a changing environment (Spoor & Kelly, 2004). Accordingly, groups with greater mood diversity benefited from greater deliberation and better decision making in a simulation using a hidden profile task (Tuncel & Doucet, 2005). Another case in which affective diversity may be helpful is when displays differ in terms of dominance versus suppression, for which complementarity is preferable to convergence (Tiedens & Fragale, 2003).

Emotional Intelligence

No review of emotion in organizations could be complete without a section on emotional intelligence (EI). Although EI is not listed in any one stage of the process framework, it is intended as an umbrella construct inclusive of the range of phenomena depicted in Figure 7.2. That said, at this point in the review, it must be clear that reducing the entire emotion process to one individual difference that aggregates "correct" performance in each of these processes is necessarily an oversimplification. At the same time that EI has captured the attention of the lay public and practitioners alike—thus, making it among the areas within organizational studies most likely to heed Hambrick's (1994) call for the Academy of Management to "matter" (p. 11)—the challenge has been to maintain scientific standards in the face of the incentives that accompany mass popularization. Researchers are pressured to create assessment tools and intervention programs at the individual level, to focus on measures that are easily scalable, and to present results that are simple and digestible—and they find that there is less interest in their work that has potentially more nuance but less marketability (Furnham, 2006).

Exhaustive reviews of EI appear elsewhere (e.g., Mayer, Roberts, & Barsade, in press). Likewise, there are detailed critiques (e.g., Fineman, 2004; Matthews et al., 2002), covering topics as diverse as conceptual clarity, divergent validity from existing constructs, psychometric shortcomings, the questionable validity of pencil-and-paper measures and scoring difficulties, notably the theoretical quandary about how to define correct performance. Many models of EI stretch far beyond the boundaries of the emotion process in Figure 7.2, including nearly everything except the proverbial kitchen sink—for example, Tett, Fox, and Wang (2005) included creativity and flexible planning, and Goleman, Boyatzis, and McKee (2002) included self-confidence, conflict management skills, fostering a service climate, and living one's values with transparency. These models are preemptive in that they presume a relationship between emotional skills and desirable qualities rather than testing it. Indeed, interpersonal skills can be used toward beneficent as well as manipulative ends (Steiner, 1959). Further, many of these models assume that individual differences across the distinct emotional processes converge into a single emotional "g," which is an empirical question that has not yet been tested beyond common method variance due to response tendencies, verbal intelligence, and other factors involved in pencil-and-paper testing. Given the distinctness of the emotion processes, researchers working within an EI paradigm should steer away from gestalt predictions about the effects of total EI and should make specific predictions about the effects of individual processes, such as expression, recognition, and regulation.

That said, there is provocative new evidence that the best existing tests of emotional intelligence do predict workplace performance, above and beyond the role of cognitive intelligence (Mayer et al., in press). For example, Côté and Miners (2006) recently demonstrated that emotional intelligence, as measured by Mayer, Salovey, and Caruso's (2002) MSCEIT test, can even compensate for low cognitive intelligence in predicting task performance and citizenship behavior.

One promising possibility for the future of EI is for researchers to address the issue of how to define correct responses by using objective laboratory-based measures.[1] Scores in current so-called ability tests (e.g., the MSCEIT) are based on the opinions of expert and peer samples. Matthews et al. (2002) argued that this practice taps into conformity and knowledge of social norms, rather than ability per se. However, by contrast, objective measures of individual emotional skills can include psychophysiological and behavioral responses, for example the response time in responding to survey scales (Brockner & Higgins, 2001), the degree of interference on stroop tasks using emotional content (Sanchez-Burks, 2005), or the speed of physiological recovery from negative events (Fredrickson & Levenson, 1998).

Another promising possibility is to focus on emotional fit rather than emotional intelligence per se. Some contexts reward emotional behaviors that others consider deficient. For example, whereas American mothers prefer children who are assertive and sociable and consider highly inhibited children to have socialization difficulties, Chinese mothers prefer inhibited children and consider bold children to be emotionally dysregulated (Campos et al., 2004). One's social interaction partner is also part of the emotional context. For example, some dyads and groups achieve greater emotion recognition accuracy than would be predicted by their individual skills (Elfenbein et al., 2006, 2007). As with other aspects of organizational culture, organizations may vary in the extent to which they prioritize affective fit—which, indeed, may or may not be uniformly beneficial, particularly when a business environment may call for employees who can represent a range of emotional styles. Emotionally intelligent behavior may truly consist of finding and shaping an environment so that one's dominant emotional responses are acceptable or even rewarded.

Culture and Emotion

Differences across cultural groups are infused into each stage of the emotion process, although it is beyond the scope of this chapter to review them in detail (for reviews, see Elfenbein & Shirako, 2006; Mesquita & Frijda, 1992). Models of the emotional registration process have been tested cross-culturally and appear to be relatively universal in their mapping of appraisal dimensions to emotional states (Ellsworth & Scherer, 2003; Scherer, 1997). However, first, cultural groups differ in the ways that they map stimuli to the appraisal dimensions. For example, members of individualistic versus collectivistic cultural groups attribute greater agency to the individual (Morris & Peng, 1994) and, thus, may evaluate events to have greater attributed personal control, resulting in greater blame and lesser uncertainty. Second, cultural groups differ in the schemas and feeling rules that guide their emotional registration, for example with members of collectivistic groups preferring emotional states that emphasize connectedness with others (Kitayama, Markus, & Kurokawa, 2000). Wide variance in the emotions typically experienced across cultural groups also results from cultural differences in the stimuli that one generally encounters as well as regulation via situation selection, situation modification, reappraisal, and experience regulation (Mesquita & Frijda, 1992). Further, once an emotion is experienced, cultural groups differ in the tightness of regulation processes, with collectivistic versus individualistic groups more likely to inhibit emotional processes for the sake of maintaining social harmony (Ekman, 1972). As discussed earlier in the section on display rules, cultural groups differ in their style of expressing particular emotions, and emotion recognition is more accurate when judging expressions posed in a culturally familiar style (Elfenbein et al., 2007). In the presence of others' emotional expressions, members of collectivistic versus individualist groups are more likely to mimic and synchronize such expressive behaviors to be congruent with those around them (Van Baaren, Maddux, Chartrand, de Bouter, & van Knippenberg, 2003). In terms of postemotional responses in the workplace, even the same emotional state can lead to different instrumental behaviors across cultural groups. For example, Bagozzi, Verbeke, and Gavino (2003) found that salespeople's senses of shame in Holland and the Philippines—operationally defined in terms of self-consciousness in interactions with customers—was similar in its experience, yet differed in its consequences. Whereas Dutch salespeople responded by withdrawing personal involvement from interactions, Filipino salespeople responded by varying their approaches to find more comfortable interaction strategies. In general, psychologists have been actively interested in cultural differences within emotion processes, which remain ripe for exploration within organizational settings.

In general, the study of emotion in organizations has tended to be more fashionable in Western cultural settings, perhaps because the value of emotion seems more counterintuitive to members of individualist versus collectivist societies. Our field would benefit from more research conducted across diverse contexts. Straightforward cross-cultural replications are necessary for a greater understanding of boundary conditions. However, beyond replication, the impact of culture on emotional processes also offers researchers the opportunity to test theory-driven hypotheses by increasing variance. Notably, Grandey, Fisk, and Steiner (2005) took advantage of differences between France and the United States in employee personal control overemotional displays in order to examine the role of personal control.

Organizational researchers should look for ideas, inspiration, and grounding in the large existing literature on cultural differences in emotion. Further, to encourage such research, we should take care not to consider Anglophone Western groups as an implicit reference point—a practice that places an unfair burden on researchers outside these settings to defend the cultural generality of their work. For example, culture is frequently listed as a boundary condition outside the United States (e.g., Butt et al., 2005), but there is rarely any mention of culture in research conducted exclusively within the United States.

What Is Next for Emotion in Organizations?

This chapter attempted to review the research literature widely conducted under the banner of emotion in organizations, and to consolidate what we know into a single coherent model to provide common ground across these disparate domains. Such a fragmented body of work is common for nascent areas of organizational scholarship (Walsh, 1995). Barsade et al. (2003) argued, however, that the field of emotion in organizations is now transforming into a mature, hybrid paradigm that draws from a variety of methods and perspectives.

The current review attempts to further Barsade et al.'s (2003) vision by presenting an integrated process framework. Emotion is a complex set of interrelated processes, and referring to any one piece as *emotion* is a misnomer. I argue that each stage matters at least in part due its interconnectedness with the other stages. For example, internal feeling rules exist to try to elicit appropriate postemotional behaviors. Emotion recognition exists because expressive cues allow us to see into others' internal states. For this reason, even if researchers are interested in one particular area, wherever possible it is valuable to examine at least one stage forward and one stage backward. The field would benefit from researchers specifying where in the process framework their phenomenon of interest lives. Although the process framework in Figure 7.2 is a first step that is inevitably a work in progress to be revised and extended, detailed searches and reviews of the existing literature suggest that it largely represents the field's existing theoretical and empirical base. Thus, it can be a starting point to situate, theorize, and test explicit mechanisms and to suggest a boundary for what organizational researchers label "emotion." The term *emotion* has been something of a Rorschach ink blot test, which at extremes can describe nearly every phenomenon within management. However, as I argued in the introduction, for emotion to mean anything, it cannot mean everything.

A number of challenges remain for affect in organizations. Staw (2005) argued that these challenges include its potentially faddish nature, its possibility of remaining relatively isolated from mainstream organizational studies, its appeal primarily to micro- versus macro- and mezzo-level organizational scholars, its use as a supplemental variable rather than a focus on its own right, and its reliance on theories from psychology without theories specific to organizations. Organizational researchers have applied these psychological theories into fruitful streams of empirical work, particularly in the areas of emotional stimuli, display rules, feeling rules and norms, the relationship between affective states and performance, and emotional contagion—all specific to organizational contexts. One gap is for organizational scholars to broaden their interests across the emotion processes, given that they have been unevenly focused on specific areas such as postemotional responses and emotional labor. Research has been less common in some areas that psychologists consider central, such as emotion recognition and emotional registration—which may, indeed, connect emotion more closely to mainstream organizational topics such as power, justice, accountability, and others. Another gap is that, until very recently, there has been relatively less focus on the processes that, indeed, have the greatest potential for Staw's (2005) call for a uniquely organizational lens—those that move beyond the individual level of analysis into dyads, groups, and even organizations. In the process framework, these interpersonal and higher levels appear primarily in terms of the norms that guide emotion regulation and the iteration of dyadic processes.

At the same time that we need organization-specific theory and research on emotion, we need organizational researchers to steep themselves in the knowledge base of the disciplines so as not to reinvent the wheel. In particular, appraisal theories of emotion are underutilized, as previously discussed. If we appraise every stimulus that is relevant to personal concerns, then any area of business becomes an emotional arena. Many topics central to organizational researchers (e.g., justice, trust, commitment, and conflict) overlap heavily with appraisal dimensions (e.g., fairness, responsibility, valence, and certainty). Indeed, most topics of intense interest to researchers are interesting precisely because organizational members relate to the phenomena as novel, intrinsically rewarding or punishing, and relevant to goals—the first three of Scherer's (1988) dimensions. Given that society creates emotional labels for frequent clusters of appraisals and behavioral intentions (Fridlund, 1994), we should expect that emotions are woven throughout existing organizational phenomena. However, their co-occurrence does not always make them the mechanism. Indeed, cognition—not emotion—was earlier proposed as the intervening step between a stimulus and a response (Walsh, 1995). Although formal mediation analyses, often using self-reported data, may frequently declare emotion to be the winner, this is often as much a methodological artifact versus phenomenon. As such, the field would benefit from a moratorium on omnibus claims to discover "the role of emotion" in existing topics, and emotions researchers should have the burden to justify—theoretically and empirically—that any emotional approach adds uniquely to what we already know.

A further challenge is for organizational work on emotion to incorporate research methods from the disciplines, where the best practices have been more rigorous. The methods that represent emotional phenomena most faithfully are often expensive and intricate, with the state of the art having moved beyond pencil and paper. Each emotional process is distinct and can be studied in different ways. Multimedia methods are amenable to organizational phenomena, and allow objective coding of recordings and the presentation to participants of actual expressive behavior. Fineman (1993) called for more focus on the "simmer and flow of everyday emotions" (p. 14), which includes sociological methods such as ethnography and qualitative examination of narratives, even if qualitative methods are sometimes passed over in the attempt for greater legitimacy from quantification (Fineman, 2004). It can be difficult to study emotion observationally because much of it is regulated and, therefore, difficult to observe (Scherer, 1984b). However, in the attempt to bypass this difficulty by relying on self-reports, we risk asking our participants to tell us more than they could know (Nisbett & Wilson, 1977). Emotion can be so implicit, so automatic, and so outside of conscious awareness that we should not rely—somewhat paradoxically—on participants' emotional awareness in order to study it. As discussed in the section on EI, valid objective measures can be developed, and examples such as response latency and psychophysiological factors are just a beginning. When self-reported data is necessary, collection in real time via experience sampling is preferable to retrospective reports. On a more mundane level, researchers using self-report measures should be particularly vigilant regarding the possibility of common method bias when they collect perceptions of the work environment, stimulus events and consequences via self-report as well, given that such perceptions may be tainted by affective personality traits (e.g., Bagozzi & Yi, 1990). Vignettes and verbal stimuli are simple to implement but do not reflect the richness of truly emotional stimuli. For example, vignette studies tap into implicit theories that may or may not reflect actual behavior. Likewise, explicitly reporting others' emotions to participants bypasses the processes that do or do not lead to their accurate recognition. Ultimately, when done well, organizational research on emotion has the potential to bring to the table the rich context that has been less prevalent in disciplinary work, without sacrificing internal validity.

The final challenge for emotion in organizations has been its mass popularization, but this is a great opportunity as well. On the one hand, scholars have been pressured to formulate their research around the commercial goals of a thirsty business public. On the other hand, it is exciting for an area of management research to attract so much attention outside of the ivory tower (Hambrick, 1994). I end this review by expressing hope that we can preserve this momentum while changing the conversation, to channel the energy around the practical implications away from evaluating individuals—with rewards for those considered to be emotionally savvy—and into improving the emotional quality of our organizations for all (e.g., Dutton, 2003; Frost, 2003).

Acknowledgments

Correspondence should be addressed to Hillary Anger Elfenbein, Haas School of Business, University of California, Berkeley, CA 94720, or via the Internet to hillary@post.harvard.edu. Preparation of this chapter was supported by National Institute of Mental Health Behavioral Science Track Award for Rapid Transition 1R03MH071294-1. I am deeply indebted to Aiwa Shirako for comments, research assistance, and her contribution to an earlier version of the process framework. For helpful comments and suggestions, I thank Sigal Barsade, Art Brief, Stéphane Côté, Kevin Fox, Gavin Kilduff, and Jim Walsh.

Endnote

1. I thank Stéphane Côté for this suggestion.

References

Albrow, M. (1992). Sine-ira-et-studio—Or do organizations have feelings. *Organization Studies, 13*, 313–329.

Allport, G. W., & Vernon, P. E. (1933). *Studies in expressive movement*. New York: Macmillan.

Allred, K. G., Mallozzi, J. S., Matsui, F., & Raia, C. P. (1997). The influence of anger and compassion on negotiation performance. *Organizational Behavior and Human Decision Processes, 70*, 175–187.

Amabile, T. M. (1983). The social psychology of creativity: A componential conceptualization. *Journal of Personality and Social Psychology, 45*, 357–376.

Amabile, T. M., Barsade, S. G., Mueller, J. S., & Staw, B. M. (2005). Affect and creativity at work. *Administrative Science Quarterly, 50*, 367–403.

Ambady, N., & Rosenthal, R. (1992). Thin slices of expressive behavior as predictors of interpersonal consequences: A meta-analysis. *Psychological Bulletin, 111*, 256–274.

Anderson, C., & Thompson, L. (2004). Affect from the top down: How powerful individuals' positive affect shapes negotiations. *Organizational Behavior and Human Decision Processes, 95*, 125–139.

Anderson, C., Keltner, D., & John, O. P. (2003). Emotional convergence between people over time. *Journal of Personality and Social Psychology, 84*, 1054–1068.

Aquino, K., Grover, S. L., Bradfield, M., & Allen, D. G. (1999). The effects of negative affectivity, hierarchical status, and self-determination on workplace victimization. *Academy of Management Journal, 42*, 260–272.

Ashby, F. G., Isen, A. M., & Turken, A. U. (1999). A neuropsychological theory of positive affect and its influence on cognition. *Psychological Review, 106*, 529–550.

Ashforth, B. E., & Humphrey, R. H. (1993). Emotional labor in service roles: The influence of identity. *Academy of Management Review, 18*, 88–115.

Ashforth, B., & Humphrey, R. (1995). Emotion in the workplace: A reappraisal. *Human Relations, 48*, 97–125.

Ashkanasy, N. M. (2003). Emotions in organizations: A multi-level perspective. *Multilevel issues in organizational behavior and strategy, 2*, 9–54.

Au, K., Chan, F., Wang, D., & Vertinsky, I. (2003). Mood in foreign exchange trading: Cognitive processes and performance. *Organizational Behavior and Human Decision Processes, 91*, 322–338.

Avolio, B. J., Howell, J. M., & Sosik, J. J. (1999). A funny thing happened on the way to the bottom line: Humor as a moderator of leadership style effects. *Academy of Management Journal, 42*, 219–227.

Bagozzi, R. P., & Yi, Y. J. (1990). Assessing method variance in multitrait multimethod matrices—The case of self-reported affect and perceptions at work. *Journal of Applied Psychology, 75*, 547–560.

Bagozzi, R., Verbeke, W., & Gavino, J. (2003). Culture moderates the self-regulation of shame and its effects on performance: The case of salespersons in the Netherlands and the Philippines. *Journal of Applied Psychology, 88*, 219–233.

Barry, B., & Oliver, R. (1996). Affect in dyadic negotiation: A model and propositions. *Organizational Behavior and Human Decision Processes, 67*, 127–143.

Barry, B., Fulmer, I. S., & Van Kleef, G. (2004). I laughed, I cried, I settled: The role of emotion in negotiation. In M. J. Gelfand, & J. M. Brett (Eds.), *The handbook of negotiation and culture: Theoretical advances and cross-cultural perspectives* (pp. 71–94). Palo Alto, CA: Stanford University Press.

Barsade, S. (2002). The ripple effect: Emotional contagion and its influence on group behavior. *Administrative Science Quarterly, 47*, 644–675.

Barsade, S. G., Brief, A. P., & Spataro, S. E. (2003). The affective revolution in organizational behavior: The emergence of a paradigm. In J. Greenberg (Ed.), *OB: The state of the science* (2nd ed., pp. 3–52). Hillsdale, NJ: Lawrence Erlbaum Associates.

Barsade, S. G., Ward, A., Turner, J., & Sonnenfeld, J. (2000). To your heart's content: A model of affective diversity in top management teams. *Administrative Science Quarterly, 45*, 802–836.

Barsade, S. G., & Gibson, D. E. (1998). Group emotion: A view from top to bottom. In D. H. Gruenfeld, B. Mannix, & M. Neale (Eds.), *Research on managing groups and teams: Composition* (Vol. 1, pp. 81–102). Greenwich, CT: JAI Press.

Bartel, C., & Saavedra, R. (2000). The collective construction of work group moods. *Administrative Science Quarterly, 45*, 197–231.

Basch, J., & Fisher, C. D. (2000). Affective events-emotion matrix: A classification of work events and associated emotions. In N. M. Ashkanasy, C. E. J. Härtel, & W. Zerbe (Eds.), *Emotions in the workplace: Research, theory, and practice* (pp. 221–235). Westport, CT: Quorum.

Beal, D. J., Weiss, H. M., Barros, E., & Macdermid, S. M. (2005). An episodic process model of affective influences on performance. *Journal of Applied Psychology, 90,* 1054–1068.

Boudens, C. J. (2005). The story of work: A narrative analysis of workplace emotion. *Organization Studies, 26,* 1285–1306.

Boyce, N. (Speaker). (2006, July 5). *Shuttle makes historic Independence Day launch* [Radio broadcast]. National Public Radio. Retrieved on July 31, 2006 from http://www.npr.org/templates/story/story.php?storyId=5534276

Brief, A. P., Butcher, A. H., & Roberson, L. (1995). Cookies, disposition, and job-attitudes: The effects of positive mood-inducing events and negative affectivity on job-satisfaction in a field experiment. *Organizational Behavior and Human Decision Processes, 62,* 55–62.

Brief, A., & Weiss, H. (2002). Organizational behavior: Affect in the workplace. *Annual Review of Psychology, 53,* 279–307.

Brockner, J., & Higgins, E. T. (2001). Regulatory focus theory: Implications for the study of emotions at work. *Organizational Behavior and Human Decision Processes, 86,* 35–66.

Brooks, I. (2003). Systemic exchange: Responsibility for angst. *Organization Studies, 24,* 125–141.

Brotheridge, C. M., & Lee, R. T. (2003). Development and validation of the emotional labour scale. *Journal of Occupational and Organizational Psychology, 76,* 365–379.

Brown, S. P., Westbrook, R. A., & Challagalla, G. (2005). Good cope, bad cope: Adaptive and maladaptive coping strategies following a critical negative work event. *Journal of Applied Psychology, 90,* 792–798.

Brunswik, E. (1955). Representative design and probabilistic theory in a functional psychology. *Psychological Review, 62,* 193–217.

Buck, R. (1984). *The communication of emotion.* New York: Guilford Press.

Buck, R. (1988). *Human motivation and emotion* (2nd ed.). New York: John Wiley & Sons.

Burke, M. J., Brief, A. P., & George, J. M. (1993). The role of negative affectivity in understanding relations between self-reports of stressors and strains—A comment on the applied-psychology literature. *Journal of Applied Psychology, 78,* 402–412.

Buss, D. M. (1987). Selection, evocation, and manipulation. *Journal of Personality and Social Psychology, 53,* 1214–1221.

Butt, A. N., Choi, J. N., & Jaeger, A. M. (2005). The effects of self-emotion, counterpart emotion, and counterpart behavior on negotiator behavior: A comparison of individual-level and dyad-level dynamics. *Journal of Organizational Behavior, 26,* 681–704.

Campos, J. J., Frankel, C. B., & Camras, L. (2004). On the nature of emotion regulation. *Child Development, 75,* 377–394.

Carnevale, P. J. D., & Isen, A. M. (1986). The influence of positive affect and visual access on the discovery of integrative solutions in bilateral negotiation. *Organizational Behavior and Human Decision Processes, 37,* 1–13.

Casciaro, T., Carley, K. M., & Krackhardt, D. (1999). Positive affectivity and accuracy in social network perception. *Motivation and Emotion, 23,* 285–306.

Clore, G. L., Schwarz, N., & Conway, M. (1994). Affective causes and consequences of social information processing. In R. S. Wyer, & T. K. Srull (Eds.), *Handbook of social cognition* (2nd ed., Vol. 1, pp. 323–417). Hillside, NJ: Lawrence Erlbaum Associates.

Collinson, D. L. (1988). Engineering humor: Masculinity, joking, and conflict in shop-floor relations. *Organization Studies, 9,* 181–199.

Conger, J. A. (1991). Inspiring others: The language of leadership. *Academy of Management Executive, 5,* 31–45.

Connolly, J. J., & Viswesvaran, C. (2000). The role of affectivity in job satisfaction: A meta-analysis. *Personality and Individual Differences, 29,* 265–281.

Cosmides, L., & Tooby, L. (2000). Evolutionary psychology and the emotions. In M. Lewis, & J. M. Haviland-Jones (Eds.), *Handbook of emotions* (2nd ed., pp. 91–115). New York: Guilford.

Côté, S. (1999). Affect and performance in organizational settings. *Current Directions in Psychological Science, 8,* 65–68.

Côté, S. (2005). A social interaction model of the effects of emotion regulation on work strain. *Academy of Management Review, 30,* 509–530.

Côté, S., & Miners, C. T. H. (2006). Emotional intelligence, cognitive intelligence, and job performance. *Administrative Science Quarterly, 51,* 2006, 1–28.

Côté, S., & Morgan, L. (2002). A longitudinal analysis of the association between emotion regulation, job satisfaction, and intentions to quit. *Journal of Organizational Behavior, 23,* 947–962.

Crites, S. L., Fabrigar, L. R., & Petty, R. E. (1994). Measuring the affective and cognitive properties of attitudes: Conceptual and methodological issues. *Personality and Social Psychology Bulletin, 20,* 619–634.

Cropanzano, R., Weiss, H., Hale, J., & Reb, J. (2003). The structure of affect: Reconsidering the relationship between negative and positive affectivity. *Journal of Management, 29,* 831–857.

Csikszentmihalyi, M. (1975). Play and intrinsic rewards. *Journal of Humanistic Psychology, 15,* 41–63.

Damasio, A. R. (1994). *Descartes' error.* New York: Grosset Putnam.

Dasborough, M. T. (2006). Cognitive asymmetry in employee emotional reactions to leadership behaviors. *Leadership Quarterly, 17,* 163–178.

Davis, P. J., & Schwartz, G. E. (1987). Repression and the inaccessibility of affective memories. *Journal Of Personality And Social Psychology, 52,* 155–162.

DePaulo, B. M., & Friedman, H. S. (1998). Nonverbal communication. In D. T. Gilbert, S. T. Fiske, & G. Lindzey (Eds.), *The handbook of social psychology* (Vol. 1, 4th ed., pp. 591–632). Boston: McGraw-Hill.

Diener, E. (2000). Subjective well-being: The science of happiness and a proposal for a national index . *American Psychologist, 55,* 34–43.

Diener, E., & Larsen, R. J. (1984). Temporal stability and cross-situational consistency of affective, behavioral, and cognitive responses. *Journal of Personality and Social Psychology, 47,* 871–883.

Diener, E., Larsen, R., & Emmons, R. (1984). Person x situation interactions: Choice of situations and congruence response models. *Journal of Personality and Social Psychology, 47,* 580–592.

Dilorio, J. A., & Nusbaumer, M. R. (1993). Securing our sanity: Anger management among abortion escorts. *Journal of Contemporary Ethnography, 21,* 411–438.

Domagalski, T. (1999). Emotion in organizations: Main currents. *Human Relations, 52,* 833–852.

Dutton, J. (2003). Breathing life into organizational studies. *Journal of Management Inquiry, 12,* 1–19.

Dutton, J., & Dukerich, J. (2006). The relational foundation of research: An underappreciated dimension of interesting research. *Academy of Management Journal, 49*(1), 21–26.

Eagley, A. H., & Chaiken, S. (1998). Attitude structure and function. In D. T. Gilbert, & S. T. Fiske (Eds.), *The handbook of social psychology* (pp. 269–322). Boston: McGraw-Hill.

Edwards, K. (1990). The interplay of affect and cognition in attitude formation and change. *Journal of Personality and Social Psychology, 59,* 202–216.

Ekman, P. (1972). Universals and cultural differences in facial expressions of emotion. In J. Cole (Ed.), *Nebraska symposium on motivation, 1971* (Vol. 19, pp. 207–282). Lincoln: University of Nebraska Press.

Ekman, P. (1984). Expression and the nature of emotion. In K. R. Scherer, & P. Ekman (Eds.), *Approaches to emotion* (pp. 319–344). Hillsdale, NJ: Erlbaum.

Ekman, P. (1992). An argument for basic emotions. *Cognition and Emotion, 6,* 169–200.

Ekman, P., & Friesen, W. V. (1969). Nonverbal leakage and clues to deception. *Psychiatry, 32,* 88–106.

Ekman, P., Sorensen, E. R., & Friesen, W. V. (1969, April 4). Pancultural elements in facial displays of emotions. *Science, 164,* 86–88.

Elfenbein, H. A., & Ambady, N. (2002a). On the universality and cultural specificity of emotion recognition: A meta-analysis. *Psychological Bulletin, 128,* 203–235.

Elfenbein, H. A., & Ambady, N. (2002b). Predicting workplace outcomes from the ability to eavesdrop on feelings. *Journal of Applied Psychology, 87,* 963–971.

Elfenbein, H. A., & Ambady, N. (2003). Universals and cultural differences in recognizing emotions. *Current Directions in Psychological Science, 12,* 159–164.

Elfenbein, H. A., & Shirako, A. (2006). An emotion process model for multicultural teams. In B. Mannix, M. Neale, & Y. R. Chen (Eds.), *Research on managing groups and teams: National culture and groups* (pp. 263–297). Amsterdam: Elsevier.

Elfenbein, H. A., Beaupré, M. G., Lévesque, M., & Hess, U. (2007). Toward a dialect theory: Cultural differences in the expression and recognition of posed facial expressions. *Emotion, 7,* 131–146.

Elfenbein, H. A., Foo, M. D., Boldry, J. G., & Tan, H. H. (2006). Dyadic effects in nonverbal communication: A variance partitioning analysis. *Cognition and Emotion, 20,* 149–159.

Elfenbein, H. A., Foo, M. D., White, J. B., Tan, H. H., & Aik, V. C. (in press). Reading your counterpart: The benefit of emotion perception ability for effectiveness in negotiation. *Journal of Nonverbal Behavior.*

Elfenbein, H. A., Polzer, J. T., & Ambady, N. (2007). Team emotion recognition accuracy and team performance. In N. M. Ashkanasy, W. J. Zerbe, & C. E. J. Härtel (Eds.), *Research on emotions in organizations* (Vol. 3, pp. 87–119). Amsterdam: Elsevier.

Ellsworth, P. C., & Scherer, K. R. (2003). Appraisal processes in emotion. In R. J. Davidson, K. R. Scherer, & H. H. Goldsmith (Eds.), *Handbook of affective sciences* (pp. 572–595). Oxford, U.K.: Oxford University Press.

Feldman Barrett, L., & Russell, J. A. (1999). The structure of current affect: Controversies and emerging consensus. *Current Directions in Psychological Science, 8*, 10–14.

Feldman, L. A. (1995). Valence focus and arousal focus: Individual differences in the structure of affective experience. *Journal of Personality and Social Psychology, 69*, 153–166.

Fineman, S. (1993). Organizations as emotional arenas. In S. Fineman (Ed.), *Emotion in organizations* (pp. 9–35). London: Sage Publications.

Fineman, S. (1996). Emotion and organizing. In S. R. Clegg, C. Hardy, & W. R. Nord (Eds.), *Handbook of organization studies* (pp. 543–564). London: Sage Publications.

Fineman, S. (2004). Getting the measure of emotion—And the cautionary tale of emotional intelligence. *Human Relations, 57*, 719–740.

Fitness, J. (2000). Anger in the workplace: An emotion script approach to anger episodes between workers and their superiors, co-workers, and subordinates. *Journal of Organizational Behavior, 21*, 147–162.

Fleeson, W. (2001). Toward a structure- and process-integrated view of personality: Traits as density distributions of states. *Journal of Personality and Social Psychology, 80*, 1011–1027.

Fong, C. T. (in press). The effects of emotional ambivalence on creativity. *Academy of Management Journal.*

Fong, C., & Tiedens, L. (2002). Dueling experiences and dual ambivalences: Emotional and motivational ambivalence of women in high status positions. *Motivation and Emotion, 26*, 105–121.

Forgas, J. (1995). Mood and judgment: The affect infusion model (AIM). *Psychological Bulletin, 117*, 39–66.

Forgas, J. P. (2003). Affective influences on attitudes and judgments. In R. J. Davidson, K. R. Scherer, & H. H. Goldsmith (Eds.), *Handbook of affective sciences* (pp. 596–618). Oxford, U.K.: Oxford University Press.

Forgas, J. P., & George, J. M. (2001) Affective influences on judgments and behavior in organizations: An information processing perspective. *Organizational Behavior and Human Decision Processes, 86*, 3–34.

Forgas, J. P. (1998). On feeling good and getting your way: Mood effects on negotiation strategies and outcomes. *Journal of Personality and Social Psychology, 74*, 565–577.

Fredrickson, B. L., & Levenson, R. W. (1998). Positive emotions speed recovery from the cardiovascular sequelae of negative emotions. *Cognition and Emotion, 12*, 191–220.

Fredrickson, B. L. (2001). The role of positive emotions in positive psychology: The broaden and build theory of positive emotions. *American Psychologist, 56*, 218–226.

Fridlund, A. J. (1994). *Human facial expression: An evolutionary view*. San Diego, CA: Academic Press.

Frijda, N. H. (1986). *The emotions*. Cambridge, U.K.: Cambridge University Press.

Frijda, N. H. (1988). The laws of emotion. *American Psychologist, 43*, 349–358.

Frijda, N. H., & Mesquita, B. (1994). The social roles and functions of emotions. In S. Kitayama, & H. R. Markus (Eds.), *Emotion and culture* (pp. 51–87). Washington, DC: American Psychological Association.

Frost, P. J. (2003). *Toxic emotions at work*. Cambridge, MA: Harvard Business School Publishing.

Fuller, J. A., Stanton, J. M., Fisher, G. G., Spitzmuller, C., Russell, S. S., & Smith, P. C. (2003). A lengthy look at the daily grind: Time series analysis of events, mood, stress, and satisfaction. *Journal of Applied Psychology, 88*, 1019–1033.

Furnham, A. (2006). Explaining the popularity of Emotional Intelligence. In K. R. Murphy (Ed.), *A critique of emotional intelligence: What are the problems and how can they be fixed?* (pp. 141–160). Mahwah, NJ: Lawrence Erlbaum Associates.

Gaddis, B., Connelly, S., & Mumford, M. D. (2004). Failure feedback as an affective event: Influences of leader affect on subordinate attitudes and performance. *Leadership Quarterly, 15*, 663–686.

Garcia-Prieto, P., Bellard, E., & Schneider, S. (2003). Experiencing diversity, conflict, and emotions in teams. *Applied Psychology—An International Review, 52*, 413–440.

Garot, R. (2004). "You're not a stone": Emotional sensitivity in a bureaucratic setting. *Journal of Contemporary Ethnography, 33*, 735–766.

George, J. M. (1990). Personality, affect, and behavior in groups. *Journal of Applied Psychology, 75*, 107–116.

George, J. M. (1991). State or trait: Effects of positive mood on prosocial behaviors at work. *Journal of Applied Psychology, 76*, 299–307.

George, J. M. (2000). Emotions and leadership: The role of emotional intelligence. *Human Relations, 53*, 1027–1055.

George, J. M., & Brief, A. P. (1992). Feeling good doing good: A conceptual analysis of the mood at work organizational spontaneity relationship. *Psychological Bulletin, 112*, 310–329.

George, J., & Brief, A. (1996). Motivational agendas in the workplace: The effects of feelings on focus of attention and work motivation. *Research in Organizational Behavior, 18*, 75–109.

George, J. M., & Jones, G. R. (2001). Towards a process model of individual change in organizations. *Human Relations, 54*, 419–444.

George, J. M., & Zhou, J. (2002). Understanding when bad moods foster creativity and good ones don't: The role of context and clarity of feelings. *Journal of Applied Psychology, 87*, 687–697.

Gibson, J. J. (1979). *The ecological approach to visual perception*. Boston: Houghton Mifflin.

Gilbert, D. T., Pinel, E. C., Wilson, T. C., Blumberg, S. J., & Wheatley, T. P. (1998). Immune neglect: A source of durability bias in affective forecasting. *Journal of Personality and Social Psychology, 75*, 617–638.

Glomb, T. M., & Hulin, C. (1997). Anger and gender effects in observed supervisor-subordinate dyadic interactions. *Organizational Behavior and Human Decision Processes, 72,* 281–307.

Glomb, T. M., Kammeyer-Mueller, J. D., & Rotundo, M. (2004). Emotional labor demands and compensating wage differentials. *Journal of Applied Psychology, 89,* 700–714.

Goleman, D. (1995). *Emotional intelligence: Why it can matter more than IQ.* New York: Bantam Books.

Goleman, D., Boyatzis, R., & McKee, A. (2002). *Primal leadership: Realizing the power of emotional intelligence.* Boston: Harvard Business School Press.

Gosserand, R. H., & Diefendorff, J. M. (2005). Emotional display rules and emotional labor: The moderating role of commitment. *Journal of Applied Psychology, 90,* 1256–1264.

Grandey, A. A. (2000). Emotion regulation in the workplace: A new way to conceptualize emotional labor. *Journal of Occupational Health Psychology, 5,* 95–110.

Grandey, A. A. (2003). When "the show must go on": Surface acting and deep acting as determinants of emotional exhaustion and peer-rated service delivery. *Academy of Management Journal, 46,* 86–96.

Grandey, A. (in press). Emotions at work: A review and research agenda. To appear in C. Cooper & J. Barling (Eds.), *Handbook of Organizational Behavior.* Oxford: Blackwell.

Grandey, A. A., Dickter, D., & Sin, H. (2004). The customer is not always right: Customer aggression and emotion regulation of service employees. *Journal of Organizational Behavior, 25,* 397–418.

Grandey, A. A., Fisk, G. M., & Steiner, D. D. (2005). Must "service with a smile" be stressful? The moderating role of personal control for American and French employees. *Journal of Applied Psychology, 90,* 893–904.

Grandey, A. A., Fisk, G. M., Mattila, A. S., Jansen, K. J., & Sideman, L. A. (2005). Is 'service with a smile' enough? Authenticity of positive displays during service encounters. *Organizational Behavior and Human Decision Processes, 96,* 38–55.

Grandey, A. A., Tam, A. P., & Brauburger, A. L. (2002). Affective states and traits in the workplace: Diary and survey data from young workers. *Motivation and Emotion, 26,* 31–55.

Gross, J. (1998a). Antecedent- and response-focused emotion regulation: Divergent consequences for experience, expression, and physiology. *Journal of Personality and Social Psychology, 74,* 224–237.

Gross, J. (1998b). The emerging field of emotion regulation: An integrative review. *Review of General Psychology, 2,* 271–299.

Gross, J. (2001). Emotion regulation in adulthood: Timing is everything. *Current Directions in Psychological Science, 10,* 214–219.

Gross, J. J., & John, O. P. (1998). Mapping the domain of expressivity: Multimethod evidence for a hierarchical model. *Journal of Personality and Social Psychology, 74,* 170–191.

Haas, J. (1977). Learning real feelings: A study of high steel ironworkers' reactions to fear and danger. *Sociology of Work and Occupations, 4,* 147–170.

Hackman, J. R., & Oldham, G. R. (1976). Motivation through the design of work: Test of a theory. *Organizational Behavior and Human Performance, 16,* 250–279.

Halberstadt, A. G. (1986). Family socialization of emotional expression and nonverbal communication styles and skills. *Journal of Personality and Social Psychology, 51*, 827–836.

Hambrick, D. C. (1994). What if the Academy actually mattered? *Academy of Management Review, 19*, 11–16.

Haselhuhn, M. P., & Mellers, B. A. (2005). Emotions and cooperation in economic games. *Cognitive Brain Research, 23*, 24–33.

Hatfield, E., Cacioppo, J. T., & Rapson, R. L. (1994). *Emotional contagion.* Cambridge, U.K.: Cambridge University Press.

Hatfield, E., Hsee, C. K., Costello, J., & Weisman, M. S. (1995). The impact of vocal feedback on emotional experience and expression. *Journal of Social Behavior and Personality, 10*, 293–312.

Heaphy, E., & Dutton, J. (in press). Positive social interactions and the human body at work: Linking organizations and physiology. *Academy of Management Review.*

Hennig-Thurau, T., Groth, M., Paul, M., & Gremler, D. D. (2006). *Are all smiles created equal? How employee-customer emotional contagion impacts service relationships.* Manuscript submitted for publication.

Hersey, R. B. (1932). Rates of production and emotional state. *Personnel Journal, 10*, 355–364.

Herzberg, F. (1966). *Work and the nature of man.* Chicago: World Publishing.

Higgins, E. T. (1998). Promotion and prevention: Regulatory focus as a motivational principle. *Advances in Experimental Social Psychology, 30*, 1–46.

Hochschild A. R. (1983). *The managed heart: Commercialization of human feeling.* Berkeley, CA: University of California Press.

Hochschild, A. R. (1979). Emotion work, feeling rules, and social structure. *American Journal of Sociology, 85*, 551–575.

Howard, D. J., & Gengler, C. (2001). Emotional contagion effects on product attitudes. *Journal of Consumer Research, 28*, 189–201.

Huy, Q. (1999). Emotional capability, emotional intelligence, and radical change. *Academy of Management Review, 24*, 325–345.

Huy, Q. N. (2002). Emotional balancing of organizational continuity and radical change: The contribution of middle managers. *Administrative Science Quarterly, 47*, 31–69.

Ilies, R., & Judge, T. A. (2002). Understanding the dynamic relationships among personality, mood, and job satisfaction: A field experience sampling study. *Organizational Behavior and Human Decision Processes, 89*, 1119–1139.

Isen, A. M. (1987). Positive affect, cognitive processes, and social behavior. *Advances in Experimental Social Psychology, 20*, 203–253.

Isen, A. M. (2001). An influence of positive affect on decision making in complex situations: Theoretical issues with practical implications. *Journal of Consumer Psychology, 11*, 75–85.

Isen, A. M., & Baron, R. A. (1991). Positive affect as a factor in organizational behavior. *Research in Organizational Behavior, 13*, 1–53.

Jackson, S. E., & Dutton, J. E. (1988). Discerning threats and opportunities. *Administrative Science Quarterly, 33*, 370–387.

James, W. (1884). What is an emotion? *Mind, 9*, 188–205.

Jehn, K. A. (1995). A multimethod examination of the benefits and detriments of intragroup conflict. *Administrative Science Quarterly, 40*, 256–282.

Judge, T. A., & Larsen, R. J. (2001). Dispositional affect and job satisfaction: A review and theoretical extension. *Organizational Behavior and Human Decision Processes, 86,* 67–98.

Judge, T. A., Scott, B. A., & Ilies, R. (2006). Hostility, job attitudes, and workplace deviance: Test of a multilevel model. *Journal of Applied Psychology, 91,* 126–138.

Judge, T. A., Thoresen, C. J., Bono, J. E., & Patton, G. K. (2001). The job satisfaction-job performance relationship: A qualitative and quantitative review. *Psychological Bulletin, 127,* 376–407.

Keith, N., & Frese, M. (2005). Self-regulation in error management training: Emotion control and metacognition as mediators of performance effects. *Journal of Applied Psychology, 90,* 677–691.

Kelly, J. R., & Barsade, S. G. (2001). Mood and emotions in small groups and work teams. *Organizational Behavior & Human Decision Processes, 86,* 99–130.

Keltner, D., Gruenfeld, D. H., & Anderson, C. (2003). Power, approach, and inhibition. *Psychological Review, 110,* 265–284.

Keltner, D., & Haidt, J. (1999). Social functions of emotions at four levels of analysis. *Cognition and Emotion, 13,* 505–521.

Kitayama, S., Markus, H., & Kurokawa, M. (2000). Culture, emotion, and well-being: Good feelings in Japan and the United States. *Cognition and Emotion, 14,* 93–124.

Kluger, A. N., & Tikochinsky, J. (2001). The error of accepting the "theoretical" null hypothesis: The rise, fall, and resurrection of commonsense hypotheses in psychology. *Psychological Bulletin, 127,* 408–423.

Knutson, B. (1996). Facial expressions of emotion influence interpersonal trait inferences. *Journal of Nonverbal Behavior, 20,* 165–182.

Lakin, J. L., Jefferis, V. E., Cheng, C. M., & Chartrand, C. L. (2003). The chameleon effect as social glue: Evidence for the evolutionary significance of nonconscious mimicry. *Journal of Nonverbal Behavior, 27,* 145–162.

Larsen, R. J., & Ketelaar, T. (1989). Extraversion, neuroticism, and susceptibility to positive and negative mood induction procedures. *Personality and Individual Differences, 10,* 1221–1228.

Larsen, R. J., & Ketelaar, T. (1991). Personality and susceptibility to positive and negative emotional states. *Journal of Personality and Social Psychology, 61,* 132–140.

Lazarus, R. S. (1991). Cognition and motivation in emotion. *American Psychologist, 46,* 352–367.

Lerner, J. S., & Keltner, D. (2001). Fear, anger, and risk. *Journal of Personality and Social Psychology, 81,* 146–159.

Lerner, J. S., Small, D. A., & Loewenstein, G. (2004). Heart strings and purse strings - carryover effects of emotions on economic decisions. *Psychological Science, 15,* 337–341.

Leventhal, H., & Scherer, K. R. (1987). The relationship of emotion to cognition: A functional approach to a semantic controversy. *Cognition and Emotion, 1,* 3–28.

Lewis, K. M. (2000). When leaders display emotion: How followers respond to negative emotional expression of male and female leaders. *Journal of Organizational Behavior, 21,* 221–234.

Lind, E. A., & Tyler, T. R. (1988). *The social psychology of procedural justice.* New York: Plenum.

Locke, K. D., & Horowitz, L. M. (1990). Satisfaction in interpersonal interactions as a function of similarity in level of dysphoria. *Journal of Personality and Social Psychology, 58*, 823–831.

Loewenstein, G., & Lerner, J. S. (2003). The role of affect in decision making. In R. J. Davidson, K. R. Scherer, & H. H. Goldsmith (Eds.), *Handbook of affective sciences* (pp. 619–642). Oxford, U.K.: Oxford University Press.

Loewenstein, G., & Schkade, D. (1999). Wouldn't it be nice? Predicting future feelings. In E. Diener, N. Schwarz, & D. Kahneman (Eds.), *Hedonic psychology: Scientific approaches to enjoyment, suffering, and well-being* (pp. 85–105). New York: Russell Sage Foundation.

Lopes, P. N., Barsade, S. G., Nezlek, J. B., Straus, R., & Salovey, P. (submitted). *Ability to read emotions in group negotiations: Help or hindrance?*

Lopes, P. N., Salovey, P., Côté, S., & Beers, M. (2005). Emotion regulation abilities and the quality of social interaction. *Emotion, 5*, 113–118.

Martin, J., Knopoff, K., & Beckman, C. (1998). An alternative to bureaucratic impersonality and emotional labor: Bounded emotionality at the body shop. *Administrative Science Quarterly, 43*, 429–469.

Maslow, A. H. (1943). A theory of human motivation. *Psychological Review, 50*, 370–396.

Matthews, G., Zeidner, M., & Roberts, R. D. (2002). *Emotional intelligence: Science and myth.* Cambridge, MA: MIT Press.

Mayer, J. D., Roberts, R. D., & Barsade, S. G. (in press). Human abilities: Emotional intelligence. *Annual Review of Psychology, 58.*

Mayer, J. D., Salovey, P., & Caruso, D. R. (2002). *Manual for the MSCEIT Mayer-Salovey-Caruso Emotional Intelligence Test.* Toronto, ON: Multi-Health Systems.

McArthur, L. Z., & Baron, R. M. (1983). Toward an ecological theory of social perception. *Psychological Review, 90*, 215–238.

Mellers, B. A. (2000). Choice and the relative pleasure of consequences. *Psychological Bulletin, 126*, 910–924.

Merton, R. K. (1952). Bureaucratic structure and personality. In R. K. Merton, B. Hockey, & H. C. Selvin (Eds.), *Reader in bureaucracy* (pp. 361–371). Glencoe, IL: Free Press.

Mesquita, B., & Frijda, N. H. (1992). Cultural variations in emotions: A review. *Psychological Bulletin, 112*, 197–204.

Mignonac, K., & Herrbach, O. (2004). Linking work events, affective states, and attitudes: An empirical study of managers' emotions. *Journal of Business and Psychology, 19*, 221 – 240.

Millar, M. G., & Millar, K. U. (1996). The effects of direct and indirect experience on affective and cognitive responses and the attitude-behavior relation. *Journal of Personality and Social Psychology, 32*, 561–579.

Miner, A. G., Glomb, T. M., & Hulin, C. (2005). Experience sampling mood and its correlates at work. *Journal of Occupational and Organizational Psychology, 78*, 171–193.

Morris, M., & Keltner, D. (2000). How emotions work: The social functions of emotional expression in negotiations. *Research in Organizational Behavior, 22*, 1–50.

Morris, M. W., & Peng, K. (1994). Culture and cause: American and Chinese attributions for social and physical events. *Journal of Personality and Social Psychology, 67*, 949–971.

Motowidlo, S. J., Packard, J. S., & Manning, M. R. (1986). Occupational stress: Its causes and consequences for job-performance. *Journal of Applied Psychology, 71*, 618–629.

Mumby, D. K., & Putnam, L. L. (1992). The politics of emotion: A feminist reading of bounded rationality. *Academy of Management Review, 17*, 465–486.

Muraven, M., & Baumeister, R. F. (2000). Self-regulation and depletion of limited resources: Does self-control resemble a muscle? *Psychological Bulletin, 126*, 247–259.

Neck, C. P., & Manz, C. C. (1996). Thought self-leadership: The impact of mental strategies training on employee cognition, behavior, and affect. *Journal of Organizational Behavior, 17*, 445–467.

Neumann, R., & Strack, F. (2000). "Mood contagion": The automatic transfer of mood between persons. *Journal of Personality and Social Psychology, 79*, 211–223.

Newcombe, M., & Ashkanasy, N. (2002). The role of affect and affective congruence in perceptions of leaders: An experimental study. *Leadership Quarterly, 13*, 601–614.

Nisbett, R. E., & Wilson, T. D. (1977). Telling more than we can know: Verbal reports on mental processes. *Psychological Review, 84*, 231–259.

O'Sullivan, M. (2005). Emotional intelligence and detecting deception: Why most people can't "read" others, but a few can. In R. Riggio, & R. Feldman (Eds.), *Applications of nonverbal communication* (pp. 215–253). Mahway, NJ: Lawrence Erlbaum Associates.

Parkinson, B. (2005). Do facial movements express emotions or communicate motives? *Personality and Social Psychology Review, 9*, 278–311.

Pennebaker, J. W., Mehl, M. R., & Niederhoffer, K. G. (2003). Psychological aspects of natural language use: Our words, our selves. *Annual Review of Psychology, 54*, 547–577.

Pescosolido, A. T. (2002). Emergent leaders as managers of group emotion. *Leadership Quarterly, 13*, 583–599.

Petty, R. E., & Wegener, D. T. (1998). Attitude change: Multiple roles for persuasion variables. In D. T. Gilbert, S. T. Fiske, & G. Lindzey (Eds.), *The handbook of social psychology* (4th ed., Vol. 1, pp. 323–390). Boston: McGraw-Hill.

Pillutla, M. M., & Murnighan, J. K. (1996). Unfairness, anger, and spite: Emotional rejections of ultimatum offers. *Organizational Behavior and Human Decision Processes, 68*, 208–224.

Pirola-Merlo, A., Hartel, C., Mann, L., & Hirst, G. (2002). How leaders influence the impact of affective events on team climate and performance in R&D teams. *Leadership Quarterly, 13*, 561–581.

Pogrebin, M. R., & Poole, E. D. (1995). Emotion management: A study of police responses to tragic events. In M. G. Flaherty, & C. Ellis (Eds.), *Social perspectives on emotion* (Vol. 3, pp. 149–168). Greenwich, CT: JAI Press.

Pratt, M. G., & Doucet, L. (2000). Ambivalent feelings in organizational relationships. In S. Fineman (Ed.), *Emotions in organizations* (2nd ed., Vol. 2, pp. 204–226). London: Sage Publications.

Pugh, S. (2001). Service with a smile: Emotional contagion in the service encounter. *Academy of Management Journal, 44,* 1018–1027.

Putnam, L. L., & Mumby, D. K. (1993). Organizations, emotion, and the myth of rationality. In S. Fineman (Ed.), *Emotion in organizations* (pp. 36–57). London: Sage Publications.

Rafaeli, A., & Sutton, R. I. (1987). Expression of emotion as part of the work role. *Academy of Management Review, 12,* 23–37.

Rafaeli, A., & Sutton, R. I. (1989). The expression of emotion in organizational life. *Research in Organizational Behavior, 11,* 1–42.

Rafaeli, A., & Vilnai-Yavetz, I. (2004). Emotion as a connection of physical artifacts and organizations. *Organization Science, 15,* 671–686.

Rafaeli, A., & Worline, M. (2001). Individual emotion in work organizations. *Social Science Information Sur Les Sciences Sociales, 40,* 95–123.

Rinn, W. E. (1984). The neuropsychology of facial expression: A review of the neurological and psychological mechanisms for producing facial expressions. *Psychological Bulletin, 95,* 52–77.

Robbins, T. L., & DeNisi, A. S. (1994). A closer look at interpersonal affect as a distinct influence on cognitive processing in performance evaluations. *Journal of Applied Psychology, 79,* 341–353.

Rosenthal, R., Hall, J. A., DiMatteo, M. R., Rogers, P. L., & Archer, D. (1979). *Sensitivity to nonverbal communication: The PONS test.* Baltimore: Johns Hopkins University Press.

Rubin, R. S., Munz, D. C., & Bommer, W. H. (2005). Leading from within: The effects of emotion recognition and personality on transformational leadership behavior. *Academy of Management Journal, 48,* 845–858.

Russell, J. A. (1994). Is there universal recognition of emotion from facial expression? A review of the cross-cultural studies. *Psychological Bulletin, 115,* 102–141.

Saavedra, R., & Kwun, S. K. (2000). Affective states in job characteristics theory. *Journal of Organizational Behavior, 21,* 131–146.

Sanchez-Burks, J. (2005). Protestant relational ideology: The cognitive underpinnings and organizational implications of an American anomaly. *Research in Organizational Behavior, 26,* 265–305.

Sandelands, L. E. (1988). The concept of work feeling. *Journal for the Theory of Social Behavior, 18,* 437–357.

Schachter, S., & Singer, J. E. (1962). Cognitive, social, and physiological determinants of emotional state. *Psychological Review, 69,* 379–399.

Scherer, K. (1984a) Emotion as a multicomponent process: A model and some cross-cultural data. In P. Shaver (Ed.), *Review of personality and social psychology* (Vol. 5, pp. 37–63). Beverley Hills, CA: Sage.

Scherer, K. R. (1984b). On the nature and function of emotion: A component process approach. In K. R. Scherer, & P. Ekman (Eds.), *Approaches to emotion.* Hillsdale, NJ: Lawrence Erlbaum Associates.

Scherer, K. R. (1988). Criteria for emotion-antecedent appraisal: A review. In V. Hamilton, G. H. Bower, & N. H. Frijda (Eds.), *Cognitive perspectives on emotion and motivation* (pp. 89–126). New York: Kluwer.

Scherer, K. R. (1995). In defense of a nomothetic approach to studying emotion-antecedent appraisal. *Psychological Inquiry, 6,* 241–248.

Scherer, K. (1997). The role of culture in emotion-antecedent appraisal. *Journal of Personality and Social Psychology, 73*, 902–922.

Scherer, K. R., & Ceschi, G. (2000). Criteria for emotion recognition from verbal and nonverbal expression: Studying baggage loss in the airport. *Personality and Social Psychology Bulletin, 26*, 327–339.

Scherer, K. R., & Tran, V. (2001). Effects of emotion on the process of organizational learning. In M. Dierkes, J. Child, & I. Nonaka (Eds.), *Handbook of organizational learning* (pp. 369–392). New York: Oxford University Press.

Scherer, K. R., & Wallbott, H. G. (1994). Evidence for universality and cultural variation of differential emotion response patterning. *Journal of Personality and Social Psychology, 66*, 310–328.

Schneider, B. (1987). The people make the place. *Personnel Psychology, 40*, 437–453.

Schwarz, N. (1990). Feeling as information: Informational and motivational functions of affective states. In E. T. Higgins, & R. M. Sorrentino (Eds.), *Handbook of motivation and cognition: Foundations of social behavior* (Vol. 2, pp. 229–264). New York: Guilford Press.

Schwarz, N., & Clore, G. L. (1983). Mood, misattribution, and judgments of well-being: Informative and directive functions of affective states. *Journal of Personality and Social Psychology, 45*, 513–523.

Schwarz, N., & Clore, G. L. (1988). How do I feel about it? Informative functions of affective states. In K. Fiedler, & J. Forgas (Eds.), *Affect, cognition, and social behavior* (pp. 44–62). Toronto, Canada: Hogrefe.

Simpson, J. A., Ickes, W., & Blackstone, T. (1995). When the head protects the heart: Empathic accuracy in dating relationships. *Journal of Personality and Social Psychology, 69*, 629–641.

Simpson, P. A., & Stroh, L. K. (2004). Gender differences: Emotional expression and feelings of personal inauthenticity. *Journal of Applied Psychology, 89*, 715–721.

Sinaceur, M., & Tiedens, L. Z. (2006). Get mad and get more than even: When and why anger expression is effective in negotiations. *Journal of Experimental Social Psychology, 42*, 314–322.

Sloan, M. (2004). The effects of occupational characteristics on the experience and expression of anger in the workplace. *Work and Occupations, 31*, 38–72.

Smith, C. A., & Ellsworth, P. C. (1985). Patterns of cognitive appraisal in emotion. *Journal of Personality and Social Psychology, 48*, 813–838.

Spoor, J. R., & Kelly, J. R. (2004). The evolutionary significance of affect in groups: Communication and group bonding. *Group Processes and Intergroup Relations, 7*, 398–412.

Staw, B. M. (2005, May). *A brief history of affect in organizations.* Keynote address to the Rotman Integrative Thinking Conference: The Role of Emotions in Organizational Life, Toronto, Canada.

Staw, B. M., Bell, N. E., & Clausen, J. A. (1986). The dispositional approach to job attitudes: A lifetime longitudinal test. *Administrative Science Quarterly, 31*, 56–77.

Staw, B., & Cohen-Charash, Y. (2005). The dispositional approach to job satisfaction: More than a mirage, but not yet an oasis. *Journal of Organizational Behavior, 26*, 59–78.

Staw, B., Sutton, R., & Pelled, L. (1994). Employee positive emotion and favorable outcomes at the workplace. *Organization Science, 5*, 51–71.

Steiner, I. D. (1955). Interpersonal behavior as influenced by accuracy of social perception. *Psychological Review, 62*, 268–274.

Steiner, I. D. (1959). Human interaction and interpersonal perception. *Sociometry, 22*, 230–235.

Sutton, R. I. (1991). Maintaining norms about expressed emotions: The case of bill collectors. *Administrative Science Quarterly, 36*, 245–268.

Sutton, R. I., & Rafaeli, A. (1988). Untangling the relationships between displayed emotions and organizational sales: The case convenience stores. *Academy of Management Journal, 31*, 461.

Swann, W. B., Jr., Stein-Seroussi, A., & McNulty, S. E. (1992). Outcasts in a white lie society: The enigmatic worlds of people with negative self-conceptions. *Journal of Personality and Social Psychology, 62*, 618–624.

Sy, T., Côté, S., & Saavedra, R. (2005). The contagious leader: Impact of the leader's mood on the mood of group members, group affective tone, and group processes. *Journal of Applied Psychology, 90*, 295–305.

Tan, H. H., Foo, M. D., & Kwek, M. H. (2004). The effects of customer personality traits on the display of positive emotions. *Academy of Management Journal, 47*, 287–296.

Taylor, F. W. (1911). *The principles of scientific management.* New York: Harper.

Taylor, S. E. (1991). Asymmetrical effects of positive and negative events: The mobilization-minimization hypothesis. *Psychological Bulletin, 110*, 67–85.

Tett, R. P., Fox, K. E., & Wang, A. (2005). Development and validation of a self-report measure of emotional intelligence as a multidimensional trait domain. *Personality and Social Psychology Bulletin, 31*, 859–888.

Thompson, L. L., Nadler, J. & Kim, P. H. (1999). Some like it hot: The case for the emotional negotiator. In L. L. Thompson, J. M. Levine, & D. M. Messick (Eds.), *Shared cognition in organizations: The management of knowledge* (pp. 139–161). Mahwah, NJ: Erlbaum.

Thompson, L. L., Valley, K. L., & Kramer, R. M. (1995). The bittersweet feeling of success: An examination of social perception in negotiation. *Journal of Experimental Social Psychology, 31*, 467–492.

Thoresen, C. J., Kaplan, S. A., Barsky, A. P., Warren, C. R., & de Chermont, K. (2003). The affective underpinnings of job perceptions and attitudes: A meta-analytic review and integration. *Psychological Bulletin, 129, 914–945*.

Tiedens, L. Z. (2001). Anger and advancement versus sadness and subjugation: The effect of negative emotion expressions on social status conferral. *Journal of Personality and Social Psychology, 80*, 86.

Tiedens, L. Z., & Fragale, A. R. (2003). Power moves: Complimentarity in dominant and submissive nonverbal behavior. *Journal of Personality and Social Psychology, 84*, 558–568.

Tiedens, L. Z., & Linton, S. (2001). Judgment under emotional certainty and uncertainty: The effects of specific emotions on information processing. *Journal of Personality and Social Psychology, 81*, 973–988.

Tomkins, S. S., & McCarter, R. (1964). What and where are the primary affects: Some evidence for a theory. *Perceptual and Motor Skills, 18*, 119–158.

Totterdell, P. (2000). Catching moods and hitting runs: Mood linkage and subjective performance in professional sport teams. *Journal of Applied Psychology, 85*, 848–859.

Totterdell, P., Kellett, S., Teuchmann, K., & Briner, R. (1998). Evidence of mood linkage in work groups. *Journal of Personality and Social Psychology, 74*, 1504–1515.

Totterdell, P., Wall, T., Holman, D., Diamond, H., & Epitropaki, O. (2004). Affect networks: A structural analysis of the relationship between work ties and job-related affect. *Journal of Applied Psychology, 89*, 854–867.

Tsai, W. C. (2001). Determinants and consequences of employee displayed positive emotions. *Journal of Management, 27*, 497–512.

Tuncel, E., & Doucet, L. (2005). *Mixed feelings: Impact of mood diversity on confirmation bias and decision accuracy in groups.* Urbana: University of Illinois at Urbana-Champaign.

Vaes, J., Paladino, M. P., Castelli, L., Leyens, J. P., & Giovanazzi, A. (2003). On the behavioral consequences of infrahumanization: The implicit role of uniquely human emotions in intergroup relations. *Journal of Personality and Social Psychology, 85*, 1016–1034.

Van Baaren, R. B., Maddux, W. W., Chartrand, T. L., de Bouter, C. & van Knippenberg, A. (2003). It takes two to mimic: Behavioral consequences of self-construals. *Journal of Personality and Social Psychology, 84*, 1093–1102.

Van Kleef, G. A., De Dreu, C. K. W., & Manstead, A. S. R. (2004a). The interpersonal effects of anger and happiness in negotiations. *Journal of Personality and Social Psychology, 86*, 57–76.

Van Kleef, G. A., De Dreu, C. K. W., & Manstead, A. S. R. (2004b). The interpersonal effects of emotions in negotiations: A motivated information processing approach. *Journal of Personality and Social Psychology, 87*, 510–528.

Van Maanen, J., & Kunda, G. (1989). Real feelings—Emotional expression and organizational culture. *Research in Organizational Behavior, 11*, 43–103.

Vescio, T. K., Gervais, S. J., Snyder, M., & Hoover, A. (2005). Power and the creation of patronizing environments: The stereotype-based behaviors of the powerful and their effects on female performance in masculine domains. *Journal of Personality and Social Psychology, 88*, 658–672.

Vince, R. (2006). Being taken over: Managers' emotions and rationalizations during a company takeover. *Journal of Management Studies, 43*, 343–365.

Walsh, J. P. (1995). Managerial and organizational cognition: Notes from a trip down memory lane. *Organization Science, 6*, 280–321.

Watson, D., & Clark, L. A. (1984). Negative affectivity: The disposition to experience aversive emotional states. *Psychological Bulletin, 96*, 465–490.

Watson, D., Clark, L. A., & Tellegen, A. (1988). Development and validation of brief measures of positive and negative affect: The PANAS scales. *Journal of Personality and Social Psychology, 54*, 1063–1070.

Wegener, D. (1986). Transactive memory: A contemporary analysis of the group mind. In B. Mullen, & G. Goethals (Eds.), *Theories of group behavior* (pp. 185–208). New York: Springer-Verlag.

Wegener, D. M., Erber, R., & Zanakos, S. (1993). Ironic processes in the mental control of mood and mood-related thought. *Journal of Personality and Social Psychology, 65*, 1093–1104.

Weick, K. E., Sutcliffe, K. M., & Obstfeld, D. (2005). Organizing and the process of sensemaking. *Organization Science, 16*, 409–421.

Weiss, H. M. (2002). Deconstructing job satisfaction: Separating evaluations, beliefs, and affective experiences. *Human Resource Management Review, 12*, 173–194.

Weiss, H. M., Nicholas, J. P., & Daus, C. S. (1999). An examination of the joint effects of affective experiences and job beliefs on job satisfaction and variations in affective experiences over time. *Organizational Behavior and Human Decision Processes, 78,* 1–24.

Weiss, H., & Cropanzano, R. (1996). Affective events theory: A theoretical discussion of the structure, causes, and consequences of affective experiences at work. *Research in Organizational Behavior, 18,* 1–74.

Wharton, A. S. (1993). The affective consequences of service work: Managing emotions on the job. *Work and Occupations, 20,* 205–232.

Wharton, A. S., & Erickson, R. J. (1993). Managing emotions on the job and at home: Understanding the consequences of multiple emotional roles. *Academy of Management Review, 18,* 457–486.

Wilk, S. L., & Moynihan, L. M. (2005). Display rule "regulators": The relationship between supervisors and worker emotional exhaustion. *Journal of Applied Psychology, 90,* 917–927.

Williams, K. J., & Alliger, G. M. (1994). Role stressors, mood spillover, and perceptions of work-family conflict in employed parents. *Academy of Management Journal, 37,* 837–868.

Williams, K. Y., & O'Reilly, C. A. (1998). Demography and diversity in organizations: A review of 40 years of research. *Research in organizational behavior, 20,* 77–140.

Wrzesniewski, A., Dutton. J., & Debebe, G. (2003). Interpersonal sensemaking and the meaning of work. *Research in Organizational Behavior, 25,* 93–135.

Xin, K. R., & Pelled, L. H. (2003). Supervisor-subordinate conflict and perceptions of leadership behavior: A field study. *Leadership Quarterly, 14,* 25–40.

Yerkes, R. M., & Dodson, J. D. (1908). The relation of strength of stimulus to rapidity of habit formation. *Journal of Comparative Neurology and Psychology, 18,* 459–482.

Yik, M. S. M., & Russell, J. A. (1999). Interpretation of faces: A cross-cultural study of a prediction from Fridlund's theory. *Cognition & Emotion, 13,* 93–104.

Yukl, G. (1999). An evaluation of conceptual weaknesses in transformational and charismatic leadership theories. *Leadership Quarterly, 10,* 285–305.

Zajonc, R. B. (1998). Emotions. In D. T. Gilbert, S. T. Fiske, & G. Lindzey (Eds.), *The handbook of social psychology* (4th ed., Vol. 1, pp. 591–632). Boston: McGraw-Hill.

8
Leadership Research in Healthcare
A Review and Roadmap

MATTIA J. GILMARTIN AND THOMAS A. D'AUNNO

INSEAD Healthcare Management Initiative

Abstract

This chapter's purpose is to advance leadership research in the healthcare field in particular and in organizational studies more broadly. Based on a review of 60 empirical papers, we conclude that leadership is positively and significantly associated with individual work satisfaction, turnover, and performance. Despite these important results, however, we argue that researchers are missing opportunities to develop general leadership theory in the health sector, for example, by (a) examining the role of professionals as leaders and (b) developing understanding of the role of gender in leadership. Nonetheless, we also argue that we are not likely to advance leadership research until we address barriers to collaborative, multidisciplinary studies that develop conceptual models of leadership that makes it neither heroic nor impotent.

Introduction

In the last several years, both managers and researchers have renewed their interest in the role that leaders and leadership play in organizations. Results from a recent analysis of trends in leadership as a research topic show that from the late 1990s until 2002, leadership research accounted for 7% of all published papers in the general management literature, up from 2–3% in the 1980s and 1990s, and surpassing the 6% mark of the 1970s (Vance & Larson, 2002).

Similar to the case for the general management literature, our review shows that research on leadership in healthcare has increased significantly in recent years; 38 of 60 empirical papers we reviewed were published between 1999 and 2005. These papers address several important questions: Given the relatively strong role that the professions play in this sector, what is the relevance of leadership? In other words, to what extent, and how, does leadership matter in highly professional organizations? Do major professional groups (physicians, nurses, managers) agree on desirable competencies for leaders? Is leadership related to important aspects of organizational behavior such as staff satisfaction and turnover? Are particular leadership styles more effective and, if so, under what conditions?

Of course, one could argue that, based on prior work, current interest in leadership is misplaced. Indeed, as Podolny, Khurana, and Hill-Popper (2005) recently noted, critics of the concept of leadership claim both that it has been too loosely defined to be useful and that individuals, including leaders, account for very little variance in organizational performance. In fact, the dominant organizational theories of the past 30 years (resource dependence, population ecology, institutional theory, transaction cost theory) assign no role to leadership.

We agree that researchers and managers may be disappointed if they expect leaders to have a significant impact at the organizational level of analysis, particularly on organizations' financial performance. Following Podolny and colleagues (2005), we argue, however, that leadership may make a significant difference at the individual and group levels of analysis. Leaders can engage in a range of behaviors that affect individual and team performance, and prior studies show good support for this view (e.g., Hackman, 2002; Pfeffer & Davis-Blake, 1986). The literature we review later also supports this view.

Thus, the time seems right to assess the current state of knowledge about leadership in the health sector. This chapter's purpose is to advance leadership research in the healthcare field in particular and in organizational studies more broadly. We aim to develop a roadmap for future research that builds on strengths and weaknesses in the literature to date. To achieve this goal, we analyze results from empirical work in the health sector as well as discuss key issues in theory and methods.

Why Study Leadership in the Healthcare Industry?

We argue that healthcare is an especially useful and important sector in which to encourage and conduct leadership research. In many nations, healthcare is the single largest industry. For example, in the United Kingdom, the National Health Service employs more than one million people, making it the largest employer in the United Kingdom. Similarly, the healthcare industry accounts for about 15% of the U.S. gross domestic product, easily making it the largest part of the U.S. economy. Moreover, the performance of healthcare and public health organizations is critical to promoting societal well-being; in turn, healthy societies are more productive societies (Sachs, 2005). In short, one could argue that health and healthcare are so important in the modern world that advancing knowledge about effective leadership in this sector is worthwhile in and of itself.

But, advancing understanding of effective leadership in the health sector is only part of this chapter's motivation. We also argue that managers' responses to challenges in the health sector provide excellent opportunities for studies that can advance general theories of leadership. Nonetheless, researchers historically have been reluctant to work in this sector due to perceptions that it is too idiosyncratic to support the development of general theory. More recently, however, several important papers have shown that empirical work in healthcare clearly can advance organizational theory (e.g., Arndt & Bigelow, 2005; Human & Provan, 2000; Scott, Reuf, Mendel, & Caronna, 2000; Westphal, Gulati, & Shortell, 1997).

We take the position that both arguments in this debate have merit. On the one hand, we agree that the healthcare sector is not so idiosyncratic as to rule out or limit its usefulness as a field in which to test and develop general social science theories. Enough common ground exists between the healthcare sector and other sectors to make it possible to develop general models of organizational behavior. For example, there is increasing pressure for cost-efficiency in healthcare systems around the world, and such pressures make the health sector more like other industries (e.g., Kimberly, de Pouvourville, & D'Aunno, in press).

On the other hand, we argue that there are some important ways in which the health sector differs from other sectors, and researchers need to take into account these differences (Ramanujam & Rousseau, in press). Specifically, perhaps more than in other sectors, managers in healthcare face inconsistent or conflicting external demands (D'Aunno, Sutton, & Price, 1991). Many of these demands stem from the relatively strong, but fragmented, institutional forces and increasingly strong market forces that healthcare organizations face (D'Aunno, Succi, & Alexander, 2000). As just noted, societies around the world are pressuring healthcare providers to reduce costs but, at the same time, stakeholders are expecting improvements in both the quality of, and access to, services.

Second, the healthcare sector is more technology-intensive than many other sectors. As a result, healthcare managers often face challenges that stem from advances in technology. These advances, ranging from new biotechnologies to complex information systems (e.g., electronic patient records), exacerbate tensions in balancing cost, quality, and access to services. Advances in anticancer treatments, for example, raise questions about affordability and access to them.

Third, a distinctive challenge for the sector is that, even with the aid of advanced technology, there remains a great deal of uncertainty in the work of healthcare organizations and their members. At base, healthcare is a human service; this entails great variability in the nature of the "inputs" and uncertain means-ends relationships in production, that, in turn, result in problems for defining and measuring organizational outcomes (Hasenfeld, 1983).

Finally, managers in the health sector must deal with powerful professionals, especially physicians, who continue to dominate many aspects of day-to-day work in healthcare organizations. Though professionals of all types have notoriously ambivalent relationships with organizations, medicine is probably the most powerful of all the professions and is widely viewed as the preeminent profession.

Of course, few organizations and industries don't experience leadership challenges that stem from powerful professionals in the workplace; competing goals and external demands; technological advances coupled with uncertainty; and problems defining performance criteria. However, the health sector sometimes lies at the extreme end of continua that characterize organizational fields, particularly in the extent to which professionals hold power and in the strength of institutional forces. Further, the combination of ways in which healthcare differs from other sectors may seem to make it unique.

In sum, the health sector is especially useful as a field to develop leadership theory not because it is essentially the same as other sectors, but because it both shares many characteristics with other sectors, and differs in the degree to which these characteristics are manifested. This means that models developed in the general literature may sometimes need to be adapted for use in healthcare. However, it also means that the health sector yields particular opportunities to advance leadership theory. To take two prominent examples that we discuss in more detail later, compared to other empirical settings, healthcare offers opportunities to (a) examine the role of leadership in professional organizations and professionals as leaders (Montgomery, 2001); and (b) develop understanding of the role of gender in leadership because there is a wide range of (sometimes atypical) patterns of gender relationships—for example, women leading women, and women leading mixed groups of followers in which women are the majority.

Unfortunately, and perhaps not surprisingly, our review reveals less than optimal cross-fertilization among leadership researchers. As discussed in more detail later in this chapter, researchers interested in developing general theories of leadership, and specialists interested in developing knowledge about healthcare organizations, have missed opportunities to promote their work by failing to take into account theories, concepts, and empirical results that originate in each camp. We seek to stimulate studies that take full advantage of what generalists and specialists have to offer, bridging the two groups.

Data and Method

We examined research on leadership in healthcare for the period 1989–2005. We focus on this period because previous reviews have examined earlier work (Altieri & Elgin, 1994; Vance & Larson, 2002). Further, in this period, environmental turbulence in the health sector increased due to changes, for example, in service payment, workforce shortages, and quality and safety concerns; these changes promoted interest in leaders' effectiveness.

We conducted searches of the EBSCO, Business Source Premier, CINAHL, and MEDLINE electronic databases using the combinations of the terms *leadership, leadership effectiveness, leadership research and leadership competencies* paired with *healthcare, healthcare professionals, physician(s), and nurse(s)(ing)* to generate an initial set of citations. This search strategy produced over 1,000 citations. We excluded the great majority of this published work because it did not consist of systematic empirical studies. More specifically, we excluded papers that were anecdotal accounts; descriptive articles introducing leadership concepts to clinical professionals; or position statements discussing the role of leadership in relation to improving clinical care, an individual's status in the profession, or organizational survival.

To learn more about these excluded papers, we read a sample of them and found some interesting similarities and differences with the literature reviewed later. For the most part, the excluded and reviewed papers focus on similar topics. Much overlap exists in concerns about what effective leadership is; what competencies are needed for effective leadership; what roles leaders should play in organizations; and how individuals can develop (or not develop) into leaders. What distinguishes the papers that we did not review is their promotion of strong leaders, and often heroic ones, including celebrity CEOs.

Further, we limited our search to empirical studies in healthcare settings, published in English, using leadership as a predictor variable. We also reviewed the table of contents of key nursing, healthcare, and general management journals likely to publish leadership research. Specifically, we examined the *Journal of Nursing Administration, Nursing Research, Medical Care Research and Review, Healthcare Management Review, Health Services Management Research, Leadership Quarterly, Academy of Management Journal, Journal of Organizational Behavior,* and *Journal of Management* to identify additional studies not captured in our electronic search. We identified 54 studies with this search method. We reviewed bibliographies to identify an additional six studies. Sixty studies met our review criteria.

Summary of the Published Research

Based on our reading of the papers, we identified four major themes or categories of research and we organize the discussion later around these four: (a) transformational and transactional leadership; (b) leadership and nurse job satisfaction, retention, and performance; (c) leader effectiveness; and (d) leadership-development programs. Of course, there are papers that fit in more than one of these categories, but they nonetheless provide a useful summary of major research topics.

Transformational and Transactional Leadership (14 Studies)

Papers focusing on transformational and transactional leadership theory comprise the largest subset of research on leadership in healthcare. Important aspects of these studies (research design, sample, conceptual foundation) are presented in Appendix 8.1. The majority of these studies were conducted in hospital settings using data from nurse managers and staff nurses. Five studies tested theory or hypotheses; in contrast, six studies were descriptive and did not test hypotheses.

We have several observations about these studies. First, results from several studies that examined key outcomes of transformational leadership show that it is positively and significantly associated with staff job satisfaction (Gellis, 2001; Medley & Larochelle, 1995; Morrison, Jones, & Fuller, 1997); extra effort (Dunham-Taylor, 2000; Gellis, 2001); perceived unit performance (Stordeur, Vandenberghe, & D'hoore, 2000); a supportive organizational climate (Corrigan, Diwan, Campion, & Rashid, 2002; Dunham-Taylor, 2000); organizational commitment; intent to stay; and staff retention (Force, 2005; Leach, 2005; McDaniel & Wolf, 1992).

Interestingly, it appears that the educational level of staff members is related to their perceptions of leadership effectiveness (Morrison et al., 1997). The amount of variance that leadership style accounted for was much greater for less-well-educated staff members (e.g., nursing assistants, clerks, and secretaries) than for more-well-educated staff; leadership appears to matter more for nonprofessionals than professionals.

Second, results from four studies, all conducted in hospital settings, support Bass' (1985) proposition that transformational leadership cascades across organizational levels. Notably, all four studies found that managers higher in the hierarchy demonstrated more transformational behaviors than those lower in the hierarchy (Hamlin, 2002; Leach, 2005; McDaniel & Wolf, 1992; Stordeur et al., 2000).

Third, a research team in the United Kingdom has challenged the applicability of Burns' (1978) and Bass' (1985) models of transactional and transformational leadership to healthcare settings because these models were developed in the United States, and in Fortune 500 companies and military organizations (Alimo-Metcalf & Alban-Metcalf, 2001; Hamlin, 2002). These researchers developed a new conceptual model of transformational leadership and, to support the model, developed an instrument to assess leadership behaviors. Drawing on a sample of men and women middle-, senior-, and top-level managers working for the U.K. government and National Health Service, the researchers established the reliability and validity of a nine-factor transformational leadership questionnaire (e.g., empowers others and develops their potential; decisiveness; and accessible and approachable). This study did not, however, compare Bass and Avolio's MLQ to the new instrument, nor has any published work examined relationships between the model's leadership behaviors and outcomes.

Fourth, despite challenges to the use of Bass' transformational leadership model in healthcare organizations, results from the papers we reviewed show that this model applies well to healthcare settings. In fact, results from a meta-analysis by Lowe, Kroeek, and Sivasubramanian (1996) showed that leaders in nonprofit organizations were more likely to use transformational leadership styles than leaders in for-profit organizations.

Nonetheless, one interesting difference is that, in nine studies involving healthcare professionals, transformational leadership was associated with leaders' use of contingent reward systems, whereas in non-healthcare studies the use of such systems is linked to a transactional leadership style. In other words, the psychometric properties of the contingent reward scale of the MLQ (Bass & Avolio, 1985) behave differently in samples of healthcare professionals (Gellis, 2001; Medley & Larochelle, 1995; Xirasagar, Samuels, & Stoskopf, 2005). Specifically, results from Lowe and colleagues' (1996) meta-analysis showed that the use of contingent reward scale was highly correlated with the transformational leadership factor of the MLQ (e.g., charisma and contingent reward = .70; based on nine studies).

To develop understanding of the underlying factor structure of the MLQ in healthcare settings, Garman, Davis-Lenane, and Corrigan (2003) examined relationships among the four different leadership styles that the MLQ assesses: active and passive forms of management-by-exception, transformational, transactional, and laissez-faire. Much like the results of Lowe and colleagues' (1996) report, Garman and colleagues' results showed a robust relationship between measures of transformational leadership and contingent reward. These authors suggested that participants perceive the use of contingent rewards as transformational behaviors because promotions, raises, or other monetary inducements to participate in organizational goal-achievement activities, have not been a traditional part of managers' repertoires in healthcare settings.

Finally, results from an innovative study (Kan & Parry, 2004) indicated that data from "paper-and-pencil" assessments of leadership styles and behavior (e.g., the MLQ) should be viewed cautiously. This study examined nurse managers who had high scores on the MLQ transformational style scale, but whose peers and subordinates perceived them to be ineffective leaders of organizational change. The study results suggest that leadership style was only one important factor in successful organizational change; organizational structure and culture, particularly resistance to change on the part of staff members, also mattered a great deal.

Summary. Studies in healthcare provide relatively strong support for transformational leadership theory. Nonetheless, there appear to be two context-specific results that suggest opportunities for theory development. First, empirical results suggest that what it means to be a transformational leader may depend on followers' expectations and context-specific norms. In healthcare, leaders typically have not given rewards contingent on performance, relying instead on staff members' professionalism to motivate them. Thus, as noted earlier, leaders who use contingent rewards are more likely to be seen as "path-breaking" because they do not conform to followers' expectations of how leaders should behave (Garman et al., 2003). Second, results show that professional staff members do not respond to transformational leadership as well as less-well-educated staff. Taken together, these results suggest that healthcare is a context in which leadership theory might be developed to better take into account followers' expectations, and to understand how and why professionals respond (or not) to different leadership styles.

Leadership and Nurse Job Satisfaction, Retention and Job Performance (12 Studies)

Similar to the research on transformational and transactional leadership, this set of studies examines links between manager's leadership styles and the outcomes of job performance, job satisfaction, and turnover. Notably, most of the participants in these studies are nurses. We found only two studies that examined relationships among leaders' behaviors and job satisfaction among health professionals other than nurses (e.g., social workers and mental-health teams) (Corrigan et al., 2002; Gellis, 2001). Key characteristics of these studies are presented in Appendix 8.2.

The major finding of this work is that there is a consistent link between manager's leadership style and staff job satisfaction, retention, and organizational commitment. More specifically, nurses desire that managers use participative (Boyle, Bott, Hansen, Woods, & Taunton, 1999; Lucas, 1991; Upenieks, 2003a), facilitative (Ingersoll, Schultz, Hoffart, & Ryan, 1996), and emotionally intelligent (McNeese-Smith, 1995) leadership styles. Managers' use of these leadership styles has been empirically linked to staff perceptions of workgroup cohesion, reduced work stress, empowerment over practice decisions, and self-efficacy—which, in turn, lead to job satisfaction and retention. Similarly, results from recent work show that units with strong leaders are more likely to have better outcomes such as lower turnover rates of newly hired staff, and recruitment of highly skilled staff (Capuano, Bokovoy, Hitchings, & Houser, 2005).

These studies are a subset of the larger literature on nurse job satisfaction and retention. Their research methods are the most sophisticated of the studies we reviewed, using path analysis models to assess relationships among the variables of interest. These well-executed studies test established leadership and management theories (e.g., Kouzes and Posner's Leadership Behaviors (1993), Kanter's Theory of Structural Empowerment (1993), and Structural Contingency Model (Charns & Tewksbury, 1993), using established instruments (e.g., Price and Muller Job Satisfaction Scale (1986); Leadership Practices Inventory (Kouzes & Posner, 1993); and the Index of Work Satisfaction (Slavitt, Stamps, Piedmont, & Hasse, 1986).

Summary. Results from these studies show relatively strong support for a variety of conceptual models that share an emphasis on using what can generally be termed participative and person-focused leadership styles. Further, results from these studies are convincing because they use strong research methods. Nonetheless, we see missed opportunity for theory development because conceptual models in this work are not linked either to the larger literature on the sociology of professions or to the more focused literature on the recruitment and retention of professionals working in organizational settings (e.g., Kraatz & Moore, 2002).

One important reason for this missed opportunity may be that healthcare researchers, policymakers, and practitioners face a pressing need to understand the causes of nursing shortages and to develop management actions to overcome them, and, as a result, theory-development has taken a "backseat" in this work. Thus, this may be an area where collaboration between healthcare and non-healthcare researchers would be useful so that studies can advance understanding of the competition for, and recruitment and retention of, professionals in general.

Leadership Effectiveness (9 Studies)

This set of studies focuses on leader effectiveness (see Appendix 8.3). Because of their diverse empirical contexts and methods, these studies are difficult to characterize. Half of the papers rely heavily on qualitative methods to examine attributes, behaviors, and values of effective leaders (Alexander, Comfort, Weiner, & Bogue, 2001; Edmondson, 2003; Upenieks 2002, 2003b). The remaining studies examine leaders' effectiveness as a function of gender, professional group (physician managers and general managers), and organizational context (public and private ownership).

Despite the qualitative studies' diverse empirical settings, there is convergence in their results concerning the attributes of effective leaders, who are characterized as flexible and collaborative in their approach; who share their power with other staff members or organizations; and who use their personal values or visions to promote high standards of performance. Unfortunately, these studies examine leadership effectiveness within highly specialized settings using small samples, thus limiting the extent to which we can generalize from them. Examples of these empirical settings include collaborative community health partnerships (Alexander et al., 2001), Magnet hospitals (Upenieks, 2002, 2003b), operating-room teams in cardiac surgery (Edmondson, 2003), and education administrators (Mansen, 1993; Womack, 1996).

Summary. Research on leadership effectiveness in healthcare supports relatively well-established theories that emphasize the importance of leaders who provide vision and performance standards, while promoting participation and being flexible in their approach. Again, there is less emphasis in these studies on theory development. Nonetheless, some studies in this set break new ground. Edmondson (2003) showed how leaders can coach team members to raise concerns within the team and to discuss issues across organizational boundaries to promote team performance. The study identifies specific mechanisms and leader behaviors (e.g., mitigating status and power differentials within a surgical operating team) that affect team-level performance. Alexander and colleagues (2001) showed how leaders can affect outcomes beyond the individual and group levels (e.g., the outcomes of multiorganizational collaboration), and, as we discuss later, in leadership research generally this is relatively rare (Yammarino, Dionne, Chun, & Dansereau, 2005).

Leadership Development: Roles, Educational Preparation, Curricula and Program Evaluation (18 Studies)

The final set of studies focuses on identifying skills for effective leaders and educational programs to develop them. The study of physicians' leadership competencies is relatively new to this literature; we reviewed papers that discuss and evaluate programs for developing physician leaders (Leslie et al., 2005; McAlearney, Fisher, Heiser, Robbins, & Kelleher, 2005a; McKenna, Gartland, & Pugno, 2004). Appendix 8.4 presents key characteristics of these papers.

Several themes are prominent in these papers. First, across the three disciplines of nursing management, public health, and health-services management, there is agreement on competencies in six areas for effective leadership. These areas are (a) interpersonal relationships, (b) communication, (c) finance and business acumen, (d) clinical knowledge, (e) collaboration and team building, (f) change management, and (g) quality improvement. This convergence is based on studies that were conducted to identify skills that should be required for leaders; these studies use survey data from practitioners, including assessments of their job descriptions (Brown & McCool, 1987; Dienemann & Schaffer, 1993; Guo, 2003; Helfand, Cherlin, & Bradley, 2005; Liang, Renard, Robinson, & Richards, 1993; Scoble & Russell, 2003; Williams & Ewell, 1996). Based on this work, two papers propose masters-degree curricula to develop better alignment between managers' academic preparation and the realities of their roles (Dienemann & Schaffer, 1993; Russell & Scoble, 2003).

Second, a handful of studies provide empirical support for the argument that managers with advanced education are more effective in leadership roles (Helfand et al, 2005; Kleinman, 2003; Sanford, 1994; Scoble & Russell, 2003). This issue has been contentious, however, featuring a debate about the relative strengths and weaknesses of advanced education (e.g., the MBA degree or Master's degree) for leadership roles (Dienemann & Schaffer, 1993; Klienman, 2003; Sanford, 1994; Scoble & Russell, 2003). The nursing literature places more emphasis than the other disciplines on the completion of formal education as a prerequisite for managerial and leadership roles.

The empirical studies also show that new managers value different competencies than more experienced managers. Specifically, new nurse managers value clinical and communication skills more than established managers who place more value on negotiation skills and business-and-management knowledge (Dienemann & Shaffer, 1993; Klienman, 2003).

Third, results are mixed from analyses of participants' use of the skills taught in executive education and training programs, and changes in their leadership ability. In contrast, four papers report positive results from participants' self-ratings of learning from executive education programs (Leslie et al., 2005; McAlearney et al., 2005a; Umble et al., 2005; Wolf, 1996).

These studies also report that the majority of participants were highly satisfied with the content of their programs. More recently, several authors (Kleinman, 2003; McAlearney et al., 2005a, in press; McKenna et al., 2004) have advocated focused, work-based executive education programs as a pragmatic method to develop leadership skills among practicing and aspiring managers.

Summary. Some overarching methods and conceptual issues are worth noting. First, the majority of the leadership-skill and education surveys are based on convenience samples of relatively small sizes (a low of 10 participants and a high of 125; see Appendix 8.4). This limits the generalizability of their results concerning both identified skills and proposed curriculum changes.

Second, the proposed leadership competencies and development programs are either atheoretical, on the one hand, or are based on well-known management and leadership models, such as the work of Mintzberg (1973), Hershey and Blanchard (1988), Kotter (1995), and Quinn (1996), on the other hand. Much like the research cited earlier, existing models were tested to determine the extent to which they hold in healthcare settings; little effort was made to advance knowledge by developing models.

Mapping Healthcare Leadership and General Leadership Research

One goal of this review is to assess the extent to which researchers studying leadership generally and those who are focusing on healthcare settings are examining the same questions, and to explore opportunities for the two communities to inform each other. We draw in part on Lowe and Gardner's (2001) review of a decade of studies published in *Leadership Quarterly* and previous reviews of the leadership literature in healthcare (Altieri & Elgin, 1994; Vance & Larson, 2002) to highlight areas in which the two literatures overlap and areas in which they diverge.

Points of Convergence

The most important point of convergence between the two literatures is that, similar to the general literature (Lowe & Gardner, 2001), transformational and transactional leadership theory is the dominant conceptual perspective in healthcare research. McDaniel and Wolf (1992) first introduced Bass' (1985) transformational leadership model into nursing-management research and, as noted earlier, it has been tested on samples of leaders in nursing, medicine, mental health, and social work. Notably, healthcare researchers have favored the models advanced by Bass and Burns (1978) over other neocharismatic theories. More recently, studies have linked transformational leadership behaviors with unit goal achievement and change management (Kan & Parry, 2004; Xirasagar et al., 2005).

Points of Divergence

There is a puzzling lack of correspondence between the healthcare and general literatures when it comes to leader-member exchange theory (Dansereau, Graen, & Haga, 1975; LMX), which has been prominent in the latter (Gerstner & Day, 1997), but totally absent in the former. One possible explanation is that healthcare professionals and researchers do not accept the contrast between in-groups and out-groups, which is central to LMX theory. In other words, it seems "unprofessional" that leaders would favor some followers more than others. Nurses in particular, who comprise the great majority of participants in healthcare leadership studies, have an egalitarian model of professional behavior.

A second point of divergence is that, in recent years, general leadership researchers have developed and tested a number of theories that fall under the broad heading of "emotional intelligence" (Goleman, 1995). These theories advance understanding of leaders' ability to attend to individuals' emotions and they focus on the outcomes of these behaviors for individuals' well-being and performance (Huy, 1999; Rafaeli & Sutton, 1987).

In contrast, emotional intelligence is a relatively neglected area of leadership research in healthcare settings. That few studies test theories of emotionally intelligent leadership in healthcare is surprising given the personal connection between healthcare professionals and patients, and the recent strategic emphasis on healthcare organizations as service providers (Eisenberg, 1997; Scott & Aiken, 1995).

We found only four studies that examined emotional intelligence or leaders' roles in managing emotions in the workplace (Cummings, 2004; Cummings, Hayduk, & Estabrooks, 2005; McNeese-Smith, 1995; Skinner & Spurgeon, 2005). Results from these studies show that emotionally intelligent, person-oriented leaders had more satisfied and committed staff members, who attended well to patient-care needs, even when they were emotionally exhausted; participants also reported fewer negative effects of organizational restructuring.

Closely related to the theories of transformational, charismatic, and emotionally intelligent leadership are emerging perspectives on positive organizational behavior (Cameron, Dutton, & Quinn, 2003; Roberts, 2006) and authentic leadership (Avolio & Gardner, 2005). Nascent theories of authentic leadership focus on how individuals draw on their experiences, beliefs, emotions, preferences, and thoughts, and use these aspects of deep self-awareness to engage followers and to shape organizational environments (Erickson, 1995; Shamir & Eilam, 2005).

Nurse researchers seem to be examining a similar leadership phenomenon, albeit from a different perspective and motivation. Arguing that existing leadership theories are not applicable to healthcare settings, some nurse researchers have conducted qualitative studies that distinguish effective and ineffective leaders on the dimensions of personal experiences, values, beliefs, and attributes (Upenieks, 2002, 2003b). This opportunity for collaboration between the general and healthcare leadership fields can advance theories of authentic leadership.

On the one hand, nurse researchers can contribute to developing theories of authentic leadership by adopting conceptual perspectives that are informed by the new work. On the other hand, healthcare organizations offer an empirical testing ground in which strong social and professional values motivate leaders and followers (Gilmartin & Freeman, 2002). These settings may be particularly useful for studies of authentic leadership—including, for example, studies that measure this construct and examine mechanisms involved in authentic leadership.

Finally, healthcare researchers are reviving the study of situational leadership, while, in the general leadership literature, trait, behavioral, and contingency approaches have waned in popularity over the last decade (Lowe & Gardner, 2001). Specifically, Laschinger and colleagues (1994, 1997, 1999; Manojlovich, 2005a, b; Patrick & Laschinger, 2006) developed a research program that takes healthcare leadership research in a promising new direction by examining situational variables as explanatory factors in models of leadership effectiveness. Built on Kanter's Theory of Structural Empowerment (1993), this research program examines situational variables in organizational contexts (e.g., position power, nature of the environment, task technology, and resources) and a range of staff and client outcomes (e.g., burnout, emotional exhaustion, and clinical errors). This work has developed knowledge about how leaders shape work environments that, in turn, promote or inhibit staff and organizational performance.

Discussion

We divide our discussion into three sections. These are (a) key conceptual issues facing leadership research in healthcare (and more generally), (b) specific contributions that leadership research in healthcare can make, and (c) notes concerning research methods.

Key Conceptual Issues

Despite progress in understanding leadership and its effects in the health sector, we argue that there remains a pressing need for a careful conceptualization of leadership that delimits what leaders are more or less likely to achieve, and specifies mechanisms by which leaders can affect unit or organizational-level behavior (perhaps through secondary or indirect means). We argue that this also is true for the general leadership literature (House & Aditya, 1997; House & Baetz, 1979; Lowe & Gardner, 2001; Yukl, 1989). Yukl (1989) captured this challenge quite well: "an accurate conception of leadership importance lies between the two extremes of heroic leader and impotent figurehead" (p. 277).

Researchers and practitioners are likely to be disappointed to the extent that they rely on expansive conceptual approaches that explicitly or implicitly assume that leadership matters significantly and consistently in organizations' financial performance or effectiveness. For example, defining leaders as individuals who develop and implement strategies to improve organizational performance in the face of difficult market and institutional conditions does not seem realistic; there is too much empirical evidence to the contrary (Pfeffer, 1977). The search for heroic leaders probably reflects societies' (and researchers') continuing romance with leadership more than anything else (Mendl, Ehrlich, & Dukerich, 1985; Podolny et al., 2005).

Searching for a Middle Ground: Theorizing Leadership and Levels of Analysis

Our pessimism about expansive definitions of leadership does not mean that conceptual and empirical work should be limited to examining the effects of leadership on individual and team-level performance, however. In fact, given the positive results reviewed earlier, continuing work in these areas may be less fruitful than it has been. Rather, we propose that it may be useful to search for a middle ground by considering how the effects of leadership can extend beyond individuals and groups, not necessarily directly, but perhaps indirectly (Lowe & Gardner, 2001). In other words, the effects of leadership may extend across levels of analysis and, under some conditions, affect organizational-level behavior and characteristics, including, for example, organizational culture and climate.

Yammarino and colleagues (2005) recently reviewed the general leadership literature and came to a similar conclusion. Their analysis specifically examined how the leadership literature deals with multilevel conceptual models, issues, and methods. Perhaps not surprisingly, they found that 70% of the papers they examined focused only on individual-level analyses. The vast majority of papers do not even examine leader-follower interaction, let alone the context in which such interaction occurs. We certainly support their conclusion that researchers should place a higher priority on developing conceptual models of leadership that take into account organizational contexts and multiple levels of analysis (see Altieri & Elgin, 1994; House & Aditya, 1997; Vance & Larson, 2002).

For example, one line of work that may be useful is to examine how leaders can affect unit and organizational-level performance by promoting shared emotions across individuals and groups. Perhaps effective leaders extend their influence beyond individuals by promoting emotional contagion and the diffusion of shared emotions in ways that affect group, unit, and organizational performance (e.g., Barsade, 2002; Huy, 1999). Studies could examine the roles that leaders may play to use emotions across groups to, for example, motivate organizational change.

Podolny and colleagues (2005) proposed another important mechanism by which the effects of leadership can extend beyond the individual level of analysis. They argue that a key, neglected function of leaders is to give meaning and value to work and organizations. Classic sociological analyses of organizations (Parsons, 1971; Selznick, 1984; Weber, 1946) focused precisely on the role of leaders in giving meaning to followers and their work and organizations. Yet, with the possible exception of neocharismatic theories, this emphasis has been lost in leadership research in the past 30 years. We not only agree that the meaning-giving function of leadership—rather than its financial effects—should be a focus of study, but we also argue that by instilling a shared sense of meaning and values in organizations, leaders can extend their influence beyond the individuals with whom they directly interact and, in so doing, exert effects on multiple levels of organizational life.

Results from a few studies in the healthcare sector show support for this view by indicating that a leader's style is related to organizational climate and culture. For example, Stordeur and colleagues (2000) reported that leaders' MLQ ratings varied by hospital, and Corrigan and colleagues (2002) reported that leaders who perceived themselves as having a transformational style also saw their organizations as transformational and cohesive. And, Spence-Laschinger's research, cited earlier, examined the role of organizational contextual factors, as well as the contribution of leadership, to individual-level outcomes. Nonetheless, these studies are only a beginning and they give relatively little attention to relationships between leaders and the contexts in which they work.

Thus, in leadership research generally, more work is needed to untangle causal relationships, if any, between leaders' behaviors and the organizational contexts they operate. Several questions need to be addressed, including to what extent do leaders create environments that contribute to, or hinder, organizational success? Or, to what extent do organizations attract, recruit and select leaders to match their culture, thus promoting or hindering their success? To what extent, and how often, do leaders change organizational culture or climate or do leaders mainly act to reinforce dominant values, norms, and behaviors (Kraatz & Moore, 2002)?

Challenges in finding the middle ground in conceptualizing leadership and its effects. Several very useful reviews of the general leadership literature have been published over the past 6 decades, including Stogdill (1948, 1974), House and Baetz (1979), Yukl (1989), House and Aditya (1997), and Lowe and Gardner (2001). One major, common theme in this work is the challenge of defining leadership precisely, distinguishing it from other relevant concepts (e.g., social influence), and clarifying assumptions about the importance of leadership in organizational life. Stogdill found, for example, 72 definitions of leadership published between 1902 and 1967.

Lowe and Gardner's (2001) more recent review showed that though researchers have given much less attention in the past decade to defining leadership per se, they are clearly still using a wide variety of leadership theories and models. In fact, all reviews of the leadership literature typically devote the great majority of their attention to studies that elaborate and test various individual-level models of leadership (e.g., contingency theories, trait theory, behavioral theories, neocharismatic theories). Nonetheless, despite this continuing lack of consensus on definitions and theories, these reviews show steadily mounting evidence that leadership can matter significantly in a range of individual and group-level outcomes, including job satisfaction, turnover, and performance.

A second major theme that these reviews have emphasized increasingly since the late 1970s is the need to understand the organizational context (defined broadly to include organizational environments) in which leadership emerges; how organizational contexts influence the leaders' behaviors and vice versa; and how, if at all, leaders can influence organizational strategy and performance. House and Aditya (1997) captured this theme well: "A problem with the current study of leadership is that it continues to focus excessively on superior-subordinate relationships to the exclusion of several functions that leaders perform and to the exclusion of organizational and environmental variables that are crucial to effective leadership performance" (p. 46).

We believe that progress on the particular challenges of defining leadership and examining its relationships with organizational context and performance has been relatively slow for at least three major reasons, one of which pushes research toward expansive views of leadership and two that make studies focus too narrowly and conservatively on individual-level effects.

First, the romance of leadership makes it difficult both to define leadership precisely and to focus attention on plausible effects that leaders can have on followers and organizations. Put simply, there is so much "hype" surrounding leadership that it is tempting to believe that leaders can do more than they actually can. We live in the age of celebrity CEOs such as Jack Welch and Carlos Ghosn. Consider, for example, that Amazon.com currently lists 42,829 books on leadership and this number has increased substantially in the last year. In this climate, one might expect varied and expansive definitions of leadership to flourish.

Second, we argue that there is a counterbalancing force to the romance of leadership: when it comes to publishing in scholarly journals, researchers are pragmatic and "trim their sails." The vast majority of published leadership studies use survey data from individuals (let alone dyads or teams) because such studies are feasible; workforce surveys that focus on individuals allow us to examine, and control for, relevant variables with a minimum of cost.

Perhaps this is why current research on leadership in healthcare tends to conflate management and leadership roles. That is, many studies in healthcare suffer from using the term "leadership" when they are actually studying individuals who simply occupy formal management positions. Similarly, Terry (1995), Podolny and colleagues (2005), and Bedeian and Hunt (2006), among others, question if researchers in the general literature are actually examining managers, rather than leaders.

Nursing research in particular continues to use data from individuals in formal managerial roles for samples of "leaders" and staff nurses for samples of "followers" (see Altieri & Elgin, 1994). Studies that examine leadership behaviors of physicians and allied health professionals do somewhat better because they tend to use participants in both formal and informal leadership roles, but this literature is nascent. For this reason and others discussed later, we want to strongly emphasize the need for more leadership studies of non-nurses, especially physicians, in the healthcare field.

As our review makes clear, to date the great majority of leadership studies in healthcare focus on nurses. There are many possible reasons for this, including the fact that there exists a branch of nursing that focuses explicitly on management research (see the *Journal of Nursing Administration*) and that, as noted earlier, there are serious, recurrent nursing shortages in the United States that fuel demand for leadership studies. But, we suspect that, consistent with our argument earlier, the ease of studying nurses as "leaders" is also driving the focus on them.

A third major barrier to improving conceptual models of leadership is that our field puts increasing pressure on researchers to specialize and we tend to reward individual scholarly contributions rather than team work. In particular, progress on conducting research that crosses levels of analysis continues to be limited by the disciplinary gap between psychologists, who have traditionally dominated the study of leadership, viewing it from individual and group-level perspectives, and sociologists, who have dominated studies of organizations and organizational contexts.

Yet, it is likely to take research teams using multiple conceptual approaches to advance leadership research. For example, researchers who specialize in leadership may not be familiar with literature on organizational culture; to the extent that this is true, we will find few studies that show how leaders can influence organizational culture. An example of a study that overcomes many of these barriers is the Project Globe study that focuses on cross-cultural leadership (Javidan & House, 2002). The study involves 170 researchers working in 62 nations.

Of course, not only leadership researchers, but the field of management research as a whole, face pressures to work individually, in discipline-defined models, and to tackle problems that will result in quick, publishable, and "safe" papers. Indeed, management researchers may take some lessons from the field of leadership. Here is an area that has had enormous attention and is clearly relevant to society, organizations, and managers and, yet, it is a field that has had difficulty making as much progress as its advocates would like.

Using Healthcare to Advance Leadership Theory: Two Examples

In the introduction, we argued that studies in the health sector could advance leadership research in two prominent areas: the role of leadership in professional organizations and professionals as leaders, and the role of gender in leadership. We begin by discussing general observations about the intersection of leadership and healthcare and then turn to the examples of gender and professionals.

Healthcare Specific Versus General Models of Leadership

We advocate that researchers attempt to strike a balance between developing healthcare-specific models of leadership and models that use the particular characteristics of the health sector (e.g., powerful professions, gender mix) as opportunities to develop general theory. Many authors of papers we reviewed are concerned that models of leadership developed in non-healthcare settings do not apply to complex and professional healthcare organizations. As discussed in the introduction, we are sympathetic to this concern. McAlearney (2005b; in press), Garman, Tyler, and Darnall (2004), Helfand and colleagues (2005), and Upenieks (2002; 2003b) provided striking examples of the complex nature of management practice and the systemic barriers that have limited leaders' effectiveness in healthcare settings.

Nonetheless, we do not agree that the practice of leadership and management is so radically different in healthcare that only context-specific models will work. Leaders in other industries face complex challenges in achieving organizational goals. The results from the papers we reviewed support our view. Results clearly show that, with the few exceptions noted earlier, leadership models and concepts developed in the general literature work well in healthcare settings. In fact, as Gilmartin and Freeman (2002) argue, leaders and managers in healthcare need to adopt more practices from general management to improve their effectiveness.

A fruitful approach may be to develop sharper conceptualizations of leadership phenomena using healthcare settings as empirical "testing grounds." Healthcare researchers themselves have a comparative strength in their careful approach to examining leaders' behaviors, skills, and values. By describing specific behaviors, studies in the health sector may provide data that allow us to more thoroughly and accurately capture leadership phenomena than currently available theories and models.

Leadership and gender. The healthcare sector provides a comparative advantage in studies of the role of gender in leadership because, as noted earlier, there is a wider range of patterns of gender relationships between leaders and followers. Indeed, gender effects seem to differ in healthcare compared to other sectors. For example, women in non-healthcare organizations tend to rate their own leadership qualities and effectiveness less highly than men, but in healthcare organizations, this difference either disappears or is less pronounced (Borman, 1993; Murray et al., 1998; Ostroff, Atwater, & Feinberg, 2004; Webster, Grusky, Podus, & Young, 1999).

It is noteworthy that the majority of the participants in these healthcare studies are women who are leading women. And, though there remains the "glass ceiling" phenomenon within senior management teams in healthcare, it is not as pronounced as in other industries (Foundation of the American College of Healthcare Executives, 2006; Weil & Kimball, 1996). Under such circumstances, do gender effects diminish, disappear, or reverse themselves (Borman, 1993; Upenieks, 2002)? If so, why? Do women leaders perceive themselves and their skills differently when leading women-dominated workforces (Helfand et al., 2005; Murray et al., 1998; Sanford, 1994)?

Similarly, because they often are women-dominated settings, healthcare organizations also provide a useful context to advance understanding of variations in leaders' behavior that are now attributed to gender (Eagly & Carli, 2003). Do women use approaches or techniques to lead others in healthcare settings that differ from non-healthcare organizational contexts (Carroll, 2005; Dunham-Taylor, 2000; Medley & Larochelle, 1995; Webster et al., 1999)? Conversely, studies can focus on male leaders in women-dominated settings, and address questions about how men's leadership behavior and effectiveness vary in such contexts.

Further, much of the non-healthcare research on gender and leadership has been conducted in laboratory settings with samples of undergraduate students

(Eagly, Johannesen-Schmidt & van Engen, 2003; Johnson, 1993; Walker, Ilardi, McMahon, & Fennell, 1996). Though these studies have yielded important insights into the nature of gender and leadership effectiveness, they may or may not be applicable to real-world settings where contextual factors such as organizational culture, characteristics of the organization's mission, or professional and occupational diversity of the workforce may affect leadership styles and approaches. Healthcare studies can address questions that untangle relationships among these factors. For example, do women lead members of their own profession differently than other types of staff?

Education, professionals and leadership. A second area of comparative advantage for leadership studies in healthcare focuses on the role of education and the professions. One stream of studies in healthcare has already produced evidence about the importance of leaders' educational preparation (e.g., having an MBA or Master's degree) and effectiveness. Specifically, there is evidence that nurses with masters degrees are more likely to see themselves as professionals (Anthony, Standing, Glick, et al., 2005), use intellectual stimulation behaviors associated with transformational leadership (Borman, 1993), have confidence in their leadership abilities (Sanford, 1994), and have the ability to attract and retain staff (Force, 2005).

Less evidence is available, however, about the contribution of educational preparation to leaders' effectiveness in samples of general managers and physicians (Helfand et al., 2005; Shipper, Pearson, & Singer, 1998). This gap raises important questions and opportunities: To what extent is advanced management education (e.g., the MBA or Master's degree) necessary for professionals to identify with leadership roles? What identity issues, and associated conflicts, exist for professionals who do (or do not) enroll in advanced management or leadership programs? More generally, and perhaps more importantly, under what conditions do physicians take leadership roles in organizations? Is it typical for physicians to become managers before they become leaders?

Similarly, are physicians less likely than others to take leadership roles because these roles threaten their view of themselves as clinical professionals? Or, does leadership come more naturally to physicians due to the authority and power that accompany their clinical role? How do physicians compare to nurses and nonclinical managers in taking leadership roles and exercising them?

Addressing these questions is important not only for healthcare practitioners, but also for developing our understanding of leadership among professionals more generally. Because professionals and organizations typically don't mix well, understanding the conditions that promote and hinder leadership among professionals in organizations is of wide interest and critical importance. Given the number and diversity of professions and occupations in the healthcare sector (Ramanujam & Rousseau, in press) it carries a unique ability to support studies that address these issues.

Further, like Mintzberg (2004), identifying the most appropriate training to support leadership effectiveness is a dominant theme in the healthcare literature. Unlike other industries, healthcare has been slow to adopt systematic organizationally based leadership-development programs (McAlerney, 2005b; in press). Instead, leadership development has been left to individuals and the professions. We observed differences in how the major disciplines—general management, medicine, and nursing—approach the issue of how best to develop current and future leaders.

Based on our review, the preferred training mode for healthcare managers is master's level education with a postgraduate training fellowship (Helfand et al., 2005); medicine has focused on executive education programs emphasizing team-based leadership skills (Leslie et al., 2005; McAlearney et al., 2005a); and nursing advocates master's or MBA degrees for middle managers, and Ph.D. degrees for executive level managers (Kleinman, 2003; Scoble & Russell, 2003). The goal of doctoral education for nurse leaders seems to be an attempt on the part of the nursing profession to equalize status differences with other professions.

The general interest of professionals in education, coupled with recent initiatives to improve leadership development, offer a number of interesting avenues for research. First, given that a variety of leadership training and development approaches are available, we may be able to gain insights about relationships between leadership training and leadership effectiveness. Does a particular curriculum or training approach improve leaders' effectiveness over time? How do leaders trained using different approaches compare to one another in terms of competencies, effectiveness, or areas of practice excellence?

Research Methods

Leadership research in healthcare (and in non-healthcare settings) needs stronger study designs. Too many studies are cross-sectional, correlational and, as noted earlier, limited to the individual level of analysis. Of course, this makes their results difficult to interpret. We need more studies that are experimental or quasi-experimental (Cook & Campbell, 1979); such studies would involve theory-based interventions that alter the nature of leadership behavior and follow up by examining the effects of leaders' actions on individual, team, unit, and organizational functioning (Ingersoll et al., 1996; Kleinman, 2004; Vance & Larson, 2002).

There are, of course, studies that examine the antecedents and effects of changes (turnover or executive succession) in leadership (e.g., Alexander, Fennel, & Halpern, 1993), but these studies treat leadership behavior as a "black box." Though we recognize that researchers do not typically have enough control in organizations to conduct intervention studies, we argue that even a few of them could contribute significantly to increasing our understanding of leadership. At the least, we need more studies that are longitudinal and multilevel (Yammarino et al., 2005). Similarly, we need more fine-grained studies that describe and analyze mechanisms involved in leadership. To remedy these shortcomings, we need more work on both informal and workgroup leaders and sharper operational definitions of "leaders" and "leadership."

Conclusions

Studies of leadership in the health sector have made important empirical contributions in the last several years. Based on work to date, we conclude that leadership is positively and significantly associated with individual and group satisfaction, retention and performance.

Nonetheless, we argue that there remain important opportunities to advance both general leadership theory and knowledge about leadership in the health sector specifically. Two key areas that should be examined are the role of (a) leadership among professionals, especially physicians, and in professional organizations, and (b) gender in leadership. In both cases, healthcare offers comparative advantages relative to other empirical settings due to the sector's work force composition that includes, of course, the world's most preeminent profession, medicine, but also a relatively high percentage of women who have a varied set of relationships with men and women as followers and leaders.

Moreover, although we focused on research questions concerning professionals and gender, other characteristics of the health sector clearly provide comparative advantages for leadership research. One of these, for example, concerns how leaders deal with the complexity that stems from multiple, inconsistent, and conflicting demands that characterize this sector. The extent to which healthcare organizations and their leaders face such demands is probably greater than in any other sector, and there we can learn much about leadership in such conditions. Similarly, healthcare organizations often face strong external demands from both institutional and market forces (D'Aunno et al., 2000), and we know very little about the role of leadership in such circumstances. Do individuals emerge as leaders because they place higher priority on responding to institutional demands (e.g., concerning maintaining access to care for low-income groups; Selznick, 1984), or are the new leaders in healthcare individuals who can deal effectively with increased financial pressures? In short, though the healthcare sector differs from other sectors, leadership researchers can use its differences to their advantage, as have organizational theorists.

At the same time, however, we identified key barriers that researchers need to overcome to advance understanding of leadership not only in healthcare, but more generally too. Societal expectations about heroic leaders and the romance of leadership threaten to make leadership an amorphous concept.

Perhaps more importantly, we believe that barriers to developing conceptually powerful leadership models, which go beyond the current focus on individuals and groups, stem from academic environments that reward specialization; individual work; and incremental, quick publication. These forces make it difficult to work in multidisciplinary teams to develop cross-level conceptual models as well as longitudinal and intervention research designs, all of which are needed to advance knowledge about leadership.

Even optimists would agree that these are significant barriers to overcome. Nonetheless, the history of leadership research shows that, at least with respect to empirical results, it has made steady progress over 6 decades. Ironically, what may be needed is a new generation of academic leaders, both in research and administration, who can seize the opportunities to develop leadership theory in the healthcare sector. At a minimum, researchers who are specialists in this sector and researchers who are generalists need to draw more effectively on each other's work. Both groups have much to gain from closer collaboration.

Appendix 8.1 Key Characteristics of Transformational and Transactional Leadership Research ($n = 14$ studies)

Author, Publication & Year	Purpose	Theory	Sample	Key Findings
McDaniel & Wolf, 1992 *Journal of Nursing Administration*	To test TF leadership theory and its shared theory in nursing departments. To ask if a site with transforming leaders also exhibits work satisfaction and retention of staff?	Transformational leadership (Burns, 1978; Bass, 1985) theory testing the cascading effects thesis	1 CNO; 77 staff nurses; 11 mid-level administrators	Staff work satisfaction highly correlated to leader-other TF scores; turnover was 10% lower with higher TF scores
Borman, 1993 *Journal of Nursing Administration*	To determine if male and female CNEs and CEOs differ in their role behaviors, skills and values?	Draws on concepts of leadership, managerial values and executive skills	127 male and 127 female CEOs; 232 female and 117 male CNEs	Education increased use of intellectual stimulation. CNEs used contingent reward more often. Men scored lower on organizational outcome and flexibility and caring behaviors. CNEs and CEOs emphasized different skills

Medley & Larochelle, 1995 *Nursing Management*	Do staff distinguish TF and TA behaviors of head nurses? Examines relationships between TF and TA behaviors and staff job satisfaction	Transformational leadership (Burns, 1978; Bass, 1985)	122 staff nurses working in 4 hospitals in southern Florida	Staff nurses could distinguish TF and TA styles in head nurses; TF leaders were likely to have more satisfied staff and a longer association with them
Morrison et al., 1997 *Journal of Nursing Administration*	To examine the relationship between leadership and empowerment and its effect on job satisfaction among nursing staff	Transformational leadership (Bass, 1985)	275 nursing staff members (all levels of personnel included)	Empowerment accounts for more variance in JS for licensed personnel; leadership style accounted for more variance in JS among unlicensed personnel
Stordeur et al., 2000 *Nursing Research*	Examine the cascading effect of TF leadership across hierarchical levels of nursing departments	Transformational leadership (Bass, 1985)	8 organizations; 41 units, 464 staff nurses, 41 head nurses, 12 associate directors	Main source of MLQ variation was the hospital; scores on TF and MBEP varied significantly as a function of hierarchical level; TF explains significant variance in staff satisfaction, extra effort and perceived effectiveness. Interaction between TF and hierarchical level significant for unit effectiveness

Appendix 8.1 Key Characteristics of Transformational and Transactional Leadership Research ($n = 14$ studies) (Continued)

Author, Publication & Year	Purpose	Theory	Sample	Key Findings
Dunham-Taylor, 2000 *Journal of Nursing Administration*	To explore TF leadership, level of power and organizational climate	Transformational leadership (Bass, 1998); Power Stage Theory (Hagberg,1994); Organizational Climate (Likert, 1976)	396 NE, 1115 direct reports, 360 NE bosses	NEs used TF often, achieved satisfied staff levels and were very effective according to bosses; staff satisfaction and work group effectiveness decreased with increased TA behaviors; higher TF scores occurred with higher education and more participative organizations
Gellis, 2000 *Social Work Research*	To evaluate TF and TA leadership in social work practice	Transformational leadership (Bass, 1984)	187 hospital social workers	Leadership behaviors were all significantly correlated with staff extra effort, leadership effectiveness and staff satisfaction with their leaders except for MBEA; TF behaviors associated with higher levels of performance and satisfaction
Alimo-Metcalfe & Alban-Metcalfe, 2001 *Journal of Occupational and Organizational Psychology*	To develop a new UK version of transformational leadership	Departs from transformational leadership (Bass, 1998) model. Focuses on social distance between leaders and followers	146 mid-level health care and local government managers	New TF questionnaire using a 360 approach produced a 9 factor solution

Source	Purpose	Theory/Model	Sample	Findings
Corrigan et al., 2002 *Administration and Policy in Mental Health*	To determine the relationship between TF and TA leadership and mental health team functioning	Bass' multifactor leadership model (1990)	54 mental health teams: 236 leaders and 620 subordinates	For leaders TF organizational culture associated with MLQ inspiration, individualized consideration and charisma; subordinates viewing culture as highly TA were less likely to rate leaders as charismatic, inspiring, intellectually stimulating, and individually considerate; group leaders showed pattern of correlations between leadership and burnout
Hamlin, 2002 *Health Services Management Research*	To identify the criteria of leadership effectiveness at the middle and front lines of management	Transformational leadership (Bass, 1985; Alimo-Metcalfe and Alban-Metcalfe, 2001); Task-cycle theory (Shipper, 2000).	Total sample size not given.	Identified eight positive criteria (e.g., organization/planning, active supportive leadership, giving support to staff) and eleven negative criteria (e.g., dictatorial/autocratic management, intimidating staff, negative approach)
Garman et al., 2003 *Journal of Organizational Behavior*	To examine the factor structure of TF leadership model in human services teams	Transformational leadership (Bass, 1985) focus on management by exception factors	263 leaders and 620 subordinates from 54 mental health teams	Exploratory factor analysis shows reasonable fit of both 5- and 8-factor models, supporting a leadership model with two distinct MBE factors

Appendix 8.1 Key Characteristics of Transformational and Transactional Leadership Research (*n* = 14 studies) (Continued)

Author, Publication & Year	Purpose	Theory	Sample	Key Findings
Leach, 2005 *Journal of Nursing Administration*	Investigate the relationship between NE leadership and organizational commitment among nurses in hospitals	Transformational leadership (Bass,1985); Organizational Involvement (Etzioni, 1975)	101 NE; 148 NMs; 651 staff nurses	Negative relationship between NE TF and RN organizational commitment; negative relationship between NE TA and RN org. commitment; positive relationship between NE TF and TA and NM TF and TA. RN moral commitment was correlated with job tenure, experience and age
Xirasagar et al., 2005 *Medical Care Research and Review*	Identify the leadership styles that influence clinical providers to practice behaviors that translate into the achievement of measurable clinical goals	Full-range leadership model (Bass & Avolio, 1990)	263 medical directors	Beyond TA and L-F styles, TF explained 21% variance with effectiveness; 31% satisfaction and 26% extra effort. Goal achievement associated with higher leader TF scores; TA leadership associated with low degree of goal achievement

Skinner & Spurgeon, 2005 *Health Services Management Research*	To examine the relationship between health managers' self-assessed empathy, their leadership behavior rated by staff, and staff's personal ratings of work satisfaction and related outcome measures	Developed an input–output model with the constructs of empathy; leadership behavior (TF & TA); and staff outcomes	96 manager; 563 staff	Overall model supported. TF and L-F styles mediate relationships between empathy and staff satisfaction, extra effort, leader effectiveness; JS, and org. commitment

Note: CEO = Chief Executive Officer; CNO = Chief Nurse Officer; NE = Nurse Executive, NM = Nurse Manager; TF = transformational leadership style; TA = transactional leadership style; L-F = laissez-faire leadership style MBEA = management by exception, active; MBEP = management by exception, passive; NHS = National Health Service; JS = job satisfaction

Appendix 8.2 Key Characteristics of Leadership Style and Nurse Practice, Job Satisfaction and retention studies (*n* = 12 studies)

Author, Publication & Year	Purpose	Theory	Final Sample	Findings
Lucas, 1991 *Journal of Professional Nursing*	Leadership styles desired by hospital nurses; examine relationship between leader style and job satisfaction	Likert's management systems (1967)	505 staff nurses	Respondents desired a participative style; style accounted for 36.6% of variance in JS scores
McNeese-Smith, 1995 *Journal of Nursing Administration*	Leadership behaviors by department managers related to difference in the employee outcomes of job satisfaction, productivity and organizational commitment	Kouzes and Posner's Model of Leadership Behaviors (1988)	Comparing results of 2 studies. Study 1: 41 managers and 471 staff; Study 2: 19 managers and 221 staff	Emotionally intelligent leadership predicted JS, productivity, and organizational commitment. Differences found between sites related to use of inspiring leader behaviors and staff org. commitment
Ingersoll et al., 1996 *Journal of Nursing Administration*	To measure the effects of an enhanced professional practice model on perceptions of work groups and nurse leaders	Structural Contingency Model (Charnes et al., 1993)	142 staff nurses experimental units (*n* = 2) and 143 staff nurses on control units (*n* = 2)	Introduction of the enhanced practice model resulted in more favorable perceptions about the work group and a desire for a more facilitative leader

Source	Purpose	Theory	Sample	Findings
Boyle et al., 1999 *American Journal of Critical Care*	To examine the direct and indirect effects of nurse manager characteristics of power, influence and leadership style on critical care nurses' intent to stay	Intent to Stay Model (Price & Mueller, 1981, 1986; Hinshaw, Smeltzer & Atwater, 1987)	225 staff nurses from 14 ICUs	The model explained 52% of variance in intent to stay and leadership style was significant at each stage
Laschinger et al., 1999 *Journal of Nursing Administration*	To test a model linking specific leader-empowering behaviors to staff nurse perceptions of workplace empowerment, occupational stress and work effectiveness in a recently merged acute care hospital	Theory of Structural Empowerment (Kanter, 1993); Leader Empowerment Process (Conger & Kanungo, 1988)	537 staff nurses	Leader-empowering behaviors significantly influenced employees' perceptions of formal and informal power and access to empowerment structures. Higher perceived access to empowerment predicted lower levels of job tension and work effectiveness. Final model explained 42% of variance

Appendix 8.2 Key Characteristics of Leadership Style and Nurse Practice, Job Satisfaction and retention studies ($n = 12$ studies) (Continued)

Author, Publication & Year	Purpose	Theory	Final Sample	Findings
Upenieks, 2003 *Health Care Manager*	To examine whether magnet hospitals are able to provide high levels of job satisfaction and empowerment among clinical nurses. To examine if differences in JS are related to leadership effectiveness provided by NEs, directors and managers at magnet and non-magnet hospitals	Theory of Structural Empowerment (Kanter, 1993)	305 staff nurses from 4 hospitals; interviews with 16 nurse leaders	Nurses employed at magnet hospitals experienced higher levels of empowerment and JS. Elements accounting for differences: leader accessibility, support for autonomous decision making and access to opportunity, information and resources
Cummings, 2004 *Nursing Leadership*	To explore how emotionally intelligent leadership mitigates adverse effects of restructuring on nurses	Emotional Intelligence Competencies (Goleman, Boyatzis & McKee, 2002)	6,526 staff nurses	Nurses working with emotionally intelligent leaders were able to attend to more patient care needs even when emotionally exhausted

Citation	Purpose	Theory/Model	Sample	Findings
Manojovich, 2005a *Journal of Nursing Administration*	Understand the effects of unit-level nursing leadership on the relationship of structural empowerment and nursing self-efficacy to professional nursing practice behaviors, job performance, specifically, quality of care	Theory of Structural Empowerment (Kanter, 1993); Social Cognitive Theory (Bandura, 1997)	251 staff nurses	Nursing leadership contributed to the effects of empowerment and self-efficacy on practice behaviors. Strong nursing leadership also contributed to an additional relationship between empowerment and self-efficacy. Nursing leadership explained 46% of the variance in nursing practice behaviors overall
Anthony et al., 2005 *Journal of Nursing Administration*	To describe the roles and skills of NMs; examine characteristics of NMs that are barriers to nurse retention and strategies to improve nurse retention	Structure/Process/Outcome Quality Care Model (Donabedian, 1966)	32 NMs from 7 hospitals	NMs with different educational preparation emphasized different roles; barriers to and strategies for retention identified
Manojovich, 2005b *Journal of Nursing Administration*	To investigate the interaction between structural empowerment, nursing leadership to determine if self-efficacy could contribute to more professional nursing behaviors	Theory of Structural Empowerment (Kanter, 1993); Social Cognitive Theory (Bandura, 1997)	376 staff nurses	Self-efficacy partially mediated the relationship between structural empowerment and professional practice behaviors

Appendix 8.2 Key Characteristics of Leadership Style and Nurse Practice, Job Satisfaction and retention studies (*n* = 12 studies) (Continued)

Author, Publication & Year	Purpose	Theory	Final Sample	Findings
Capuano et al., 2005 *Health Care Management Review*	To understand the microlevel of nurse staffing and outcomes through an evaluation of the work environment at one hospital	No theory identified. Tested a structural equation model: leadership, resources, staff expertise, staff stability, teamwork, patient outcomes and workload	283 staff nurses	Strong leaders had more stable staff and higher proportion of experienced nurses
Cummings et al., 2005 *Nursing Research*	To develop a theoretical model of the impact of hospital restructuring on nurses to determine the extent to which EI nursing leadership mitigated these effects	Causal Model. Emotional Intelligence Competencies (Goleman, Boyatzis & McKee, 2002).	6,526 staff nurses	All nurses felt the effects of hospital restructuring. Nurses who worked with emotionally intelligent leader reported fewer negative effects

Note: ICU = intensive care units; EI = emotional intelligence, NM = nurse managers; JS = job satisfaction

Appendix 8.3 Key characteristics leadership effectiveness studies ($n = 9$ studies)

Author, Publication and Year	Purpose	Theory	Final Sample	Findings
Mansen, 1993 *Journal of Professional Nursing*	To examine the relationship between role-taking abilities of nurse administrators and the perceptions of their leadership effectiveness	Role-taking (Conway, 1988); Transformational and Transactional Leadership Theory (Bass 1981; Burns 1978); Initiating structure and showing consideration (Hoy and Miskel, 1987)	30 administrators and 176 faculty members	Faculty ratings of JS accounted for 22% of variance in administrators ratings of consideration. Initiating structure was predicted by faculty perceptions of formalization
Womak, 1996 *Journal of Professional Nursing*	Identify the relationship between self-perceived leadership styles and scholarly productivity of nursing department chairpersons	Situational Leadership (Hershey & Blanchard, 1988)	106 faculty chairpersons	No support for the situational leadership model
Murray et al., 1998 *Journal of Nursing Administration*	To describe the leadership roles of practicing NEs	No specific theory identified	45 NEs plus one person identified by NE as having a positive or negative influence on them	Majority of CNEs were women, majority of influential others were male. Less than half of CNEs reported substantial involvement in organization-level decision making

Appendix 8.3 Key characteristics leadership effectiveness studies ($n = 9$ studies) (Continued)

Author, Publication and Year	Purpose	Theory	Final Sample	Findings
Shipper et al., 1998 *Health Services Management Research*	To study the leadership skills of successful managers in a healthcare setting	Task-cycle theory (Shipper, 1991); Interpersonal and Initiating behaviors (Yukl, 1994); Transactional and Transformational Theory (Bass, 1985)	229 managers: men and women, general and physician managers	Significant differences between high and low performing managers on 10 of 18 scales. No significant differences between frequency of physician and general managers in leadership skills clusters
Webster et al., 1999 *Administration and Policy in Mental Health*	To examine structural differences in the leadership of women and men	Social Network Analysis (Salancik, 1994) with an emphasis on gender differences	10 case management teams of 112 people and 8 supervisors	Centralization depends on leader gender and team gender
Alexander et al., 2001 *Nonprofit Management and Leadership*	Describes leadership in community health partnerships and offers guidelines for effective leadership	Collaborative Leadership Theory (Bennis, 1999)	4 case study sites, 4–5 informants in each site, total of 115 interviews	Five themes of effective collaborative leadership: systems thinking, vision-based leadership, collateral leadership, power sharing, and process-based leadership

Citation	Purpose	Theory	Sample	Findings
Upenieks, 2002 *Journal of Nursing Administration*	To examine the types of organizational structures that create conditions for NE job effectiveness and leadership success	Kanter's Theory of Structural Empowerment (1993)	16 nurse managers: 12 at manager level and 4 at NE level	83% of NEs interviewed validated the structures of Kanter's theory. New subcategories identified
Upenieks, 2003b *Journal of Nursing Administration*	To describe leadership traits considered valuable in today's healthcare environment, and to identify differences in nurse leaders magnet and non-magnet hospitals	No specific theory identified	16 nurse leaders: 7 magnet and 9 non-magnet hospitals	Global attributes of leader effectiveness: honesty, credibility, supportiveness and visibility, having a passion for nursing, working collaboratively with others, flexibility, knowledgeable of clinical standards, state and national trends / Differences found between nurse leaders in magnet and non-magnet hospitals
Edmondson, 2003 *Journal of Management Studies*	To explore what leaders of action teams do to promote speaking up and other proactive coordination behaviors	Develops a mid-range theory of learning in interdisciplinary action teams with a focus on leader behaviors	165 interviews with 16 surgical teams in 16 hospitals	The most effective leaders helped teams to learn by communicating a motivating rationale for change by minimizing concerns about power and status differences to promote speaking up in the service of learning

Note: CNE = Chief Nurse Executives; NE = Nurse Executive

Appendix 8.4 Leadership Development: Roles, competencies, curricula and program evaluations ($n = 18$ studies)

Author, Publication & Date	Purpose	Theory	Final Sample	Findings
Brown & McCool, 1987 *Health Care Management Review*	To identify attributes of high performing healthcare managers for the 1990s	None specified	Not specified	Leader traits: healthy, high energy, giving, hard working, creative, mission oriented and visionary Leader types: networked, the boss, resource builder, analyzer, synthesizer, evaluator, implementer, and people-oriented
Liang et al., 1993 *Public Health Reports*	Conduct a training needs assessment to identify perceived KSAs judged most essential for prospective or new state health officers	None specified	38 territorial or public health officers	Top competencies: policy development and program planning, agency management, interpersonal skills, personnel management, communications, financial planning, public image and legal issues

Dienemann & Shaffer, 1993 *Nursing Connections*	To determine the perceptions of nurse unit managers about the relative importance of the characteristics and skills identified by Freund (1985) for effective performance	None specified. Freund's (1985) 7-item taxonomy of NE effectiveness	73 NMs & 48 managers from 6 hospitals; 25 managers from 2 community health agencies	Differences in rank ordering of skills between new and experienced NMs. More experienced NMs ranked political savvy and business skills as more important than new NMs. New NMs ranked communication and clinical skills as most important
Williams & Ewell, 1996 *Health Care Management Review*	Examine leaders skills of medical staffs' medical executive committee	None specified	65 hospital medical staff specialist and 65 chiefs of staff	Top 5 skills for chiefs of staff success: listening, being objective, communicating, making decisions and facilitating exchange of ideas
				Top 5 self-reported skills: listener, team player, confident, physician advocate and quality oriented
				Top 5 self-reported weaknesses: reactive, hesitant, talker, process oriented, rigid

Appendix 8.4 Leadership Development: Roles, competencies, curricula and program evaluations ($n = 18$ studies) (Continued)

Author, Publication & Date	Purpose	Theory	Final Sample	Findings
				Desirable traits for medical executive committee members: demonstrated achievement in medicine, objectivity, ability to work with others, support from medical staff, experience on other committees
Wolf, 1996 *Journal of Continuing Education in Nursing*	Program evaluation of the Leadership Training Institute for nurse managers	Situational Leadership Theory (Hershey & Blanchard, 1988)	144 NMs	Primary leadership scores changed toward participating and delegating styles after training. Significant increases in leadership adaptability after training
Scoble & Russell, 2003 (part 1) Russell & Scoble, 2003 (part 2) *Journal of Nursing Administration*	To develop a profile of future NMs based on the opinions of seasoned nurse	None specified	43 nurses who participated in an invitational leadership conference	Preferred educational preparation: MSN, PhD, MSN/ MBA, MSN or MBA, BSN/MBA Curricula content (top 5): business administration, leadership, financial management, human resources and management

Kleinman, 2003 *Journal of Nursing Administration*	To assess the role preparation, competencies and education required for NE and NM roles	None specified	35 NMs and 93 NEs (*n* = 128)	Key competencies (top 5): leadership behaviors and skills, financial/budgeting, business acumen, management skills, communication skills Competencies: both NMs and NEs agreed staffing, scheduling, management and human resources are most important for NMs Preferred education: for NMs 20% perceived MSN, 17% dual MSN/MBA as preferred education; for NEs 34% perceived MSN/MBA, 20% MSN with administration emphasis as preferred education
Guo, 2003 *Health Care Manager*	To analyze skills and roles of senior-level managers	Managers' roles proposed by Zuckerman & Dowling (1997); Mintzberg (1973); Quinn (1996); Guo (2001)	10 senior leaders	Six essential roles for managers derived from semi-structured interviews and selection from a list Roles: leaders, liaison, monitor, disturbance handler, resource allocator and strategist

Appendix 8.4 Leadership Development: Roles, competencies, curricula and program evaluations ($n = 18$ studies) (Continued)

Author, Publication & Date	Purpose	Theory	Final Sample	Findings
Garman et al., 2004 *Journal of Healthcare Management*	To develop a job-relevant, multi-source feedback survey for use in healthcare administration	None specified	12 executive search consultants generate competencies; instrument validated on tested on 125 graduate students and 168 senior-level NEs	Competencies: charting the course; developing work relationships; broad influence; structuring the work environment; inspiring commitment; communication; self-management

Instrument adaptable for early, mid and senior careerists |
| McKenna et al., 2004 *Journal of Health Administration Education* | To explore the relative importance of various leadership competencies and perceptions of the methods by which such leadership competencies are developed as related to dominant behavioral styles | None specified. Core competencies defined by the Accreditation Council for Graduate Medical Education (ACGME) | 110 physicians, physician leaders, educators, and medical students | Preferred learning method: coaching or mentoring and on the job experience in a management position.

Behavioral styles: compliance to policies and proceedures under conditions of stress.

Decreased assertiveness and less direct under conditions of stress; high influencing behavior under conditions of stress

Motivated by theoretical and social values |

Source	Description	Model	Sample	Outcomes
Umble et al, 2005 *American Journal of Public Health*	Program evaluation of the National Public Health Leadership Institute	None specified	43 teams of 2–4 senior PH officers; interview with 1 person from each team (n = 25) 12–18 months after; final reports from cohort 3	Individual outcomes: 92% assumed new leadership roles after attending program Network outcomes: 96% increased number and contacts with others to discuss challenges; 86% talked with program team mates; 46% talked with other participants
McAlearney et al, 2005a *Hospital Topics*	Presents a model leadership program and evaluation to train pediatricians	Kotter's (1996) Change Process Model	28 physicians at one Academic Medical Center	Participant satisfaction: (scale 1–5, 5 excellent). Avg. 4.7 satisfaction of needs; 4.8 quality of information; 4.6 practice impact. 1 year post-program: (scale 1–5, 5 strongly agree) M = 4.2 strongly agreed more effective in current role; M = 4.0 strongly agreed more effective working in teams, M = 4.3 strongly agrees better able to lead teams. M = 4.0 had opportunities to assume or expand leadership roles

Appendix 8.4 Leadership Development: Roles, competencies, curricula and program evaluations ($n = 18$ studies) (Continued)

Author, Publication & Date	Purpose	Theory	Final Sample	Findings
Leslie et al., 2005 *Pediatrics*	To conduct a needs assessment of young pediatricians and present results of a program evaluation	None specified. Competencies ($n = 20$) in categories of self-management, system management and team management	56 pediatricians who attended a National Leadership Development Program	Evaluation of participants' satisfaction at end of each day and program T1 & T2, positive changes in scores on 20 program competencies T1, T2 & T3 (at 4 months) Also positive outcomes for career progression, further education, networking with other participants and mentoring others
Helfand et al., 2005 *Journal of Health Administration Education*	To describe administrative fellow and resident's self-rated competencies in a number of key areas	None specified. Various management and leadership competencies	78 postgraduate administrative fellows and residents in ACHE programs	Men and women reported differences in self-rated abilities; prior work experience was negatively associated with development and fundraising skills

McAlarney, 2005b *Career Development International*	To improve understanding of mentoring and other leadership development practice in healthcare organizations	Draws on concepts from mentoring, leadership development and management learning	160 key informant interviews from industry and academic plus 125 representatives from 43 hospitals and health systems; survey of 844 hospital CEOs	No interviewed CEOs and less than one quarter of survey respondents reported participating in a formal mentoring program as a protégé; 1 in 3 surveyed CEOs reported formal mentoring programs in their organizations. Only 3 respondents reported mentoring programs existing for more than 5 years
McAlearney, in press *Journal of Organizational Behavior*	To present a framework on barriers to leadership development in healthcare organizations	Conceptual framework of HC leadership needs, development practices, and areas for development	35 expert interviews, 55 organizational case studies including 160 in-depth semi-structured interviews	6 themes inhibiting leadership development: industry lag, representiveness of community and patient population, professional conflicts, time constraints; technical hurdles, financial constraints

*NM = nurse manager; NE = Nurse executive; ACHE = American College of Healthcare Executives; PH = Public Health; MSN= master's of science, nursing; MBA = Master's of Business Administration; HC = health care; M = mean score; CEO = chief executive officer

References

Alexander, J. A., Comfort, M. B., Weiner, B. J., & Bogue, R. (2001). Leadership in collaborative community health partnerships. *Nonprofit Management & Leadership, 12,* 159–175.

Alexander, J. A., Fennell, M. L., & Halpern, M. T. (1993). Leadership instability in hospitals: The influence of board: CEO relations and organization growth and decline. *Administrative Science Quarterly, 38,* 74–99.

Alimo-Metcalfe, B., & Alban-Metcalfe, R. J. (2001). The development of a new transformational leadership questionnaire. *Journal of Occupational and Organizational Psychology, 74,* 1–27.

Altieri, L. B., & Elgin, P. A. (1994). A decade of nursing leadership research. *Holistic Nursing Practice, 9,* 75–82.

Anthony, M. K., Standing, T. S., Glick, J., Duffy, M., Paschall, F., Sauer, M. R., et al. (2005). Leadership and nurse retention: The pivotal role of nurse managers. *Journal of Nursing Administration, 35,* 146–155.

Arndt, M., & Bigelow, B. (2005). Professionalizing and masculinizing a female occupation: The reconceptualization of hospital administration in the early 1900s. *Administrative Science Quarterly, 50,* 233–261.

Avolio, B. J., & Gardner, W. L. (2005). Authentic leadership development: getting to the root of positive forms of leadership. *Leadership Quarterly, 16,* 315–338.

Barsade, S. G. (2002). The ripple effect: Emotional contagion and its influence on group behavior. *Administrative Science Quarterly, 47,* 644–675.

Bass, B. M. (1985). *Leadership and performance beyond expectations.* New York: Free Press/Collier Macmillan.

Bass, B. M., & Avolio, B. J. (1985). *The multifactor leadership questionnaire.* Palo Alto, CA: Consulting Psychologists Press.

Bedeian, A. G., & Hunt, J. G. (2006). Academic amnesia and vestigial assumptions of our forefathers. *Leadership Quarterly, 17,* 190–205.

Borman, J. S. (1993). Women and nurse executives. Finally, some advantages. *Journal of Nursing Administration, 23,* 34–41.

Boyle, D. K., Bott, M. J., Hansen, H. E., Woods, C. Q., & Taunton, R. L. (1999). Managers' leadership and critical care nurses' intent to stay. *American Journal of Critical Care, 8,* 361–371.

Brown, M., & McCool, B. P. (1987). High-performing managers: Leadership attributes for the 1990s. *Healthcare Management Review, 12,* 69–75.

Burns, J. M. (1978). *Leadership.* New York: Harper & Row.

Cameron, K. S., Dutton, J. E., & Quinn, R. E. (2003). *Positive organizational scholarship: Foundations of a new discipline.* San Francisco : Barrett-Koehler.

Capuano, T., Bokovoy, J., Hitchings, K., & Houser, J. (2005). Use of a validated model to evaluate the impact of the work environment on outcomes at a magnet hospital. *Healthcare Management Review, 30,* 229–236.

Carroll, T. L. (2005). Leadership skills and attributes of women and nurse executives. Challenges for the 21st Century. *Nursing Administration Quarterly, 29,* 146–153.

Charns, M. P., & Tewksbury, L. J. S. (1993). *Collaborative management in healthcare.* San Francisco: Jossey-Bass.

Cook, T. D., & Campbell, D. T. (1979). *Quasi-experimentation: Design and analysis issues for field settings.* New York: Houghton Mifflin.

Corrigan, P. W., Diwan, S., Campion, J., & Rashid, F. (2002). Transformational leadership and the mental health team. *Administration and Policy in Mental Health, 30*, 97–108.

Cummings, G. (2004). Investing relational energy: The hallmark of resonant leadership. *Canadian Journal of Nursing Leadership, 17*, 76–87.

Cummings, G., Hayduk, L., & Estabrooks, C. (2005). Mitigating the impact of hospital restructuring on nurses: The responsibility of emotionally intelligent leadership. *Nursing Research, 54*, 2–12.

Dansereau, F., Graen, G., & Haga, W. J. (1975). A vertical dyad linkage approach to leadership within formal organizations: A longitudinal investigation of the role making process. *Organizational Behavior and Human Performance, 13*, 46–78.

D'Aunno, T., Succi, M., & Alexander, J. A. (2000). The role of institutional and market forces in divergent organizational change. *Administrative Science Quarterly, 45*, 679–703.

D'Aunno, T., Sutton, R. I., & Price, R. H. (1991). Isomorphism and external support in conflicting institutional environments: A study of drug abuse treatment units. *Academy of Management Journal, 34*, 636–661.

Dienemann, J., & Shaffer, C. (1993). Nurse manager characteristics and skills: Curriculum implications. *Nursing Connections, 6*, 15–23.

Dunham-Taylor, J. (2000). Nurse executive transformational leadership found in participative organizations. *Journal of Nursing Administration, 30*, 241–250.

Eagly, A. H., & Carli, L. L. (2003). Finding gender advantage and disadvantage: Systematic research integration is the solution. *Leadership Quarterly, 14*, 851–859.

Eagly, A. H., Johannesen-Schmidt, M. C., & Van Engen, M. L. (2003). Transformational, transactional, and laissez-faire leadership: A meta-analysis comparing women and men. *Psychological Bulletin, 129*, 569–592.

Edmonsdon, A. C. (2003). Speaking up in the operating room: How team leaders promote learning in interdisciplinary teams. *Journal of Management Studies, 40*, 1419–1452.

Eisenberg, B. (1997). Customer service in healthcare: A new era. *Hospitals and Health Services Administration, 42*, 17–32.

Erickson, R. J. (1995). The importance of authenticity for self and society. *Symbolic Interaction, 18*, 121–144.

Force, M. (2005). The relationship between effective nurse managers and nursing retention. *Journal of Nursing Administration, 35*, 336–341.

Foundation of the American College of Healthcare Executives. (2006). *A comparison of career attainments of men and women healthcare executives. Findings of a national survey of healthcare executives.* Retrieved August 28, 2006, from http://www.ache.org/pubs/research/genderstudy_executivesummary.cfm

Garman, A., Davis-Lenane, D., & Corrigan, P. (2003). Factor structure of the transformational leadership model in human service teams. *Journal of Organizational Behavior, 24*, 803–812.

Garman, A. N., Tyler, J. L., & Darnall, J. (2004). Development and validation of a 360-degree-feedback instrument for healthcare administrators. *Journal of Healthcare Management, 49*, 299–321.

Gellis, Z. D. (2001). Social work perceptions of transformational and transactional leadership in healthcare. *Social Work Research, 25*, 17–26.

Gerstner, C. R., & Day, D. V. (1997). Meta-analytic review of leader-member exchange theory: Correlated and construct issues. *Journal of Applied Psychology, 82,* 827–844.

Gilmartin, M. J., & Freeman, R. E. (2002). Business ethics and healthcare: A stakeholder perspective. *Healthcare Management Review, 27,* 52–65.

Goleman, D. (1995). *Emotional intelligence: Why it can matter more than I.Q.* London: Bloomsbury.

Guo, K. L. (2003). A study of the skills and roles of senior-level healthcare managers. *Healthcare Manager, 22,* 152–158.

Hackman, J. R. (2002). *Leading teams: Setting the stage for great performance.* Boston, MA: Harvard Business School Press.

Hamlin, R. G. (2002). A study and comparative analysis of managerial and leadership effectiveness in the National Health Service: An empirical factor analytic study within an NHS Trust hospital. *Health Services Management Research, 15,* 245–263.

Hasenfeld, Y. (1983). Human service organizations. Englewood Cliffs, NJ: Prentice Hall.

Helfand, B., Cherlin, E., & Bradley, E. H. (2005). Next generation leadership: A profile of self-rated competencies among administrative resident and fellows. *Journal of Health Administration Education, 22,* 85–105.

Hershey, P., & Blanchard, K. (1988). *Leadership effectiveness and adaptability description.* San Diego, CA: Leadership Studies, Inc.

House, R. J., & Aditya, R. N. (1997). The social scientific study of leadership: Quo vadis? *Journal of Management, 23,* 409– 474.

House, R. J., & Baetz, M. L. (1979). Leadership: Some empirical generalizations and new research directions. *Research in Organizational Behavior, 1,* 341–423.

Human, S. E., & Provan, K. G. (2000). Legitimacy building in the evolution of small-firm multilateral networks: A comparative study of success and demise. *Administrative Science Quarterly, 45,* 327–365.

Huy, Q. N. (1999). Emotional capability, emotional intelligence, and radical change. *Academy of Management Review, 24,* 325–346.

Ingersoll, G. L., Schultz, A. W., Hoffart, N., & Ryan, S. A. (1996). The effect of a professional practice model on staff nurse perception of work groups and nurse leaders. *Journal of Nursing Administration, 26,* 52–60.

Javidan, M., & House, R. J. (2002). Leadership and cultures from around the world: Findings from GLOBE. An introduction to the special issue. *Journal of World Business, 37,* 1–2.

Johnson, C. (1993). Gender and formal authority. *Social Psychology Quarterly, 56,* 193–210.

Kan, M. M., & Parry, K. W. (2004). Identifying paradox: A grounded theory of leadership in overcoming resistance to change. *Leadership Quarterly, 15,* 467–491.

Kanter, R. M. (1993). *Men and women of the corporation* (2nd ed.). New York: Basic Books.

Kimberly, J. R., de Pouvourville, G., & D'Aunno, T. (in press). *The globalization of managerial innovation in healthcare.* London: Cambridge University Press.

Kleinman, C. S. (2004). Leadership and retention: Research needed. *Journal of Nursing Administration, 34,* 111–113.

Kleinman, K. (2003). Leadership roles, competencies, and education: How prepared are our nurse managers? *Journal of Nursing Administration, 33,* 451–455.

Kotter, J. P. (1995). Leading Change: Why transformation efforts fail. *Harvard Business Review, 73,* 59–68.

Kouzes, J. W., & Posner, B. Z. (1993). *Psychometric properties of the leadership practices inventory.* San Diego, CA: Pfeiffer & Company.

Kraatz, M. A., & Moore, J. H. (2002). Executive migration and institutional change. *Academy of Management Journal, 45,* 120–145.

Laschinger, H. K. S., Sabiston, J. A., & Kutzscher, L. (1997). Empowerment and staff nurse decision involvement in nursing work environments: Testing Kanter's theory of structural power in organizations. *Research in Nursing and Health, 20,* 341–352.

Laschinger, H. K. S., & Shamian, J. (1994). Staff nurses' and nurse managers' perceptions of job related empowerment and managerial self-efficacy. *Journal of Nursing Administration, 24,* 38–47.

Laschinger, H. K. S., Wong, C., McMahon, L., & Kaufmann, C. (1999). Leader behavior, impact on staff nurse empowerment, job tension, and work effectiveness. *Journal of Nursing Administration, 29,* 28–39.

Leach, L. S. (2005). Nurse executive transformational leadership and organizational commitment. *Journal of Nursing Administration, 35,* 228–237.

Leslie, L. K., Miotto, M. B., Liu, G. C., Ziemnik, S., Cabrera, A. G., Calma, S., et al. (2005). Training young pediatricians as leaders for the 21st century. *Pediatrics, 115,* 765–773.

Liang, A. P., Renard, P. G., Robinson, C., & Richards, T. B. (1993). Survey of leadership skills needed for state and territorial health officers, United States. *Public Health Reports. 108,* 116–120.

Lowe, K. B., & Gardner, W. L. (2001). Ten years of the *Leadership Quarterly*: Contributions and challenges for the future. *Leadership Quarterly, 11,* 459–514.

Lowe, K. B., Kroeek, K. G., & Sivasubramanian, N. (1996). Effectiveness correlates of transformational and transactional leadership: A meta-analytic review of the MLQ literature. *Leadership Quarterly, 7,* 385–425.

Lucas, M. D. (1991). Management style and staff nurse job satisfaction. *Journal of Professional Nursing, 7,* 119–125.

Manojlovich, M. (2005a). Promoting nurses' self-efficacy: A leadership strategy to improve practice. *Journal of Nursing Administration, 35,* 271–278.

Manojlovich, M. (2005b). The effect of nursing leadership on hospital nurses' professional practice behaviors. *Journal of Nursing Administration, 35,* 366–374.

Mansen, T. J. (1993). Role-taking abilities of nursing education administrators and their perceived leadership effectiveness. *Journal of Professional Nursing, 9,* 347–357.

McAlearney, A. S., Fisher, D., Heiser, K., Robbins, D., & Kelleher, K. (2005a). Developing effective physician leaders: Changing cultures and transforming organizations. *Hospital Topics, 83,* 11–18.

McAlearney, A. S. (2005b). Exploring mentoring and leadership development in healthcare organizations. Experience and opportunities. *Career Development International, 10,* 493–511.

McAlearney, A. S. (in press). Leadership development in healthcare: A qualitative study. *Journal of Organizational Behavior.*

McDaniel, C., & Wolf, G. (1992). Transformational leadership in nursing service. A test of theory. *Journal of Nursing Administration, 22,* 60–65.

McKenna, M. K., Gartland, M. P., & Pugno, P. A. (2004). Defining and developing physician leadership competencies: Perceptions of physician leaders, physician educators, and medical students. *Journal of Health Administration Education, 5,* 8–13.

McNeese-Smith, D. (1995). Job satisfaction, productivity and organizational commitment: The results of leadership. *Journal of Nursing Administration, 25,* 17–26.

Medley, F., & Larochelle, D. R. (1995). Transformational leadership and job satisfaction. *Nursing Management, 26,* 64–64.

Mendl, J. R., Ehrlich, S., & Dukerich, J. M. (1985). The romance of leadership. *Administrative Science Quarterly, 30,* 78–103.

Mintzberg, H. (1973). *The nature of managerial work.* New York: Harper-Row.

Mintzberg, H. (2004). *Managers not MBAs: A hard look at the soft practice of managing and management development.* San Francisco: Barrett-Koehler.

Montgomery, K. (2001). Physician executives: The evolution and impact of a hybrid profession. *Advances in Healthcare Management, 2,* 215–241.

Morrison, R. S., Jones, L., & Fuller, B. (1997). The relation between leadership style and empowerment on job satisfaction of nurses. *Journal of Nursing Administration, 27,* 27–34.

Murray, B. P., Fosbinder, D., Parsons, R. J., Dwore, R. B., Dalley, K., Gustafson, G., et al. (1998). Nurse executives' leadership roles. Perceptions of incumbents and influential colleagues. *Journal of Nursing Administration, 28,* 17–24.

Ostroff, C., Atwater, L. E., & Feinberg, B. J. (2004). Understanding self-other agreement: A look at rater and ratee characteristics, context and outcomes. *Personnel Psychology, 57,* 333–375.

Parsons, T. (1971). *The system of modern societies.* New York: Prentice Hall.

Patrick, A., & Laschinger, H. K. (2006). The effects of structural empowerment and perceived organizational support on middle level nurse managers' role satisfaction. *Journal of Nursing Management, 14,* 13–22.

Pfeffer, J. (1977). The ambiguity of leadership. *Academy of Management Review, 2,* 104–112.

Pfeffer, J., & Davis-Blake, A. (1986). Administrative succession and organizational performance: How administrator experience mediates the succession effect. *Academy of Management Journal, 29,* 72–83.

Podolny, J. M., Khurana, R., & Hill-Popper, M. (2005). Revisiting the meaning of leadership. *Research in Organizational Behavior, 26,* 1–36.

Price, J. L., & Mueller, C. W. (1986). *Absenteeism and turnover of hospital employees.* Greenwich, CT: JAI Press.

Quinn, R. E. (1996). *Becoming a master manager: A competencies framework* (2nd ed). New York: Wiley.

Rafaeli, A., & Sutton, R. I. (1987). Expression of emotion as part of work role. *Academy of Management Review, 12,* 23–37.

Ramanujam, R., & Rousseau, D. M. (in press). The challenges are organizational not just clinical. *Journal of Organizational Behavior.*

Roberts, L. M. (2006). Shifting the lens on organizational life: The added value of positive scholarship. *Academy of Management Review, 31,* 292–305.

Russell, K. B., & Scoble, G. R. (2003). Vision 2020, part 2: Educational preparation for the future nurse manager. *Journal of Nursing Administration, 33,* 404–409.

Sachs, J. (2005). *The end of poverty: How we can make it happen in our lifetime.* London: Penguin.

Sanford, K. (1994). Future education: What do nurse executives need? *Nursing Economics, 12,* 126–130.

Scoble, G. R., & Russell, K. B. (2003). Vision 2020, part I: Profile of the future nurse leader. *Journal of Nursing Administration, 33,* 324–330.

Scott, R. A., & Aiken, L. H. (1995). Organizational aspects of caring. *Milbank Quarterly, 73,* 77–96.

Scott R. W., Reuf, M., Mendel, P., & Caronna, C. (2000). *Institutional change and healthcare organizations: From professional dominance to managed care.* Chicago: The University of Chicago Press.

Selznick, P. (1984). *Leadership in administration: A sociological interpretation.* Berkeley: University of California Press.

Shamir, B., & Eilam, G. (2005). "What's your story?" A life-stories approach to authentic leadership development. *Leadership Quarterly, 16,* 395–417.

Shipper, F., Pearson, D. A., & Singer, D. (1998). A study and comparative analysis of effective and ineffective leadership skills of physician and non-physician healthcare administrators. *Health Services Management Research, 11,* 124–135.

Skinner, C., & Spurgeon, P. (2005). Valuing empathy and emotional intelligence in health leadership: A study of empathy, leadership behaviour and outcome effectiveness. *Health Services Management Research, 18,* 1–12.

Slavitt, D., Stamps, P., Piedmont, E., & Hasse, A. (1986). *Index of work satisfaction.* Ann Arbor, MI: University of Michigan Press.

Stogdill, R. M. (1948). Personal factors associated with leadership: A survey of the literature. *Journal of Psychology, 25,* 35–71.

Stogdill, R. M. (1974). *Handbook of leadership: A survey of theory and research.* New York: Free Press.

Stordeur, S., Vandenberghe, C., & D'hoore, W. (2000). Leadership styles across hierarchical levels in nursing departments. *Nursing Research, 49,* 37–43.

Terry, L. D. (1995). The leadership-management distinction: The domiance and displacement of mechanistic and organismic theories. *Leadership Quarterly, 6,* 515–527.

Umble, K., Steffen, D., Porter, J., Miller, D., Hummer-McLaughlin, K., Lowman, A., et al. (1995). The national public health leadership institute: Evaluation of a team-based approach to developing collaborative public health leaders. *American Journal of Public Health, 95,* 641–644.

Upenieks, V. V. (2002). What constitutes successful nurse leadership?: A qualitative approach utilizing Kanter's theory of organizational behavior. *Journal of Nursing Administration, 32,* 622–632.

Upenieks, V. V. (2003a). The interrelationship of organizational characteristics of magnet hospitals, nursing leadership, and nursing job satisfaction. *Healthcare Manager, 22,* 83–99.

Upenieks, V. V. (2003b). What constitutes effective leadership?: Perceptions of magnet and non-magnet nurse leaders. *Journal of Nursing Administration, 33,* 456–467.

Vance, C., & Larson, E. (2002). Leadership research in business and healthcare. *Image, Journal of Nursing Scholarship, 34,* 165–171.

Walker, H. A., Ilardi, B. C., McMahon, A. M., & Fennell, M. L. (1996). Gender, interaction, and leadership. *Social Psychology Quarterly, 59,* 255–272.

Weber, M. (1946). *From Max Weber: Essays in sociology* (H. H. Gerth & C. Wright Mills, Eds.). New York: Oxford University Press.

Webster, C., Grusky, O., Podus, D., & Young, A. (1999). Team leadership: Network differences in women's and men's instrumental and expressive relations. *Administrative Policy in Mental Health, 26,* 169–190.

Weil, P., & Kimball, P. (1996). Gender and compensation in healthcare management. *Healthcare Management Review, 21,* 19–33.

Westphal, J. D., Gulati, R., & Shortell, S. M. (1997). Customization or conformity? An institutional and network perspective on the content and consequences of TQM adoption. *Administrative Science Quarterly, 42,* 366–394.

Williams, S. J., & Ewell, C. M. (1996). Medical staff leadership: A national panel survey. *Healthcare Management Review, 21,* 29–38.

Wolf, M. S. (1996). Changes in leadership styles as a function of a four-day leadership training institute for nurse managers: A perspective on continuing education program evaluation. *Journal of Continuing Education in Nursing, 27,* 245–252.

Womack, R. B. (1996). Measuring the leadership styles and scholarly productivity of nursing department chairpersons. *Journal of Professional Nursing, 12,* 133–140.

Xirasagar, S., Samuels, M. E., & Stoskopf, C. H. (2005). Physician leadership styles and effectiveness: An empirical study. *Medical Care Research and Review, 62,* 720–740.

Yammarino, F. J., Dionne, S. D., Chun, J. U., & Dansereau, F. (2005). Leadership and levels of analysis: A state-of-the-science review. *Leadership Quarterly, 16,* 879–919.

Yulk, G. (1989). Managerial leadership: A review of theory and research. *Journal of Management, 15,* 251–289.

9
Creativity in Organizations

JENNIFER M. GEORGE

Jesse H. Jones Graduate School of Management, Rice University

Abstract

In this chapter, I review contemporary theories and research on creativity in organizations. After discussing key definitional issues in this domain, I review the contemporary scholarly literature proceeding from the most molecular of perspectives focusing on within-individual processes to the more molar perspective of the collective creativity that can take place in work groups. While the within-individual process featured most prominently in the extant literature is intrinsic motivation, after a treatment of some fundamental issues surrounding the intrinsic motivation construct, I review research on conscious and unconscious thinking and positive and negative affect as key internal processes relevant to understanding creativity. Next, I focus on contextual influences on creativity including safety signals, creativity prompts, supervisors, leadership, and networks. Lastly, I focus on creativity in groups (from both an input and a process perspective). In closing, I reiterate a recurrent theme throughout the review. This is an exciting era for research on creativity in organizations with many intriguing questions awaiting future scholarly inquiry.

Introduction

Creativity is being increasingly recognized as a critical means by which organizations and their members can create meaningful, lasting value for their multiple stakeholders in today's dynamically changing environment (e.g., Amabile, 1988; George & Zhou, 2001, 2002). Thus, not surprisingly, popular business magazines such as *Business Week, Fast Company,* and *Fortune* regularly have features highlighting creativity in organizations, and practitioner-oriented publications such as *Harvard Business Review* frequently publish articles on how and why managers often inadvertently thwart creativity and on ways they can and should seek to promote it (e.g., Amabile, 1998; Amabile,

Hadley, & Kramer, 2002; Florida & Goodnight, 2005). Scholarly research on creativity in organizations, the subject of this review, is burgeoning.

Interestingly, and perhaps reflective of the nature of this elusive construct, theorizing and research on creativity is proceeding in anything but a linear fashion. Rather, just as new buds on a tree seem to sprout in seemingly random directions that nonetheless might have some underlying order that could be discerned, creativity research is developing in a variety of different promising directions that, while building from the common ground of the existing literature, are not necessarily reflective of a unified paradigmatic thrust. This is most likely a good thing given the very nature of creativity and given how little we currently know about it.

Underscoring the timeliness of this topic in the minds of academics and practitioners alike, in conducting research for this chapter, I uncovered a remarkable number of recent reviews of the literature. For example, in the 2004 Annual Review issue of the *Journal of Management*, Shalley, Zhou, and Oldham provided an extensive and comprehensive review of empirical research on how personal and contextual characteristics, individually and in interaction, influence creativity in organizations. Personal characteristics in their review include the Five Factor personality traits, creative potential (as assessed by Gough's, 1979, Creative Personality Scale [CPC]), and cognitive style (based on Kirton's, 1976, 1994, Adaptation-Innovation Theory). Contextual characteristics included job complexity, relations with supervisors and coworkers, goals and deadlines, evaluation and reward structures, and the physical work environment.

As another example, in *Research in Personnel and Human Resource Management*, Zhou and Shalley (2003) reviewed (a) theoretical frameworks underlying creativity research such as Amabile's (1988) componential model, interactionist perspectives (e.g., Woodman, Sawyer, & Griffin, 1993), and more recent theoretical models and approaches (e.g., Drazin, Glynn, & Kazanjian, 1999; Ford, 1996; Mainemelis, 2001; Perry-Smith & Shalley, 2003; Unsworth, 2001); (b) research design and measurement issues and challenges in creativity research; (c) contextual antecedents of creativity; and (d) person antecedents of creativity. Contextual characteristics covered in their review included productivity and creativity goals, performance evaluation and feedback, social influence, supervisor behaviors, leadership, and job design. Person antecedents include CPC, the Five Factor personality traits, and creative self-efficacy.

Coinciding with these reviews in the management literature, the 2004 *Annual Review of Psychology* included a chapter on creativity by Runco. This review focused on the person, product, press, and process of creativity (Rhodes, 1961, 1987), disciplinary approaches (e.g., behavioral, biological, developmental, and organizational), and other topical areas (e.g., implicit theories of creativity, problem finding, and evolutionary approaches). Additional reviews pertaining to creativity have also appeared in other journals (e.g., Anderson, De Dreu, & Nijstad, 2004; Egan, 2005; Rank, Pace, & Frese, 2004).

The existence of these excellent, comprehensive, and relatively recent reviews of creativity theorizing and research affords me a certain luxury in this chapter. That is, it gives me the opportunity to focus in more depth on the most contemporary and perhaps especially intriguing new directions that creativity theorizing and research is taking. I will not review research that has already been reviewed elsewhere (e.g., Runco, 2004; Shalley et al., 2004; Zhou & Shalley, 2003) unless it is particularly pertinent to set the stage for the theorizing and research on which I do focus. Work reviewed in this chapter was identified by both manual and electronic searches of the scholarly literature in management, organizational behavior, psychology, and related disciplines.

The chapter unfolds as follows. After addressing definitional issues, I review contemporary theorizing and research relevant to creativity in organizations proceeding from the most molecular of approaches focused on internal processes within individuals to the influence of contextual factors to more molar approaches addressing creativity at a collective level within and across work groups. Even this very crude approach to organizing the review is inherently fuzzy, as will likely become clearer in the following sections. That is, consistent with the tenets of interactionism (e.g., Carson, 1989; George, 1992; Kenrick & Funder, 1988; Pervin, 1985; Pervin & Lewis, 1978; Rowe, 1987), even the most internal and molecular of processes occurs in a social and organizational context that cannot be ignored and interacts with these internal processes to shape behavior. Analogously, when considering creativity at more molar levels such as the collective creativity that can take place in work groups, this creativity stems, in part, from internal processes within individual group members in the context of their group membership and interactions. Thus, an ongoing dynamic interplay between more molecular and more molar influences on creativity will be a unifying thread throughout the chapter.

Creativity Defined: Charting the Domain

Creativity is typically defined as the generation or production of ideas that are both novel and useful (e.g., Amabile, 1988, 1996; Oldham & Cummings, 1996; Scott & Bruce, 1994). Thus, to be considered creative, ideas must be both new and seen as having the potential to create value for organizations in the short or long run. Creativity is typically viewed as a key precursor to innovation (the successful implementation of creative ideas) and is increasingly being recognized as an important ingredient for effectiveness in all kinds of work and organizations (e.g., Amabile, 1988, 1996; George & Zhou, 2007; Oldham & Cummings, 1996). Creative ideas can relate to work procedures, products, services, and organizing structures and can vary in terms of the degree to which the idea reflects an incremental versus radical departure from the status quo (Mumford & Gustafson, 1988; Shalley et al., 2004). Creative ideas can also vary in terms of scope or the range of their value-creating potential. Thus, creativity occurs, for example, when a nurse develops a novel approach to scheduling shifts in a hospital that alleviates recurring staff shortages while affording nurses more flexibility to deal with unforeseen nonwork demands, when an administrative assistant develops a new electronic filing system, or when a research scientist develops a promising new drug. As vastly different as these examples of new and useful ideas are, they fall under the rubrics of creativity.

Considering that both novelty and usefulness must be present for ideas to be considered creative helps to distinguish what is creative from what is not creative. Outlandish, wild ideas can be creative but they are not necessarily so; they must also be seen as being useful in an organization or having the potential to create value to be considered creative. Novelty for novelty's sake, therefore, is not the same thing as creativity. Similarly, effective problem solving is certainly useful in organizations but does not necessarily reflect creativity; in order for problem solving to be creative, generated solutions must be novel. Thus, creativity is not the same thing as problem solving (Runco, 2004).

Interestingly, theorizing and research on creativity tends to make the implicit assumption that the same causal factors will operate in a similar manner regardless of the type of creativity that occurs or that researchers are studying, with some exceptions (e.g., Elsbach & Hargadon, 2006). Thus, as Shalley and colleagues (2004) noted, "In the extant literature, the concept of creativity is generally discussed as if it were a unitary construct" (p. 949). Recently, this implicit assumption was challenged. For example, Unsworth (2001) theorized that four types of creativity could be distinguished based upon two dimensions: (a) whether initial engagement in idea generation is driven internally or externally, and (b) whether the task domain or problem type is open or closed. She theorized that causal determinants and underlying processes contributing to creativity might differ depending upon the type of creativity under consideration. As another example, Elsbach and Hargadon suggested that one needs to take the nature of jobs and workdays into account in understanding factors that might promote or inhibit creativity. They theorized that, while increasing levels of autonomy and job complexity on relatively routine jobs with predictable workdays might facilitate intrinsic motivation and creativity, the creativity of professionals who are overworked, face numerous time pressures, and already have high level of job complexity on an ongoing basis might be facilitated by scheduling periods of relatively routine "mindless" work into their workdays.

Think about the jobs and workdays of production workers, nurses, secretaries, teachers, physicians, lawyers, college professors, stockbrokers, advertising executives, engineers, managers, and chefs. The potential for creativity resides in each of these jobs and for each of these types of jobholders. Will the same causal factors and processes contribute to creativity in the same ways in these various contexts? Clearly, this is an important issue for future theorizing and research to address.

Another implicit assumption that seems to underlie creativity theorizing and research is that "usefulness" as criteria for creative ideas is without controversy. Clearly, organizations have multiple stakeholders whose interests are often competing. What is useful and creates value for one stakeholder group might harm one or more other stakeholder groups. Essentially, a "creative idea" from the perspective of one stakeholder group might be bad decision making from the perspective of other groups. For example, a top administrator of a for-profit hospital chain might come up with new ideas for ways to increase profitability for the chain that have implications for both patients and staff. From the perspective of shareholders, these ideas would likely be viewed as creative as they are new, and they may create value in terms of increased profitability. However, these very same ideas might have negative repercussions for both staff and patients. From the perspective of these two stakeholder groups, the ideas are not only useless but also potentially harmful. In this case, what is creative from one vantage point is potentially destructive from other vantage points. Thus, perhaps more attention needs to be paid to what is meant by "useful" in this literature and the question of "useful for whom" needs to be addressed.

The notion of "useful for whom" actually relates to a broader observation with regards to the creativity literature. That is, creativity is typically thought of as an outcome (e.g., dependent variable) and attention has focused exclusively on understanding what factors can promote or inhibit it. An implicit assumption perhaps being that creativity is always "a good thing," leads to innovation and other positive outcomes (and does not lead to negative outcomes), and thus, attention is appropriately focused on how to facilitate it in organizations. As Shalley and colleagues (2004) noted, however, research has not tended to focus on the assumed benefits of creativity in organizations (or potential unintended negative consequences of creativity), and "it is not yet clear that boosting creativity at work will necessarily result in more innovative organizations that respond effectively to dynamic market conditions" (p. 952). Interestingly, in their review of the innovation literature, Anderson and colleagues (2004) made the same observation and suggested that, to significantly advance research on innovation, "it will be necessary for researchers to reconceptualize the process as one in which innovation may be the cause of multiple, spin-off outcome effects at different levels of analysis. That is, to begin to treat innovation as the independent rather than dependent variable" (p. 160). Thus, future theorizing and research might benefit from considering creativity not only as a dependent variable but also as an independent variable with multiple potential ramifications for organizations and their members. For example, all organizations need some degree of predictability, control, and reliability. Creativity, by nature, is unpredictable, and thus has the potential to reduce levels of predictability and reliability. Anderson and colleagues (2004) proposed a model of creativity and innovation in which some form of distress (at the individual, group, or organizational level) is viewed as triggering creativity and innovation in a cyclical manner; perhaps, when individuals, groups, and organizations experience some form of distress, it signals the need for change (and a concomitant reduction in predictability and control).

Within-Individual Internal Processes

People generate creative ideas, and thus, attention has been focused on the internal processes that might lead to creative insights (and/or processes that can inhibit creativity). In the organizational literature, the internal process that has garnered perhaps the most significant attention (albeit, more often than not, as a theoretical and unmeasured mediating process) is intrinsic motivation (e.g., Amabile, 1988, 1996; Shalley et al., 2004). Juxtaposed against intrinsic motivation is extrinsic motivation, which is thought to be dampening of creativity (e.g., Amabile, 1988, 1996).

Intrinsic motivation stems from the work itself and positive engagement in tasks; motivation arises and it is maintained through performing work tasks including developing creative ideas (Amabile, 1996). Extrinsic motivation stems from sources external to the performance of work tasks themselves such as external pressures, job requirements, and influences from others (Amabile, 1996). The distinction between intrinsic motivation, as a facilitating internal process for creativity, and extrinsic motivation, as an inhibiting internal process (albeit one driven most typically by external forces), was prominently featured in more recent reviews of the creativity literature (e.g., Shalley et al., 2004; Zhou & Shalley, 2003), and I will not address it in depth in this chapter.

Some observations are nonetheless in order with regards to the intrinsic-extrinsic motivation distinction and intrinsic motivation as a key internal process responsible for creativity. First, as Shalley and colleagues indicated in their reviews (e.g., Shalley et al., 2004; Zhou & Shalley, 2003), very few studies directly examined to what extent intrinsic motivation is an explanatory mediating process, and the few that directly tested this proposition yielded inconsistent results (e.g., Amabile, 1979; Amabile, Goldfarb, & Brackfield, 1990; Shalley & Perry-Smith, 2001; Shin & Zhou, 2003). Thus, research has yet to support consistently and rigorously the intuitively appealing premise that intrinsic motivation underlies creativity.

Second, given the prominence of Deci and Ryan's (1985) cognitive evaluation theory in explanations of how and why intrinsic motivation mediates the effects of various factors (e.g., contextual characteristics) on creativity (Shalley et al., 2004), recent developments in the former vein might be better integrated into creativity research (e.g., Deci, Eghrari, Patrick, & Leone, 1994; Deci & Ryan, 2000; Gagne & Deci, 2005; Ryan & Deci, 2000).

Third, recognition should be given to the fact that there might be very real sources of extrinsic motivation for creativity in organizations (George, 2007). Organizational members know that problems need to be solved, opportunities need to be taken advantage of, and their creative ideas need to be "useful." All of these external pressures can motivate individuals, and they are not clearly and necessarily negative influences on creativity.

Lastly, researchers might want to consider to what extent a singular mediating process such as intrinsic motivation can account for various types of creativity. For example, workers performing relatively routine jobs that by most counts would not be considered intrinsically motivating can and do nonetheless come up with creative ideas for improvements in work processes and procedures. As another example, academics conducting research, writing, and seeking to publish scholarly journal articles are presumably often intrinsically motivated by their work. Yet, one wonders to what extent they would carry on these often difficult and time-consuming activities were they not employed by universities and expected to engage in these very activities as part of their jobs. Clearly, these and other unanswered questions regarding the motivation for creativity suggest that, rather than assume that intrinsic motivation underlies creativity, researchers need to tackle this theorized linkage more directly and in more depth.

In the remainder of this section, I focus on the ways in which the internal processes of thinking and feeling have the potential to influence creativity in organizations. While cognition and affect are also highly interdependent and reciprocally related, for ease of exposition, I discuss each in turn with the following caveat. The literature on cognition and affect are vast, and I can by no means attempt to do justice, in this chapter, to the many ways in which cognitive and affective processes underlie creativity. I will nonetheless touch upon certain salient developments that I hope will spur organizational scholars to explore in more depth how the workings of the mind play out in creativity in organizations.

Conscious and Unconscious Thinking

Given that organizations are goal driven and that the behavior of their members is presumably purposively oriented around the ultimate achievement of organizational goals, it is perhaps not surprising that contemporary work on creativity in organizations emphasizes the role of the conscious mind and conscious thought. Models of the creative process in the organizational literature have a decidedly rational flavor (e.g., Amabile, 1988). Contextual factors thought to be promotive of creativity presumably operate through increasing employees' active engagement in their work and intrinsic motivation (e.g., Amabile, 1988, 1996; Shalley et al., 2004). The current literature paints a picture in which creativity comes about by putting into place a variety of factors (e.g., person and contextual characteristics) that will consciously lead employees to develop new ideas to solve problems and create new opportunities.

Such an approach seems to make all the more sense given that creativity does entail much hard work and sustained effort over time (e.g., Ross, 2004; Staw, 1995). It also often requires domain-specific knowledge that is acquired through effortful processes (e.g., Amabile, 1988, 1996). Just as a management scholar would be unlikely to come up with a paradigm-changing theory of behavior in organizations without knowledge of existing work in the area, a research scientist needs to be intimately familiar with theory and research findings in his or her area to come up with a scientific breakthrough, and a machinist needs to understand the functioning of mechanized parts to creatively solve a recurrent breakdown in a mechanized process. Thus, the literature focuses on how to create a set of circumstances in which the kinds of conscious thought processes that will lead to creativity will flourish.

And yet, we are all familiar with the sudden insights in the shower or on the drive to work, how putting aside a vexing problem for a while and returning to it later can lead to better insights than persistently and doggedly plugging away at it, and the stories of how famous creatives seem to have arrived at their major breakthroughs through rather unusual routes (e.g., Adams, 2001; Burke, 1978; Claxton, 1997, 2005; Dijksterhuis & Meurs, 2006). What these anecdotes suggest is that creativity is not just a product of conscious thought…something else is going on.

This something else is often thought of in terms of the rather elusive construct of incubation. Writings on incubation suggest that when trying to find creative solutions to problems and come up with new ideas, it can be beneficial to take a break from task-related activities (Jett & George, 2003) as during these breaks, the mind still may be at work (without conscious awareness; e.g., Csikszentmihalyi & Sawyer, 1995; Leonard & Swap, 1999). Until recently, however, understanding what might being going on during these breaks and periods of incubation has been a challenge to isolate (Dijkesterhuis & Meurs, 2006; Olton, 1979).

One explanation for potential benefits of incubation suggests that sometimes when people are consciously working on a task, they are blocked from considering alternative perspectives, different assumptions, or even evaluating the veracity of the information they are relying on (Dijkesterhuis & Meurs, 2006; Schooler & Melcher, 1995; Smith, 2003). That is, people consciously approach tasks with a certain mental set of heuristics, schemas, assumptions, and biases that can limit their creative insights. Taking a break from a task requiring creativity or engaging in some kind of different activity may be beneficial, as when people return to the focal task, they may approach it with a different mental set and prior blocks to creative ideas might no longer exist (Dijkesterhuis & Meurs, 2006; Schooler & Melcher, 1995; Smith, 2003). Breaks and time away from active engagement in a particular task allows one to approach it anew upon returning to it and potentially from a different vantage point or mental set from which new information and insights might come to light. This explanation essentially suggests that incubation operates through a passive process of freeing the mind from a given mental set through distractions or breaks (Dijkesterhuis & Meurs, 2006; Jett & George, 2003).

Interestingly, and in support of anecdotal evidence that incubation entails something more than just a passive process of shifting mind-sets, growing evidence suggests that during periods of incubation, a much more active process is actually taking place (e.g., Claxton, 1997, 2005). In particular, unconscious-thought theory (UTT) and supportive empirical evidence suggests that active and beneficial "thinking" takes place during incubation, and that this kind of thinking might not even be possible when one remains consciously focused on a task (e.g., Dijksterhuis, 2004; Dijksterhuis & Meurs, 2006; Dijksterhuis & Nordgren, 2006). Importantly, UTT has significant implications for understanding creativity in organizations as it calls into question a theme in the extant literature that creativity necessarily benefits from a kind of intense and encompassing engagement in work tasks (e.g., intrinsic motivation), and to spur creativity, we need to increase levels of task complexity and engagement in work tasks. It also suggests that incubation itself might need to play a bigger role in the scholarly literature on creativity in organizations than it has to date (e.g., recent reviews are largely silent on this topic given the paucity of empirical research).

According to UCT, *conscious thought* refers to "object-relevant or task-relevant cognitive or affective thought processes that occur while the object or task is the focus of one's conscious attention" (Dijksterhuis & Nordgren, 2006, p. 96). For example, when organizational members are trying to creatively solve problems, think of improvements, or seize opportunities, and they are focused on the task or problem at hand, they are engaged in conscious thought. The scholarly literature on creativity in organizations implicitly tends to assume that conscious thought is *the* precursor to creativity—only by consciously thinking about problems and ways to improve things and only by consciously trying to come up with new ideas for products, processes, and procedures will creativity actually occur. Thus, to spur creativity, we should try to promote organizational members' active engagement and involvement in their work tasks (e.g., Amabile, 1988, 1996).

In UCT, *unconscious* thought refers to "object-relevant or task-relevant cognitive or affective thought processes that occur while conscious attention is directed elsewhere" (Dijksterhuis & Nordgren, 2006, p. 96). Essentially, conscious thought is thinking with attention being paid to the object of thought or the task; unconscious thought is thinking that takes place without attention or with attention being focused on something else. UCT and supportive research suggests that much thinking takes place without conscious awareness, that unconscious thought is actually better suited for certain kinds of tasks, problems, and decisions (e.g., complex and difficult problems or tasks in which much disparate information needs to be taken into account and tasks requiring creativity), and that conscious and unconscious thought processes work together (e.g., Dijksterhuis, 2004; Dijksterhuis & Meurs, 2006; Dijksterhuis & Nordgren, 2006).

For example, suppose a professor has had an idea for a new theoretical approach to a substantive research area and seeks to write a conceptual, theory-building paper. The professor has a rough, general sense of what she wants to say and what literatures can be integrated to build the argument and she immerses herself in reading these and related literatures. However, as she progresses reading, a sense of frustration kicks in as she can't figure out how to integrate the disparate approaches and themes into a coherent and compelling story, and she begins to worry that she is wasting time and spinning wheels (and, unfortunately forgetting material read early on in the process). Nonetheless, not yet ready to give up, the professor continues to consciously work on the idea, engages in further reading, and plays with different ways of telling the story that still do not pass muster. While driving to pick up her children from school, a "big-picture story" suddenly pops into her head. She sees how these various and disparate literatures can be integrated to tell the story she thought was there, and she has a real sense of how it all fits together to shed new light on the substantive area (and actually how to write the paper and tell the story). As another example, imagine a developer is trying to come up with an initial prototype for a new concept and line of dishwashers. While consciously working on this task, the developer identifies a number of features of form and function and options for the line that seem viable but not terribly exciting or unique. Not under a pressing deadline, the developer decides to put the project aside for a while and complete other tasks with deadlines. While putting together an unrelated PowerPoint presentation a few days later, an idea for the prototype that combines elements of the previously identified options in a unique manner pops into his mind. In each of these cases and countless examples from our own experience, conscious and unconscious thought work together. Consciously thinking about a problem, decision, or an opportunity helps us acquire information and parameters. When the task is complex, however, integrating this information and arriving at a decision, solution, or creative idea can be difficult. UCT suggests that while not consciously thinking about the task and directing attention elsewhere, the unconscious continues to "think." At some point later on, the appropriate decision, solution, or creative idea seems to just pop into the decision-maker's consciousness out of the blue (Dijksterhuis & Nordgren, 2006).

UCT and supportive empirical research suggests a number of reasons why unconscious thought might be particularly important for creativity and why reliance on conscious thought alone might be inferior. First, unconscious thought has much higher capacity than conscious thought (Dijksterhuis & Nordgren, 2006). Conscious thought engages with only one thing at a time and is generally limited to temporarily remembering and taking into account approximately seven elements (Dijksterhuis & Nordgren, 2006; Miller, 1956). In fact, the processing capacity of consciousness is just a small fraction of the processing capacity of the mind (e.g., Dijkesterhuis, Aarts, & Smith, 2005; Norretranders, 1998; Wilson, 2002) and the limits of consciousness for decision making on complex tasks have long been recognized in the literature (e.g. Kahneman, 2003; Simon, 1955; Tversky & Kahneman, 1974; Wilson & Schooler, 1991). Returning to our frustrated professor, when she is consciously reading a variety of disparate literatures, she has a sense that they can be woven together to yield new insights, yet how it is to be done alludes her. It is hard enough to master and remember all of what she has read, yet alone integrate and weave it together to say something new.

Second, conscious thought tends to operate in a focused, top-down manner and rely on expectations, schemas, and preconceived notions. It tends to be more convergent, while unconscious thought operates in a bottom-up manner and tends to be more divergent (Dijksterhuis & Nordgren, 2006). Thus, for example, when consciously thinking about the paper and ways to frame it, none of the approaches that come to the professor's mind reflect the new insight she believes might be there. Rather, they almost seem to be rather formulaic variations on preexisting themes in the literature. Third, unconscious thought works slowly to combine and weigh information to form a meaningful and organized whole (Dijksterhuis & Nordgren, 2006). Continuing with this running example, when engaged in unconscious thought, the professor's mind takes the time it needs to bring together and incorporate disparate approaches to yield an integrative story that represents a truly new approach to the topic rather than "old wine in a new bottle." Lastly, conscious thought can follow rules whereas unconscious thought does not follow rules and operates more in terms of estimates (Dijksterhuis & Nordgren, 2006). Thus, our professor, when engaged in unconscious thought, can focus on the bigger picture and how all the disparate pieces come together. She does not get bogged down in the details of how to convincingly challenge conventional wisdom in the area.

While research in a variety of areas supports the tenets of UCT (Dijksterhuis & Nordgren, 2006), given that it is recent and also the many complexities of the mind that remain unanswered (e.g., how and when does thought that is unconscious become crystallized and pop into consciousness in terms of a decision, solution, or new idea), clearly much more research is needed in this area. In any case, though, experimental social-psychology research tends to support the notion that on relatively complex tasks, allowing time for unconscious thought leads to better outcomes than relying exclusively on conscious thought (Dijksterhuis & Nordgren, 2006). For example, in a series of studies,

Dijksterhuis (2004) presented participants with complex judgment tasks in which they had to either evaluate or choose among apartments or roommates after being provided with information on multiple attributes of the apartments or roommates in question (one alternative being relatively superior, one alternative being relatively inferior, and an additional one or two alternatives being relatively neutral). After being presented with the information, participants (a) had to immediately make their judgments (immediate condition), (b) were given some time to think about the task (conscious-thought condition), or (c) worked on another unrelated task for the same amount of time as in the conscious-thought condition prior to returning to the focal task (unconscious-thought condition). Participants who were distracted from the focal task (those in the unconscious-thought condition) performed better than those who engaged in conscious thought about the task and those who were given no opportunity for unconscious thought (the immediate condition).

In thinking about creativity in organizations and the kinds of tasks in which employees are actually likely to have the opportunity to be creative (e.g., George & Zhou, 2001), future theorizing and research should focus on how conscious and unconscious thought, together, can lead to creative insights. It should also consider the extent to which the creativity of overextended employees performing complex tasks might actually be inhibited by time pressures and deadlines and highly complex work, which allow little or no time for unconscious thought.

Consistent with this reasoning, Elsbach and Hargadon (2006) turned traditional job design notions on their head by proposing that, for overstretched professionals, design should focus on workdays, and in particular, scheduled periods of "mindless" work (e.g., work that is low in both cognitive difficulty and performance pressure, yet is necessary for effective functioning) should be injected into workdays. As they indicated, "…tasks that are low in cognitive difficulty do not require that workers come up with creative ideas on the spot. Instead they provide the attention capacity that allows creative thinking to be an unexpected by-product of work. That is, they let creativity happen, rather than force it to be done" (p. 477). UCT takes this idea a step further. That is, for professionals performing complex tasks for which creativity is desired but often not demonstrated (Elsbach & Hargadon, 2006), scheduled periods of mindless work might be beneficial precisely because they distract attention away from complex problems in need of creative solutions and provide needed time for unconscious thought. Scheduled and unscheduled breaks might serve much the same function (Jett & George, 2003). However, for overstretched employees with multiple time pressures, deliberately taking breaks might not be feasible and may even seem nonsensical. Mindless work, on the other hand, encompasses tasks that do need to be performed in organizations and is thus a more realistic alternative to breaks.

Similarly, Ohly, Sonnentag, and Pluntke (2006) reasoned that while routinization is often thought of as detracting from creativity (e.g., Ford & Gioia, 2000), it may actually help to foster creativity as it can save time and free employees' minds to think about their work and creative ideas. Essentially, when some aspects of work are covered by routines, employees have additional cognitive resources to think about other aspects of their work that might benefit from creativity. In a field study of employees of a high-technology company working in diverse functional areas and departments (e.g., sales, marketing, production, and R&D), the researchers found that routinization was positively associated with self-reported creativity after controlling a number of other factors (e.g., control variables, other work characteristics, and curvilinear time pressure).

Positive and Negative Affect

Pioneering studies conducted by Isen in the 1980s (e.g., Isen, Daubman, & Nowicki, 1987; Isen, Johnson, Mertz, & Robinson, 1985) prompted interest in the link between affective states and creativity, and in particular between positive affect or mood and creativity. A somewhat coherent theme has emerged in the literature suggesting that positive affective states or moods are conducive to creativity as they promote more flexible, divergent thinking and related cognitive processes that should facilitate the generation of new and useful ideas (e.g., Greene & Noice, 1988; Hirt, McDonald, & Melton, 1996; Isen, Johnson, et al., 1985, Isen, Daubman, et al., 1987). Most recently, in a longitudinal field study of professionals working on project teams, Amabile, Barsade, Mueller, and Staw (2005) found that affective reactions characterized by pleasantness were positively associated with creativity.

Some recent theorizing and research, however, has turned the tables in terms of thinking more seriously about negative mood states, ways in which they might be promotive of creativity, and how both mood states might interact over time to influence creativity. For example, based on Martin and colleagues mood-as-input model (e.g., Martin, Abend, Sedikides, & Green, 1977; Martin, Achee, Ward, & Harlow, 1993; Martin, Ward, Achee, & Wyer, 1993; Martin & Stoner, 1996), George and Zhou (2002) theorized about conditions under which negative moods might be positively associated with creativity (and positive moods might be negatively related to creativity).

The mood-as-input model proceeds from the fundamental premise that moods provide people with information (e.g., Clore, Schwarz, & Conway, 1994; Schwarz & Clore, 1988). Recognizing that the effects of mood states are often context-dependent (e.g., Forgas, 1995), the model suggests that the nature and consequences of the information provided by one's current mood state depends upon the context (Martin & Stoner, 1996). George and Zhou (2002, p. 689) reasoned that people are most likely to use their mood as input to determine how well they are doing and how much effort to exert when the context provides cues or signals that there is an overall objective to be achieved, but while engaged in work activities, people decide for themselves how well they are doing on this overall objective and how much effort to exert.

Positive moods provide information or signal that all is well, good progress has been made, and current efforts are sufficient (Johnson & Tversky, 1983; Kavanagh & Bower, 1985). Alternatively, negative moods provide information that current efforts might be insufficient and thus, lead to lower levels of confidence in the progress that has been made on creative-idea generation (Martin & Stoner, 1996; Martin et al., 1993). Thus, using their mood as input, people in negative moods might exert high levels of effort to come up with truly creative ideas. George and Zhou (2002) hypothesized and found that when perceived recognition and rewards for creativity and clarity of feelings were high, negative moods were positively associated with creativity and positive moods were negatively associated with creativity in a sample of employees in a new product/process development center of a manufacturer.

Importantly, context-dependent effects of mood states and the mood-as-input model do not imply that a certain mood state will always have a positive or negative relation with an outcome or behavior such as creativity. Rather, the effects of either mood state hinge on the context, and both have the potential to have positive (or negative) effects on creativity.

More recently, and based again on mood-as-information theory, George and Zhou (2007) developed a dual-tuning perspective concerning how the combined experience of both mood states (experienced at different times) might be facilitative of creativity. That is, mood-as-information theory suggests that moods exert tuning effects on cognition. In providing information and signaling that all is well and the task environment is unproblematic, positive moods lead to less systematic and careful information processing, greater use of top-down simplifying strategies, heuristics, and schemas, and also more expansive, divergent thinking (e.g., Clore et al., 2001; Fiedler, 1988; Kaufmann, 2003; Schwarz, 2002; Schwarz & Clore, 2003). Negative moods provide information that the task environment is problematic and thus encourage people to exert high levels of effort to figure out what's wrong and improve matters (e.g., George & Zhou, 2002; Kaufmann, 2003; Martin & Stoner, 1996; Schwarz, 2002). As such, negative moods tune cognitive processes to a bottom-up, detail-oriented approach to understanding the facts at hand focused on analyzing the realities of the current situation rather than relying on top-down schemas and heuristics (e.g., Kaufmann, 2003; Schwarz & Clore, 2003). Based on this reasoning, George and Zhou (2007) hypothesized and found that in a supportive context, negative moods had the most positive relation to creativity when positive moods were high, with creativity being the highest when both mood states were high and the context was supportive in a field study of employees in an oil-field services company.

Recap: Within Individual Processes

Clearly, it is not possible to do justice to the complex array of within-individual internal processes that underlie creativity in organizations. And while, in focusing on a diverse subset of internal processes (e.g., motivation, conscious/ unconscious thought, and affective experience), I have raised more questions than I have provided tentative answers, an interesting theme emerges from consideration of these internal processes. That is, future theorizing and research may benefit from considering internal processes in a dialectical fashion rather than seeking to identify one process as a key facilitator of creativity and its seeming "opponent" process as a detractor (George, 2007). Rather, seemingly opponent processes exist for a reason, and it is through their complex interplay in the mind of the creator that creativity comes to fruition.

To date, theorizing and research was dominated by a quest to determine singular internal processes responsible for creativity. Perhaps a more nuanced and complex view of the mind is called for. Clearly, intrinsic motivation is a good thing and one would be hard pressed to make a convincing argument that it is not a good thing when it comes to creativity in organizations. Yet, at the same time, extrinsic motivation is a powerful force (problems need to be identified and solved, novel ideas need to be "useful," work serves important economic functions in most people's multidimensional lives). Appreciating and understanding how both intrinsic and extrinsic motivation can contribute to creativity and how it is through their complex interplay that creativity emerges might bear more fruit than positing that a singular motivational process facilitates creativity (e.g., intrinsic motivation) and another singular, seemingly opposing process (e.g., extrinsic motivation) detracts from it.

Similarly, one would be hard pressed to convincingly argue that conscious thought is not necessary for creativity or that a certain rationality does not underlie the creative process. However, "rational" models of the creative process emphasizing conscious thought (e.g., Amabile, 1988) ignore the critical role of unconscious thought in human endeavors in general, and in creative endeavors, in particular (e.g., Bechara, Damasio, Tranel, & Damasio, 1997; Claxton, 1997, 2005; Dijksterhuis, 2004; Dijksterhuis & Meurs, 2006; Dijksterhuis & Nordgren, 2006). Perhaps, as Dijksterhuis and Nordgren (2006) suggested, "Consciousness should be used to gather information and the unconscious be used to work on it" (p. 107).

Lastly, clearly positive moods have the potential to promote creativity through a variety of means—expansive, divergent thinking, playfulness, and confidence (e.g., Clore et al., 2001; Fiedler, 1988; Kaufmann, 2003; Schwarz, 2002; Schwarz & Clore, 2003). Yet, a dominant and singular focus on positive affect as a precursor of creativity ignores the important functions that negative affect serves in people's lives in general and in facilitating creativity (e.g., Frijda, 1988; George & Zhou, 2007; Kaufman, 2003; Schwarz, 2002). For example, when people are in negative moods, they are more likely to identify problems and performance shortfalls in need of creative solutions, they are more likely to push themselves to exert high levels of effort to come up with truly new and useful ideas, and they are more likely to pay attention to detail and the facts at hand rather than rely on preexisting schemas, assumptions, and mental sets that may be faulty or inaccurate (e.g., George & Zhou, 2002, 2007; Kaufmann, 2003; Martin & Stoner, 1996; Schwarz, 2002; Schwarz & Clore, 2003). Mood-as-information theory, dual-tuning effects of both moods states, and theorizing and research in diverse areas suggest that positive and negative moods serve important functions and contribute to effective functioning in different ways (e.g., George & Zhou, 2007; Schwarz, 2002; Schwarz & Clore, 2003). Thus, research focused on the affect-creativity link might benefit from considering the combined effects of both mood states.

Contextual Influences

As mentioned earlier, Shalley and colleagues (2004) and Zhou and Shalley (2003) reviewed theorizing and research on a variety of contextual factors as potential facilitators or detractors of creativity in organizations (e.g., job complexity, relations with supervisors and coworkers, goals and deadlines, evaluation and reward structures, physical work environment, and leadership). The more recent literature on contextual influences not only focuses on some of these same kinds of contextual influences, but also branches off in a number of intriguing directions. For ease of exposition, I have grouped contextual influences into four main categories: (a) signals of safety, (b) creativity prompts, (c) supervisors and leaders, and (d) social networks. Before proceeding, clearly some of these factors are not purely contextual influences. From an interactional perspective, organizational members most likely contribute often to creating the context, which, in turn, influences their behavior. For example, the kinds of networks and network ties organizational members develop are clearly a function, at least in part, of their personal characteristics. And, of course, from a measurement perspective, given that self-reports of contextual characteristics are often relied upon, the contextual characteristics that are perceived are partially a function of the nature of the perceiver.

Signals of Safety

Creativity is often a risky endeavor for organizational members as it may entail some kind of challenge to the status quo. Given that organizational structures and routines are developed to enhance predictability and control, creativity can be seen as raising levels of uncertainty and reducing predictability and control. Creativity also can be risky as there is always an associated risk of failure and mistakes. Generating creative ideas often means coming up with many ideas, some of which end up not being new and some of which are not really useful (George & Zhou, 2007). Thus, creativity may be discouraged to the extent that a work context signals that potential negative repercussions might accompany creative ideas. Alternatively, creativity may be encouraged to the extent that signals of safety are present.

One signal of safety that is of much contemporary concern in both business and government circles is information privacy. Alge, Ballinger, Tangirala, and Oakely (2006) suggested, "Information privacy entails the degree of control that an organization affords its employees over practices relating to collection, storage, dissemination, and use of their personal information (including their actions and behaviors) and the extent that such practices are perceived as legitimate" (p. 222). Alge and colleagues (2006) theorized that information privacy enhances levels of intrinsic motivation by increasing levels of psychological empowerment and hypothesized that information privacy would be positively associated with creativity and operate through the mediating mechanism of psychological empowerment. They reasoned that privacy enables employees to generate and develop ideas without fear of critical scrutiny (Westin, 1967) and also gives employees a sense of having time to think on their own without evaluation pressure, which can foster experimentation (Pedersen, 1997). Privacy also potentially entails a lack of close monitoring, which can be detrimental for creativity (George & Zhou, 2001). Relying on data from two field studies, Alge and colleagues (2006) found that while psychological empowerment was positively associated with creativity and perceived information privacy contributed to feelings of empowerment, information privacy per se was not positively associated with creativity. Perhaps, as these authors suggested, direct links between information privacy and creativity may be context dependent. For example, to the extent that privacy concerns or assurances relate more directly to creative endeavors, stronger relations might be uncovered. Clearly, this is an important topic for future research given the increasing ease with which a variety of organizations are able to gather personal information and the increasing public concerns about the extent to which such information gathering is necessary and legitimate or capricious and in violation of important rights to privacy.

Based on the premise that psychological safety can encourage experimentation and lessen concerns about failure (Edmondson, 1999, 2003), Lee, Edmondson, Thomke, and Worline (2004) explored to what extent inconsistency among contextual conditions (normative values, instrumental rewards, and evaluation pressures) influences experimentation, an often critical contributor to creativity (Ciborra, 1996; Thomke, 2003; Vincente, 1990). They reasoned that inconsistency can reduce psychological safety because it may increase employees' levels of uncertainty about how their actions will be perceived and responded to, can be a significant source of stress, and might lead to confusion, distrust, and potential "threat rigidity" effects (Argyris, 1990;

Masserman, 1971; Staw, Sandelands, & Dutton, 1981). In a field and laboratory study, they found that when evaluation pressures were high, people facing inconsistent values and rewards regarding experimentation had lower levels of experimentation whereas when evaluation pressures were low, inconsistent values and norms lead to higher levels of experimentation.

These findings suggest that future theorizing and research might benefit from adopting what Lee and colleagues (2004) referred to as a *combinational perspective* regarding contextual conditions with the potential to influence creativity in organizations rather than following the *componential perspective* that is currently dominant in the literature. The combinational approach suggests the need to look at how contextual conditions interact with each other (e.g., their consistency or inconsistency) while the combinational perspective considers independent effects with the implicit or explicit assumption that such effects are additive (and not interactive). Consistent with this reasoning, George and Zhou (2001) found that task characteristics (unclear ends and unclear means) interacted with feedback valence and the five-factor personality trait of openness to explain creativity—such that creativity was highest when individuals were high on openness to experience, worked on heuristic tasks (ends were unclear or means were unclear), and received positive feedback—than when any other combination of openness and these two contextual factors existed. They also determined that having unsupportive coworkers and supervisors who engaged in close monitoring interacted with conscientiousness to explain creativity such that it was lowest when individuals high on conscientiousness had unsupportive coworkers (e.g., coworkers provided inaccurate communication, coworkers did not provide constructive help, or coworkers provided a negative work environment) and supervisors engaged in close monitoring than when any other combination of conscientiousness and these two contextual factors existed.

Creativity Prompts

In addition to signaling that it is safe to be creative, organizational contexts can also more directly prompt creative behavior. While prior reviews have highlighted factors, such as creativity goals and recognition and rewards for creativity that can prompt creativity (e.g., Shalley et al., 2004), Unsworth, Wall, and Carter (2005) suggested that the creativity requirement of a job might be a more proximal influence on creativity. They defined creativity requirement as "the perception that one is expected, or needs to generate work-related ideas….the experienced, psychological aspect of both explicit requirements (e.g., being told to be creative) and other cues (e.g., as a response to task demands)" (p. 542). In a field study of health-service employees, they found that creativity requirement fully mediated the effects of leadership and role requirements on creativity (assessed via self-report) and partially mediated the effects of empowerment and time demands on creativity. While Unsworth and colleagues suggested that including a creativity requirement in jobs in which creativity is desired may be a simpler way to encourage creativity than, for example, other approaches such as altering job design, Lee and colleagues's (2004) combinational perspective suggested that other contextual factors still need to be taken into account and addressed. For example, a creativity requirement on a job with low levels of autonomy and discretion and in which supervisors engage in close monitoring could potentially backfire as the requirement is inconsistent with other contextual factors linked to creativity.

Another creativity prompt (which is sometimes viewed as a creativity detractor) is time pressure. In fact, time pressure has typically been viewed as a deterrent to creativity because it discourages exploration and increases reliance on established ways of doing things (e.g., Amabile, 1996; Andrews & Smith, 1996). Nonetheless, results from prior research have tended to be weak or inconclusive (e.g., Amabile, Conti, Coon, Lazenby, & Herron, 1996; Madjar & Oldham, 2006).

Baer and Oldham (2006) sought to advance our understanding of time pressure as a potential creativity prompt and provided an explanation for inconclusive prior research in this area in a field study of employees in a manufacturer. They reasoned that one potential explanation for inconclusive prior research findings on the time pressure-creativity link is that prior studies have typically assessed overall time pressure experienced on a job, instead of time pressure as it pertains to creative activities. In particular, for jobs that are not necessarily in creative domains, employees, could, for example, not experience time pressure on the job in terms of performing their day-to-day activities, yet have little leftover time during the workday for creative endeavors. Hence, they focused on time pressure specifically as it relates to not having time for creativity-related pursuits. Additionally, they hypothesized that the relation between creativity time pressure and creativity is curvilinear (e.g., an inverted U) based on activation theory (Gardner & Cummings, 1988) and that openness to experience and support for creativity would moderate this inverted U relation. They did not find support for a curvilinear relation between creativity time pressure and creativity. They also did not find support for the hypothesized moderating effects of openness to experience on this relation. However, they did find support for a moderated curvilinear relation between creativity time pressure and creativity (moderated by support), and in a post hoc analysis, for a three-way interaction between curvilinear creativity time pressure, openness to experience, and support.

Consistent with these results, Ohly and colleagues (2006) found a curvilinear relationship between time pressure and creativity after controlling for the effects of control variables and job characteristics. Again, this hypothesized relation was based on the tenets of activation theory (Gardner, 1986; Scott, 1966), which suggests that up until some optimal point, time pressure increases levels of activation, which allows for more cognitive resources to be devoted to creative idea generation.

Supervisors and Leaders

Supervisors and leaders have long been recognized for their critical role in providing a work context that is either supportive of or discouraging of creativity (e.g., Oldham & Cummings, 1996; Shalley et al., 2004), and researchers have continued to explore the ways in which managers can either encourage or thwart creativity. In a study linking goal orientation (e.g., mastery goal orientation and performance-goal orientation) to performance and satisfaction via the mediating mechanism of leader-member exchange, Janssen and Van Yperen (2004) included in the performance domain a measure of what they referred to as *innovative job performance*. Their measure of innovative job performance (Janssen, 2000, 2001) included items assessing both idea generation and items measuring idea promotion and realization. Thus, it appears to tap into both creativity and aspects of innovation (or the implementation of creative ideas).

Janssen and Van Yperen (2004) theorized that mastery-goal orientations lead employees to develop high-quality relations with their supervisors, which, in turn, positively affect behaviors and attitudes, whereas performance-goal orientations prevent the establishment of high-quality leader-member exchanges. In a field study of employees of a Dutch energy supply company holding a variety of jobs in diverse functional areas, they found that a mastery-goal orientation was positively associated with innovative job performance and that leader-member exchange mediated this relation. Contrary to their expectations, however, performance-goal orientation was not found to be significantly associated with innovation job performance.

The role of supervisor support has also been addressed in other recent studies (e.g., Janssen, 2005; Rice, 2006) that also support some of the ways in which supervisors can provide a supportive work environment for creativity identified in prior research (e.g., by providing developmental feedback; George & Zhou, 2007). George and Zhou (2007) identified two additional ways in which supervisors can provide a supportive environment for creativity that, while receiving widespread attention in their respective literatures (e.g., Bies, 2005; Greenberg, 1993; Lewis & Weigert, 1985; McAllister, 1995; Niehoff & Moorman, 1993), have not previously been linked to creativity. More specifically, they identified (a) interactional justice and (b) cognitive trust as two additional ways that supervisors can provide a supportive work context for creativity. They found that these forms of justice and trust interacted with employee positive and negative mood to explain creativity. Perhaps when supervisors display interactional justice and are trustworthy, they contribute to creating a secure environment for creative idea generation and can serve as a prompt to creativity. For example, when employees are treated with dignity, kindness, and respect (e.g., interactional justice is high), they may be more likely to take the risks that accompany creativity. As another example, when employees believe that their supervisors are knowledgeable, competent, professional, and dedicated (e.g., cognitive trust is high), this may prompt them to generate ideas for improvements, because they are more likely to be confident that their supervisors can be depended upon to respond to and follow through on creative ideas.

Clearly, supervisors and leaders play a critical role in providing a context that encourages or stifles creativity (Shalley et al., 2004). Research also continues to explore some of the ways in which managers can provide a supportive context and the mechanisms through which such support operates to stimulate creativity. Yet, at the same time, one gets the sense that the literature assumes that creativity is something that supervisors either allow and encourage or discourage. Perhaps this is actually the case for jobs that are not in creative domains or do not necessarily require that employees come up with new and useful ideas to perform effectively. However, for jobs that do require creativity, the same supervisory behavior that potentially can encourage creativity in noncreative jobs might actually inhibit creativity. For example, if a designer is trying to discover a new concept for a dishwasher, developmental feedback from a supervisor might actually inhibit creativity as the feedback could potentially serve to block or constrain the designer's creativity and lead to fixation along more conventional and well-trodden paths (Smith, 2003). Thus, whether or not supervisors do play a critical role in creativity might depend upon the actual nature of jobs and work tasks and it might be the case, that on certain tasks that are by nature creative, supervisors may be well advised to just stay out of the picture all together. Perhaps this is the reason why some organizations in which creativity is explicitly desired give employees specific times where they can pursue their own ideas without having to answer questions.

Networks

Recognizing the importance of social influence from others, contemporary research has also sought to further our understanding of how various properties and characteristics of individuals' social networks influence their creativity. In particular, Uzzi and Spiro (2005) explored how the small-world networks of creative artists influenced the Broadway musicals they produced (e.g., the artistic and financial performance of the musicals) from 1945 to 1989. As these authors indicated, "a small world is a network structure that is both highly locally clustered *and* has a short path length" (p. 448), conditions that "enable the creative material in separate clusters to circulate to other clusters as well as to gain the kind of credibility that unfamiliar material needs to be regarded as valuable in new contexts" (p. 449). Uzzi and Spiro (2005) found an inverted U-shape relationship between networks' small-world typologies and the artistic and financial performance of musicals. They reasoned that up until a certain point, small-world features are beneficial for creativity as they facilitate the spread of information and material across clusters. However, when small worldliness becomes very high, a homogenizing effect takes place, which makes it more difficult to come up with novel ideas representing a departure from preexisting mind-sets.

In a field study of researchers working in two laboratories, Perry-Smith (2006) discovered that weak network ties were beneficial for creativity (and strong ties were not) and that weak ties may facilitate creativity by providing individuals with a more heterogeneous group of contacts. She also found that closeness centrality ("the distance between an actor and all other actors in the network," p. 88) within an organizational network interacted with ties outside the network to explain creativity such that centrality had a positive relation to creativity when outside ties were low. Under these conditions, individuals in central positions might have more confidence to take risks (Perry-Smith & Shalley, 2003) and might have access to different clusters within the network. However, they are not distracted by having too many contacts and disparate sources of information.

Clearly, the burgeoning interest in social networks during the past several decades (e.g., Brass, 1984, 1995; Burt, 1992; Granovetter, 1982), and the increasing acknowledgment of the social side of creativity (e.g., Perry-Smith, 2006; Perry-Smith & Shalley, 2003; Simonton, 1984), suggests that further research is needed to understand the complex interrelations between social networks and creativity. In particular, to answer the questions: Why do some individuals have social networks that appear to foster creativity to a greater extent than other individuals? Through what processes do social networks exert their potential effects? Some, so far unexplained, causal factor might be responsible for both the kinds of networks individuals develop over time and their levels of creativity. For example, one might conjecture that individuals with broader, more wide-ranging interests (or perhaps individuals high on the personality trait of openness to experience) might develop networks with weaker ties and might not develop networks that are overly small-worldish in typology.

Recap: Contextual Influences

Progress continues to be made in terms of identifying and understanding how the work context can signal that it is safe to be creative, how the work context can prompt creativity, and the role of supervisors and social networks in facilitating creativity. Information privacy, a growing concern in both private and public sectors, has the potential to signal safety as it can reduce fears concerning close monitoring and critical scrutiny of time use and behavior that may discourage employees from generating new and useful ideas (e.g., Alge et al., 2006; George & Zhou, 2001; Pedersen, 1997; Westin, 1967). While Alge and colleagues (2006) did not find information privacy to have a direct association with creativity, they did find that information privacy contributed to feelings of psychological empowerment, and that psychological empowerment was positively associated with creativity. Future research on information privacy and other contextual influences may be advanced by Lee and colleagues's

(2004) proposed combinational perspective. That is, rather than assuming that contextual factors have additive or main effects on creativity, researchers should consider potential interactive effects. In particular, to the extent that contextual factors are consistent with each other, safety may be signaled whereas inconsistency may signal the absence of a safe environment for generating new and useful ideas (Lee et al., 2004). Thus, for example, the effects of creativity prompts such as the creativity requirement of jobs (Unsworth et al., 2005) might depend upon the extent to which a creativity requirement is consistent or inconsistent with other contextual factors such as close monitoring and levels of autonomy.

In an era when time pressures on many jobs seem to be exponentially increasing, the relation between such pressures and creativity has received increased attention in literature. While clearly much more research is needed in this area, there is some initial support for a potential curvilinear relation between time pressure and creativity (Baer & Oldham, 2006; Ohly et al., 2006); however, it appears that to understand this relation, a number of additional factors need to be taken into account such as the nature of the time pressure, support, personality, and job characteristics (Baer & Oldham, 2006; Ohly et al., 2006).

High-quality relations between supervisors and subordinates and supervisor support have long been recognized as important contributors to creativity (e.g., Shalley et al., 2004). What contributes to high-quality relations and supervisor support for creativity? Research has focused on answering this fundamental question from the perspective of both the subordinate and the supervisor. In particular, Janssen and Van Yperen (2004) found that subordinates with mastery-goal orientations were more likely to have high-quality relations with their supervisors which, in turn, were positively associated with innovative job performance. From the perspective of the supervisor, George and Zhou (2007) suggested that displaying interactional justice and being trustworthy are important ways in which supervisors can provide a supportive work environment for creativity. Clearly, supervisors and subordinates influence each other and thus, supervisor support for creativity may be partially influenced by subordinates' own behavior.

Research on the relation between social networks and creativity suggests that network characteristics that promote the sharing and spreading of heterogeneous information and perspectives promote creativity. In particular, networks with a moderate small-world typology might be more advantageous for creativity than networks with low or high degrees of small worldiness, because they may lead to rapid sharing of information that is not homogeneous or redundant (Uzzi & Spiro, 2005). Similarly, weak network ties might be advantageous for creativity because they lead to more heterogeneous contacts and sources of information (Perry-Smith, 2006).

In terms of these and other contextual characteristics, it is important for future research not only to consider how contextual factors might interact with each other to support or discourage creativity (Lee et al., 2004) but also how person factors interact with the context in a multitude of ways. At a very basic level, person factors may play a role in creating the contextual conditions existing at any given time.

Group Creativity

In their review, Shalley and colleagues (2004) concluded that research has tended to focus on individual creativity, with little empirical research focused on creativity at the group or team level. This appears to continue to be true for organizational research on group creativity. While psychologists are intrigued by group creativity and are working to understand creativity as a collective phenomenon (Paulus & Nijstad, 2003), organizational research has been focused on the individual level of analysis (Shalley et al., 2004). This is somewhat paradoxical given the increasing reliance of organizations on flatter, more flexible, team-based structures (e.g., Applebaum & Batt, 1994; Ilgen, 1999; Mannix & Neale, 2005), but it is perhaps understandable given that the study of creativity in organizations is a relatively new and emerging area of research and the very real challenges of studying creativity in ongoing teams in organizations. Nonetheless, progress is being made in this area and research has focused on understanding the inputs and conditions that foster or hinder creativity in groups and the kinds of processes that take place in groups resulting in creativity. This is reminiscent of the input-process-outcome paradigm existing in group research (e.g., Cohen & Bailey, 1997).

Inputs and Conditions

Inputs and conditions for creativity in groups include both compositional and contextual factors that presumably influence group processes in ways that can serve to promote or hinder creativity. At a very basic level, who is in a group influences what the group does. Conventional wisdom in the popular business press as well as among organizational scholars suggests that groups composed of diverse members should be more creative than more homogenous groups because they presumably can call upon a greater diversity of knowledge, skills, expertise, and perspectives to generate new and useful ideas (Mannix & Neale, 2005). Adopting a broad definition of diversity (e.g., variation arising from any characteristic that a person can use to distinguish one group member from another; Jackson, 1992; Williams & O'Reilly, 1998), Mannix and Neale (2005) reviewed 50 years of research on the effects of diversity in teams and concluded that there is

a tension between the promise and the reality of diversity in team process and performance...surface-level social-category differences such as race/ethnicity, gender, or age tend to be more likely than underlying differences to have negative effects on the ability of groups to function effectively....Underlying differences, such as differences in functional background, education or personality, are more often positively related to performance, for example, in terms of creativity or group problem solving, but only when the group process is carefully controlled...However, the actual evidence for the input—process—outcome linkage is not as strong as one might like. (pp. 31, 43)

Mannix and Neale (2005) suggested that future research in this area will benefit from considering moderating factors such as contextual conditions, considering additional forms or types of diversity, and paying more attention to theorized mediating processes.

Choi and Thompson (2005) addressed group composition vis-à-vis the effects of membership change and the introduction of newcomers in groups. They suggested that membership change might promote creativity in groups by increasing task focus (e.g., Ziller, 1965; Ziller, Behringer, & Goodchilds, 1962) and the heterogeneity of knowledge, perspectives, and viewpoints in a group (e.g., Levine & Choi, 2004; Staw, 1980), and by establishing more dynamic group processes such as minority dissent (e.g., Nemeth, 1992; Nemeth & Owens, 1996). In two laboratory experiments, Choi and Thompson (2005) found that membership change resulted in groups generating ideas that were more fluent and flexible and that the creativity of old-timers in groups was enhanced by the introduction of newcomers.

In another laboratory experiment, Goncalo and Staw (2006) explored to what extent groups with an individualist orientation would outperform groups with a collectivist orientation given established links between collectivism and conformity (e.g., Bond & Smith, 1996; Kim & Markus, 1999) and factors that may moderate the cultural orientation-creativity relation. While they did not find a significant effect for cultural orientation, they found that groups with an individualistic orientation that were instructed to be creative were actually more creative than collectivist groups given the same creativity instructions.

Group Processes

In a qualitative study involving six professional service firms, Hargadon and Bechky (2006) identified when interactions within groups led to "moments of collective creativity," which they nonetheless characterized as "a rare and fleeing phenomenon even in the most creative of organizations" (p. 494). Essentially, they identified the kinds of interactions that yield collective creativity, the latter resulting from coming up with new ways to combine old or existing ideas, procedures, and processes to arrive at creative solutions to problems (e.g., Amabile, 1988; Hargadon & Sutton, 1997; Weick, 1979). When individuals with diverse backgrounds and experiences come together to solve a problem creatively or develop a new product design, what is it about their interactions that enables them to combine aspects of their differential areas of expertise and knowledge in new ways to creatively solve a problem or come up a new idea for a product? Based on their field data, they theorized that four sets of interrelated behavior patterns yield moments of collective creativity: (a) help seeking, (b) help giving, (c) reflective reframing, and (d) reinforcing.

Help seeking includes all of the activities individuals engage in to obtain the assistance of others in solving a problem. In the organizations studied, this appeared to be a dynamic and changing process with the result that ultimately creative solutions depended upon whose help was sought to arrive at them. Help giving, the flip side of help seeking, includes spontaneously devoting attention, time, and effort to assist others and is reminiscent of treatments of organizational citizenship behavior and related constructs such as organizational spontaneity (e.g., Bateman & Organ, 1983; George & Brief, 1992). Reflective reframing "represents the mindful behavior of all participants in an interaction, where each respectfully attends to and build upon the comments and actions of others" (Hargadon & Bechky, 2006, p. 489) and seems to represent how ideas evolve through reciprocal interactions to be truly collective. Reinforcing encompasses all of the activities that echo organizational values to encourage help seeking, help giving, and reflective reframing. In professional service firms like those studied by Hargadon and Bechky (2006; e.g., IDEO) such values were likely prevalent, and reinforcing perpetuated and maintained both the values and the behaviors they encourage (e.g., help seeking, help giving, and reflective reframing). Interesting questions for future research are, (a) How can the behaviors underlying collective creativity be encouraged in other kinds of organizations (e.g., those more bureaucratic in nature)? and (b) How might mounting pressures in many such organizations mitigate against collective creativity? That is, in an era of seemingly never-ending layoffs and downsizings, overstretched employees face considerable time pressures to accomplish increasing workloads. Under such conditions, employees might be reluctant to seek help from others because they know that others are also overstretched with their own work tasks. Those being asked for help might not have the time or energy to spontaneously offer it. Reflective reframing may be particularly likely to suffer under such conditions, as those not specifically assigned to solve a problem in need of a creative solution might not have the time or energy for active involvement in reframing.

Clearly, help seeking, help giving, and reflective reframing take place in an affective context. Specifically, the moods and emotions group members experience are reciprocally related to both their thought processes and behaviors. In fact, based on George's (1990) theorizing that affect may be a meaningful construct at the group level of analysis, research has focused on understanding the antecedents and consequences of group affective tone (e.g., Bartel

& Saavedra, 2000; George, 1995; Grawitch, Munz, Elliot, & Mathis, 2003; Grawitch, Munz, & Kramer, 2003; Mason & Griffin, 2003; Totterdell, Kellett, Teuchmann, & Briner, 1998), defined as relatively consistent or homogeneous affective reactions within a group. An implicit, and at times explicit, assumption in the literature on group affective tone is that a positive affective tone is functional for groups and their members (George & King, 2007).

George and King (2007) theorized that in order to understand the potential consequences of group affective tone, researchers need to consider the kinds of tasks and information that groups deal with. Specifically, they proposed that for groups dealing with complex, equivocal information, problems, and opportunities and for those who need to come up with creative solutions to problems and responses to opportunities, a positive affective tone may be dysfunctional and group functioning may be better served by heterogeneity in moods states within groups (George & King, 2007; Tiedens, Sutton, & Fong, 2004).

George and King (2007) theorized that a positive affective tone might be dysfunctional for such groups, because it may lead to groups developing a single shared reality (Hardin & Conley, 2000; Hardin & Higgins, 1996; Levine & Higgins, 2001) concerning goals and objectives, problems and opportunities, cause-and-effect relations, parameters of problems, and the task environment which, due to its shared nature and collective verification, might come to take on a seemingly "objective" status for the group (Baron et al., 1996; Goethals & Darley, 1977; Levine & Higgins, 2001; Sniezek, 1992). For groups facing equivocal, dynamic, and uncertain conditions in which creative solutions to problems and responses to opportunities are desired, multiple shared realities rather than a single shared reality might lead to superior outcomes. Moreover, a positive affective tone might lead to group centrism and an emphasis on coherence in the group (Kruglanski, Pierro, Mannetti, & De Grada, 2006). These posited effects of a positive affective tone were theorized to operate through the collective effects of positive mood effects on cognition and information processing (e.g., Abele, 1992; Fiedler, 1988, 2000; Hirt et al., 1996; Kaufmann, 2003; Kaufmann & Vosburg, 1997; Schwarz, 2002; Vosburg, 1998a,b).

Thus, George and King (2007) proposed that for groups engaged in creative activities, and for those that need to develop creative solutions to problems and responses to opportunities, heterogeneity in affect within the group rather than homogeneity (or an affective tone) might be desired. Mood as information theory (e.g., Schwarz, 2002; Schwarz & Clore, 1983, 1996, 2003), and dual-tuning effects of positive and negative mood (George & Zhou, 2007), while focused on the individual level of analysis, suggest ways in which heterogeneity in affect within groups might promote creativity (George & King, 2007).

Recap: Group Creativity

Perhaps what is most striking about the literature on group creativity is how much we currently do not know about the creativity of ongoing groups in organizations. And, even things we thought we might have known (e.g., diversity in groups fosters creativity) are much more nuanced than commonly thought (Mannix & Neale, 2005). Interestingly, of the scholarly work reviewed here, only one study actually explores creativity in ongoing groups in an organizational context (Hargadon & Bechky, 2006). What does seem to be clear is that more research is needed focusing on what actually takes place in groups or group processes and this research needs to consider the context in which groups function.

Conclusions

Clearly, it is an exciting time for theorizing about and researching creativity in organizations. Not only is creativity increasingly being recognized as critical for organizational effectiveness, but also the existing literature is at a point where there are many interesting questions in need of research to answer them. Moreover, when one considers that many of the factors and relations covered in this chapter have the potential to interact with each other (e.g., within individual affective and cognitive processes occur within collective organizational contexts), ever more intriguing questions arise.

And yet in reviewing this literature, one might wonder to what extent the literature on creativity is succumbing to a certain single-mindedness or routinization (Anderson et al., 2004) that, while enriching our understanding of creativity in incremental ways, is not leading to the kinds of breakthrough advances that are the true marks of creativity in the scholarly domain. While perhaps a harsh overstatement, the existing literature has approached creativity in ways that do not always do justice to the very nature of creative endeavors. That is, creativity, especially in complex, modern organizations, often arises through the interaction of opposing dualities, paradoxes, or contradictions (George, 2007; Runco, 1994). For example, in contrast to the somewhat dominant focus on the importance of pleasurable intrinsic motivation in the creativity literature, Runco (1994) suggested, "Some kind of tension must precede the intrinsic motivation that characterizes creative effort" (p. 102).

The current literature assumes that creativity is a unitary construct (Shalley et al., 2004), that the "usefulness" condition for ideas to be considered creative is uncontested, and that creativity is a universally desired outcome that should be promoted. While there is merit to each of these positions, consideration of presumably opposing perspectives suggests potentially interesting questions for future research. Might not the nature of creativity be fundamentally different depending upon the nature of jobs and organizations under consideration? From whose perspective are creative ideas considered useful, and when are useful ideas for one stakeholder group harmful for another? What are the positive and negative consequences of creativity in organizations, and how are they differentially borne by various stakeholder groups? For example, creativity often requires considerable hard work, effort, and sacrifices on the part of creators, and can have both positive and negative consequences for them personally and professionally (e.g., Janssen, 2003; Ross, 2004; Staw, 1995); perhaps a more nuanced perspective on creativity is called for that acknowledges not only the benefits of creativity but also its potential hidden costs (Ross, 2004).

In terms of individual processes, perhaps rather than focusing on singular processes such as intrinsic motivation, conscious thought, and positive affect as presumed facilitators of creativity, research should consider how seemingly opposing processes interact to bring about creativity. How might extrinsic pressures bring about intrinsic involvement and how does intrinsic involvement uncover extrinsic pressures (e.g., via problem finding)? How do conscious and unconscious thought work together? How are alternating experiences of positive and negative affect both antecedents and consequences of creativity?

Contextual antecedents of creativity typically are viewed as exogenous factors that can serve to promote or inhibit the generation of new and useful ideas. Yet, perhaps these contextual antecedents are reflective of broader forces with their own implications. If signals of safety are not present, for example, and employees are closely monitored, perhaps this is because the presumed need for control in an organization is higher than the desire for creativity. If supervisors are unsupportive or if time pressures are overwhelming, perhaps this is because supervisors do not really want or trust employees to generate organizationally useful new ideas and real work pressures mitigate against employees taking the time to be creative.

Essentially, there are deep-rooted paradoxes of context embedded in all organizations, and how these play out determines the extent to which a work context is supportive of creativity. On the one hand, organizations require predictability, control, and reliable performance and are dependent on collective learning whereby solutions to problems become embedded in organizational routines (or the wheel is not reinvented repeatedly in slightly different forms). On the other hand, organizations face dynamically changing environments, the nature of problems and opportunities change, and creative responses are required. Understanding how work contexts can support or inhibit creativity might be enhanced by considering the broader issue of the mechanisms by which organizations balance competing pressures for collective learning, predictability, and control with pressures for creative responses to new problems and opportunities and dynamically changing circumstances.

As another example, in thinking about job and workday design, clearly autonomy, interesting work, and heuristic tasks have the potential to facilitate creativity; yet, so, too, does having the opportunity to think, acquire knowledge and information, and process that information consciously and unconsciously. While job complexity is presumed to foster creativity via intrinsic motivation (Shalley et al., 2004), highly complex jobs in today's economy often result in very taxing demands on already overstretched workers who perhaps simply do not have the time to be creative (Elsbach & Hargadon, 2006; Gini, 2001). Thus, research might benefit from considering potential paradoxical effects of contextual factors (e.g., job design) on creativity.

And while much research continues to focus on creativity in groups and teams, perhaps research in this area will benefit from consideration of how groups manage the fundamental paradox of needing both a coming together and meeting of the minds that fosters collective endeavors and divergent opinions and perspectives, meaningful dissent, and distinctive contributions that enable the achievement of real synergies and creative approaches.

Thus, perhaps, a more nuanced approach to creativity is called for which reflects the fundamental paradoxes surrounding this elusive construct. Now, more than ever, we might need some big-picture thinking about creativity in organizations. And, such thinking might only come about by considering the very complex nature of creativity in organizations.

Acknowledgment

I am very grateful to Art Brief and Jim Walsh for their very helpful comments on a prior draft of this chapter.

References

Abele, A. (1992). Positive vs. negative mood influences on problem solving: A review. *Polish Psychological Bulletin, 23*, 187–202.

Adams, J. L. (2001). *Conceptual blockbusting: A guide to better ideas* (4th ed.). New York: Perseus Books.

Alge, B. J., Ballinger, G. A., Tangirala, S., & Oakely, J. L. (2006). Information privacy in organizations: Empowering creative and extrarole performance. *Journal of Applied Psychology, 9*, 221–232.

Amabile, T. M. (1979). Effects of external evaluation on artistic creativity. *Journal of Personality and Social Psychology, 37*, 221–233.

Amabile, T. M. (1988). A model of creativity and innovation in organizations. In B. M. Staw, & L. L. Cummings (Eds.), *Research in organizational behavior* (Vol. 10, pp. 123–167). Greenwich, CT: JAI Press.

Amabile, T. M. (1996). *Creativity in context*. Boulder, CO: Westview Press.

Amabile, T. M. (1998, September-October). How to kill creativity. *Harvard Business Review*, 77–87.

Amabile, T. M., Barsade, S. G., Mueller, J. S., & Staw, B. M. (2005). Affect and creativity at work. *Administrative Science Quarterly, 50*, 367–403.

Amabile, T. M., Conti, R., Coon, H., Lazenby, J., & Herron, M. (1996). Assessing the work environment for creativity. *Academy of Management Journal, 39*, 1154–1184.

Amabile, T. M., Goldfarb, P., & Brackfield, S. C. (1990). Social influences on creativity: Evaluation, coaction, and surveillance. *Creativity Research Journal, 3,* 6–21.

Amabile, T. M., Hadley, C. N., & Kramer, S. J. (2002). Creativity under the gun. *Harvard Business Review, 80*(8), 52–61.

Anderson, N., DeDreu, C. K. W., & Nijstad, B. A. (2004). The routinization of innovation research: A constructively critical review of the state-of-the-science. *Journal of Organizational Behavior, 25,* 147–173.

Andrews, J., & Smith, D. C. (1996). In search of the marketing imagination: Factors affecting the creativity of marketing programs for mature products. *Journal of Marketing Research, 33,* 174–187.

Applebaum, E., & Batt, R. (1994). *The new American workplace.* Ithaca, NY: ILR Press.

Argyris, C. (1990). *Knowledge for action: Changing the status quo.* San Francisco: Jossey-Bass.

Baer, M., & Oldham, G. R. (2006). The curvilinear relation between experienced creative time pressure and creativity: Moderating effects of openness to experience and support for creativity. *Journal of Applied Psychology, 91,* 963–970.

Baron, R. S., Hoppe, S. I., Kao, C. F., Brunsman, B., Linneweh, B., & Rogers, D. (1996). Social corroboration and opinion extremity. *Journal of Experimental Social Psychology, 32,* 537–560.

Bartel, C. A., & Saavedra, R. (2000). The collective construction of work group moods. *Administrative Science Quarterly, 45,* 197–231.

Bateman, T. S., & Organ, D. W. (1983). Job satisfaction and the good soldier: The relationship between affect and employee "citizenship". *Academy of Management Journal, 26,* 587–595.

Bechara, A., Damasio, H., Tranel, D., & Damasio, A. R. (1997). Deciding advantageously before knowing the advantageous strategy. *Science, 275,* 1293–1295.

Bies, R. J. (2005). Are procedural justice and interactional justice conceptually distinct? In J. Greenberg, & J. A. Colquitt (Eds.), *Handbook of organizational justice* (pp. 85–112). Mahwah, NJ: Erlbaum.

Bond, R., & Smith, P. B. (1996). Culture and conformity: A meta-analysis of studies using Asch's (1952b, 1956) line judgment task. *Psychological Bulletin, 119,* 111–137.

Brass, D. J. (1984). Being in the right place: A structural analysis of individual influence in an organization. *Administrative Science Quarterly, 29,* 518–539.

Brass, D. J. (1995). Creativity: It's all in your social network. In C. M. Ford, & D. A. Gioia (Eds.), *Creative action in organizations* (pp. 94–99). Thousand Oaks, CA: Sage.

Burke, J. (1978). *Connections.* Boston: Little, Brown.

Burt, R. S. (1992). *Structural holes.* Cambridge, MA: Harvard University Press.

Carson, R. C. (1989). Personality. *Annual Review of Psychology, 40,* 227–248.

Choi, H.-S., & Thompson, L. (2005). Old wine in a new bottle: Impact of membership change on group creativity. *Organizational Behavior and Human Decision Processes, 98,* 121–132.

Ciborra, C. (1996). The platform organization: Recombining strategies, structures, and surprises. *Organization Science, 7,* 103–118.

Claxton, G. (1997). *Hare brain tortoise mind: Why intelligence increases when you think less.* London: Fourth Estate.

Claxton, G. (2005). *The wayward mind: An intimate history of the unconscious*. London: Little, Brown.

Clore, G. L., Gaspar, K., & Garvin, E. (2001). Affect as information. In J. P. Forgas (Ed.), *Handbook of affect and cognition* (pp. 121–144). Mahwah, NJ: Erlbaum.

Clore, G. L., Schwarz, N., & Conway, M. (1994). Affective causes and consequences of social information processing. In R. S. Wyer & T. K. Srull (Eds.) *Handbook of social cognition* (2nd. ed., Vol. 1, pp. 323–417). Hillsdale, NJ: Erlbaum.

Cohen, S. G., & Bailey, D. E. (1997). What makes teams work: Group effectiveness research from the shop floor to the executive suite. *Journal of Management, 23,* 239–290.

Csikszentmihalyi, M., & Sawyer, K. (1995). Creative insight: The social dimension of a solitary moment. In R. J. Sternberg, & J. E. Davidson (Eds.), *The nature of insight* (pp. 329–363). Cambridge, MA: MIT Press.

Deci, E. L., Eghrari, H., Patrick, B. C., & Leone, D. R. (1994). Facilitating internalization: The self-determination theory perspective. *Journal of Personality, 62,* 119–142.

Deci, E. L., & Ryan, R. M. (1985). *Intrinsic motivation and self-determination in human behavior*. New York: Plenum.

Deci, E. L., & Ryan, R. M. (2000). The "what" and "why" of goal pursuits: Human needs and the self-determination of behavior. *Psychological Inquiry, 11,* 227–268.

Dijksterhuis, A. (2004). Think different: The merits of unconscious thought in preference development and decision making. *Journal of Personality and Social Psychology, 87,* 586–598.

Dijksterhuis, A., Aarts, H., & Smith, P. K. (2005). The power of the subliminal: Perception and possible applications. In R. Hassin, J. Uleman, & J. A. Bargh (Eds.), *The new unconscious* (pp. 77–106). New York: Oxford University Press.

Dijksterhuis, A., & Meurs, T. (2006). Where creativity resides: The generative power of unconscious thought. *Consciousness and Cognition, 15,* 135–146.

Dijksterhuis, A., & Nordgren, L. R. (2006). A theory of unconscious thought. *Perspectives on Psychological Science, 1,* 95–109.

Drazin, R., Glynn, M. A., & Kazanjian, R. K. (1999). Multilevel theorizing about creativity in organizations: A sensemaking perspective. *Academy of Management Review, 24,* 286–307.

Edmondson, A. C. (1999). Psychological safety and learning behavior in work teams. *Administrative Science Quarterly, 44,* 350–383.

Edmondson, A. C. (2003). Speaking up in the operating room: How team leaders promote learning in interdisciplinary action teams. *Journal of Management Studies, 40,* 1419–1452.

Egan, T. M. (2005). Factors influencing individual creativity in the workplace: An examination of quantitative empirical research. *Advances in Developing Human Resources, 7,* 160–181.

Elsbach, K. D., & Hargadon, A. B. (2006). Enhancing creativity through "mindless" work: A framework of workday design. *Organization Science, 17,* 470–483.

Fiedler, K. (1988). Emotional mood, cognitive style, and behavior regulation. In K. Fiedler, & J. Forgas (Eds.), *Affect, cognition, and social behavior* (pp. 101–119). Toronto, Canada: J. Hogrefe.

Fiedler, K. (2000). Toward an account of affect and cognition phenomena using the BIAS computer algorithm. In J. P. Forgas (Ed.), *Feeling and thinking: The role of affect in social cognition* (pp. 223–252). Paris: Cambridge University Press.

Florida, R., & Goodnight, J. (2005, July-August). Managing for creativity. *Harvard Business Review,* 125–131.

Ford, C. (1996). A theory of individual creative action in multiple social domains. *Academy of Management Review, 21,* 1112–1142.

Ford, C. M., & Gioia, D. A. (2000). Factors influencing creativity in the domain of managerial decision making. *Journal of Management, 26,* 705–732.

Forgas, J. P. (1995). Mood and judgment: The affect infusion model. *Psychological Bulletin, 117,* 39–66.

Frijda, N. H. (1988). The laws of emotion. *American Psychologist, 43,* 349–358.

Gagne, M., & Deci, E. L. (2005). Self-determination theory and work motivation. *Journal of Organizational Behavior, 26,* 331–362.

Gardner, D. G. (1986). Activation theory and task design: An empirical test of several new predictions. *Journal of Applied Psychology, 71,* 411–418.

Gardner, D. G., & Cummings, L. L. (1988). Activation theory and job design: Review and reconceptualization. In B. M. Staw, & L. L. Cummings (Eds.), *Research in organizational behavior* (Vol.10, pp. 81–122). Greenwich, CT: JAI Press.

George, J. M. (1990). Personality, affect, and behavior in groups. *Journal of Applied Psychology, 75,* 107–116.

George, J. M. (1992). The role of personality in organizational life: Issues and evidence. *Journal of Management, 18,* 185–213.

George, J. M. (2007). Dialectics of creativity in complex organizations. In T. Davila, M. J. Epstein, & R. Shelton (Eds.), *The creative enterprise: Managing innovative organizations and people,* (Vol. 2, pp. 1–15). Westport, CT: Praeger.

George, J. M., & Brief, A. P. (1992). Feeling good—Doing good: A conceptual analysis of the mood at work-organizational spontaneity relationship. *Psychological Bulletin, 112,* 310–329.

George, J. M., & King, E. B. (2007). Potential pitfalls of affect convergence in teams: Functions and dysfunctions of group affective tone. In E. A. Mannix, M. A. Neale, & C. P. Anderson (Eds.), *Research on managing groups and teams: Affect and groups* (Vol. 10, pp. 97–123). New York: Elsevier.

George, J. M., & Zhou, J. (2001). When openness to experience and conscientiousness are related to creative behavior: An interactional approach. *Journal of Applied Psychology, 86,* 513–524.

George, J. M., & Zhou, J. (2002). Understanding when bad moods foster creativity and good ones don't: The role of context and clarity of feelings. *Journal of Applied Psychology, 87,* 687–697.

George, J. M., & Zhou, J. (2007). Dual tuning in a supportive context: Joint contributions of positive mood, negative mood, and supervisory behaviors to employee creativity. *Academy of Management Journal, 50,* 605–622.

Gini, A. (2001). *My job, my self: Work and the creation of the modern individual.* New York: Routledge.

Goethals, G. R., & Darley, J. M. (1977). Social comparison theory: An attributional approach. In J. M. Suls, & R. L. Miller (Eds.), *Social comparison processes: Theoretical and empirical perspectives* (pp. 259–278). Washington, DC: Hemisphere Publishing.

Goncalo, J. A., & Staw, B. M. (2006). Individualism—Collectivism and group creativity. *Organizational Behavior and Human Decision Processes, 100,* 96–109.

Gough, H. G. (1979). A creative personality scale for the adjective check list. *Journal of Personality and Social Psychology, 37,* 1398–1405.

Granovetter, M. S. (1982). The strength of weak ties: A network theory revisited. In P. V. Marsden, & N. Lin (Eds.), *Social structure and network analysis* (pp. 105–130). Beverly Hills, CA: Sage.

Grawitch, M. J., Munz, D. C., Elliott, E. K., & Mathis, A. (2003). Promoting creativity in temporary problem-solving groups: The effects of positive mood and autonomy in problem definition on idea-generating performance. *Group Dynamics: Theory, Research, and Practice, 7,* 200–213.

Grawitch, M. J., Munz, D. C., & Kramer, T. J. (2003). Effects of member mood states on creative performance in temporary work groups. *Group Dynamics: Theory, Research, and Practice, 7,* 41–54.

Greenberg, J. (1993). The social side of fairness: Interpersonal and informational classes of justice. In R. Cropanzano (Ed.), *Justice in the workplace: Approaching fairness in human resource management* (pp. 79–103). Hillsdale, NJ: Erlbaum.

Greene, T. R., & Noice, H. (1988). Influence of positive affect upon creative thinking and problem solving in children. *Psychological Reports, 63,* 895–898.

Hardin, C. D., & Conley, T. D. (2000). A relational approach to cognition: Shared experience and relationship affirmation in social cognition. In G. B. Moscowitz (Ed.), *Future directions in social cognition* (pp. 3– 17). Hillsdale, NJ: Erlbaum.

Hardin, C. D., & Higgins, E. T. (1996). Shared reality: How social verification makes the subjective objective. In E. T. Higgins (Ed.), *Handbook of motivation and cognition* (Vol. 3, pp. 28–84). New York: Guilford Press.

Hargadon, A. B., & Bechky, B. A. (2006). When collections of creatives become creative collectives: A field study of problem solving at work. *Organization Science, 17,* 484–500.

Hargadon, A. B., & Sutton, R. I. (1997). Technology brokering and innovation in a product development firm. *Administrative Science Quarterly, 42,* 716–749.

Hirt, E. R., McDonald, H. E., & Melton, R. J. (1996). Processing goals and the affect-performance link: Mood as main effect or mood as input? In L. L. Martin, & A. Tesser (Eds.), *Striving and feeling: Interactions among goals, affect, and self-regulation* (pp. 303–328). Mahwah, NJ: Elrbaum.

Ilgen, D. (1999). Teams embedded in organizations: Some implications. *American Psychologist, 54,* 129–139.

Isen, A. M., Daubman, K. A., & Nowicki, G. P. (1987). Positive affect facilitates creative problem solving. *Journal of Personality and Social Psychology, 52,* 1122–1131.

Isen, A. M., Johnson, M. M. S., Mertz, E., & Robinson, G. R. (1985). The influence of positive affect on the unusualness of word associations. *Journal of Personality and Social Psychology, 48,* 1413–1426.

Jackson, S. (1992). Team composition in organizations. In S. Worchel, W. Wood, & J. Simpson (Eds.), *Group process and productivity* (pp. 138–173). Newbury Park, CA: Sage.

Janssen, O. (2000). Job demands, perceptions of effort-reward fairness, and innovative work behavior. *Journal of Occupational and Organizational Psychology, 73,* 287–302.

Janssen, O. (2001). Fairness perceptions as a moderator in the curvilinear relationships between job demands, and job performance and job satisfaction. *Academy of Management Journal, 44,* 1039–1050.

Janssen, O. (2003). Innovative behavior and job involvement at the price of conflict and less satisfactory relations with co-workers. *Journal of Occupational and Organizational Psychology, 76,* 347–364.

Janssen, O. (2005). The joint impact of perceived influence and supervisor supportiveness on employee innovative behavior. *Journal of Occupational and Organizational Psychology, 78,* 573–579.

Janssen, O., & Van Yperen, N. W. (2004). Employees' goal orientations, the quality of leader-member exchange, and the outcomes of job performance and job satisfaction. *Academy of Management Journal, 47,* 368–384.

Jett, Q. R., & George, J. M. (2003). Work interrupted: A closer look at the role of interruptions in organizational life. *Academy of Management Review, 28,* 494–507.

Johnson, E., & Tversky, A. (1983). Affect, generalization, and the perception of risk. *Journal of Personality and Social Psychology, 45,* 20–31.

Kahneman, D. (2003). A perceptive on judgment and choice: Mapping bounded rationality. *American Psychologist, 58,* 697–720.

Kaufmann, G. (2003). The effect of mood on creativity in the innovation process. In L. V. Shavinina (Ed.), *The international handbook on innovation* (pp. 191–203). Oxford, U.K.: Elsevier Science.

Kaufmann, G., & Vosburg, S. K. (1997). 'Paradoxical' mood effects on creative problem-solving. *Cognition and Emotion, 11,* 151–170.

Kavanaugh, D. J., & Bower, G. H. (1985). Mood and self-efficacy: Impact of joy and sadness on perceived capabilities. *Cognitive Therapy and Research, 9,* 507–525.

Kenrick, D. T., & Funder, D. C. (1988). Profiting from controversy: Lessons from the person-situation debate. *American Psychologist, 43,* 23–34.

Kim, H., & Markus, H. R. (1999). Deviance or uniqueness, harmony or conformity: A cultural analysis. *Journal of Personality and Social Psychology, 77,* 785–800.

Kirton, M. J. (1976). Adaptors and innovators: A description and measure. *Journal of Applied Psychology, 61,* 622–629.

Kirton, M. J. (1994). *Adaptors and innovators: Styles of creativity and problem solving* (2nd ed.). New York: Routledge.

Kruglanski, A. W., Pierro, A., Mannetti, L., & De Grada, E. (2006). Groups as epistemic providers: Need for closure and the unfolding of group-centrism. *Psychological Review, 113,* 84–100.

Lee, F., Edmondson, A. C., Thomke, S., & Worline, M. (2004). The mixed effects of inconsistence on experimentation in organizations. *Organization Science, 15,* 310–326.

Leonard, D., & Swap, W. (1999). *When sparks fly: Igniting creativity in groups.* Boston: Harvard Business School Press.

Levine, J. M., & Choi, H.-S. (2004). Impact of personnel turnover on team performance and cognition. In E. Salas & S. M. Fiore (Eds.), *Team cognition: Process and performance at the interindividual level* (pp. 163–176). Washington, D.C.: American Psychological Association.

Levine, J. M., & Higgins, E. T. (2001). Shared reality and social influence in groups and organizations. In F. Butera, & G. Mugny (Eds.), *Social influence in social reality* (pp. 33–53). Seattle, WA: Hogrefe & Huber.

Lewis, J. D., & Weigert, A. (1985). Trust as a social reality. *Social Forces, 63,* 967–985.

Madjar, N., & Oldham, G. R. (2006). Task rotation and polychronicity: Effects on individuals' creativity. *Human Performance, 19,* 117–131.

Mainemelis, C. (2001). When the muse takes it all: A model for the experience of timelessness in organizations. *Academy of Management Review, 26,* 548–565.

Mannix, E., & Neale, M. A. (2005). What differences make a difference: The promise and reality of diverse teams in organizations. *Psychological Science in the Public Interest, 6*(2), 31–55.

Martin, L. L., Abend, T., Sedikides, C., & Green, J. D. (1997). How would I feel if...? Mood as input to a role fulfillment evaluation process. *Journal of Personality and Social Psychology, 73,* 242–253.

Martin, L. L., Achee, J. W., Ward, D. W., & Harlow, T. F. (1993). The role of cognition and effort in the use of emotions to guide behavior. In R. W. Wyer, & T. K. Srull (Eds.), *Advances in social cognition,* (Vol. 6, pp. 147–157). Hillsdale, NJ: Erlbaum.

Martin, L. L. &, Stoner, P. (1996). Mood as input: What we think about how we feel determines how we think. In L. L. Martin, & A. Tesser (Eds.), *Striving and feeling: Interactions among goals, affect, and self-regulation* 279–301. Mahwah, NJ: Erlbaum.

Martin, L. L., Ward, D. W., Achee, J. W., & Wyer, R. S. (1993). Mood as input: People have to interpret the motivational implications of their moods. *Journal of Personality and Social Psychology, 64,* 317–326.

Mason, C. M., & Griffin, M. A. (2003). Group absenteeism and positive affective tone: A longitudinal study. *Journal of Organizational Behavior, 24,* 667–687.

Masserman, J. H. (1971). The principle of uncertainty in neurotigenesis. In H. D. Kimmel (Ed.), *Experimental psychopathology: Recent research and theory* (pp. 13–32). San Diego: Academic Press.

McAllister, D. J. (1995). Affect- and cognition-based trust as foundations for interpersonal cooperation in organizations. *Academy of Management Journal, 38,* 24–59.

Miller, G. A. (1956). Information theory. *Scientific American, 195,* 42–46.

Mumford, M., & Gustafson, S. (1988). Creativity syndrome: Integration, application, and innovation. *Psychological Bulletin, 103,* 27–43.

Nemeth, C. J. (1992). Minority dissent as a stimulant to group performance. In S. P. Worchel, W. Wood, & J. L. Simpson (Eds.), *Productivity and process in groups* (pp. 95–111). Newbury Park, CA: Sage.

Nemeth, C. J., & Owens, P. (1996). Making work groups more effective: The value of minority dissent. In M. A. West (Ed.), *Handbook of work group psychology* (pp. 125–142). Chichester, U.K.: Wiley.

Niehoff, B. P., & Moorman, R. H. (1993). Justice as a mediator of the relationship between methods of monitoring and organizational citizenship behavior. *Academy of Management Journal, 36,* 527–556.

Norretranders, T. (1998). *The user illusion: Cutting consciousness down to size.* New York: Viking.

Ohly, S., Sonnentag, S., & Pluntke, F. (2006). Routinization, work characteristics and their relationships with creative and proactive behaviors. *Journal of Organizational Behavior, 27,* 257–279.

Oldham, G. R., & Cummings, A. (1996). Employee creativity: Personal and contextual factors at work. *Academy of Management Journal, 39,* 607–634.

Olton, R. (1979). Experimental studies of incubation: Searching for the elusive. *Journal of Creative Behavior, 13,* 9–22.

Paulus, P. B., & Nijstad, B. A. (Eds.). (2003). *Group creativity: Innovation through collaboration.* New York: Oxford University Press.

Pedersen, D. M. (1997). Psychological functions of privacy. *Journal of Environmental Psychology, 17,* 147–156.

Perry-Smith, J. E. (2006). Social yet creative: The role of social relationships in facilitating individual creativity. *Academy of Management Journal, 49,* 85–101.

Perry- Smith, J. E., & Shalley, C. E. (2003). The social side of creativity: A static and dynamic social network perspective. *Academy of Management Review, 28,* 89–106.

Pervin, L. A. (1985). Personality: Current controversies, issues, and directions. *Annual Review of Psychology, 36,* 83–114.

Pervin, L. A., & Lewis, M. (1978). Overview of the internal-external issue. In L. A. Pervin, & M. Lewis (Eds.), *Perspectives in interactional psychology* (pp. 1–22). New York: Plenum.

Rank, J., Pace, V. L., & Frese, M. (2004). Three avenues for future research on creativity, innovation, and initiative. *Applied Psychology: An International Review, 53,* 518–528.

Rhodes, M. (1961/1987). An analysis of creativity. In S. G. Isaksen (Ed.), *Frontiers of creativity research: Beyond the basics* (pp. 216–222). Buffalo, NY: Bearly.

Rice, G. (2006). Individual values, organizational context, and self-perceptions of employee creativity: Evidence from Egyptian organizations. *Journal of Business Research, 59,* 233–241.

Ross, A. (2004). *No collar—The humane workplace and its hidden costs.* Philadelphia: Temple University Press.

Rowe, D. C. (1987). Resolving the person-situation debate: Invitation to an interdisciplinary dialogue. *American Psychologist, 42,* 218–227.

Runco, M. A. (1994). Creativity and its discontents. In M. P. Shaw, & M. A. Runco (Eds.), *Creativity and affect* (pp. 102–123). Norwood, NJ: Ablex.

Runco, M. A. (2004). Creativity. *Annual Review of Psychology, 55,* 657–687.

Ryan, R. M., & Deci, E. L. (2000). The darker and brighter sides of human existence: Basic psychological needs as a unifying concept. *Psychological Inquiry, 11,* 319–338.

Schooler, J. W., & Melcher, J. (1995). The ineffability of insight. In S. M. Smith, T. B. Ward, & R. A. Finke (Eds.), *The creative cognition approach* (pp. 97–134). Cambridge, MA: MIT Press.

Schwarz, N. (2002). Situated cognition and the wisdom of feelings: Cognitive tuning. In L. Feldman Barrett, & P. Salovey (Eds.), *The wisdom in feelings* (pp. 144–166). New York: Guilford.

Schwarz, N., & Clore, G. L. (1983). Mood, misattribution, and judgments of well-being: Informative and directive functions of affective states. *Journal of Personality and Social Psychology, 45,* 13–23.

Schwarz, N., & Clore, G. L. (1988). How do I feel about it? The information function of affective states. In. K. Fiedler & J. Forgas (Eds.), *Affect, cognition, and social behavior* (pp. 44–62). Toronto: C. J. Hogrefe.

Schwarz, N., & Clore, G. L. (1996). Feelings and phenomenal experiences. In E. T. Higgins, & A. Kruglanski (Eds.), *Social psychology: Handbook of basic principles* (pp. 433–465). New York: Guilford.

Schwarz, N., & Clore, G. L. (2003). Mood as information: 20 years later. *Psychological Inquiry, 14,* 296–303.

Scott, S. G., & Bruce, R. A. (1994). Determinants of innovative behavior: A path model of individual innovation in the workplace. *Academy of Management Journal, 37,* 580–607.

Scott, W. E. J. (1966). Activation theory and task design. *Organizational Behavior and Human Performance, 1,* 3–30.

Shalley, C. E., & Perry-Smith, J. E. (2001). Effects of social-psychological factors on creative performance: The role of informational and controlling expected evaluation and modeling experience. *Organizational Behavior and Human Decision Processes, 84,* 1–22.

Shalley, C. E., Zhou, J., & Oldham, G. R. (2004). Effects of personal and contextual characteristics on creativity: Where should we go from here? *Journal of Management, 30,* 933–958.

Shin, S., & Zhou, J. (2003). Transformational leadership, conservation, and creativity: Evidence from Korea. *Academy of Management Journal, 46,* 703–714.

Simon, H. A. (1955). A behavioral model of rational choice. *Quarterly Journal of Economics, 69,* 99–118.

Simonton, D. K. (1984). Artistic creativity and interpersonal relationships across and within generations. *Journal of Personality and Social Psychology, 46,* 1273–1286.

Smith, S. M. (2003). The constraining effects of initial ideas. In P. B. Paulus, & B. A. Nijstad (Eds.), *Group creativity: Innovation through collaboration* (pp. 15–31). New York: Oxford University Press.

Sniezek, J. A. (1992). Groups under uncertainty: An examination of confidence in group decision making. *Organizational Behavior and Human Decision Processes, 52,* 124–155.

Staw, B. M. (1980). The consequences of turnover. *Journal of Occupational Behavior, 1,* 253–273.

Staw, B. M. (1995). Why no one really wants creativity. In C. M. Ford, & D. A. Gioia (Eds.), *Creative action in organizations* (pp. 161–166). Thousand Oaks, CA: Sage.

Staw, B. M., Sandelands, L. E., & Dutton, J. E. (1981). Threat-rigidity effects in organizational behavior: A multilevel analysis. *Administrative Science Quarterly, 26,* 501–524.

Thomke, S. (2003). *Experimentation matters: Unlocking the potential of new technologies for innovation.* Boston: Harvard Business School Press.

Tiedens, L. Z., Sutton, R. I., & Fong, C. T. (2004). Emotional variation in work groups: Causes and performance consequences. In L. Z. Tiedens, & C. W. Leach (Eds.), *The social life of emotions* (pp. 164–186). New York: Cambridge University Press.

Totterdell, P., Kellett, S., Teuchmann, K., & Briner, R. B. (1998). Evidence of mood linkage in work groups. *Journal of Personality and Social Psychology, 74,* 1504–1515.

Tversky, A., & Kahneman, D. (1974). Judgment under uncertainty: Heuristics and biases. *Science, 185,* 1124–1131.

Unsworth, K. (2001). Unpacking creativity. *Academy of Management Review, 26,* 289–297.

Unsworth, K. L., Wall, T. D., & Carter, A. (2005). Creative requirement: A neglected construct in the study of employee creativity? *Group and Organization Management, 30,* 541–560.

Uzzi, B., & Spiro, J. (2005). Collaboration and creativity: The small world problem. *The American Journal of Sociology, 111,* 447–504.

Vincente, W. (1990). *What engineers know and how they know it.* Baltimore: John Hopkins University Press.

Vosburg, S. K. (1998a). The effects of positive and negative mood on divergent thinking performance. *Creativity Research Journal, 11,* 165–172.

Vosburg, S. K. (1998b). Mood and the quantity and quality of ideas. *Creativity Research Journal, 11,* 315–324.

Weick, K. E. (1979). *The social psychology of organizing.* Reading, MA: Addison-Wesley.

Westin, A. F. (1967). *Privacy and freedom.* New York: Atheneum.

Williams, K., & O'Reilly, C. (1998). The complexity of diversity: A review of forty years of research. In B. Staw, & R. Sutton (Eds.), *Research in organizational behavior* (Vol. 21, pp. 77–140). Greenwich, CT: JAI Press.

Wilson, T. D. (2002). *Strangers to ourselves: Discovering the adaptive unconscious.* Cambridge, MA: Harvard University Press.

Wilson, T. D., & Schooler, J. W. (1991). Thinking too much: Introspection can reduce the quality of preferences and decisions. *Journal of Personality and Social Psychology, 60,* 181–192.

Woodman, R. W., Sawyer, J. E., & Griffin, R. W. (1993). Toward a theory of organizational creativity. *Academy of Management Review, 18,* 293–321.

Zhou, J., & Shalley, C. E. (2003). Research on employee creativity: A critical review and directions for future research. In J. J. Martocchio, & G. R. Ferris (Eds.), *Research in Personnel and Human Resource Management* (Vol. 22, pp. 165–217). Oxford, U.K.: Elsevier Science.

Ziller, R. C. (1965). Toward a theory of open and closed groups. *Psychological Bulletin, 65,* 164–182.

Ziller, R. C., Behringer, R. D., & Goodchilds, J. D. (1962). Group creativity under conditions of success or failure and variations in group stability. *Journal of Applied Psychology, 46,* 43–49.

10
Learning and Strategic Alliances

ANDREW C. INKPEN

Thunderbird

ERIC W. K. TSANG

University of Texas at Dallas

Abstract

Various researchers have suggested that an important explanatory factor for the growth in strategic alliances is that alliances provide a platform for organizational learning, giving firms access to the knowledge of their partners. The notion that alliances are a vehicle for learning is the basis for an important and cross-disciplinary stream of research. This chapter examines theoretical and empirical research in the alliance learning area. We have two central objectives. The first is to integrate a large body of research by examining the key research questions addressed. The second objective is to critically examine the existing research as the basis for establishing a research agenda. Although the alliance learning area has generated a substantial amount of research interest and spawned wide-ranging types of inquiry, many important and substantive managerial issues remain underexplored.

Introduction

Since the early 1980s, there has been a global proliferation of strategic alliances of many different forms. The essence of strategic alliances is that a collaborative effort provides incentives for a firm to combine its own competencies with the competencies of its partners and, in the process, achieve strategic benefits that the partners can share (Makino & Inkpen, 2003). Alliances offer several benefits. First, they enable an increase in operating efficiencies by pooling economic activities, such as raw-materials supply, manufacturing, and marketing and distribution (Kogut, 1988). Second, alliances also reduce risk and promote stability. Strategic alliances may be an attractive option as a vehicle to manage risk in large, complex projects (Ghoshal, 1987). A third benefit is that alliances can help reduce demand or competitive uncertainties (Burgers, Hill, & Kim, 1993). A fourth benefit, and the subject of this chapter, is that alliances provide a platform for organizational learning, giving the alliance and partner firms access to new knowledge. Through the shared execution of the alliance task, mutual interdependence and problem solving, and observation of alliance activities and outcomes, firms can learn with and from their partners. Unlike other learning contexts, the formation of an alliance reduces the risk that the knowledge will dissipate quickly (Powell, 1987) because the creation of an alliance results in a new organizational entity. Thus, alliances provide an ideal platform for learning. Two or more organizations are brought together because of their different skills, knowledge, and strategic complementarity. The differences in partner skills and knowledge provide the catalyst for learning by both the alliance organization and by the parent firms.

Until about two decades ago, research dealing with strategic alliances primarily focused on areas such as governance forms and task structures. The issue of learning was largely unexamined. Today, the notion that alliances are a vehicle for learning is the basis for an important and cross-disciplinary stream of research, which has evolved alongside of the important emphasis in the management arena on organizational-learning capability and knowledge management. More than a decade ago, researchers accurately predicted that learning capability and learning organization would become two key concepts of future management thinking (Ulrich, Von Glinow, & Jick, 1993). Today, it is well accepted that organizational knowledge is perhaps the most valuable firm resource and that an organization's ability to learn is crucial for its competitive success.

As a subfield within the broader field of organizational learning, the literature on alliance learning has evolved into a well-developed and legitimate research area. In considering this body of work, the current chapter has two main purposes. The first is to review what is known about alliances and learning. After providing some background material on the nature of alliance learning and knowledge, we examine the evolution of the field and discuss the main research areas. The second purpose of this chapter is to argue that although the alliance learning area has generated a substantial amount of research interest and spawned wide-ranging types of inquiry, many important and substantive issues remain underexplored. These issues are examined as the basis for establishing a research agenda.

Types of Alliance Learning

Managing strategic alliances is a multifaceted and interrelated process involving a variety of organizational challenges (Glaister, Husan, & Buckley, 2003).

As starting point in examining alliances and learning, we classify four types of alliance learning.

Learning about alliance management. Firms can learn about alliances and acquire knowledge useful in the design and management of other alliances (Gulati, 1999; Gupta & Misra, 2000; Lyles, 1988; Simonin, 1997). This collaborative know-how may be applied to the management of future alliances. Parkhe (1991) argued that alliances can become stronger when the partners learn to analyze their diversity and to devise solutions to accommodate the differences. Other studies have found evidence that firms with experience in alliances are more likely to replicate that behavior than are firms pursuing autonomous strategies (Gulati, 1999; Pennings, Barkema, & Douma, 1994). There is also some evidence that alliance-experienced firms learn to manage alliances more effectively over time (Anand & Khanna, 2000; Barkema, Shenkar, Vermeulen, & Bell, 1997; Tsang, 2002). Lyles' (1988) study of four joint-venture sophisticated firms found that what the firms had learned from their experience led managers to be effective in developing partner rapport and understanding the life cycle of a joint venture. Similarly, Varadarajan, and Cunningham (1995) argued that a firm's accumulated learning from its past involvement in strategic alliances is likely to have an impact on the effectiveness of its future alliances. A caveat suggested by Sampson's (2005) study of R&D alliances in the telecom-equipment industry is that the benefits of prior alliance experience may depreciate rapidly over time.

Learning about an alliance partner. Doz and Hamel (1998) referred to learning about an alliance partner as skill familiarity that supports the alliance partner's ability to jointly create value. The knowledge obtained can be central to the evolution of the alliance (Ariño & De La Torre, 1998; Doz, 1996). Such knowledge plays a particularly important role when the partners of an alliance jointly enter a new business area and develop new capabilities. Compared with acquiring the alliance-management skills just discussed, the learning activity here is more partner-specific, although both learning activities will support effective alliance management. Thus, this type of learning should not be viewed as an alliance motive, but rather, as a factor that supports effective alliance management.

Learning with an alliance partner. Learning with a partner can occur when the partners jointly enter into a new business area and develop new capabilities. With this type of learning, called "reciprocal learning" by Lubatkin, Florin, and Lane (2001), the goal is complementary specialization rather than knowledge transfer because each alliance partner continues to operate in its own area of expertise (Mowery, Oxley, & Silverman, 2002). In other words, each partner learns about and from the other partner without intending to acquire the other's capabilities. Grant and Baden-Fuller (2002) argued that this learning pattern represents the advantages of alliances over both markets and firms due to the efficiency with which knowledge is utilized. Airbus is a typical example of such an alliance whose member firms specialize in the design and manufacture of specific parts of the overall aircraft. The empirical study conducted by Mowery and colleagues (2002) indicated that familiarity with an alliance partner's capabilities facilitated coordination and integration of the activities undertaken by alliance partners, and partner-specific absorptive capacity played a significant role in the organization and outcome of this type of alliance.

Learning from an alliance partner.   Alliances, by definition, involve collaborative activities by two or more firms. In working together, firms have the opportunity to learn from their partners and gain access to knowledge that would otherwise be inaccessible. Access to an alliance partner's knowledge can be viewed from several strategic perspectives. Firms may seek access to other firms' knowledge and skills but not necessarily with a goal of integrating the knowledge in their own operations. When firms seek to combine their skills in an alliance, the partners contribute knowledge to the alliance, and then this knowledge will be adapted to suit the firm and industry characteristics of the alliance. This learning and knowledge transfer process must occur to some degree if a viable alliance is to be created. If parents do not transfer knowledge to the new alliance entity, the alliance has little reason to exist as a collaborative vehicle.

Alliances also create opportunities for the parent firms to acquire knowledge that can be used to enhance parent strategy and operations in areas unrelated to the alliance activities. This knowledge, which is the focus of this chapter, constitutes the private benefits that a firm can earn unilaterally by acquiring skills from its partner (Khanna, Gulati, & Nohria, 1998). Unlike knowledge dealing with how to manage alliances or knowledge about the partner, this type of knowledge is directly associated with the skills of the partner firm(s) and has value to the parent outside the alliance agreement, which means that the knowledge can be internalized by the parent and applied to new geographic markets, products, and businesses. This potentially useful knowledge is knowledge the parent would not have had access to without forming the alliance. Useful knowledge may be knowledge transferred by an alliance partner to the alliance. It may exist because the alliance creates a forum for interactions between the partners. The alliance may also independently create useful knowledge through its interactions with customers, competitors, and other firms.

The first three learning types—(1) learning about alliance management, (2) learning about an alliance partner, and (3) learning with an alliance partner—can be called "partner learning from a strategic-alliance experience."

Once an alliance is formed, some of this learning will occur if the alliance is to succeed, although only learning about an alliance partner will have a direct effect on alliance performance. The fourth type of learning—(d) learning from an alliance partner—is far from inevitable and might even be explicitly blocked by an alliance partner. It is this type of learning that has generated the most research interest and, consequently, will provide the major focus for this chapter. To learn through an alliance, a firm must have access to partner knowledge and must work closely with its partner. As a result, both collaborative process and firm-specific perspectives must be understood.

Various different strategic rationales may motivate firms to form learning-oriented alliances. A typical situation in alliances with strong learning objectives is that cooperation is preferable because the sought-after skills and capabilities are too costly to develop internally. Forming an alliance can also provide an opportunity to acquire highly tacit knowledge. As elaborated next, if the knowledge is tacit, it may be acquirable only by close observation and interactions with the owners/managers of the tacit knowledge. Thus, an alliance may provide access to this knowledge. General Motors' acquisition of knowledge from its NUMMI joint venture would fit this model (Inkpen, 2005). Alliances may also function as a viable alternative to acquisitions. Kogut (1991) suggested that alliances may be investments that provide firms with expansion opportunities. Faced with uncertainty and a desire to learn, firms may prefer an alliance to acquisition. If one partner has the option to purchase the other's equity in the venture, that partner can utilize the alliance as a means of acquiring complex knowledge about the business. Once the party with the option to buy has acquired (i.e., learned) the skills of the partner firm, further investment in the venture might not be warranted. At this point, the buy option may be exercised and the alliance terminated.

In focusing on alliance learning, we assume that learning is both a function of access to new knowledge and the capabilities for using and building on such knowledge (Powell, Koput, & Smith-Doerr, 1996). We also adopt the perspective that alliances are mixed-motive structural forms. Alliances can also be a zero-sum game in which the partner learning the fastest dominates the relationship (Hamel, 1991) and alliances can be the platform for mutual value creation. In the messy world of practice, it is not easy to separate these two positions because partner skill appropriation and the alliance as community are intertwined.

The Learning Context

Alliance Form

A strategic alliance is a long-term cooperative arrangement between two or more independent firms that engage in business activities for mutual economic gain. Multiple organizational forms can legitimately be called strategic alliances, such as equity joint ventures, minority equity relationships, licensing agreements, and an array of nonequity contractual arrangements, including collaborative R&D, coproduction agreements, technology sharing, and shared marketing and distribution deals. Alliance researchers must recognize that different alliance forms have unique organizational and strategic attributes and, therefore, a one-size-fits-all approach to alliance theory will rarely be useful or valid. Geppert (1996) argued that managerial learning is embedded in a specific social context. Different alliance forms constitute different contexts in which learning occurs. In this chapter, where appropriate, we will identify alliance forms and theoretical issues that arise when different forms are involved.

Hagedoorn and Narula's (1996) analysis of the MERIT-Cooperative Agreements and Technology Indicators database indicated that high-technology sectors tend to have a higher share of nonequity alliances than medium- or low-tech sectors. In situations of high-tech complexities, there are high uncertainties about both the outcomes of technological changes as well as the market structural consequences of these changes. Under such unstable conditions, the more flexible, evolution-oriented, nonequity alliances provide a more effective environment for reciprocal information exchange and discovery of new knowledge than equity forms. In a more stable industry structure combined with less dynamic technological changes, organizational control over information flows and new technological applications with a long life cycle becomes more relevant and, thus, equity alliances are often preferred.

Moreover, it should be noted that research-intensive cooperation often involves the management of tacit knowledge that is not easily transferable or codifiable (Osborn & Hagedoorn, 1997). Organically structured nonequity alliances may not provide as suitable an environment for learning as hierarchically structured equity forms. Consider, for example, the contrast between equity joint ventures and licensing agreements, the two common channels through which one firm can transfer technology to another. Equity joint ventures allow more intimate human interactions between partner firms than licensing agreements, making them suitable for transferring more complicated and organizationally embedded technologies (Kogut, 1988; Tsang, 1997a). Mowery, Oxley, and Silverman's (1996) patent citation analysis of strategic alliances formed by U.S. firms found that equity joint ventures appeared to be more effective conduits for the transfer of complex capabilities than nonequity alliances, such as licensing agreements.

Cross-Border Versus Domestic Alliances

In conjunction with the force of globalization, strategic alliances are increasingly formed between firms located in different countries. In addition to cross-border alliances established by firms from developed countries, during the last two decades, countries such as Russia, China, Vietnam, and nations in Eastern Europe have opened their economies to foreign investments. A popular market-entry mode in these emerging economies is the international joint venture and a prevalent type of learning takes the form of knowledge transfer from multinational corporations (MNCs) to local firms. In general, foreign partners come from countries with more sophisticated business environments and possess more advanced management and technological expertise. At least during the initial stage of operation, the foreign partner needs to actively transfer its expertise to the venture in order to develop the venture's competitive advantage in the local and international markets.

When commenting on learning in strategic alliances, Osborn and Hagedoorn (1997) stated, "If organizational learning within a corporate hierarchy is problematic, surely such learning is much more complex in the context of a cooperative effort" (p. 270). To extend their argument, if learning in domestic alliances is complicated, it will be more so in the case of international alliances where geographic distance and cultural differences generate additional difficulties and challenges for managers. Culture reflects the ideas, values, norms, and meanings shared by members of a society (Hofstede, 1980). In a learning context, culture influences how people process, interpret, and make use of a body of knowledge. Thus, complications may arise when knowledge is transferred across dissimilar cultures. Bhagat, Kedia, Harveston, and Triandis (2002) defined four transacting cultural patterns in terms of individualism–collectivism and verticalness–horizontalness and proposed a theoretical framework for understanding the influence of these patterns in moderating the effectiveness of cross-border transfer of organizational knowledge.

Cultural differences generally strengthen the social identities of managers working in international strategic alliances. For instance, in Sino-foreign joint ventures, the terms "the Chinese side" (or, *Zhongfang* in Chinese) and "the foreign side" (*waifang*) are frequently used by both local and expatriate managers when they described the situations in the ventures (Tsang, 2001). Social identity, in turn, affects the perceived social distance between the parties involved. In the context of international joint ventures, Child and Rodrigues (1996) argued that if the perceived social distance is great, knowledge transfer is likely to be impeded. Lyles and Salk (1996) maintained that cultural misunderstandings among managers in international joint ventures hinder flows of information and learning. They tested this hypothesis in a sample of international joint ventures established in Hungary and found that cultural misunderstandings affected knowledge acquisition only in shared-management joint ventures. Mowery and colleagues' (1996) study found that international alliances formed by U.S. firms resulted in lower levels of technology transfer than domestic alliances. They attributed this finding to geographical distance and cultural differences between partners.

Closely related to cultural differences is the issue of language differences. Effective communication is a precondition for learning. Communication between individuals is more than a simple activity, involving both the decoding and encoding of messages (Ko, Kirsch, & King, 2005). Communication is hindered if the sender and receiver of a message use different languages. Although interpreters can ease this problem, an in-depth understanding of the true meaning of a message often requires the use of a common language. When managers of a strategic alliance fail to speak the same language, a negative impact on learning can result. In a study of post-acquisition managerial learning in Central East Europe, Villinger (1996) found that language difficulties were the most frequently cited barrier to successful learning by both local and expatriate managers, followed by problems due to pronounced differences in cultures and systems, mentalities, and ways of thinking. Similarly, Tsang's (2001) case study of foreign-invested enterprises in China found that local employees' lack of English proficiency was an oft-cited problem by expatriate managers. Even with the help of interpreters, a communication barrier existed between local and expatriate managers when they could not accurately translate ideas.

Knowledge Characteristics
Learning in strategic alliances involves the creation, transfer, and absorption of knowledge. While there are different ways of classifying knowledge, the most common distinction is between tacit and explicit knowledge. Tacit knowledge is unarticulated, highly personal, and difficult to communicate whereas explicit knowledge is codified and transmittable in formal, systematic language (Nonaka, 1994; Polanyi, 1967). Empirically, Kogut and Zander (1993) developed three scales, namely (a) codifiability, (b) teachability, and (c) complexity, to measure knowledge tacitness. The distinction between tacit and explicit knowledge should not be regarded as a dichotomy, but rather as a spectrum, with the two knowledge types at the ends (Inkpen & Dinur, 1998).

Dhanaraj, Lyles, Steensma, and Tihanyi (2004) argued that while explicit knowledge provides the building blocks, tacit knowledge provides the glue and lends meaning to many explicit routines in an organization. Hence, in the context of an international joint venture, the tacit knowledge learned from a parent will assist the venture in acquiring explicit knowledge. Dhanaraj and colleagues' survey of international joint ventures formed in Hungary confirmed that the transfer of tacit knowledge from the foreign parent had a positive impact on explicit knowledge among the mature ventures. In a survey of large and medium-sized U.S. firms, Simonin (1999) found that two attributes of knowledge—(a) tacitness and (b) ambiguity—were positively related and ambiguity had a negative impact on knowledge transfer. In a case study of the China-Singapore Suzhou Industrial Park, an alliance involving the Chinese and Singaporean governments, their agencies, and various private sector organizations, Inkpen and Wang (2006) found that tacit knowledge was difficult to value and, consequently, the learning partner focused on the more easily transferable (and less valuable) explicit knowledge.

Simonin (1999) investigated the role played by knowledge ambiguity in the process of knowledge transfer between strategic alliance partners. Simonin (2004) defined knowledge ambiguity as a "lack of understanding of the logical linkages between actions and outcomes, inputs and outputs, and causes and effects that are related to technological or process know-how" (p. 413), and proposed seven antecedents of ambiguity: (a) tacitness, (b) asset specificity, (c) complexity, (d) experience, (e) partner protectiveness, (f) cultural distance, and (g) organizational distance.

Embeddedness is another attribute of knowledge that affects learning. Unlike tacitness, embeddedness is a less known and researched concept. Its meaning can be illustrated by the distinction between physical and organizational technologies, which some researchers label as *hard* and *soft* technologies, respectively (e.g., Morgan, 1991; Von Glinow & Teagarden, 1988). Compared with physical technologies, organizational technologies are more embedded in the broader fabric of the organization. Embeddedness limits the transferability of knowledge. Collinson's (1999) case study of a technical alliance between British Steel and Nippon Steel found that some of the latter's knowledge management practices were difficult to transfer because they were deeply embedded and highly dependent on broader contextual factors such as knowledge resources, organizational structure, and culture. Similarly, Tsang's (2001) case study found that foreign investors generally faced greater challenges when they tried to transfer organizational technologies to China. These challenges arose partly because the transfer involved changes in organizational systems and the mind-sets of local managers, and partly because it was often difficult to conclusively demonstrate that a given organizational technology was unquestionably more effective and efficient than its alternative.

In summary, the learning process and outcome is influenced by a variety of alliance contextual factors. We identified three key factors: (a) alliance form, (b) cultural and distance factors associated with cross-border alliances, and (c) knowledge characteristics. In addition to these factors, other alliance contextual factors can impact the learning process, such as alliance industry, the competitive and regulatory environment, intellectual property agreements and control, and the linkages between the focal alliance and a larger knowledge network.

Partner Characteristics and Their Influence on Learning

Von Hippel (1994) coined the term *stickiness* to connote the difficulty of transferring knowledge from one unit to another within an organization, or from one organization to another. Von Hippel argued that in addition to the nature of information itself, attributes related to the information seeker and provider influence information stickiness. In this section, we discuss how the characteristics of the learning and teaching partners affect how learning takes place in strategic alliances.

Learning Partner

In their survey of Canadian and U.S. firms engaging in production-based international joint ventures, Beamish and Berdrow (2003) found that while the ventures were not formed under a learning imperative, the partners often gained important skills and knowledge. Yet in the majority of cases, effective learning from an alliance partner occurs by design rather than by default. An important precondition for successful learning is the learning partner's recognition of the need or intent to learn (Goold, Campbell, & Alexander, 1994). *Intent to learn* refers to "the level of desire and will of the parent (firm) with respect to learning from the joint venturing experience" (Tsang, 2002, p. 839). In a case study of strategic alliances between Western and Japanese firms, Hamel (1991) found that Western firms generally viewed collaboration as a stable division of roles based on the unique capabilities of each partner. Thus, they lacked intent to learn from their Japanese partners. In contrast, Japanese firms considered collaboration a temporary vehicle for improving their own competitiveness through acquiring and internalizing skills possessed by their Western partners. In addition to the attitude toward collaboration, the partners' relative resource positions also impacts learning intent. Tsang (1999) argued that in strategic alliances formed by developed country firms with emerging market local partners, the developed country partners have little motivation to learn specific management and technological skills from their local partners. This view was confirmed by the findings of Tsang's (2002) survey of Singapore and Hong Kong firms with respect to their joint venture operations in China, and Wang and Nicholas' (2005) survey of contractual joint ventures formed by Hong Kong firms in China. Based on a case study of American-Japanese joint ventures located in North America, Inkpen (1996) argued further that if the initial learning objective is based on an incorrect assessment of partner competencies, subsequent learning efforts may be ineffective. Learning objectives, therefore, must be flexible enough to adapt to unexpected changes in the alliance and to allow for a revised valuation of the payoff from learning.

In addition to recognizing the need to learn, another prerequisite for learning is an attitude of receptivity. When the general attitude toward learning is positive, a firm is willing to develop mechanisms and make accommodations for learning activities. Tsang, Nguyen, and Erramilli (2004) defined *receptivity* as the readiness of the learning partner to appreciate and receive the knowledge brought in by the teaching partner. Their survey of international joint ventures formed in Vietnam found that local partner receptivity helped reduce the intensity of conflict between parents and facilitated knowledge acquisition by the local parent. Hamel's (1991) case study suggested that generating an attitude of receptivity among operating employees depended largely on whether the firm entered the alliance as a latecomer or as a laggard. In the former case, employees were motivated to learn and to close the gap of skills with the teaching partner. When a firm has come to think of itself as a laggard, its employees are likely to acquiesce to relying on the teaching partner. Such a sense of resignation will not be conducive to receptivity. In their case study of North American-Japanese joint ventures in the automotive industry, Inkpen and Crossan (1995) examined receptivity at the individual, group, and organization levels and found that linkages between these levels were required for learning to take place. For instance, even if receptivity exists at the individual level, its absence at the organizational level may suggest that the learning partner's senior managers are not receptive to the teaching partner's skills and knowledge; this attitude becomes a barrier to learning.

Access to knowledge via an alliance does not guarantee acquisition. Thus, while learning-partner receptivity and learning intent involve the general desire to learn, *absorptive capacity* concerns the ability to learn. Cohen and Levinthal (1990) used the term absorptive capacity to describe the ability of a firm to recognize the value of new knowledge and to assimilate and use the knowledge. The premise is that the firm needs prior related knowledge to utilize new knowledge. In the alliance context, Lane and Lubatkin's (1998) study of R&D capability transfer between U.S. pharmaceutical and biotechnology firms examined the concept of relative absorptive capacity and found that the ability of one firm to learn from another depends on the similarity of both firms' knowledge bases, organizational structures, compensation policies, and dominant logics. Moreover, they showed that their measure of relative absorptive capacity had greater explanatory power than the usual measure of absolute absorptive capacity by R&D spending. In a study of international joint ventures formed in Hungary, Lane, Salk, and Lyles (2001) tested a model of joint venture learning and performance that segmented relative absorptive capacity into three components: the ability of the venture to (a) understand, (b) assimilate, and (c) apply the knowledge offered by the foreign partner firm. They found that the first and third components positively related to extent of knowledge learned from the foreign parent firm and to joint venture performance, respectively, while the hypothesized effect of the second component on learning was mixed. Pak and Park's (2004) survey of international joint ventures established in Korea showed that the transfer of new product-development knowledge and manufacturing/processing skills to local firms directly related to the level of absorptive capacity. Finally, Inkpen's (1996) study suggested that the top management of the learning partner should play the role of architect and catalyst in the learning process. Such leadership commitment is especially important in initiating linkages between parent and alliance strategies. Even if there is an intent to learn, the required resources may not be forthcoming due to a lack of commitment from top management.

Teaching Partner

The characteristics of the teaching partner have received less attention than those of the learning partner. Pisano (1988) argued that the ability of a firm to learn through joint ventures depends not only on its own absorptive capacity, but also on the willingness of its partner to fully cooperate. In other words, the degree of protectiveness that the teaching partner desires, vis-à-vis its knowledge base, is a determinant of the potential for learning. The adoption of strict policies or the deployment of shielding mechanisms can protect key competencies (Inkpen & Beamish, 1997). For example, in many alliances, tasks are carefully partitioned and experts are physically separated in order to control the potential outflow of proprietary technology. Moreover, assigning gatekeepers to filter information access and disclosure at the alliance interface reduces the unintended dissemination of knowledge (Baughn, Denekamp, Stevens, & Obsorn, 1997). We discuss protectiveness in more detail later in the chapter.

While protectiveness refers to the willingness, or lack thereof, to share knowledge, transparency may not be the outcome of any intentional actions. For a variety of reasons, some partners are more open and accessible than others. Hamel's (1991) study found systematic asymmetries in transparency between Western and Japanese partners, with the former being far more transparent than the latter. Hamel attributed this difference to the openness of Western cultural and organizational contexts, the clannish attitude of Japanese managers, and the fact that the manufacturing competence that the Japanese partners brought to the alliances was deeply embedded in the social context of the firm. Other factors affecting transparency included the extent to which the nature of joint tasks required regular and intensive intermingling of staff from both partners, and one partner's speed of innovation relative to the other's pace of absorption.

In a study of technology transfer, Teece (1977) found that alliances incurred substantial costs when transferring technology from one country to another. In the context of a strategic alliance, the teaching partner has to commit not only physical assets, but more importantly, the training and support required to make the transfer of knowledge a success. Inkpen and Wang (2006) described the extensive efforts of the Singapore government to transfer knowledge in its Suzhou Industrial Park alliance. Tsang and colleagues' (2004) survey of international joint ventures in Vietnam found that the level of foreign parent commitment was positively related to the amount of knowledge that a joint venture acquired from its foreign parent. In a case study of foreign-invested enterprises in China, Tsang (2001) found that the foreign investor's commitment of human resources, in terms of the quantity and quality of expatriate managers assigned to China, affected how managerial learning took place in these operations. In general, the greater the commitment shown, the more likely that learning would be facilitated. For instance, some managers were assigned to China on a part-time basis. The problem with using part-time expatriate managers is that most of the managers did not have proper management positions and titles in the operations. In a study of Sino-Swedish joint ventures, Sharma and Wallström-Pan (1997) quoted one expatriate manager as saying, "Experts who sit on the side to help production but are not actually supervisors do not get any respect from the Chinese. . . . No one goes to them for advice, unless they have some kind of position or title" (p. 377). Not surprisingly, part-time expatriate managers often faced difficulties when they tried to pass their knowledge on to local staff in China. Similarly, Lyles and Salk's (1996) survey of international joint ventures in Hungary found that foreign partners' provision of training, technology, and managerial expertise was positively associated with the extent to which knowledge was acquired by the ventures.

Related to resource commitment is the teaching partner's control over the alliance operation. Makhija and Ganesh (1997) argued that control mechanisms at the outset of a joint venture based on balanced bargaining power are better able to satisfy the learning needs of partners. For international joint ventures formed in emerging economies where foreign partners often play the teaching role, however, Lin (2005) maintained that control is a vehicle foreign partners use to transfer knowledge to their local counterparts. In a study of Sino-U.S. joint ventures, Lin found supporting evidence that U.S. management control had a direct, positive impact on knowledge acquisition by Chinese partners. Similarly, Yan and Child's (2002) study of Sino-British joint ventures found a positive association between the transfer of the British partner's proprietary technology to the venture and the partner's influence over decisions related to the implementation and localization of the technology.

Interpartner and Partner Alliance Relationships

The dynamics of learning within an alliance become complicated when considering the interactions of the different aspects of learning by the alliance partners. Consider the case of learning associated with an alliance between partners from an emerging economy and a developed country. When there is a large gap of interpartner technical competence, the partners are likely to focus on very different learning activities. If the foreign partner is from a developed economy and is transferring technology to the alliance, this firm will be primarily interested in learning about the host country. Some of this learning could come naturally through participation in the alliance, and some could occur via a systematic attempt to acquire the local partner's skills in areas such as the regulatory environment and local human-resource practices. The local partner will seek to become familiar with and internalize the foreign partner's skills at various activities. For several decades, this learning pattern has played a key role in the strategies of MNCs. Thousands of Western companies have established joint ventures and other forms of strategic alliances in emerging economies such as China, India, Russia, and Eastern Europe. The emerging-economy companies seek to import modern technology by collaborating with Western companies, which, in turn, try to take advantage of the low labor cost and sizable market of these economies.

Learning and Bargaining Power Between Alliance Partners

In the alliance type discussed in the previous paragraph, issues of bargaining power become paramount because each side is seeking to enhance its skill base. Bargaining power in alliances arises out of the relative urgency of cooperation, available resources, commitments, other alternatives, and the strengths and weaknesses of each partner. The pace of knowledge acquisition by one alliance partner is a dimension in the bargaining power relationship because, as Hamel (1991) argued, this dimension is very much within the firm's control. Because of this controllability, Hamel identified learning as the most important element in determining relative bargaining power. When learning shifts the dependency relationship, the cooperative basis for the alliance may erode, and venture instability may result. If one partner acquires knowledge faster than the other, the faster learning partner no longer has the same need, which can lead to a situation of partner asymmetry (Makhija & Ganesh, 1997).

Inkpen and Beamish (1997) examined the root causes of instability in international joint ventures and argued that once the partners form the venture, if the foreign partner attaches a high value to the acquisition of local knowledge and has the ability to acquire the knowledge, the probability of instability increases. In a survey of Indian joint ventures, Kale and Anand (2006) found that MNCs had a much greater learning intent and more capabilities than their local counterparts and, in some cases, were actively using these capabilities to take greater control of their joint ventures. Once a foreign partner has acquired local knowledge, unless the local partner is contributing other valuable and nonimitable skills to the alliance, the rationale for cooperation will be eliminated. Instability may result, although relationship attributes between the partners may moderate the shifts in bargaining power. Thus, the acquisition of local knowledge is an enabling device for the foreign partner to operate autonomously. Yan and Gray's (1994) case study of bargaining power and control in Sino-U.S. joint ventures identified both resource-based and context-based components of bargaining power. They found that the main resource contributed by the local partners was local knowledge in areas such as local sourcing, domestic distribution, and personnel management.

Interestingly, Kale and Anand (2006) suggested that many local firms have become aware of MNCs' attempts to exploit learning opportunities. As a result, local firms may become wary about forming joint ventures and will seek to strengthen their own learning capabilities. Kale and Anand also found that in India, the number of joint ventures has declined because MNCs have taken advantage of deregulation to outlearn their local partners and shift their investments to wholly owned subsidiaries.

Alliances Between Competitors

Alliances between competitors are commonplace in many industries. Partners of these alliances often use the alliances as an expedient means of strengthening their competitiveness in the marketplace. In other words, collaboration between partners takes place under the shadow of competition. In some industries, such as biotechnology (Owen-Smith & Powell, 2004) or clothing (Uzzi, 1997), ties between a network of competitors play a key role in the movement of information and knowledge between and among these firms. Owen-Smith and Powell argued that "formal alliances among diverse organizations in a science-based industry may convey innovation benefits, either as diffuse channels for information spillovers or as proprietary pathways for directed information and resource transfer between partners" (p. 6).

Trust, "the mutual confidence among the partners that none of them will exploit another's vulnerabilities" (Tsang, 1999, p. 220), is a particularly salient issue in competitor alliances. Hamel, Doz, and Prahalad (1989) gave the following advice to companies that partner with competitors: "Successful companies never forget that their new partners may be out to disarm them" (p. 134). If all partners of an alliance subscribe to this "conspiracy view," rampant suspicions will leave little room for developing interpartner trust. No alliance contract can cover all of the possible contingencies. Trust is important because it represents a willingness of partners to work things out through mutual problem solving (Uzzi, 1997). As learning often requires informal give-and-take between partners, a relationship built on a contract only may not suffice for effective knowledge transfer to take place. Trust facilitates learning by creating a sense of security that the knowledge concerned will not be exploited beyond what is initially intended (Dhanaraj et al., 2004).

The difficulty of establishing trust in competitor alliances constitutes a barrier to learning. More specifically, conventional wisdom suggests that competitors would have limited incentive to share knowledge and would possibly go to great lengths to prevent knowledge spillovers. For instance, Fey and Birkinshaw's (2005) study of R&D activities of large firms based in the United Kingdom and Sweden found that partnering with universities, as opposed to potential competitors, had a positive impact on R&D performance. They attributed this finding to the possibility of better knowledge sharing in alliances with universities, which would not be competing with the local firm. On the other hand, Dussauge, Garrette, and Mitchell (2002) argued that link alliances (alliances to which partner firms make complementary contributions) between competitors tend to create contexts that particularly favor interpartner learning. Their rationale was that the competitor partners have complementary resource endowments and the combination of resources through a link alliance creates new learning opportunities. In another study, Simonin (2004) found no difference in levels of perceived protectiveness between partners that are strong direct competitors and partners that are not competitors. Larsson, Bengtsson, Henriksson, and Sparks (1998) extended the notion of competitive learning by developing a framework examining how partners can manage the collective learning process and deal with opportunistic learning strategies.

To help capture the dynamics of alliances between competitors, Hamel (1991) coined the notion of a race to learn between alliance partners.. Under this scenario, alliance partners seek to out-learn their respective partners. As discussed, when one partner internalizes another's skills, the partners' relative bargaining power will shift within the alliance, as will their competitive positions outside the alliance. This bargaining power shift has been depicted as a win-lose race to learn. The race to learn concept is intriguing and has found its way into various studies. However, empirical evidence of a race to learn is mixed. In their study of Japanese-American alliances, for instance, Hennart, Roehl, and Zietlow (1999) found no evidence of a race to learn. In sum, validation of this concept awaits further research.

Alliance Learning Processes

The questions of how alliance learning and knowledge transfer actually happen over a longitudinal period, how knowledge reshapes the nature of partner relationships, and how alliance learning changes the competitive position of the learning firm are all questions involving complex organizational processes. Relative to some of the other areas discussed in this chapter, these research questions have received limited attention (Inkpen, 2002). Huber (2006) noted, "The organization design field is without elaboration of the multiple processes through which firms acquire knowledge from their environment or a field-research grounded set of design guidelines concerning organizational practices likely to result in timely and reliable knowledge acquisition via these processes" (p. 221). One of the research challenges in this area is methodological. As Badaracco (1991) noted, "For one organization to secure embedded knowledge from another, its personnel must have direct, intimate, and extensive exposure to the social relationships of the other organization" (p. 98). To develop an understanding of complex alliance learning processes, the researcher must have deep and extensive access to the actual working of the alliance and alliance-partner interactions.

Most of the process research involves case studies. Lam's (1997) case study of a high-tech collaboration between two firms compared the Japanese organizational model and the British professional model and the models' influence over the organization of knowledge. Lam argued that the difficulties in the transfer of knowledge arose not just from the tacit nature of knowledge itself, but also from differences in the degree of tacitness of knowledge and the way in which it is formed, structured, and utilized between firms in different countries. These differences not only cause serious operational difficulties in cross-border collaborative work, but also lead to asymmetry in knowledge transfer. Using data from longitudinal case studies of North American-based joint ventures between North American and Japanese firms, Inkpen and Dinur (1998) identified four critical knowledge management processes: technology sharing, alliance-parent interaction, personnel transfers, and strategic integration. The four processes share a conceptual underpinning in that each represents a knowledge connection, which creates the potential for individuals to share their observations and experiences. Using Spender's (1996) typology of knowledge, they linked the knowledge management processes with types of knowledge. They then linked the processes and primary knowledge types to organizational levels in the parent firms. Inkpen and Dinur generated four broad conclusions. First, knowledge creation can be a significant payoff from alliances. Second, each alliance partner has knowledge that, at least in part, should be considered valuable by the other partner(s). Third, knowledge creation is a dynamic process involving interactions at various organizational levels and an expanding community of individuals that enlarge, amplify, and internalize the alliance knowledge. Finally, knowledge creation and the upward movement of knowledge through the different organizational levels can be responsive to managerial influence.

To develop an in-depth understanding of the management processes used to transfer knowledge from an alliance to a parent, Inkpen (2005) examined General Motors (GM) and NUMMI, GM's California-based alliance with Toyota. The study described the formation of NUMMI, GM's initial struggles to learn, and the learning process that eventually emerged. The study also identified specific organizational factors that facilitated effective learning and knowledge transfer along with an analysis of how GM was able to overcome various obstacles to learning. Inkpen and Wang's (2006) case study of the China-Singapore Suzhou Industrial Park described the workings of an alliance in which knowledge transfer was a deliberate and specific alliance objective. The study found that partner competitive behavior, coupled with partner relationship challenges, had important influences on the knowledge transfer process.

Doz's (1996) examination of alliance evolutionary processes in alliances is one of the most important pieces of process research in the alliance area. Although the study mainly focused on evolutionary learning about the partner, as opposed to knowledge transfer between the partners, Doz addressed an important managerial issue: what happens when firms form alliances with little knowledge of their partners and how they operate? Using a case research approach, the study identifies the initial conditions that shape alliances and examines how initial conditions evolve as the partners interact and learn about each other. Doz argued that learning processes are central to the evolution of an alliance and that learning and adjustment by the partners are key determinants of alliance longevity and the avoidance of premature dissolution. This proposition about the relationship between learning and alliance performance challenges research in the alliance area dealing with concepts such as partner control, firm experience, and bargaining power. If firms can learn to be better partners, and in doing so learn about their partners, the result will be structured approaches to dealing with the inherent uncertainty and ambiguity that exists in most strategic alliances. Unfortunately, this proposition remains largely untested and the alliance field has not responded to Doz in a significant way. Several factors could account for the lack of follow-up work, with the primary reason being the challenges and costs of doing this type of research, which Doz (1996) called "unavoidably onerous" (p. 80).

The notion that alliance learning involves coevolutionary processes has been conceptually examined in a few studies. In their study of reciprocal learning, Lubatkin and colleagues (2001) suggested that as partner trust and expectations develop, each partner becomes more willing to increase their commitment to the partnership through a flow of specific and irreversible investments that are independently valuable. However, progression toward the final developmental stage of an interfirm knowledge structure can rapidly reverse should one firm stop acting in good faith, which could lead to an adversarial relationship. Inkpen and Currall (2004) used a coevolutionary approach to develop a conceptual framework showing how initial conditions give way to evolved conditions as joint venture partners develop an understanding of each other and adjust the collaborative process. Inkpen and Currall argued that learning processes are central to evolving joint venture dynamics. Once the joint venture is formed, and if the initial conditions support continued collaboration, learning processes will be central to evolving alliance dynamics.

Tsang's (2003) case study of Sino-foreign joint ventures provided evidence of unlearning processes. Tsang noticed that many Sino-foreign joint ventures were set up by acquiring existing state enterprises and the original staff continued to work in the ventures after the change of ownership. This arrangement was in contrast with greenfield joint ventures based on new operations and staff. The distinction between greenfield and acquisition joint ventures, which is generalizable beyond China, is important because for the latter, the foreign partner normally has to adopt a strategy of dismantling or restructuring the existing management systems and installing its own. This means that local employees have to unlearn their ways of doing things and learn to use the new practices brought in by the foreign partner. Tsang found that learning processes in acquisition joint ventures were hindered by problems arising from unlearning because of local employees' resistance to change.

In summary, Simonin (2004) stated that the actual learning process in alliances is dynamic and more intricate than often assumed or represented in the literature. What this suggests is that there is a definite need in the alliance area to devote more effort to understanding how alliance learning processes transform organizations, as well as how these processes unfold over time. Although there is a wealth of conceptual work on alliance processes, the limited amount of solid empirical work is a significant shortcoming in the area.

Methodological Issues

The measurement of learning has been problematic in organizational research. Researchers have often used performance measures as proxies for learning. Vermeulen and Barkema (2001) used subsidiary success to measure the degree to which acquisitions broadened a firm's knowledge base. McGrath (2001) argued that to the extent that members of an organization produced desired outcomes, they can be said to have developed specific knowledge and competence. McGrath measured learning effectiveness by project teams by assessing results achieved by the projects. Pennings and colleagues (1994) measured the learning associated with firm-diversification projects using a moving average of project longevity, which was in turn used as a proxy for the firms' diversification success. Szulanski, Cappetta, and Jensen (2004) used a survey to measure the effectiveness of knowledge transfer, which was operationalized by evaluating how accurately the recipient reproduced a replica of the template.

In the alliance area, researchers have employed various methodologies to study learning. Many have used questionnaire methodologies in their studies (e.g., Inkpen, 1995; Simonin, 1997; Tsang 2002). These studies usually measure learning by asking respondents questions related to the extent and types of knowledge acquired by the alliance or by the partner. This learning measure captures the respondent's perception of learning, which is inevitably subjective and varies from one respondent to another. Lane and Lubatkin (1998) used a card-sorting technique to address a series of learning questions. Several studies of R&D-based alliances have used patent citation data on the premise that the codified knowledge represented by patents is a complement of tacit knowledge (e.g., Almeida, Song, & Grant, 2002; Mowery et al., 1996). Using patent citations as a proxy for the flow of technological knowledge between firms, Gomes-Casseres, Hagedoorn, and Jaffe (2006) found solid evidence that knowledge flows between alliance partners are greater than flows between pairs of non-allied firms. Other studies have inferred that learning has occurred because of the nature of the learning opportunity created. For example, Powell and colleagues (1996) studied R&D ties and assumed that certain types of ties resulted in learning. Sakakibara (1997) used a questionnaire to determine the importance of learning motives for alliance formation. However, learning and knowledge flows were not empirically measured in either study. Inkpen (1995) gathered data on learning efforts and concluded that the strength of the learning effort was a proxy for learning itself. Makino and Delios (1996) examined local knowledge acquisition by the joint venture and the foreign partner but could only infer that learning was occurring by examining venture performance and local partner relationships.

Case study research (e.g., Dodgson, 1993; Hamel, 1991; Inkpen, 2005; Inkpen & Dinur, 1998; Tsang, 2001; Yan & Gray, 1994) has played a prominent role in addressing process-related learning issues, although as discussed earlier, the number of process-based studies is not high. Moreover, the case studies are generally silent, or weak, in addressing the question of "how do you know learning has occurred?" In Inkpen's (2005) case study of the NUMMI alliance, the measure of learning was based on a combination of statements from senior management and objective data on manufacturing productivity. The study was unable to definitively rule out alternative explanations besides learning for the improvements in productivity. In summary, the alliance learning area needs some methodological innovation to develop better understanding of the learning concept. In particular, innovation is needed to address the critical questions surrounding alliance learning and its impact on organizational change and performance.

The Other Side of Learning: Protecting Knowledge

Learning from an alliance partner may lead to negative outcomes for the partner whose knowledge is appropriated (Lorange, 1997). A loss of knowledge by one partner via asymmetrical learning may result in the creation of a new or stronger competitor. Various studies have considered the unintended loss of knowledge by Western firms in technology sharing alliances with Japanese firms (e.g., Pucik, 1988; Reich & Mankin, 1986; Teramoto, Richter, & Iwasaki, 1993). Other research has considered the dangers of outsourcing and manufacturing-based alliances in leading to knowledge appropriation (Bettis, Bradley, & Hamel, 1992; Lei & Slocum, 1992). Given these scenarios of knowledge loss, the protection of knowledge is an important issue for many firms involved in alliances.

Simonin (2004) found that partner protectiveness had a significant direct effect on knowledge transfer. Baughn and colleagues (1997) argued that a firm's inattentiveness to the learning potential of its partners as well as its over-reliance on structural and contractual means of protection often fail to effectively regulate the flow of skills to a partner. They proposed that the unintended transfer of intellectual capital can be contained by structuring alliances with both a clear focus and defined boundaries in scope and duration. They described a framework for monitoring the collaborative interface in strategic alliances to balance the requirements for learning and information sharing with protection of intellectual capital. Using large-sample survey data, Kale, Singh, & Perlmutter (2000) provided empirical evidence that when firms build relational capital in conjunction with an integrative approach to managing conflict, they are able to achieve both learning and knowledge protection objectives simultaneously. Norman's (2002) survey of U.S. firms found that firms are more protective when the capabilities they contribute to the alliance are highly tacit and core, when their partners have a strong learning intent, and when the firm and its partner have highly similar resources.

Using a sample of R&D alliances, Oxley and Sampson (2004) considered the choice of alliance scope as an alternative way to control the threat of knowledge leakage and protect technological assets. Establishing the scope of activities for an R&D alliance involves decisions such as whether to restrict joint activity to pre-competitive R&D only or to extend it to include manufacturing and/or marketing. Their results suggested that partnering firms narrow the scope of their alliance activities in response to competitive threats and the fear of knowledge leakage. When the monitoring of alliance activities and delineation of property rights is more complex, the alliance partners may choose to embed their activities in a protective alliance structure such as an equity joint venture. Norman's (2004) finding that equity alliances had the lowest level of knowledge loss supports this argument.

Alliance Learning and the Organizational Learning Field

Over the past decade and a half, organizational learning as a concept has spawned an enormous, diverse and interdisciplinary range of research literatures. Organizations increasingly form alliances with the specific intention of acquiring new knowledge. Even when alliances are formed for reasons other than knowledge acquisition, such acquisition is often a desirable and unintended by-product. With the rapidly increasing volume of research on alliance learning, this stream of research has become one of the most important subfields within the broader field of organizational learning. Alliance learning is also a primary research area within the strategic management fields. Mintzberg (1990), an ardent proponent of strategy as a learning process, argued that "strategy making must above all take the form of a process of learning over time . . . The learning proceeds in emergent fashion through behavior that stimulates thinking retrospectively, so that sense is made of action" (p. 154). Mintzberg also suggested that strategic initiatives may be left to develop or flounder on their own, or they may be championed by managers higher up in the organization who integrate them with elements of existing strategy. The initiatives create experiences, actions, and strategic choices which provide the basis for learning. The formation of an alliance is a specific strategic initiative and the alliance experience can be the action that triggers learning.

Compared with unitary organizations, alliances provide an interesting and rich contextual base for studying organizational learning. They also provide the opportunity to explore many different facets of organizational learning in a controlled setting. For example, using case studies of hotel alliances in Cuba, De Holan, and Phillips (2004) explored organizational forgetting and its role in organizations, arguing that forgetting is a critical aspect of knowledge processes. They categorized four modes of organizational forgetting along two dimensions, namely the intentionality of the forgetting process and the newness of the forgotten knowledge. The roles assumed by the partners in their alliance cases were clear—the international partner providing the expertise necessary to develop a world-class hotel catering for foreign tourists in Cuba; the Cuban partner providing labor, managerial systems, and knowledge about doing business in the local context. The selection of cases provided the authors with "the opportunity to observe a kind of natural experiment in the dynamics of organizational knowledge" (De Holan & Phillips, 2004, p. 1606). New knowledge was transferred to the cases while some established knowledge was discarded. Such a rich learning environment enabled the authors to readily study all four modes of organizational forgetting.

As the earlier sections indicate, alliance learning is complicated by interpartner dynamics, which do not exist in unitary organizations. Consequently, alliance learning researchers face some interesting challenges related to interorganization dynamics, such as trust, control, and bargaining power. For instance, Levin and Cross (2004) argued that on a personal level, competence- and benevolence-based trust mediate the link between tie strength and receipt of useful knowledge. They tested their model by surveying employees in three companies and found supporting results, which have significant implications for organizational learning. The issue of trust in strategic alliances is complicated. While employees of an organization are likely to work toward a common corporate goal, share an overarching corporate culture, and trust one another, trust between partners, who are often having a competitive-collaborate relationship, affects trust between employees (Inkpen & Tsang, 2005). This dual position is one indicator of the potential complexities that researchers need to deal with in their empirical study of alliance learning and learning in general.

In addition to adopting concepts in the general literature of organizational learning, researchers of alliance learning have developed some interesting new concepts with implications beyond alliances, such as organizational transparency (Hamel, 1991) and partner learning asymmetry (Makhija & Ganesh, 1997). The complicated nature of alliance learning also provides opportunities for further developing concepts that originate from the broader field of organizational learning. Consider, for example, the construct of absorptive capacity discussed earlier. Cohen and Levinthal (1990) used the term to describe the ability of a firm to value, assimilate, and utilize new external knowledge. According to Lane and Lubatkin (1998), this definition suggests that a firm has the same capacity to learn from all other organizations and, thus, fails to take into account interfirm dynamics in alliance learning. They argued that "the ability of a firm to learn from another firm is jointly determined by the relative characteristics of the student firm *and* the teacher firm" (p. 462), and reconceptualized absorptive capacity (a firm-level construct) as relative absorptive capacity (a dyad-level construct). Lane and Lubatkin's work is a step forward in developing the conceptual foundation of organizational learning theories and suggests further opportunities for alliance learning research to inform the broader field of organizational learning.

A Research Agenda

Organizational research has made notable steps in developing an understanding of alliances, learning, and knowledge transfer. That said, much remains to be done to more fully understand the complexities and dynamics of alliance learning. In this section, we develop a research agenda of areas that warrant further study. While some of these areas are natural extensions of the existing research discussed above, some are relatively new topics that have received little attention. We have grouped the areas around the following three themes.

Learning and Its Impact on Other Variables

Organizational processes. As discussed in the section on learning processes, many questions surrounding organizational processes remain unanswered. For example, alliance learning that is deliberate and linked with strategic objectives can become the basis for an organizational change process. Examining this question could involve linking partner learning to specific outcomes within an organizational change framework. Although a challenging exercise, it has the potential for significant managerial interest. Further research into the impact of alliance learning on other organizational processes, such as strategy creation and strategic change, could also add valuable insights.

Bargaining power. The nature of bargaining-power shifts has been conceptually discussed; however, with a few exceptions (e.g., Yan & Gray, 1994), empirical understanding of how power is gained, exploited, and managed is limited. As well, we do not know what efforts firms may take to prevent power from eroding and how power shifts influence the partners to change their alliance commitments and willingness to maintain collaborative objectives. Given that the possession or absence of knowledge, to a large degree (possibly the largest, according to some authors), drives the ability to exert power, the study of bargaining power shifts should be of great interest for alliance learning scholars.

Alliance stability. Alliances are inherently unstable organizational forms, and as discussed, learning plays an important role in influencing stability. The learning outcomes of alliance partners and the alliance itself often determine whether the partners will continue or terminate the alliance. When the partners subscribe to the notion of a race to learn, learning takes on a particularly important role. With a few exceptions, such as Doz's (1996) exemplar study, most of the work examining how learning shifts the balance of bargaining power between partners and impacts the stability of international joint ventures has been conceptual. For example, Grant and Baden-Fuller (2004) argued that an alliances-as-knowledge accessing thesis predicts higher stability than an alliances-as-knowledge acquisition thesis. Various questions require further empirical study, such as, "What are the types of learning most likely to destabilize an alliance?" and "Why do some alliances rapidly become unstable while others, such as NUMMI in which partner learning occurs for many years, remain in existence for an extended period?"

Firm competitiveness and protecting knowledge. The actual mechanisms used to protect knowledge and their effectiveness could be an interesting research avenue. Since alliances between competitors are common and firms may be reluctant to enter into these alliances because of worries over knowledge protection, this is a research area that has obvious practical implications. In addition, Kale and Anand (2006) suggested that firms in emerging economies are concerned about asymmetric learning and are seeking to improve their learning capabilities. Using enhanced knowledge capabilities to counterbalance a partner's learning efforts intersects with the knowledge-protection issue. Investigation into the specific learning capabilities of emerging-economy firms would help these firms and their partners better understand the path to mutual value creation.

Where and How Does Learning Occur?

Unlearning. While discussions of the concept of organizational learning have been advancing, our understanding of organizational unlearning has languished (Bettis & Prahalad, 1995) and received limited attention in the literature (Akgün, Lynn, & Byrne, 2006). This is unfortunate, as clarity about the nature of organizational unlearning helps develop strategies for effective change and renewal (Starbuck, 1996). In the alliance area, unlearning may be necessary before learning can occur, which means that unlearning can be a key determinant of learning outcomes. As discussed, acquisition joint ventures are obvious examples where unlearning occurs; more subtle, yet common, cases also exist. For instance, unlearning may be required when a parent brings in a practice that replaces an existing practice used by the other parent. When studying learning processes, researchers must pay attention to clues that suggest the existence of unlearning. This may provide insights into learning barriers or failures.

Levels issues. The reality in all alliances is that relationships between managers will determine much of what occurs in terms of partner interactions; however, most alliance theory in the learning area operates at the firm level. Some potentially interesting issues involve the managerial (e.g., individual) level and the parent (e.g., firm) level. For example, in an alliance formed between keen competitors who are wary of divulging valuable knowledge to one another, social ties between managers assigned to the alliance by the partners are likely to be cautious and tense (Inkpen & Tsang, 2005). On the other hand, allowing managers to work together and gradually form close friendships may help to reduce the suspicion between partners. In brief, our understanding of levels issues remains shallow.

Learning alliance. The notion of learning organization, which can be concisely defined as an organization that is good at learning (Tsang, 1997b), has been gaining currency, especially among management consultants and managers, since the publication of Senge's (1990) The Fifth Discipline. With few exceptions, such as Kandemir and Hult's (2005) conceptual discussion of organizational learning culture in international joint ventures, virtually all discussions of how to develop a learning organization are based in the context of unitary organizations and may not be applicable to alliances where the dynamics of learning can be very different. "Can a learning alliance be developed in the same way as a unitary learning organization?" is an important research question worth investigating; the findings would inform both theory and practice.

Learning Within a Larger Community of Firms

Learning and network effects. Social network researchers (e.g. Marsden & Friedkin, 1994; Pastor, Meindl, & Mayo, 2002) use the term network effects to describe the process whereby individuals in a social network converge in their views and behaviors to the extent that they have exposure to other people in the network. Social influence processes and the proximity of followers to leaders contribute to network effects. Given the role of individuals in shaping the alliance learning process, more research is necessary to understand how networks of alliance-exposed individuals come to be and how they contribute to the process of knowledge internalization. For example, Inkpen (2005) described how over time, GM managers who had rotated through NUMMI created a network within GM that became an important resource for strengthening GM's manufacturing capabilities. Inkpen and Wang (2006) described how managers from China were exposed in large groups to Singapore's industrial park knowledge. More work is also necessary to understand how ties at the firm level influence learning and knowledge transfer. In one of the few studies that investigate this question, McEvily and Marcus (2005) concluded that embedded ties affect the acquisition of competitive capabilities, which suggest that a firm's capacity to compete is a function of the types of alliance partners with whom it creates embedded ties, as well as the quality of its interfirm relationships. Using a dual-networks perspective, Zhao, Anand, and Mitchell (2005) investigated the transfer of R&D capabilities to international joint ventures in the Chinese automotive industry and considered the learning and teaching partner networks.

Repeatedness and learning. There is a need for further research into the question of how repeated alliance-partner ties and types of alliances impact the learning process. When firms repeat transactions with partners over time, as they will when they have multiple alliances, it creates opportunities for learning about the partner that, in turn, can lead to the development of interpartner trust. In alliances, increased interpartner trust should emerge between partners when they have successfully completed transactions in the past and they perceive one another as complying with norms of equity and reciprocity (Ring & Van de Ven, 1992). Successfully completed transactions are those that are congruent with alliance objectives. Repeated cycles of exchange, risk taking, and successful fulfillment of expectations strengthen the willingness of parties to allow learning to occur. The study by Goerzen and Beamish (2005) found that exploiting the benefits of network diversity was difficult, which suggests that repeatedness among partners may yield more positive knowledge benefits. Among the few empirical studies on repeatedness, Zollo, Reuer, and Singh (2002) found that among biotechnology firms, prior experience with the partner improved the performance of the current alliance for the focal firm. We must note, however, that the performance was measured as a perceptual construct with no reflection on the financial performance of the focal firm.

Conclusion

From its beginning as a handful of papers 15 years ago to a broad, diverse, and multidisciplinary field of study, the alliance learning research area provides an example of how a field expands almost linearly with the growth of a phenomena; in this case, alliance is used as a strategic weapon for acquiring knowledge and developing capabilities. The popularity of strategic alliances has been fueled by globalization and the opening up of former socialist economies. This increases the complexity of alliance learning, as partners may come from countries of very different social, political, and economic systems. As indicated by our review, alliance learning is a complex phenomenon that has spawned a diverse and fruitful body of research. This chapter provides an overview of the current status of research and develops a research agenda that deals with issues of theoretical and managerial significance.

Research efforts over the years have resulted in a distinct domain of alliance learning knowledge, which consists of some compelling findings and provides important insights for the broader field of alliance management. Firms that seek to exploit the learning opportunities created by their alliances have a wealth of research from which to seek guidance. We hope that scholars will continue to address alliance learning questions because, as we have identified, there are many interesting areas for which further research is needed. Although it is difficult to predict whether future research will break new ground, we believe that alliance learning will continue to be an important and evolving phenomenon for years to come.

References

Akgün, A. E., Lynn, G. S., & Byrne, J. C. (2006). Antecedents and consequences of unlearning in new product development teams. *Journal of Product Innovation Management, 23*, 73–88.

Almeida, P., Song, J., & Grant, R. M. (2002). Are firms superior to alliances and markets? An empirical test of cross-border knowledge transfer. *Organization Science, 13*, 147–161.

Anand, B. N., & Khanna, T. (2000). Do firms learn to create value? The case of alliances. *Strategic Management Journal, 21*, 295–315.

Ariño, A., & De La Torre, J. (1998). Learning from failure: Towards an evolutionary model of collective ventures. *Organization Science, 9*, 306–325.

Badaracco, J. L. (1991). *The knowledge link.* Boston, MA: Harvard Business School Press.

Barkema, H. G., Shenkar, O., Vermeulen, F., & Bell, J. H. J. (1997). Working abroad, working with others: How firms learn to operate international joint ventures. *Academy of Management Journal, 40*, 426–442.

Baughn, C., Denekamp, J. G., Stevens, J. H., & Osborn, R. N. (1997). Protecting intellectual capital in international alliances. *Journal of World Business, 32*, 103–117.

Beamish, P., & Berdrow, I. (2003). Learning from IJVs: The unintended outcome. *Long Range Planning, 36*, 285–303.

Bettis, R. A., Bradley, S. P., & Hamel, G. (1992). Outsourcing and industrial decline. *The Executive, 6*(1), 7–22.

Bettis, R. A., & Prahalad, C. K. (1995). The dominant logic: Retrospective and extension. *Strategic Management Journal, 16*, 5–14.

Bhagat, R. S., Kedia, B. L., Harveston, P. D., & Triandis, H. C. (2002). Cultural variations in the cross-border transfer of organizational knowledge: An integrative framework. *Academy of Management Review, 27*, 204–221.

Burgers, W. P., Hill, C. W. L., & Kim, W. C. (1993). A theory of global strategic alliances: The case of the global auto industry. *Strategic Management Journal, 14*, 419–432.

Child, J., & Rodrigues, S. (1996). The role of social identity in the international transfer of knowledge through joint ventures. In S. R. Clegg, & G. Palmer (Eds.), *The politics of management knowledge* (pp. 46–68). London: Sage.

Cohen, W. M., & Levinthal, D. A. (1990). Absorptive capacity: A new perspective on learning and innovation. *Administrative Science Quarterly, 35*, 128–152.

Collinson, S. (1999). Knowledge management capabilities for steel makers: A British-Japanese corporate alliance for organizational learning. *Technology Analysis and Strategic Management, 11*, 337–358.

De Holan, P. M., & Phillips, N. (2004). Remembrance of things past? The dynamics of organizational forgetting. *Management Science, 50*, 1603–1613.

Dhanaraj, C., Lyles, M. A., Steensma, H. K., & Tihanyi, L. (2004). Managing tacit and explicit knowledge transfer in IJVs: The role of relational embeddedness and the impact on performance. *Journal of International Business Studies, 35*, 428–442.

Dodgson, M. (1993). Learning, trust, and technological collaboration. *Human Relations, 46*, 77–95.

Doz, Y. L. (1996). The evolution of cooperation in strategic alliances: Initial conditions or learning processes? [Summer special issue]. *Strategic Management Journal, 17*, 55–83.

Doz, Y. L., & Hamel, G. (1998). *Alliance advantage: The art of creating value through partnering*. Boston: Harvard Business School Press.

Dussauge, P., Garrette, B., & Mitchell, W. (2002). The market share impact of inter-partner learning in alliances: Evidence from the global auto industry. In F. J. Contractor, & P. Lorange (Eds.), *Cooperative strategies and alliances*, (pp. 707–727). Oxford, U.K.: Elsevier Science.

Fey, C. F., & Birkinshaw, J. (2005). External sources of knowledge, governance mode, and R&D performance. *Journal of Management, 31,* 597–621.

Geppert, M. (1996). Paths of managerial learning in the East German context. *Organization Studies, 17,* 249–268.

Ghoshal, S. (1987). Global strategy: An organizing framework. *Strategic Management Journal, 8,* 425–440.

Glaister, K. W., Husan, R., & Buckley, P. J. (2003). Learning to manage international joint ventures. *International Business Review, 12,* 83–108.

Goerzen, A., & Beamish, P. W. (2005). The effect of alliance network diversity on multinational enterprise performance. *Strategic Management Journal, 26,* 333–354.

Gomes-Casseres, B., Hagedoorn, J., & Jaffe, A. B. (2006). Do alliances promote knowledge flows? *Journal of Financial Economics, 80,* 5–33.

Goold, M., Campbell, A., & Alexander, M. (1994). *Corporate-level strategy: Creating value in the multibusiness company*. New York: Wiley.

Grant, R. M., & Baden-Fuller, C. (2002). The knowledge-based view of strategic alliance formation: Knowledge accessing *versus* organizational learning. In F. J. Contractor, & P. Lorange (Eds.), *Cooperative strategies and alliances* (pp. 419–436). Oxford, U.K.: Elsevier Science.

Grant, R. M., & Baden-Fuller, C. (2004). A knowledge accessing theory of strategic alliances. *Journal of Management Studies, 41,* 61–84.

Gulati, R., (1999). Network location and learning: The influence of network resources and firm capabilities on alliance formation. *Strategic Management Journal, 20,* 397–420.

Gupta, A., & Misra, L. (2000). The value of experiential learning by organizations: Evidence from international joint ventures. *Journal of Financial Research, 23,* 77–102.

Hagedoorn, J., & Narula, R. (1996). Choosing organizational modes of strategic technology partnering: International and sectoral differences. *Journal of International Business Studies, 27,* 265–284.

Hamel, G. (1991). Competition for competence and inter-partner learning within international strategic alliances [Special issue]. *Strategic Management Journal, 12,* 83–104.

Hamel, G., Doz, Y. L., & Prahalad, C. K. (1989). Collaborate with your competitors—And win. *Harvard Business Review, 67*(1), 133–139.

Hennart, J.-F., Roehl, T., & Zietlow, D. S. (1999). "Trojan Horse" or "workhorse"? The evolution of U.S.-Japanese joint ventures in the United States. *Strategic Management Journal, 20,* 15–29.

Hofstede, G. (1980). *Culture's consequences: International differences in work-related values*. Beverly Hills, CA: Sage.

Huber, G. P. (2006). Designing firms for knowledge acquisition and absorptive capacity. In R. M. Burtn, B. Eriksen, D. D. Hakonsson, & C. C. Snow (Eds.), *Organization design: The evolving state of the art* (pp. 219–242). New York: Springer Science.

Inkpen, A. C. (1995). *The management of international joint ventures: An organizational learning perspective.* London: Routledge.

Inkpen, A. C. (1996). Creating knowledge through collaboration. *California Management Review, 39*(1), 123–140.

Inkpen, A. C. (2002). Learning, knowledge management, and strategic alliances: So many studies, so many unanswered questions. In P. Lorange, & F. Contractor (Eds.), *Cooperative strategies and alliances* (pp. 267–289). Oxford, U.K.: Elsevier Science.

Inkpen, A. C. (2005). Learning through alliances: General Motors and NUMMI. *California Management Review, 47*(4), 114–136.

Inkpen, A. C., & Beamish, P. W. (1997). Knowledge, bargaining power and international joint venture stability. *Academy of Management Review, 22,* 177–202.

Inkpen, A. C., & Crossan, M. M. (1995). Believing is seeing: Joint ventures and organization learning. *Journal of Management Studies, 32,* 595–618.

Inkpen, A. C., & Currall, S. C. (2004). The co-evolution of trust, control, and learning in joint ventures. *Organization Science, 15,* 586–599.

Inkpen, A. C., & Dinur, A. (1998). Knowledge management processes and international joint ventures. *Organization Science, 9,* 454–468.

Inkpen, A. C., & Tsang, E. W. K. (2005). Social capital, networks, and knowledge transfer. *Academy of Management Review, 30,* 146–165.

Inkpen, A. C., & Wang, P. (2006). The China-Singapore Suzhou Industrial Park: A knowledge transfer network. *Journal of Management Studies, 43,* 779–811.

Kale, P., & Anand, J. (2006). The decline of emerging economy joint ventures: The case of India. *California Management Review, 48*(3), 62–76.

Kale, P., Singh, H., & Perlmutter, H. (2000). Learning and protection of proprietary assets in strategic alliances: Building relational capital. *Strategic Management Journal, 21,* 217–237.

Kandemir, D., & Hult, T. M. (2005). A conceptualization of an organizational learning culture in international joint ventures. *Industrial Marketing Management, 34,* 430–439.

Khanna, T., Gulati, R., & Nohria, N. (1998). The dynamics of learning alliances: Competition, cooperation, and relative scope. *Strategic Management Journal, 19,* 193–210.

Ko, D. G., Kirsch, L. J., & King, W. R. (2005). Antecedents for knowledge transfer from consultants to clients in enterprise system implementations. *MIS Quarterly, 29,* 59–85.

Kogut, B. (1988). A study of the life cycle of joint ventures [Special issue]. *Management International Review, 28,* 39–52.

Kogut, B. (1991). Joint ventures and the option to expand and acquire. *Management Science, 37,* 19–33.

Kogut, B., & Zander, U. (1993). Knowledge of the firm and the evolutionary theory of the multinational corporation. *Journal of International Business Studies, 24,* 625–645.

Lam, A. (1997). Embedded firms, embedded knowledge: Problems of collaboration and knowledge transfer in global cooperative ventures. *Organization Studies, 18,* 973–996.

Lane, P. J., & Lubatkin, M. (1998). Relative absorptive capacity and interorganizational learning. *Strategic Management Journal, 19,* 461–477.

Lane, P. J., Salk, J. E., & Lyles, M. A. (2001). Absorptive capacity, learning, and performance in international joint ventures. *Strategic Management Journal, 22,* 1139–1161.

Larsson, R., Bengtsson, L., Henriksson, K., & Sparks, J. (1998). The interorganizational learning dilemma: Collective knowledge development in strategic alliances. *Organization Science, 9,* 285–305.

Lei, D., & Slocum, J. W. (1992). Global strategy, competence-building, and strategic alliances. *California Management Review, 35*(1), 81–97.

Levin, D. Z., & Cross, R. (2004). The strength of weak ties you can trust: The mediating role of trust in effective knowledge transfer. *Management Science, 50,* 1477–1490.

Lin, X. (2005). Local partner acquisition of managerial knowledge in international joint ventures: Focusing on foreign management control. *Management International Review, 45,* 219–237.

Lorange, P. (1997). Black-box protection of your core competencies in strategic alliances. In P. W. Beamish, & J. P. Killing (Eds.), *Cooperative strategies: European perspectives* (pp. 59–73). San Francisco: New Lexington.

Lubatkin, M., Florin, J., & Lane, P. (2001). Learning together and apart: A model of reciprocal interfirm learning. *Human Relations, 54,* 1353–1382.

Lyles, M. A. (1988). Learning among joint venture sophisticated firms [Special Issue]. *Management International Review, 28,* 85–97.

Lyles, M. A., & Salk, J. E. (1996). Knowledge acquisition from foreign parents in international joint ventures: An empirical examination in the Hungarian context. *Journal of International Business Studies, 27,* 877–903.

Makhija, M. V., & Ganesh, U. (1997). The relationship between control and partner learning in learning-related joint ventures. *Organization Science, 5,* 508–520.

Makino, S., & Delios, A. (1996). Local knowledge transfer and performance implications for alliance formation in Asia. *Journal of International Business Studies, 27,* 905–927.

Makino, S., & Inkpen, A. C. (2003). Knowledge seeking FDI and learning across borders. In M. Easterby-Smith, & M. A. Lyles (Eds.), *The Blackwell handbook of organizational learning and knowledge management* (pp. 233–252). Oxford, U.K.: Blackwell.

Marsden, P. V., & Friedkin, N. (1994). Network studies on social influence. In S. Wasserman, & J. Galaskiewicz (Eds.), *Advances in social network analysis* (pp. 3–25). Thousand Oaks, CA: Sage.

McEvily, B., & Marcus, A. (2005). Embedded ties and the acquisition of competitive capabilities. *Strategic Management Journal, 26,* 1033–1055.

McGrath, R. G. (2001). Exploratory learning, innovative capacity, and managerial oversight. *Academy of Management Journal, 44,* 18–131.

Mintzberg, H. (1990). Strategy formation: Schools of thought. In J. Frederickson (Ed.), *Perspectives of strategic management* (pp. 105–235). New York: Harper Business.

Morgan, B. (1991). Transferring soft technology. In R. D. Robinson (Ed.), *The international communication of technology: A book of readings* (pp. 149–166). New York: Taylor & Francis.

Mowery, D. C., Oxley, J. E., & Silverman, B. S. (1996). Strategic alliances and interfirm knowledge transfer [Special issue]. *Strategic Management Journal, 17,* 77–91.

Mowery, D. C., Oxley, J. E., & Silverman, B. S. (2002). The two faces of partner-specific absorptive capacity: Learning and cospecialization in strategic alliances. In F. J. Contractor, & P. Lorange (Eds.), *Cooperative strategies and alliances* (pp. 291–319). Oxford, U.K.: Elsevier Science.

Nonaka, I. (1994). A dynamic theory of organizational knowledge creation. *Organization Science, 5,* 14–37.

Norman, P. M. (2002). Protecting knowledge in strategic alliances: Resource and relational characteristics. *Journal of High Technology Management Research, 13,* 177–203.

Norman, P. M. (2004). Knowledge acquisition, knowledge loss, and satisfaction in high technology alliances. *Journal of Business Research, 57,* 610–619.

Osborn, R. N., & Hagedoorn, J. (1997). The institutionalization and evolutionary dynamics of interorganizational alliances and networks. *Academy of Management Journal, 40,* 261–278.

Owen-Smith, J., & Powell, W. W. (2004). Knowledge networks as channels and conduits: The effects of spillovers in the Boston biotechnology community. *Organization Science, 15,* 5–21.

Oxley, J. E., & Sampson, R. C. (2004). The scope and governance of international R&D alliances. *Strategic Management Journal, 25,* 723–749.

Pak, Y. S., & Park, Y.-R. (2004). A framework of knowledge transfer in cross-border joint ventures: An empirical test of the Korean context. *Management International Review, 44,* 417–434.

Parkhe, A. (1991). Interfirm diversity, organizational learning, and longevity in global strategic alliances. *Journal of International Business Studies, 22,* 579–601.

Pastor, J. C., Meindl, J., & Mayo, M. (2002). A network effects model of charisma attributions. *Academy of Management Journal, 45,* 410–420.

Pennings, J. M., Barkema, H., & Douma, S. (1994). Organizational learning and diversification. *Academy of Management Journal, 37,* 608–640.

Pisano, A. (1988). *Innovation through markets, hierarchies, and joint ventures: Technology, strategy and collaborative arrangements in the biotechnology industry.* Unpublished doctoral dissertation. University of California, Berkeley.

Polanyi, M. (1967). *The tacit dimension.* London: Routledge & Kegan Paul.

Powell, W. W. (1987). Hybrid organizational arrangements: New form or transitional development? *California Management Review, 30*(1), 67–86.

Powell, W. W., Koput, K. W., & Smith-Doerr, L. (1996). Interorganizational collaboration and the locus of innovation: Networks of learning in biotechnology. *Administrative Science Quarterly, 41,* 116–145.

Pucik, V. (1988). Strategic alliances, organizational learning, and competitive advantage: The HRM agenda. *Human Resource Management, 27,* 77–93.

Reich, R. B., & Mankin, E. D. (1986). Joint ventures with Japan give away our future. *Harvard Business Review, 64*(2), 78–86.

Ring, P. S., & Van de Ven, A. (1992). Structuring cooperative relationships between organizations. *Strategic Management Journal, 13,* 483–498.

Sakakibara, M. (1997). Heterogeneity of firm capabilities and cooperative research and development: An empirical examination of motives [Special issue]. *Strategic Management Journal, 18,* 143–164.

Sampson, R. C. (2005). Experience effects and collaborative returns in R&D alliances. *Strategic Management Journal, 26,* 1009–1031.

Senge, P. M. (1990). *The fifth discipline.* London: Century Business.

Sharma, D. D., & Wallström-Pan, C. (1997). Internal management of Sino-Swedish joint ventures. In I. Björkman, & M. Forsgren (Eds.), *The nature of the international firm* (pp. 363–390). Copenhagen, Denmark: Copenhagen Business School Press.

Simonin, B. L. (1997). The importance of collaborative know-how: An empirical test of the learning organization. *Academy of Management Journal, 40,* 1150–1174.

Simonin, B. L. (1999). Ambiguity and the process of knowledge transfer in strategic alliances. *Strategic Management Journal, 20,* 595–623.

Simonin, B. L. (2004). An empirical investigation of the process of knowledge transfer in international strategic alliances. *Journal of International Business Studies, 35,* 407–427.

Spender, J. C. (1996). Organizational knowledge, learning, and memory: Three concepts in search of a theory. *Journal of Organizational Change Management, 9,* 63–78.

Starbuck, W. H. (1996). Unlearning ineffective or obsolete technologies. *International Journal of Technology Management, 11,* 725–737.

Szulanski, G., Cappetta, R., & Jensen, R. J. (2004). When and how trustworthiness matters: Knowledge transfer and the moderating effect of causal ambiguity. *Organization Science, 15,* 600–613.

Teece, D. J. (1977). Technology transfer by multinational firms: The resource cost of transferring technological know-how. *Economic Journal, 87,* 242–261.

Teramoto, Y., Richter, F., & Iwasaki, N. (1993). Learning to succeed: What European firms can learn from Japanese approaches to strategic alliances. *Creativity and Innovation Management, 2,* 114–121.

Tsang, E. W. K. (1997a). Choice of international technology transfer mode: A resource-based view. *Management International Review, 37,* 151–168.

Tsang, E. W. K. (1997b). Organizational learning and the learning organization: A dichotomy between descriptive and prescriptive research. *Human Relations, 50,* 73–89.

Tsang, E. W. K. (1999). A preliminary typology of learning in international strategic alliances. *Journal of World Business, 34,* 211–229.

Tsang, E. W. K. (2001). Managerial learning in foreign-invested enterprises of China. *Management International Review, 41,* 29–51.

Tsang, E. W. K. (2002). Acquiring knowledge by foreign partners from international joint ventures in a transition economy: Learning-by-doing and learning myopia. *Strategic Management Journal, 23,* 835–854.

Tsang, E. W. K. (2003). Resistance to restructuring in Sino-foreign joint ventures: Toward a preliminary model. *Journal of Organizational Change Management, 16,* 205–222.

Tsang, E. W. K., Nguyen, D. T., & Erramilli, M. K. (2004). Knowledge acquisition and performance of international joint ventures in a transition economy. *Journal of International Marketing, 12*(2), 82–103.

Ulrich, D., Von Glinow, M. A., & Jick, T. (1993). High-impact learning: Building and diffusing learning capability. *Organizational Dynamics, 22*(2), 52–66.

Uzzi, B. (1997). Social structure and competition in interfirm networks: The paradox of embeddness. *Administrative Science Quarterly, 42,* 35–67.

Varadarajan, P. R., & Cunningham, M. H. (1995). Strategic alliances: A synthesis of conceptual foundations. *Journal of the Academy of Marketing Science, 23,* 282–296.

Vermeulen, F., & Barkema, H. (2001). Learning through acquisitions. *Academy of Management Journal, 44,* 457–476.

Villinger, R. (1996). Post-acquisition managerial learning in Central East Europe. *Organization Studies, 17,* 181–206.

Von Glinow, M. A. &, Teagarden, M. B. (1988). The transfer of human resource management technology in Sino-U.S. cooperative ventures: Problems and solutions. *Human Resource Management, 27,* 201–229.

Von Hippel, E. (1994). "Sticky information" and the locus of problem solving: Implications for innovation. *Management Science, 40,* 429–439.

Wang, Y., & Nicholas, S. (2005). Knowledge transfer, knowledge replication, and learning in non-equity alliances: Operating contractual joint ventures in China. *Management International Review, 45,* 99–118.

Yan, A., & Gray, B. (1994). Bargaining power, management control, and performance in United States-China joint ventures: A comparative case study. *Academy of Management Journal, 37,* 1478–1517.

Yan, Y., & Child, J. (2002). An analysis of strategic determinants, learning, and decision-making in Sino-British joint ventures. *British Journal of Management, 13,* 109–122.

Zhao, Z., Anand, J., & Mitchell, W. (2005). A dual networks perspective on inter-organizational transfer of R&D capabilities: International joint ventures in the Chinese automotive industry. *Journal of Management Studies, 42,* 127–160.

Zollo, M., Reuer, J. J., & Singh, H. (2002). Interorganizational routines and performance in strategic alliances. *Organization Science, 13,* 701–713.

11
Postcards from the Edge
A Review of the Business and Environment Literature

LUCA BERCHICCI

Ecole Polytechnique Fédérale de Lausanne

ANDREW KING

Tuck School of Business at Dartmouth College

Abstract

Environmental issues, while of growing interest, have been outside the main focus of business scholarship. This position on the periphery may have been a good thing. It allowed scholars of business and the environment to consider unusual theories and evaluate overlooked phenomenon. In doing so, they have created a body of research providing new insights into two topics of mainstream interest: (a) the sources of competitive advantage and (b) the origin and function of self-regulatory institutions.

Introduction

During the last 20 years, a research agenda has emerged that is often termed *business and the environment* (B&E). Special issues in several leading management journals have advanced this agenda and it now represents a growing part of the management literature. Yet, the boundaries of this research agenda, and even the definition of its central term, remain unclear. At one time, the word *environment* was understood to mean *nature*, but scholars have realized that this definition is overly narrow and possibly meaningless. Nature has been bound together with human activity for so long that there is little left of any primordial nature. Today, the word environment refers to everything from the health of the community to the appearance of a neighbor's yard.

The meaning of the word environment, as used by many of the scholars reviewed in this chapter, is best understood through its connection to the economic concept of externality. In classic economic analysis, costs and benefits accrue to the transacting parties—or they spill over as externalities to unconsidered others. As a result, the effect of economic activity can be divided into internalities and externalities—into business and environment (B&E).

By definition then, the B&E literature should be of little interest to business academics. The purpose of business is to maximize internal returns, and the role of business scholars is to understand how they do so. Government, not business, has the responsibility of correcting problems caused by externalities. Thus, people interested in the environment should be in schools of government or public policy.

As you might guess, we argue in this chapter that this perspective is wrong. What you may not expect, however, is that we do so for different reasons than most other authors. We do not argue that the environment is in such terrible shape that every scholar should consider ways to protect it (though this may indeed be true). Instead, we argue that B&E literature is important because it provides new insights on topics of interest to most business scholars.

The B&E literature provides these insights, ironically enough, precisely because it has been peripheral to mainstream management literature. This position has encouraged its scholars to consider unusual problems, implausible explanations, and unimportant data. This freedom has allowed the literature to peer into some of the dark corners of management theory. Unfortunately, it also has allowed B&E scholarship to disperse so widely that it is not possible for us to review it all. To manage this diversity, we have chosen to limit our review to just two areas and send quick overviews—academic postcards if you will—that provide a sense of the research being conducted by B&E scholars. For our postcards, we have chosen research that is being conducted to answer two questions: (a) Can firms compete more successfully by protecting the environment? and (b) Can firms create a competition where protecting the environment leads to success?

Research on the first question, which we will call the "pays-to-be-green" (PTGB) literature, grew out of natural experiments caused by increased environmental regulation. According to accepted economic theory, regulation should hurt firms, because it increases costs and constrains the choices available to managers. Yet, in the early 1990s, anecdotal evidence appeared suggesting that some regulations provided unexpected benefits and revealed that some firms chose voluntarily to go "beyond compliance." Why would they do this? Are such benefits sustainable? What are the implications for theory? In our first postcard review, we consider how scholars have attempted to answer these questions.

Research on the second question arose from observation that firms sometimes assume the role of government and attempt to self-regulate environmental problems. Institutions for supporting such self-regulation have become visible and important. These new institutions are neither markets, nor hierarchies, nor public norms of behavior. What is their function? What causes them to arise? When do they work effectively? In our second postcard, we consider emerging scholarship that attempts to answer these questions.

Each of our two sections can be considered independently. You are welcome to consider both or one. In our conclusion, we bring together the two literatures and argue that they share some common approaches and themes. We discuss some limitations on generalization from B&E scholarship and consider implications for future investigation.

Postcard 1: Pays to Be Green

A postcard-length synopsis of the PTBG literature might read, *"scholars investigate the proposal that firms profit by further protecting the environment."* With a bit more space, we might also note that it is remarkable that serious scholars are even willing to consider such an implausible claim. According to mainstream economic theory, there are two strikes against the idea: (a) firms gain little by providing public goods (e.g., clean water or air), and (b) market pressure should drive firms to make profit-maximizing choices about when and how much to provide.

The PTBG literature began to take shape in the early 1990s when reports surfaced stating that regulation had spurred some companies to uncover cost-saving measures (Berube, Nash, Maxwell, & Ehrenfeld, 1992). According to these reports, these innovations would have benefited the company even if the regulation had never been promulgated (Repetto, 1995; U.S. Congress; Office of Technology Assessment, 1994). As it was, they partially or fully offset the cost of complying with the regulation.

Such reports might have been dismissed and ignored, were it not for their endorsement by two notable authorities. In a path-breaking article, Michael Porter and Claus van der Linde (1995a) proposed that "by stimulating innovation, strict environmental regulations can actually enhance competitiveness" and therefore "partially or more than fully offset the costs" of compliance (Porter & Van der Linde, 1995a, p. 98). Known as the Porter Hypothesis (PH), this claim stimulated and organized research in the field.

The Porter Hypothesis includes two provocative elements. First, it assumes that firms are missing opportunities to make money. More critically, it states that firms are doing so in a *systematic* way (Palmer, Oates, & Portney, 1995). Firms miss profit opportunities, Porter and van der Linde (1995a, b) reasoned, by using too many environmental resources or by ignoring ways to reduce the firm's consumption. Such choices are bad both for public welfare and for the firm. Social returns are a by-product, not a motive force, in the Porter Hypothesis.

The second provocative claim is that external stakeholders can provide information or incentives that will improve the efficiency of most firms. In the words of Porter and van der Linde (1995b): "The belief that companies will pick up on profitable opportunities without a regulatory push makes a false assumption about competitive reality—namely, that all profitable opportunities for innovation have already been discovered, that all managers have perfect information about them, and that organizational incentives are aligned with innovating" (p. 127).

The notion that it might "pay to be green" attracted further attention when scholars linked it to the Resource Based View (RBV) (Hart, 1995; Rugman & Verbeke, 1998). Where the Porter Hypothesis is a theory of how environmental performance helps industries or nations gain competitive advantage, the Natural Resource Based View (NRBV) is a theory of how an individual firm might gain a competitive advantage by going green. The typical RBV proceeds as follows. Prior to investing (*ex-ante*) in resources, managers make varying estimations of the resource's future value. As a result of these varying estimations, firms make differing investments in resources. After investing (*ex-post*), factor immobility and barriers to competition from substitute products or services prevent those that made inferior decisions from adjusting. Thus, some firms gain a sustainable competitive advantage (Barney, 1991; Peteraf, 1993). As an addition to the RBV, the NRBV focuses on those resources that will allow the firm to manufacture environmentally friendly products or generate fewer harmful by-products.

The NRBV differs also from classic RBV analysis by borrowing two ideas from the Porter Hypothesis. First, it assumes that managers not only make heterogeneous investments in resources, but also, in the case of resources needed to protect the environment, systematically invest too little (McWilliams & Siegel, 2001). Like the Porter Hypothesis, it therefore assumes that an average firm can achieve a competitive advantage by improving its environmental performance. Second, the NRBV differs from the RBV by arguing (like the Porter Hypothesis) that external actors can be instrumental in stimulating firms to achieve superior performance. The NRBV emphasizes different agents as sources of stimuli for change and has tended to explore the role played by nongovernmental stakeholders rather than government regulation.

Contributions of the PTBG Literature

The provocative claims made in both the Porter Hypothesis and the NRBV are hotly debated. In particular, scholars have evaluated (a) the assumption that managers systematically miss profit opportunities, and (b) the expectation that external actors can stimulate firms to superior financial performance. In doing so, they have extended existing theories of the source of competitive advantage.

Investigation of the first claim has focused attention on an ambiguity in the existing RBV theory (Denrell, Fang, & Winter, 2003). As formulated by Barney and Arikan (2001), the RBV theory assumes that ex-ante expectations differ, but it does not assume that managers make systematic errors (e.g., repeatedly invest too little in a particular type of resource). Other strands of the theory, however, are more open to the potential for systematic error. For example,

Denrell and colleagues (2003) suggested that prices for some resources are systematically suppressed by ignorance of untried activities.

Investigation of the second claim has provided an opportunity to consider a topic that has been neglected in the standard RBV literature—the role of external actors in stimulating comparative advantage. Although there are both theoretical and empirical reasons to believe that regulation and stakeholders could play an important role in spurring innovation that leads to competitive advantage, the literature on the issue remains slight.

In the following section, we discuss research on these two claims. We first consider theories and evidence for systematically overlooked profit opportunities. We then consider research on the role of exogenous actors in spurring competitive advantage.

Systematically Overlooked Opportunities
Many scholars dislike claims that decision makers overlook profit opportunities, and any such claim must be justified both theoretically and empirically (Walley & Whitehead, 1994). Over the last 10 years, scholars in the PTBG literature have attempted to piece together such an explanation, and while it remains inchoate, its general shape now can be discerned. In brief, scholars argue that the difficulty of evaluating the value (and cost) of environmental performance weakens the force of objective analysis and encourages managers to resort to rules of thumb. Biases in these heuristics then cause some types of profit opportunities to be systematically overlooked.

Valuation difficulties. Scholars have given three reasons as to why environmental performance is particularly hard to value. First, market prices usually do not exist for environmental goods and services (Reinhardt, 2000). Lacking price information (and all that is embedded in it), managers must perform their own analyses to estimate the value of environmental performance.[1] For example, they may need to estimate how improvements in performance will reduce the threat of lawsuits or regulatory pressure. Such estimates are highly uncertain and contain attributions regarding the potential behavior of regulators, activist groups, and other actors.

Second, managers may receive incomplete or biased information about the cost of environmental performance because agents with such information may not have a clear incentive to communicate it. Since many aspects of environmental performance—such as the prevention of oil spills or chemical accidents—are particularly difficult to observe or monitor (Reinhardt, 2000), it is often very difficult to design effective incentive systems to encourage agents to engage in environmental improvements. Given the lack of such systems, agents may even have an incentive to misreport both their activities and the cost of these activities (Ambec & Barla, 2002). Such distortion could mean that decision makers use inaccurate information in making investment decisions.

Third, organizational structures may impede the flow of information about ways to profit by improving environmental performance (DeCanio & Watkins, 1998). Most existing organizations were created when environmental resources were thought to have little value. As a result, organizations are often staffed and structured to gather and transfer information about other factors, but not for environmental ones (Cebon, 1992).

Testing the previously mentioned relationships empirically has proven difficult. Many scholars have investigated whether organizations with better information-gathering abilities are more likely to identify ways to profit from improved environmental performance. Many of these studies have drawn inspiration from classic theories of organizational design (Galbraith, 1973; Thompson, 1967) and more recent theories based on "lean production" (Womack, Jones, & Roos, 1991). For example, Cebon (1992) and Ashford and Heaton (1983) found case evidence that the creation of specialized environmental departments can buffer the organization from new demands and, thus, restrict information flow about possible improvements. Klassen and Whybark (1999) used surveys from 83 firms to investigate the effect of investment in end-of-pipe buffers (e.g., pollution-control equipment). They found investments in end-of-pipe controls to be associated with lower performance, while investments in pollution prevention to be associated with better manufacturing performance.

Later research reinterpreted the effect of dedicated environmental departments and pollution-control equipment and argued that they could act as potential sources of information. King (1995, 1999) and Rothenberg (2003) found that specialized environmental units and operators of waste-treatment equipment often discover or transfer information about profitable, but unrealized, waste-reduction opportunities. Melnyk, Sroufe, and Calantone (2003a) reported that specialized structures and personnel, such as formal environmental-management systems, allow managers to gain information about impacts well beyond pollution abatement and bring real benefits on many aspects of operation performance (Melnyk et al., 2003a). Florida and Davison (2001) found that firms adopting environmental-management systems were able to gather more accurate information on their activities resulting in reduced environmental risks for the community.

A particularly fruitful avenue for empirical research on the role of organizational structure in unleashing unrealized profit opportunities has investigated parallels between "lean production" and "green" production. Theories of lean production suggest that by limiting inventory stocks (and other types of buffers) in production, managers can expose production problems and change agent incentives. Evidence on lean production, suggests that until recently, managers have tended to systematically invest too much in inventory (or too little in inventory reduction) (Macduffie, 1995). Noting parallels between lean production and green production ideas, PTBG scholars have argued that (a) the use of lean production will inform managers of the value of waste reduction efforts (Klassen, 2000), or (b) the idea of reduced inventory can be extended to cover the benefits derived from reduced inventory buffers that will also accrue from reduced waste treatment buffers. Consistent with this idea, Rothenberg, Pil, and Maxwell (2001) discovered that the use of lean production reveals ways to minimize waste and make better use of production inputs. Klassen (2000) reported that "quality-related organizational systems" were associated with greater investment in pollution prevention and recycling. Pil and Rothenberg (2003) found that environmental and manufacturing improvement efforts are "synergistic and reciprocal". King and Lenox (2001) also discovered evidence that adoption of lean production is related to environmental-performance improvement.

While the studies just discussed suggest that differences in organizational or operational designs influence the transfer of valuable information and the discovery of profit opportunities, they cannot rule out unobserved firm differences as a possible explanation of observed behavior. To control for fixed organizational characteristics, Lenox and King (2004) used panel data to investigate behavior before and after the creation of corporate environmental information provision offices. They found that the creation of such offices anticipates the adoption of environmentally beneficial practices. Yet, their study did not distinguish the effect of information from potentially confounding changes in incentives.

Cognitive heuristics and biases. The difficulties managers face in determining the value of environmental performance (just described above) do not provide a complete theory as to why managers might overlook opportunities to increase profits while protecting the environment. Managers with unconstrained reasoning power should be able to anticipate the potential for missing or biased information and adjust their decisions accordingly. Practically, however, the difficulties make it less likely that managers will use "hard" numbers in making decisions and more likely they will rely on intuition or rules of thumb. It is these heuristics, PTBG scholars have argued, that cause managers to miss win–win opportunities to improve both environmental and financial performance.

Scholars have suggested that there are several sources of bias in decision making that explain systematic underinvestment in environmental resources (Kleindorfer, 1999). In concert with the previous section, scholars argue that the availability of information about the value of environmental performance influences the degree of investment. Since, as just discussed, managers often lack accurate information about environmental costs and benefits, an "availability bias" could cause managers to discount excessively the value of investments in environmental resources (Kleindorfer, 1999; Tversky & Kahneman, 1973).

Other scholars have noted that other known cognitive biases may reduce investment in environmental resources. Bazerman and Hoffman (1999) suggested that individuals tend to use irrationally high discount rates and argued that such a bias suppresses investment in factors that provide deferred returns—a case that is common for environmental performance. Hoffman and colleagues (1999) argued that biased decisions result from the tendency of managers to view environmental and financial performance as a "fixed pie," in which gain on one dimension necessitates loss on an other. Finally, Mylonadis (1993) argued that commonly used metaphors can influence the framing of problems and influence investment. Both Mylonadis and Hoffman used case studies to test their claims, and both found evidence that framing environmental performance as problem of disposal or waste treatment tended to distract managers from the potential strategic and financial value of environmental performance.

Tenbrunsel, Wade-Benzoni, Messick, and Bazerman (2000) argued that certain types of regulation may trigger damaging heuristics and biases. They argued that the existence of a government standard acts as an anchoring mechanism for decision making. Even if the standard is not required or enforced, the mere existence of a standard causes people to perceive conforming solutions as more desirable than nonconforming ones (Tenbrunsel et al., 2000). Employing an experimental research design, they found that subjects give greater value to a particular option when it is presented as a standard. They inferred that framing something as a standard causes cognitive distortions that increase "the attractiveness of standard-conforming solutions over that of nonconforming solutions" (Tenbrunsel et al., 2000, p. 854).

Finally, Kunreuther and Pauly (2004) argued that people often underestimate the cost of rare events. For this reason, they contended, people fail to buy the optimal amount of insurance against natural disasters such as earthquakes, hurricanes, and so on. Kunreuther and Bowman (1997) and Kleindorfer and Saad (2005) argued that similar difficulties in evaluating rare events like chemical accidents and spills could cause managers to systematically underinvest in the prevention of such accidents.

The Role of Exogenous Actors in Creating Sustainable Advantage
The second claim of the Porter Hypothesis and NRBV theory—that external actors can stimulate firms to superior financial performance—has received almost as much attention as the notion that managers might systematically overlook profit opportunities (discussed in the last section). Scholars have long agreed that government and stakeholders can affect the value of environmental goods and services. What is much more controversial is the possibility that external actors might be able to foster better decision making, and thereby cause managers to uncover hidden value. Research on this possibility

has emphasized the role of government or stakeholders, and we will subdivide our review accordingly.

Government stimuli. A prominent argument for a possible beneficial effect of government stimuli is that government can facilitate the flow of information to decision makers. If, as discussed in the previous section, a lack of information causes managers to overlook profit opportunities, government may be able to encourage improvement by publicizing information about the costs and benefits of certain activities. Government programs such as Green Lights and Energy Star are examples of such a strategy. DeCanio (1998) found that the returns to investments made as a result of the Green Lights program were higher than for other investments of comparable risk. He concluded that managers had failed to recognize these opportunities and that government-provided information stimulated their discovery. Consistent with Decanio's finding, Howarth, Haddad, and Paton (2000) also observed that other types of governmental programs induce firms to investment in cost-saving opportunities. Yet, neither study measured how expensive the discovery of these improvements would have been without the free government-provided information, and thus did not demonstrate that managers should have expended the necessary effort to find the opportunities themselves.

A second way that government can facilitate the flow of information to decision makers is by reducing transaction costs that may impede information transfer. For example, government requirements that oblige firms to report waste byproducts can reduce the cost of finding potential buyers of these byproducts (King & Shaver, 2001). Government disclosure requirements also may help alleviate problems caused by misaligned incentives between principals and agents. As discussed in the previous section, agents may have an incentive to inflate cost estimates to obtain additional funds for pollution reduction. By precluding this possibility, regulation can facilitate better investment decisions (Ambec & Barla, 2002).

Scholars have also investigated whether more traditional types of regulation (e.g., emissions levels or technological requirements) can cause firms to uncover unrealized profit opportunities. Jaffe and Palmer (1997) found that regulation leads to R&D expenditure but not necessarily to patent innovation, while Nameroff, Garant, and Albert (2004) found significant evidence that regulation leads to patenting innovation. Brunnermeier and Cohen (2003) found that regulation (as measured by pollution-control costs) leads to a higher rate of patenting, but found no evidence that greater enforcement or monitoring causes innovation. King (1995) reported that equipment purchased to comply with regulation also revealed the causes of hidden production problems and helped firms to realize significant operational improvements.

Other studies have sought to determine if the realized cost of stringent regulation matches ex-ante predictions. Majumdar and Marcus (2001) found that stringent regulation, if well designed, positively influences productivity. Morgenstern, Pizer, and Shih (2002) found no evidence that it harms employment. Using data-envelopment analysis, Managi, Opaluch, Jin, and Grigalunas (2005) suggested that environmental regulations reduce productivity in the short term, but lead to long-term increases in total-factor productivity. Isaksson (2005) found that among 114 facilities, reductions in nitrous-oxide emissions were accomplished at little or no cost, and he inferred evidence for extensive ex-ante production inefficiencies. Yet, he concluded that regulation allowed the discovery of "low-hanging fruit," but did not provide competitive advantage.[2]

Stakeholder stimuli. Governmental stimuli may help explain the competitiveness of industries, but cannot easily explain competitive heterogeneity among firms. Researchers with interest in the NRBV propose that environmental stakeholders can sometimes fulfill this role.

One explanation for stakeholder influence on innovation follows a logic first proposed by Coase (1960). Stakeholders wish to encourage firms to improve their performance but are impeded from doing so by transaction costs. One way to overcome this problem is for stakeholders to invest in innovations that are both valuable and better for the environment. Stafford, Polonsky, and Hartman (2000) reported an example that precisely matches this story. Concerned by the effect of CFC refrigerants, the environmental group Greenpeace helped design and market a CFC free "greenfreeze" refrigerator (Stafford et al., 2000). They first transferred the technology to one firm and then to the rest of the industry. Outside of the United States, this technology now controls the majority of the market (Stafford et al., 2000).

Several authors have reported a relationship between stakeholder involvement and performance improvement. Anton, Deltas, and Khanna (2004) reported that stakeholders often encourage the adoption of environmental management systems and find these systems to be associated with performance improvement. Klassen and Vachon (2003) found that customer-initiated collaborative activities increased waste prevention. Roome and Wijen (2006) reported that stakeholder involvement can facilitate learning and improvement. Stafford and colleagues (2000) suggested that environmental groups can provide firms with extended networks, thereby enhancing firm "bridging" capabilities. Some evidence suggests that such close stakeholder connections can lead to greater financial performance. Hillman and Keim (2001) found that stakeholder management can improve shareholder value—particularly when those shareholders represent suppliers and local communities.

Stakeholders may also be able to help firms resolve market imperfections that prevent them being rewarded for superior performance. By acting as credible conduits for unobserved information, stakeholders may allow firms to charge a premium for environmental attributes (Reinhardt, 2000). We further consider this role in the second half of this chapter.

The Bottom Line: Does It Pay to Be Green?

Ultimately, whether it pays to be green is a question that must be answered by empirical analysis of the link between environmental and financial performance. Elsewhere, Margolis and Walsh (2001, 2003), Allouche and Laroche (2005), and Koehler, Bennett, Norris, and Spengler (2005) have reviewed this literature, and we provide only a brief summary of it here.

In general, studies have employed three different types of tests. Some studies have looked for a contemporaneous association between environmental and economic performance. To correct for the possibility that unobserved heterogeneity might explain observed relationships, some scholars have investigated the relationship between changes in environmental and financial performance. Finally, some scholars have used event-study methodologies to explore the response of financial markets to new information about environmental performance.

Konar and Cohen (2001) performed a cross-sectional analysis of the association between environmental performance and financial performance (Tobin's q). They found evidence of a negative relationship between toxic emissions and firm valuation. However, they recognized that unobserved firm attributes could account for the relationship. To partially rule out unobserved factors, Hart and Ahuja (1996) and Russo and Fouts (1997) evaluated the relationship between changes in environmental performance and changes in financial performance; both found evidence of a strong positive relationship. King and Lenox (2002) argued that such findings may be explained by misspecified models or constructs. Employing a 10-year panel and more conservative specifications, they found no significant relationship between emissions and financial performance. Yet, they did find a modest causal relationship between waste reduction and financial performance. Other scholars have investigated the investment timing, where early investments in environmental innovation could allow firms to gain and maintain a competitive advantage over late movers. Exploring the paper industry Nehrt (1996) found that early pollution-reducing technology investments by first movers boosted profit growth, while late movers were not able to catch up, despite of copious investments.

Finally, several scholars have suggested contingencies for PTBG arguments. Nehrt (1996) argued that the timing of investments determines their financial impact. Exploring the paper industry, he found that early pollution-reducing technology investments by first movers boosted profit growth, while late movers were not able to catch up despite copious investments. Christmann (2000) argued that profitable green can occur only if the firm has the complementary assets to protect its advantage.

Other scholars have used event-study methodologies to evaluate stock-market responses to the release of information on environmental performance or news of an environmentally significant event. Several scholars have investigated how markets respond on the day that government data on toxic releases are announced, and they found that such announcements are associated with significant losses (Hamilton, 1995; Khanna, Quimio, & Bojilova, 1998). However, Koehler and Cram (2001) argued that such studies fail to account for contemporaneous correlation in stock-price movements. Reanalyzing data on market responses to toxic release inventory reports, Koehler and Cram found a statistically significant but weak relationship.

Summarizing the findings, Margolis and Walsh (2001, 2003) reported evidence of a generally positive relationship between social (including environmental) and financial performance. Orlitzky, Schmidt, and Rynes (2003) criticized their methodology and performed an alternative meta-analysis on 52 studies. Yet, they, too, concluded that environmental performance is positively correlated with financial performance. Moreover, they reported a causal relationship in both directions: firms with slack resources invest more in environmental and social practices, but green practices help them to be more efficient and competitive. Most recently, Allouche and Laroche (2005) again found evidence of a positive relationship. They argued that their meta-analytic technique allowed a better estimate of the economic effect of the relationship, and helped them identify firm and location characteristics that moderate its strength.

Summary and Future Directions

This section represents a quick postcard of research on the radical idea that it might pay to be green. We discussed progress made by researchers in understanding (a) what might cause managers to systematically overlook profit opportunities and (b) what role external agents might play in stimulating the discovery of such opportunities. By focusing attention on these issues, PTBG scholarship has helped advance understanding of the sources of competitive advantage.

PTBG research has created the outlines of one theory for why managers might systematically miss profit opportunities. This research suggests that for new performance criteria that are not priced by markets and for which organizations lack information-gathering systems, managers tend to use heuristics in making investment decisions. Biases in these heuristics can cause systematic underinvestment.

PTBG research has also identified conditions where governments or stakeholders can provide an important stimulus for improvement. By assuaging organizational barriers, by reducing transaction costs or by directly providing information, government can increase the flow of information available to managers and improve their decision making. Stakeholders can also act as information conduits to firms or can directly negotiate mutually beneficial changes in corporate practice.

Yet, these summaries veil a growing divergence among scholars about the potential of win-win improvements to provide meaningful environmental and financial gains. Some scholars have drawn parallels between neo-Schumpeterian theories of new market entry and PTBG theory to suggest that firms can profit while improving economic, social, and environmental conditions in the developing world (Hart & Christensen, 2002). These scholars argue that organizational and cognitive factors cause managers to systematically undervalue the market potential of the world's 4 billion poorest people (London & Hart, 2004; Prahalad & Hammond, 2002). They argue that such underinvestment creates enormous potential for profit, and those firms that address these markets will find fortunes hidden at the "base of the pyramid." Moreover, the economic activity that generates these profits will also improve the environmental and social conditions of these desperately poor people.

Other scholars have become skeptical of any "rule of riches" that suggests firms can always profit by increasing their environmental performance. Such optimism, so clearly evident in early studies, has given way to a more moderate position that environmental-performance improvement may pay only for some firms, or in certain cases, or in certain time frames. Continuing research on such contingencies, we believe, will prove useful theoretical and practical insight.

Finally, evidence of a contingent or economically marginal relationship between environmental and financial performance suggests to some scholars that meaningful gains in environmental performance will require more than the resolution of overlooked profit opportunities (Orsato, 2006; Zadek, 2001). Real gains will entail changing the business climate and the rules of competition. Clearly, such change could come from government and national institutions. Increasingly, however, scholars also have suggested that firms themselves can play an important role in setting rules that support a "greener" competition. How firms do this is the topic of our second academic postcard.

Postcard II: Self-Regulation

In the previous section, we considered whether, given the existing rules of competition, firms could profit from improving their environmental performance. Now, we consider whether firms themselves can create rules that allow a better and greener competition. In so doing, we shift the attention away from potential inefficiencies in a firm's operational choices to potential inefficiencies in market competition.

A postcard-length synopsis of this section might read: "*Leviathans not needed. Researchers study how firms use a little-known type of institution to solve common problems.*" With a bit more space, we might add that it is rather surprising that these self-regulatory institutions are so little known, because they have been hiding in plain sight. And, we might add that the B&E literature has contributed to broader management theory by increasing awareness and consideration of these institutions.

The Role of Institutions in Preventing the Tragedy of the Commons

Institutions are the "humanly devised constraints that structure political, economic and social interaction" (North, 1990, p. 97). For anyone interested in environmental issues, "the tragedy of the commons" famously illustrates the need for such institutions. According to Hardin (1968), "the inherent logic" of common ownership "remorselessly" leads to collective ruin. As actors attempt to maximize their own return, they impoverish themselves. Common fields are overrun with sheep, common fisheries are driven to exhaustion, and even common atmospheres are damaged by pollution.

To prevent such common tragedy, Hardin reasoned, a central authority—what Hobbes called a "leviathan"—should control use of the common resource. Attempts by actors to self-regulate solutions without recourse to this authority should be viewed with skepticism. Self-regulation creates public value, and thus again causes a kind of commons problem. Each firm would like another to abide by common rules, but each also has an incentive to defect.

But is self-regulation indeed impossible? The scholars reviewed in this section think not. They investigate instances where the actors themselves try to solve common problems by creating self-regulatory institutions. Neither markets nor hierarchies, these institutions present exciting new problems for theory (in Karl Popper's sense of the phrase) that can help refine and extend existing theories of how institutions form and operate (Popper, 1968).

Self-Regulatory Institutions: Lost and Found

Institutions come in a diverse array of forms. They can be private (e.g., firms) or public (e.g., governments), and they can be hierarchical or decentralized. The self-regulatory institutions that we consider in this section are usually classified as private (because it is possible for participants to opt in or out), and decentralized (because they have flat structures of authority and little or no system of central enforcement).

Self-regulatory institutions (SRIs) are often thought of as rare and new when in fact, they are neither. Examples include voluntary codes of conduct, trade association-sponsored standards, and management-certification programs. They have been documented in industries as diverse as accounting, electronics, computer software, agriculture, and banking (Furger, 1997). Why have they been neglected by management scholars?

One explanation is that the two dominant strands of institutional theory do not provide a comfortable home for self-regulatory institutions. For one strand of theory, institutional choice lies along a line between markets and hierarchies—leaving little room for self-regulation (Coase, 1960; Williamson, 1975). For a second strand of theory, institutions obtain their authority through their very constancy. Thus, the idea that agents can self-regulate solutions conflicts with the mechanisms thought to infuse institutions with power. A final explanation was previously discussed: scholars remain influenced by the metaphor of "the tragedy of the commons" and it's message about the impossibility of self-regulation.

In the 1980s and 1990s, growing empirical evidence began to change these perspectives. Case studies, histories, and experimental research appeared that provided evidence that actors using common resources, despite their misaligned incentives, were able to coordinate solutions (cf., Khanna, 2001; Ostrom, 1990). Much of this work was conducted, supported, or inspired by Elinor Ostrom. Using numerous theoretical perspectives and methods, she explored how participants could self-regulate common-pool resource problems and avoid the "tragedy of the commons" (cf., Ostrom, Gardner, & Walker, 1994).[3]

Drivers of Self-Regulation in Modern Industries

Common-pool resources, like the ones discussed in "the tragedy of the commons" and investigated by Elinor Ostrom, conjure up images of meadows and fish ponds, but common-pool resource problems exist in modern industrial economies as well. Modern corporations use open-access fisheries (Schlager & Ostrom, 1992), access shared water or energy resources (Dayton-Johnson, 2000; Hanna, 1997), contribute to shared knowledge resources (Furman & Stern, 2006), and so on. Self-regulatory institutions exist in these settings, but many more occur in industries with no apparent common-pool resource (cf., Khanna, 2001). What could explain the need for self-regulation in these settings? An important area of research for business and environment scholars has been to theorize and empirically test possible drivers of self-regulation. This research has identified common sanctions and asymmetric information as particularly important causes.

Common sanctions. To explain the emergence of self-regulatory institutions in industries that do not share a common physical resource, some authors have argued that common problems can arise from interaction with other institutions or institutional actors. Blunt application of force by governments or stakeholders can unite the fate of all firms in an industry. For example, if regulation is determined by an industry's collective performance, a classic social dilemma is created in which each firm wishes others to improve, but has little incentive to do so itself (Dawson & Segerson, 2005; Maxwell, Lyon, & Hackett, 2000). Likewise, stakeholder's inability to differentiate performance among firms can cause a common risk of sanctions. For example, the Earth Island Institute initiated a boycott of all albacore tuna—despite the fact that some companies sourced their tuna from locations where porpoises were not put at risk by tuna fishing (Reinhardt & Vietor, 1996).

Several studies have quantified this industry commons by investigating if the behavior of one firm influences the perceived value of another firm in the industry. Research has demonstrated that an accident at one firm can influence the stock price of another (Hill & Schneeweis, 1983). Likewise, product recalls at one pharmaceutical firm or automaker influence the value of other firms (Jarrell & Peltzman, 1985). This *sanction commons* increases the more similar the firms are (Blacconiere & Patten, 1994).

Dawson and Segerson (2005) proposed that a common risk of government regulation can drive the formation of self-regulatory institutions. They asserted that such institutions forestall government regulation by helping coordinate collective improvement. In concert with this idea, Barnett and King (2006) found evidence that an important example of self-regulation in the chemical industry (the Responsible Care Program) arose after a deadly accident in Bhopal, India increased the importance of a reputation commons. They reported that after the Bhopal accident, investors punished firms similar to those where an accident had occurred, and they found that these joint sanctions diminished after the formation of the program.

Asymmetric information. Since Akerlof (1970), scholars have recognized that asymmetric information can cause a collective problem by creating an inefficient "market for lemons" in which only low-quality products can be sold. To solve this problem, firms must credibly communicate the quality of their goods and services. Doing so does not necessarily create the need for collective action. In some cases, firms can differentiate themselves from their peers by engaging in visible acts that reveal their unobserved quality. However, business and environment scholars have argued that for many environmental problems, such unilateral solutions are not feasible (cf., Reinhardt, 2000).

The environmental aspects of a good or service—how its production affects the environment or how it will decompose over time—are usually hidden attributes. Customers cannot determine by inspection whether the cotton in a pair of trousers was grown in an organic manner or a pound of coffee beans was grown under a natural-forest canopy. For these types of goods, a warrantee or a reputation is still suspect, because the stakeholder may never know whether he or she has been deceived (Reinhardt, 2000). To provide a credible means of communicating the unobserved quality of these "credence goods," firms often need to set up a common infrastructure for inspection and certification (Darnall & Carmin, 2005). Scholars have proposed that many of the self-regulatory institutions that require changes in behavior and certification of these changes help firms communicate unobserved attributes of their products or processes to customers (King, Lenox, & Barnett, 2002).

Sponsors and Origins

Given the drivers of self-regulation just presented, how do self-regulatory institutions form? Who sponsors them? How do they emerge? What conditions enable them to operate? Early work in the business and environment literature sought to categorize the numerous sponsors of self-regulatory institutions (cf.,

Nash & Ehrenfeld, 1997). Corporations, trade associations, international organizations, and stakeholders all have been prime movers behind the creation of one or more examples. Some programs, like the Marine Stewardship Council, were formed by the collaboration of corporations and groups of stakeholders (Reinhardt, 2000). Still international organizations like the International Organization for Standardization (e.g., ISO 14001) created other programs. In some cases, several types of actors have played an entrepreneurial role. For example, the chemical industry's Responsible Care program was influenced by the Canadian CAER program, the Chemical Manufacturer's Association, and personal sponsorship by Robert Kennedy, CEO of Union Carbide (Rees, 1997).

Other work has explored the historical process through which SRIs emerge. Several studies have identified shocks or scandals as playing a particularly important role in catalyzing formative action. For example, Rees (1988) reported that the accident at Three Mile Island helped spur the formation of the nuclear industry's INPO program (Rees, 1994). Similarly, the accident at Bhopal played a critical role in driving the formation of the Chemical Industry's Responsible Care Program (Barnett, 2004; Rees, 1997). In the petroleum industry, the Valdez accident encouraged the development of both the Valdez Principles and the STEP program (Lenox & Nash, 2003). A smuggled video of dolphins being caught and tortured on tuna boats provided impetus for the creation of the dolphin-safe certification system (Reinhardt, 2000).

Other scholars have argued that industry shocks are just part of a more continuous process of field-level institutional change leading to the creation of more formal self-regulatory structures. Hoffman (1999) argued that frames of perception in the chemical industry evolved as new metaphors appeared for how firms interact with their surroundings. Early metaphors of pollution as a problem of regulatory compliance gradually changed to ones of corporate strategy and profitability. As shared frames of perception changed, responses included more strategic considerations, and firm interaction with stakeholders took on new forms. Yet, Hoffman also argued that "change can emerge suddenly and unpredictably" (p. 366) as exogenous events (e.g., the publication of Rachel Carson's *Silent Spring*) or endogenous events (accidents and spills) influence taken-for-granted assumptions (Carson, 1962). Hoffman and Ocasio (2001) argued that such events have greater impact when they violate existing norms and frames.

Research on the conditions needed to allow effective self-regulation has emphasized the importance of monitoring and sanctions. Based on the history of Responsible Care and the Institute of Nuclear Power Operations (INPO), Rees (1997) argued that self-regulation is more likely to take hold when the industry is closely connected (incestuous in his language) so that important actors can monitor behavior. Moreover, he argued, self-regulation is fostered by a central forum for communicating and discussing governance issues. Furger (1997) argued that overlapping oversight by different institutional actors allowed monitoring of conformance to self-regulatory safety institutions in the maritime shipping industry. He further argued that sanctions and rewards from insurance companies provided incentives to conform with agreed-upon standards. He found that when market pressure and new industry entrants eroded these conditions, self-regulatory institutions lost the power to control behavior. Lenox and Nash (2003) echoed the importance of sanctioning mechanisms and empirically confirmed their effect.

Sanctioning mechanisms—emphasized by the authors just discussed—represent a critical challenge for self-regulatory institutions, because in many countries group-level coercion is illegal. Antitrust regulation designed to prevent anticompetitive behavior also restricts the ability of firms to coordinate sanctions against other firms. In a few cases, self-regulatory structures can call on state government to provide enforcement (cf., Rees, 1994), but that is not usually possible. How then do self-regulatory structures coordinate action? The next section considers research on this issue.

Sources of Power

Most of the research by business and environmental scholars on environmental self-regulatory institutions has investigated how these institutions obtain the power to influence behavior. Because this is both a large and difficult question, scholars have emphasized two broadly differing perspectives. One argues that institutions obtain power by becoming institutionalized in social settings. Because of this process, agent cognition and choice are constrained, and certain opportunistic behaviors are prevented. Another perspective argues that agents continue to have the freedom to behave opportunistically, but are constrained from doing so by their choice to cooperate to advance their own self-interest.

From the first perspective, self-regulatory institutions represent preconscious or postconscious constraints on strategic behavior. Preconscious constraints occur because institutions include taken-for-granted elements that create powerful schema or frames for decision making (Berger & Luckmann, 1966). These elements influence what decision makers perceive and what choices they consider. Postconscious constraints "directly or indirectly divert design adoption away from the proposed dynamic in transaction cost economics (e.g., comparative efficiency) and toward the dynamic of legitimacy" (Roberts & Greenwood, 1997, p. 355). These constraints "cause actors who do recognize and try to act on their interests to be unable to do so effectively" (Dimaggio, 1988, p. 5).

From the second perspective, self-regulatory institutions represent nothing more than the manifest outcome of strategic interactions. Drawing on the theory of cartels and clubs, scholars have developed many formal models of self-regulatory institutions (Barrett, 1994; Dawson & Segerson, 2005; Potoski

& Prakash, 2005b). In most of these models, actors propose rules for the group to which the group responds by deciding whether to participate and how to behave. In making these decisions, each actor considers how all others will behave and how different options will influence the decisions of other actors. By considering this process in detail, scholars identify one or more equilibrium where each actor will be making his or her best decision (given what he expects everyone else to do). The "institution" as it is observed in business practice is the expression of this equilibrium.

To explore these two perspectives, business and environment scholars have sought to evaluate the predictive power of the above two broad strands of institutionalism. Most commonly, these studies have sought to develop models of (a) who participates in self-regulatory institutions and (b) how participation influences performance.

The three pillars. In search of evidence of pre- and postconscious constraints applied by self-regulatory institutions, several authors have investigated whether cognitive, normative, or coercive pressures influence participation in self-regulatory institutions. Delmas (2002) found that "regulatory, normative, and cognitive aspects of a country's institutional environment greatly impact the costs and potential benefits of the ISO 14001 [environmental management] standard and therefore explain the differences in adoption across countries" (Delmas, 2002, p. 91).[4] Several authors found that government regulation or support was an important determinant of participation in a self-regulatory institution (Chan & Wong, 2006; Rivera, 2004; Rivera & de Leon, 2004; Rivera, De Leon, & Koerber, 2006; Shin, 2005). Neumayer and Perkins (2004) found that participation in ISO 14001 is influenced by pressure from local wealthy stakeholders, civil society, and foreign customers in Europe and Japan. Albuquerque, Bronnenberg, and Corbett (2004) found evidence that national–cultural differences influence the diffusion of ISO 14001 among countries.

Many studies, including several designed to test economic models of institutions, reported a link between participation in one SRI and involvement in another. Such a connection is difficult to interpret, but it might suggest evidence of normative pressure or mimetic behavior. Corbett and Kirsch (2004) found that "patterns of international certification to ISO 14000 are strongly correlated with those to ISO 9000" (p. 339). King and Lenox (2001) found a strong relationship between ISO 9000 adoption and ISO 14000 adoption. Viadiu, Fa, and Saizarbitoria (2006) found that the diffusion pattern of ISO 14000 matches that of ISO 9000. In contrast, using a different diffusion model, Melnyk, Sroufe, and Calantone (2003b) found that adoption of ISO 9000 was not associated with adoption of ISO 14000.

Jiang and Bansal (2003) made an important distinction between adoption of the underlying technical aspects of self-regulatory institutions and visible association with the emblem of the institution. Based on interviews with managers at 16 companies, they concluded that regulatory and social forces tend to predict adoption of environmental management systems, but that strategic choice drives the decision to certify these systems under ISO 14001. They found that when tasks were less visible or the outcome of these tasks was more "opaque" to viewers, managers sought to demonstrate their actions by certifying with ISO14000. King, Lenox, and Terlaak (2005) quantitatively tested this idea in a larger setting and found corroborating results.

Strategic choice. To investigate the predictive power of the second brand of institutional theory (that strategic action shapes the functioning of institutions), several authors have looked for standard signs of opportunism. These authors predict that programs without strict entry rules fall victim to adverse selection, and programs without means of enforcing compliance will suffer from moral hazard.

King and Lenox (2000) demonstrated that the Chemical Industry's Responsible Care program suffered from both adverse selection and moral hazard. Participating firms tended to pollute more than comparable firms in the same industry, and their rates of improvement slowed after the creation of the program (King & Lenox, 2000). Howard, Nash, and Ehrenfeld (2000) found evidence consistent with these findings in interviews in 16 firms; they concluded that participation of Responsible Care provided "a poor indicator that any particular standard practices will be followed" (p. 281).

In three important studies, Rivera and de Leon demonstrated that self-regulatory programs with weak enforcement also exhibited telltale signs of strategic opportunism. They showed that participants in a hotel eco-label in Costa Rica did not have superior environmental performance (Rivera & De Leon, 2005). They also found that participants in a self-regulatory program among ski areas (the Sustainable Slopes program) had lower performance than nonmembers (Rivera & de Leon, 2004; Rivera et al., 2006). Moreover, they found no indication that this deficit had been resolved 5 years after the program's initiation.

Studies on programs that include stronger sanctions or that can draw on sanctions from another institution have revealed fewer signs of opportunism. Rees (1994) attributed the success of self-regulation among nuclear power-plant operators (INPO) to their ability to use the threat of sanctions from government regulators to prevent free riding. In a study of a voluntary initiative between government and industry—the 33/50 program[5]—Khanna and Damon (1999) predicted that the governmental oversight on the program would reduce the tendency for firms to free ride. In support of this idea, they found that participants in the program improved their performance more than nonparticipants. Lenox and Nash (2003) compared four self-regulatory programs and claimed that the more successful ones included internal sanctioning mechanisms to prevent free riding.

Equilibrium outcomes. A true test of a strategic-equilibrium theory of institutions would do more than show evidence of strategic choice, it would demonstrate that a calculated equilibrium accurately predicts observed behavior.

Tests of incentive-compatible equilibria can be accomplished most easily for institutions that appear to help firms "signal" unobserved firm or facility attributes. Most commonly, scholars have investigated whether, as predicted by signaling models, participants have higher performance than nonparticipants on some performance dimension that is not readily observable to customers (or other important stakeholders).

Evidence suggests that validation and certification systems are important determinants of the signaling potential of SRIs. As just discussed, for two programs with weak validation and certification systems, Rivera and de Leon (2004; 2005) found that participation did not provide evidence of superior performance. In contrast, for the ISO 14000 standard, which does entail certification by an approved third party, several authors found evidence that certification could be a market signal. Yet, these authors did not find evidence for the simplest signaling story—that certification provides evidence of relatively superior performance. Instead, they argued that certification provides evidence of superior efforts to improve or superior improvement rates. Potoski and Prakash (2005a, b) and Toffel (2004, 2006) found that firms improve their performance after certifying with ISO 14000. King and colleagues (2005) found that firms certify with ISO 14000 when they need to communicate the existence of internal environmental-management systems to distant or foreign-exchange partners.

Tests of equilibrium market-signaling models of SRIs have also investigated the financial performance of participants and nonparticipants. Signaling models suggest that participants in SRIs should benefit financially, because the signal allows them to charge customers for superior quality. Because ISO 14000 has been adopted by a relatively small number of facilities (at least in the United States), scholars have turned their attention to its close cousin—the ISO 9000 Quality Management Standard. Terlaak and King (2006) reported that certification is associated with a moderate increase in production—suggesting that certification helps attract marginal customers. Corbett, Montes-Sancho, and Kirsch (2005) found that ISO 9000 certification is associated with substantially higher financial returns.

Equilibrium models of cartel-like self-regulatory institutions are much harder to test. Depending on the precise structure of these models, multiple equilibria may exist and different static hypotheses can be generated. In general, however, these models suggest that (a) participants should benefit from participating, (b) nonparticipants should benefit from not participating, and (c) the institution should provide some welfare benefit to the participants (Barrett, 1994; Dutta & Radner, 2004). These models usually suggest, moreover, that the biggest gains should accrue to the nonparticipants, because these free riders appropriate the value of the program without accruing any of the cost. These expectations have been best explored with respect to the Responsible Care program. Lenox (2006) found that the creation of the program provided dramatic financial benefits to most firms in the industry, and he found that nonparticipating firms benefited considerably more. Barnett and King (2006) found that the devastating chemical accident in Bhopal, India, created a common sensitivity to accidents such that an event at one firm would influence the stock price of another. They found evidence that the self-regulatory program reduced this tendency, but benefited nonparticipants more than participants.

A theoretical problem for many researchers exploring equilibrium models of self-regulatory institutions is that the evidence for environmental and financial consequences often provides contradictory insights. For example, scholars have tended to argue that the Responsible Care Program represents a means of forestalling government regulation (Dawson & Segerson, 2005; Rees, 1997). If so, participants should improve their environmental performance, because the program helps them cooperate to prevent regulation. However, as discussed earlier, just the opposite seems to be true—after joining the program, participants slowed the rate at which they reduced their emissions. Financial benefits from such a program may suggest credulous stakeholders who ascribe meaning to a program without a rational basis. Alternatively, studies demonstrating adverse selection and moral hazard may have missed important variables of interest to stakeholders (like accident prevention) upon which the participants did improve.

Another problem for theory is that some self-regulatory institutions seem to be designed in such a way as to provide conflicting incentives. Darnall and Carmin (2005) suggested that variability in the rules and mechanisms among self-regulatory institutions confuses interpretation of participation. Surveying 61 examples, they found great variation in the purposes, design concepts, and rules. They suggested that if stakeholders (or researchers) lump programs together, they tend to respond inefficiently to the programs. Terlaak (2007) argued that some programs actually contain conflicting design objectives. She argued that some programs hope to provide both useful best-practice guidelines and a means of distinguishing high- and low-performing firms. The problem, she noted, is that the worst firms stand to gain the most from the guidelines, and this can lead to an adverse selection of firms. Such conflicting objectives, she noted, can destroy the usefulness of certification as a means of identifying organizations with better hidden attributes.

Summary and Future Directions

The management literature has largely neglected the potential for firms to use self-regulatory institutions to solve common problems. This oversight stems in part from a poor fit with existing dominant theories in the literature. It also results in part from pessimism—as expressed in the metaphor of the tragedy of the commons—about the ability of actors to solve environmental problems without the aid of a leviathan (Thompson, 2000). Recent research on self-regulatory institutions is beginning to change these expectations. This research reveals a world of possibility, not one of inevitable tragedy—one in which the effected parties look for institutional solutions of their own creation.

Empirical research on self-regulatory institutions reveals that both streams of institutional theory have some predictive power. The strategic pursuit of individual gain plays a central role in the creation of these institutions and determines how they are understood and used. These decentralized forms are not just "customs in common" that guide our interactions by creating pre and postconscious constraints. They are governance structures of our own making into which we enter so that they may constrain us.

Yet, this research also seems to reveal that these institutions are not the product of fully rational actors. As of this writing, there is reason to doubt that these institutions represent a manifestation of an incentive-compatible equilibrium. Yes, the evidence suggests that the actors in these institutions are strategic, but to our eyes it also suggests that they are only limitedly so. They appear to guess what others will do and respond to these expectations, but they are also unable to guess all possible strategic interactions. At least for a time, behaviors can be contradictory and inconsistent—systems can be out of equilibrium. And, institutions can take on a larger, richer, and different meaning than that justified by purely economic rationale. Programs that fail to improve performance or differentiate better performers, nonetheless grant financial benefits to their participants.

Clearly more research is needed to explore the contradictions, and some efficiency argument may eventually be found to explain these contradictions. However, we believe that the research also suggests the need to consider how these institutions might operate if they are formed by strategic actors whose decisions reflect both a limited ability to anticipate consequences and a bias toward certain interpretations of institutions.

We are not suggesting that fully rational models of institutions should play no role. The precise analysis and prescriptions of these methods will continue to provide a useful benchmark for theoretical and empirical study. Yet, we expect that models including more limited actors will provide higher fidelity predictions. From this perspective, we believe it will be possible to pose questions that are otherwise unacceptable. We hope it will also be possible to develop theories and interpret data free from restriction to particular academic dogma. Therefore, from this narrow ledge between theories, we would like to pose some eccentric questions. We hope you will indulge us.

First, how do innate and public norms influence how actors interpret and engage self-regulatory institutions? Numerous studies have shown that people in many cultures have a propensity to behave "fairly," which cannot be easily explained by rational behavior. These tendencies have been well documented in studies of people in cultures that benefit from fair dealings (Fehr & Fischbacher, 2003). A potential evolutionary origin for these tendencies has even been suggested by studies of animals (Gintis, Bowles, Boyd, & Fehr, 2003). Do these tendencies also color how actors interpret new institutional forms? If so, could institutions that seem to enshrine fairness garner value that they do not deserve?

Second, how do institutional entrepreneurs understand the institutions that they help to create? Evidence from some of the studies just mentioned suggests that the sponsors of some programs envisioned them to play a different role than they eventually came to have. What causes such inconsistency? Can a formal model with rational actors explain such results? Much more research is needed on how institutions might evolve over time. Two of the programs discussed in this review have evolved from leniency to greater oversight and enforcement. Can a model with rational actors explain such an evolution? We think it can, and we suspect that it might even help connect economic concepts with the idea of "legitimization."

Third, existing research has sought to understand the determinants of self-regulation versus no regulation at all. Are the self-regulatory structures reviewed in this section always a second-best alternative to hierarchy or are their some cases where they are preferred? What are the determinants of the choice to employ self-regulation rather than firm or state hierarchy?

Many more questions can be formulated from the literature reviewed in this chapter. Indeed, the most important contribution of the reviewed literature is that it provides precedence for asking such questions within the field of management.

Conclusion

In this chapter, we send two quick postcards about some of the research being done by B&E scholars. We argue that in these two areas, B&E scholars are developing new theories and evidence that should be of interest to more mainstream management researchers. Given the relatively small size of the B&E community and the common perception that they are located at the periphery of the management literature, what might explain this unexpected role? To provide a possible explanation and illustrate some possible dangers that the literature holds, we hope you will indulge us in one last metaphor.

Near the little town of Patagonia, Arizona, there is a picnic table that is famous among birdwatchers and ornithologists. It seems that one day, a traveling birdwatcher stopped to eat lunch and happened to spot a rare bird. As is common in the community, he immediately let his friends know of the sighting, and people gathered at the table to see if they could spot this unusual species. As the group stood searching with their binoculars, someone spotted an even rarer bird, and after careful evaluation by the others at the site, the sighting was confirmed. A little while later, another uncommon species was spotted. It, too, was considered with skepticism, but eventually confirmed. By the end of the afternoon, the group had compiled a long list of rare or locally uncommon species.

You might think that these birders were imagining things, but almost every bird-watcher has experienced something similar. Birds tend to congregate in particular habitats, so the sighting of an interesting bird is often a sign that others are around. Moreover, if you gather together a bunch of sharp-eyed people all looking carefully, they often discover a whole string of species. Among birders, the phenomenon even has a name—"the Patagonia picnic table effect."

We propose that much the same thing has happened in environmental literature. A few unfamiliar "birds" (e.g. regulation-driven innovation, the Porter Hypothesis, examples of self-regulation, and so on) focused the attention of B&E scholars. Once organized, these researchers then discovered other examples and related phenomenon. They began to extend and develop theories about these observations. In the end, they developed growing research agendas—two of which we have sent to you in a postcard (from Patagonia, if you will).

Of course, our metaphor breaks down eventually. B&E scholars have tended to study more carefully a few phenomena, rather than identify entirely "new birds." Yet, the metaphor illustrates both why this literature may be important and why it must be viewed with some caution.

The birders in the story all brought with them their own unique expertise, and thus the many-binoculared monster they formed on the picnic table was vastly more knowledgeable and sensitive than any individual could ever be. Just the same is true for B&E scholarship. Drawn by their interest in environmental issues, B&E scholars have come from backgrounds in sociology, economics, psychology, and so on. Working together, they have shared notes and perspectives, and this has modified the way in which they have investigated the phenomena. As a result, B&E scholars have been willing both to consider the unexpected and to subject it to skeptical scrutiny. Three examples stand out in our review of the literature.

First, B&E scholars have been willing to break from orthodox disciplinary perspectives. For example, the PTBG literature is fundamentally based in economics, but unlike usual economic models, it considers the possibility that the system under consideration is far from equilibrium. It postulates that decision makers make choices that are systematically biased and that firms operate distant from efficiency frontiers. Yet, many B&E scholars also view this conjecture skeptically and subject it to rigorous econometric analysis. Similarly, the B&E literature on self-regulatory institutions includes many competing theories. As a result, its scholars evaluate both whether economic actors use institutions strategically and whether these institutions place preconscious limits on such behavior. The same scholars who have investigated whether institutions represent strategic equilibria have also investigated whether these institutions are "off-the-equilibrium path." As a result, B&E scholars are helping to develop theories of "thin rationality" in institutions (to use Ostrom's terminology) that combine economic models with institutional constraints and nonrational behavior.

Second, B&E scholars have been willing to rethink what is endogenous and what is exogenous. For the PTBG literature, this has meant that scholars have considered the possibility that forces exogenous to the industry can be sources of innovation and comparative advantage. For example, the literature on the Porter Hypothesis considers governments as "information gatekeepers" whose regulation may provide better information and help the industry improve performance and efficiency. The Natural Resource Based View postulates that suppliers and consumers can be sources of valuable innovations. For the literature on self-regulatory institutions, in contrast, B&E scholars have been willing to consider the possibility that institutional formation and change could be endogenous. Solution to collective-action problems need not come from outside leviathan, these scholars admit, they can be created endogenously by the effected parties themselves. As with the PTBG literature, information has played a central role in the analysis. SRI scholars have considered the use of institutions as a double-edged weapon that can hide information or reveal it to stakeholders.

Finally, given their contemporaneous observation of important changes, B&E scholars have been unusually focused on time. Organizational studies in general and the RBV in particular have tended to neglect time (Ancona, Goodman, Lawrence, & Tushman, 2001; Priem & Butler, 2001). In contrast, both PTBG and SRI literature consider time as both an important theoretical and empirical factor. The PTBG literature postulates set time periods that lead to competitive advantage. For the B&E literature on self-regulatory institutions, time has been an important variable of interest. Models of new institutions include periods of decision making (formation, entry, behavior, etc.), and empirical studies have explicitly separated these stages. In both streams, scholars have employed powerful longitudinal methods to study temporal changes.

Yet, for all of its merit, there is reason to be cautious in drawing general conclusions from the B&E literature. Our metaphor of the Patagonia picnic table again illustrates the problem. The people in the story are spotting birds because they are experts on rare birds, and they are working together and looking hard—not necessarily because a picnic table in Patagonia, Arizona, is the best place to look. The story provides a reminder that discoveries can arise from focused attention, and not always from a particularly valuable vantage point. Thus, it is possible that focused attention on PTBG possibilities or attempts at self-regulation has exaggerated or biased the theories and findings reviewed in this chapter. Seeking to understand unexpected innovation or self-regulation, scholars may have inadvertently overstated the importance of both. Skepticism, we believe, is vital to the health of the field. Every sighting of a new bird species, as it were, should be evaluated carefully and confirmed by others before it is put on our list.

We are also confident, however, that environmental issues may indeed represent a good place for scholarly focus. One reason for our confidence is that the "view" of these phenomena is particularly sharp. Regulatory requirements for disclosure of environmental and business information allow a clear view of contemporaneous changes in competitive advantage. Information on self-regulatory institutions that might otherwise be kept secret (e.g., information about a cartel) are willingly revealed by regulators or by participants. Another reason for our confidence is that environmental issues are both currently important and clearly representative of future business conditions. Finally, environmental problems are not restricted to those arising from nature. Common property problems, hidden-quality attributes, and the importance of extramural knowledge as a source of competitive advantage are all of growing importance in the information age. Evaluating how firms address these challenges will require scholars to rethink disciplinary boundaries, reconsider what is exogenous and endogenous, and reevaluate the fundamental roles of business and governing institutions. Business and environmental scholarship should inform such research.

In summary, we believe studies of business and environment have provided and will continue to provide new insight for mainstream management scholarship. In other words, we think there just might be something unique or even inspiring about the view from this particular picnic table.

Endnotes

1. To facilitate exposition, we will use "environmental performance" to refer to the degree to which firms harm or help the natural environment.
2. Several scholars propose that the potentially beneficial effects of regulation are contingent on the design of the regulation or on the match between regulation and other organizational and institutional factors. This extensive literature is not reviewed here. See Hahn and Stavins (1991) for a complete review.
3. Among management scholars, Ostrom's work has had the greatest impact on researchers investigating human decision-making in experimental strategy games – particularly social dilemmas (Weber, Kopelman, & Messick, 2001). For the rest of the academy, Ostrom's work in particular, and self-regulation in general, has been slow to take hold. Business and environment scholars were among the first to draw inspiration from her research.
4. To specify the management system standards that became ISO 9000 and ISO 14000, the International Organization for Standardization (ISO) convened technical advisory committees comprised of representatives of numerous companies, NGOs, and governments. ISO 9000 is primarily concerned with quality management and ISO 14000 with environmental management. Collectively, over 800,000 organizations in 161 countries have been certified as having adopted these standard management practices.
5. Firms voluntarily pledged to reduce their emissions of 17 key chemicals by 33% and then 50%.

References

Akerlof, G. A. (1970). Market for 'lemons': Quality uncertainty and market mechanism. *Quarterly Journal of Economics, 84*(3), 488–500.

Albuquerque, P., Bronnenberg, B., & Corbett, C. J. (2004). *A spatio-temporal analysis of the global diffusion of ISO 9000 and ISO 14000 certification.* Los Angeles: University of California.

Allouche, J., & Laroche, P. (2005). A meta-analytical investigation of the relationship between corporate social and financial performance. *Revue de gestion des ressources humaines, 57,* 18–41.

Ambec, S., & Barla, P. (2002). A theoretical foundation of the Porter hypothesis. *Economics Letters, 75*(3), 355–360.

Ancona, D. G., Goodman, P. S., Lawrence, B. S., & Tushman, M. L. (2001). Time: A new research lens. *Academy of Management Review, 26*(4), 645–663.

Anton, W. R. Q., Deltas, G., & Khanna, M. (2004). Incentives for environmental self-regulation and implications for environmental performance. *Journal of Environmental Economics and Management, 48*(1), 632–654.

Ashford, N. A., & Heaton, G. R. (1983). Regulation and technological innovation in the chemical-industry. *Law and Contemporary Problems, 46*(3), 109–157.

Barnett, M. L. (2004). *Cooperation among rivals in pursuit of institutional change: Three essays on the antecedents, process, and outcome.* New York: New York University.

Barnett, M. L., & King, A. A. (2006). *Good fences make good neighbors: An institutional explanation of industry self-regulation.* Paper presented at the Academy of Management Best Paper Proceedings, Atlanta, GA.

Barney, J. (1991). Special theory forum the resource-based model of the firm—Origins, implications, and prospects. *Journal of Management, 17*(1), 97–98.

Barney, J., & Arikan, A. (2001). The resource-based view: Origins and implications. In M. A. Hitt, R. E. Freeman, & J. S. Harrison (Eds.), *The Blackwell handbook of strategic management* (pp. 124–188). Oxford, U.K.: Blackwell Business.

Barrett, S. (1994). Self-enforcing international environmental agreements. *Oxford Economic Papers-New Series, 46,* 878–894.

Bazerman, M. H., & Hoffman, A. J. (1999). Sources of environmentally destructive behavior: Individual, organizational, and institutional perspective. In R. I. Sutton (Ed.) *Research in organizational behavior* (Vol. 21, pp. 39–79). Stamford: Jai Press Inc.

Berger, P., & Luckmann, T. (1966). *The social construction of reality.* New York: Doubleday.

Berube, M., Nash, J., Maxwell, J., & Ehrenfeld, J. (1992). From pollution control to zero discharge: How the robbins company overcame the obstacles. *Pollution Prevention Review, 22,* 189–207.

Blacconiere, W. G., & Patten, D. M. (1994). Environmental disclosures, regulatory costs, and changes in firm value. *Journal of Accounting & Economics, 18*(3), 357–377.

Brunnermeier, S. B., & Cohen, M. A. (2003). Determinants of environmental innovation in U.S. manufacturing industries. *Journal of Environmental Economics and Management, 45*(2), 278–293.

Carson, R. (1962). *Silent spring.* Boston: Houghton Mifflin Company.

Cebon, P. B. (1992). Organizational-behavior, technical prediction, and conservation practice. *Energy Policy, 20*(9), 802–814.

Chan, E. S. W., & Wong, S. C. K. (2006). Motivations for ISO 14001 in the hotel industry. *Tourism Management, 27*(3), 481–492.

Christmann, P. (2000). Effects of "best practices" of environmental management on cost advantage: The role of complementary assets. *Academy of Management Journal, 43*(4), 663–680.

Coase, R. H. (1960, October). The problem of social cost. *Journal of Law & Economics, 3*, 1–44.

Corbett, C. J., & Kirsch, D. A. (2004). Response to "Revisiting ISO 14000 diffusion: A new 'look' at the drivers of certification". *Production and Operations Management, 13*(3), 268–271.

Corbett, C. J., Montes-Sancho, M. J., & Kirsch, D. A. (2005). The financial impact of ISO 9000 certification in the United States: An empirical analysis. *Management Science, 51*(7), 1046–1059.

Darnall, N., & Carmin, J. (2005). Greener and cleaner? The signaling accuracy of US voluntary environmental programs. *Policy Sciences, 38*(2–3), 71–90.

Dawson, N. L., & Segerson, K. (2005). *Voluntary environmental agreements with industries: Participation incentives with industry-wide targets.* Storrs: University of Connecticut.

Dayton-Johnson, J. (2000). Choosing rules to govern the commons: A model with evidence from Mexico. *Journal of Economic Behavior & Organization, 42*(1), 19–41.

DeCanio, S. J. (1998). The efficiency paradox: Bureaucratic and organizational barriers to profitable energy-saving investments. *Energy Policy, 26*(5), 441–454.

DeCanio, S. J., & Watkins, W. E. (1998). Information processing and organizational structure. *Journal of Economic Behavior & Organization, 36*(3), 275–294.

Delmas, M. A. (2002). The diffusion of environmental management standards in Europe and in the United States: An institutional perspective. *Policy Sciences, 35*(1), 91–119.

Denrell, J., Fang, C., & Winter, S. G. (2003). The economics of strategic opportunity. *Strategic Management Journal, 24*(10), 977–990.

Dimaggio, P. J. (1988). Interest and agency in institutional theory. In L. Zucker (Ed.), *Institutional patterns and organizations* (pp. 3–21). Cambridge, MA: Ballinger.

Dutta, P. K., & Radner, R. (2004). Self-enforcing climate-change treaties. *Proc. Nat. Acad. Sci. U.S., 101*, 4746–4751.

Fehr, E., & Fischbacher, U. (2003). The nature of human altruism. *Nature, 425*(6960),785–791.

Florida, R., & Davison, D. (2001). Gaining from green management: Environmental management systems inside and outside the factory. *California Management Review, 43*(3), 64–84.

Furger, F. (1997). Accountability and systems of self-governance: The case of the maritime industry. *Law & Policy, 19*(4), 445–476.

Furman, J., & Stern, S. (2006). *Climbing atop the shoulders of giants: The impact of institutions on cumulative research.* Boston: Boston University/Kellogg School of Management.

Galbraith, J. (1973). *Designing complex organizations.* Boston: Addison-Wesley.

Gintis, H., Bowles, S., Boyd, R., & Fehr, E. (2003). Explaining altruistic behavior in humans. *Evolution and Human Behavior, 24*(3), 153–172.

Hahn, R. W., & Stavins, R. N. (1991). Incentive-based environmental-regulation: A new era from an old idea. *Ecology Law Quarterly, 18*(1), 1–42.

Hamilton, J. T. (1995). Pollution as news: Media and stock-market reactions to the toxics release inventory data. *Journal of Environmental Economics and Management, 28*(1), 98–113.

Hanna, S. S. (1997). The new frontier of American fisheries governance. *Ecological Economics, 20*(3), 221–233.

Hardin, G. (1968). Tragedy of commons. *Science, 162*(3859), 1243–1248.

Hart, S. L. (1995). A natural-resource-based view of the firm. *Academy of Management Review, 20*(4), 986–1014.

Hart, S. L., & Ahuja, G. (1996). Does it pay to be green? An empirical examination of the relationship between emission reduction and firm performance. *Business Strategy and the Environment, 5*(1), 30–37.

Hart, S. L., & Christensen, C. M. (2002). The great leap: Driving innovation from the base of the pyramid. *Mit Sloan Management Review, 44*(1), 51–56.

Hill, J., & Schneeweis, T. (1983). The effect of Three-Mile-Island on electric utility stock-prices—a note. *Journal of Finance, 38*(4), 1285–1292.

Hillman, A. J., & Keim, G. D. (2001). Shareholder value, stakeholder management, and social issues: What's the bottom line? *Strategic Management Journal, 22*(2), 125–139.

Hoffman, A. J. (1999). Institutional evolution and change: Environmentalism and the US chemical industry. *Academy of Management Journal, 42*(4), 351–371.

Hoffman, A. J., Gillespie, J. H., Moore, D. A., Wade-Benzoni, K. A., Thompson, L. L., & Bazerman, M. H. (1999). A mixed-motive perspective on the economics versus environment debate. *American Behavioral Scientist, 42*(8), 1254–1276.

Hoffman, A. J., & Ocasio, W. (2001). Not all events are attended equally: Toward a middle-range theory of industry attention to external events. *Organization Science, 12*(4), 414–434.

Howard, J., Nash, J., & Ehrenfeld, J. (2000). Standard or smokescreen? Implementation of a voluntary environmental code. *California Management Review, 42*(2), 63–82.

Howarth, R. B., Haddad, B. M., & Paton, B. (2000). The economics of energy efficiency: Insights from voluntary participation programs. *Energy Policy, 28*, 477–486.

Isaksson, L. H. (2005). Abatement costs in response to the Swedish charge on nitrogen oxide emissions. *Journal of Environmental Economics and Management, 50*(1), 102–120.

Jaffe, A. B., & Palmer, K. (1997). Environmental regulation and innovation: A panel data study. *Review of Economics and Statistics, 79*(4), 610–619.

Jarrell, G., & Peltzman, S. (1985). The impact of product recalls on the wealth of sellers. *Journal of Political Economy, 93*(3), 512–536.

Jiang, R. H. J., & Bansal, P. (2003). Seeing the need for ISO 14001. *Journal of Management Studies, 40*(4), 1047–1067.

Khanna, M. (2001). Non-mandatory approaches to environmental protection. *Journal of Economic Surveys, 15*(3), 291–324.

Khanna, M., & Damon, L. A. (1999). EPA's voluntary 33/50 Program: Impact on toxic releases and economic performance of firms. *Journal of Environmental Economics and Management, 37*(1), 1–25.

Khanna, M., Quimio, W. R. H., & Bojilova, D. (1998). Toxics release information: A policy tool for environmental protection. *Journal of Environmental Economics and Management, 36*(3), 243–266.

King, A. (1995). Innovation from differentiation: Pollution control departments and innovation in the printed circuit industry. *IEEE Transactions on Engineering Management, 42*(3), 270–277.

King, A. (1999). Retrieving and transferring embodied data: Implications for the management of interdependence within organizations. *Management Science, 45*(7), 918–935.

King, A. A., & Lenox, M. J. (2000). Industry self-regulation without sanctions: The chemical industry's responsible care program. *Academy of Management Journal, 43*(4), 698–716.

King, A. A., & Lenox, M. J. (2001). Lean and green? An empirical examination of the relationship between lean production and environmental performance. *Production and Operations Management, 10*(3), 244–256.

King, A., & Lenox, M. (2002). Exploring the locus of profitable pollution reduction. *Management Science, 48*(2), 289–299.

King, A., Lenox, M. J., & Barnett, M. L. (2002). Policy and the natural environment: Institutional and strategic perspectives. In A. Hoffman, & M. Ventresca (Eds.), *Organizations, policy, and the natural environment: Institutional and strategic perspectives* (pp. 393–406). Stanford, CA: University Press.

King, A. A., Lenox, M. J., & Terlaak, A. (2005). The strategic use of decentralized institutions: Exploring certification with the ISO 14001 management standard. *Academy of Management Journal, 48*(6), 1091–1106.

King, A. A., & Shaver, J. M. (2001). Are aliens green? Assessing foreign establishments' environmental conduct in the United States. *Strategic Management Journal, 22*(11), 1069–1085.

Klassen, R. D. (2000). Exploring the linkage between investment in manufacturing and environmental technologies. *International Journal of Operations & Production Management, 20*(2), 127–147.

Klassen, R. D., & Vachon, S. (2003). Collaboration and evaluation in the supply chain: The impact on plant-level environmental investment. *Production and Operations Management, 12*(3), 336–352.

Klassen, R. D., & Whybark, D. C. (1999). The impact of environmental technologies on manufacturing performance. *Academy of Management Journal, 42*(6), 599–615.

Kleindorfer, P. R. (1999). Understanding individuals' environmental decisions: A decision sciences approach. In K. Sexton, A. A. Marcus, K. W. Easter, & T. D. Burkhardt (Eds.), *Better environmental decisions: Strategies for governments, businesses, and communities* (pp. 37–56). Washington, DC: Island Press.

Kleindorfer, P. R., & Saad, G. H. (2005). Managing disruption risks in supply chains. *Production and Operations Management, 14*(1), 53–68.

Koehler, D. A., Bennett, D. H., Norris, G. A., & Spengler, J. D. (2005). Rethinking environmental performance from a public health perspective: A comparative industry analysis. *Journal of Industrial Ecology, 9*(3), 143–167.

Koehler, D. A., & Cram, D. (2001). *The financial impact of corporate environmental performance: A review of the evidence of the link between environmental and financial performance.* Boston: Harvard School of Public Health.

Konar, S., & Cohen, M. A. (2001). Does the market value environmental performance? *Review of Economics and Statistics, 83*(2), 281–289.

Kunreuther, H., & Bowman, E. H. (1997). A dynamic model of organizational decision making: Chemco revisited six years after Bhopal. *Organization Science, 8*(4), 404–413.

Kunreuther, H., & Pauly, M. (2004). Neglecting disaster: Why don't people insure against large losses? *Journal of Risk and Uncertainty, 28*(1), 5–21.

Lenox, M. (in press). The role of private, decentralized institutions in sustaining industry self-regulation. *Organization Science.*

Lenox, M., & King, A. (2004). Prospects for developing absorptive capacity through internal information provision. *Strategic Management Journal, 25*(4), 331–345.

Lenox, M., & Nash, J. (2003). Industry self-regulation and adverse selection: A comparison across four trade association programs. *Business Strategy and Environment, 12*(6), 343–356.

London, T., & Hart, S. L. (2004). Reinventing strategies for emerging markets: Beyond the transnational model. *Journal of International Business Studies, 35*(5), 350–370.

Macduffie, J. P. (1995). Human-resource bundles and manufacturing performance: Organizational logic and flexible production systems in the world auto industry. *Industrial & Labor Relations Review, 48*(2), 197–221.

Majumdar, S. K., & Marcus, A. A. (2001). Rules versus discretion: The productivity consequences of flexible regulation. *Academy of Management Journal, 44*(1), 170–179.

Managi, S., Opaluch, J. J., Jin, D., & Grigalunas, T. A. (2005). Environmental regulations and technological change in the offshore oil and gas industry. *Land Economics, 81*(2), 303–319.

Margolis, J. D., & Walsh, J. P. (2001). *People and profits?: The search for a link between a company's social and financial performance.* Mahwah, NJ: Lawrence Erlbaum Associates.

Margolis, J. D., & Walsh, J. P. (2003). Misery loves companies: Rethinking social initiatives by business. *Administrative Science Quarterly, 48*(2), 268–305.

Maxwell, J. W., Lyon, T. P., & Hackett, S. C. (2000). Self-regulation and social welfare: The political economy of corporate environmentalism. *Journal of Law & Economics, 43*(2), 583–617.

McWilliams, A., & Siegel, D. (2001). Corporate social responsibility: A theory of the firm perspective. *Academy of Management Review, 26*(1), 117–127.

Melnyk, S. A., Sroufe, R. P., & Calantone, R. (2003a). Assessing the impact of environmental management systems on corporate and environmental performance. *Journal of Operations Management, 21*(3), 329–351.

Melnyk, S. A., Sroufe, R. P., & Calantone, R. J. (2003b). A model of site-specific antecedents of ISO 14001 certification. *Production and Operations Management, 12*(3), 369–385.

Morgenstern, R. D., Pizer, W. A., & Shih, J. S. (2002). Jobs versus the environment: An industry-level perspective. *Journal of Environmental Economics and Management, 43*(3), 412–436.

Mylonadis, Y. (1993). *The 'green' challenge to the industrial enterprise mindset: Survival threat or strategic opportunity?* Cambridge, MA: Massachusetts Institute of Technology.

Nameroff, T. J., Garant, R. J., & Albert, M. B. (2004). Adoption of green chemistry: An analysis based on US patents. *Research Policy, 33*(6–7), 959–974.

Nash, J., & Ehrenfeld, J. (1997). Codes of environmental management practice: Assessing their potential as a tool for change. *Annual Review of Energy and the Environment, 22,* 487–535.

Nehrt, C. (1996). Timing and intensity effects of environmental investments. *Strategic Management Journal, 17*(7), 535–547.

Neumayer, E., & Perkins, R. (2004). What explains the uneven take-up of ISO 14001 at the global level? A panel-data analysis. *Environment and Planning A, 36*(5), 823–839.

North, D. C. (1990). *Institutions, institutional change, and economic performance.* Cambridge, U.K.: Cambridge University Press.

Orlitzky, M., Schmidt, F. L., & Rynes, S. L. (2003). Corporate social and financial performance: A meta-analysis. *Organization Studies, 24*(3), 403–441.

Orsato, R. J. (2006). Competitive environmental strategies: When does it pay to be green? *California Management Review, 48*(2), 127–143.

Ostrom, E. (1990). *Governing the commons: The evolution of institutions for collective action.* Cambridge, U.K.: Cambridge University Press.

Ostrom, E., Gardner, R., & Walker, J. (1994). *Rules, games, and common-pool resources.* Ann Arbor: University of Michigan Press.

Palmer, K., Oates, W. E., & Portney, P. R. (1995). Tightening environmental standards: The benefit-cost or the no-cost paradigm. *Journal of Economic Perspectives, 9*(4), 119–132.

Peteraf, M. A. (1993). The cornerstones of competitive advantage: A resource-based view. *Strategic Management Journal, 14*(3), 179–191.

Pil, F. K., & Rothenberg, S. (2003). Environmental performance as a driver of superior quality. *Production and Operations Management, 12*(3), 404–415.

Popper, K. (1968). *The logic of scientific discovery* (Rev. ed.). London: Hutchinson.

Porter, M. E., & Van der Linde, C. (1995a). Toward a new conception of the environment–competitiveness relationship. *Journal of Economic Perspectives, 9*(4), 97–118.

Porter, M. E., & Van der Linde, C. (1995b). Green and competitive—Ending the stalemate. *Harvard Business Review, 73*(5), 120–134.

Potoski, M., & Prakash, A. (2005a). Covenants with weak swords: ISO 14001 and facilities' environmental performance. *Journal of Policy Analysis and Management, 24*(4), 745–769.

Potoski, M., & Prakash, A. (2005b). Green clubs and voluntary governance: ISO 14001 and firms' regulatory compliance. *American Journal of Political Science, 49*(2), 235–248.

Prahalad, C. K., & Hammond, A. (2002). Serving the world's poor, profitably. *Harvard Business Review, 80*(9), 48–57.

Priem, R. L., & Butler, J. E. (2001). Is the resource-based "view" a useful perspective for strategic management research? *Academy of Management Review, 26*(1), 22–40.

Rees, J. (1988). Self regulation: An effective alternative to direct regulation by OSHA. *Policy Studies Journal, 16*(3), 602–614.

Rees, J. (1994). *Hostages of each other: The transformation of nuclear safety since Three Mile Island.* Chicago: University of Chicago Press.

Rees, J. (1997). Development of communitarian regulation in the chemical industry. *Law and Policy, 19,* 477–528.

Reinhardt, F. L. (2000). *Down to earth: Applying business principles to environmental management.* Boston: Harvard Business School Press.

Reinhardt, F. L., & Vietor, R. H. K. (1996). *Business management and the natural environment: Cases and text.* Cincinnati, OH: Southwestern Publishing Company.

Repetto, R. (1995). *Jobs, competitiveness, and environmental regulation: What are the real issues?* Washington, DC: World Resources Institute.

Rivera, J. (2004). Institutional pressures and voluntary environmental behavior in developing countries: Evidence from the Costa Rican hotel industry. *Society & Natural Resources, 17*(9), 779–797.

Rivera, J., & de Leon, P. (2004). Is greener whiter? Voluntary environmental performance of western ski areas. *Policy Studies Journal, 32*(3), 417–437.

Rivera, J., & de Leon, P. (2005). Chief executive officers and voluntary environmental performance: Costa Rica's certification for sustainable tourism. *Policy Sciences, 38*(2–3), 107–127.

Rivera, J., de Leon, P., & Koerber, C. (2006). Is greener whiter yet? The sustainable slopes program after five years. *Policy Studies Journal, 34*(2), 195–221.

Roberts, P. W., & Greenwood, R. (1997). Integrating transaction cost and institutional theories: Toward a constrained-efficiency framework for understanding organizational design adoption. *Academy of Management Review, 22*(2), 346–373.

Roome, N., & Wijen, F. (2006). Stakeholder power and organizational learning in corporate environmental management. *Organization Studies, 27*(2), 235–263.

Rothenberg, S. (2003). Knowledge content and worker participation in environmental management at NUMMI. *Journal of Management Studies, 40*(7), 1783–1802.

Rothenberg, S., Pil, F. K., & Maxwell, J. (2001). Lean, green, and the quest for superior environmental performance. *Production and Operations Management, 10*(3), 228–243.

Rugman, A. M., & Verbeke, A. (1998). Corporate strategies and environmental regulations: An organizing framework. *Strategic Management Journal, 19*(4), 363–375.

Russo, M. V., & Fouts, P. A. (1997). A resource-based perspective on corporate environmental performance and profitability. *Academy of Management Journal, 40*(3), 534–559.

Schlager, E., & Ostrom, E. (1992). Property-rights regimes and natural-resources: A conceptual analysis. *Land Economics, 68*(3), 249–262.

Shin, S. (2005). The role of the government in voluntary environmental protection schemes: The case of ISO 14001 in China. *Issues & Studies, 41*(4), 141–173.

Stafford, E. R., Polonsky, M. J., & Hartman, C. L. (2000). Environmental NGO-business collaboration and strategic bridging: A case analysis of the Greenpeace-Foron Alliance. *Business Strategy and the Environment, 9*(2), 122–135.

Tenbrunsel, A. E., Wade-Benzoni, K. A., Messick, D. M., & Bazerman, M. H. (2000). Understanding the influence of environmental standards on judgments and choices. *Academy of Management Journal, 43*(5), 854–866.

Terlaak, A. (2007). Order without law: The role of certified management standards in shaping socially desired firm behaviors. *Academy of Management Review, 32*(3), 968–985.

Terlaak, A., & King, A. A. (2006). The effect of certification with the ISO 9000 quality management standard: A signaling approach. *Journal of Economic Behavior and Organization, 60*(4), 579–602.

Thompson, B. H. (2000). Tragically difficult: The obstacles to overcoming the commons. *Environmental Law, 30,* 241–278.

Thompson, J. D. (1967). *Organizations in action: Social science bases of administrative theory.* New York: McGraw-Hill.

Toffel, M. W. (2004). Strategic management of product recovery. *California Management Review, 46*(2), 120–141.

Toffel, M. W. (2006). *Resolving information asymmetries in markets: The role of certified management programs.* Cambridge, MA: Harvard Business School.

Tversky, A., & Kahneman, D. (1973). Availability: A heuristic for judging frequency and probability. *Cognitive Psychology, 5,* 207–232.

U.S. Congress Office of Technology Assessment. (1994). *Industry, technology, and the environment competitive challenges and business opportunities.* OTA-586. Washington, DC.

Viadiu, F. M., Fa, M. C., & Saizarbitoria, M. H. (2006). ISO 9000 and ISO 14000 standards: An international diffusion model. *International Journal of Operations & Production Management, 26*(1–2), 141–165.

Walley, N., & Whitehead, B. (1994). It's not easy being green. *Harvard Business Review, 72*(3), 46–51.

Weber, J. M., Kopelman, S., & Messick, D. M. (2001). *A conceptual review of decision-making in social dilemmas: Applying a logic of appropriateness.* Evanston, IL: Kellogg School of Management.

Williamson, O. E. (1975). *Markets and hierarchies, analysis and antitrust implications: A study in the economics of internal organization.* New York: Free Press.

Womack, J. P., Jones, D. T., & Roos, D. (1991). *The machine that changed the world: How Japan's secret weapon in the global auto wars will revolutionize Western industry* (1st ed.). New York: HarperPerennial.

Zadek, S. (2001). *The civil corporation: The new economy of corporate citizenship.* Sterling, VA: Earthscan Publications Ltd.

12
HRM and Distributed Work
Managing People Across Distances

JOHN PAUL MACDUFFIE

Wharton School, University of Pennsylvania

Abstract

The phenomenon of managing work that is distributed over geographical distance is not new but is increasing in both frequency and intentionality as a function of globalization and knowledge-centric strategies. I review the literature on geographically distributed work, both that which highlights liabilities of loss of proximity and more recent research that emphasizes "virtual teams" as an intentional organizing device. I explore the adaptations, remedies, and countervailing strategies deployed to support such teams, contrasting those that minimize distance with those that increase individual and group capacity for coping with distance. I also emphasize that other dimensions of distance — cultural, administrative, and economic — affect the organization of work, the experiences of those doing the work, and individual and organizational outcomes. Here I highlight the "blended workforce" in which standard (traditional employees) and nonstandard (temporary and contract) workers are organized to accomplish interdependent tasks — and again contrast problems of distance with emergent adaptations. Finally, I explore the implications for human resource management (HRM), first considering which HR systems are best suited to work distributed over different types of distance, and then reviewing literature on specific HR practices — selection, training, task/job design, compensation, and performance appraisal. I close by arguing that HRM research must reach beyond its past focus on managing employees within a single firm over a prolonged career under collocated conditions. As the world generates countless new distance-related phenomena, our research must tackle the challenges of managing both standard and non-standard workers engaged in interdependent tasks of limited duration across multiple employers/clients and involving multiple dimensions of distance.

Introduction

> It is now possible for more people than ever to collaborate and compete in real time with more other people on more different kinds of work from more different corners of the planet and on a more equal footing than at any previous time in the history of the world. (Thomas Friedman, *The World Is Flat*, 2005)

The new realities of work and its distribution over geographical distance confront us daily as we scan what is happening in the world. News of the latest investment by a multinational corporation (MNC) in a foreign R&D facility is followed by predictions of the high numbers of developed-economy workers whose jobs may be displaced by offshoring to low-labor-cost countries. This news can both surprise and disorient us when it challenges our sense of what work firms can plausibly distribute over geographic distance and our assumptions about why and when firms decide to keep particular activities collocated versus disaggregating them for distribution over time and space.

The phenomenon of geographically distributed work is not new but it has received increased attention in recent years. Three trends are particularly noteworthy:

1. Both large and small companies in developed countries have increased their outsourcing of tasks to suppliers and contractors in other countries, thus combining externalization of economic activity with geographic dispersion in the phenomenon known as "offshoring." Following an initial emphasis on offshoring manufacturing tasks, where the numerical impact has been greatest, the current accelerating trend is the offshoring of knowledge-based impersonal services (Dossani & Kenney, 2006; Farrell, Laboissiere, & Rosenfeld, 2006).

2. Multinational corporations have shifted employment within the firm's boundaries. In an internal analogue to "offshoring," they are decreasing employment at their "home base" facilities in high-cost developed countries while increasing employment at their sites in lower-cost developing countries. Furthermore, they are also increasing their employment in developed countries, outside their home country, through new investments designed to provide more market opportunities. Harrison and McMillan (2006) documented this trend for U.S. MNCs; however, this appears to be a general trend.

3. Even within a given country, firms of all kinds take advantage of lower costs and improved performance of information and communications technology (ICT) to distribute more work over distance,

both within the firm (e.g., assigning more tasks to "virtual teams"; allowing more employees to perform telework away from the central office; acquiring firms whose employees are located too far away to allow for geographic consolidation) and across firms (e.g., utilizing a wide array of organizational arrangements to carry out interdependent tasks involving both the firm's employees and employees of suppliers, customers, or alliance partners).

The combination of these trends—together with the "three billion new capitalists" (Prestowitz, 2005) entering the global labor market from countries such as China and India—has stimulated public imagination and caused considerable media attention. Solid research is only slowly emerging, and it often focuses on the impact of these trends on employment, wages, and standard of living in the developed countries.[1] Much less attention has been paid to the actual challenges of carrying out diverse interdependent work tasks over geographical distance. One goal of the current chapter is to summarize what we know about geographically distributed work and how it is different from (or similar to) collocated work.

The debate over the positive and negative features of geographically distributed work is both intellectually and emotionally compelling. I would argue, however, that we risk giving disproportionate attention to geographical distance while neglecting other issues of distance less perceptually salient, yet possibly having a larger impact on how work is accomplished in today's organizations. Calling attention to work distributed over different types of distance is a second goal of this chapter.

To address this goal, I will modify the CAGE framework that Ghemawat (2001) developed to analyze the challenges of cultural, administrative/political, geographical, and economic distance for the multinational/global firm. I will argue that by considering various kinds of distance and how they interact, we can understand more deeply the opportunities and liabilities of distributed work. In particular, I will argue that distance associated with employment status (the "E" in my modified framework) can be highly problematic whenever regular employees and nonstandard (temporary or contract) workers interact while accomplishing interdependent tasks—but that this type of distance has not received sufficient attention from managers or scholars (see, however, Ashford, George, & Blatt, chapter 2, this volume).

My third goal is to highlight the human resource (HR) challenges of managing people over distance. I will first consider what the strategic human resource management (SHRM) literature suggests about the HR systems best suited to different types of distributed work. I next examine the research on specific HR practices—for example, selection, training, task/job design, compensation, and performance appraisal—in relation to distributed work. Then I will shift the focus from HR practices of the firm to employment policies at higher levels of analysis—for example, industry, region, or country. Many employers still premise employment policies on the idea of employees that work for long continuous periods for a single employer at a common location under direct supervision by management. The proliferation of different types of distributed work makes many of these policies obsolete at best and harmful at worst.

Much research on distributed work emphasizes the many problems that can result from different types of distance. I will briefly summarize this research, but I will devote more attention to adaptations, remedies, and countervailing strategies, developed by individual, groups, and organizations, in response to those problems. One kind of adaptation seeks to *minimize distance*, either physically (e.g., bringing team members together for face-to-face meetings) or in the structuring of work (e.g., defining tasks to be modular with standardized interfaces that minimize coordination requirements). Another kind of adaptation seeks to *increase individual and group capacity for coping with distance*. This capacity is best increased, the literature suggests, by enhancing shared understanding of the work task/context and developing some level of shared or collective identity among those working together on the task. My fourth goal for this chapter is to highlight these two approaches in relation to various types of distance.

I organize the chapter into four sections. First, I will define *distributed work*, categorize different types of distance, and assess the incidence of these phenomena. Second, I will summarize what we know about distributed work, highlighting two phenomena: (a) virtual teams, consisting of members separated by geographical distance whose interactions are primarily ICT-mediated; and (b) the blended workforce, consisting of a mixture of regular employees and nonstandard temporary or contract workers. Third, I will draw out the implications of applying strategic HRM theories to managing people over distance, and then spotlight HR practices and employment policies relevant to the management of virtual teams and blended workforces. The fourth section will suggest the limitations of the research carried out so far on these topics, as well as a future research agenda.

Exploring the Phenomenon of Distributed Work

What Is Work Distributed Over Distance(s)?

To say that work is distributed immediately conjures up an image of geographic distance; however, distributed work potentially involves more than this one kind of distance. The Webster's definition of *distribute* includes the following: (a) to divide among several or many: apportion; (b) to spread out to cover something: scatter; (c) to separate, especially into kinds. *Distribute* conveys a broader meaning than divide; it is said to apply to any manner of separating into parts or spreading out, equally or systematically or merely at random, whereas divide connotes the initial separation of the whole before giving out the parts. Our images of division of labor, going back to Adam Smith, involve a preplanned, rational separation into parts for the purpose of efficiency. The realities of distributed work are more complex. It may take many forms, from systematic to more random; both separation into parts and spreading out may occur along more dimensions than geography; and motivations include achieving cost savings but also connecting to expertise, exploring new knowledge domains, and enabling personal networks.

A Google search on distributed work quickly turns up definitions that reflect this complexity. The author of one Weblog (http://futuretense.corante. com/archives/2005/09/14) stated

> We consider work to be distributed if *any of the following conditions* are met [emphasis added]: Individual workers are located in different physical locations; most normal communications and interactions, even with colleagues in the next office, are asynchronous. That is, they do not occur simultaneously, or the individual workers are not all working for the same organization, or are working within distinctively different parts of the same parent organization. They may have widely different terms of employment.

Ghemawat (2001) provided a useful framework for thinking about such multiple forms of distance in the context of globalization. He called it CAGE, referring to cultural, administrative/political, geographical, and economic distance, and developed the argument that the type of distance affects different businesses in different ways. I have modified this framework to suit my purposes, as shown in Table 12.1. As previously noted, the most significant modification is the replacement of "economic distance" with "employment status" distance.

I will use this typology to consider the challenges of managing distributed work across distance, defined along cultural, administrative, geographical, and employment status dimensions, following the premise that different types of distance will affect this management task in different ways.

Why Is Distributed Work Important?

We can link the realities of distributed work to a number of broader trends affecting today's organizations. One trend highlighted by Walsh, Meyer, and Schoonhoven (2006) is "transnational emergence," referring to the rapid growth and increased impact of transnational corporations.[2] As Walsh and colleagues (2006) reported, transnational organizations are big—and getting bigger (employment at U.S.-based transnationals grew by 34% between 1991 and 2001, with 42% of their employees living outside of the United States by 2001). They operate in a huge number of countries (an average of 93 countries for the top 10 firms in the 2005 *Fortune* 500), and much of this growth is accomplished via cross-border mergers and acquisitions (increasing from

Table 12.1   Different Types of Distance

	Ghemawat (2001)	Definitions Used Here
C: Cultural	Affects how people interact, with common (linguistic) language as the most obvious factor; however, also social norms and assumptions about "how we do things" that are more subtle but still powerful	Same; however, considered at both national and organizational levels of analysis
A: Administrative/ Political	Historical and political associations, including (a) colony/colonizer relations and presence (or absence) of common currency, (b) trading bloc, (c) political union, and (d) other factors that can facilitate interaction	The relationship of focal organization to others; for example, is one organization a supplier, a contractor, or a customer of another? Did one organization acquire or merge with another? How many administrative boundaries must be crossed in doing distributed work? How many different organizational identities are salient to interacting individuals?
G: Geographic	Miles/kilometers separating those interacting; size of country; average within-country distance to borders; access to waterways; transportation and communications infrastructure	Physical location; size of location (number of employees); proximity or dispersion of other locations associated with focal organization; proximity or dispersion of locations of affiliated firms
E: Economic (modified here to cover Employment Status)	The extent to which a rich country is trading with another rich country or a poor country is trading with another poor country, vs. a rich country trading with a poor country; the influence of disparities on the frequency and intensity of interaction	The extent to which interactions involve individuals of the same or different employment status in relation to focal organization; for example, a full-time employee versus a part-time employee, or a temporary employee versus a full or part-time contract worker (potentially hired through a third party or broker)

less than $100 billion in 1987 to $720 billion in 1999) and strategic alliances (increasing from roughly 2,500 in 1990 to 4,350 in 2000).

The need to coordinate the work of employees operating within the same transnational firm, but separated by geographical distance, is certainly one consequence of this trend. These firms increasingly organize virtual teams to work on specific projects, with members chosen for their distinctive expertise or knowledge. These firms also pursue competitive advantage by continually reconfiguring their value chains. They may partner with a supplier or customer on a collaborative project, outsource certain activities completely, or decide to strengthen a competence and bring activities back into the firm (called "insourcing"). The resulting fluidity and complexity of organizational and employment arrangements often generates multiple forms of distance. These forms of distance become layered, one upon another, and interact in ways that we largely do not understand.

A second trend highlighted by Walsh and colleagues (2006) is disaggregation—that is, the fragmentation of organizations, careers, and jobs. This is a by-product of firms pursuing the strategies previously described and seeking flexibility in order to cope with the volatility and uncertainty of being part of a global economy. Disaggregation also results from related changes in the nature of work (Arthur & Rousseau, 2001; Barley & Kunda, 2001; Bradley, Schipani, Sundaram, & Walsh, 1999; DiMaggio, 2001; Heckscher & Adler, 2006; Kalleberg, 2000; Kanter, 1990; Maccoby, 2006; Powell, 2001; Smith, 1997, 1998). These include

- The increased value placed on knowledge as a source of value creation (vs. simply owning physical assets of land, capital, or equipment)
- The increased value placed on employee adaptability, learning capabilities, and interpersonal skills (vs. specific specialized expertise)
- The increased reliance on projects as the basic unit for organizing work, with an individual's work life organized around a stream of projects (vs. job ladders and fixed periods between promotions as the building blocks of an individual's work life)
- The increased emphasis on peer-based, informal social controls and horizontal/lateral coordination mechanisms (vs. hierarchical forms of organizational control and vertical coordination mechanisms embedded in formal organizational structure)
- The increased prevalence of market-based influences on individual employment contracts and career paths that span organizations (vs. internal labor markets that shield employees from market forces, coupled with employment security)

In addition, the pursuit of strategic flexibility and lower costs in the face of global competition means that firms are essentially engaged in a continuous process of restructuring. This restructuring can lead to hiring as well as layoffs;

it is not confined to periods of economic distress, but results from ongoing deliberations about which activities/businesses to maintain and which to out-source or eliminate. This constant state of flux accelerates the disaggregation process, as firms are less willing to hire permanent employees (who expect long-term careers and steady growth in both salary and employee benefits). Firms are also more willing to engage contingent workers (whose attachment to the firm is time-limited, whose pay is often hourly and negotiated by a third-party broker, and whose skills are often technically specialized, yet not firm specific). Employees end up with a much higher sense of job insecurity and often have less trust in management and less commitment to the firm (Cappelli, 1999; Morris, Cascio, & Young, 1999).

Under these conditions, many firms end up with "blended" workforces of employees and contractors that can be challenging to manage. These differences in employment status can create distance, even among individuals working side by side, whose consequences can be more destructive to effective coordination and collaboration than many miles of physical separation.[3] Where standard and nonstandard workers have shared responsibility for interdependent tasks and the consequences of poor performance are significant—for example, in contexts that present high risks and require high reliability—these negative consequences of employment status distance can actually be dangerous for workers (Kochan, Smith, Wells, & Rebitzer, 1994), customers, and citizens/communities (Rousseau & Libuser, 1997). Few problems facing virtual teams are as potentially serious, yet the challenges of managing such teams draw far more attention than those associated with the blended workforce.

How Extensive Is Distributed Work?

The term distributed work covers a very wide range of organizational and individual activity, including intraorganizational virtual teams, offshoring, nonstandard work arrangements, teleworking (telecommuting), and any combination of these categories. For example, interorganizational virtual teams involving employees from a focal firm and employees from its suppliers; or a contract worker who is located offshore; or telecommuting arrangements that allow a contract worker to work from home.

Estimates of activity in any of these categories are likely to be based on imprecise, varied definitions and limited in scope—that is, based on a single country, a limited number of industries, or a limited sample of (usually large) companies. With those caveats, here are some admittedly scattershot statistics:

Intraorganizational Virtual Teams

- The *Wall Street Journal* reports that more than half of U.S. companies with more than 5,000 employees use virtual teams (de Lisser, 1999).

- A Gartner Group survey found that more than 60% of professional employees surveyed reported working in a virtual team (Jones, 2004; Yoo, Kanawattanachai, & Citurs, 2002).
- McDonough, Kahn, and Griffin (1999) surveyed a sample of Fortune 500 companies to inquire about their use of global new product development teams (GNPDT). The sample included 22 projects from 13 business units at 10 corporations: 8 headquartered in the United States, 1 headquartered in Japan, and 1 headquartered in France. All SBUs were using GNPDTs. Out of 13 SBUs, 6 reported using GNPDTs extensively, with at least 10 teams in operation. The rest of the SBUs were using fewer than five GNPDTs. The average project consisted of 15 core team members from four functions residing in four countries. Team members from 3 projects were collocated for more than 50% of the time. Team members from the remaining 19 projects spent on average 7.5% of their time collocated.

Offshoring

- The McKinsey Global Institute study of offshoring, based on assessing eight industries, estimates that 11% of service jobs around the world could be carried out remotely, considering those tasks that require "neither substantial local knowledge nor physical or complex interaction between an employee and customers or colleagues" (Farrell et al., 2006, p. 24). Extrapolated to all nonagricultural employment, this is equivalent to 160 million jobs. (Farrell et al., 2006).
- Alan Blinder (2006) considered the portion of current U.S. employment that could be classified as "impersonal services" and estimated that, "while large swaths of the U.S. labor market look to be immune," the number of current U.S. service sector jobs that could be susceptible to offshoring is two to three times the total number of current manufacturing jobs, or 30–40 million (p. 120).
- In 2004, the Ministry of Economic Affairs in Taiwan reported on the percentage of personal-computer and laptop production outsourced to a handful of Taiwanese contract manufacturers operating in Taiwan and China. The list ranges from 100% for Apple, HP, NEC, and Acer, to 92% for Dell, to 50–70% for Fujitsu, Sony, and Toshiba. IBM's PC business is now entirely owned by the Chinese company Lenovo (Yang & Hsia, 2004).

Nonstandard Work Arrangements

- U.S. employment in the temporary-help industry grew by 58% between 1992 and 1996 (Kunda, Barley, & Evans, 2002), and accounted for 10% of net job creation between 1990 and 2000 (Autor, 2001).
- According to the 1995 and 1997 Current Population Surveys, roughly 18% of the U.S. labor force work under nonstandard arrangements, either as independent contractors (~7%), self-employed workers (~5%), temporary agency employees (~3%), or on-call workers (3%) (Polivka, Cohany, & Hipple, 2000; p. 44).

Teleworking

- According to the 2004 Gartner Group report, "Teleworking: The Quiet Revolution," by 2008, 41 million corporate employees globally may spend at least one day a week teleworking, and 100 million will work from home at least one day a month. The highest proportion of these will be U.S. workers.
- A 2004 report from the U.S. Census identified a rapid increase in work from home, based on data from 2000. In the year 2000, 4.2 million (19%) of Americans did some or all of their work at home (the percentage that are employees is not identified). This is an increase of 800,000 (23%) from 1990 to 2000, twice the growth rate of the overall workforce.

I will not treat all of these types of distributed work in detail; in particular, I will say little specifically on the topic of individual teleworking (see Bailey & Kurland, 2002, for a recent review). My focus on multiple types of distance does encompass all the other categories and their potential combinations. I will seek to find common ways to think about dealing with these different types of distance and suggest what this means for research on distributed work.

What We Know About Distributed Work

I will start this section by summarizing social psychological research on the benefits of proximity for work groups and how those benefits are disrupted by geographical distance. I will next highlight research on virtual teams, first summarizing the many problems they potentially face, and then devoting considerable attention to the *adaptations, remedies, and countervailing strategies* (hereafter, ARCS) that individuals and groups have developed to cope with these problems. Finally, I turn to research on the "blended workforce" to more closely examine employment status distance. Again, I will start with a review of problems from combining regular (standard) and contingent (nonstandard) workers, and then report on the ARCS for this type of distance.

Benefits of Proximity

In their review of social psychological literature, Sara Kiesler and Jonathon Cummings (2002) amassed extensive evidence that closer proximity in work groups is highly beneficial vis-à-vis a variety of individual and group outcomes.[4] The relationship is marked by three threshold effects. First, individuals are uncomfortable when physical proximity is too close because this violates a sense of personal space (Freedman, 1975). Second, the consequences of proximity known as "social facilitation"—triggered by a person's awareness of others, concern with what others think, and sense of involvement with a group—are heavily dependent on the ongoing physical presence of others (Forsyth, 1998). Third, frequency of communication and informal interaction are both highly dependent on proximity. When distance increases to the point that the costs of getting together rise, both communication and interaction drop dramatically (Allen, 1977; Kraut & Streeter, 1995); a distance of 30–50 meters of physical separation appears to be the boundary condition.

Table 12.2 is an abridged summary of the effects of proximity from Kiesler and Cummings (2002). While the mere presence of others can increase distraction and stress in the performance of difficult tasks (as people prefer privacy for these), most social facilitation effects of observing and gaining familiarity with others in your immediate presence are positive. Performance on many tasks improves, imitation and conformity behaviors increase, liking of others grows, and an incipient group identity emerges, leading to commitment and greater contributions to the group.

The effects of face-to-face communication are even more positive. Felt commitment, interpersonal attraction, information exchange, feedback, and persuasion all increase, leading to greater cooperation, participation, and mutual adjustment on interdependent tasks, as well as a stronger group identity, a decrease in conflict and misunderstanding, and greater contribution by and consensus among individual group members. When this communication recurrently takes place in a shared social setting, shared norms and expectations increase, as does work satisfaction, and role behaviors become increasingly well-matched to task and situational requirements. Finally, individuals who repeatedly experience a shared space will, over time, mark it (and defend it) as group territory; group identity and cohesion both strengthen quickly under such conditions.

Proximity within the 30–50 meter threshold leads to spontaneous communication, which is valuable because of its links to group creativity and innovation. When individuals can bump into each other in the hallways, at the cafeteria, in the coffee room, or around the mailboxes, information exchange and feedback increase, as does interpersonal attraction. At the group level, interdependent tasks are more often created, group meetings and decisions are more frequent, and shared understanding increases. Group identity is

Table 12.2 Concepts and Research Findings Related to Proximity

Concept	Psychological Effects	Behavioral and Group Effects	Effects on Work	Related Factors
Mere presence of others	Evaluation of apprehension ↑ Sense of privacy ↓	Stress ↑ Distraction ↑ Effort ↑	Performance of automated tasks ↑ Performance of difficult tasks ↓	Work complexity
	Observation of and attention to those present ↑ Social pressure ↑	Involvement ↑ Imitation ↑ Social influence ↑ Conformity ↑	Urgency of proximate task, time spent on proximate group's work ↑	Competing tasks and deadlines
	Familiarity ↑ (mere exposure effect)	Liking, positive responding ↑ Group identity ↑	Contributions to group ↑	Time spent in presence of others
Face-to-face communication	Felt social contract (commitment) ↑	Cooperation ↑ Conflict ↓	Agreements ↑ Contributions to group ↑	
	Interpersonal attraction ↑	Group identity ↑	Agreements ↑ Contributions to group ↑	Type of task
	Information exchange, mutual observation, and backchannel and direct feedback ↑	Task adjustments, decisions ↑	Coordination ↑ Learning and overlapping expertise ↑	
	Perceived participation ↑ Social pressure ↑ Persuasion ↑	Participation ↑ Group identity ↑	Conformity ↑ Consensus ↑ Work satisfaction ↑	Decision rules (e.g., majority)

Shared social setting	Shared expectations and norms ↑	Roles and behaviors matched to situation ↑	Enactment of expected work behavior and roles ↑	Cues that demark situations and territories
	Territoriality ↑	Demarcation and protection of territory ↑	Control of work and access within the territory ↑	
	Group identity ↑	Interaction ↑	Work satisfaction ↑	
Spontaneous communication	Information exchange, mutual observation, and backchannel and direct feedback ↑	Group meetings and decisions ↑	Task adjustments ↑	Work interdependence
		Creation of interdependent tasks ↑	Know-how and overlapping expertise ↑	
		Mutual understanding ↑	Social support ↑	
	Interpersonal attraction ↑	Group identity ↑	Likelihood of collaboration ↑	
		Close ties ↑		
		Intentional contact ↑		

Source: Kiesler & Cummings, 2002, pp. 60–61.
Note: Adjacent cells along the same row represent relationships shown in the research literature.
Arrows up = more of this quality increases the proximity effect
Arrows down = more of this quality reduces the proximity effect

reinforced, more overlapping know-how and expertise is generated, social support is provided more often, and the overall likelihood of intentional contact and collaborative behavior increases.

This early research on proximity found that distance caused the loss of these benefits. Kiesler and Cummings (2002) summarized what happens to distributed workers at geographical distances greater than 30–50 meters[5]:

> Distributed workers will have more difficulty forming close collaborations, dealing flexibly with one another, and expanding the breadth of relationships through unplanned mutual experiences. Strong ties will be more difficult to forge and to sustain in the distributed than in the collocated work group. When ties are weak (Hansen, 1999), transfer of complex knowledge from one location to another becomes more difficult. (p. 67)

Loss of Proximity—Cues Filtered Out

Research following this emphasis on the benefits of proximity has tended to emphasize what is lost when ICT-mediated interaction replaces face-to-face interaction. ICT-mediated communication eliminates nonlinguistic cues that amplify understanding of speech, constrains conversational strategies that put people at ease (e.g., small talk) or draw out their ideas (e.g., Socratic questioning), and restricts spontaneous social activities. Axtell, Fleck, and Turner (2004) identified this (following Culnan & Markus, 1987) as the "cues filtered out" perspective and linked it to theorizing about media richness (e.g., Daft & Lengel, 1986). Here, the emphasis is on the characteristics of different communications media, with face-to-face communication having the greatest richness due to the availability of visual and verbal cues that signal understanding and convey nuance, telephone having intermediate richness due to the presence of verbal cues, and e-mail, lacking both cues, having the least richness.[6]

Sproull and Kiesler's (1986) Lack of Social Context hypothesis suggested that the consequence of minimal social cues is deindividuation, so that individuals pay less attention to themselves and to others, are therefore less socially inhibited (hence, more likely to engage in antisocial behavior) and are less likely to establish close, interpersonal relationships. As noted next, support for this hypothesis has been mixed, yet this image of depersonalized communication remains prominent in our views about work distributed over geographic distance.

Much of this research was based on ad hoc teams of student volunteers under experimental lab conditions, whose members had no expectation of an ongoing relationship. As such, it did not consider the context in which real-world distributed work occurs. Kiesler and Cummings (2002) acknowledged the ramifications: "Distributed work does not drop from the sky on hapless groups. Surely it matters whether the antecedents of collocation or great distance include chance, management decision, personal choice, technology investment, the architecture of the task, or side effects of some other problem such as resource dependence" (p. 73).

This shortcoming began to receive attention beginning in the late 1990s with the wave of research on virtual teams.

Virtual Teams: Defined

The term *virtual teams* became common in management literature beginning in the late 1990s. This literature emphasizes geographically distributed teams explicitly created to leverage unique combinations of knowledge across various organizational and cultural boundaries, and hence, coming into existence with the reality of operating over distance as a founding condition.

Gibson and Cohen (2003) defined virtual teams as follows:

1. They are real teams, using classic definitional criteria (e.g., Hackman, Wageman, Ruddy, & Ray, 2000)—namely, a collection of individuals who are interdependent in their tasks, share responsibility for outcomes, see themselves (and viewed by others) as an intact social unit embedded in one or more social systems, and collectively manage their relationships across boundaries.
2. They work while separated by geographic distance.
3. Work is done virtually, via ICT-mediation, rather than face-to-face (p. 8).

Virtuality, from this perspective, is a continuum that has two dimensions: (a) extent of geographical dispersion and (b) extent of dependence on ICT (see also Griffith & Neale, 2001; Axtell et al., 2004). Virtual team members may all come from the same function or organization—or all belong to different organizations. Heterogeneity in the characteristics of individual members adds complexity to the task of managing the virtual team, but these differences do not define virtual teams because they also exist in collocated teams. Virtual teams deal with many of the same issues as collocated teams do, with virtuality amplifying both the benefits and the difficulties experienced by face-to-face teams.

The research reviewed here emphasizes the importance of studying virtual teams (a) over time, (b) that have relatively stable memberships, and (c) with significant tasks that provide the basis for selecting members.[7] Such teams still face the difficulties created by geographical/physical distance. Indeed, much virtual-teams research has emphasized the "cues filtered out" issues identified in past proximity-focused studies and the problems related to cohesion, conflict, trust, causal attributions, mutual contextual knowledge, and accessing dispersed knowledge. I will briefly address each of these problems here.

More thorough treatments can be found in Axtell and colleagues (2004), and Griffith and Neale (2001).

Virtual Teams: Problems

Cohesion. From a proximity perspective, the premise here is that since geographically distributed team members interact less often and use less rich forms of communication than face-to-face team members, interpersonal attraction and friendship are less likely to occur, stereotyping of remote others is more likely, and members are less likely to identify with the team (e.g., McGrath and Hollingshead, 1994). Viewed from the perspective of social categorization, cohesion is linked to shared identity—that is, the extent of team-member attraction to the idea of the group and, hence, the extent to which they are likely to identify themselves with the group (Hogg, 1992). Just because individuals are assigned to be members of a work team does not automatically mean that they will perceive all team members as "in-group" (Hinds & Mortensen, 2002). When individuals have out-group feelings toward teammates, the consequences can be (a) decreased satisfaction with the team, (b) increased turnover, (c) lowered levels of cohesiveness, (d) reduced cooperation, and (e) higher levels of conflict (Williams & O'Reilly, 1998).

Trust. From the perspective of the benefits of proximity, virtual teams should have difficulty in establishing trust; Handy's phrase (1995) captures the hypothesis concisely: "trust needs touch." Clearly, trust in any group is emergent and evolutionary. McKnight, Cummings, and Chervany (1998) suggested that trust can often be strong at the beginning of any team's work, even when there are no preexisting relationships, as a function of individuals' general inclination to trust and assurances provided by the institutional context. Since this trust is based on assumptions and attributions rather than experience, it can unravel quickly in the presence of any negative information about the trustworthiness of the partner. Thus, if virtual teams are more likely to experience conflict and mistaken attributions, as the research reviewed in the following section would suggest, they would be more vulnerable to damaging this fragile trust.

Empirical research on trust at different points in a team's life cycle has produced mixed results. Zheng, Bos, Olson, & Olson (2001) found that trust was attainable by virtual teams with no face-to-face interaction among members in the context of an electronic prisoners' dilemma game. The "high-trust," globally dispersed student teams in Jarvenpaa and Leidner (1999) achieved that condition using only electronic communication. Furthermore, the high-trust teams in Jarvenpaa and Leidner's study had better group processes and performance outcomes than "low-trust" teams. Some of their high-trust teams started from a condition of low trust, but the reverse was also true, with teams that reported initially high trust seeing deterioration over time.

Child (2001) pointed out that the calculative initial stage of trust is often based on either traditional bases of relationship, such as kinship or ethnicity ties, or on institutional assurances, provided by law or custom. A multinational team of diverse members may find little basis for establishing this initial trust and will thus be more dependent on building trust through their task-oriented activities. In line with Meyerson, Weick, and Kramer's (1996) notion of "swift trust," such teams will do best when members' roles are defined around technical specialties—reputations that they are motivated to uphold—and only moderate levels of task interdependence (Mannix, Griffith, & Neale, 2002). Jarvenpaa and Leidner (1999) found that in their student virtual teams, initial trust depended heavily on how much personal information team members shared at the start of their project, while the continuity of trust throughout the project depended more on the level of task-related communications.

Conflict. Many theories predict that conflict will be higher for virtual teams than it will be for collocated teams. Lack of proximity should bring less closeness and affinity (Kiesler & Cummings, 2002). Diversity of membership, along multiple dimensions, should weaken collective identity (Griffith & Neale, 2001). Mutual contextual awareness will be reduced (Cramton, 2001). Communication through a less rich media may filter out social cues and make it feel more impersonal (Sproull and Kiesler, 1986).

Hinds and Bailey (2003) developed a comprehensive model of conflict in virtual teams and have predicted that distance and ICT-mediated communication will each generate antecedents of all three types of conflict—(a) task, (b) affective/interpersonal, and (c) process—identified by Jehn (1997; Jehn, Northcraft, & Neale, 1999). While early studies found a potentially positive (actually an inverse U-shaped) relationship between task conflict and performance (e.g., Pelled, Eisenhardt, & Xin, 1999), others argued that individuals cannot necessarily distinguish among types of conflict (Williams & O'Reilly, 1998). Furthermore, recent meta-analyses suggest that teams engaged in complex tasks perform more poorly in the presence of any types of conflict, separately or combined (DeDreu & Weingart, 2003).

Only a few studies have actually compared distributed and collocated teams. In the first of a series of studies, Mortensen and Hinds (2001) found no differences in interpersonal or task conflict when comparing 12 dispersed teams and 12 collocated teams. They observed that teams became more harmonious over time as they developed familiarity and shared processes. Yet, in a different setting, Hinds and Mortensen (2005) noted that distributed teams reported more task and interpersonal conflict than collocated teams within the same multinational corporation. Here, they found that these differences were reduced or eliminated when moderated by shared understanding and shared context. Clearly, it is important to understand not only potential antecedents to conflict, but also conflict management strategies that any given virtual team may utilize.

Causal attribution. Cramton (2002) thoroughly examined the premise that the fundamental attribution error is likely to be exacerbated for distributed work. According to her summary, "working across dispersed locations typically reduces the situational information that collaborators have about each other, affects how they process information, and fosters the development of in-groups and out-groups based on locations. These processes bias perceptions of causes of behavior toward dispositional explanations rather than situational explanations" (p. 191). Among the potentially negative consequences are blunting of the capacity to learn; failure to meet expectations of others; and damage to interpersonal trust. The mechanism is consistent with past attribution research—that because actors have more information about their situation than others do, they attribute their own behavior to the situation, but when they do not have equivalent information for others, they tend to attribute cause for behavior to the disposition of the individual. So the relative lack of contextual information about remote others in distributed work (common, as described next) can lead to conflict-inciting attributions.

Mutual knowledge of context and accessing dispersed knowledge. Cramton (2001) focused on the "mutual knowledge" problem. For a group to access its collective knowledge, each member must have a good sense of not only the collective information known to all, but also what other members uniquely know. Cramton found that dispersed collaborators lack mutual knowledge of important aspects of each other's context; they do not guess/figure out what they need to explain about their own context; they find it difficult to develop a picture of their collaborator's context in their minds; they tend to forget what is communicated to them about this context; thus causing conflict. The negative consequences of these conflicts can be severe. What is salient in one context may have little meaning in another context; a team member may miss what is most crucial in a message; thus, it can be hard to know if everyone is operating from the same information. Furthermore, lack of contextual information can create a tendency toward dispositional rather than situational attributions.

Collocated groups often give more attention to commonly held information and ignore the unique knowledge of its individual members (Stasser & Titus, 1985). Distributed work may exacerbate this problem, because virtual team members may have less opportunity or capability to learn "who knows what" and may not even realize what unique information they hold.

The system by which a group organizes its knowledge about who knows what is called its "transactive memory" (Hollingshead, 1998; Wegner, 1987). For the previously stated reasons, a virtual team is likely to have a more difficult time developing its transactive memory than a collocated team

(Hollingshead, Fulk, & Monge, 2002; Liang, Moreland, & Argote, 1995). Since familiarity from frequent interaction helps individuals cognitively organize their own knowledge of who knows what, the lessened interaction among virtual team members could block this process.

Virtual Teams: Adaptations, Remedies, and Countervailing Strategies

This list of potential problems with distributed work in virtual teams is long and daunting.[8] The mechanisms that affect virtual teams, however, are often no different from those that affect any collocated work group. Indeed, in some cases, features of the virtual work or the distributed work may prompt stronger, earlier, more appropriate action to prevent or circumvent these problems.

In this section, I will focus on the adaptations, remedies, and countervailing strategies (ARCS) created by individuals, work groups, and managers to cope with the problems of distributed work. These include (a) learning to recognize and react to the "cues left in" computer-mediated communication, (b) reducing coordination requirements and task interdependence through modularization and work restructuring, and (c) increasing shared understanding and shared identity.

Cues left in. The "cues left in" perspective takes issue with the implicit technological determinism in the media richness and "lack of social context" literature by showing how virtual team members adapt and respond to a different set of social cues when face-to-face cues are not available. From this perspective, technology does not completely eliminate social cues, but rather, causes them to take a different form (such as with e-mail messages). Over time, individuals learn to pick up cues from the content and language of the message, its timing, and even its typography and style (Walther & D'Addario, 2001; Walther & Tidwell, 1995).

In line with Walther's (1992) Social Information Processing theory, virtual team members seem to take longer to socialize and establish process norms and other ground rules, but eventually, these stages of group formation do happen. Given an expectation of future interaction, communications tend to remain personal and friendly, in contrast with earlier findings of impersonal, ICT-mediated communication among ad hoc, short-term groups. Essentially, media richness is not seen as an attribute of a given technology or communications mode, but rather, as a perception that can be enhanced over time through experience with the technology/communications mode, but also with the topic, the context, and the communication partners (Carlson & Zmud, 1999).

Another kind of adaptation occurs in the absence of cues providing individuating information about group members. Spears and Lea (1992, 1994) suggested that in visually anonymous distributed groups, attention is shifted away from individual differences toward those cues that help establish a common group identity; indeed, group members may grab onto the shared identity quickly and strongly (Postmes, Spears, & Lea, 1998). Similarly, Bhappu, Griffith, and Northcraft (1997) found that in the absence of visual cues, ascriptive differences such as gender were less salient to virtual team members.

Walther (1996, 1997) proposed a "hyper-personal" perspective: Given the limited information about an individual revealed through ICT-mediated communications, whatever is revealed becomes intensified as a basis for forming impressions. Group-identity cues may be more salient than individual-identity cues related to ascriptive characteristics such as gender, race, or age. The individual information that is available may be exaggerated, either positively or negatively.

Status differences, more than ascriptive characteristics, appear to be a "cue left in," according to several studies. Owens, Neale, and Sutton (2000) examined interactions among low-, medium-, and high-status group members of project teams in an R&D organization and found that teams tend to reproduce organizationally defined categories, hierarchies, and status differentials when working virtually.

Metiu (2006) highlighted the difficulties when distributed work involves cooperation among remote groups differing in status, a common phenomenon at a time of frequent outsourcing to lower labor cost countries. She found that status is both an input and an output of intergroup relations, and that cooperation often breaks down as status differentials are enacted. The U.S.-based, high-status software development group often refused to engage with the lower status group in India; this closure deepened perceived status differentials. The status dynamic was reinforced by the implicit competition between the two locations in the software industry. Clearly, status is highly relevant for situations in which geographical distance coincides with other types of distance.

Modularization and work structuring. Both modularization and work restructuring reduce task interdependence among individual team members as a coordination-minimizing approach to dealing with the challenges of distributed work. These strategies facilitate effective performance for geographically distributed teams by standardizing task boundaries and interface requirements, making extensive interaction unnecessary when completing assigned tasks.

Modularity is at once an attribute of product architecture and an organizational principle. When module boundaries, interface requirements, and hand-off processes are preestablished, individuals can work in relative autonomy with knowledge that their output will synchronize, by design, in the end. Software development and physical product development methodologies are now well-elaborated to pursue modularization as a solution for minimizing coordination complexity (Fixson, 2005; MacDuffie & Helper, 2006; Schilling, 2000; Sosa, Eppinger, Pich, McKendrick, & Stout, 2002; Ulrich, 1995).

The limits of modularization are confronted whenever either external customer requirements or internal changes in technical content or organizational resources force a redrawing of module boundaries. Such boundary changes often involve intensive discussion and negotiation, and they increase task interdependence and communication requirements dramatically until new specifications are defined.

Similar to modularization, work restructuring aims to reduce interdependence through task decomposition. Eppinger (2001) argued that for complex, tightly coupled tasks such as product development, task sequences should be restructured to reduce interdependencies and minimize necessary information exchange. Even when a product design and the associated organizational structure cannot be modularized, careful attention to how tasks are allocated to different subgroups operating over distance can reduce the amount of information each group needs about the work of the other.

Work structuring has distinct limitations where geographical distance is involved. Lack of knowledge of what others are doing (in terms of mutual knowledge of context and the who knows what of transactive memory) can lead to confusion and lack of shared understanding of goals, as well as insufficient development of expertise or matching of expertise to task. Formalization tends to rely upon bureaucratic procedures, often adding costs and layers that impede speed. The reduction in interpersonal interaction that accompanies task segmentation can also increase the risk of different *thought worlds*, Dougherty's (1992) term for the different cognitive frames that arise naturally in functionally differentiated settings. Perspectives on the shared tasks and habits of work can harden in this segmented state.

Shared understanding and shared identity. Increasing shared understanding and shared identity is a capacity-enhancing approach to dealing with distance that can lessen the likelihood (or magnitude) of problems in virtual teams. *Shared understanding* is defined as the degree of cognitive overlap and commonality in beliefs, expectations, and perceptions about goals, tasks, processes, and members' knowledge, skills, and abilities; it is primarily concerned with task-related information and knowledge. *Shared identity* is defined as the degree of commonality in perceiving oneself as a member of an established and esteemed in-group with a particular identity, set of values, norms, and routines; it is primarily concerned with social categorization processes. These two conditions rarely occur independently. This dual emphasis is consistent with the perspective that group effectiveness is affected by both task characteristics and by the dynamics of interpersonal relations (Jehn et al., 1999; McGrath, 1984; Williams & O'Reilly, 1998).

Shared understanding is perhaps the most frequently identified factor necessary for the achievement of distributed work involving interdependent tasks (Hinds & Mortensen, 2005; Hinds & Weisband, 2003). This *cognitive* factor has both informational and interpretative content. With respect to information, group members doing work over distance need to have (or acquire) congruent information in relation to the common task—not identical, but substantially overlapping and cognitively consistent across the group. With respect to interpretation, group members must possess a common language, a common grounding in the issues, problems, challenges facing the organization and team, and a shared frame of reference. Shared understanding should help individuals engaged in separate but interdependent tasks to coordinate their actions more effectively (Kogut & Zander, 1992). In product development settings, for example, design engineers can coordinate their separate tasks if they share some knowledge about the technical subsystem within which each task is embedded (Postrel, 2002).

Hinds and Weisband (2003) emphasized several ways in which shared understanding contributes to the work of virtual teams:

1. It makes the behavior of others predictable, so that one can make assumptions about what is being done and what needs to be done without having to extensively monitor others (Mathieu, Goodwin, Heffner, Salas, & Cannon-Bowers, 2000).
2. It facilities the efficient use of resources and effort, both by avoiding risk-averse precautions in which individuals hedge their bets as they wait to observe the actions of others, and by knowing what expertise resides in which of the other team members—that is, transactive memory (Liang et al., 1995).
3. It reduces implementation problems and errors by helping a group resolve inevitable misunderstandings more quickly and with less interpersonal damage.
4. It increases satisfaction and motivation (and reduces frustration and conflict) of team members. In particular, shared understanding of goals and task requirements focuses attention on the specific goal-focused behaviors that will lead to positive outcomes and associated rewards.

As just noted, work distributed over distance can make shared understanding more complicated due to lack of mutual knowledge of context (Cramton, 2002) and difficulty accessing dispersed knowledge (Axtell et al., 2004). Sole and Edmondson (2002) found that with geographic distance, team members are not only less likely to know the expertise of members at a distant location, but they are also likely to view going to those members for task-appropriate knowledge as onerous. Given distance, members may make assumptions about others' knowledge based on social categorization, such as occupation, status, organizational membership, or location (Krauss & Fussell, 1990; Krauss, Fussell, Brennan, & Siegel, 2002). Even if shared understanding is constrained, groups may still tend to rely too heavily on the knowledge that they *know* is shared and underexploit the unique knowledge present in individual group members.

On the other hand, a virtual team selected explicitly to bring together individuals with unique and relevant knowledge may already be proactively focused on making all members aware of who knows what, as well as how to access remote knowledge. Experimental evidence suggests that explicitly identifying and locating the expertise of each team member greatly reduces information-sharing problems (Stasser, Vaughan, & Stewart, 2000).

Shared identity emerges from processes of social comparison (Sokol, 1992) and self-categorization (Turner, Hogg, Oakes, Reicher, & Whetherell, 1987)— that is, categorizing the self in relation to proximate others—in which individuals regularly engage. In-group versus out-group categorizations emerge, resulting in a more positive view of in-group members. As noted earlier, there is ample basis to predict a weakening of shared identity when group members are geographically remote from each other (Wiesenfeld, Raghuram, & Garud, 1999). From the "cues left in" perspective, however, the absence of individuating information may reduce friendship, but intensify identification with the group.

This raises the issue of how salient membership in a particular virtual team is for an individual. In a work context, individuals may belong to multiple teams, some collocated and some virtual. The physical presence of collocated team members will make identification with that group more salient and may interfere with identification with a virtual team. Indeed, dispersed group members often identify more strongly with their location or site than they do with their organizational function (Mortensen & Hinds, 2002). On the other hand, when virtual teams are formed to draw together specialized, complementary expertise for a particular task of great significance, membership is likely to have high salience for individuals and become the basis for a strong group identity.

Shared identity contributes to positive outcomes in a distributed group in the following ways. When a shared group identity is salient, team members are inclined to be more loyal, more trusting, and more concerned about promoting the welfare of the group (Brewer & Miller, 1996). In the presence of a shared team identity, distant team members may have more faith in other members and be more likely to talk through issues that arise (Hinds and Bailey, 2003). Shared identity will minimize in-group/out-group distinctions and will limit the stereotyping and attributions that tend to accompany them. Shared identity may mitigate—although it may not eliminate—the negative impact of status differences on interpersonal dynamics within a distributed team.

Shared understanding and shared identity interact in a variety of ways. Cramton (2001) found that in the absence of shared understanding, and with little knowledge of what distant colleagues do and do not know, members of dispersed teams at one location tend to rely on out-group categorizations to interpret the actions of remote-located teammates, and then make attributions about problems accordingly. The "cues left in" perspective predicts that the absence of individuating cues in virtual teams could intensify identification with the group (Spears & Lea, 1992). This could boost shared identity, but increase the common knowledge bias, which could cause the group to sub-optimize the scope of shared understanding by not drawing out the unique knowledge of each member.

Hinds and Mortensen (2005) have performed one of the few empirical tests of these interrelated effects of these two factors; their design is also rare in that it compares virtual and collocated teams doing similar tasks in a common organizational context. They conceptualized both shared understanding and shared identity as moderators of conflict in distributed teams. They found that shared identity moderated the effects of distributed work on *interpersonal* conflict, while shared understanding moderated the effects of distributed work on *task* conflict. A measure of "spontaneous communication"—an important construct from the tradition of proximity-focused research, defined here as informal, unplanned interactions that occur among team members—was associated with a stronger shared identity and more shared understanding, and also mitigated the effect of distributed work on both kinds of conflict.

Given the importance of shared understanding and shared identity to the effectiveness of virtual teams, how are they created? The answers are unlikely to be mutually exclusive; the following list is drawn from literature on both variables (particularly, Hinds & Weisband, 2003; also Cramton, 2002; Hinds & Bailey, 2003; Hinds & Mortensen, 2005). Shared understanding and shared identity will increase on the basis of

1. Similarity—People who share similar demographic characteristics, occupation, national culture, and so forth, can often establish a shared identity and shared understandings more quickly and easily.
2. Shared experience—When people share experiences, they learn things about each other while also building transactive memory and establishing a common history as a referent for shared understanding and shared identity in the future.
3. Team cohesion—Greater cohesion helps build shared understanding by orienting team members toward getting to know and supporting each other. It also increases one aspect of similarity (same team) and creates a positive incentive to pursue shared experiences, both of which reinforce a shared team identity.
4. Information distribution/sharing—When routinely pursued and reinforced with group norms about open access to information/data, this can improve the shared understanding of group members. In distributed teams, it is particularly important to make sure that all information shared at one location (e.g., in a meeting) is actively communicated to all team members at another location.

5. Spontaneous communication—This informal, unplanned communication happens naturally among proximate team members, but must be created through concerted action in virtual teams. Such communication, often dyadic, helps amplify the impact of the other four variables. Shared understanding increases because missing pieces of context can be filled in, as needed, by a particular individual; shared identity increases because spontaneous communication creates stronger social bonds between team members.

Little is known about the degree to which shared understanding and shared identity can compensate for one another; this may be task- or context-specific. Furthermore, certain individual differences precede—and will endure well beyond—virtual team membership.

Collocated teams also face challenges of building shared understanding and shared identity, but these can often emerge naturally from well-managed group processes. For virtual teams, intentional proactive efforts to build these collective resources from a team's very founding can provide a powerful countervailing force to the potential liabilities of operating over geographical distance, thereby building goodwill and psychological safety among team members, and generating resilience for the team as a whole.

Two case studies of automotive product development illustrate many of these points. Vaccaro and Veloso (2006) have provided a longitudinal case study of a geographically dispersed product-development team for a light commercial vehicle at a European original equipment manufacturer (OEM). In a multistage process, engineers first work from separate locations, then physically come together for the core design phase, and then disperse again. While separated, common experiences of training on the OEM's virtual design tools and the collective building of a database of technical documents helped develop shared understanding among project team members and became an early reference point for shared identity. While collocated, engineers drew design sketches of components and posted them for other engineers to see:

> Designers working at the same time on the same computer system began, after a brief period of collaboration, to share and develop a heterogeneous group of experiences, technological concepts, and ideas at a tacit level. [They] exploited virtual environments as a place to freely share complex experimentation and design activities. (Vaccaro & Veloso, 2006, p. 16)

This design collaboration continued with relative ease once engineers were again dispersed. The virtual design tools also helped designers do their jobs better (e.g., with more precision, visual flexibility, reusability, and a faster and wider search). During the final two stages of documentation and testing, team members independently completed most tasks from separate locations, and their work was then verified asynchronously by remote testers.

Helper and Khambete (2006) offered a longitudinal case study of a firm in India that provides contract engineering support for a U.S. supplier working on a U.S. OEM's automotive-vehicle project. All of the CAGE types of distance were present. The contract engineering firm created a team of two engineers, one in the U.S. and one in India, that worked together to support the automotive glass supplier to the OEM. The U.S.-based engineer, a specialist, met face-to-face with the vehicle design team at the OEM and sent certain tasks to his generalist counterpart in India. A 3-month training period for the Indian engineer, in the United States, allowed a personal relationship to develop and provided shared understanding of the context. Once the Indian engineer returned home, mutual use of collaborative project-management software and the OEM's visual design tools supported information exchange for interdependent tasks. Norms and routines for handling problems and weekly conference calls helped keep the two engineers synchronized and engaged in joint problem solving. Financial incentives tied to the completion of project tasks encouraged the U.S. engineer to rely frequently on his Indian counterpart for routine tasks, while pay and working conditions were highly desirable for the Indian engineer.

Earlier in this chapter, I focused on virtual teams and geographical distance, even though other forms of distance (e.g., cultural) may also have been operative. Now I will examine the phenomenon of blended workforces that combine regular (standard) employees and contingent (nonstandard) workers to explore whether the adaptations, remedies, and countervailing strategies utilized for geographical distance also apply to employment status distance.

Blended Workforce: Defined

A blended workforce combines individuals in standard (regular employees) and nonstandard (contingent/contract, temporary/part-time) work arrangements. The definitional issues surround how we define each category, as well as what constitutes "blending." Kalleberg, Reskin, and Hudson (2000) defined standard work as "work done on a fixed schedule—usually full-time—at the employer's place of business, under the employer's control, and with the mutual expectation of continued employment" (p. 258), and nonstandard work as lacking one or more of these attributes.

Ashford and colleagues (chapter 2, this volume) adopted the same definition, noting the value (see also Cappelli, 1999) of an implicit contrast between a normative, "standard" arrangement and a counternormative, "nonstandard" arrangement, and pointing out the consistency with Pfeffer and Baron's (1988) influential typology of three types of attachments between workers and organizations. Pfeffer and Baron's typology also maps well onto the CAGE categories used here. They distinguish attachment based on physical proximity (equivalent to geographical distance), administrative control (equivalent to administrative distance), or expected duration of employment (equivalent to employment status distance).

Broschak and Davis-Blake (2006) elaborated one further distinction, following Befort (2003), between those nonstandard workers who have no legal basis whatsoever to be classified as an "employee" of the organization for which they provide services (e.g., contract workers, independent contractors) and those who either do have legal status as employees (e.g., part-time or direct-hire temporary workers) or can more easily make claims to that status (under U.S. law) under coemployment doctrine (e.g., agency-provided temporary workers). The latter category will possess a status more equivalent to standard workers (or regular employees), hence they are less separated in terms of employment status distance than are contract workers.

Blended Workforce: Problems

Employment status distance has powerful consequences when nonstandard and standard workers are proximate. According to Broschak and Davis-Blake (2006)

> Past research has shown that the mere presence of nonstandard workers can affect standard workers and is associated with increased conflict and poorer relations between coworkers, decreased organizational loyalty and increased turnover (exit) intentions among standard workers, and poorer relationships between managers and standard workers. (p. 372; see also Davis-Blake, Broschak, & George, 2003; Geary, 1992: Pearce, 1993; Smith, 1994)

They go on to demonstrate that these negative consequences (specifically, propensity to turnover, more negative relations with their supervisor and their peers, and less work-related helping behaviors) have a greater magnitude as the proportion of nonstandard workers in the work group increased. Clearly, in this context, the negative consequences of employment status distance overwhelm the usual benefits of proximity (minimal geographical distance).

The reasons for these consistently negative findings are multiple. The presence of nonstandard workers may cause standard workers to worry about their own employment security; threaten their career prospects; increase their workload; violate their trust in the organization that employs them; offend their sense of fairness; and weaken the norm of reciprocity that can motivate work-related helping and organizational citizenship behaviors. What is striking is that these effects are pervasive. Not only do they (predictably) generate negative feelings toward the nonstandard workers themselves, but they also negatively affect relations with supervisors and peers (e.g., standard workers/regular employees) as well as overall attachment to the organization.

Broschak and Davis-Blake (2006) argued that employment status is an organizationally determined characteristic of high salience to both standard and nonstandard workers. The strong consequences of these status distinctions (e.g., employment status distance) support Reskin's (2003) argument that organization-initiated actions that create difference can have the same effects on attitudes and behavior as differences based on ascriptive characteristics (gender, race, age)—namely, negative feelings, stereotyping, and dispositional attributions.[9] The offshoring of software development studied by Metiu (2006) bears this out. Barley and Kunda's (2004) ethnography of itinerant IT contractors (summarized in the following section) found a slightly different dynamic. Contractors faced client-initiated status differentials meant to demonstrate (for the benefit of regular employees) that they were "outsiders," yet this was partially offset by the client's high need for their specialized expertise, which caused managers to integrate them into core work routines.

Blended Workforce: Adaptations, Remedies, and Countervailing Strategies

Here I briefly summarize research also identifying adaptations and policies that can potentially deal with problems of the blended workforce. Here we can again differentiate between actions/strategies that minimize distance and those that enhance capacity for dealing with distance.

Work restructuring falls in the first category. Broschak and Davis-Blake (2006) found that task-related interaction between standard and nonstandard workers often leads to negative supervisor-subordinate relations because of tensions around the allocation of work tasks, the consequences for work load, and the quality/efficiency of task completion. They suggested that supervisors can structure work to minimize interdependence between workers with different employment status, or even physically segregate them on separate production lines or in separate facilities. (Here, intriguingly, increased geographical distance is hypothesized to help with reducing problems of employment status distance.)

Allowing/encouraging more social interaction between standard and nonstandard workers appears to enhance individual and group capacity to deal with employment status distance. Broschak and Davis-Blake (2006) found that such social interaction—explicitly informal, deliberately not task-oriented; intended to develop interpersonal relationships—increases work group and organizational cohesion and expressions of social support, reduces tensions, and boosts work-related helping behaviors.

Broschak and Davis-Blake (2006) found that the tensions are greatest between nonstandard workers and lower level standard workers. This is very likely attributable to policies that allow the best-performing temporary workers to win full-time jobs as regular employees. Eliminating the prospect of direct competition for future jobs is a potential remedy. Another suggestion is to offer equivalent training opportunities to both standard and nonstandard workers. Combining these groups in training classes may reduce the salience of employment arrangements; this also allows for increased non-task-related social interaction.

Both of these examples are approaches that aim to increase shared understanding and shared identity. Nonstandard workers engaged in an organization's central activities on an ongoing (and physically proximate) basis face an ambiguous situation vis-à-vis their identity. Shared identity in this context, where employment status distance separates the two types of workers, may take the form of feelings of belonging to the broader organization. As Ashford and colleagues (chapter 2, this volume) pointed out,

> It is through relationships that nonstandard workers come to understand who they are relative to the organization. Their *experience* of belongingness (or perceived insider status) …is sensed not through the objective details of their work arrangement but in their daily encounters with others who grant them a sense of organizational membership and acknowledge their claims that they belong to the social fabric of the organizations. (p. 95)

It is in this sense that both informal social interaction and mutual training help build a sense of shared identity.

Similarly, when nonstandard workers perceive the organization's values as aligning with their own, their identification with the organization is stronger (George & Chattopadhyay, 2005). Increasing a nonstandard worker's sense of identification with the organization for which she or he provides services does not necessarily eliminate employment status distance (unless it has the effect of raising expectations, e.g., of shifting from temporary to permanent employment status). It does appear, however, to increase a nonstandard worker's capacity for handling this distance.

Case studies and ethnographies of blended workforces doing information technology (IT) work illustrate many of these dynamics. The companies that are the largest users of IT services use several types of IT employees simultaneously: their own IT staff, independent contractors, and consultants (who may also use a mix of their own staff and contractors). They choose this mix both for numerical flexibility (contractors and consultants can be managed as variable costs, with contracts ended or cut back when business conditions dictate) and for access to specialized skills (Abraham & Taylor, 1996; Houseman, 2001).

Bidwell (2006a, b) provided a longitudinal case study of IT consultants and independent contractors working side by side with regular employees of their customer, a large financial services firm. He found that these different types of IT workers were often managed by the firm's IT department in very similar ways. The firm often employed consultants and contractors alike for lengthy periods; while the average was 3 years, many had worked for 10 years or more. Almost all projects were staffed with a mix of all three types of workers. Employment status had little impact on the work performed by individuals, or on how the individuals were perceived. Nonemployees were as likely as employees were to be staffed on projects said to be most important to the organization or having the longest term consequences. Managers saw consultants/contractors as being equally motivated and committed as regular employees were, as well as having equivalent levels of firm-specific skills. The managers also disagreed with the idea that they had more control over their regular employees. The fact of physical proximity combined with the firm's high dependence on the contractors' specialized knowledge appears to have overcome the high level of employment status and cultural distance between the employees and the contract workers.

Barley and Kunda (2004, 2006) examined IT contractors as a new kind of professional. Their ethnographic data suggest that these contractors do experience employment status distance that imposes barriers on their integration into the task work of their client organizations. Whether doing distributed work from a cubicle at the client's office, or from their home, contractors confront many ambiguities and contradictions.

> Although a contractor's position in a client's organization was usually defined well enough in legal terms, how he or she actually fit into the social fabric of organizational life was problematic. Because everyday life in most firms was still governed by traditional notions of employment, the people with whom contractors worked struggled with conflicting images of the contractors' rightful place and the mixed feelings these images generated.

> To make the most of the contractors' skills, hiring managers discovered they had to integrate the contractor into the flow of activities and the network of relationships.... At the same time....contractors knew that no matter how appreciated, accepted, and integrated they became, they were still outsiders. Firms repeatedly drove this fact home in countless, symbolic ways, from the color of the contractors' badges to the size and location of their office space. (p. 49)

Yet Barley and Kunda (2004) also discovered that regular IT employees and IT contractors can coordinate their efforts on interdependent tasks with relative ease. The regular IT employees can be viewed as "corporate professionals," who perform their professional duties as full-time employees. Many contractors had held such positions themselves and had exited corporate life to seek an alternative. When contractors come back into corporate settings, the two groups can relate, at some level, as fellow professionals. These occupational bonds between itinerant IT contractors and corporate IT professionals create shared understanding, although their interaction also highlights the organizational privileges and benefits enjoyed by employees and the temporal flexibility and (often) higher pay of the contractors, creating barriers to shared identity.

Summary: Doing a Distance Inventory

To summarize this section, I provide, in Table 12.3, a "distance inventory" that shows, for the types of distance in the modified CAGE framework, those adaptations, remedies, and countervailing strategies (ARCS) that are distance-minimizing and those that enhance individual, group, or organizational capacity to deal with distance.

Managing People Over Distance: HRM Practices and Employment Policies

Previously, I examined the problems that arise when managing people over distance—geographical and otherwise—and potential adaptations, remedies, and countervailing strategies. In this section, I focus on HRM practices and employment policies that can potentially support these adaptations, remedies, and countervailing strategies, continuing to compare the same two contexts: (a) virtual teams and (b) blended workforces of standard and nonstandard workers. First, I offer a conceptualization of how to think about managing people over distances that draws on the literature of strategic human resources management (SHRM).

Distance From a Strategic HRM (SHRM) Perspective

Research on SHRM seeks to identify particular configurations of HR practices that are well-aligned, both externally—with organizational strategies (in order to develop capabilities, knowledge, and social capital needed to achieve competitive advantage)—and also internally—such that practices are logically consistent and mutually reinforcing (in order to achieve systemic and synergistic benefits that are difficult to imitate and thus sustain competitive advantage). Much SHRM research searches for these configurations in relation to organizational performance. Sometimes one (or more) "bundles" of HR practices are identified that predict performance well for a sample of organizations/establishments in a specific context (Batt, 1999; Delery & Doty, 1996; Huselid, 1995; Ichniowski, Shaw, & Prennushi, 1997; MacDuffie, 1995), and sometimes successful firms are studied to inductively extract the common patterns in their HR practices (O'Reilly & Pfeffer, 2000; Pfeffer, 1994, 1998). The resulting portrayal of "high performance work systems" often provides what appear as a set of "best practices" whose benefits are argued to be broadly applicable, at least to the context under examination.

The literature on "high performance work systems" (HPWS) has faced several challenges and criticisms. First, the practices that are said to predict

Table 12.3 Distance Inventory for Managing Over Distance

	Distance Characteristics	Distance-Minimizing Actions	Actions to Maximize Capacity for Handling Distance
C: Cultural	Mix of national and organizational culture	Cultural homogeneity of interacting individuals	Select for cultural awareness; set norms of discussing cultural issues; direct exposure by visiting different locations; shared experiences in cross-cultural groups
A: Administrative	Relationship among organizations (e.g., supplier-customer? Merger or acquisition?)	Collocation of all individuals at focal organization, applying the same administrative procedures as much as possible	Common access to the same administrative and communications systems; common/shared training on those systems; anchoring discussions on shared information, particularly visualizations
G: Geographic	Physical proximity or dispersion; distribution of individuals across various locations	Periodic face-to-face meetings, ideally rotated across locations	Norms of communicating contextual information related to location; encouraging spontaneous and informal dyadic communication
E: Employment Status	Mix of standard & nonstandard workers	Minimize status markers and differentials; collocation when possible	Encourage informal interaction; emphasize contract worker's identification with goals and values of the firm; common/shared training

superior performance (and even sustainable competitive advantage) have diffused much less widely than economic theory would predict (Osterman, 1994; Pil & MacDuffie, 1996). In addition, while visible economic benefits may accrue from certain configurations of HR practices, implementing these practices may also incur additional costs, yielding a questionable contribution to profitability (Batt, 2002; Cappelli & Neumark, 2001). Third, even where outcomes of HPWS are entirely positive for the firm, the consequences for the employees who are involved—in terms of workload, share of productivity gain received as compensation, morale, stress, and so forth—may be negative (Applebaum & Batt, 1994; Osterman, 2000). In addition, the "one size fits all" prescriptions of much of this literature do not match the proliferation of employment arrangements and work contracts found at most contemporary firms (Lepak & Snell, 1999; Matusik & Hill, 1998).

Scholars have responded by offering frameworks of contingent relationships between various HR approaches and particular business strategies (Arthur, 1992; Delery & Doty, 1996; Snell & Youndt, 1995). These are relevant to our inquiry into managing people over distances in two ways. First, organizations seek different things in distributing work over distance, and strategies for best managing the people involved in distributed work should depend on those organizational purposes. Second, for a given purpose, different HR configurations might be better aligned with managing particular types of distance (C, A, G, and/or E). A full examination of these issues is beyond the scope of this chapter, but I will examine one such contingency framework to assess its applicability to virtual teams and the blended workforce.

Just as predictions about the diffusion of high performance work systems have not always held up, contingency frameworks have also struggled to incorporate the diversity of work and employment arrangements in this period of disaggregation of jobs, careers, and firms. Early SHRM contingency theories built directly on the resource-based view of the firm and the argument that firms should develop a particular "core competence" that provides competitive advantage and externalizes all "noncore" activities. Translated into employment arrangements and HR practices, this meant managing "core" employees (those with human and social capital crucial to the firm's core capability) in a way that would stimulate their motivation, win their commitment, and strengthen/prolong their attachment to the firm, while either externalizing (outsourcing to another firm) or peripheralizing (hiring noncore employees whose value to the firm is less) those activities not related to the core capability.

While some firms have followed this pattern, many others have taken actions that contradict the anticipated contingencies, such as outsourcing activities considered core (Azoulay, 2004), assigning core activities to contractors or other nonstandard workers (Bidwell, 2006a, b), managing core employees in ways that weaken their attachment (Cappelli, 1999), or acquiring firms for their employees'

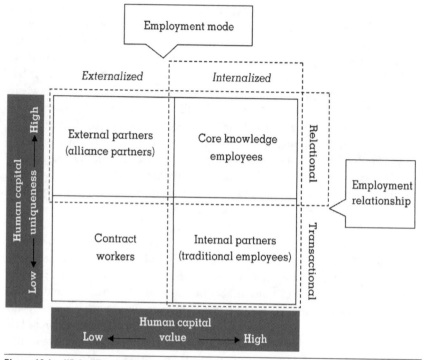

Figure 12.1 HR Architecture

human and social capital, and then managing the integration process in ways that prompt most of those employees to leave the firm (Hitt, Ireland, & Harrison, 1991). These contradictory actions can be fruitfully juxtaposed with the contingency frameworks to see what can be learned.

Lepak and Snell (1999) and Kang, Morris, and Snell (2007) presented contingency frameworks relevant to my purposes. Lepak and Snell set out a "human resource architecture" that shows a portfolio of different approaches to managing stocks of human capital depending on their value and uniqueness in relation to achieving the firm's strategy (Figure 12.1). The resulting four approaches are differentiated in terms of employment mode (internalized vs. externalized) and employment *relationship* (relational vs. transactional).

For human capital that is highly valuable and highly unique, their framework specifies investing in the development of core employees managed for high commitment and a long-term relationship with the firm (internalized and relational). In the opposite case—human capital of low value and low uniqueness—it points toward contracting out through transaction-oriented arrangements that are managed for contract compliance (externalized and transactional).

For human capital that is unique and scarce, yet not central to the firm's strategy of value creation, the framework specifies establishing alliances with external partners (individuals or firms) and investing heavily in establishing an effective collaborative relationship (externalized and relational), rather than internalizing the human capital through an employment relationship. Finally, for human capital possessing skills and knowledge high in value for achieving the firm's strategy, but relatively abundant and easy to access, the framework specifies hiring individuals as regular employees, but not anticipating long-term employment or making efforts to develop firm-specific expertise (internalized and transactional); this employment relationship is designed to last only as long as it serves the needs of both parties.

Applying the framework to the two contexts I have used in this chapter, intraorganizational virtual teams would typically be deployed in one of the two "internalized" quadrants: either (a) entirely among core employees managed for a long-term relationship under a high commitment approach, or (b) between such core employees and other internal employees possessing other necessary, value-added skills. The blended workforce context would be managed according to one of the two "externalized" quadrants, either (a) between core employees and external alliance partners possessing unique and complementary expertise, under a collaborative relationship in which the focal firm invests heavily, or (b) between regular employees and contract workers governed by a well-defined transactional contract.

Kang and colleagues (2007) expanded on the HR architecture framework, focusing on knowledge flows (Table 12.4b). They argue that when firms want to pursue exploitation-related learning, they take a "cooperative" approach to the underlying social relations, emphasizing intensive interactions between core-knowledge employees and regular employees within a strong/dense network, drawing on the generalized trust that comes from a shared collective identity and shared understanding of the firm's knowledge architecture—that is, the links among components of specialized knowledge. In contrast, when firms want to pursue exploration-related learning, they take an "entrepreneurial" approach to social relations, emphasizing dispersed interactions between core-knowledge employees and external alliance partners within a weak/nonredundant network, working to building resilient dyadic trust and emphasizing exchanges of complementary, cospecialized knowledge that can potentially generate something new and innovative.

It makes sense that firms would think of "intraorganizational virtual teams" from an internalized, cooperative perspective, expecting that the work of such teams should be facilitated by the shared identity of being employees of the same firm and the shared understanding that comes from knowing how the firm organizes its core knowledge. From the perspective of the Kang and colleagues (2007) framework, virtual teams are often managed as if the cooperative social context available for collocated core employees is a resource upon which team members can readily draw. This includes a dense network of relationships with overlapping/redundant ties, the easy (even swift)

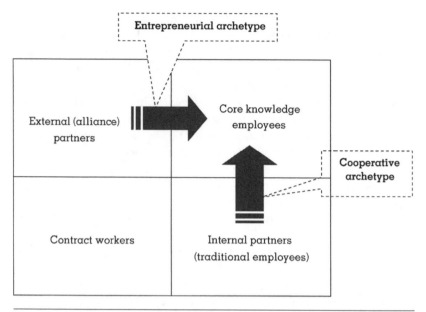

Figure 12.2 Relational Archetypes in the HR Architecture

institutionalized trust from a shared organizational membership, and awareness of who knows what within the firm's knowledge system.

Similarly, it makes sense that firms would think of a blended workforce as involving externalized relationships that should either be managed as arm's-length contracts around prespecified tasks or as collaborations on a project basis involving complementary and cospecialized knowledge assets. In terms of the Kang and colleagues (2007) framework, where rare or unique knowledge is involved, the blended workforce requires significant investments in the relationship between core-knowledge employees and external partners. This is done in order to tap the unique knowledge that lies outside the firm's internal network, to build dyadic trust, and to deepen shared expertise for the project; otherwise, where little unique knowledge is involved, the external contracting arrangement can be approached as a simple transaction with no relational consequences.

Yet, much of what has previously been reviewed from the literature on virtual teams and blended workforces suggests the opposite. The loss of proximity affecting intraorganizational virtual teams means that shared understanding and shared identity are weakened and strained. Virtual teams perform best when their members are highly aware that they must thoroughly explain their context and clearly articulate their special knowledge, making sure that communications have cues left in. This may actually be easier to do if one frames the virtual team as an alliance among various partners, each with valuable and complementary knowledge assets, because this will prompt explicit and careful attention to developing a highly collaborative relationship and filling in missing bits of context knowledge. Put differently, a powerful way to deal with the problems of geographical distance is to act as if fellow team members are highly valuable collaborators who do not (yet) know you well, with payoffs that will remain high as long as everyone works very hard to establish an effective working relationship.

In turn, with the blended workforce, when organizations reinforce the externalized nature of the relationship, either with alliance partners or transactional contracts, the consequences of making these differences salient can be strongly negative. The literature reviewed earlier in this chapter suggests that nonstandard work arrangements are best managed through minimizing the salience of employment status distance and increasing the sense of shared understanding and shared identity. Put differently, a powerful way to deal with the problems of employment status distance is to treat nonstandard workers more like regular employees and to encourage informal social interaction and collective problem-solving between these two groups.

Ultimately, choices about managing people over distance must wrestle with the same issues found in the SHRM literature. Choices about what kinds of human/social capital are needed and how HR systems should be implemented to develop capabilities should be contingent upon what the firm needs to achieve with a particular strategy.

Yet there may be certain approaches to developing HR capabilities with universal applicability (as the HPWS research suggests) because they respond to something fundamental about how people are motivated, how they learn, how they interact with others, how they draw upon tacit and articulated knowledge, how they develop trust and handle conflict, and how they respond to change. In particular, when managing people over distance, developing communication channels and norms that emphasize cues left in, and increasing the level of shared understanding and shared identity among individuals and groups, may both be universal best practices that should be applied in relation to any kind of distance. The need to deal with these fundamentals of human behavior within employment and work relationships may trump the logic associated with a contingency framework.

Keeping in mind this SHRM perspective on managing people over distance, I now turn to a detailed examination of HR practices in key areas.

HR Practices for Managing People in Work Distributed Over Distances

For both virtual teams and the blended workforce, the literature review and case examples previously examined in this chapter display the problems of managing work distributed over cultural, administrative, geographical, and/or employment status distance. In this section, I will focus on remedies for those problems, focusing on five key HR areas: (a) selection, (b) training and development, (c) task design, (d) compensation, and (e) performance management. Most of the available literature reviewed here focuses on virtual teams, but I will devote attention to the "blended workforce" as well, even if only speculatively.

Selection. In the context of virtual teams, careful selection of the individuals involved may be possible if a new team is being created around a particular project. In other cases, the membership of virtual teams may not be something a manager can realistically control; the task may dictate that certain individuals be chosen. In either case, the composition of the virtual team will affect its work processes and outcomes.

Most authors agree that virtual teams will benefit from selecting for the same general attributes that characterize members of effective face-to-face teams—namely, general cognitive abilities, task-related attributes (e.g., conscientiousness, integrity), and socioemotional attributes (e.g., extroversion, emotional stability, agreeableness) (Barrick, Stewart, Neubert, & Mount, 1998; Neuman & Wright, 1999; Stevens & Campion, 1994). Others argue, however, that teams that are high on a dimension of "virtualness" (e.g., high separation by geographical distance and high reliance on ICT to accomplish team tasks) will require members with additional attributes.

Blackburn, Furst, and Rosen (2003) urged consideration of the KSAs (knowledge, skills, abilities) required by the particular distributed work situation, such as

1. Self-management—self-starting, able to set personal goals and fulfill them in the absence of close supervision, to work in isolation with sporadic feedback, and so forth
2. Communications—sending communications effectively so they are thoroughly understood; choosing the medium in accordance with the nature of the inquiry, task, and timeframe; and proactively gathering and utilizing feedback
3. Cultural sensitivity—actively learning about cultural differences, paying attention to how they might affect group process, and developing norms that foster discussion of cultural differences and how they may be affecting the shared understanding of the problem
4. Technology—a comfort level with the technologies needed to communicate and coordinate over distance, and a willingness to adopt new technologies as needed

These authors also speculated about how personality testing could help with the staffing of virtual teams, suggesting three clusters of traits that would be particularly applicable: (a) ability to set personal goals, take initiative, and work autonomously; (b) capacity for emotional control, high tolerance of ambiguity, and openness to new experience; and (c) listening empathically and cross-cultural sensitivity.

Hertel, Konradt, and Orlikowski (2004) compared attributes of team members in more and less effective virtual teams of an Internet provider company. The authors developed a multiscale questionnaire covering task-related, team-related, and telecommunicating-related attributes and obtained team effectiveness assessments from managers overseeing the teams. These scales showed good reliability and a composite measure, the Virtual Team Competency Inventory, showed a relatively strong correlation (r = 0.40) with team effectiveness measures. Among individual items, measures of self-management skills, intercultural skills, and perceived interpersonal trust made particularly strong contributions.

Diversity of team members is often a central concern at the point of selection. In this context, team members for virtual teams are often selected because of their unique perspective or expertise, as well as knowledge that may itself be derived in part from their geographical location (e.g., about a particular market). Griffith and Neale (2001) proposed that virtual teams will generally have greater diversity than teams whose members are more physically and temporally proximate on three dimensions: (a) informational diversity, (b) social category diversity, and (c) values diversity. Geographical dispersion and functional heterogeneity (common on virtual teams), in combination, will generate both informational and social category diversity. In their view, values diversity arises not due to selection/composition, but because virtual teams may have more difficulty establishing shared values, or at least will require more time for this to be achieved.

Jarvenpaa and Leidner (1999) explored whether certain cultural backgrounds might fit the requirements of virtual teams better than others might. Specifically, they hypothesized that team members from individualistic cultures might be more prone to trust than members from collectivistic cultures because the former have a greater willingness to respond to ambiguous messages. They identified a counterhypothesis: that members from collectivistic cultures might be quicker to identify with a group and hence achieve a shared group identity more readily than individualistic members. Their empirical work showed no effects in either direction. Hertel, Giester, and Konradt (2005) speculated that both individualistic and collectivistic cultures may offer advantages for virtual teamwork; the physical isolation that members may experience during distributed work might be easier for the former group to tolerate, yet the latter group might more frequently initiate interpersonal contact with other team members to alleviate this condition.

Axtell and colleagues (2004) argued that the strongest effects of diversity resulting from selection of virtual team members may come from the combination of multiple dimensions of diversity. This is similar to the notion of multiple sources of distance identified by the CAGE framework. Most research on diversity suggests a U-shaped relationship between degree of differences among team members and team effectiveness; too much diversity can lead to both relationship- and task-related conflict that can be difficult to manage (Pelled et al., 1999; Williams & O'Reilly, 1998).

Furthermore, where members of virtual teams are clustered in different locations, the group at each location is likely to share attributes along multiple dimensions (e.g., nationality, language, function, educational background, socialization experiences) and to strongly differ from the group at another location. This increases the risk of what Lau and Murnighan (1998) called a compositional "faultline"; strong faultlines increase the likelihood of subgroup formation and conflict among subgroups, which can reduce team effectiveness. Hence, there is value in avoiding too much homogeneity at any one location; a moderate level of diversity along multiple dimensions should be sought at each geographical location.

Heckscher and Adler (2006), along with Maccoby (2006), emphasized the importance of selecting individuals that have an "ethic of contribution" and an "interactive social character." "Ethic of contribution" combines two elements: (a) an individual's commitment to contributing to the group's purposes and not simply fulfilling one's own job responsibilities, and (b) a similar commitment to contributing to the success of others, based on understanding their concrete interests and identities and helping them to achieve their personal goals as well as those of the group. Interactive social character is internalized in an individual's motivational system and is manifest in "interdependent self-construals: rather than orienting to a single source of morality and authority, the personality must reconcile multiple conflicting identities and construct a sense of wholeness from competing attachments and interactions" (Heckscher & Adler, p. 17). Whether these traits can be assessed in advance or only become apparent from an individual's performance during a collaborative project is not specified, but clearly, an individual with a track record demonstrating these qualities would be an excellent choice for collaborative distributed work.

I found no literature dealing directly with the selection of contingent, nonstandard workers. Undoubtedly, the specialized knowledge of a high-skilled nonstandard worker is typically the primary basis for selection, while pursuing low cost in choosing nonstandard workers for routine, noncore tasks may dominate any selection considerations. Still, the analysis discussed earlier in this chapter suggests that similarity along certain dimensions can aid the development of shared understanding and shared identity; the common occupational identity of IT contractors and corporate IT professionals is one example. The risk of faultlines between standard and nonstandard workers is high if there is too much homogeneity within each type of worker and too much heterogeneity across the two types.

Training and development.   Blackburn and colleagues (2003) called attention to a variety of areas for training that can support the work of virtual teams: (a) helping teams develop their social capital, learn to use technologies that will help them communicate, and become proactive about monitoring group processes, (b) offering feedback, and (c) checking on group members that seem to be dropping out (inactive, no communication) or not fulfilling responsibilities (tasks not completed on time, or poorly done).

Relatively little research has investigated the impact of training of this kind. Warkentin and Beranek (1999) reported an exploratory study of student teams working on an eight-week project, some of whom received initial face-to-face training on communications aspects of virtual teams. While teams that received this training reported higher cohesion and member satisfaction than the control group, no impact on team performance was found. Hertel and colleagues (2004) reported results from a special 2-day training provided to 10 virtual procurement teams within the same large company. This training focused on three areas: (a) clarification of team goals, (b) effective use of different communications media, and (c) reaching early agreement on team norms and processes (e.g., for project management, conflict resolution, routine communications). Three months later, team members indicated significant improvements in the trained areas and perceived improvements in team performance and team morale/climate. This limited evidence suggests that training designed to support the unique aspects of distributed work, particularly in areas where virtual teams are known to have greater difficulties than face-to-face teams, can be effective.

Research on transactive memory has found that groups whose members have trained together have more developed cognitive systems for organizing their knowledge of who knows what (Liang et al., 1995; Moreland, Argote, & Krishnan, 1998). While this is particularly relevant for virtual teams, it also has implications for a blended workforce. As previously noted, Broschak and Davis-Blake (2006) found that shared training is one way to make employment status differences between standard and nonstandard employees less salient, and hence, to facilitate both shared understanding and shared identity for the two groups.

Toyota and other Japanese companies have greatly increased their use of contract workers in their assembly plants in Japan, to levels as high as 30–35%, in an effort to preserve employment continuity for its core employees while being able to respond to unpredictable swings in market demand. Toyota trains regular and contract workers together and intermingles them on the assembly line (although certain jobs are assigned to younger vs. older workers based on physical demands, and more of the former are contract workers); their uniforms do not identify their employment status (author's field notes). Given the importance of shop-floor problem solving in support of continuous improvement (*kaizen*) to Toyota's core capability of achieving both high quality and high productivity, the company has given careful attention to how to effectively integrate standard and nonstandard workers.

Task design. Research based on experimental designs that compare face-to-face and computer-mediated groups reveals intriguing differences in performance on different kinds of tasks, based on McGrath's (1984) typology of generating (e.g., brainstorming), choosing (e.g., decision making), negotiating, and execution tasks.

Many studies have examined methodologies for electronic brainstorming. This low interdependence task appears to work well when members are physically separated. The software to support electronic brainstorming typically gathers a first set of ideas from all individuals, and then presents each participant with a random set of ideas from the aggregated group, in order to stimulate further idea contributions. Early studies concluded that this approach leads to higher performance because it prevents known motivation and coordination problems associated with proximity (Dennis & Valacich, 1993), such as production blocking (e.g., turn-taking behavior—since only one person can speak at a time—that may prevent someone from voicing their idea) and evaluation apprehension (fear of what others will think of your idea).

Later studies argued against these findings (Pinsonneault, Barki, Gallupe, & Hoppen, 1999; Ziegler, Diehl, & Zijlstra, 2000). Being presented with a list of ideas from other group members early in the brainstorming process may channel subsequent ideas in a particular direction. The anonymity of the process may reduce evaluation apprehensiveness, but it may also reduce engagement in the task and commitment to the group. Finally, the best brainstorming performance (e.g., that which generates the highest number of unique ideas) continues to be demonstrated by nominal groups (e.g., individuals do not actually interact at all during the brainstorming; rather, each individual generates his or her own list, and then these lists are aggregated).

Research on decision-making tasks focuses on computer-mediated processes that allow discussion and multiple rounds of voting to reach a decision. In a 2002 meta-analysis, Baltes, Dickson, Sherman, Bauer, & LaGanke (2002) concluded that computer-mediated decision processes have a number of disadvantages: they take more time, less information is exchanged, and the satisfaction of team members is low. Others argue against this conclusion, because these results are based on ad-hoc teams carrying out a one-time task under experimental conditions. Real virtual teams, with more time to adjust to the effects of geographical dispersion on their decision processes and to learn how best to use technology in support of decision making, might have a different result (Hollingshead & McGrath, 1995; Walther, 2002).

Negotiating tasks are regarded as highly complex, with high interdependence and high needs for communications bandwidth, all of which are provided best in face-to-face situations. Similarly, execution tasks often have a physical logic of collocation, so virtual teams do not usually perform them. Of the relatively few studies conducted on these tasks, results are inconclusive.

The general theme connecting these studies of task design is that virtual teams are well-suited to certain tasks (e.g., idea generation) and not to others (e.g., decision-making)—suggesting that the degree of interdependence of a task may be the critical underlying dimension. High task interdependence requires a great deal of communication and coordination among team members and makes the performance of one member dependent on the performance of other members. Given that virtual teams need to make more effort to communicate and coordinate than face-to-face teams, because of less unplanned interaction and spontaneous communication, less information content, and fewer interpersonal cues during each interaction, virtual teams may do better where less task interdependence is involved. Indeed, as previously noted in this chapter, the modularization of system/product designs and the structuring of work to minimize coordination requirements are primary remedies to problems of geographical distance.

Yet at the same time, high team interdependence tends to be highly associated with team cohesion, trust, and the sense of indispensability of personal contributions to the team. This suggests a possible U-shaped relationship between task interdependence and team performance, with low performance associated with too little or too much interdependence (Kirkman, Rosen, Tesluk, & Gibson, 2004). Hertel and colleagues (2004) investigated this relationship for different stages of a team's development, hypothesizing that high interdependence may be helpful at the start of a team's activities, when norms and routines are being established, whereas at a later stage, teams could benefit from less interdependence so individuals could shift effort from coordination to task completion. They found that interdependence had a strong positive relationship to team effectiveness during the first 12 months, but that the relationship diminished after that point.

For the blended workforce, work structuring is often chosen as a means of reducing task interdependence between standard and nonstandard workers. The same advantages and disadvantages should apply; less task interdependence means minimizing social relations problems, but also less opportunity to build shared understanding and shared identity.

In summary, distributed work characterized by highly interdependent tasks may pose large challenges of coordination and communication, but these tasks may also help those doing the work develop a high degree of shared understanding and shared identity, essentially increasing the capacity to deal with these challenges. Given that it is exactly to accomplish knowledge-intensive, communications-rich collaborative tasks that distributed work is often established, this latter perspective may be most helpful as a guide to practice.

Compensation. Edward Lawler (2003) examined methods for adapting pay/reward systems to the challenges of virtual teams. He distinguished between four types of teams and the reward systems that suit each best: (a) parallel, (b) production/service, (c) project, and (d) management teams. The types most likely to be established as virtual teams are production/service and project teams.[10]

The key differences between production/service and project teams is that the former are often made up of employees who share a particular expertise and perform similar work on an ongoing basis, whereas as the latter are deliberately made up of employees from different areas of expertise (indeed, even different organizations). Each person contributes something different, but according to common goals and processes. For production and service teams, a team bonus is appropriate if the team's tasks are independent, versus if those tasks are heavily interdependent with those of other parts of the organization, in which case a business unit bonus is more appropriate. The risk of maintaining individualized pay for members of production/service teams is that insufficient attention will be paid to the activities that may reduce individual task output but boost the team's overall performance.

Project teams—by far the most common form of virtual team—pose particular compensation challenges. While members are often chosen for their specialized expertise, they often need to learn new things from fellow team members to be able to work with them. Accordingly, project teams are particularly well-suited to knowledge-based (vs. traditional job-based) pay systems. In addition, because projects follow their own timetable, rewards should be tied to achievement of project goals, rather than the traditional approach of a fixed schedule, such as annual performance appraisals and bonus awards. Basing bonuses on objective performance metrics is best, to facilitate goal setting and strengthen performance-to-outcome expectancies.

Where social integration and shared identity are important, team and organizational bonuses are more appropriate than individual bonuses. Lawler (2003) argued that when virtual team members come from different organizations, rewarding team performance may be particularly important. Since most incentives will be aligned to each member's respective organization, such a bonus can reinforce both shared identity and joint accountability for results. This should still be supplemental to rewards provided through each member's home organization, so that there are proper incentives for the member to achieve each organization's goals as well.

In the blended workforce, differentiation in compensation method is often central to the distinction between standard and nonstandard workers (Lautsch, 2003), with the latter often paid on an hourly basis for specified tasks on a particular project and not receiving performance-based pay or any nonmonetary compensation (e.g., benefits, awards, etc.). This difference, along with the ability to end the contract at any time, is central to the flexibility that nonstandard workers provide the firm.

Barley and Kunda (2004) wrote about the tensions between standard and nonstandard workers caused by compensation issues; these become particularly inflamed when IT contractors are collocated and the details of their much-higher (on an hourly basis) pay becomes known to the regular employees. Proximity generally heightens equity comparisons for a relevant and accessible comparative other, and the shared occupational identity between "corporate professionals" and IT contractors that can often facilitate their mutual work here increases the likelihood of perceived inequities.

Performance management. All indications are that virtual teams benefit as much as face-to-face teams from having clear goals and objectives, participating in setting those goals, and receiving performance-related feedback. Explicit feedback from a performance-management system may be particularly important for virtual teams where information about the goal achievements of geographically distributed members is difficult to obtain and opportunities for informal feedback during unscheduled face-to-face encounters are few. Shepherd, Briggs, Reinig, Yen, and Nunamaker (1996) found that including graphical performance feedback in electronic brainstorming groups led to higher performance.

Providing peer assessments as part of this feedback can be helpful in building a stronger sense of group identity. Peer-based performance feedback can help build trust and prevent feelings of exploitation. While a lack of process feedback in computer-mediated groups yields a reduction in social exchange, the provision of such feedback can increase motivation, satisfaction, and performance (Weisband, 2002).

Performance management is rarely a formalized process with respect to nonstandard workers, and regular employees often perceive contract workers as being less committed to the quality of the work being done than are the regular employees (Broschak & Davis-Blake, 2006). In fact, however, contract workers' desire for an ongoing relationship (either a return engagement as a contractor or being hired as a regular employee) makes them potentially very responsive to feedback. Where nonstandard workers are integrated with standard workers on a project, it may be relatively straightforward to engage them in performance-management activities (postproject appraisal by supervisor; peer evaluations). However, this could raise anxieties of regular employees about potential negative consequences for their job or career from this comparative appraisal, and these negative effects may outweigh the positive benefits of feedback to nonstandard workers. This suggests that it may be better to keep appraisal processes of standard and nonstandard workers separate.

Summary. This brief review of HR practices that can support distributed work reveals that, in many cases, the findings are not tremendously different for virtual versus face-to-face teams, nor are they for standard versus nonstandard workers. Furthermore, while there is ample speculation about why the conditions of virtual teams or nonstandard workers might point toward particular choices of HR policies, there is relatively little research at this point to guide those choices.

The Bigger Picture: Employment Policy and Managing Across Distance

The vast array of new approaches to managing distributed work highlighted earlier in this chapter poses important challenges to the prevailing mindsets, regulatory frameworks, and laws associated with employment policy. I will provide a series of examples. The U.S. examples focus on how employment policies are out of step with the reality of blended workforces marked by high employment status distance, while the international examples focus on the challenges of managing employment issues when work is distributed both across geographical and administrative/political distance.

Burton, Bidwell, Fernandez-Mateo, and Kochan (2004) described how U.S. employment policy, with its roots in 1930s New Deal legislation, has taken the individual male breadwinner as the focal employee and the individual employer as a focal actor through which social benefits reach that employee:

> The individual employer is held accountable for complying with the full range of labor and employment laws such as labor relations, health and safety, equal employment opportunity, family and medical leave, etc. Moreover, since the New Deal framework was put in place, individual firms have been expected to provide other functions and benefits, such as health insurance, pensions, and training and development. All of these are predicated on (a) a long-term, ongoing employment relationship; (b) a clear definition of who is the responsible employer; and (c) a clear definition of who is and who is not an employee. (p. 20)

The varying employment relationships now evident in the organizing of distributed work create ambiguity around all of these core definitions.

The consequences of this ambiguity are illustrated by two U.S.-based examples: (a) worker safety in the petrochemical industry and (b) independent contractors in the information technology (IT) industry.

Worker safety in the petrochemical industry. In this setting, negative aspects of the working relationships between regular employees and contractors have resulted in extreme safety violations and deaths (Kochan et al., 1994). Heavy equipment in this highly capital-intensive industry requires regular shutdown periods for maintenance and retooling. Firms hire contractors to supplement maintenance crews and minimize downtime without adding to their full-time workforce. During the 1970s and 1980s, labor costs began to diverge between unionized, full-time employees and nonunion contractors; by 1990, the use of contractors had increased by 15%.

A wide range of employment and labor relations conflicts followed that, according to Burton and colleagues (2004), resulted from petrochemical firms following the advice of their labor lawyers.

> To avoid being liable as the employer or as a co-employer [following the so-called "co-employment doctrine"], there should be a clear separation of the full range of HRM functions (recruitment, selection, training, supervision, labor relations, and compensation) between the regular and contract workforce. This, not surprisingly, led unions in the industry to argue that the growth of contract workers threatened the employment security of their members and indeed the safety of their plants. These debates came to a head in the aftermath of a tragic accident in a Phillips Chemical plant in Pasadena, Texas that killed 22 workers and injured another 220 employees. Contract workers were working on the vessel that exploded and caused the accidents.

> A study commissioned by Congress and the Occupational Safety and Health Administration (OSHA) found that contract workers [in the petrochemical industry] were more likely to experience accidents and injuries in large part because they were less experienced and less well trained than regular employees. Moreover, case-study evidence indicated that many plant managers were aware of the risks associated with increased use of contract workers. These managers, however, were strongly advised to not extend their well-developed safety training and supervisory oversight models to contract workers lest they violate the co-employment doctrine and make their firm liable for the full range of responsibilities (coverage under OSHA [safety], NLRA [worker representation], ERISA [pensions]). Thus, while these oil and chemical companies arguably have some of the most comprehensive and sophisticated safety and health programs in the world, managers were constrained from applying them to the growing subset of workers who were doing some of the most dangerous tasks in their plants. (p. 21)

This study highlights not only the distortions introduced by legal concerns about the co-employment doctrine but also the complex relations that can emerge between regular employees and contractors, working side by side and yet separated by employment status, administrative/political, and cultural distance—in this case, with tragic consequences. Proximity in this situation was not enough to produce either shared understanding or shared identity; instead, it is likely that there was considerable hostility between regular employees and contractors. Not only was the training absent, but the conversations that should have taken place in order to prevent accidents when dealing with dangerous conditions never happened.

Ample evidence can still be found that these problems of distance between regular and contract employees, working side by side, can have catastrophic consequences. The 2005 explosion at a British Petroleum refinery in Texas killed 15 people, all contractors, under conditions similar to those identified in Kochan and colleagues (1994). According to the *Houston Chronicle* (Olsen, 2005),

Increasingly, the accuracy of government safety statistics is undermined by the changing work force. These days, up to half of refinery workers are contractors, who generally get some of the most dangerous jobs. .... The way the U.S. safety statistics are kept, a work site will not generally get a black mark if contractors from other companies are killed or injured there—only if a permanent employee dies or gets hurt. Even though it is contract workers who are often injured or killed, refinery employees are often intimately involved in creating or monitoring working conditions.... If the usual guidelines are followed, none of the 15 people who lost their lives in the refinery fire in Texas City—one of the worst refinery accidents in decades—would be counted as refinery deaths since none worked directly for BP, the refinery owner. (p. A1)

This is not a situation in which regular employees were treated substantially better than contractors. According to the report released by a panel of experts headed by former Secretary of State James A. Baker III,

BP's training of its workers—who operate and oversee some of the most dangerous equipment in the country—falls short of providing them with the expertise they need to safely do their jobs. (Belli, 2007, p. A1)

Tensions and communications breakdowns between regular and contract employees have also been implicated in aviation safety problems, as in the accidents due to inadequate maintenance that shut down Valu-Jet. Rousseau and Libuser (1997) identified two primary ways in which employment status distance can be dangerous in high-risk environments. First, the contingent workers themselves tend to be younger, less experienced, and less well-trained, unfamiliar with both the technical and social systems that underlie task performance in a particular context. Second, organizations often substitute contingent workers for core workers while both maintaining the same organizational structure (without new mechanisms of oversight) and applying HR policies in differentiated fashion to the two groups of workers (contingent workers excluded from practices designed for core workers).

Independent contractors in the IT industry. The rise of itinerant IT professionals working as contractors, documented in Barley and Kunda (2004), poses several policy questions. Contingent employment status in the United States is overwhelmingly characterized by difficulty in obtaining benefits equivalent to those available to full-time employees. This is particularly true with regard to low-skilled temporary workers; data from the Current Population Survey shows that they are much less likely to have either health insurance or pension coverage (Hipple & Stewart, 1996). Barley and Kunda reported that the IT contractors they studied could sometimes obtain health insurance through a spouse, but rarely had any structured means of saving for retirement, whether through a pension plan, a 401k offered through an agency, or individual IRAs, Keogh, and SEP-IRA accounts. While contract agencies do sometimes offer participation in benefit plans to attract contractors, they typically impose a minimum period of working for the agency in order to qualify that is longer than the typical project. Since most contractors do not work continuously with one agency, they often do not qualify.

In the United States, the role of staffing agencies—even for skilled professionals doing repeated engagements with clients they know—has grown tremendously in recent years. Client firms increasingly prefer that contractors have such agencies as an "employer of record." Firms do not want to be held accountable, under the co-employment doctrine, for providing benefits and training to contractors; they also want to avoid IRS scrutiny on whether they are evading payroll taxes by hiring contractors. Given that firms are more reluctant to hire contractors directly and that contractors face high costs if they want to incorporate (so their contracting business can be treated legally as a firm), staffing agencies have a great deal of leverage to demand high fees and markups from both clients and contractors. Hence, the current legal and regulatory environment privileges staffing agencies and disadvantages contractors (Barley & Kunda, 2005).

In contrast, I will now provide two international examples involving challenges for multinational firms in managing their "extended enterprise" across geographical and/or administrative/political boundaries: first, "supplier parks" in the global automotive industry, and second, working conditions at developing country factories in the footwear industry.

Supplier parks in the automotive industry. An interesting variant on the combination of geographical proximity with employment status distance can be found in the rise of supplier parks or "industrial consortium" models of collocated production in the auto industry. In these settings, regular employees of an automaker work in close proximity with regular employees of multiple suppliers, either in separate buildings on the same physical site or at the extreme, side by side on a final assembly line, with each supplier adding their own component and the automaker overseeing quality assurance.

Among these individuals, equity comparisons on wages, benefits, and working conditions happen readily. In some cases, the automaker with administrative responsibility for this clustered production site has found it necessary to impose a single set of employment policies for the site in order to avoid the negative consequences of unfavorable comparisons that lead to worker discontent. This has usually taken the form of moving to the greatest—rather than the lowest—common denominator, with supplier employees receiving the same wages and benefits as automaker employees (Sako, 2004). At times, governments—which are often asked to subsidize the creation of these sites—require common conditions for all employees vis-à-vis access to training, and so forth. Here, geographical proximity creates pressure for minimizing employment status and administrative distance in relation to employment policies.

Working conditions in footwear factories. A very different employment policy issue concerns the responsibilities of a firm that has distributed work to suppliers in other countries for the labor standards experienced by the employees of those suppliers. As more and more firms subcontract their manufacturing to low-cost suppliers, concerns about the exploitative conditions that may lie behind the production of high-margin branded products have caught the attention of nongovernmental organizations (NGOs) and, increasingly, the public. There is no clear regulatory jurisdiction over this issue, although countries that are signatories to certain United Nations declarations and International Labor Organization (ILO) covenants have ostensibly made some commitment to minimal labor standards.

Nevertheless, some multinational corporations (MNCs), such as Nike, stung by the negative effects of publicity about sweatshop factories making their products, have established labor codes of conduct for their suppliers, and then either worked with NGO watchdog groups, or directly established their own staff to monitor supplier compliance with these codes (Locke & Ramis, 2007). The effectiveness of these monitoring activities is still unclear; however, some recent research suggests that when MNCs involve their suppliers in programs to improve quality and productivity through the application of new operations processes and human resource methods, labor conditions improve more quickly than with monitoring alone (Locke, Qin, & Brause, 2006). This occurs, arguably, because the high level of interaction between MNCs and suppliers on these operational issues replaces a low-trust environment of monitoring and compliance with richer forms of communication to achieve mutually beneficial goals, while highlighting the importance of how workers are managed to achieving those goals. Furthermore, this interaction is well-designed to build both shared understanding and shared identity.

Summary. The multiplicity of new employment arrangements associated with distributed work makes it imperative to reexamine employment policies based on old assumptions about a primary breadwinner working at a single employer throughout a long career. The United States and other advanced economies will need new policies supporting work engagements of shorter duration, across multiple employers/clients, and involving different kinds of employment status that do not neglect the important social benefits provided to individuals and their families—and hence, to the stability of communities and societies—associated with the old model.

Looking Ahead: The Research Agenda for Managing People Over Multiple Types of Distance

What Is Missing/Lacking in the Current Literature

The most fundamental critique that this chapter makes of the existing research on distributed work is that it does not explicitly take into account multiple types of distance. This is primarily by design, in order to focus on one type of distance and to facilitate operationalization of variables. Clearly, many researchers are aware of the phenomenon; this quote from Metiu (2006) is representative: "In distributed work, geographical distance and social distance can reinforce each other, with negative consequences for intergroup cooperation" (p. 420).

Researchers studying conflict in virtual teams are particularly aware of the consequences of diversity of team membership along multiple dimensions—that is, national and organizational cultural differences as well as ascriptive characteristics of gender, race, or age (e.g., Mannix et al., 2002). Researchers of nonstandard work do explore issues of employment status distance between regular employees and contingent workers, although they tend to frame this issue more in terms of conflict and the consequences for organizational commitment, citizenship behaviors, propensity to turnover (e.g., George, 2003). The consequences of distance, however, in any of these dimensions, are both cognitive and affective; distance makes it difficult to attain both shared understanding (of task, context, where knowledge resides) and shared identity (which, in turn, affects motivation, commitment, and discretionary effort). It is critical, in my view, to develop a twinned cognitive and affective focus for the consequences of distance and the adaptations, remedies, and strategies for countering distance.

Greater attention to the coinciding and overlapping of multiple forms of distance is also needed. I would argue that the CAGE typology and "distance inventory" mechanism can be helpful to researchers attempting to understand these new phenomena. Important issues will have to be addressed for these to have value in empirical research, for example, how to reliably measure these different types of distance, how to define them distinctly in a way that will have traction across diverse settings, and how they interact with each other. The concept of administrative distance—my adaptation of Ghemawat's administrative/political distance in the context of a country-level analysis—seems particularly complicated to more precisely define, as well as operationalize, but it responds directly to the important phenomenon of organizational disaggregation that has spawned a huge array of new interorganizational work arrangements. None of the other types quite pick up what administrative distance does—namely, the consequences of having to carry out distributed work across many layers of administrative systems and multiple organizational boundaries.

Implicit in the discussion of adaptations, remedies, and countervailing strategies is the idea that dealing effectively with one type of distance (either through minimizing it or through increasing capacity for dealing with it) can *compensate* for the negative effects of other types of distance. This idea needs considerable development, both conceptually and in terms of measurement issues. To what extent (and in what situations) does a given remedy help in dealing with multiple types of distance simultaneously, and to what extent are there tradeoffs? Framing issues of distance in this way may allow for contingent hypothesizing that comes closer to addressing the variegated and ever-evolving phenomena of distributed work.

In terms of research design, it is imperative that more studies be done that directly compare two situations that vary with respect to distance, but otherwise share a context (e.g., task or organization). It is striking how many studies of virtual teams compare differences within a sample of such teams, but do not make any comparison to collocated teams. In such a design, it is easy to exaggerate the effects of distance (in this case, geographical distance). By now, there is ample evidence that virtual teams can be understood within the set of constructs and theories developed for face-to-face groups, so designs that allow comparison along the dimension of distance are critical to advance research on distributed work. Methodologically, research designs that allow for tests of moderating or mediating effects are important, particularly in light of the emphasis here on both distance-minimizing and capacity-enhancing ways of dealing with distance. The series of studies by Hinds and Mortensen (2002, 2005) are exemplary illustrations of such an approach.

A final suggestion on dealing with the complexity of multiple forms of distance is to frame the issue differently. Given the reality of work distributed across multiple forms of distance, what does it take to create the conditions for individuals and groups to interact effectively? Put differently, if we imagine these interactions as "conversations," how can managers make sure that good conversations happen, among the right mix of the right people at the right time, in order to accomplish knowledge-intensive collaborative tasks?

A growing body of research focuses on managerial work as conversations, which can be a resource for creative new approaches to studying distance. I would particularly recommend Lester and Piore (2004) on the role of conversations in innovation; Hardy, Lawrence, and Grant (2005) on how shared identity emerges from conversations to facilitate interorganizational collaborations; Quinn and Dutton (2005) on coordination as "energy-in-conversation," with their emphasis on the emotional and affective—as well as cognitive—components of coordinating distributed work; Gratton and Ghoshal (2002) on creating higher quality conversations, in which people can learn something new about themselves or others, or arrive at creative solutions to problems; Helper,

MacDuffie, and Sabel (2000) on "pragmatic collaboration" in supplier relations in the global automotive industry, with in its emphasis on how conversations leading to effective collaboration can take place even in the absence of preexisting trust or shared norms and values; and Kellogg, Orlikowski, and Yates' (2006) ethnographic study highlighting the role of a "trading zone" (see also Galison, 1997) in facilitating coordination of ideas and actions.

Promising Questions and High-Priority Issues for Further Study

This chapter hopes to leave the reader more aware of what we do know about managing people over distance, as well as what we do not know. We know a lot about the beneficial effects of proximity for small group process, but we do not have a good way to think about the difficulties that arise when other forms of distance (e.g., cultural, employment status) exist among collocated individuals. We know a lot about what is more difficult for virtual teams than for face-to-face teams, but not as much about how virtual teams may adapt and innovate over time in response to these difficulties, both by finding ways to minimize distance and ways to increase their capacity to handle distance. We know that the different kinds of distance often coexist in a given situation, but not as much about how they interact, whether particular clusters of distance characteristics have distinctive consequences, or the extent to which minimizing one type of distance may compensate for the continued presence of other types of distance.

Certain themes recur in this examination of distributed work. Having a shared experience (e.g., training, looking at a design, creating a shared database) can build both shared understanding and shared identity among those working on a distributed task. Certain social cues are lost when virtual teams do their work, but in their absence, other social dimensions of the group process—including identification with the team—can intensify. Trust and shared values can provide an important foundation for meaningful conversations that bridge various types of distance, yet it is possible to create a context, ground rules, and a set of interdependent task processes that allow trust to emerge and strengthen over time, even where it does not exist in advance.

When it comes to HR policies, much of what we know about selection, training, compensation, and performance management seems to be applicable to distributed work once we correctly identify characteristics of the task being carried out. Complex interdependent tasks are difficult for virtual teams, yet these are the tasks that we most often need such teams to perform. In addition, working together on such tasks helps team members develop shared understanding and shared identity more rapidly than easily separable tasks. Employment policies are still primarily keyed to long-term relationships between a single firm and a full-time employee, yet they are rendered irrelevant at best and dysfunctional at worst by the bewildering range of new ways of organizing work. These new forms are short-term and project-focused, involve multiple firms, and combine contractors (independent and brokered) and employees (full-time and part-time, new and high-seniority) in countless permutations.

Clearly, the issues discussed here reach well beyond the scope of the HR function, as it is usually conceived. Managers can take a variety of steps to deal effectively with different types of distance, many of which could not easily be delegated to HR or incorporated into ongoing HR processes. Among these are the following:

1. During selection, when facing heterogeneity on some dimensions (e.g., national origin, company affiliation, demographic characteristics), look for similarity on other attributes (e.g., education, occupational identity, hobbies).

2. In the face of geographical distance, arrange for members of a virtual team to share certain experiences (e.g., combined training; learning collaborator-specific routines and preferences; simultaneous scrutiny of a digitalized design).

3. Over a multistage project, make careful choices about when to apply the power of proximity (e.g., intensive face-to-face interaction, not only at the start but when shared understanding and shared identity are sufficiently well-developed and task interdependence is at its highest point).

4. Choose to maintain an ongoing—if episodic—work relationship with nonstandard workers (rather than accepting high churn in order to minimize costs), to maintain access to their knowledge and to preserve their working relationships with other key full-time employees.

All of these situations require managerial judgment, attentiveness to the dynamics of distributed work, and awareness of the implications of different types of distance.

Thinking imaginatively about distance also requires creativity and a willingness to embrace the apparent paradoxes of distributed work—to make sense of situations where these familiar statements about distance can all be true: "so near, yet so far," "out of sight, out of mind," and "absence makes the heart grow fonder." The world is generating new distance-related phenomena for us to study with each passing day. We have rich traditions of research, ample theories, a versatile array of methods, and an ever-deeper appreciation of the adaptive capacities of individuals, groups, and organizations, all of which we can draw upon for this important endeavor. We had better get going if we hope to keep up!

Endnotes

1. Some studies attempt global assessments of these impacts (e.g., the McKinsey Global Institute study; Farrell et al., 2006), while others take a domestic focus (e.g., forthcoming National Academy of Sciences and National Academy of Engineering studies of the impact of offshoring on both the United States economy's innovation capability and labor market and career prospects for U.S. engineers).

2. *Transnational* is Bartlett and Ghoshal's (1998) terminology for an approach to structuring a global company—moving beyond "multidomestic" and "multinational" approaches—that combines legal consolidation and geographical dispersion.

3. For a more extended treatment of the research issues surrounding nonstandard work, see Ashford, George, and Blatt, chapter 2, in this volume.

4. Kiesler and Cummings (2002) opened their review with an intriguing historical observation. In the early days of group dynamics research pioneered by Kurt Lewin and his colleagues, social psychologists were deeply immersed in understanding the microdynamics of interaction in small, collocated, face-to-face groups. "A social psychologist in the 1960s, when speaking of proximity, might be talking about the seating arrangements at a table of diners, among a jury, or a committee" (p. 58). From this starting point, it was natural to devote a great deal of research attention to the role of proximity in small groups.

5. That such a threshold effect exists means that the effects of geographical distance do not increase monotonically, as we might assume. In terms of spontaneous communication and unplanned interaction, the other side of the city (or campus) can be as far away as halfway around the world—although the potential for planned/intentional face-to-face interaction is obviously more directly related to physical distance.

6. This literature predicted that videoconferencing would provide a richer medium for dealing with geographical distance by providing both visual and verbal cues, albeit accompanied by nuance-defeating side effects such as delay, fuzzy resolution, limited visual scope, and so forth. Subsequent research, however, has found videoconferencing to have disappointing and, at times, negative effects, even as the technology has improved. Indeed, this research shows that teleconferencing phone calls—once all participants recognize each other's voices—can be more effective at communicating nuances of meaning and emotion than videoconferencing. Whether Internet 2-powered videoconferencing (the new buzzword is "telepresence") can achieve more nuanced communication among distributed work groups remains to be seen.

7. I will focus primarily on what is possible in this "best-case scenario" for virtual teams, in terms of problems and related adaptations/remedies for those problems. At the same time, it should be acknowledged that many individuals may experience virtual teams as short-term and unstable, may not be aware of who is and is not a member (Mortensen & Hinds, 2002), and could even be members of multiple virtual teams (as well as collocated teams) at the same time, each making competing demands. The problems of virtual teams reported here are certainly going to be much exacerbated under such volatile conditions—but collocated teams might also suffer under these conditions.

8. Virtual teams are still a relatively new phenomenon and some of these problems could be regarded as those of an immature organizational form. Armstrong and Cole (1995) provided an early in-depth study of virtual teams that revealed a staggering number of problems. In an addendum to a reprint of this study, Armstrong and Cole (2002) stated that "most distributed groups do not attain the ideal of being a real team: a work group with a stable and defined membership that has established a shared working process in the pursuit of a common goal that they can only achieve together (Hackman et al., 2000)" (p. 189). At the same time, "we have been impressed with the qualities of those distributed groups that *have* become real teams..., modest in size and stable over time so the members get to know each other and establish a track record" (p. 189). Similarly, many of the "lack of social context" findings from the early research on e-mail (e.g., Constant, Sproull, & Kiesler, 1986)—for example, the high incidence of uninhibited "flaming"—seem to be moderated in today's e-mail usage, given the developments of norms for e-mail that are either reinforced by ongoing personal relationships or enforced by institutionally established means (from Web site monitors to automated filters).

9. Given that organizations often determine or influence the location where an employee works, Reskin's (2003) argument may also help explain why individual self-identification tied to site/location is so powerful and often competes successfully with virtual team membership to influence an individual's sense of shared identity.

10. Parallel teams carry out part-time activities involving specific problem-solving activities, such as quality circles or suggestion teams, whereas management teams are collectively responsible for supervising particular activities or people; both rarely appear as virtual teams.

References

Abraham, K. G., & Taylor, S. K. (1996). Firms' use of outside contractors: Theory and evidence. *Journal of Labor Economics, 14,* 394–434.

Allen, T. (1977). *Managing the flow of technology.* Cambridge, MA: MIT Press.

Applebaum, E., & Batt, R. (1994). *Transforming work systems in the United States.* Ithaca, NY: ILR Press.

Armstrong, D. J., & Cole, P. (1995). Managing distances and differences in geographically distributed work groups. In S. E. Jackson, & M. N. Ruderman (Eds.), *Diversity in work teams: Research paradigms for a changing workplace* (pp. 187–215). Washington, DC: American Psychological Association.

Armstrong, D. J., & Cole, P. (2002). Managing distances and differences in geographically distributed work groups. In P. Hinds, & S. Kiesler (Eds.), *Distributed work* (pp. 167–186). Cambridge, MA: MIT Press.

Arthur, J. B. (1992). The link between business strategy and industrial relations systems in American steel minimills. *Industrial and Labor Relations Review, 45,* 488–506.

Arthur, M. B., & Rousseau, D. M. (Eds.). (2001). *The boundaryless career: A new employment principle for a new organizational era.* New York: Oxford University Press.

Ashford, S. J., George, E., & Blatt, R. (2007). Old assumptions, new work: The opportunities and challenges of research on nonstandard employment. In J. P. Walsh, & A. Brief (Eds.), *Annals of the Academy of Management* (Vol. 1, pp. 65–118). New York: LEA.

Autor, D. H. (2001). Why do temporary help firms provide free general skills training? *Quarterly Journal of Economics, 116,* 1409–1449.

Axtell, C. M., Fleck, S. J., & Turner, N. (2004). Virtual teams: Collaborating across distance. In C. L. Cooper, & I. T. Robertson (Eds.), *International review of industrial and organizational psychology* (Vol. 19, pp. 205–248). Chichester, U.K.: Wiley.

Azoulay, P. (2004). Capturing knowledge within and across firm boundaries: Evidence from clinical development. *American Economic Review, 94,* 1591–1612.

Bailey, D. E., & Kurland, N. B. (2002). A review of telework research: Findings, new directions, and lessons for the study of modern work. *Journal of Organizational Behavior, 23,* 383–400.

Baltes, B. B., Dickson, M. W., Sherman, M. P., Bauer, C. C., & LaGanke, J. S. (2002). Computer-mediated communication and group decision making: A meta-analysis. *Organizational Behavior and Human Decision Processes, 87,* 156–179.

Barley, S. R., & Kunda, G. (2001). Bringing work back in. *Organization Science, 12,* 76–95.

Barley, S. R., & Kunda, G. (2004). *Gurus, hired guns, and warm bodies: Itinerant experts in a knowledge economy.* Princeton, NJ: Princeton University Press.

Barley, S. R., & Kunda, G. (2006). Contracting: A new form of professional practice. *Academy of Management Perspective, 19,* 1–19.

Barrick, M. R., Stewart, G. L., Neubert, M. J., & Mount, M. K. (1998). Relating member ability and personality to work-team processes and team effectiveness. *Journal of Applied Psychology, 83,* 377–391.

Bartlett, C. A., & Ghoshal, S. (1998). *Managing across borders: The transnational solution.* (2nd ed.) Boston: Harvard Business School Press.

Batt, R. (1999). Work organization, technology, and performance in customer service and sales. *Industrial and Labor Relations Review, 52,* 539–564.

Batt, R. (2002). Managing customer services: Human resource practices, quit rates, and sales growth. *Academy of Management Journal, 45,* 587–597.

Befort, R. S. (2003). Revisiting the black hole of workplace regulation: A historical and comparative perspective of contingent work. *Berkeley Journal of Employment and Labor Law, 24,* 153–179.

Belli, A. (2007, January, 21). BP workers ill-trained for dangers, report says: Baker panel criticizes lack of hands-on exercises. *Houston Chronicle,* p. A1.

Bhappu, A., Griffith, T. L., & Northcraft, G. B. (1997). Media effects and communication bias in diverse groups. *Organizational Behavior and Human Decision Processes, 70,* 199–205.

Bidwell, M. (2006a). *Do peripheral workers do peripheral work? A test of internal labor market theory using information technology consultants.* Fontainebleau, France: INSEAD.

Bidwell, M. (2006b). *Reworking contingent employment.* Fontainebleau, France: INSEAD.

Blackburn, R., Furst, S., & Rosen, B. (2003). Building a winning virtual team. KSAs, selection, training, and evaluation. In C. B. Gibson, & S. G. Cohen (Eds.), *Virtual teams that work: Creating conditions for virtual team effectiveness* (pp. 95–120). San Francisco: Jossey-Bass.

Blinder, A. S. (2006). Offshoring: The next industrial revolution. *Foreign Affairs, 85*, 113.

Bradley, M., Schipani, C. A., Sundaram, A. K., & Walsh, J. P. (1999). The purposes and accountability of the corporation in contemporary society: Corporate governance at a crossroads. *Law Contemporary Problems, 62*, 9–85.

Brewer, M. B., & Miller, N. (1996). *Intergroup relations*. Buckingham, U.K.: Open University Press.

Broschak, J. P., & Davis-Blake, A. (2006). Mixing standard work and nonstandard deals: The consequences of heterogeneity in employment arrangements. *Academy of Management Journal, 49*, 371–393.

Burton, D., Bidwell, M., Fernandez-Mateo, I., & Kochan, T. A. (2004). *HRM challenges for managing varied employment relationships: IT employees, independent contractors, and consultants*. Cambridge, MA: MIT Institute of Work and Employment Relations.

Cappelli, P. (1999). *The new deal at work: Managing the market-driven workforce*. Boston: Harvard Business School Press.

Cappelli, P., & Neumark, D. (2001). Do "high performance" work practices improve establishment-level outcomes? *Industrial and Labor Relations Review, 54*, 737–775.

Carlson, J. R., & Zmud, R. W. (1999). Channel expansion theory and the experiential nature of media richness perceptions. *Academy of Management Journal, 42*, 153–170.

Child, J. (2001). Trust—the fundamental bond in global collaboration. *Organizational Dynamics, 29*, 274–288.

Constant, D., Sproull, L., & Kiesler, S. (1996). The kindness of strangers: On the usefulness of weak ties for technical advice. *Organization Science, 7*, 119–135.

Cramton, C. D. (2001). The mutual knowledge problem and its consequences for dispersed collaboration. *Organization Science, 12*, 346–371.

Cramton, C. D. (2002). Finding common ground in dispersed collaboration. *Organizational Dynamics, 30*, 356–367.

Culnan, M. J., & Markus, L. M. (1987). Information technologies. In F. M. Jablin, L. L. Putnam, K. H. Roberts, & L. W. Porter (Eds.), *Handbook of organizational communication: An interdisciplinary perspective* (pp. 420–443). London: Sage.

Daft, R., and Lengel, R. (1986). Organizational information requirements, media richness, and structural design. *Management Science, 32*, 554–571.

Davis-Blake, A., Broschak, J. P., & George, E. (2003). Happy together? How using nonstandard workers affects exit, voice, and loyalty among standard employees. *Academy of Management Journal, 46*, 475–485.

De Dreu, C. K. W., & Weingart, L. R. (2003). Task versus relationship conflict and team effectiveness: A meta analysis. *Journal of Applied Psychology, 88*, 741–749.

Delery, J. E., & Doty, D. H. (1996). Modes of theorizing in strategic human resource management: Tests of universalistic, contingency, and configurational performance predictions. *Academy of Management Journal, 39*, 802–835.

de Lisser, E. (1999, October 5). Update on small business: Firms with virtual environments appeal to workers. *Wall Street Journal*, B2.

Dennis, A. R., & Valacich, J. S. (1993). Computer brainstorms: More heads are better than one. *Journal of Applied Psychology, 4*, 531–537.

DiMaggio, P. (2001). *The twenty-first century firm: Changing economic organization in international perspective*. Princeton, NJ: Princeton University Press.

Dossani, R., & Kenney, M. (2006). Reflections upon "sizing the emerging global labor market." *Academy of Management Perspectives, 20*, 35–41.

Dougherty, D. (1992). Interpretive barriers to successful product innovation in large firms. *Organization Science, 13*, 77–92.

Eppinger, S. D. (2001). Innovation at the speed of information. *Harvard Business Review, 79*, 149–158.

Farrell, D., Laboissiere, M. A., & Rosenfeld, J. (2006, November). Sizing the emerging global labor market: Rational behavior from both companies and countries can help it work more efficiently. *Academy of Management Perspectives*, 23–34.

Fixson, S. (2005). Product architecture assessment: A tool to link product, process, and supply chain design decisions. *Journal of Operations Management, 23*, 345–369.

Forsyth, D. (1998). *Group dynamics*. Pacific Grove, CA: Brooks/Cole.

Freedman, J. L. (1975). *Crowding and behavior*. San Francisco: Freeman.

Friedman, T. L. (2005). *The world is flat*. New York: Farrar, Straus, and Giroux.

Galison, P. (1997). *Image and logic: A material culture of microphysics*. Chicago: University of Chicago Press.

Geary, J. F. (1992). Employment flexibility and human resource management: The case of three American electronics plants. *Work, Employment and Society, 7*, 213–225.

George, E. (2003). External solutions and internal problems: The effects of employment externalization on internal workers' attitudes. *Organization Science, 14*, 386–402.

George, E., & Chattopadhyay, P. (2005). One foot in each camp: The dual identification of contract workers. *Administrative Science Quarterly, 50*, 68–99.

Ghemawat, P. (2001, September). Distance still matters: The hard reality of global expansion. *Harvard Business Review*, 1–10.

Gibson, C. B., & Cohen, S. G. (Eds.). (2003). *Virtual teams that work: Creating conditions for virtual team effectiveness*. San Francisco: Jossey-Bass.

Gratton, L., & Ghoshal, S. (2002). Improving the quality of conversations. *Organizational Dynamics, 31*, 209–223.

Griffith, T. L., & Neale, M. A. (2001). Information processing in traditional, hybrid, and virtual teams: From nascent knowledge to transactive memory. In M. A. Neale, E. A. Mannix, and T. L. Griffith (Eds.), *Research in organizational behavior* (Vol. 23, pp. 379–421). Amsterdam: Jai-Elsevier Science.

Hackman, J. R., Wageman, R., Ruddy, T. M., & Ray, C. R. (2000). Team effectiveness in theory and practice. In C. Cooper, & E. A. Locke (Eds.), *Industrial and organizational psychology: Theory and practice* (pp. 109–129). Oxford, U.K.: Blackwell.

Handy, C. (1995). Trust and the virtual organization. *Harvard Business Review, 73*, 40–50.

Hansen, M. (1999). The search-transfer problem: The role of weak ties in sharing knowledge across organization subunits. *Administrative Science Quarterly, 44*, 82–111.

Hardy, C., Lawrence, T., & Grant, D. (2005). Discourse and collaboration: The role of conversations and collective identity. *Academy of Management Review, 30*, 58–77.

Harrison, A. E., & McMillan, M. S. (2006). Dispelling some myths about offshoring. *Academy of Management Perspectives, 20*, 6–22.

Heckscher, C., & Adler, P. A. (Eds.). (2006). *The form as collaborative community: Reconstructing trust in the knowledge economy.* Oxford, U.K.: Oxford University Press.

Helper, S., & Khambete, S. (2006). *Off-shoring, interfaces, and collaboration across the supply chain: A case study in automotive product development.* Cleveland, OH: Case Western Reserve University.

Helper, S., MacDuffie, J. P., & Sabel, C. (2000). Pragmatic collaborations: Advancing knowledge while controlling opportunism. *Industrial and Corporate Change, 9*, 443–487.

Hertel, G., Giester, S., & Konradt, U. (2005). Managing virtual teams: A review of current empirical research. *Human Resource Management Review, 15*, 69–95.

Hertel, G., Konradt, U., & Orlikowski, B. (2004). Managing distance by interdependence: Goal setting, task interdependence, and team-based rewards in virtual teams. *European Journal of Work and Organizational Psychology, 13*, 1–28.

Hinds, P., & Bailey, D. (2003). Out of sight, out of sync: Understanding conflict in distributed teams. *Organization Science, 14*, 615–632.

Hinds, P., & Mortensen, M. (2002). *Distributed work.* Cambridge, MA: MIT Press.

Hinds, P., & Mortensen, M. (2005). Understanding conflict in distributed teams: An empirical investigation. *Organization Science, 16*, 290–307.

Hinds, P. J., & Weisband, S. P. (2003). Knowledge sharing and shared understanding in virtual teams. In C. B. Gibson, & S. G. Cohen (Eds.), *Virtual teams that work: Creating conditions for effective virtual teams* (pp. 21–36). San Francisco: Jossey-Bass.

Hipple, S., & Stewart, J. (1996). Earnings and benefits of workers in alternative work arrangements. *Monthly Labor Review, 119*, 46–54.

Hitt, M. A., Ireland, R. D., & Harrison, J. S. (1991). Effects of acquisitions on R&D inputs and outputs. *Academy of Management Journal, 34*, 693–706.

Hogg, M. A. (1992). *The social psychology of group cohesiveness: From attraction to social identity.* New York: New York University Press.

Hollingshead, A. B. (1998). Retrieval processes in transactive memory systems. *Journal of Personality and Social Psychology, 74*, 659–671.

Hollingshead, A. B., Fulk, J., & Monge, P. (2002). Fostering intranet knowledge sharing: An integration of transactive memory and public goods approaches. In P. Hinds, & S. Kiesler (Eds.), *Distributed work* (pp. 335–356). Cambridge, MA: MIT Press.

Hollingshead, A., & McGrath, J. (1995). Computer-assisted groups: A critical review of the empirical research. In R. Guzzo, & E. Salas (Eds.), *Team Effectiveness and decision-making in organizations* (pp. 46–78). San Francisco: Jossey-Bass.

Houseman, S. N. (2001). Why employers use flexible staffing arrangements: Evidence from an establishment survey. *Industrial and Labor Relations Review, 55,* 149–170.

Huselid, M. A. (1995). The impact of human resource management practices on turnover, productivity, and corporate financial performance. *Academy of Management Journal, 38,* 635–672.

Ichniowski, C., Shaw, K., & Prennushi, G. (1997). The effects of human resource management practices on productivity. *American Economic Review, 87,* 291–313.

Jarvenpaa, S. L., & Leidner, D. E. (1999). Communication and trust in global virtual teams. *Organization Science, 10,* 791–815.

Jehn, K. A. (1997). Qualitative analysis of conflict types and dimensions in organizational groups. *Administrative Science Quarterly, 42,* 530–557.

Jehn, K. A., Northcraft, G. B., & Neale, M. A. (1999). Why differences make a difference: A field study of diversity, conflict, and performance in workgroups. *Administrative Sciences Quarterly, 44,* 741–763.

Jones, C. (2004). *Teleworking: The quiet revolution.* Report published by The Gartner Group.

Kalleberg, A. (2000). Nonstandard employment relations: Part-time, temporary, and contract work. *Annual Review of Sociology, 26,* 341–65.

Kalleberg, A. L., Reskin, B., & Hudson, K. (2000). Bad jobs in America: Standard and nonstandard employment relations and job quality in the United States. *American Sociological Review, 65,* 256–278.

Kang, S., Morris, S. S., & Snell, S. A. (2007). Relational archetypes, organizational learning, and value creation: Extending the human resource architecture. *Academy of Management Review, 32,* 236–256.

Kanter, R. M. (1990). The new managerial work. *Harvard Business Review, 67,* 85–92.

Kellogg, K. C., Orlikowski, W. J., & Yates, J. (2006). Life in the trading zone: Structuring coordination across boundaries in postbureaucratic organizations. *Organization Science, 17,* 22–44.

Kiesler, S., & Cummings, J. N. (2002). What do we know about proximity and distance in work groups? A legacy of research. In P. Hinds, & S. Kiesler (Eds.), *Distributed work* (pp. 57–82). Cambridge, MA: MIT Press.

Kirkman, B. L., Rosen, B., Tesluk, P. E., & Gibson, C. B. (2004). The impact of team empowerment on virtual team performance: The moderating role of face-to-face interaction. *Academy of Management Journal, 47,* 175–192.

Kochan, T. A., Smith, M., Wells, J. C., & Rebitzer, J. B. (1994). Human resource strategies and contingent workers: The case of safety and health in the petrochemical industry. *Human Resource Management, 33,* 55–77.

Kogut, B., & Zander, U. (1992). Knowledge of the firm, combinative capabilities, and the replication of technology. *Organization Science, 3,* 383–397.

Krauss, R. M., & Fussell, S. R. (1990). Mutual knowledge and communicative effectiveness. In J. Galegher, R. E. Kraut, & C. Egido (Eds.), *Intellectual teamwork: Social and technical bases of collaborative work* (pp. 111–146). Hillsdale, NJ: Erlbaum.

Krauss, R. E., Fussell, S. R., Brennan, S. E., & Siegel, J. (2002). Understanding effects of proximity on collaboration: Implications for technologies to support remote collaborative work. In P. Hinds, & S. Kiesler (Eds.), *Distributed work* (pp. 137–164). Cambridge, MA: MIT Press.

Kraut, R., & Streeter, L. (1995). Coordination in software development. *Communications of the ACM, 38*, 69–81.

Kunda, G., Barley, S. R., & Evans, J. (2002). Why do contractors contract? The experience of highly skilled technical professionals in a contingent labor market. *Industrial & Labor Relations Review, 55*, 234–261.

Lau, D., & Murnighan, K. (1998). Demographic diversity and faultlines: The compositional dynamics of organizational groups. *Academy of Management Review, 23*, 325–240.

Lautsch, B. (2003). The influence of regular work systems on compensation for contingent workers. *Industrial Relations, 42*, 565–588.

Lawler, E. E., III (2003). Pay systems for virtual teams. In C. B. Gibson, & S. G. Cohen (Eds.), *Virtual teams that work: Creating conditions for effective virtual teams* (pp. 121–144). San Francisco: Jossey-Bass.

Lepak, D. P., & Snell, S. A. (1999). The human resource architecture: Toward a theory of human capital allocation and development. *Academy of Management Review, 24*, 31–48.

Lester, R. K., & Piore, M. J. (2004). *Innovation: The missing dimension.* Boston: Harvard University Press.

Liang, D. W., Moreland, R., & Argote, L. (1995). Group versus individual training and group performance: The mediating factor of transactive memory. *Personality and Social Psychology Bulletin, 21*, 384–393.

Locke, R., Qin, F., & Brause, A. (2006). *Does monitoring improve labor standards? Lessons from Nike* (Working Paper No. 4612–06). Cambridge, MA: MIT Sloan School of Management.

Locke, R., & Ramis, M. (2007). Improving work conditions in a global supply chain. *MIT Sloan Management Review, 48*, 54–62.

Maccoby, M. (2006). The self in transition: From bureaucratic to interactive social character. In C. Heckscher, & P. A. Adler (Eds.), *The form as collaborative community: Reconstructing trust in the knowledge economy* (pp. 157–176). Oxford, U.K.: Oxford University Press.

MacDuffie, J. P. (1995). Human resource bundles and manufacturing performance: Organizational logic and flexible production systems in the world auto industry. *Industrial and Labor Relations Review, 48*, 197–221.

MacDuffie, J. P., and Helper, S. (2006). Collaboration in supply chains: With and without trust. In C. Heckscher, & P. A. Adler (Eds.), *The form as collaborative community: Reconstructing trust in the knowledge economy* (pp. 417–466). Oxford, U.K.: Oxford University Press.

Mannix, E. A., Griffith, T., & Neale, M. (2002). The phenomenonology of conflict in distributed work teams. In P. Hinds, & S. Kiesler (Eds.), *Distributed work* (pp. 213–234). Cambridge, MA: MIT Press.

Mathieu, J., Goodwin, G. F., Heffner, T. S., Salas, E., & Cannon-Bowers, J. A. (2000). The influence of shared mental models on team process and performance. *Journal of Applied Psychology, 85*, 273–283.

Matusik, S. F., & Hill, C. W. L. (1998). The utilization of contingent work, knowledge creation, and competitive advantage. *Academy of Management Review, 23*, 680–697.

McDonough, E. F., Kahn, K. B., & Griffin, A. (1999). Managing communication in global product development teams. *IEEE Transactions on Engineering Management, 46*, 375–386.

McGrath, J. E. (1984). *Groups: Interaction and performance*. Englewood Cliffs, NJ: Prentice-Hall.

McGrath, J. E., & Hollingshead, A. B. (1994). *Groups interacting with technology: Ideas, evidence, issues, and an agenda*. Thousand Oaks, CA: Sage.

McKnight, D. H., Cummings, L. L., & Chervany, N. L. (1998). Initial trust formation in new organizational relationships. *Academy of Management Review, 23*, 473–490.

Metiu, A. (2006). Owning the code: Status closure in distributed groups. *Organization Science, 17*, 418–436.

Meyerson, D., Weick, K. E., & Kramer, R. M. (1996). Swift trust and temporary groups. In R. M. Kramer, & T. R. Tyler (Eds.), *Trust in organizations: Frontiers of theory and research* (pp. 166–195). Thousand Oaks, CA: Sage.

Moreland, R. L., Argote, L., & Krishnan, R. (1998). Training people to work in groups. In R. S. Tindale et al. (Eds.), *Applications of theory and research on groups to social issues* (pp. 36–60). New York: Plenium.

Morris, J., Cascio, W., & Young, C. (1999, Winter). Downsizing after all these years: Questions and answers about who did it, how many did it, and who benefited from it. *Organizational Dynamics*, 78–87.

Mortensen, M., & Hinds, P. (2001). Conflict and shared identity in geographically distributed teams. *International Journal of Conflict Management, 12*, 212–238.

Mortensen, M., & Hinds, P. (2002). Fuzzy teams: Boundary disagreement in distributed and collocated teams. In P. Hinds, & S. Kiesler (Eds.), *Distributed work* (pp. 283–308). Cambridge, MA: MIT Press.

Neuman, G. A., & Wright, J. (1999). Team effectiveness: Beyond skills and cognitive ability. *Journal of Applied Psychology, 84*, 376–389.

Olsen, L. (2005, May 16). Murky stats mask plant deaths: Government safety figures are misleading on contract workers at U.S. refineries. *Houston Chronicle*, http://www.chron.com/disp/story.mpl/special/05/blast/3183356.html

O'Reilly, C. A., & Pfeffer, J. (2000). *Hidden value: How great companies achieve extraordinary results with ordinary people*. Boston: Harvard University Press.

Osterman, P. (1994). How common is workplace transformation and who adopts it? *Industrial & Labor Relations Review, 47*, 173–188.

Osterman, P. (2000). Work reorganization in an era of restructuring: Trends in diffusion and effects on employee welfare. *Industrial & Labor Relations Review, 53*, 179–196.

Owens, D. A. Neale, M. A., & Sutton, R. I. (2000). Technologies of status negotiation: Status dynamics in email discussion groups. In M. A. Neale, E. A. Mannix, & D. H. Gruenfeld (Eds.), *Research on managing groups and teams: Technology* (Vol. 3, pp. 205–230). Stamford, CT: JAI Press.

Pearce, J. L. (1993). Toward an organizational behavior of contract laborers: Their psychological involvement and effects on employee coworkers. *Academy of Management Journal, 36,* 1082–1096.

Pelled, L., Eisenhardt, K., and Xin, K. (1999). Exploring the black box: An analysis of work group diversity, conflict, and performance. *Administrative Science Quarterly, 44,* 1–28.

Pfeffer, J. (1994). *Competitive advantage through people: Unleashing the power of the work force.* Boston: Harvard Business School Press.

Pfeffer, J. (1998). *The human equation: Building profits by putting people first.* Boston: Harvard Business School Press.

Pfeffer, J., & Baron, J. (1988). Taking the workers back out: Recent trends in the structuring of employment. In L. L. Cummings, & B. M. Staw (Eds.), *Research in organizational behavior* (Vol. 10, pp. 257–303). Greenwich, CT: JAI Press.

Pil, F. K., & MacDuffie, J. P. (1996). The adoption of high involvement work practices. *Industrial Relations, 35,* 423–455.

Pinsonneault, A., Barki, H., Gallupe, R. B., & Hoppen, N. (1999). Electronic brainstorming: The illusion of productivity. *Information Systems Research, 10,* 110–133.

Polivka, A. E., Cohany, S. R., & Hipple, S. (2000). Definition, composition, and economic consequences of the nonstandard workforce. In F. Carre et al. (Eds.), *Nonstandard work: The nature and challenges of changing employment arrangements* (pp. 41–94). Champaign, IL: IRRA.

Postmes, T., Spears, R., & Lea, M. (1998). Breachng or building social boundaries? SIDE-effects of computer-mediated communications. *Communication Research, 25,* 689–715.

Postrel, S. (2002). Islands of shared knowledge: Specialization and mutual understanding in problem-solving teams. *Organization Science, 13,* 303–320.

Powell, W. (2001). The capitalist firm in the twenty-first century: Emerging patterns in western enterprise. In P. DiMaggio (Ed.), *The twenty-first century firm: Changing economic organization in international perspective* (pp. 33–68). Princeton, NJ: Princeton University Press.

Prestowitz, C. (2005). *Three billion new capitalists: The great shift of wealth and power to the east.* New York: Basic Books.

Quinn, R. W., & Dutton, J. E. (2005). Coordination as energy-in-conversation. *Academy of Management Review, 30,* 36–57.

Reskin, B. F. (2003). Including mechanisms in our models of ascriptive inequality. *American Sociological Review, 68,* 1–21.

Rousseau, D. M., & Libuser, C. (1997). Contingent workers in high risk environments. *California Management Review, 39,* 103–123.

Sako, M. (2004). Modularity and outsourcing: The nature of co-evolution of product architecture and organizational architecture in the global automotive industry. In A. Principe, A. Davies, & M. Hobday (Eds.), *The business of systems integration* (pp. 229–254). Oxford, U.K.: Oxford University Press.

Schilling, M. A. (2000). Towards a general modular systems theory and its application to inter-firm product modularity. *Academy of Management Review, 25,* 312–334.

Shepherd, M. M., Briggs, R. O., Reinig, B. A., Yen, J., & Nunamaker, J. F. (1996). Invoking social comparison to improve electronic brainstorming: Beyond anonymity. *Journal of Management Information Systems, 12,* 155–170.

Smith, V. (1994). Institutionalizing flexibility in a service firm: Multiple contingencies and hidden hierarchies. *Work and Occupations, 21,* 284–307.

Smith, V. (1997). New forms of work organization. *Annual Review of Sociology, 23,* 315–39.

Smith, V. (1998). The fractured world of the temporary worker: Power, participation, and fragmentation in the contemporary workplace. *Social Problems, 45,* 411–430.

Snell, S. A., & Youndt, M. A. (1995). Human resource management and firm performance: Testing a contingency model of executive controls. *Journal of Management, 21,* 711–737.

Sokol, M. B. (1992). A theory of social comparison processes. *Human Relations, 7,* 117–140.

Sole, D., & Edmundson, A. (2002). Situated knowledge and learning in dispersed teams. *British Journal of Management, 13,* S17–S34.

Sosa, M. E., Eppinger, S. D., Pich, M., McKendrick, D. G., & Stout, S. K. (2002). Factors that influence technical communication in distributed product development: An empirical study in the telecommunications industry. *IEEE Transactions on Engineering Management, 49,* 45–58.

Spears, R., & Lea, M. (1992). Social influence and the influence of the 'social' in computer-mediated communication. In L. Martin (Ed.), *Contexts of computer-mediated communication* (pp. 33–65). London: Harvester Wheatsheaf.

Spears, R., & Lea, M. (1994). Panacea or panopticon—The hidden power in computer-mediated communication. *Communication Research,* 427–459.

Sproull, L., & Kiesler, S. (1986). Reducing social-context cues—Electronic mail in organizational communication. *Management Science, 32*(11), 1492–1512.

Stasser, G., & Titus, W. (1985). Pooling of unshared information in group decision making: Biased information sampling during discussion. *Journal of Personality and Social Psychology, 48,* 1467–1478.

Stasser, G., Vaughan, S. I., & Stewart, D. (2000). Pooling unshared information: The benefits of knowing how access to information is distributed among group members. *Organisational Behavior and Human Decision Processes, 82,* 102–116.

Stevens, M. J., & Campion, M. A. (1994). The knowledge, skill, and ability requirements for teamwork: Implications for human resource management. *Journal of Management, 20,* 503–530.

Turner, J. C., Hogg, M. A., Oakes, P. J., Reicher, S. D., & Whetherell, M. (Eds.). (1987). *Rediscovering the social group: A self-categorization theory.* New York: Basil Blackwell.

Ulrich, K. (1995). The role of product architecture in the manufacturing firm. *Research Policy, 24,* 419–440.

Vaccaro, A., & Veloso, F. (2006). *The virtualization of firms' knowledge creation processes: An empirical investigation.* Pittsburgh, PA: Carnegie Mellon University.

Walsh, J. P., Meyer, A. D., & Schoonhoven, C. B. (2006). A future for organization theory: Living in and living with changing organizations. *Organization Science, 17,* 657–671.

Walther, J. B. (1992). Interpersonal effects in computer-mediated interaction—A relational perspective. *Communication Research, 19,* 52–90.

Walther, J. B. (1996). Computer-mediated communication: Impersonal, interpersonal, and hyperpersonal interaction. *Communication Research, 23,* 3–43.

Walther, J. B. (1997). Group and interpersonal effects in international computer-mediated collaboration. *Human Communication Research, 23,* 342–369.

Walther, J. B. (2002). Time effects in computer-mediated groups: Past, present, and future. In P. Hinds, & S. Kiesler (Eds.), *Distributed work* (pp. 235–258). Cambridge, MA: MIT Press.

Walther, J. B., & D'Addario, K. P. (2001). The impacts of emoticons on message interpretation in computer-mediated communication. *Social Science Computer Review, 19,* 324–347.

Walther, J. B., & Tidwell, L. C. (1995). Nonverbal cues in computer-mediated communication, and the effect of chronemics on relational communication. *Journal of Organizational Computing, 5,* 355–378.

Warkentin, M., & Beranek, P. M. (1999). Training to improve virtual team communication. *Information Systems Journal, 9,* 271–289.

Wegner, D. M. (1987). Transactive memory: A contemporary analysis of the group mind. In B. Mullen, & G. R. Goethals (Eds.), *Theories of group behavior* (pp. 185–208). New York: Springer-Verlag.

Weisband, S. (2002). Maintaining awareness in distributed team collaboration: Implications for leadership and performance. In P. Hinds, & S. Kiesler (Eds.), *Distributed work.* Cambridge, MA: MIT Press.

Wiesenfeld, B. M., Raghuram, S., & Garud, R. (1999). Communication patterns as determinants of organizational identification in a virtual organization. *Organization Science, 10,* 777–790.

Williams, K. Y., & O'Reilly, C. A. I. (1998). Demography and diversity in organizations: A review of 40 years of research. In B. M. Staw, & L. L. Cummings (Eds.), *Research in organizational behavior* (Vol. 20, 77–140). Stamford, CT: JAI Press.

Yang, Y. R., & Hsia, C. J. (2004). Local clustering and organizational governance of trans-border production networks: A case study of Taiwanese IT companies in the greater Suzhou area. *Journal of Geographical Science, 36,* 23–54.

Yoo, Y., Kanawattanachai, P., & Citurs, A. (2002). Forging into the wired wilderness: A case study of a technology-mediated distributed discussion-based class. *Journal of Management Education, 26,* 139–163.

Zheng, J., Bos, N., Olson, J. S., & Olson, G. M. (2001). *Trust without touch: Jump-start trust with social chat.* Paper presented at CHI-01 Conference on Human Factors in Computing Systems. Seattle, WA.

Ziegler, R., Diehl, M., & Zijlstra, G. (2000). Idea production in nominal and virtual groups: Does computer-mediated communication improve group brainstorming? *Group Processes and Intergroup Relations, 3,* 141–158.

13

When Group Identities Matter

Bias in Performance Appraisal

LORIANN ROBERSON

Teachers College, Columbia University

BENJAMIN M. GALVIN

Arizona State University

ATIRA CHERISE CHARLES

Arizona State University

Abstract

Performance appraisals are a critical part of organizational life, and bias in appraisals is consistently mentioned as a barrier to advancement for diverse workers. This chapter reviews the literature on rater bias in performance appraisals, defined as effects on performance ratings due to ratee category membership. We focus on the major theoretical frameworks (e.g., stereotype fit and relational demography) used in the study of bias, organizing the research findings by the four most commonly studied demographic categories: gender, race, age, and disability. The review allows better understanding of the gaps in our knowledge and identifies needed future research directions in this literature stream. We conclude the chapter with several concerns including a lack of empirical research testing propositions concerning the effect of organizational variables on bias.

Introduction

Organizational diversity and equal employment opportunity (EEO) initiatives have emphasized entry and recruitment as a first step in creating a diverse work force (Avery & McKay, 2006). The success of these efforts can perhaps most dramatically be seen in the changes in rates of entry of women and people of color into managerial and professional positions. For example, the number of African American women entering management positions increased by 79% from 1986 to 1996 (Combs, 2003). Recent figures show that the representation of women and people of color in managerial and professional positions is becoming closer to their representation in the labor force (Catalyst, Inc., 2006).

But still, disparities remain, particularly in rates of advancement into top leadership positions. A recent study by Catalyst, Inc. (2006) found that 37% of managers, but only 16% of corporate officers, were female and that the rate of growth for women into top positions has slowed in the last three years. A similar picture was found for people, particularly women, of color. Other studies have documented slower rates of advancement for men and women of color than for their White peers, even for those who eventually reach upper echelons (Bell & Nkomo, 2001; D. A. Thomas & Gabarro, 1999). Thus, a ceiling—be it glass, concrete (Catalyst, Inc., 1999), or bamboo (Hyun, 2006)—continues to be a reality of organizational life. Attention has shifted from organizational entry to advancement as the most important diversity challenge facing organizations (Kilian, Hukai, & McCarty, 2005). Disparate advancement rates mean limited career paths for women and minorities and are believed to contribute to higher turnover for members of these groups (Kilian et al., 2005).

A number of possible reasons for these disparities have been identified including a lack of mentors or early job challenge, and exclusion from informal networks (Kilian et al., 2005). But also included in the list of probable causes is a set of factors related to performance evaluation and appraisal such as stereotypes, low expectations, and double standards (Catalyst, Inc., 2006; Kilian et al., 2005). For example, 41% of African American female managers surveyed by Bell and Nkomo (2001) expressed concern with double standards, saying that they had to perform better than their male colleagues had to. Concern with appraisal bias as a potential contributor to outcome disparities (Dipboye, 1985; Nieva & Gutek, 1980) has spurred and maintained interest in research on this issue and interest in the development of theories to explain when, why, and how bias in appraisal can occur.

What is bias in appraisal? Finding greater disparities between the representation of women and men or of Whites and people of color at upper management levels does not demonstrate unequivocally that performance evaluations (on which promotions are often based) are biased. Nor do employee concerns about discrimination in appraisals and promotions; nor does the existence of mean differences (e.g., women vs. men; Black vs. White) in the appraisals themselves. While ideally we might hope to see no differences in outcomes by group memberships, observed differences in level of attainment or performance could be the result of differences in skills, abilities, education, or experience. Fiske (2002) defined bias as "reacting to a person on the basis of perceived membership in a single human category, ignoring other category attributes" (p. 123). In terms of performance appraisal, this means a systematic effect due to category membership (e.g., gender, race, age, disability), unrelated to actual performance (Colella, DeNisi, & Varma, 1998; Ilgen & Youtz, 1986; Nieva & Gutek, 1980; Stauffer & Buckley, 2005). Finding this effect in research can be accomplished (or attempted) in several ways. In the laboratory, the actual work behaviors and outputs seen by evaluators can be equated. In the field, other major contributors to performance (e.g., ability or experience) or objective performance level can be statistically controlled. Some studies use within-subjects designs, so that ratees and performance are constant across raters. When performance or its other causes are controlled, and effects due to category membership remain—when group identities still matter—bias is said to exist.

This chapter reviews literature on bias in performance appraisals. In reviewing the literature, we concentrated on management and applied psychology journals, but we included work in basic or social psychology that considered performance evaluations in organizational contexts. Our review is structured around the major theoretical frameworks used to study and explain bias in the management literature. We consider work for four commonly studied demographic categories: gender, race, age, and disability. While we focus on the theories of bias for each of these categories, we also briefly summarize recent (i.e., post-1990) results of empirical studies based on these perspectives. Finally, we reflect on the state of our knowledge and the field, and offer suggestions for future research.

History and Overview

Because of their importance for administrative decisions and employee development, as well as their perceived vulnerability to error and inaccuracy (Landy & Farr, 1980), performance evaluations have been a subject of study since the early days of industrial and organizational psychology. Research was conducted on rating errors, formats, and rater and ratee demographics (mostly race, sex, and age) as sources of rating variance. Thus, the study and reporting of group differences in appraisals, especially for gender and race, have a long history. The 1980 review of Landy and Farr reported two common findings from research. First, in occupations perceived as masculine, ratings of females tended to be lower than males. This pattern suggested that gender bias may be a function of role incongruity (Nieva & Gutek, 1980). Second, raters were often found to give more favorable evaluations to same-race ratees. This pattern received less explanation. As noted by Ilgen and Youtz (1986), in the study of race and performance appraisal, scholars seemed content to document the existence of differences rather than seek to explain why they might be occurring. The rise of the cognitive models of person perception in social psychology and their application to the performance appraisal process set the stage for more theoretical approaches to the study of bias in appraisal.

Using a cognitive approach, Heilman (1983) presented the lack-of-fit model to explain the pattern of findings for gender. Tsui and O'Reilly (1989) introduced the relational demography approach, providing a theoretical basis for understanding similarity effects on ratings. These two papers formed the foundation for the two major theoretical approaches to the study of bias today. In the last 15 to 20 years, work within these frameworks on gender and race bias has continued, and models of age and disability bias have appeared as well.

Models of bias utilize either or both of the two theoretical frameworks. One (perhaps the predominant) theoretical model is what we will refer to as "stereotype fit" (Dipboye, 1985). This type of model proposes a matching process such that evaluators compare their stereotype (e.g., the beliefs about the attributes or characteristics associated with an identity group; Dovidio & Hebl, 2005) of a ratee with another stereotype of the perceived requirements of the ratee's job or role. These models argue that some jobs and roles become "typed," in that the attributes believed necessary for success are those associated with a particular group. Bias is predicted to occur when there is little fit between the two, and the stereotype of a ratee's group is incongruous with the stereotype of his or her job. Incongruity is hypothesized to affect performance evaluations negatively through expectations of success. Theories based largely on stereotype fit models have been proposed to explain both selection and appraisal bias for gender (e.g., Eagly & Karau, 2002; Heilman, 1983, 2001; Perry, 1997; Perry, Blake-Davis, & Kulik, 1994), age (e.g., Perry, 1997; Perry & Finkelstein, 1999) and disability (e.g., Colella, DeNisi, & Varma, 1997; D. L. Stone & Colella, 1996).

The second major theoretical framework used to predict bias in appraisal comes from relational demography. The relational demography approach investigates the effects of an individual's demographic similarity-dissimilarity relative to others in a dyad or group (Tsui & Gutek, 1999). This model proposes that demographic dissimilarity of a ratee from his or her rater or work group will result in less favorable performance evaluations. Researchers have used the demography framework to explain appraisal bias for gender (Tsui & O'Reilly, 1989), race (Mount, Sytsma, Hazucha, & Holt, 1997), age (Tsui, Porter, & Egan, 2002), and disability (Colella et al., 1997).

These two theoretical frameworks (stereotype fit and relational demography) specify the general conditions under which bias will occur (an incongruous job or a dissimilar rater/work group) and, thus, specify where researchers should investigate bias. Within these general frameworks, researchers have studied a number of other theories of smaller scope that seek to explain in greater detail the process through which bias is manifested in evaluations—how expectancies or dissimilarity influence ratings. These process models, developed in social psychology, are often invoked to explain or predict particular patterns of ratings.

We begin by discussing the general frameworks and briefly summarize the research evidence for the four demographic categories. Then, we discuss the process models and the role of individual and of contextual factors in bias.

The Stereotype Fit Framework

Models of bias relying on the stereotype fit framework predict that bias occurs when the stereotype of a ratee's group is incongruous with the stereotype of his or her job. As the lack of fit model for gender states, "[T]he presumed lack of fit that arises from a perceived attributes-job requirements incongruity underlies each of the many varieties of sex-bias encountered in the work world" (Heilman, 1983, p. 280). This framework rests on the assumption that both jobs or roles, and identity groups are stereotyped. Accordingly, research has documented the existence and content of stereotypes for gender, disability, and age groups (Colella, 1996; Heilman, 2001; Kulik, Perry, & Bourhis, 2000; Wittenbrink, Judd, & Park, 1997), as well as evidence for the sex and age typing of jobs (Perry & Bourhis, 1998; Saks & Waldman, 1998). Research on disability has shown that people hold different expectations of success for various disability job categories (Colella, 1996).

Stereotype fit models also rely on a large body of social cognition research to predict that incongruity between the job and ratee group stereotypes negatively affects performance evaluations through expectations of success. Stereotypes create expectations about the likely characteristics and behaviors of group members (Higgins & Bargh, 1987). Social cognition research has shown how stereotype-based expectancies can bias the perception, processing, and recall of information (Dovidio & Hebl, 2005). For example, in the absence of information perceivers fill in details consistent with their expectations (Kulik & Bainbridge, 2005). Research has also tested the central hypothesis of the fit model: that bias in evaluation for a particular demographic group depends on the typing of the job, typically indicated by a target demographic by job interaction (Kulik & Bainbridge, 2005). Although most of this research has focused on evaluations of job applicants in selection contexts, evidence supporting the hypothesis for performance evaluations has been found for several demographic categories. Much of the strongest evidence in support of the model concerns gender (Davison & Burke, 2000; Eagly & Karau, 2002), the category with which job congruity effects on appraisals were first noted. As predicted, women tend to be evaluated as less effective than men are in male-dominated leader roles and roles perceived as masculine. Women tend to be perceived as more effective than men are in roles perceived as feminine (Eagly, Karau, & Makhijani, 1995).

Models of age bias (Perry & Finkelstein, 1999) also incorporate the stereotype fit hypothesis, and much of the empirical research on age bias has been guided by this framework (Gordon & Arvey, 2004). Empirical results suggest that older ratees in "young-typed" jobs are penalized more than younger ratees are in "old-typed" jobs. For example, Finkelstein, Burke, and Raju's (1995) meta-analysis of studies that tested the fit hypothesis revealed that younger workers received slightly higher ratings than older workers did for young-type jobs, but there was little difference in ratings of younger and older workers on old-type jobs. This pattern of results is consistent with some variations of the fit model specific to age. Lawrence (1988) proposed that age bias involved a matching process but argued that raters make comparisons not based on perceived attributes of the group and job, but based on the age of the ratee relative to perceived organizational norms for career progression (beliefs about the typical age of people in a role). Ratees whose age is similar to the norm are deemed "on schedule" and those younger than the norm are deemed "ahead of schedule." Performance expectations and ratings will be positive for these individuals, particularly for those judged "ahead of schedule." However, ratees older than the norm are deemed "behind schedule," and this is predicted to have a negative impact on expectations and ratings. Maurer, Wrenn, and Weiss (2003) also proposed a fit process to predict appraisal bias affecting older and not younger workers. They suggested that the common stereotype that older workers are less motivated or able to learn (Chiu, Chan, Snape, & Redman, 2001) can negatively affect performance evaluations of older workers on jobs that are viewed as having a learning component.

D. L. Stone and Colella (1996) and Colella et al. (1997) also propose stereotype fit as one of the important processes affecting the evaluation of disabled ratees. The few empirical studies of the stereotype fit hypothesis for disability show mixed results. In Colella et al. (1998), negative bias for disabled ratees was seen under poor job fit conditions, but only on rankings and not on performance ratings. Colella and Varma (1999) also found that performance ratings were not affected by fit (or disability), but performance expectancies and reward recommendations were negatively affected for disabled ratees under poor fit conditions. In Lynch and Finkelstein (2006), fit had no impact on ratings of disabled ratees.

Given the popularity of the stereotype fit model, it is somewhat striking that it has not been used to explain race bias in appraisals. In their article examining factors affecting evaluations of minorities, Ilgen and Youtz (1986) argued that, although stereotype fit models appeared useful for explaining gender bias, they were less relevant when considering race bias, as jobs are not race typed to the extent that they are sex typed. However, status characteristics theory (Wagner & Berger, 1997) suggests that similar processes are involved in both race and gender bias. Gender and race are both viewed as diffuse status characteristics, which means that stereotypes about these groups contain beliefs about their status position and about member competence with regard to a wide range of abilities (Ridgeway, 2001). These assumptions about competence and social significance influence performance expectancies. Status characteristics theory proposes that these characteristics will be used to form expectancies when they are salient in the situation (i.e., in mixed groups, or when they are relevant to the task). Thus, the results of tests of the stereotype fit model for gender are also viewed as consistent with status characteristics theory (Ridgeway, 2001). If race is also associated with status, then race bias in appraisals should be seen on higher status roles or jobs. Although work in social psychology has utilized this perspective for explaining race bias, in the management literature most research on race bias in appraisals has been guided by the next framework.

The Relational Demography Framework

The relational demography approach investigates the effects of an individual's demographic similarity/dissimilarity relative to others in a dyad, group, or organization (Riordan, Schaffer, & Stewart, 2005; Tsui & Gutek, 1999). This framework proposes that demographic dissimilarity of a ratee from a rater or work group will result in less favorable performance evaluations.

The relational demography framework relies on three theories to predict the effects of similarity and dissimilarity on processes and outcomes: social identity theory (Hogg & Abrams, 1988), self-categorization theory (Tajfel, 1982), and the similarity-attraction paradigm (Byrne, 1971). These theories explain the tendency to perceive others in terms of in-groups and out-groups and an individual's attraction to and preference for similar others (Tsui, Egan, & O'Reilly, 1992). At the dyadic level, these theories predict that demographic dissimilarity of a ratee to a rater will result in less favorable performance evaluations, with liking or attraction as the mediator of these effects (Riordan, 2000). At the work group level, in addition to similarity-attraction, social identity, and social categorization theories, Kanter's (1977) theory of tokenism is used to predict the effect of similarity/dissimilarity to the group on appraisals (Riordan et al., 2005). Kanter proposed that when members of one group make up 15% or less of the total, the salience of group memberships and associated stereotypes increases, and the behavior and performance of token individuals receive greater levels of scrutiny. The theoretical implication for appraisals is that individuals who are dissimilar to the group, particularly those who are members of low-status groups, are more likely to be given lower appraisals by the dominant group (Bettencourt & Bartholow, 1998). Here we will look at evidence for dyadic and group similarity effects on appraisals.

Dyadic Similarity

The more popular approach to investigating appraisal bias involves examining dyadic rater–ratee similarity and its effects on appraisals. Rater–ratee similarity effects have been reported for gender (Biernat, Crandall, Young, Kobrynowicz, & Halpin, 1998; Furnham & Stringfield, 2001; Tsui & O'Reilly, 1989; Tsui et al., 2002; Varma & Stroh, 2001). Results tend to show that gender similarity positively predicts performance ratings. There is some indication that males and females may vary in the extent of in-group favoritism, although the direction of the relationship is unclear. In Biernat et al. (1998), male raters showed more in-group bias than female raters did, but in Tsui and O'Reilly, female raters showed greater similarity effects than males.

For age, results have been mixed. In Liden, Stilwell, and Ferris (1996) and Tsui and O'Reilly (1989), age similarity had no effect on performance ratings. Other findings suggest that the direction of the age difference may be important (Tsui & O'Reilly, 1989). Tsui et al. (2002) found that similarity in age between subordinates and employees was positively related to performance ratings and that older subordinates, relative to the supervisor, received the lowest performance scores. Shore, Cleveland, and Goldberg (2003) found predicted similarity effects on manager rated potential but not on performance ratings. On ratings, results opposite to those predicted were found. While older and younger managers rated the performance of younger employees similarly, older employees were rated more favorably by younger managers than they were by older managers.

In 1980, Landy and Farr noted race similarity effects on appraisals. In general, subsequent examinations of race have also reported rater–ratee similarity effects, with the bulk of studies examining Black and White groups (Biernat et al., 1998; Elvira & Town, 2001; Kraiger & Ford, 1985; Mount et al., 1997; Stauffer & Buckley, 2005). Tsui and O'Reilly (1989) found no evidence for race (Black–White) dissimilarity effects on performance ratings, but Tsui et al. (2002) reported that race dissimilarity affected ratings of extrarole performance. Several studies suggest a greater negative effect of racial dissimilarity on ratings made by White evaluators. In Mount et al. (1997), both Black and White superiors assigned more favorable ratings to same race ratees, with the greatest difference between raters for Black ratees. Stauffer and Buckley (2005) found that higher ratings were given to White ratees by both White and Black supervisors. However, White supervisors rated Black ratees much lower than Black supervisors did. Biernat et al. (1998) reported that racial similarity effects were stronger for White raters than they were for non-White raters.

Group Similarity

Some studies of group similarity effects have utilized the compositional demography approach, which examines performance ratings as a function of the relative proportions of social identity groups in a work group or organizational unit. Studies of the effect of group composition on appraisals have been more common for gender than for other demographic variables (Reskin, McBrier, & Kmec, 1999), and the evidence is stronger. For example, Pazy and Oron (2001) explored the relationship between the proportion of women in military units and performance evaluation outcomes for high-ranking officers in the Israeli Defense Force. When women made up less than 10% of a unit, they received lower overall ratings than men did. In groups in which women made up more than 10% of the unit, they generally received superior ratings to the men. In contrast, men's overall performance ratings did not vary with the proportion of women in the unit. Sackett, Du Bois, and Noe (1991) similarly reported that women received lower ratings than men did when they made up less than 20% of a group, but received higher evaluations than men did when they made up more than 50% of the group. Sackett et al. (1991) also examined the effect of race work group composition on Black-White rating differences. The proportion of Blacks in the work group had no significant influence on ratings.

For age and disability, there have been few, if any, studies of the effects of group similarity on performance evaluations. Lawrence (1988) found that performance ratings were significantly related to deviations from age norms, not deviations from the age composition of those in the role. Lawrence concluded that, although demographic composition is often used as a proxy for age norms, the two are not identical and deviation from age norms is the important predictor of bias. However, age norms may be partly a function of age composition. A study of selection bias (Cleveland, Festa, & Montgomery, 1988) found that perceived age norms for the job and age typing of the job were related to the proportion of older individuals in the applicant pool. Similar to the findings of Lawrence, age composition was not related to evaluations when holding perceptions of age norms constant.

In summary, the stereotype fit and relational demography approaches provide broad frameworks that indicate where and when rating bias will occur, and thus where to look for it. Models of bias in management utilize either or both of these frameworks. For example, Colella et al.'s (1997) model of appraisal bias for disabled employees includes predictions derived from both stereotype fit and relational demography frameworks. The two frameworks are not inconsistent with each other. It has been proposed that the demographic composition of a job or role is one contribution to its typing (Perry, 1997), and the study of Cleveland et al. (1988) supports this for age. If so, the findings of a relationship of ratings for a particular group to its representation in the job are consistent with the stereotype fit and status characteristics predictions.

Evidence exists to support the central predictions of each framework, although overall, results are mixed. But mixed results are not surprising, as models of bias also propose a number of contextual and individual difference variables that can influence the extent to which bias occurs. Overwhelmingly, empirical research has not considered or measured proposed moderators, but rather tests basic hypotheses concerning congruency or similarity effects on evaluations. In addition, research has tended to define and to look for bias in appraisals in terms of lower, less favorable ratings for members of the target group. But as discussed in the next section, bias does not always mean lower ratings.

Process Theories

The stereotype fit and relational demography frameworks specify basic mechanisms through which bias occurs: through expectancies in the stereotype fit framework and through attraction/liking in the relational demography approach. However, within the theoretical bases of the two frameworks, other theories have been developed that provide greater detail on particular processes that are involved in bias. Here we review some of these process theories that explain in more detail how bias is manifested, and why "bias" does not always mean "lower ratings."

Performance Attributions

In both the stereotype fit and relational demography frameworks, performance attributions are one mechanism through which bias is hypothesized to occur. Within the stereotype fit framework, low expectations for success result in rater attribution of high performance to instable or external factors instead of internal factors such as ability. For example, models of gender bias argue that when a woman's level of performance is high, incongruity (which results in low expectations) results in denying women credit for their success (Eagly & Karau, 2002; Heilman, 2001). Heilman predicted this attribution pattern to be more likely in situations where individual contributions to success are ambiguous such as in team settings. Colella et al. (1997) also suggested that attributions contribute to appraisal bias for disabled ratees, arguing that raters would be expected to attribute poor performance to stable, uncontrollable, internal factors (the disability), but high performance to unstable causes.

Relevant to the relational demography framework, intergroup theory also proposes that attributions differ for in-group versus out-group members, consistent with the in-group bias predicted by social identity theory. Sometimes referred to as the ultimate attribution error (Pettigrew, 1979), successes of in-group members tend to be attributed to internal factors, and their failures to external factors. For out-group members, attributions show an opposite pattern, such that successes are attributed to external factors and failures are attributed to internal factors.

Research on attributions in social psychology has tended to corroborate these patterns. Predicted differential attributions for in-groups versus out-groups have been found (Beal, Ruscher, & Schnake, 2001). Gender effects on attributions also support predictions. A meta-analysis (Swim & Sanna, 1996) suggested that the more masculine a task is, the more likely it is that females' failures are attributed to stable causes such as low ability and task difficulty, while males' failures are more likely to be attributed to unstable factors such as low effort and bad luck.

Some empirical work in management has examined the role of attributions in appraisals. Heilman and Haynes (2005) used written scenarios of mixed sex dyads completing a traditionally male task to manipulate clarity of contributions by varying task structure, information about individual contribution levels, and evidence of past performance. Consistent with predictions, when contributions and past performance were unclear, women were rated as less competent and influential and were viewed as being less likely to have filled the leadership role. When the task was structured in a manner that increased the clarity of contributions, gender effects on ratings were reduced. Greenhaus and Parasuraman (1993), studying race, found that relative to White managers, Black managers were less likely to have their work performance attributed to their effort and ability, and more likely to have their performance attributed to help from others. Thus, attributional patterns may be one of the processes through which ratings are affected.

Norm Violation (Backlash)

Eagly and Karau's (2002) and Heilman's (2001) stereotype fit models of gender bias further argue that evaluations of high-performing women in male sex-typed jobs are biased downward because such women are viewed as violating prescriptive aspects of the gender stereotype. Gender role stereotypes contain not only descriptive elements that describe how men and women are (e.g., men are agentic; women are communal), but also normative, prescriptive elements that specify what men and women should or ought to do (e.g., women *should* be communal; men *should* be agentic; Rudman & Glick, 2001). Rudman and Glick (1999) argue that because agency and communality are seen as opposing traits, a woman who succeeds in a male role may be viewed as agentic, but she is also likely to be viewed as *not* communal, and therefore as violating the prescriptive norm. Such individuals are more likely to be derogated and disliked. Status characteristics theory also predicts that norm violations by low-status group members result in derogation of the target. Prescriptive elements of the stereotype are predicted to be strong when the dominant group is dependent on the subordinate group and therefore has a strong interest in maintaining its own superiority and dominance. Negative reactions to violations are responses to a threat to the status quo (Ridgeway, 2001). Because a woman's role violation is a greater threat to the status quo than a man's is, there should be asymmetrical effects of role violation, such that women are penalized more for not being communal than men are for not being agentic (Rudman & Glick, 2001).

There is some evidence in support of this prediction. Heilman, Wallen, Fuchs, and Tamkins (2004) reported that successful women in a male sex-typed role were less liked by evaluators and more likely to be personally derogated than successful males. Being disliked had a negative impact on performance evaluations. They also found weaker evidence that successful men in female and neutral-typed jobs were disliked. In Rudman and Glick (1999, 2001) asymmetric effects were also reported. For women but not men, being seen as agentic had a negative impact on perceptions of communality. Agentic females were rated as equally competent to but less socially skilled than agentic men were. These evaluations influenced perceived hireability ratings when job descriptions stressed interpersonal skills as well as competence. Rudman and Glick (2001) concluded that ironically including interpersonal dimensions as criteria for hiring and promotion may result in more and not less discrimination against women.

Double Standards and Extremity Effects

Bias is often thought of in terms of lower, less favorable evaluations. But another process involved in appraisal bias, concerns double standards for evaluating performance, which may not always result in lower evaluations. Stereotype fit and status characteristics theories argue that because group stereotypes carry expectations of competence, the level of performance needed for judging an individual as highly competent or capable will be higher for low-status than high-status group members (Eagly & Karau, 2002). Successful performance by a low-status individual (e.g., woman, person of color) will be assessed by a stricter standard than similar performance by a high-status person (Foschi, 2000). The shifting standards model (Biernat & Kobrynowicz, 1997; Biernat & Manis, 1994) further proposes that judgments of minimum competence are also affected by double standards. For low-status groups, the level of performance needed for a judgment of minimum competence will be lower than it will be for high-status groups, again because of low expectations.

These arguments suggest that in general, high performance by a low-status or job-incongruent group member will not be rated as favorably as a similar performance by a high-status group member; and conversely, that poor performance by a low-status group member will be rated more favorably than the same performance by a high-status group member will be rated. Some studies in the management literature have reported this pattern of ratings. Gundersen, Tinsley, and Terpstra (1996) had senior business students play the role of a retail store manager appraising a subordinate's performance based upon a performance log and a video. Female subordinates were given lower ratings than males were under high-performance conditions and higher ratings than males were under low-performance conditions. Similarly, Lynch and Finkelstein (2006) found that for poor performance there was a positive bias, but for high performance, a negative bias for disabled ratees.

However, research has sometimes reported an opposite pattern, such that ratings of stigmatized targets are polarized or extrematized in the direction of their performance (Fleming, Petty, & White, 2005). There are several explanations of this extremity effect. Expectancy violation theory argues that high performance by a low-status group member is rated more favorably than high performance by a high-status group member because high performance violates low expectations for the low-status person (Jussim, Coleman, & Lerch,

1987). Expectancy violation theory also predicts that among low performers, in-group members may receive lower evaluations than out-group members may because low performance by the in-group violates high expectations. In addition, social identity theory suggests that derogation of a negative in-group member can be one strategy to maintain the positive distinctiveness of the in-group (Tajfel, 1982). This "Black Sheep effect" predicts more negative ratings for in-group members than for out-group members at low levels of performance (Marques, Yzerbyt, & Leyens, 1988). Complexity-extremity theory (Linville, 1982) proposes that evaluations of out-group members are more extreme because raters have less contact with and thus a simpler cognitive schema of out-group members than of in-group members. Raters view the performance of an out-group member using fewer dimensions, leading to more extreme evaluations. Ambivalence-response amplification theory (Katz & Glass, 1979) argues that raters are ambivalent in their attitudes toward the stigmatized. These ambivalent feelings threaten the rater's sense of self, and extrematized responses occur as a way to resolve identity threat (D. L. Stone & Colella, 1996).

These theories have been variously discussed in models of bias to explain the positive bias sometimes found for ratings of disabled (Colella et al., 1997; Lynch & Finkelstein, 2006; D. L. Stone & Colella, 1996) and Black (E. F. Stone, D. L. Stone, & Dipboye, 1992) ratees, but little empirical work in management has directly examined predictions.

Shifting standards theory (Biernat & Manis, 1994) proposes that the response scale used by raters may determine if extremity effects occur. This model argues that on subjective (i.e., Likert) scales, which are often used for performance evaluations, raters will use within-category standards when judging ratee performance. So, for example, a woman's competence will be rated relative to the rater's (low) standards for women, while a man's competence will be rated relative to the rater's (high) standards for men. Thus, on subjective scales, the ratings of both high- and low-status groups can appear to be equally "good," as the scale conceals the double standards. This can produce the positive bias often seen for high-performing, low-status, or stigmatized ratees. The shifting standards model proposes that the effects of stereotypes (i.e., lower ratings for high performers; higher ratings for low performers) are more likely to be seen on objective scales or rankings (Biernat & Fuegen, 2001). Because these types of measures force raters to use the same scale to evaluate members of both groups, they are more likely to reveal the influence of stereotypes (Biernat & Kobrinowicz, 1997).

Biernat and her colleagues have conducted several examinations of shifting standards in performance appraisal contexts. In Biernat and Vescio (2002), participants played the role of coed softball team managers, judging the batting and fielding performance of male and female players. Although the information provided to participants equated athleticism for male and female players, evidence of shifting standards was found on ratings of batting performance. Men were more likely to be rated as better batters on objective than subjective scales. However, no evidence of shifting standards was found on another dimension; the rating scale used did not moderate gender effects on ratings of fielding performance. Biernat et al. (1998) examined shifting standards for both race and gender in a sample of U.S. Army officers. As predicted, gender differences favoring males were found in rankings but not ratings of leader competence. However, there was no evidence for the use of different standards by race. Rather, both ratings and rankings favored Whites over non-Whites. The authors suggested that these results may have occurred due to the U.S. Army's explicit policy against using different standards based on race.

Research on bias in the management literature has not examined shifting standards directly. However, some results are suggestive. For example, Colella et al. (1998) found a negative bias only in rankings, not ratings, of disabled ratees, consistent with shifting standards theory.

Emotion and Affect

Dipboye (1985) noted that models of bias in the management literature emphasized cognitive processes while tending to ignore affective and emotional factors that might contribute to bias in appraisal. Although in general this is still true of models of bias, affect and emotion are hypothesized to play a role in the two major theoretical frameworks we have reviewed. We have seen that the stereotype fit model of gender bias and status characteristics theory propose negative affect toward those who violate status norms and threaten the dominant group's status. There is some evidence supporting this for gender. The relational demography approach suggests liking and positive affect as a mediator of similarity effects on judgments. There is also some evidence for this predicted role of affect. Tsui and O'Reilly (1989) reported that gender dissimilarity had a negative impact on liking as well as performance evaluations. Using structural equation modeling, Ferris, Judge, Rowland, and Fitzgibbons (1994) found that supervisor affect mediated the relationship of demographic (e.g., race, age, and function) similarity to supervisor ratings of subordinate performance.

Models of disability bias have given emotion a larger role, and theorists have expanded the consideration of emotional responses beyond positive and negative reactions and their effect on appraisals. D. L. Stone and Colella (1996) and Colella and D. L. Stone (2005) propose that disabilities evoke a variety of emotional responses in perceivers, ranging from mild discomfort to disgust or fear, or to pity and compassion, and that these emotions can have different effects on ratings. For example, pity and paternalism may result in a positive bias in ratings (Colella & D. L. Stone, 2005), while anxiety may have negative effects. However, we found no empirical studies of the role of emotions on appraisals for disabled ratees.

Recent work in social psychology has also examined the specific emotions associated with stereotypes of different groups. Fiske, Cuddy, Glick, and Xu (2002) proposed that stereotype content varies on two dimensions of warmth and competence. Groups considered high on both of these dimensions (e.g., one's in-group) are liked; groups seen as warm but not competent (e.g., elderly, disabled) receive pity; groups viewed as low warmth but high competence (e.g., Asian Americans) evoke envy; and groups viewed as low on both dimensions (e.g., poor people) evoke disgust. Cottrell and Neuberg (2005) argued that when social identities are salient, people will view out-groups in terms of the potential harm or benefit for one's in-group. The emotional response evoked by different out-groups is based on the type of perceived threat that the particular group poses to the in-group. An empirical study supported predictions, finding that out-groups seen as a threat to personal safety evoked fear; those seen as unable to reciprocate in exchange relationships due to an inability to respond evoked pity, and groups perceived as threatening values evoked disgust. These perceptions of threat and opportunity arise not only from the historical relations between the groups, but also current group relations (Cottrell & Neuberg, 2005).

These models move from consideration of a simple positive-negative reaction associated with a single in-group/out-group distinction to greater differentiation of emotions associated with specific groups, and also imply that emotional responses are inextricably linked to the content of stereotypes. Cottrell and Neuberg's (2005) theory of emotional responses as dependent on the threats posed by a particular out-group is consistent with status characteristics theory, which argues that the negative emotional reactions to some groups (norm violators) are due to perceived threats to the dominant group's power and status.

In summary, theory and research on processes presents a muddier picture given many theories, some with competing predictions. However, it seems likely that several processes are involved in bias. Evidence exists for the role of differential attributions and backlash against agentic women. For double and shifting standards, evidence exists but questions remain about the conditions under which effects will be seen. Most of the empirical work has concerned gender. Thus, one question concerns the extent to which these processes generalize to other categories. Extremity effects and differences in attribution patterns have also been reported for race (Black-White groups). Rudman and Glick (2001) propose that backlash against norm violators is unique to gender. They argue that communality (niceness) as a prescriptive norm is particularly strong for women because of men's dependence on women to fulfill important subordinate roles, which gives men a strong incentive to control women to maintain their status. When Black-White relations were also characterized by a similar close dependence between groups (e.g., in the pre-Civil War southern United States), communality was also prescribed for Blacks, and violators more likely to be derogated or punished. However, societal changes that have enhanced the status of Blacks and decreased the dependency of Whites on Blacks have weakened the prescriptive stereotype for Blacks, while men continue to rely on women (Rudman & Glick, 2001). Therefore, prescriptive stereotypes for women remain strong.

However, Tsui, Xin, and Egan (1995) and Perry, Kulik, and Zhou (1999) suggested that violation of status norms may also contribute to age dissimilarity effects on evaluations. Since age is often used to infer wisdom and knowledge, an older subordinate may perceive a younger supervisor as lacking a legitimate basis of authority. One effect of this is that younger supervisors may view older subordinates as a threat to their higher status, leading to less liking and lower evaluations.

Evidence also exists for the predicted role of affect (e.g., liking) in similarity effects, but other predicted processes such as attributions and extremity effects have not been examined within the relational demography framework in management research.

Contextual Factors Affecting Bias

One of the unique contributions of the models of appraisal bias in management is their organizational focus. Although based on social cognition, the models move beyond a sole focus on cognitive processes to delineate contextual factors influencing bias (Kulik & Bainbridge, 2005). This organizational focus is important for not only understanding how and when bias occurs, but also identifying interventions that can reduce bias in appraisals.

The models of bias within the stereotype fit framework include contextual factors that affect the activation and use of stereotypes in making judgments. As the models are based on social cognitive theory and research, many of the contextual factors incorporated have also been derived from work in social cognition. For example, cognitive research has found that the amount of time available to decision makers, cognitive busyness, the amount, and quality of information available, and outside accountability can all influence the extent of stereotypic processing (Kulik & Bainbridge, 2005). These factors are included in several models of bias (e.g., Eagly & Karau, 2002; Heilman, 1983, 1995; Perry, 1997; Perry et al., 1994; Perry, Kulik, & Bourhis, 1996).

Beyond directly incorporating context variables found to be important in social cognitive research, models of appraisal bias delineate how these contextual variables can be influenced by organizational factors. For example, studies have found that rater accountability can decrease reliance on stereotypic processing (Perry et al., 1994). Models propose that rater accountability will increase, and bias decrease with the strength of the EEO culture, awareness of legislation (Colella et al., 1997; Powell & Butterfield, 2002; D. L. Stone & Colella, 1996), firm visibility, and the amount of external scrutiny received by the firm (Perry & Finkelstein, 1999). Both D. L. Stone and Colella (1996) and Perry and Finkelstein (1999) propose that organizational technology will influence the extent of bias against disabled and older workers, respectively. Technology can influence the degree to which disabled employees are viewed as suitable for jobs by affecting the flexibility with which jobs can be performed (D. L. Stone & Colella, 1996). High-technology firms and jobs are likely to have a greater concentration of young workers than low-technology firms are, affecting the degree to which jobs are age typed and the salience of age in the setting (Perry & Finkelstein, 1999). The presence of internal labor markets has also been proposed to affect the salience of age, to the extent that older employees are in the minority in the incumbent populations of entry and lower level jobs. This may increase the activation of age stereotypes (Perry & Finkelstein, 1999). Heilman (1995) suggested that the presence of programs that target women as a group (e.g., mentoring, work arrangement, or affirmative action programs) will increase the salience of gender in the organization, and the extent of bias in appraisals and treatment.

Organizational culture, climate, and values are also proposed as influences on the salience of identity group memberships and the activation of stereotypes. For example, Perry and Finkelstein (1999) propose that age will be more salient in organizations that value age-associated traits such as flexibility, adaptability, and creativity. Ely and Meyerson (2000) and Cleveland, Vescio, and Barnes-Farrell (2005) argue that organizational cultures can be "gendered" in that informal and social patterns implicitly place a higher value on male identity and traits. Some examples of such gendered patterns are the use of time spent at work as a measure of organizational commitment and contributions, crisis oriented work patterns, and the portrayal of ideal workers as individualistic, assertive, and independent (Ely & Meyerson, 2000), as all of these value the male over the female identity. These patterns increase the salience of gender and contribute to the sex typing of jobs, increasing the probability of appraisal bias. Cox (1994) also proposed that the values of the dominant group are reflected in formal and informal work policies and practices, which he labeled institutional bias. This serves to disadvantage culturally different organizational members. D. L. Stone and Colella (1996) proposed that organizational values of competitiveness, individualism, and assertiveness may decrease the extent to which disabled workers are viewed as suitable for jobs, by implicitly valuing traits associated with "able" individuals.

Thus, models of appraisal bias have adapted and extended the results of social-cognitive research to develop rich and detailed predictions about how organizational factors may influence cognitive processing and bias. However, empirical research has not examined predictions regarding organizational variables. Instead research has examined if and how the contextual factors identified by social-cognitive work as influencing cognitive processing similarly influence the performance appraisal process. For example, for age, race, and gender, studies have shown that differences in ratings are less significant when clear performance information is provided to raters (Finkelstein et al., 1995; Gaertner & Dovidio, 2000; Robbins & DeNisi, 1993; Weiss & Maurer, 2004). Cognitive busyness, the extent to which the rater is engaged in competing tasks, appears to make stereotyping more likely (Martell, 1996; Perry et al., 1996). So, rich theory but little evidence exists about how organizational factors influence cognitive processing and bias in appraisals.

Theoretical work on contextual and organizational variables influencing bias has been less apparent in the relational demography framework (Riordan et al, 2005). Tsui et al. (1992) argued that ratee tenure with a manager or group will moderate the effects of similarity on outcomes. They suggested that, with increasing time together, individuals have more opportunities to observe and collect accurate performance information, which should result in less reliance on stereotypes in making judgments. However, theories of intergroup relations argue that mere time together will be insufficient to improve cross-group relationships and decrease stereotyping (Dovidio, Gaertner, & Kawakami, 2003). The Contact Hypothesis (Allport, 1954) posits that intergroup interaction must occur under certain conditions: equal status, cooperation toward shared goals, opportunities for friendship, and support of authorities to decrease the tendency toward in-group/out-group categorization and the use of stereotypes (Allport, 1954; Dovidio et al., 2003). The proposal of Riordan et al. (2005) that interdependence may moderate similarity effects reflects this position. In addition, some work suggests that cooperative or collectivist cultures weaken similarity effects in groups (Chatman, Polzer, Barsade, & Neale, 1998). If as proposed, an emphasis on collectivist values decreases the salience of demographic categories as a basis for identification, collectivist values and culture may also moderate the effect of dyadic similarity on appraisals.

Tsui et al. (1995) proposed that work group heterogeneity moderates the effect of dyadic similarity. For example, for a female superior, they argued that the effect of subordinate similarity will be weaker when the work group is largely female, and stronger when the work group is largely male. When the work group is largely female, there are more opportunities to identify and interact with similar others, weakening attraction to particular subordinates. In contrast, when the work group is largely male, there may be greater attraction and identification with the few females in the group.

There has been little empirical investigation of these proposed contextual influences on similarity effects and performance evaluations. However, one longitudinal study found that similarity effects for White and male raters increased, rather than decreased over time (Biernat et al., 1998).

Individual Differences Affecting Bias

Rater individual differences are also included in models of bias. Theories of gender bias propose endorsement of traditional gender norms as a moderator of the backlash effect—negative reactions to women succeeding in traditionally male roles (Eagly & Karau, 2002). Negative reactions are proposed to be greater for those who endorse traditional gender roles. Findings have partially supported this theory. Glick, Diebold, Bailey-Warner, and Zhu (1997) distinguished among several dimensions of sexism. Male endorsement of traditional gender norms that idealize women (benevolent sexism) did not result in lower overall evaluations of career women. However, views of women as inferior in ways that legitimize male social control (hostile sexism) predicted negative overall evaluations of career women for male raters. It may be that beliefs that women are inferior and should be socially controlled by men rather than the idealizing of women into certain traditionally feminine roles results in bias toward nontraditional women. Among female raters, ambivalent sexism (endorsement of both traditional gender norms that idealize women and views of women as inferior in ways that legitimize male control) predicted negative overall evaluations of career women.

Other models using the stereotype fit framework include individual differences as an influence on the activation and use of stereotypes. For example, Perry (1997) proposed rater authoritarianism and prejudice against older workers as affecting the extent to which age stereotypes will be activated and used in decision making. D. L. Stone and Colella (1996) and Colella et al. (1997) suggested that previous contact with the disabled should influence the use of stereotypes. Those with more previous contact are more likely to seek individuating information about the disabled, rather than to rely on stereotypes. In addition, personality variables such as self-esteem, ethnocentrism, and tolerance for ambiguity are predicted to influence attitudes toward disabled workers (D. L. Stone & Colella, 1996). These predictions have not received much empirical attention in the appraisal context. Perry et al. (1996) measured the extent of rater endorsement of age stereotypes and their impact on selection decisions. Those with higher stereotype endorsement evaluated age congruent job applicants more favorably than they did age incongruent applicants, with the greatest difference in evaluations on young-typed jobs.

Historically, most research on race bias has ignored individual differences (Roberson & Block, 2001). However, Brief and his colleagues (Brief, 1998; Brief & Hayes, 1997) have argued the importance of studying racism for understanding race discrimination in the workplace. They suggest that race bias and discrimination can be explained in part by modern racism (McConahay, 1983), a subtle form of bigotry which influences behavior only when actions can be attributed to a nonracial justification. Brief, Dietz, Cohen, Pugh, and Vaslow (2000) found that only when White participants were given a business justification to discriminate (the boss's belief that the race composition of the sales force should match that of the customer base), did modern racism predict selection bias against Black applicants. Aquino, Stewart, and Reed (2005) suggested social dominance orientation as a factor in appraisal bias. Those high in social dominance orientation believe in group hierarchies and unequal social outcomes, and tend to be prejudiced toward a variety of groups (Dovidio & Hebl, 2005; Pratto, Sidanius, Stallworth, & Malle, 1994). Aquino et al. (2005) found that people high in social dominance orientation evaluated Black ratees more negatively than people with low social dominance orientation. This effect was stronger when the respondents believed that the Black ratee had been hired through an affirmative action process.

Although there has been little attention to individual differences in theory and research on relational demography (Riordan et al., 2005), some research in social psychology suggests individual differences that may moderate effects of similarity on appraisals. Branscombe, Wann, Noel, and Coleman (1993) and Biernat, Vescio, and Billings (1999) found that polarization of in-group ratings, including the tendency to derogate low-performing in-group members, was highest for those who identify strongly with their in-group. Biernat et al. (1999) proposed that high identification with the in-group activates high expectations for in-group members. When these are violated, negative evaluations result. These results suggest that rater level of in-group identification should influence the effect of similarity on evaluations such that similarity should have a stronger impact on the ratings of highly identified raters.

Interventions to Reduce Appraisal Bias

In 1980, Landy and Farr concluded that not enough was known concerning the dynamics underlying race and gender effects on performance appraisal to recommend interventions to eliminate biases. The past 25 years of research have increased our knowledge of the dynamics involved. Based on the research, we can conclude that giving raters more performance information, uninterrupted time to make appraisals, as well as increasing rater accountability are likely to decrease bias (Arthur & Doverspike, 2005).

In addition, several studies have examined the extent to which raters can reduce bias by using deliberate processing strategies. The effects of stereotypes on judgment are believed to be greatest when individuals rely on quick heuristic processing (Fiske & Neuberg, 1990), and use of a more deliberate, controlled strategy may decrease the extent to which stereotypes are used in judgments. Bauer and Baltes (2002) and Baltes and Parker (2000) used a structured free recall intervention to reduce rater reliance on heuristics. Raters were instructed to recall observed behaviors and use that information in making judgments. In Bauer and Baltes, this strategy decreased the impact of gender stereotypes on accuracy and level of performance ratings. In Baltes and Parker, free recall was also effective in reducing the performance cue effect, which occurs when performance expectations or past ratings of a ratee influence current ratings. Kulik et al. (2000) examined instructions for raters to suppress stereotypic thoughts. Previous research in social psychology had found that efforts to suppress stereotypes can backfire, making them more and not less likely to influence impressions at a later time (Macrae, Bodenhausen, & Milne, 1998).

Consistent with predictions, they found that raters who received instructions to suppress age-related thoughts and were cognitively busy during the rating task evaluated older job applicants most negatively.

Conclusions

By the 1990s many appraisal scholars had started to question the contributions of the psychological, cognitive approach to understanding performance evaluations (Arvey & Murphy, 1998). However, in the study of appraisal bias, cognitive models still have theoretical dominance and psychological theories have enhanced our understanding of bias (Kulik & Bainbridge, 2005). Our review finds support for both theoretical frameworks. The results of the review are shown in Table 13.1, which summarizes both theoretical and empirical research efforts so far. The left hand column shows, for each theoretical framework, the process theories, and moderators proposed as relevant for appraisal bias. The cells indicate, for each identity group, where empirical work has been conducted in a performance appraisal context.

For the stereotype fit framework, the central hypothesis (an interaction between job and ratee group membership) has been tested for each demographic variable with the exception of race. Although as we mentioned, status characteristics theory is relevant to race, no stereotype fit model of race bias has been proposed, perhaps reflecting the early skepticism of this model's relevance for race (Ilgen & Youtz, 1987). This table shows that regarding processes, most empirical work has involved gender. For this variable, theory and research are most advanced, and they have benefited from research attention in other fields such as social psychology and sociology. Regarding the other demographic variables, it is clear that the processes involved in bias need more attention. This is particularly true for emotion and affect. Stereotype fit models have focused on the content of the stereotype as important for bias. Recent work linking stereotype content to emotions for various groups (Cottrell & Neuberg, 2005; Fiske et al., 2002) offers some directions for exploring the interplay of cognition and affect on bias in appraisals.

Looking at research on moderators, a few individual differences have been empirically examined, but many more have been proposed as relevant. However, the biggest gap between theory and research concerns organizational moderator variables. The table shows that the empirical study of situational moderators has exclusively involved testing the effects of contextual variables that influence cognitive processing. Research has investigated the amount/clarity of performance information, cognitive busyness, and the effects of rater strategies such as suppression and structured recall. However, an important contribution of management research to the study of bias has been to specify organizational factors that influence cognitive processing. Unfortunately, empirical research testing propositions about organizational variables and their effects on cognitive processing and appraisal bias is

Table 13.1 Summary Table of Research on the Stereotype Fit and Relational Demography Frameworks by Demographic Variable in Management Literature

Theories & Moderators	Stereotype Fit Framework Demographic Variables				Relational Demography Framework Demographic Variables			
	Gender	Race	Age	Disability	Gender	Race	Age	Disability
Central Hypothesis	Empirical Testing		Empirical Testing	Empirical Testing	Empirical Testing	Empirical Testing	Empirical Testing	
Processes								
Performance Attributions	Empirical Testing	Empirical Testing						
Norm Violation	Empirical Testing							
Double/shifting Standards and Extremity effects	Empirical Testing	Empirical Testing		Empirical Testing				
Emotion & Affect					Empirical Testing	Empirical Testing	Empirical Testing	
Moderating Variables								
Contextual Variables Influencing Cognitive Processing	Empirical Testing	Empirical Testing	Empirical Testing		Empirical Testing	Empirical Testing		
Organizational Variables Influencing Cognitive Processing								
Individual Differences	Empirical Testing	Empirical Testing	Empirical Testing					

Empirical Testing—indicates that there has been theoretical development followed by empirical testing of the theory or moderating variable for the demographic variable listed in the column heading virtually nonexistent. When organizational factors are mentioned, they seem to be invoked post hoc in an attempt to explain empirical findings. Kulik and Bainbridge (2005) noted that scholars fail to take advantage of opportunities to measure contextual variables in organizational settings, which would help explain the mixed results of research—why bias is seen in some but not all settings. Here we note that scholars also fail to take full advantage of the extensive theoretical work done in our field.

For the relational demography framework, the central hypothesis that rater–ratee similarity influences ratings has been tested for most of the demographic variables. However, this table shows that there has been little research on processes. Although the role of affect as a mediator has been explored in a few studies, other proposed processes such as extremity effects or differential attributions have not received attention in the management literature.

In contrast to the stereotype fit framework, very little work within the relational demography framework has examined potential moderators of similarity effects. Models of intergroup relations and the work of Cottrell and Neuberg (2005) point to the functional relationships between groups as a determinant of attitudes and stereotyping (Dovidio & Hebl, 2005; K. M. Thomas & Chrobot-Mason, 2005). Thus, intergroup relations within the organization should be important moderators of similarity effects. Further, Brief, Butz, and Deitch (2005) argued that perceived group relations outside the organization also influence relations in the workplace. Brief, Umpress, et al. (2005) found that the closer proximity with which White employees lived to Blacks, and the higher their perceptions of interethnic conflict in their community, the more negative their responses to a racially diverse workplace. Although appraisals were not studied, similarity effects may be stronger when intergroup relations in the external environment are poor.

Unlike gender, age, and disability, for race there has been less theoretical work in the appraisal literature on organizational factors that moderate the specific processes involved in appraisal bias. The diversity literature stresses the importance of organizational culture and climate for diversity as influencing outcomes for people of color, but the impact of these organizational factors on cognitive processing is not typically emphasized. For example, Cox (1994) argues that organizations pressuring assimilation of organizational members will result in poor outcomes for the culturally different. Might the extent of emphasis on assimilation also moderate the effect of similarity on appraisals? Dass and Parker (1999) proposed that some organizations are characterized by a climate "resistant" to diversity. In such organizations where diversity is viewed as a threat, perhaps out-group stereotypes are more salient and associated with greater negative affect. In addition, the research of Brief and his colleagues on the effects of racism and contextual factors on racial attitudes and discrimination is relevant to the appraisal context.

The theoretical frameworks have also proved useful in designing interventions to reduce bias in appraisals. Research suggests that raters be given information, time, and cognitive resources and also suggests that rater training might profitably teach strategies such as structured recall (Bauer & Baltes, 2002) prior to conducting appraisals. The study by Kulik et al. (2000) demonstrated the limitations of thought suppression instructions in a selection task. This suggests that organizations recommending stereotype suppression must also ensure that raters have sufficient cognitive resources when doing appraisals. However, information on organizational moderators of bias is also critical for designing interventions and settings to decrease bias in appraisal. For example, D. L. Stone and Colella (1996) proposed that when job technology constrains flexibility, disabled employees are less likely to be seen as suitable for a position, and bias in appraisal and selection are therefore more likely. Technology that enhances job flexibility should have the opposite effect. The implication is that technology can be used to design jobs that minimize bias. Others have proposed that attention to EEO legislation should decrease bias as it enhances rater accountability (Powell & Butterfield, 2000). On the other hand, if attention to EEO legislation results in greater salience of demographic categories to evaluators, this may increase the possibility of stereotyping and bias (Heilman, 1995).

From a relational demography perspective, research suggests that contexts which meet the conditions of the contact hypothesis (interdependence, cooperation) may decrease bias. In addition, a suggestion for rater training was found in a study by Crisp and Beck (2005), who evaluated an intervention rooted in the logic of social identity and social categorization theories. Their two experiments tested an intervention to reduce differentiation, the tendency of individuals to create cognitive distance between in-groups and out-groups, which in turn makes differences more salient. The manipulated intervention asked participants to think about the characteristics that are shared between the in-group and out-group before making judgments. This proved to reduce in-group favoritism on attitudes and resource allocation decisions, especially for low-identifying participants. The impact of this strategy on appraisal bias warrants investigation.

Limitations

This review was limited to a relatively narrow view of bias, defined as effects on performance ratings due to category membership. The two theoretical frameworks addressed in this chapter focus on rater effects—how similarity or job incongruence influences ratings through raters. In recent years, the concept of bias has been extended to include group differences in perceived fairness and justice in appraisals (Chen & DiTomaso, 1996), provision of feedback across group identities (Harber, 1998), and employee reactions to performance appraisal (Arvey & Murphy, 1998). In addition, some have examined how rater bias may occur through ratee behavior. For example, Ferris and King (1992) proposed that age effects on performance appraisal operate through political behavior and ingratiation tactics used by ratees, which influence rater liking. Tsui et al. (1995) and Colella et al. (1997) have argued that the exchange relationship between superiors and subordinates also mediates the effect of similarity on outcomes. Similarity not only increases liking and in-group classification, it fosters a more favorable leader-member exchange. This can influence performance appraisals and performance level, as superiors give more support, information, and feedback in more favorable exchange relationships and subordinates respond with greater contributions and cooperation (Tsui et al., 1995). These broader issues of bias are important for understanding the effects of appraisals. For example, even if ratings themselves are not biased, appraisal feedback may be given differently, and may have differential impact across groups, which can affect outcomes such as advancement. To understand barriers to advancement fully, we need to know about bias in the broader appraisal system and feedback process as well as in the rating process.

In addition, we considered mostly research conducted in the United States and group identities important in the U.S. context. Bias is not unique to the United States, but the particular identities stigmatized or viewed as high or low status are likely to be culture specific. However, Schein (2001) found evidence of sex typing of the management role using Chinese, Japanese, British, and German samples. Role congruity (Rojahn & Willemsen, 1994) and similarity effects (Gibson, Zerbe, & Franken, 1993; Lindeman & Sundvik, 1995) have received some support through empirical testing outside of the United States, suggesting that the two theoretical frameworks are most likely generalizable.

Research also suggests that the factors salient for social identification differ by cultural context. Pelled and Xin (2000) found that age similarity had negative effects on relationship quality in their Mexican sample, but not in their U.S. sample. In addition, gender similarity had a stronger positive impact on trust in Mexico than it did in the United States, while it had a stronger positive impact on the leader-member exchange in the United States than it did in Mexico. Farh, Tsui, Xin, and Cheng (1998) examined relational demography predictions in the Chinese context and found positive effects of education similarity between rater and ratee; but not for age and gender similarity. They proposed that in China other factors such as *guanxi* (particularistic ties) may play a more dominant role in social identification than demographic variables. Other countries and cultures may demonstrate further differences.

Unique racial/ethnic compositions and historical contexts also provide a fertile ground for extending and generalizing theory such as in Western Europe where numerous excolonials, "guest workers," refugees, and other immigrants have settled in recent decades and face unique challenges in the work setting (Pettigrew, 1998). Similarly, research in countries with different views on gender roles and beliefs about age may lend new insights into our understanding of bias.

In summary, understanding bias in appraisals is not only an issue of theoretical importance, but one of practical relevance. Where bias exists—where group identities matter—potential benefits of diversity for organizations cannot be fully realized and opportunities for individuals are limited. Management scholars have started to understand the dynamics of bias in appraisals. However, we do not yet know the extent to which bias limits the advancement of diverse workers, nor do we know how large a role appraisal bias plays in relation to the other mentioned barriers, such as lack of mentors or exclusion from networks. But models of bias argue that these barriers are likely to be related: the conditions that lead to appraisal bias are also hypothesized to lead to other forms of differential treatment that influence outcomes. For this reason, it is critical to give more research attention to the organizational conditions that influence the salience and use of stereotypes and similarity effects.

Acknowledgments

We wish to thank Elissa Perry for her comments and suggestions on an earlier draft of this chapter.

References

Allport, G. W. (1954). *The nature of prejudice*. New York: Doubleday.

Aquino, K., Stewart, M. M., & Reed, A., II. (2005). How social dominance orientation and job status influence perceptions of African-American affirmative action beneficiaries. *Personnel Psychology, 58,* 703–744.

Arthur, W., Jr., & Doverspike, D. (2005). Achieving diversity and reducing discrimination in the workplace through human resource management practices: Implications of research and theory for staffing, training, and rewarding performance. In R. L. Dipboye & A. Colella (Eds.), *Discrimination at work: The psychological and organizational bases* (pp. 305–327). Mahwah, NJ: Lawrence Erlbaum Associates.

Arvey, R. D., & Murphy, K. R. (1998). Performance evaluation in work settings. *Annual Review of Psychology, 49,* 141–168.

Avery, D. R., & McKay, P. F. (2006). Target practice: An organizational impression management approach to attracting minority and female job applicants. *Personnel Psychology, 59,* 157–187.

Baltes, B. B., & Parker, C. P. (2000). Reducing the effects of performance expectations on behavioral ratings. *Organizational Behavior and Human Decision Processes, 82,* 237–267.

Bauer, C. C., & Baltes, B. B. (2002). Reducing the effects of gender stereotypes on performance evaluations. *Sex Roles, 47,* 465–476.

Beal, D. J., Ruscher, J. B., & Schnake, S. B. (2001). No benefit of the doubt: Intergroup bias in understanding causal explanation. *British Journal of Social Psychology, 40,* 531–543.

Bell, E. L., & Nkomo, S. M. (2001). *Our separate ways: Black and White women and the struggle for professional identity*. Boston: Harvard Business School Press.

Bettencourt, B. A., & Bartholow, B. D. (1998). The importance of status legitimacy for intergroup attitudes among numerical minorities. *Journal of Social Issues, 54,* 759–775.

Biernat, M., Crandall, C. S., Young, L. V., Kobrynowicz, D., & Halpin, S. M. (1998). All that you can be: Stereotyping of self and others in a military context. *Journal of Personality and Social Psychology, 75,* 301–317.

Biernat, M., & Fuegen, K. (2001). Shifting standards and the evaluation of competence: Complexity in gender-based judgment and decision making. *Journal of Social Issues, 57,* 707–724.

Biernat, M., & Kobrynowicz, D. (1997). Gender- and race-based standards of competence: Lower minimum standards but higher ability standards for devalued groups. *Journal of Personality and Social Psychology, 72,* 544–557.

Biernat, M., & Manis, M. (1994). Shifting standards and stereotype-based judgments. *Journal of Personality and Social Psychology, 66,* 5–20.

Biernat, M., & Vescio, T. K. (2002). She swings, she hits, she's great, she's benched: Shifting judgment standards and behavior. *Personality and Social Psychology Bulletin, 28,* 66–76.

Biernat, M., Vescio, T. K., & Billings, L. S. (1999). Black sheep and expectancy violation: Integrating two models of social judgment. *European Journal of Social Psychology, 29,* 523–542.

Branscombe, N. R., Wann, D. L., Noel, J. G., & Coleman, J. (1993). In-group or out-group extremity: Importance of the threatened social identity. *Personality and Social Psychology Bulletin, 19,* 381–388.

Brief, A. P. (1998). *Attitudes in and around organizations.* Thousand Oaks, CA: Sage.

Brief, A. P., Butz, R. M., & Deitch, E. A. (2005). Organizations as reflections of their environments: The case of race composition. In R. L. Dipboye & A. Colella (Eds.), Discrimination at work: The psychological and organizational bases (pp. 119–148). Mahwah, NJ: Lawrence Erlbaum Associates.

Brief, A. P., Dietz, J., Cohen, R. R., Pugh, S. D., & Vaslow, J. B. (2000). Just doing business: Modern racism and obedience to authority as explanations for employment discrimination. *Organizational Behavior and Human Decision Processes, 81,* 72–97.

Brief, A. P., & Hayes, E. L. (1997). The continuing "American dilemma": Studying racism in organizations. In C. L. Cooper & D. M. Rousseau (Eds.), *Trends in organizational behavior* (pp. 89–105). Chichester, U.K.: John Wiley & Sons.

Brief, A. P., Umphress, E. E., Dietz, J., Burrows, J. W., Butz, R. M., & Scholten, L. (2005). Community matters: Realistic group conflict theory and the impact of diversity. *Academy of Management Journal, 48,* 830–844.

Byrne, D. (1971). *The attraction paradigm.* New York: Academic Press.

Catalyst, Inc. (1999). *Women of color in corporate management: Opportunities and barriers.* New York: Author.

Catalyst, Inc. (2006). *The 2005 Catalyst census of woman corporate officers and top earners of the Fortune 500.* New York: Author.

Chatman, J. A., Polzer, J. T., Barsade, S. G., & Neale, M. A. (1998). Being different yet feeling similar: The influence of demographic composition and organizational culture on work processes and outcomes. *Administrative Science Quarterly, 43,* 749–780.

Chen, C. C., & DiTomaso, N. (1996). Performance appraisal and demographic diversity: Issues regarding appraisals, appraisers, and appraising. In E. E. Kossek & S. A. Lobel (Eds.), *Managing diversity: Human resource strategies for transforming the workplace* (pp. 137–163). Cambridge, MA: Blackwell.

Chiu, W. C. K., Chan, A. W., Snape, E., & Redman, T. (2001). Age stereotypes and discriminatory attitudes towards older workers: An east-west comparison. *Human Relations, 54,* 629–661.

Cleveland, J. N., Festa, R. M., & Montgomery, L. (1988). Applicant pool composition and job perceptions: Impact on decisions regarding an older applicant. *Journal of Vocational Behavior, 32,* 112–125.

Cleveland, J. N., Vescio, T. K., & Barnes-Farrell, J. L. (2005). Gender discrimination in organizations. In R. L. Dipboye & A. Colella (Eds.), *Discrimination at work: The psychological and organizational bases* (pp. 149–176). Mahwah, NJ: Lawrence Erlbaum Associates.

Colella, A. (1996). Organizational socialization of newcomers with disabilities: A framework for future research. *Research in Personnel and Human Resources Management, 14,* 351–417.

Colella, A., DeNisi, A. S., & Varma, A. (1997). Appraising the performance of employees with disabilities: A review and model. *Human Resource Management Review, 7,* 27–53.

Colella, A., DeNisi, A. S., & Varma, A. (1998). The impact of ratee's disability on performance judgments and choice as partner: The role of disability-job fit stereotypes and interdependence of rewards. *Journal of Applied Psychology, 83,* 102–111.

Colella, A., & Stone, D. L. (2005). Workplace discrimination toward persons with disabilities: A call for some new research directions. In R. L. Dipboye & A. Colella (Eds.), *Discrimination at work: The psychological and organizational bases* (pp. 227–254). Mahwah, NJ: Lawrence Erlbaum Associates.

Colella, A., & Varma, A. (1999). Disability-job fit stereotypes and the evaluation of persons with disabilities at work. *Journal of Occupational Rehabilitation, 9,* 79–95.

Combs, G. M. (2003). The duality of race and gender for managerial African American women: Implications of informal social networks on career advancement. *Human Resource Development Review, 2,* 385–405.

Cottrell, C. A., & Neuberg, S. L. (2005). Different emotional reactions to different groups: A sociofunctional threat-based approach to "prejudice." *Journal of Personality and Social Psychology, 88,* 770–789.

Cox, T. (1994). *Cultural diversity in organizations: Theory, research, and practice.* San Francisco: Berrett-Koehler.

Crisp, R. J., & Beck, S. R. (2005). Reducing intergroup bias: The moderating role of ingroup identification. *Group Processes & Intergroup Relations, 8,* 173–185.

Dass, P., & Parker, B. (1999). Strategies for managing human resource diversity: From resistance to learning. *Academy of Management Executive, 13,* 68–80.

Davison, H. K., & Burke, M. J. (2000). Sex discrimination in simulated employment contexts: A meta-analytic investigation. *Journal of Vocational Behavior, 56,* 225–248.

Dipboye, R. L. (1985). Some neglected variables in research on discrimination in appraisals. *Academy of Management Review, 10,* 116–127.

Dovidio, J. F., & Gaertner, S. L. (2000). Aversive racism in selection decisions: 1989 and 1999. *Psychological Science, 11,* 315–319.

Dovidio, J. F., Gaertner, S. L., & Kawakami, K. (2003). Intergroup contact: The past, present, and the future. *Group Processes and Intergroup Relations, 6,* 5–21.

Dovidio, J. F., & Hebl, M. R. (2005). Discrimination at the level of the individual: Cognitive and affective factors. In R. L. Dipboye & A. Colella (Eds.), *Discrimination at work: The psychological and organizational bases* (pp. 11–36). Mahwah, NJ: Lawrence Erlbaum Associates.

Eagly, A. H., & Karau, S. J. (2002). Role congruity theory of prejudice toward female leaders. *Psychological Review, 109,* 573–598.

Eagly, A. H., Karau, S. J., & Makhijani, M. G. (1995). Gender and the effectiveness of leaders: A meta-analysis. *Psychological Bulletin, 117,* 125–145.

Elvira, M., & Town, R. (2001). The effects of race and worker productivity on performance evaluations. *Industrial Relations, 40,* 571–591.

Ely, R. J., & Meyerson, D. E. (2000). Theories of gender in organizations: A new approach to organizational analysis and change. *Research in Organizational Behavior, 22,* 103–151.

Farh, J., Tsui, A. S., Xin, K., & Cheng, B. (1998). The influence of relational demography and guanxi: The Chinese case. *Organization Science, 9,* 471–488.

Ferris, G. R., Judge, T. A., Rowland, K. M., & Fitzgibbons, D. E. (1994). Subordinate influence and the performance evaluation process: Test of a model. *Organizational Behavior and Human Decision Processes, 58,* 101–136.

Ferris, G. R., & King, T. R. (1992). The politics of age discrimination in organizations. *Journal of Business Ethics, 11,* 341–350.

Finkelstein, L. M., Burke, M. J., & Raju, N. S. (1995). Age discrimination in simulated employment contexts: An integrative analysis. *Journal of Applied Psychology, 80,* 652–663.

Fiske, S. T. (2002). What we know now about bias and intergroup conflict, the problem of the century. *Current Directions in Psychological Science, 11,* 123–128.

Fiske, S. T., Cuddy, A. J. C., Glick, P., & Xu, J. (2002). A model of (often mixed) stereotype content: Competence and warmth respectively follow from perceived status and competition. *Journal of Personality and Social Psychology, 82,* 878–902.

Fiske, S. T., & Neuberg, S. L. (1990). A continuum of impression formation, from category-based to individuating processes: Influences of information and motivation on attention and interpretation. In M. P. Zanna (Ed.), *Advances in experimental social psychology* (pp. 1–74). New York: Academic Press.

Fleming, M. A., Petty, R. E., & White, P. H. (2005). Stigmatized targets and evaluation: Prejudice as a determinant of attribute scrutiny and polarization. *Personality and Social Psychology Bulletin, 31,* 496–507.

Foschi, M. (2000). Double standards for competence: Theory and research. *Annual Review of Sociology, 26,* 21–42.

Furnham, A., & Stringfield, P. (2001). Gender differences in rating reports: Female managers are harsher raters, particularly of males. *Journal of Managerial Psychology, 16,* 281–288.

Gaertner, S. L., & Dovidio, J. F. (2000). *Reducing ingroup bias: The common ingroup identity model.* Philadelphia: The Psychology Press.

Gibson, K. J., Zerbe, W. J., & Franken, R. E. (1993). The influence of rater and ratee age on judgments of work-related attributes. *The Journal of Psychology, 127,* 271–280.

Glick, P., Diebold, J., Bailey-Warner, B., & Zhu, L. (1997). The two faces of Adam: Ambivalent sexism and polarized attitudes towards women. *Personality and Social Psychology Bulletin, 23,* 1323–1334.

Gordon, R. A., & Arvey, R. D. (2004). Age bias in laboratory and field settings: A meta-analytic investigation. *Journal of Applied Social Psychology, 34,* 468–492.

Greenhaus, J. H., & Parasuraman, S. (1993). Job performance attributions and career advancement prospects: An examination of gender and race effects. *Organizational Behavior and Human Decision Processes, 55,* 273–297.

Gundersen, D. E., Tinsley, D. B., & Terpstra, D. E. (1996). Empirical assessment of impression management biases: The potential for performance appraisal error. *Journal of Social Behavior & Personality, 11,* 57–76.

Harber, K. D. (1998). Feedback to minorities: Evidence of a positive bias. *Journal of Personality and Social Psychology, 74,* 622–628.

Heilman, M. E. (1983). Sex bias in work settings: The lack of fit model. *Research in Organizational Behavior, 5,* 269–298.

Heilman, M. E. (1995). Sex stereotypes and their effects in the workplace: What we know and what we don't know. *Journal of Social Behavior and Personality, 10,* 3–26.

Heilman, M. E. (2001). Description and prescription: How gender stereotypes prevent women's ascent up the organizational ladder. *Journal of Social Issues, 57,* 657–674.

Heilman, M. E., & Haynes, M. C. (2005). No credit where credit is due: Attributional rationalization of women's success in male-female teams. *Journal of Applied Psychology, 90,* 905–916.

Heilman, M.E., Wallen, A. S., Fuchs, D., & Tamkins, M. M. (2004). Penalities for success: Reactions to women who succeed at male gender-typed tasks, *Journal of Applied Psychology, 89,* 416–427.

Higgins, E. T., & Bargh, J. A. (1987). Social cognition and social perception. *Annual Review of Psychology, 38,* 369–425.

Hogg, M., & Abrams, D. (1988). *Social identification.* London: Routledge.

Hyun, J. (2006). *Breaking the bamboo ceiling: Career strategies for Asians.* New York: Harper Collins.

Ilgen, D. R., & Youtz, M. A. (1986). Factors affecting the evaluation and development of minorities in organizations. In K. Rowland & G. Ferris (Eds.), *Research in personnel and human resource management* (pp. 307–337). Greenwich, CT: JAI Press.

Jussim, L., Coleman, L. M., & Lerch, L. (1987). The nature of stereotypes: A comparison and integration of three theories. *Journal of Personality and Social Psychology, 52,* 536–546.

Kanter, R. M. (1977). *Men and women of the corporation.* New York: Basic Books.

Katz, I., & Glass, D. C. (1979). An ambivalence-amplification theory of behavior toward the stigmatized. In W. Austin & S. Worchel (Eds.), *The psychology of intergroup relations* (pp. 55–70). Monterey, CA: Brooks/Cole.

Kilian, C. M., Hukai, D., & McCarty, C. E. (2005). Building diversity in the pipeline to corporate leadership. *Journal of Management Development, 24,* 155–168.

Kraiger, K., & Ford, J. K. (1985). A meta-analysis of ratee race effects in performance ratings. *Journal of Applied Psychology, 70,* 56–65.

Kulik, C. T., & Bainbridge, H. T. J. (2005). Psychological perspectives on workplace diversity. In A. M. Konrad, P. Prasad, & J. K. Pringle (Eds.), *Handbook of workplace diversity* (pp. 25–52). Thousand Oaks, CA: Sage.

Kulik, C. T., Perry, E. L., & Bourhis, A. C. (2000). Ironic evaluation processes: Effects of thought suppression on evaluations of older job applicants. *Journal of Organizational Behavior, 21,* 689–711.

Landy, F. J., & Farr, J. L. (1980). Performance rating. *Psychological Bulletin, 87,* 72–107.

Lawrence, B. S. (1988). New wrinkles in the theory of age: Demography, norms, and performance ratings. *Academy of Management Journal, 31,* 309–337.

Liden, R. C., Stilwell, D., & Ferris, G. R. (1996). The effects of supervisor and subordinate age on objective performance and subjective performance ratings. *Human Relations, 49,* 327–347.

Lindeman, M., & Sundvik, L. (1995). Evaluation bias and self-enhancement among gender groups. *European Journal of Social Psychology, 25,* 269–280.

Linville, P. W. (1982). The complexity-extremity effect and age-based stereotyping. *Journal of Personality and Social Psychology, 42,* 193–211.

Lynch, J. E., & Finkelstein, L. M. (2006, May). *Employee disability: Its effect on the performance evaluation process.* Paper presented at the 21st annual conference of the Society for Industrial and Organizational Psychology, Dallas, TX.

Macrae, C. N., Bodenhausen, G. V., & Milne, A. B. (1998). Saying no to unwanted thoughts: Self-focus and the regulation of mental life. *Journal of Personality and Social Psychology, 74,* 578–589.

Marques, J. M., Yzerbyt, V. Y., & Leyens, J. P. (1988). The black sheep effect: Judgmental extremity towards ingroup members as a function of group identification. *European Journal of Social Psychology, 18,* 1–16.

Martell, R. F. (1996). What mediates gender bias in work behavior ratings? *Sex Roles, 35,* 153–169.

Maurer, T. J., Wrenn, K. A., & Weiss, E. M. (2003). Toward understanding and managing stereotypical beliefs about older workers' ability and desire for learning and development. *Research in Personnel and Human Resources Management, 22,* 253–285.

McConahay, J. B. (1983). Modern racism and modern discrimination: The effects of race, racial attitudes, and context on simulated hiring decisions. *Personality and Social Psychology Bulletin, 9,* 551–558.

Mount, M. K., Sytsma, M. R., Hazucha, J .F., & Holt, K. E. (1997). Rater–ratee race effects in developmental performance ratings of managers. *Personnel Psychology, 50,* 51–69.

Nieva, V. F., & Gutek, B. A. (1980). Sex effects on evaluations. *Academy of Management Review, 5,* 267–276.

Pazy, A., & Oron, I. (2001). Sex proportion and performance evaluation among high-ranking military officers. *Journal of Organizational Behavior, 22,* 689–702.

Pelled, L. H., & Xin, K. R. (2000). Relational demography and relationship quality in two cultures. *Organization Studies, 21,* 1077–1094.

Perry, E. (1997). A cognitive approach to understanding discrimination: A closer look at applicant gender and age. *Research in Personnel and Human Resources Management, 15*, 175–240.

Perry, E. L., Blake-Davis, A., & Kulik, C. T. (1994). Explaining gender-based selection decisions: A synthesis of contextual and cognitive approaches. *Academy of Management Review, 19*, 786–820.

Perry, E. L., & Bourhis, A. C. (1998). A closer look at the role of applicant age in selection decisions. *Journal of Applied Social Psychology, 28*, 1670–1697.

Perry, E. L., & Finkelstein, L.M. (1999). Toward a broader view of age discrimination in employment-related decisions: A joint consideration of organizational factors and cognitive processes. *Human Resource Management Review, 9*, 21–49.

Perry, E. L., Kulik, C. T., & Bourhis, A. C. (1996). Moderating effects of personal and contextual factors in age discrimination. *Journal of Applied Psychology, 81*, 628–647.

Perry, E. L., Kulik, C. T., & Zhou, J. (1999). A closer look at the effects of subordinate-supervisor age differences. *Journal of Organizational Behavior, 20*, 341–357.

Pettigrew, T. F. (1979). The ultimate attribution error: Extending Allport's cognitive analysis of prejudice. *Personality and Social Psychology Bulletin, 5*, 461–476.

Pettigrew, T. F. (1998). Reactions toward the new minorities of Western Europe. *Annual Review of Sociology, 24*, 77–103.

Powell, G. N., & Butterfield, D. A. (2002). Exploring the influence of decision makers' race and gender on actual promotions to top management. *Personnel Psychology, 55*, 397–428.

Pratto, F., Sidanius, J., Stallworth, L. M., & Malle, B. F. (1994). Social dominance orientation: A personality variable predicting social and political attitudes. *Journal of Personality and Social Psychology, 67*, 741–763.

Reskin, B. F., McBrier, D. B., & Kmec, J.A. (1999). The determinants and consequences of workplace sex and race composition. *Annual Review of Sociology, 25*, 335–361.

Ridgeway, C. L. (2001). Gender, status, and leadership. *Journal of Social Issues, 57*, 637–655.

Riordan, C. M. (2000). Relational demography within groups: Past developments, contradictions, and new directions. In G. R. Ferris (Ed.), *Research in personnel and human resources management* (pp. 131–173). New York: JAI Press.

Riordan, C. M., Schaffer, B. S., & Stewart, M. M. (2005). Relational demography within groups: Through the lens of discrimination. In R. L. Dipboye & A. Colella (Eds.), *Discrimination at work: The psychological and organizational bases* (pp. 37–62). Mahwah, NJ: Lawrence Erlbaum Associates.

Robbins, T. L., & DeNisi, A. S. (1993). Moderators of sex bias in the performance appraisal process: A cognitive analysis. *Journal of Management, 19*, 113–126.

Roberson, L., & Block, C. J. (2001). Explaining racioethnic group differences in performance and related outcomes: A review of theoretical perspectives. In B. Staw & R. Sutton (Eds.), *Research in organizational behavior* (pp. 247–325). New York: JAI Press.

Rojahn, K., & Willemsen, T. M. (1994). The evaluation of effectiveness and likability of gender-role congruent and gender-role incongruent leaders. *Sex Roles, 30*, 109–119.

Rudman, L. A., & Glick, P. (1999). Feminized management and backlash toward agentic women: The hidden costs to women of a kinder, gentler image of middle managers. *Journal of Personality and Social Psychology, 77,* 1004–1010.

Rudman, L. A., & Glick, P. (2001). Prescriptive gender stereotypes and backlash toward agentic women. *Journal of Social Issues, 57,* 743–762.

Sackett, P. R., DuBois, C. L. Z., & Noe, A. W. (1991). Tokenism in performance evaluation: The effects of work group representation on male-female and White-Black differences in performance ratings. *Journal of Applied Psychology, 76,* 263–267.

Saks, A. M., & Waldman, D. A. (1998). The relationship between age and job performance evaluations for entry-level professionals. *Journal of Organizational Behavior, 19,* 409–419.

Schein, V. E. (2001). A global look at psychological barriers to women's progress in management. *Journal of Social Issues, 57,* 675–688.

Shore, L. M., Cleveland, J. N., & Goldberg, C. B. (2003). Work attitudes and decisions as a function of manager age and employee age. *Journal of Applied Psychology, 88,* 529–537.

Stauffer, J. M., & Buckley, M. R. (2005). The existence and nature of racial bias in supervisory ratings. *Journal of Applied Psychology, 90,* 586–591.

Stone, D. L., & Colella, A. (1996). A model of factors affecting the treatment of disabled individuals in organizations. *Academy of Management Review, 21,* 352–401.

Stone, E. F., Stone, D. L., & Dipboye, R. L. (1992). Stigmas in organizations: Race, handicaps, and physical unattractiveness. In K. Kelley (Ed.), *Issues, theory, and research in industrial and organizational psychology* (pp. 385–444). Amsterdam: Elsevier.

Swim, J. K., & Sanna, L. J. (1996). He's skilled, she's lucky: A meta-analysis of observers' attributions for women's and men's successes and failures. *Personality and Social Psychology Bulletin, 22,* 507–519.

Tajfel, H. (1982). Social psychology of intergroup relations. *Annual review of psychology, 33,* 1–39.

Thomas, D. A., & Gabarro, J. J. (1999). *Breaking through: The making of minority executives in corporate America.* Boston: Harvard Business School Press.

Thomas, K. M., & Chrobot-Mason, D. (2005). Group-level explanations of workplace discrimination. In R. L. Dipboye & A. Colella (Eds.), *Discrimination at work: The psychological and organizational bases* (pp. 63–88). Mahwah, NJ: Lawrence Erlbaum Associates.

Tsui, A. S. & O'Reilly, C. A. (1989). Beyond simple demographic effects: The importance of relational demography in superior-subordinate dyads. *Academy of Management Journal, 32,* 402–423.

Tsui, A. S., Egan, T., & O'Reilly, C. (1992). Being different: Relational demography and organizational attachment. *Administrative Science Quarterly, 37,* 549–579.

Tsui, A. S., & Gutek, B. A. (1999). *Demographic differences in organizations: Current research and future directions.* Lanham, MD: Lexington Books.

Tsui, A. S., Porter, L. W., & Egan, T. D. (2002). When both similarities and dissimilarities matter: Extending the concept of relational demography. *Human Relations, 55,* 899–907.

Tsui, A. S., Xin, K. R., & Egan, T. D. (1995). Relational demography: The missing link in vertical dyad linkage. In S. Jackson & M. Ruderman (Eds.), *Diversity in work teams: Research paradigms for a changing workplace* (pp. 97–129). Washington, DC: American Psychological Association.

Varma, A., & Stroh, L. K. (2001). The impact of same-sex LMX dyads on performance evaluations. *Human Resource Management, 40,* 309–320.

Wagner, D. G., & Berger, J. B. (1997). Gender and interpersonal task behaviors: Status expectation accounts. *Sociological Perspectives, 40,* 1–32.

Weiss, E.M., & Maurer, T. J. (2004). Age discrimination in personnel decisions: A reexamination. *Journal of Applied Social Psychology, 34,* 1551–1562.

Wittenbrink, B., Judd, C. M., & Park, B. (1997). Implicit racial stereotypes and prejudice and their relationships with questionnaire measures: We know what we think. *Journal of Personality and Social Psychology, 72,* 262–274.

Author Index

651

Johannesen-Schmidt, M.C., 406
John, O.P., 332, 362, 363
John of Salisbury, 35
Johns, G., 101, 102
Johnson, C., 406
Johnson, D.R., 102
Johnson, D.W., 8
Johnson, E., 452
Johnson, J.L., 7, 11, 12, 13, 44n.27, 44n.29
Johnson, K., 103
Johnson, M., 286
Johnson, M.M.S., 451
Johnson, P., 128, 160
Johnson, P.E., 147, 150, 161
Johnson, R.A., 22, 30
Johnson, S.A., 71
Jones, C., 159, 557
Jones, D.G., 250
Jones, D.T., 518
Jones, E.E., 201
Jones, G.R., 325, 334
Jones, L., 392, 411
Jordan, A.T., 84
Jordan, J.W., 79, 82, 83
Joyce, P.G., 245
Judd, C.M., 621
Judge, T.A., 324, 329, 337, 345, 346, 347, 352, 630
Julian, S., 151
Jundt, D., 286
Jurik, N.C., 80, 83, 85
Jurkiewicz, C.L., 249
Jussim, L., 628

K

Kaboolian, L., 240
Kaeufer, K., 301, 305, 307
Kahn, K.B., 557
Kahn, R.L., 126
Kahn, W.A., 297
Kahneman, D., 31, 213, 214n., 449, 520
Kahnweiler, W., 79, 83
Kale, P., 492, 498, 502
Kalleberg, A., 160
Kalleberg, A.L., 68, 73, 76, 77, 78, 79, 83, 86, 92, 98, 100, 555, 574
Kallinikos, J., 95

Kamens, D., 126
Kammeyer-Mueller, J.D., 339, 341
Kamp, D., 185, 186, 192, 217n.
Kan, M.M., 393, 398
Kanawattanachai, P., 557
Kandemir, D., 503
Kang, E., 13
Kang, S., 582, 583, 584
Kanter, R.M., 36, 67, 154, 395, 417, 418, 419, 423, 555, 623
Kanungo, R., 417
Kao, C.F., 465
Kaplan, A., 38, 184
Kaplan, R.S., 257n.45
Kaplan, S.A., 345
Karamanou, I., 44n.27
Karasek, R.A., 196
Karau, S.J., 620, 621, 626, 627, 628, 632, 635
Karmel, R.S., 7, 20, 23, 41, 46n.46
Kasznik, R., 18
Katz, D., 126
Katz, I., 629
Katz, J.A., 79, 80, 81
Katz, J.P., 17
Kauffmann, C., 399, 417
Kaufman, A., 11, 36, 39
Kaufman, H., 229
Kaufmann, G., 452, 453, 454, 465
Kavanaugh, D.J., 452
Kawakami, K., 634
Kayes, D.C., 139
Kazanjian, R.K., 440
Kearns, F., 143
Kedia, B.L., 485
Kedia, S., 18
Keep, E., 160
Keim, G.D., 522
Keith, N., 335
Kelleher, K., 396, 397, 407, 429
Kellett, S., 359, 362, 363, 465
Kellogg, K.C., 601
Kelly, J., 124
Kelly, J.R., 320, 326, 334, 343, 356, 359, 360, 361, 363, 364
Kelly, L., 191
Kelman, S.J., 228, 237, 240, 247, 251

Subject Index